DIARIES OF FIELD MARSHAL MOHAMMAD AYUB KHAN

1966–1972

DIARIES OF FIELD MARSHAL MOHAMMAD AYUB KHAN

1966–1972

b. Nov 1905
d. 20 April 1974

Edited and Annotated by
CRAIG BAXTER

OXFORD
UNIVERSITY PRESS

OXFORD

UNIVERSITY PRESS

Great Clarendon Street, Oxford OX2 6DP

Oxford University Press is a department of the University of Oxford.
It furthers the University's objective of excellence in research, scholarship,
and education by publishing worldwide in

Oxford New York

Auckland Cape Town Dar es Salaam Hong Kong Karachi
Kuala Lumpur Madrid Melbourne Mexico City Nairobi
New Delhi Shanghai Taipei Toronto

with offices in

Argentina Austria Brazil Chile Czech Republic France Greece
Guatemala Hungary Italy Japan Poland Portugal Singapore
South Korea Switzerland Turkey Ukraine Vietnam

Oxford is a registered trade mark of Oxford University Press
in the UK and in certain other countries

ISBN 978-0-19-547442-8

Second Impression 2007

Typeset in Adobe Garamond Pro
Printed in Pakistan by
Kagzi Printers, Karachi.
Published by
Ameena Saiyid, Oxford University Press
No. 38, Sector 15, Korangi Industrial Area, PO Box 8214
Karachi-74900, Pakistan.

Contents

Preface by Craig Baxter   vii

Author's Note   ix

Editor's Note   x

DIARY 1966   1

DIARY 1967   41

DIARY 1968   197

DIARY 1969   295

DIARY 1970   355

DIARY 1971   433

DIARY 1972   511

Appendices   545

Notes   551

Bibliography   588

Index   589

Preface

Field Marshal Mohammad Ayub Khan began his diary in September 1966, and ended his record in October 1972, when his health began to fail and he was unable to maintain his record of the events of the period and his comments on, and interpretations of them. The period covered by the diaries includes such events as Ayub's resignation from the presidency, the assumption of power by Yahya Khan, the division of Pakistan, and the replacement of Yahya by Zulfiqar Ali Bhutto.

As he stated in the author's note, the contents would require safe-keeping for a specified time before release or publishing because many entries contain information or opinions that could be detrimental to individuals and institutions that were involved in the events he describes. The diaries were, therefore, embargoed for more than thirty years after the final entry.

The diaries were retained by Ayub Khan's son, Gohar Ayub and it was always the intention of Ayub Khan and his son that the diaries would be released and published. Ayub Khan further intended that the diaries would be edited by Altaf Gauhar. Since the death of Altaf Gauhar occurred before the anticipated lifting of the embargo, Gohar Ayub entrusted the editing and publishing to Oxford University Press (OUP), Karachi.

OUP asked me to undertake the editing of the diaries. Although I was able to gather much information from published works (and some, admittedly, from my memory), I was greatly assisted by friends in Pakistan, Bangladesh and the United States who have responded kindly and helpfully to my frequent questions.

CRAIG BAXTER

Author's Note

Ever since assumption of the responsible office of C-in-C of the Army on 17 January 1951, I, apart from becoming responsible for the defence of the country, also came into contact with the higher functionaries of the government at the policy making level. So, I have had the opportunity of seeing the history of Pakistan in the making and later making it myself in the capacity of President. I was often asked by friends to record my experiences for the benefit of future generations and myself felt the need for it, but somehow I never got round to writing my diary, more through lack of habit than anything else. However, when I came to writing my book *Friends not Masters*,[1] I had to do it through memory. This was a very taxing and tiresome job. So, I forced myself to start writing my diary in case it was decided to write another book or use it as reference material. But one thing is clear: that this material cannot be used for a long time to come as it is bound to contain sensitive material affecting personalities or events having a bearing or relationship with, or influence on, the affairs of Pakistan. In making my comments or observations, I will do so as I honestly felt at the time. But these are liable to be misunderstood and can cause a lot of harm if divulged prematurely. Hence, the need for deferment of publication of this material until such time as it ceases to be part of contemporary history.[2]

MOHAMMAD AYUB KHAN
Field Marshal
1 September 1966

Editor's Note

The month and year of each diary is given at the top of each page and the day is given above each entry. No editorial changes, save any additions within square brackets, have been made.

📖 Signifies an entry
[…] Word missing
[abcd] Editor's additions

DIARY 1966

2 | FRIDAY

📖 Draft letter for the Governor, West Pakistan (Malik Amir Mohammad Khan)[1]

I have given a very serious thought to the proposal made by you during our meeting on 1st September and have come to the conclusion that an alternative solution will have to be found. My reasons are that before the EBDO[2] is lifted, bringing in its wake new problems, the man in charge should be well in the saddle; otherwise it would not be fair to him. Secondly, there are far too many disturbing stories circulating, which have even penetrated the Armed Forces and which will gain momentum with the passage of time, creating more problems. Therefore, the need for early change, unfortunately, is apparent.

An alternative has occurred to me, which I put forward for your consideration; you proceed on leave abroad for check up, as you intended doing later. Your relief will remain acting or officiating (constitution permitting) for the duration of your leave.

True that the weather will get colder in Europe as time goes on, but it is no great problem with modern conveniences like central heating etc.

The objection that this change may look like the outcome of pressure by certain officials can't hold any water because people know that I am not easily influenced by such tactics, and besides, this so-called pressure is not a new phenomenon. If it had not worked before, why should it do so now?

Please be assured that I am making this proposal just as much to uphold your honour and dignity as to serve the interest of the state. If there is anything else I can do for you, I shall be delighted to do so.

I hope you would let me have a reply soon.

With best wishes
Mohammad Ayub Khan

📖 Zulfiqar Bhutto[3] left the cabinet in early July. He was given notice to quit in January at his own house in Larkana. Yet he complains that he was given 24 hours notice.

When he left, the leftist elements and a certain section of student community made a lot of fuss. I was accused of turning him out because of his pro-China and anti-USA tendencies. Some said that he went under American pressure and that the American aid was conditional on this.

None of these things are there. He went because during last year or so, something perceptible went wrong with him.

He started using provocative language even on international platforms and started behaving in an irresponsible and objectionable manner. He was working fast in the direction of becoming another Krishna Menon or Subandrio.[4] Demagogy became his stock in trade. Several warnings went unheeded. So, there was no alternative but to tell him to go. Besides, he started drinking himself into a stupor and led a very loose life. It is a pity that a man of considerable talent went astray. I offered him a foreign assignment, but he was not interested.

His real trouble was that he started running a personal policy assisted by a few elements in the Foreign Office instead of the national policy; also he was distrusted and disliked in most capitals.

📖 The American ambassador[5] came to see me today. Gave me a letter from President Johnson in reply to my request for spare parts etc. for the American type of military equipment. It was evasive.

It is quite obvious that the Americans are very reluctant to do anything that will annoy India. Our argument that we have a much smaller force than India and are no threat to it cuts no ice with them. It looks that they even expect us to deny ourselves the right of self-defence.

📖 Played a game of golf. Did well. Even surprised myself.

3 | SATURDAY

📖 The Iranian Ambassador, Hassan Pakravan, came to present his credentials. Spoke about the F-86 Canadian aircraft bought from Germany. Said that India and others are putting pressure on them and that could some aircraft be sent back to Iran. Told him not to get frightened. These protests are formal and will die down in due course. He said that the Shahinshah was very anxious to see RCD[6] succeed and that joint ventures be started on realistic basis. I heartily agreed, as RCD is my brainchild. I told him to remain in touch with M.M. Ahmed,[7] our chief planner. I also told him that if they genuinely believed that the future of Iran and Pakistan was common, then why not think in terms of political tie up which will benefit both. He promised to pass on my view to the Shahinshah.

Both Iran and Pakistan have a great deal to gain if such tie up comes into being. Maybe others in the Middle East will also be attracted.

4 | SUNDAY

📖 Proposed six points programme for the Muslim League.[8]

a. Unity of nation based on a strong centre, considerable measure of provincial autonomy, decentralisation of provincial administration. In other words, support of the present constitution and counter disruption.

b. Security of the country through unity of the nation, strong and prosperous Pakistan and maintaining requisite armed strength and have sound and purposeful foreign policy.

c. Development in education, industry and agriculture. Maintaining parity between the two wings and giving fair deal to backward areas. Like treatment for urban and rural peoples.

d. Ideology of Islam: Inculcate it and make it play a positive role in attaining unity, and higher spiritual and moral values. Also, make it a prime mover in attaining our objective of progress, prosperity and social justice. Help the needy and poor personnel, organizations on governmental basis.

e. Approach problems of life with maturity, pragmatism and realism. Emotions and passions have a place, but they must be tempered with reason. The way to progress and salvation lies through critical inquiry and rational approach. When emotions take charge reason goes out and when reason goes out all hopes of attaining worthwhile results evaporate. In other words be kind, but be hard-headed and have your feet firmly on the ground. Avoid talking in the air.

f. Eliminate extravaganza and the un-Islamic customs.

6 | TUESDAY

📖 Confucius—true name Kung Fu-Tzu—liked advising politicians as follows:

a. Common herd should be led with kindness, justice, and paternalism—Golden Rule.
b. The cautious seldom err.
c. Not more surely does the grass bend before the wind than the masses yield to the will of those above them.
d. Exalt the straight, set aside the crooked, the people will be loyal.

📖 Sahibzada Faizul Hasan, though an ex-Ahrar[9] is an enlightened *alim*. Somehow he has developed an attachment with me. This is known to the other ulema, as such they are very jealous of him. He came to see me yesterday and told me that the followers of Maududi,[10] the Deoband group,[11] the Ahrars, etc. are spreading all sorts of disaffection against me. They are criticizing the family law which has brought so much relief to the poor women, orphans and helpless people, and the family planning scheme. The idiots or rascals are calling these things anti-Islamic.

The point is, why do they do these things? There are two reasons: one, belonging to a parasitical profession they can only flourish on the ignorance of people. Their art is to arouse people and retain their attention and passions so that they (people) remain willing victims. Secondly, this class of people have been dead against the creation of Pakistan and acted as willing and servile tools in the hands of Congress before partition. Now that Pakistan is formed and has given them asylum, and they are eating its salt, their efforts are diverted towards its disruption. Also, they are the deadliest enemy of the educated Muslim. They cannot bear such people being the leaders and have the responsibility of running the country. In the name of Islam, they are dead against progress and society having the right to think for itself. Their religion and philosophy has not the slightest affinity into the true spirit of Islam. No wonder the thinking peoples are running away from religion. This is a great pity. It was this spirit of jealousy that caused such people to defame and even dub as *kafir* those that tried to bring enlightenment and salvation of the Muslim *millat*. Look at what they did to Sir Syed,[12] Jinnah[13] and Iqbal.[14] But these great men, imbued with the spirit of dedication, carried on their mission. The Muslim *millat* owes so much to them.

📖 Told the principal secretary to constitute a committee to determine the sequence of events leading to fighting in Kashmir and the Indian attack against Pakistan.[15]

8 | THURSDAY

📖 My draft letter was delivered to the governor, West Pakistan, yesterday. He sent in a reply today asking to be relieved of his responsibilities. The arrangement is that he will attend certain conferences here during the course of next week and then depart for Kalabagh. He wants the announcement of the change to be made then. This will deprive me giving him a proper send off, but I don't want to hurt his sensibilities.

He has been a governor for seven years or so and has done a very good job except during the last couple of years when he deviously started changing and in a way trying to demolish my image. In the Karachi by-election for the National Assembly he openly operated against the Muslim League candidate though he was nominated with his concurrence. A betrayal is unforgivable and I was forced to let him to go.

The lesson is that in politics hundred per cent reliability is unattainable and thus keeping a man in one place for too long is not a sound policy.

I intend appointing General Musa[16] as governor. He is loyal, trustworthy and has vast experience of administration. I think he should do well. But I told him plainly that there must be perfect freedom for both of us to part from each should we feel so inclined at any time.

📖 On the inauguration of National Refinery in Karachi met a man called Taraki from Saudi Arabia now employed by the Kuwait government. He lives in Beirut. He told me to hurry up and take oil-prospecting licenses in Iraq, Kuwait, and Saudi Arabia. There are some promising areas still available and it may be possible to go in for joint ventures with these governments. And they may well be induced to accept us, as Pakistan is such a big and expanding oil market. Libya is another place where we should make soundings. I have told the industries minister and the secretary to be ready to proceed to these countries for making enquiries.

There is a talk of having a joint oil venture in the Moghan area in Iran, but the Iranian terms are very stiff. In fact, they are almost unreasonable. Also, they are not prepared to give us oil on the Persian Gulf in lieu of our share of oil found in Kagmin area. If I happen to meet the Shah, I might mention this to him.

📖 The Sui gas, and later, gas from Marri and also from Sari will be used for power generation. It is used as fuel. I have told the experts that you are wasting gas pressure at the source. Why can't that pressure be used for turning turbines for power production? They took my suggestion with great scepticism. But today they came and told me that is a perfectly feasible proposition. I think this should remobilise power production from gas and bring down the cost considerably.

📖 I understand the 1400th anniversary of the first revelation of Quran is due next year. A few ulema have approached me to call ulema of other countries to celebrate the occasion. In order that such a meeting is purposeful the Islamic Research Institute[17] should play the host and set certain subjects to be discussed in the form of seminar, otherwise it will be just a repetition of orthodoxy and dogma. These subjects should be searching and relate to the problems that the Muslim countries are faced with in the twentieth century. An effort should be made to show how the teachings of Quran can help in resolution of these problems.

📖 I have caused word to be passed on to all my children that there must be no promiscuous breeding of children. The quota is two or three children per couple. Anything more will be frowned upon.

9 | FRIDAY

📖 In our foreign missions abroad, there is far too much emphasis on politics. This is all right up to a point and in some cases even necessary, but the emphasis should be on commercial dealings, because this is a commercial world. Unless the people's basic needs are met how can any country maintain stability and progress? So our representatives abroad should be commercially oriented. These people should get thorough grounding in the commercial field before departure abroad.

10 | SATURDAY

A report came about the *jashan* in Kabul. It was celebrated with great fervour. Some 15,000 Pakistanis also went and were received with courtesy on an occasion when the king visited the fireworks. All the dignitaries and diplomats were presented to the king, Abdul Ghaffar Khan[18] leading. He is doing a lot of mischief there against Pakistan. He is trying to persuade the Afghans to allow him to set up a provisional government of Pakhtoonistan. He is supposed to have told a friend, 'the king of Afghanistan calls me uncle and so does the President of Pakistan, but the trouble is that my nephews won't listen to me'. Who can listen to such a man.

15 | THURSDAY

Briefing to General Musa on taking over the governorship of West Pakistan.

a. As a governor he will be my personal representative, head of the administration and almost the head of the Muslim League party.
b. Duties as my personal representative:

i.   Act as a link between the province and me.
ii. Act as link between the Central Government and the province.
iii. Come and discuss policy with me. Thereafter have complete freedom to carry it out. Don't let people know even if we differ on any thing

c. Duties as the head of the administration:

i.   Be fair, just and firm.
ii.   See that the administrative organs that are created function properly. In other words, instead of the administration being personal, institutionalise it. In other words, give directives to the ministers and the officials and see that they carry them out.
iii. Some departure is sometimes necessary, but by and large don't allow the administration to be used for political ends or interfered with.
iv.   Encourage good people, but don't hesitate to go for those who are not pulling their weight.
v.   Allow autonomous bodies freedom to operate within their charter, but carry out personal supervision constantly to ensure optimum efficiency.
vi.   Get to know the background of the ministers, officials and public men and their mutual relationship. Don't allow anyone to mislead you. When in doubt check up with some reliable and knowledgeable people or with me.
vii. Allow the relationship between the central and provincial ministers to operate on institutional basis, so that the coordination of effort and implementation of policy is constant and natural amongst them.

viii. A large number of people would want to see you. That is necessary. You can't always fulfil their demands, but if you listen patiently, they will get some satisfaction. Be a good listener.

ix. See your ministers and their secretaries on a regular basis.

x. Maintain good relationship with the High Court.

xi. See that the government cases whenever instituted are carefully prepared. This will need correct manning and supervision of the Law Ministry and Home Ministry.

xii. Get to know the background of the opposition parties and their leaders, their intentions and activities. By and large their activities will be agitational, so a constant watch over them is necessary and so is the need to deal with them timely if they unduly transgress. They will be especially active when the EBDO is lifted.

xiii. Keep a watch on the press and the student community.

xiv. Watch sectarianism.

xv. See that the administration is development oriented and assigned to promote progress. Quick decisions and implementation necessary.

xvi. Industries in private sector should be broad-based and diversified. Emphasis on industrialisation, increased agriculture output, and family planning.

xvii. Study literature on reforms and organisational matters. Have a sound knowledge of the constitution. Know something about preventive laws.

d. Political responsibilities:

i. Mother the Muslim League. It is in the process of reorganisation. Help its sound formation and function as the representative of the people.

ii. Beware of regional susceptibilities, but remember that the welfare of the people of West Pakistan lies in remaining together.

iii. Get to know the party MNAs and MPAs and their background. Attend to their legitimate demands, but also keep them under control.

iv. Look to the welfare of the masses. Meet public representatives and political masses.

v. See that the government point of view is properly and constantly projected before the people. After all the object of this administration is their welfare.

e. Meet once or twice a month to discuss problems.

f. From today you are a civilian. Your successor is now responsible for running of the Army. It is imperative that his undivided authority is established and upheld. An Army can only work under ONE master. So, all your contacts with the Army from now should be through the Commander-in-Chief.

📖 Timetable for the induction of the new governor:

a. D-day: Swearing-in in Rawalpindi. Send for the chief justice of the West Pakistan High Court to be present in time.

b. D+7 days and so on: Orientation in the functioning of the Central Government and how the agencies of the Central Government and the provincial government dovetail with each other.
c. He should have a session with the:

    i.   Principal Secretary
    ii.   Finance Ministry
    iii. Planning Commission
    iv.   Information and Interior Ministries and the Director of the Intelligence Bureau.
    v.   Cabinet and Establishment Secretariat.
          Any others considered necessary. Principal Secretary to arrange.

d. Have final briefing with me if need be.

📖 Discuss with the principal secretary and the information people as what is to be put out on retirement of Malik Amir Mohammad Khan. Also send a letter of commendation to him.

16 | FRIDAY

📖 Draft of the letter to be sent to Malik Amir Mohammad Khan, Governor, West Pakistan:

> I acknowledge with thanks your letter of ___ asking to be relieved of your responsibilities because of your domestic problem and the kind and noble sentiments you have expressed therein. I am deeply moved by them.
>   I reluctantly accept your resignation, which will become effective from 18th September. In doing so, I should like to assure you of the highest appreciation of the work you have done and my deep regard for you. I hope and pray that you will be happy and prosperous and that we shall continue to meet as good friends as hitherto for.

📖 Last two days were spent on discussion of several important matters in the governors' conference: Recommendation of Hamood-ur-Rahman's Commission on the educational problems;[19] the system of giving licenses for different type of industries; fixation of rice procurement price in West Pakistan; the food situation; and financing of works programme.

The laxity of discipline in our educational institutions is a big problem: My answer is that education standards must be given spiritual, moral and ethical content; bad teachers and students should be got rid of; bad students should be denied scholarship; and laws should be formulated to deal with the politicians who are misusing the students.

It was decided that industrialists who don't give any dividends should be refused any further licenses for industries.

Food situation is bleak. We shall have to make large-scale purchases out of our cash. I have suggested that amongst other things, potatoes should be grown at a large scale. The problem is preservation, for which cold storages are required. An idea has come to my mind that underground storages might do, as the underground temperature stays constant at 79°F.

Works programme is a must: we must have something for our rural people. And it should form part of the annual development programme. In the past we used to get funds free for the works programme from PL 480[20] earnings. Since the Americans have decided to sell these commodities against dollars in future, these funds will no longer be available as a grant, which the provinces insisted upon. I am afraid we can't comply with this request. So the need of this programme will have to be met out of the total resources made available to the provinces.

📖 Held a reception for the diplomats and as a send off for Governor Amir Mohammad Khan. He seemed rather downcast. The reality is probably dawning that it does not pay to betray your best benefactor.

17 | SATURDAY

📖 Announced General Musa's appointment as Governor, West Pakistan. Also gave a detailed briefing. He is an honest, sincere and a just man. I believe he will do well. I understand his appointment has been received well.

18 | SUNDAY

📖 Musa was sworn in today in my house. And Yahya[21] was appointed as Commander-in-Chief of the Army.

📖 A German TV team came to interview. They grilled for an hour and a half.

📖 I caused an Army unit to give a demonstration of mass P.T. to be given to Germans and others to show this could be practiced in schools and colleges within a limited space and small expenditure, if taken up seriously. I have no doubt that it will improve student discipline, build their bodies and quicken their minds.

📖 Saw a Chinese acrobatic show this evening. The Chinese Ambassador started talking about their Cultural Revolution. He said the western press was misrepresenting that it was related to the Chinese foreign policy. This was far from the truth. The reality was that it was purely an internal movement. No change in leadership had taken place. He said that stories about desecration of Muslim mosques were not true. It was quite possible that some Muslims had been dealt with but that was purely on a personal basis and for any error they may have committed.
I told him that ill treatment of Muslims will have wider repercussions in Sinkiang, Central Asia, and Pakistan. He should, therefore, inform his government of the danger. He promised to do so. I hope this effort helps the poor Muslims in China in some measure and saves them from the tyranny and excesses of the majority.

📖 I am getting reports from several sources that Governor Amir Mohammad Khan had been acting in a disloyal manner to me in his subtle and devious way. I believe the people have heaved a sigh of relief on his departure.

📖 Had a discussion with Musa on the formation of his cabinet. He wanted to await announcement until he was ready with the complete list. I told him that delay will cause unnecessary confusion and speculation. He should appoint some ministers quickly. He agreed.

It is quite obvious that for various reasons Memon, Tamman, Masood Sadiq and Habibullah Khan should be dropped. There is no hurry about replacements. They can be found in due course.

📖 Arshad Hussain,[22] our High Commissioner in Delhi, came to see me. Said that economic, food, and law and order situation in India was bad. During the course of the recent session of Lok Sabha, the government and especially Indira Gandhi was bitterly attacked. Corruption charges were levelled against the prime minister, some other ministers and even the speaker. The coming elections were worrying the Congress, as were internal fights and power struggle. They were expected to win the centre, but might lose majority in four or five provinces.

He said that the recent vilification of Pakistan and accusations that we were preparing to attack India were deliberately engineered to put the Americans and the Russians off from selling arms to us and also to find an excuse to put off elections in the Western Province. Their deployment of number of divisions against us had an adverse effect of jittering their population further. Large number left the border areas. However, our commander-in-chief visited Delhi and met the Indian counterpart. This may lead to some lowering of tension.

He said that India had built up a vast military machine beyond their economic capacity. They cannot maintain it for long, certainly not for more than two or three years. They may well use this force against us during this period. So, the next couple of years or so are going to be critical for Pakistan.

21 | WEDNESDAY

📖 We have so far received no reply from the Russians on request for sale of arms, though this request was made on behest of Kosygin. I am causing a reminder to be sent to him.

22 | THURSDAY

📖 Came to Swat for a week's rest. Met Air Marshal Nur Khan[23] on the way in Peshawar and also saw my brother Mohammad Iqbal, who is convalescing in Lady Reading Hospital. He suffered a heart attack.

Nur Khan told me that the Americans are not playing the game in supply of spares for even non-lethal equipment. All sorts of excuses are being made for delay.

23 | FRIDAY

📖 I have always been fascinated by Professor Parkinson's writings. His book on the future history of mankind is most revealing. His latest publication is Parkinson's *Law of Delay*. In every organization there is 'Abominable No Man'. Says 'No' to everything, because to say 'Yes' requires an obligation to carry out something. No good arguing with 'No Man'. Raise the level and get to 'Yes Man', which every organization has. And so on.

26 | MONDAY

📖 The deputy foreign minister of the Soviet Union, Nikolai Pavlovich Firyubin, came to see me in Swat. His objective was to gain support on the stand they are taking on different world problems in the current General Assembly. Problems like disarmament, non-proliferation of nuclear weapons, Vietnam, decolonisation, future of Southwest Africa, etc. are involved. Our views are not dissimilar.

I brought up the question of more economic aid, supply of arms and the danger of arming India to such an extent. He took note of these things and promised to convey my views to his government. The general impression one gets is that the Soviets are happy about the manner in which our relations are developing and so are we. It is in our interest that our relations with the Soviets should gain depth. We can then develop greater leverage with the USA and India.

The Soviets seem to be hesitant in supplying us arms even though Kosygin had repeatedly promised to me. I am sending him a letter of reminder.

27 | TUESDAY

📖 Went to the Kalam Valley at the head of Swat Valley for a day. In fact, there are two main valleys from the village of Kalam with beautiful rivers flowing through them. We motored up these valleys part of the way. The scenery was fantastic. The roads have made all the difference to the life of the people. They can get their products out and get their requirements in so cheaply. All villages are connected by a bus service. They hardly had any winter crop in the past. Now the agriculture department has developed a strain of wheat for them which does well on those heights. All this has remobilised the life of the people. There are schools, dispensaries and rest houses in all places of note.

On the way to Kalam, we found many signs of progress and prosperity. The Wali[24] has done a lot for his people. There is a great influx of tourists, especially in the summer. Small hotels and rest houses are, therefore, springing up everywhere. The trouble with the Wali is that he is not interested in agriculture and horticulture and is not prepared to take advice or learn. If he did, a lot of development could take place increasing the income of the people and the state manifold.

The drive up the valley of Swat is by itself soul satisfying, but the beauty of the side valleys, which are many, is fantastic and breathtaking. There are good shingle roads to practically all of them.

28 | WEDNESDAY

📖 Attended a luncheon party given by the Wali's father,[25] who is now about 85 and not in very good state of health, though mentally still alert. In traditional old Pathan style the guest and the servants all sat on the same table and had the same food. One can't help being moved by such demonstration of basic equality in Muslim society. But that is why ruling or leading Muslims is so much more different, because the leader is regarded just a senior amongst equals. This sounds good, but has been responsible for the virtues of Muslim leaders not being recognized in their lifetime. They are revered when dead and of no use.

📖 Dictated to Altaf Gauhar[26] my views on the problems modern Muslim societies face in harmonizing the requirements of technological and scientific age with the precepts of Islam as expected to be applied by the priest class. This is meant to go as a chapter in the book. I am writing my views which may arouse controversy, but it should be of some interest to thinking people.

📖 Held a session with the Commissioner and the Political Agents of Dir and Malakand on the problems of these areas. Dir state is in a mess. There are several intricate problems to be resolved. This is going to be a time consuming affair.

📖 General Musa has announced the names of his new cabinet. He has only retained six out of the old ministers. There is a vacancy for four more. So, the chase by the prospective candidates, who are many, is on: I am the quarry.

29 | THURSDAY

📖 Returned to Rawalpindi. Dropped into the Centre Mess of the Punjab Regiment. Met JCOs and officers. They are an impressive lot.

📖 Have received a communication from the Chinese Ambassador that his government would like to assure us that the Chinese Muslims will not be allowed to be molested by the Red Guards. This is in response to the concern I had expressed to him some time ago. I am glad that I have been able to serve the cause of Chinese Muslims in a small way.

2 | SUNDAY

📖 Musa came to see me today. We discussed:

a. Completion of his cabinet.
b. Situation in Balochistan.
c. Countering Maududi's nefarious activities.
d. Treatment to detainees who have wilfully broken the law in spite of repeated warnings.
e. Problems of Dir and Bajaur and Swat.

I think he is getting into his job. The administration is feeling relieved and as someone put it, they feel that they have been reinstated.

📖 I have been very concerned about the cyclone in East Pakistan. We don't yet know what is the extent of damage, but it must be considerable. All the coastal districts have been badly hit.

📖 Attended General Habibullah's[27] daughter's wedding in Peshawar.

📖 The Saudi ambassador came and delivered a letter from King Faisal in reply to one I sent him. He is very thankful for the Air Force team we sent him to examine his air defence problems and agreed to see how else the two Air Forces could be of assistance to each other. My objective is to see what assistance we can get from them in case of trouble.

3 | MONDAY

📖 There has been a devastating cyclone again in East Pakistan affecting several coastal districts. Chittagong town has been worst hit. A lot of loss of human life and cattle, crops and property has been reported. I have sanctioned Rs 10 lakhs for relief work. I feel sorry for the people of East Pakistan. They suffer one calamity after another, but also admire their courage and the way they bear it. Last winter their crops failed through a long drought, then two bouts of extensive floods and now this cyclone.

📖 For the coming year or so we are going to go through a difficult period on account of food shortage. Some two and a half million tons have to be procured, mostly against our cash, as the Americans are getting very tight fisted with PL 480 issues. This is going to be a big drain on the country's resources on top of enhanced defence procurements.

📖 Attended a farewell dinner by General Yahya for General Musa.

6 | THURSDAY

📖 The American ambassador[28] came to see me and discussed the following points:

a. The Americans mean no ill will to Pakistan and especially East Pakistan. Any suspicions about the bona fides of the Americans intentions is ill-founded.

b. Gave their programme of PL 480 issues. Said that they have now decided to give 30,000 tons of edible oils.

c. Gave me a summary of their assessment of the food problem in East Pakistan and the means to be adopted to meet the situation.

d. Said that it would be a good thing if we continue with the works programme. Being new he was not fully conversant with the scheme, but he was told that it was doing a lot of good to the countryside and helping the regime in maintaining stability. I told him that it was doing a lot of good to their prestige too as people knew that these resources come from PL 480 proceeds. If PL 480 commodities are put on loan basis as the Congress intends doing, I have no doubt that the American image in the eyes of the people will suffer. I hoped that he would convey this to President Johnson and to the Congressmen. I have promised to send him a paper on this.

e. Said that Washington's assessment was that the Pakistani press was still bad on Vietnam etc. I told him that people's minds are inflamed on Vietnam and this inevitably gets reflected in the press. We do attempt to counsel restraint, but we don't have absolute control over the press and some of it is in opposition. They even write against us. And what about the lies the American press writes against us?

My assessment that the present ambassador is a good man. He is doing his best to improve relations.

📖 Interviewed seven candidates for judgeship for West Pakistan High Court in conjunction with the law minister and the governor. Only two were selected against the requirement of three. The material produced was poor. It is surprising that it should be so in a profession which is so over-manned.

---

7 | FRIDAY

📖 Mr Bhutto recently passed through Rawalpindi after a visit to almost all the capitals in Europe and the Middle East. He has been in, so to say, expectation of extensive conquest. Apart from anything else, where does he get this much foreign exchange from I don't know. The British have a notion that he is being paid heavily by a foreign power.

Some people went to see him in Pindi. The impression they got was that he is very bitter against me. Said that he was not going to contest presidential elections in 1970. He is still young and can wait till 1975 or 1980. He seems to have a feeling of insecurity. He has unbounded ambition, but NO firm political base in his district or Sindh. Sindhis don't trust him and are happy that he is out of power. So, he is going to concentrate on the student community and the leftists.

📖 Shahab[29] has returned from The Hague and has taken over as Secretary of Education. Briefed him on his duties. It is essential that the educational reforms should be fully implemented. The textbooks should be centrally prepared and change over to Urdu or Bengali, as the medium of instruction should be done rationally and scientifically. Shahab has a literary bent of mind. He should do well.

📖 President Cevdet Sunay of Turkey arrived with his entourage from Tehran on a five-day state visit. I had met him before when he was the Chief of Staff of the Turkish Army. He seems a mature and balanced man. He was given a rousing reception on arrival.

8 | SATURDAY

📖 Took President Sunay to Peshawar in the morning. He was given a big welcome. The Peshawar University conferred upon him the LLD degree. He was then taken around the campus, which is new, and was deeply impressed. After lunch at Government House, which was given by the governor, we returned to Pindi. Saw Islamabad. Gave him a briefing on the war between India and Pakistan. There was a return banquet by him in the evening. The Turks felt relaxed. They all wanted photographs taken with me. Before departure for Peshawar, there was discussion for an hour or so. President Sunay explained their foreign policy, attitude to CENTO[30] and the RCD. Their foreign policy is based on adherence to NATO, friendship with the West, at the same time normalizing relations with the Soviet bloc whilst remaining apprehensive of Communism. They also want to have a measure of understanding with the Arab world. They would like CENTO to be strengthened. They have firm belief in RCD and promised full support to it. On Cyprus they would be satisfied if given satisfaction on treaty rights. Occasional talks between them and the Greeks seem to go on, though they are not very optimistic of the outcome.

I told them we value Turkish friendship and we shall do everything possible to strengthen RCD, but we have no faith in CENTO. And how can we when no one came to our assistance during Indian aggression? The Americans failed to honour their written commitment to Pakistan. Not only that, they stopped military supplies and even now won't sell us spare parts, etc. However, we have no intention of giving up CENTO and that is out of consideration for the Turks and the Iranians.

Then I told them why it was necessary to normalize relations with China and the Soviet Union. We cannot afford to antagonize them after what the Americans have done to us. Then I gave them my impressions of communism. It is not an exportable or importable commodity. It is an internal growth of a society, which is mismanaged, has lost hope and faith, and is shattered. Wherever such conditions exist communism will come. That is what happened in Russia and China. So, as long as we ensure that conditions in our countries remain satisfactory, we don't have to fear much through physical contact with communism. President Sunay did not quite agree, but it set him thinking.

9 | SUNDAY

📖 Saw President Sunay off. He was flying to Lahore.

📖 Took a plane to Lyallpur and then flew into Karachi. I saw the Ayub Agriculture Research Institute at Lyallpur. This institute was started only in 1961. Only one laboratory is functioning so far. Others are being built and will be occupied and operated in due course.

Whatever work has been done so far is of a very superior quality. They have achieved a breakthrough in wheat, cotton, maize and fodder crops. New strain of high yield quality have been developed. I am impressing on the Agriculture Department to universalise their use through the Union Councils; unless we do that we are not going to solve the food problem.

📖 Mr Uqaili[31] came to see me in the evening. He just came back from US. Told me of his efforts to obtain more food and support for the Tarbela dam project. The food situation is worrying. There is a deficiency of some 2.3 million tons. In terms of money its cash would be about 100 crores. How can this poor country bear such a burden?

Chances of support for Tarbela are bright. His impression was that in the matter of goods supply, the Americans were playing politics with us. They complain that our press is not sympathetic on Vietnam. Curious people. How can we muzzle the press on an emotional matter like Vietnam? Have they been able to muzzle theirs? Besides, our press, at times, is just as critical of us and some portion of it deliberately and maliciously so. They talk loud about the freedom of press in their country and imagine that other people are not listening.

📖 Saw a person called Akhund from Hyderabad. Interviewed him as a prospective minister in West Pakistan. He is a man of about fifty years old, very well educated, presentable and stable. Has sound ideas inspiring confidence. At present principal of the law college. I was very pleased to see him and have recommended him to the governor for acceptance. I have also approved of the appointment of Allah Yar, from Khunda, Sarwar Khan from Dera Ismail Khan, and Ahmed Saeed Kirmani from Lahore as ministers. They are all good and loyal people. In the presidential form of government, people will accept a mediocre as a minister, but not a rogue, however brilliant.

10 | MONDAY

📖 Spent the morning on the beaches of Sandspit. The sea is much calmer because the monsoon winds are dropping. It was nice and cool and very pleasant.

11 | TUESDAY

📖 Received President Sunay after his return from East Pakistan. He was very impressed with the greenery, colour and rivers in East Pakistan. He was also impressed with what was going on in China. This he was told by Governor Monem Khan,[32] who has just returned from a visit to China.

📖 Altaf Gauhar gave me details of the contract which the Oxford University Press has offered for the publication of my book. I have agreed with them. They have got the right of publication other than Urdu and Bengali. But when you come to think of it, there is very little money in book writing. They give you a very small percentage of the proceeds. However, moneymaking is not my concern. I have written this book for the satisfaction of the people of Pakistan.

12 | WEDNESDAY

📖 Another session of talks took place with President Sunay and his foreign minister. The Turks were after finding out whether we were on the side of the WEST or not. I said the answer was YES if the Middle East was attacked. But we cannot ignore the Soviets and the Chinese as the Americans have been found to be unreliable friends. They support India, our avowed enemy, against us. The Turks were lucky: They have only one neighbour, whereas we have three. In view of the American lukewarmness toward us, we cannot afford to antagonize the communist powers. This is a compulsion of geography and circumstances, which all those who wish to have friendship with us must understand.

I told them that our mutual friendship was progressing satisfactorily, but friendship was not divisible between peace and war time. I wanted to know what the Turks could do for us in the event of aggression by India. They asked for time to consider the matter and be ready to discuss at the foreign minister's level during the next RCD meeting.

President Sunay and party left for Turkey. They were given a rousing send off.

13 | THURSDAY

Dr Ishtiaq Hussain Qureshi,[33] Vice Chancellor, Karachi University, came to see me. Amongst other things, he talked of the Muslim League records that were seized by the police at the time of declaration of Martial Law. They are still in the possession of the police. He was deeply concerned about their safety and future. They are records of immense importance to the history of Muslims in the subcontinent and must be preserved. So I am arranging for them to be handed over to the Karachi University for sorting and categorization.

Our food position is getting critical. Substantial drought followed by the devastating floods and cyclonic systems have played havoc with food production. Therefore, our stocks are getting dangerously low. So I have written a personal letter to the agriculture minister to the USA to expedite deliveries of promised grain and also meet our total requirements. I know Freeman;[34] he might play.

14 | FRIDAY

Flew into Tehran and was received by the Shahinshah, who showed considerable warmth and also regard for Pakistan for self-preservation. He realises that if he were to succumb to Indian pressure, his country's turn will come next. After the usual guard of honour, saw a large number of Pakistanis in festive mood. Our community here is increasing.

I am put up in a house belonging to the sister of the Shah in the compound of the former Saadabad Palace in Shimran, where the Shah and Queen are also staying. This is an ultra-modern house designed by an American. Looks fragile and complicated. I would not like to live here for any length of time. Went for a drive around Tehran. Tremendous development is taking place. New modern colonies are being built and the roads are full of vehicles. At rush hour, traffic jams as in Europe are experienced.

On arrival in Tehran, was taken to the opening ceremony of a mosque built in the university campus. Met the university and the Iranian dignitaries. It was a simple and impressive ceremony. The mosque is designed by an Iranian architect to blend the traditional and the modern. The result is pleasing to the eye. The main building has a large dome supported not on side walls but on pillars set at an angle with Quranic inscriptions written in crevices on them.

The Shah and the Queen came to dinner with me. The prime minister and our ambassador with their wives were also present. By a very happy coincidence, it was the Queen's birthday. I proposed her health. She is a very fine person indeed and feels very relaxed in my presence. She is a lady of pleasing and human qualities. After dinner, the Shah and I went out into the compound. He pointed out the house he had built for his mother-in-law and also a house his brother had built for himself. It is a twenty-room house but not occupied because the prince divorced his wife one month after marriage. I am told divorce is a common occurrence in Iran. It is certainly not frowned upon. The Shah complained that his brother now insists that the Shah should buy his house. I told him that this is the way of useless relations all over the world. They like you to suffer for their folly.

16 | SUNDAY

The day before leaving Karachi I had received a telegram from our foreign minister before leaving New York in which he gave the gist of Indian foreign minister's talk with him. Apparently Swaran Singh asked to see Pirzada. Swaran Singh proposed that we hold talks in a quiet place like Geneva on settlement of Kashmir and other disputes and reduction of armed forces. They have realised that Pandit Nehru was wrong in not accepting my advice which I gave him from time to time. He asked if someone from amongst them could meet me in London during the state visit. He also sought our cooperation on the Security Council seat. If we support them this time, they promised to support us next year when the Japanese vacate their seat.

I don't know how genuine the Indians are. Past experiences do not encourage optimism. However, it would not be wise to reject this proposal. Maybe something may come out of it.

Meeting in Geneva will do no good. My view is that such meetings should take place in Delhi, the source of mischief. Our high commissioner could meet the Indians at any level.

17 | MONDAY

The Shah is also disenchanted with CENTO like us. He thinks it has lost its value, but we should not quit it until we replace it with something worthwhile which will have to be regional. He thinks the answer is for Afghanistan, Pakistan and Iran to get together in as many fields as possible. But will the Afghans listen and will the Russians allow them to do so.

Had further discussions with the Shah at his residence. Mr [Amir Abbas] Hoveida and a representative of the General Staff were also present. After discussion, it was agreed that our foreign minister should meet the Iranian foreign minister and the prime minister under the chairmanship of the Shah on 10th December to discuss respective foreign policies and to determine the circumstances under which military aid would be required for each country. The military comity should then be formed to work out details under the heads I have described earlier. I regard this as a very satisfactory start.

The Shah also promises to get his people to look into the problem of oil exploration concession for us on preferential basis. Mr Yousaf has had lengthy discussions with the head of INOC [Iranian National Oil Compay]. He was very helpful. The correct answer is that we should join as partners with the Iranians, without paying any royalty in return for an assured market of oil in Pakistan. Our annual imports of oil amount to approximately six million tonnes. This will increase as time goes on. So it should be a great inducement for the Iranians. The question of joint projects under the RCD came up for discussion. The Turks for several reasons are reluctant to participate. The answer is for us to work on bilateral service with India and the Turks wherever possible.

Whenever the question of political tie-up between the two countries comes up, the Shah, in a diplomatic way, expresses doubts about the intentions of the Bengalis. He said, 'Why do they say and do suicidal things.' I wish those Bengalis who behave irresponsibly would realise the damage they are doing themselves and Pakistan. I kept on reassuring that only a lunatic fringe talks in those terms.

18 | TUESDAY

📖 The Iranian Air Force celebrated their day. A large number of people gathered together on the air-field. The Shah and the Queen took me with them to the display. Iran has now a sizable air force, mostly bought by their own resources. They perform well. Given this pace, they should be an effective service in due course.

The notable event was the participation of twenty-four Pakistani aircrafts in this display. This was done secretly to demonstrate that the Canadian aircraft bought from Germany by Iran for us had gone back after refit in Pakistan. Apart from that, it demonstrated how quickly and without any difficulty a sizable air force can be shifted from one country to another. I hope the Shah felt reassured.

During talks with the Shah, the future of India came under discussion. He felt India is bound to split up if they go on the way they are going. I have my doubts. It is not easy to break up a country which has managed to establish a central government and raise a centrally controlled army. Such a country can only split up if the army splits up and that is not likely to happen unless the army takes over political control resulting in rivalries and jealousy amongst members of the armed forces from different parts of the country. It must be remembered that regional loyalties, class and caste prejudices are very strong and basic in Indian society. Its nature is evasive. Besides, there are strong forces that would like to see India remain in one piece. United States, Russia and Britain are certainly interested to see India united. As far as Pakistan is concerned, it will have to live on mobilisation basis so long as India is to remain an independent country. There are no indications so far that India will let us live in peace.

22 | SATURDAY

📖 In contacts with the Chinese, I found that while they regard America as the enemy, they are very bitter against the Russians. Several reasons are advanced, but they do add up to extreme bitterness. The real reason probably is that the Russians denied them atomic secrets, withdrew large number of technicians en bloc and do not wish to see China develop into a power which can challenge their supremacy in the communist world, Asia and the world at large.

I happened to inquire from Mr Kosygin the cause of estrangement with China. He said that Mao Tse-tung wants to be regarded as the Buddha of Communism and wants to dictate to us as how we should run our affairs. Also, the Chinese malign us without any justification for collusion with the Americans. This is most galling and unbelievable.

Whatever may be the reasons Russia–China conflict had an extremely adverse affect on our security. Both the Russian and the American policy have coincided in making India strong as a bulwark against China. I don't think they will succeed in that but they have succeeded in making India a real menace for us.

Mr Kosygin told me that would it not be wonderful if the Soviet Union, India, and Pakistan got together. The combination of some 800 million people would be formidable. I understand the reason for their growing interest in the subcontinent.

📖 When in Iran, I was anxious to find out that whereas the friendship and understanding of the Iranian government with us was wholehearted, was this the case with the people also. I was told that this was largely true. The reason is that except with Pakistan, their relation with other neighbours due to past history and present tensions are not good. So they do find comfort in our company. Besides, all those who go back after visiting Pakistan are full of admiration. The Iranians have a working arrangement with the Turks, but there is no real trust. This is due to past history, but also due to the Turkish attitude. They are too keen to be recognized as Europeans.

2 | WEDNESDAY

📖 Mr Harriman, the roving US Ambassador, came to see me to explain on President Johnson's behalf as to what transpired at the Manila conference. He said that US was prepared to withdraw its forces from South Vietnam within six months if North Vietnam promised to do the same and ceased hostilities. But it seems that North Vietnam is not prepared to agree to this. The Manila Communiqué may be considered vague, but it was negotiable on the conference table. They are even prepared to discuss the North Vietnamese four-point proposal. But it seems that North Vietnam is not yet prepared to come to the conference table.

Mr Harriman said that a demand was made that the Americans should cease bombing of North Vietnam without pre-conditions to give that country the time to come forward with a constructive proposal to end hostilities. This, the President of USA was not prepared to do unless he had some indication of reciprocity on the part of Hanoi. He was compelled to take this stand politically and militarily. When bombing was stopped last time, Hanoi used the opportunity to send large-scale war materials and men to South Vietnam.

He said that initially things were improving but this problem is not susceptible to a military solution. There will have to be a political solution and the President is anxious to find it, if only Hanoi would come to the conference table. He said the US objective was limited. They had no intention of extending the war to China. And yet the US military build-up in Vietnam continues. There is talk of increasing US forces to 750,000 in a year or so. People like President Eisenhower are advocating an all out war to win victory.

I told Mr Harriman that if their intention was to win a military victory, and have a government of their liking, then they must be prepared to stay in Vietnam for another twenty-five years or so, but if they did not want this then they should allow the Vietnamese to have a government of their own choice.

Obviously there will have to be two Vietnams in the beginning but thereafter it is up to the people of the two countries to decide whether they wish to join each other or not. My belief is that Vietnamese are fighting for their freedom. They have been doing this for a long time. Once they are free, they are not going to allow another power to have a say in their affairs. So any fear of Chinese or Russian dominance is ill-founded. I told him to tell this to his President.

Mr Harriman was critical of General de Gaulle. He said that the General would have been constructive if he had given advice to both sides. Instead, he hurled everything on the USA. He was also critical of the statement made in Delhi, as he put it, by two men and a woman recently. He was obviously referring to the Tito-Nasser-Indira statement.

He is an amazing old man. During the last couple of days, he visited Manila, Jakarta, Colombo, Delhi and Rawalpindi. After seeing me, he moved on to Tehran to see the Shah and intends to reach Rome tomorrow morning to see the Pope.

With Harriman was Mr Locke, the US Ambassador in Pakistan. He said that his government told him to tell us that US was considering opening military aid to us. But before doing so, the following points will have to be discussed:

a. US policy was that there should be peace between India and Pakistan and that any military conflict should be avoided.

b. There should be proportionate reduction in the armed forces of the two countries.
c. Secret talks should open between the two countries to discuss the above.
d. US does not expect Pakistan to discontinue relations with China but does not want China to be the chief supplier of arms to Pakistan.

I told him that I can agree with a, b and c straight away. Further details can be discussed with our foreign minister and foreign secretary. But about d, the position can be stated very simply. When India attacked and USA refused to come to our assistance despite their solemn undertaking, we had to go to China for military aid which they generously gave. Bulk of it has arrived, and some more has to come. But it is limited in quantity as their production capacity is limited. And moreover, they don't produce sophisticated stuff, so we have gone for those to Russia. So if the Americans don't open up military aid in the near future, we shall have no option but to go to Russia.

Mr Locke said that US regards Pakistan and India as friends but they are not prepared to give one or the other the power of veto over them. I told him that we have no intention of dictating US policy, but we have a right to expect them not to build up India against us or our interests.

5 | SATURDAY

📖 After discussing with the foreign minister and the foreign secretary, I caused the following message to be given verbally to the American ambassador:

a. We are prepared to enter into negotiations with India on armament reduction but at the same time, there must be meaningful talks on Kashmir too. The best venue is Delhi. Our High Commissioner will represent us.
b. There are definite monetary limitations on armament supplies from China. The bulk of the equipment has arrived. The rest will take some time.
c. If the Americans don't open up armament supplies to us soon, we shall have to go to Russia. Also, the supplies must be on disposal rates.
d. The Americans should not stand in our way in purchasing surplus equipment of American origin from Germany.
e. It seems that the Americans are playing politics with us on food supply. Whereas to India they have delivered 10 million tonnes and have promised another 8 million. With us, they are quibbling over small quantities.

📖 Maulana Rashid Turabi[35] came to see me this morning. He had been to Iran recently and had long discussions with the ulema there. He was very surprised to find them hostile to the Shah even though they got enormous allowances from the government. He told them how unjust they were in operating against the man who was doing his best for the country. If, by any chance he went, there would be nothing but chaos in Iran. But he also felt that the condition of the masses is deplorable. There is hardly any middle class in the country. In this lies the danger for Iran.

Rashid Turabi has been asking for the conference of world ulema to be called next year. I have put this matter in the hands of the law minister and I want that purposeful discussion should take place. This is to discuss problems that face Muslim societies and how Islam can help in their resolution.

The Saudi ambassador came and delivered a verbal message on behalf of the king and his government. They are very pleased by the stand taken by our foreign minister on Arab affairs in the General Assembly as they were pleased with his decision not to attend the banquet of the mayor of New York who cancelled the dinner party arranged in honour of King Faisal during his stay in USA. They were happy also that we had withdrawn in favour of Syria for the Security Council seat which the Arabs claimed to be theirs.

I have told Altaf Gauhar that he should induce the press to publish:

a. Competitive prices of commodities in Pakistan and adjoining countries.
b. An article daily, on one or the other projects either under construction or executed. These should be of great informative value to the people.

6 | SUNDAY

Being a Sunday, I wanted to go out to sea for fishing but the Navy advised against it as there was a bit of a swell in the sea, so went to beaches with my wife and the grandchildren. Spent the morning and came back for lunch.

Flew to Hyderabad for a stay and shoot with Ijaz Talpur[36] at Tando Mohammad Khan. Went to see my farm at Kolab in the evening. The sugarcane and wheat crop looked good. Colonel Sadiq looks after the farm very well.

Met a large number of Sindhi friends at dinner. They were Ijaz's guests. It is always a pleasure to be with those people and listen to their lovely music. How reliable they are I don't know, but they are very hospitable and generous. Some of the most enjoyable parts of my life I have spent in Sindh. I shall never forget those times. My first Sindhi friend was Ali Gohar Mahar from Khangarh, Sukkur. He was a jewel of a man. Though uneducated, I used to be fascinated by his company. He died a few years ago.

7 | MONDAY

Tando Mohammad Khan: shot partridge at Kula, Kabalpur. Farooq, Gohar, and Tahir, Amirzeb[37] and Major General Rafi accompanied me, shot for about four hours, my bag was 76.

Discovered that the army wanted 1,000 units of a certain type of truck. The director of purchases asked for tenders specifying a vehicle of Japanese make, there being only one agent of the make, Ahmad Jaffer. The price quoted was 3000 dollars above the real price. I was naturally burnt up with this swindle. I called Major General Rafi to ring up the defence minister to check up and let me know why this happened. Luckily he got my message an hour before the letter of intention was going to be signed.

I believe Ghulam Faruque,[38] who was the defence advisor until lately, knew about this case. I am surprised that he took no cognisance or corrective action. Or that is the trouble with Faruque. He has very little regard for public funds. I hope my action will enable the army to buy 1,600 vehicles instead of 1,000 with the same money.

8 | TUESDAY

📖 Did a duck shoot beyond Sajawal, total bag 305 birds. I shot 85 and Tahir Ayub 71. Spent the night in the Sajawal rest house.

9 | WEDNESDAY

📖 Went back to the same area for a partridge shoot. Total bag 109. I shot 63 birds. Came to Tando Mohammad Khan for the night.

📖 Attended a meeting of Muslim League workers of Hyderabad district, basic democrats and other notables. Mir Ijaz read out an address. Though the Muslim League reorganization work is going on well, they had a lot of problems connected with land and agriculture. This area, apart from being saline and waterlogged, is full of pests and insects. Very few crops flourish here except sugarcane and wheat. And sugarcane prices have fallen because of our high production of sugar during the last season. This is naturally disturbing the farmers. However, they are offered rupees 2 per maund of sugarcane which is not bad. They made several other demands too expecting all sorts of concessions, which the government cannot make.

I pleaded for vigorous efforts in involvement for the Muslim League. Grow more food and taking active part in the family planning campaign.

It was a happy and cheerful gathering and Mir Ijaz had made good arrangements. I am happy to see this lad shaping so well.

📖 Motored to Tando Jam near Hyderabad and inspected the agriculture research institute and the college and later the agricultural atomic research centre. Very good research work is going on in both the places. New strains of seeds of high yield qualities are being developed and the answer found to some of the crop diseases. The requirement is for these results to be applied in the fields very intelligently and actively and extensive work is needed. I was told that the scientists in these places, although doing complementary work, are not even on speaking terms with each other let alone comparing experiments with each other. I told Mr Farooqui to see that this gets tied up. It is surprising how perfectly sensible people can behave like children.

📖 Flew into Karachi.

📖 Chaudhry Zafarullah,[39] a judge of the World Court, came to see me. He emphasized the need for putting more and more emphasis on economics. Also pleaded the cause of Dr Ashiq Hussain Batalvi,[40] who is a very old Muslim Leaguer and lives in London. He is carrying out research there on the Pakistan movement and has written one or two books too. He is financially not well off.

📖 Called Admiral Ahsan[41] and told him to examine the possibility of extending the Karachi harbour by walling in the open sea where depths are suitable. He promised to examine this in conjunction with the port trust. Some such arrangement will have to be made and quickly as the existing capacity of Karachi harbour is employed to the full. TV services in Pakistan are going to be extended shortly. This facility is a potent instrument for getting out mass education. To ensure this is necessary, a suitable committee should be set up to lay down and supervise programmes.

📖 Large numbers of people pester me for interviews. I accommodate as many as I can, but it is becoming a tiresome business. They do not seem to realize that I could well spend this time to their better advantage in other ways.

11 | FRIDAY

📖 The defence adviser explained the case of purchase of 3-ton vehicles from Japan. He is satisfied that all possible precautions have been taken to ensure that the price paid is reasonable. He also showed me the gist of discussions that took place with a French firm regarding the purchase of Mirage III. This is a very expensive aircraft costing nearly rupees two crores each and the terms offered by the French are hard. He wanted me to take this matter up with the French in Paris.

12 | SATURDAY

📖 Held a meeting with the governors and ministers. The following points were discussed:

a. Amendments to the basic democracies law to simplify the method of preparation and amendment of the electoral rules.
b. Review of the laws concerning the volunteers and workers for the political parties. The demand is to put them in some sort of uniform and drill them to instil discipline. East Pakistan governor was particularly insistent. As the matter is not free from danger, it was decided to let East Pakistan examine its future and bring it up for discussion and decision during the National Assembly session in Dacca.
c. Uniformity of law in both the provinces concerning the removal of an undesirable chairman of a union council and committee. It was decided that no removal motion be allowed during the first year. That after 'no removal motion' before the expiry of one year from the previous one. The idea is that whilst providing for the removal of an undesirable chairman, the institution should not be allowed to become unstable through continued harassment.
d. Mr Altaf Hussain[42] has just returned from a visit to Saudi Arabia, Kuwait, Iraq, and Libya after exploring the possibilities of joint exploration of oil in these countries. He has brought back an encouraging report from Saudi Arabia and Libya who are very kind and considerate with him.
e. Several other points of minor nature were also discussed.

The finance minister, deputy chairman, planning commission, and the finance secretary gave a review of foreign exchange earnings. They expect a considerable shortfall from the earlier estimates and also greater outlay on food procurement. In consequence, it is inevitable that imports will have to be curtailed. We gave a lunch party to those attending the meeting.

📖 A four-man Jordanian mission headed by a minister arrived to escort me to Jordan tomorrow. I was deeply touched by this gesture. Apparently this is a well known Arab custom.

📖 Attended the silver jubilee of Habib Bank[43] and laid the foundation stone of their new building which is going to be twenty-one stories high. Later attended a banquet given by them. Some 2,000 guests were present. Habibs are very fine people. Deeply religious, humble, good businessmen, but thoroughly honest. They take care of their small investors. They and the Dawoods[44] are the only two firms that do that. The rest of the business community or at least the ones I know, are nothing short of scoundrels. They black market, fudge on taxation and are most reluctant to pay dividends to their shareholders. Of course, the taxation law too is to blame. Once the dividend is declared the tax becomes due. What should happen is that the individuals should be taxed on receipt of dividends. I have told this when the finance minister[45] comes. He has promised to make the necessary change.

13 | SUNDAY

📖 Took off for Jordan at 8:30 a.m. Reached Amman at 10:20 local time. Was met by King Hussein and other dignitaries. Inspected a combined Guard of Honour. Was impressed by their turn out. They looked tough and well-trained.

On arrival at the palace, was told of an Israeli attack-brigade strike supported by tanks and air on a Jordanian post of company strength covering a number of villages which were Israeli objectives. After a sharp clash, the Israelis withdrew. Jordanians suffered a brigadier, a major and five other ranks killed and several wounded. Israeli casualties are claimed to be much larger in men and matériel. Two Israeli and one Jordanian planes were shot down.

The king told me that this was the largest clash that had taken place for a long time. Though the Jordanian policy is not to cause unnecessary provocation, some Arabs, perhaps from Syria, occasionally carry out sabotage in Israel. The Israelis claim to have acted in retaliation. They may also have been emboldened by feuds amongst the Arab countries. I caused our foreign minister to issue a statement of sympathy for Jordan and for condemnation of Israel.

Called on the king at his villa. I found the king natural, easy to get on with, courteous and warm-hearted. His physical bravery is, of course, well known.

I told the king that only if there was unity among the Arab countries and they were ready to engage the Israelis from all directions, the Israelis would think twice before doing anything against any one of them. For instance, on this occasion, why could Egypt not send its MIG-21s to engage its Mirages. He said they were busy with Muslims in Yemen.

14 | MONDAY

📖 Went straight to Bait-ul-Mukaddas and was introduced to a large of number of people including Christian priests of different denominations. We saw the Dome of the Rock, Masjid al-Aqsa, and the tomb of Maulana Mohammad Ali Jauhar.

15 | TUESDAY

📖 Thanked [King Hussein] for the reception and the support Jordan gave us during the war with India. This is what we expect from a brother Muslim country and that is what they can expect from us.

Explained our foreign policy towards the big powers, India, and the Muslim world. On Muslim Summit Conference, the need is apparent but should be held when large numbers of Muslim countries agree to attend.

Specific points of cooperation between Pakistan and Jordan:

a.   Army: A team of experts has been sent for. They will look into matters connected with organization, equipment and tactical concepts of the Jordanian army.
b.   Air Force: A team has already looked into the defence problem. Other training facilities required are being looked into.
c.   Economic: We can buy 26,000 tonnes of phosphate increasing to 600,000 tonnes but Jordan will have to give us the same tariff concessions on our goods as to those of Lebanon and Syria. The Jordanians agreed to consider.
d.   Joint Ventures: Opening of a bank, establishment of jute, cotton and sugar mills are under consideration. Also under consideration are avoidance of double taxation, Treaty of Friendship and Commerce, and establishment of air ceilings.
e.   Cultural: We shall consider giving more scholarships to Jordanian students.

17 | THURSDAY

📖 Landed at London airport at 2 p.m. The Duke of Edinburgh received me. He seemed very relaxed and cheerful. I inspected a guard of honour provided by the air force; saw a lot of our people who had come to welcome me at the airport. They were in a festive mood. Motored to the Tate Gallery where the Queen and leading military and civil leaders received me. Field Marshal Lord Alexander was also present. He greeted me with *asalaamul-aleikum*. I inspected the guard of honour provided by the Scots Guards. The courtesies over, we all mounted horse carriages escorted by the Horse Guard and moved to Buckingham Palace where I was to spend the night.

The route was tastefully decorated by the Union Jack and Pakistan flags and a large number of people lined the route in spite of the fact that it was working hours. They were cheering and smiling. Every now and then a Pakistani would shout 'Pakistan Zindabad'. A British friend remarked that they have never seen the British crowd so cheerful. It was the weather, the pageantry and the sight of a foreigner who did not look so different to them—I was in uniform—made them relax.

On arrival at the palace, the Queen introduced me to her staff. I, in turn, introduced my staff to her. She took me to my living quarters and took a lot of care in explaining facilities. She too was in an unusually cheerful mood. Everyone noticed and remarked on it. She would come every now and then to my room to see that my kit was laid out properly and everything was in order.

Soon after arrival, I called on the Queen Mother. She took me and Naseem [Ayub Khan's daughter] to a separate room for tea. She is one of the most remarkable personalities I have ever met in my life. She is the embodiment of human kindness and warmth. It was a pleasure to be in her company. The other persons I can think of who can equal her is Shareen, wife of Agha Mustafa from Lahore and the other is the sister of General Cariappa.

I was taken to St. James Palace where the mayor and councillors of the Greater London Council and the mayor and councillors of the Westminster Council presented me with an address. I replied in suitable terms. This was followed by a banquet in the palace at night. I met a large number of my friends.

The Queen, during the dinner, spoke about her children, most of whom I knew. The youngest is only two and a half years old. When his father went to his room one morning, he shouted to him, 'Papa, hands up.' He probably learnt it from TV.

18 | FRIDAY

Harold Wilson called on me in the morning. Spoke about Vietnam, common market, Rhodesia and the Non-Proliferation Treaty. It does not look as if the solution to any of these problems is around the corner.

Visited the Engineers Exhibition accompanied by the Queen. Also gave an address. Attended a lunch given by the Commonwealth Secretary. He felt that the appointment of Mr Chagla as foreign minister was an indication that India wants to settle Kashmir with us. I said, on the contrary, our belief is that he had been hired to say things against us that Hindus would not like to say themselves.

Gave a talk on 'Pakistan Today' at the International Affairs Institute. The talk was followed by a large number of questions. I think it went off well and the audience seemed appreciative.

Attended a banquet given by the prime minister at Lancaster House. This was followed by a reception. A large number of people were invited. Harold Wilson was in good form. Showed his happiness on the appointment of Mr Pirzada as foreign minister. Thought that he was a gentleman and a loyal person. Did well at the prime minister's conference. He spoke about his own foreign minister, George Brown. Thought he was an intelligent and knowledgeable person who was doing a good job, but drinks too much and loses control of his tongue.

He said, 'I'm glad you got rid of Bhutto. He was not trustworthy.' Then he turned to me and said, 'Would you like a power reactor? I'll give you one. Ours are more efficient than others.' I said, 'It's going to cost about 16 million pounds.' He said, 'I understand.' I gratefully accepted the offer and caused a signal to be sent to Dr Usmani to come and meet me in London before departure.

21 | MONDAY

Saw atomic energy works directed to peaceful uses in the industrial estate outside Edinburgh. Was shown how radiation can be used in medicine, mineral and oil survey, etc.

22 | TUESDAY

📖 Visited Calder Hall, the first atomic plant in Britain. It has been operational for the past ten years. The scientists are very pleased with its performance. Next door at Wind Scale is a more modern reactor and it is called an advanced gas cooled reactor. This is supposed to be much more efficient and economical. Alongside this is a plutonium plant. What happens here is that used uranium from different plants in Britain and even outside is brought here in casings of lead and other metals. Uranium is then put into a crucible of chemicals which dissolves it. Then being put through several processes, plutonium and uranium is separated and stored separately and dispatched to different installations for use again.

This plant produces one tonne of plutonium a year, which is enough to produce about 350 atomic bombs. Uranium, however, is produced in large quantities. Plutonium is regarded as a very poisonous and dangerous metal and is handled with great care. Its packing and storage also needs great supervision.

23 | WEDNESDAY

📖 Visited Carrington Works of Shell Chemical where they make plastics of all description. It is a huge complex costing about 100 crore rupees. I was especially interested in its operation, because we too are going to embark on the manufacture of petrochemicals.

24 | THURSDAY

📖 Dr Usmani and Mr Akhtar, our ambassador in Paris, came to see me. I had asked them to come. We discussed financing problems of a nuclear station in Rupoor and also the British offer for a nuclear plant. The points for discussion with General de Gaulle were also discussed.

📖 Attended a conference with the prime minister and his colleagues at 10 Downing Street. Vietnam, Rhodesia and Indo-Pakistan relationships were discussed. Wilson asked me if there was any chance of solution of Kashmir. I said I see no sign; on the contrary, India is piling up arms and talking of introducing selective conscription. He was non-committal on Tarbela, but he told me that he was awaiting World Bank recommendations on Tarbela. When received, he will do his best to help. I think he might do something on the power reactor too.

25 | FRIDAY

📖 Went to see a factory where computers are manufactured. The British are quite well up in this technology. It is amazing what these machines can do at such a pace. It is a great time saving device in running big business or for that matter any complicated organization. I think we should adopt it more and more for the efficient running of our industry and installations.

26 | SATURDAY

📖 Shot pheasant at the Queen's estate with the Duke. The total bag was 479 birds shot among seven guns. I shot about 150 birds. The weather was wet and cold. It was a very enjoyable day all the same. These birds fly fast especially with a following wind, but I found no difficulty in shooting them.

28 | MONDAY

📖 Took leave of my hosts in Britain and flew to Paris in the evening. Stayed at the embassy. It is a palatial place and is the property of the government of Pakistan. It was bought cheaply some years ago. I wish we had the same everywhere, but perhaps finding ready cash was the problem.

29 | TUESDAY

📖 Met President De Gaulle at the Elysee Palace. He received me with warmth and asked me what the problems of Pakistan were. I told him in detail that our main problem was India. To get them to live at peace with us. All our attempts to this end have proved fruitless. Instead she is piling up arms beyond her needs or means. Consequently, we had to divert valuable resources for creation of a military deterrent. This is a suicidal game for both of us but India does not realise this. De Gaulle surprised me by saying that would not India disintegrate if Kashmir were settled. This is the usual Indian line which most countries have swallowed. I told him that that was not so. Kashmir was an international dispute recognised as such since the inception of India and Pakistan, whereas demand for autonomy or independence by a part of India was an internal problem. If India was so fragile, then what is the good of attempting to hold it together?

Our second problem is economic development and in that respect we find French credit very hard. The repayment period is short and the interest rate is very high. Entrepreneurs are reluctant to pick these credits. Currently, we are negotiating purchase of Mirage aircraft for the air force. The terms offered are very unsuitable. Same with other military orders. I told him how other countries were being very humane. Their terms are very soft. He promised to have this looked into.

We touched on Vietnam and power struggle amongst the super powers. He said he had tried hard with the Americans, but they won't listen. I told him that that was the trouble. No country in the world had decisive influence over the super powers; therefore, they feel they can do whatever they like. This is what makes today's world so dangerous.

The talks were followed by a luncheon party. De Gaulle gave a speech to which I replied. I invited him to come to Pakistan. He promised to do so.

30 | WEDNESDAY

📖 Took off from Paris at 10 a.m. by PIA Boeing and landed at Karachi at 2115 hours local time. Large number of people came to receive me.

📖 These long and fast journeys play havoc with a man's inner time clock. The sleep and eating time gets completely upset. However, I took a pill and managed to sleep a bit.

1 | THURSDAY

Ayub Awan[46] and the governor of West Pakistan and the defence minister[47] came to see me to transact business. Bhutto's acrobatics on politics were brought up by every one of them.

Mr Farooqui and the architect showed me the plan and model of president's house in Islamabad. It looked very attractive. I told them that the cost should be kept as low as possible.

Gave a reception to the dignitaries of the Colombo Plan. The conference was held in Karachi. About seventy guests attended.

I saw a telegram from the ambassador in New Delhi that Chagla had gone back on his earlier desire to meet our foreign minister in Geneva. He refuses to discuss Kashmir. It just shows what twisters the Hindus are. They have no word of honour.

2 | FRIDAY

Went to Nawabshah for a day shoot in the Pai forest. The bag was 135 partridges. I shot 79. It was a poor shoot. Something has gone wrong. There are not so many birds there now.

Large number of people had come to see me at the airport. An address was read out inviting me to accept presidentship for twenty years. I told them that was wrong. People must exercise their right of choice every five years in accordance with the constitution. Little do they know that I should be very happy if they find someone else to replace me provided he is suitable and does not bring to naught what I have done.

3 | SATURDAY

Mr Pirzada,[48] the foreign minister, saw me on return from Geneva where he had gone to meet our team who are fighting the Rann of Kutch case[49] with India before the tribunal. It is understood that the Indians, finding their case weak, are now trying to gain time and influence the tribunal by other means. They have suggested to the tribunal to visit India for sightseeing and inspection of the Rann. Mr Pirzada was instructed to tell our representative on the tribunal to warn the president of the danger of this. If they listen to the Indians, they will only be exposing themselves to the charge of being bought.

Laid the foundation stone of Tibbi Institute being sponsored by Hakim Saeed.[50] The doctors are very perturbed. They think that quacks are being given unnecessary encouragement. I warned in my address that unless Tibbis modernize their science and allow their research to be subjected to critical analysis, they would not be able to bluff their way through.

📖 Attended a banquet given by the Pakistan British and Commonwealth Medical Council. It also included eminent scientists from several other countries. I had the pleasure of meeting several medical celebrities.

4 | SUNDAY

📖 Being a Sunday, I took the opportunity to go out to sea with the Admiral for fishing. We tried very hard but the fish proved cleverer than we. We did not catch anything.

📖 Flew to Mohenjodaro[51] for two days' stay in Larkana. This airfield is newly built and is a great boon to tourists and the locals. PIA runs two services on weekends. We saw the museum built a couple of years ago. The exhibits are magnificent. I wanted to go and see the ruins too but unfortunately there was no time. It is tragic to see the ruins being eroded by waterlogging and salinity. The water level has almost come to the surface. To counter this, I was even able to get the assistance of two experts from UNESCO. They are advising installation of tube wells around the area.

📖 A large number of Sindhi friends came to receive me at the airport and then again on the railway station. Some of them were Zulfiqar Ali Bhutto's relatives.

5 | MONDAY

📖 Larkana: Went for a duck shoot in the Lung Jheel. It belongs to my friend Hussain Ali. He is a delightful man, very affectionate, but his trouble is that he drinks too much. A friend of his told me that in anticipation of my arrival he was given liquor mixed with three quarters water so that he remains reasonably sober. His brother, Hassan Ali, on the other hand, is a very sensible man. His son Deedar is a very good singer. He and his troupe sang Shah Latif's famous *Kafi*.

📖 Whenever I go to my Sindhi friends for shoots, the occasions are turned into regular festivals. Large numbers of singers, musicians and people turn out. They are very hospitable and kind, at least to me. I went to see the Mohenjodaro ruins in the afternoon. It was a great and educative experience. The layout of the city's drainage and evolution system is fantastic and extensive. The burnt bricks of 5000 years ago are still intact. These ruins should have advanced the Indus Valley civilization and I felt it is tragic that the bullock cart used today in this area is no different to what it was 5000 years ago. It would be worth examining why such a wonderful civilization came to a halt and stagnation.

8 | THURSDAY

📖 Held official talks with Marshal Amer [of Egypt] in Rawalpindi. I spoke to him on our foreign policy, our attitude towards the Muslim and foreign world, our deteriorating relationship with India and our attitude towards the Muslim Summit Conference. I appealed to him for cessation of hostilities in Yemen, improvement of relations with King Faisal and the Shah of Iran. I offered to play host to them should they meet these people. He assured that they want to settle Yemen, improve relations with Faisal and the Shah.

About the Islamic Summit, I told him that unless the Muslim world got together, at least on an Islamic and social basis, they will have no bargaining position left and become satellites of one or the other power. As I said elsewhere, he is a cool, calm, calculated man, stable with considerable foresight. Left to himself he could command confidence and be a big factor for peace and cohesion in the Middle East.

📖 Certain documents were brought to my notice which gave the Indian plan for invasion of East and West Pakistan under certain contingencies. It shows how alert we have got to be.

10 | SATURDAY

📖 Our High Commissioner in India, Arshad Hussain came to see me and explained political and economic situation in India. Things seem to be pretty bad and there is no one in sight who can put them right. Economic distress, privation and suffering are rampant. There is universal disillusionment and frustration in the country. Some talk of military take over or precisely, a civilian regime backed by the army. The election fever is on and lawlessness is prevalent. The Congress is divided amongst itself but so is the opposition. Chances are that the Congress will lose in some provinces but will get a majority in the centre, with reduced numbers.

📖 On Kashmir, the Indians have gone back on their design as expressed by Swaran Singh to our foreign minister at the United Nations to discuss Kashmir meaningfully. That is the trouble with the Indians. They lack integrity and scruples and indulge in duplicity and deceit.

11 | SUNDAY

📖 Flew to Lahore and stayed at the Government House for a few hours before proceeding to Dacca. General Musa raised several problems. He is, of course, very worried about the food situation like all of us, and proposed that priority of the government Five Year Plan should be reoriented to greater food production. I have, therefore, ordered this matter to be discussed on the National Economic Council. I told him to also look into the processes through which food passes from the port or the *mandies* to the consumer and to see that bottlenecks and other issues are eliminated.

Rapid rise of water table in the new Guddu Barrage area is another matter of deep concern. This must be attended to quickly or otherwise assets worth thousands or crores would be lost.

He showed concern on the conduct of Mr Bucha[52] who is a minister, leader of the house and the president of the provincial league. We may have to divest him of some of these responsibilities provided a suitable man can be found. Qazi Ijaz's name was mentioned. He is an old Leaguer but his trouble is that he has no financial sense or scruples.

📖 Flew into Dacca in the evening, was met by a large number of MNAs, officers and members of the Muslim League. Marshal Amer of UAR who is on a visit to East Pakistan was also present. Later attended a reception given by him. Thereafter he departed for Karachi en route to Cairo.

📖 News of cyclone storm in the Bay of Bengal was coming in. It was supposed to be getting ominous and in the morning heading in the direction of Cox's Bazaar and Chittagong. It hit these areas in the middle of the night accompanied by torrential rain. Luckily its velocity was not very great and did no great damage. These cyclones are a curse on East Pakistan and do an enormous amount of damage to life and property. The arrival in the month of December is unprecedented. The experts say that their currents are somehow connected with the spots on the sun which face this area periodically.

12 | MONDAY

📖 I had a quiet day today, stayed in my residence except for attending a banquet at the Intercontinental Hotel recently opened in Dacca. It is a great amenity for the people and foreign visitors. Dacca is very short of good accommodation for visitors.

📖 Governor Monem Khan showed me the result of the elections of the vice chairmen of municipalities. Muslim League candidates have secured most of the seats.

14 | WEDNESDAY

📖 The meeting of the National Economic Council was held to review the Five Year Plan in the light of changed economic circumstances. It was decided to put more emphasis on food production whilst maintaining the magnitude of the plan. The provinces were told to review their developmental programmes and suggest which items could be given up in favour of the agricultural sector.

15 | THURSDAY

📖 I held a governors' conference. Several important questions were discussed.

a. Food. Decided to buy 3 lakh more tons of wheat from Australia against own cash to stave of shortage in West Pakistan.
b. A formula was evolved to see that better quality of young men were recruited to the Police Service of Pakistan. At present, they only get second-raters.
c. Aim to grow more potatoes to fill the food gap and install more cold storages.
d. To reduce corruption, the law calling upon officers living beyond their means should be applied.
e. MNAs and MPAs should be given due consideration by the local administration, but they must not be allowed to disrupt administration.

📖 Attended an *iftar* party at the house of Mr Kabir, the IG police, in celebration of his daughter's marriage.[53] The son-in-law is in Foreign Service. His complaint was that they are not given home leave at government expense often enough. He said he was very attached to his parents and would like to see them more often. It is a fact Bengalis are very mother-attached.

📖 Attended a dinner party at Mr Doha's[54] place. The food was excellent. His wife is a very good cook and housekeeper.

16 | FRIDAY

📖 Presided over the working committee of the Muslim League. Representatives from East and West Pakistan attended. Useful discussions took place on:

a. Treatment of EBDOed politicians. Those that are prepared to join the Muslim League unconditionally will be considered.
b. Subcommittees at different places to guide students and labourers.
c. How to combat Bhutto's nefarious activities.
d. Set up propaganda committees in Dacca, Lahore and Karachi to counter hostile propaganda, project Muslim League programme and think out future trends.
e. Set up a separate organization for the women.

📖 The provincial Muslim League parliamentary party gave a banquet at the Shahbagh Hotel. Some 3,000 people were present. I was told that the expense was borne by a MPA who is very anxious to become a minister.

📖 Maulana Ather Ali[55] came to see me. He is a clever and cunning old fox. Told me that he had given up politics and apologized for opposing me. This is in spite of what I did to help him in building his Dar-ul-Uloom. Also asked me for assistance over so many defamation cases pending against him. He made a statement that is not easy to believe: that Bengalis are very ungenerous and uncharitable people and treat each other like a bit of dirt and with severity. Formally they are very religious but they know very little about the philosophy and spirit of Islam as they did not take to the language, i.e. Urdu, in which it is expressed in this subcontinent.

17 | SATURDAY

📖 Flew to Shivganj airfield in Dinajpur district. Inspected the Thakurgaon tube well and surface pumping stations. This field, plus one or two others when completed, will irrigate about 180,000 acres of land. So far 13 acres of land are being irrigated because the farmers are not yet in a habit to irrigate the land. The land in this area is sandy, loamy and capable of producing anything if properly tended. I was surprised to hear that the population in this area is sparse and that is why the people are not willing to go in for intensive agriculture. I was also told that they were law abiding and loyal citizens not like some of the other districts which bred agitators.

There was a public meeting at Thakurgaon. It was well arranged and largely attended. Apparently people had started celebrating from the time of *sehri*. I spoke on the need for maintaining political and economic stability. No change in the constitution, maintenance of developmental tempo, increase in food production and protecting birth control. Also warned them against the [...] of the opposition parties. Their sole aim was to exploit the people for their selfish ends. I was happy to see people well turned out with clean clothes, looking cheerful and behaving in a disciplined manner.

18 | SUNDAY

📖 Went to Manikganj by road where I addressed a public meeting. There was a crowd of about 60,000 to 70,000 people. Very orderly and disciplined. The arrangements were first class. I was called upon to switch on the local power station that has just been installed. This proved a great boon to the people.

After the public meeting drove onto Aricha on the Brahmaputra where we took a boat for a cruise up the river. Later got on to the *Mary Anderson*, this is the steamer of the governor, where we spent the night. It was very pleasant except that the power generating plant was located close to my bedroom and kept thumping away the whole night. I slept in fits and starts.

I was going up the river. We did some duck shooting. It was a proverbial wild goose chase at the open ocean of water. The birds could see us miles away and never allowed us to get within shooting range. However, I managed to shoot three birds at long range. The road to Aricha had been recently built, and in fact, connects Dacca with North Bengal on one side and Jessore on the other with ferrying arrangements over the big rivers. However, it has a vast number of bridges as it has to cross so many waterways. It must be one of the very expensive roads we have.

The people of North Bengal sometimes talk deeply of a bridge over the river Brahmaputra about four to five miles wide in summer. This is a utopian idea, will cost about 200 crores and take twenty years to build and I doubt if it would hold as there is no solid foundation. The answer is to have several modern ferries for quick crossing.

19 | MONDAY

📖 Cruised back to Aricha in the morning and then motored to Dacca. Attended an *iftar* party given by the Dacca Municipal Committee in the afternoon. It was a largely attended function. I was presented with a silver *hookah* of about 100 years old. Pity I have given up smoking and so would not be able to make use of this great luxury reserved for nawabs.

📖 The law minister, Mr Zafar,[56] came to give me his impressions of thinking in Bengal. He felt that people have regard for me as I have done so much for them but they have no great feeling for the people of West Pakistan[…] desire to make a strong and unified nation. Their strategy is to get whatever concessions they can out of me as after me West Pakistanis will not let them get away with things.

The law minister has recently come under criticism by the section of Bengalis of secessionist and parochial tendencies for having dubbed such people as traitors and enemies of the country. I am glad he has let them have it, as this is the sort of language in which they should be spoken to. The time for mincing words has gone. During my stay in East Pakistan, I found ample evidence of the good work being done by Governor Monem Khan. He has got electrified with what he saw in China. He is putting great emphasis on respect for my leadership and is propagating my sayings on different national issues at a large scale in the form of booklets and posters etc. and pamphlets. He is also putting great emphasis on growing more food and on family planning.

I know some people criticize him for twisting their tail but the law-abiding people are happy because he is deeply religious, God fearing, brave and tough. He has good grip over the administration and has a lot of political sense and foresight. He loses no opportunity in exposing the opposition leaders for their inefficiency and selfishness and having done nothing for East Pakistan when they were in power.

📖 Flew to Karachi reaching midnight.

20 | TUESDAY

📖 Flew to Sukkur and stayed at Khairpur with His Highness the Mir. He seems to have come on in a sense that he is more forthcoming and less shy. He is also a proud father of a son.

21 | WEDNESDAY

📖 Shot partridges at Ranipur. The Mir had made very good arrangements. My bag was 153 on morning shoots. I returned to Karachi in the evening.

24 | SATURDAY

📖 Went to the area of Mirpur Sakro for a duck shoot. This *jheel* originally belonged to a family of Sindhi friends but is now being acquired by the government and improved considerably. The owners had been given land elsewhere in lieu but they still look after the birds. This place is unique in the sense that it is covered with tall reeds where ducks hover. The way to shoot them is to go about in a small boat and shoot them when flushed. The reeds are so thick that many birds are lost. Although there were a number of birds, my bag was only 73 out of which 52 were mallards. I shot badly. It is not easy to explain why one goes off sometimes.

📖 Moved on to Kalri lake after the shoot and stayed for two nights in one of the huts built by the government. It is a beautiful place worth visiting. Major General Haq Nawaz, the head of the ADC (Agriculture Development Corporation) and his staff came and explained the rate of development in Ghulam Mohammad Barrage area. Also measures are being adopted to combat waterlogging and salinity. I was impressed with what they are doing.

26 | MONDAY

📖 Went to Ladio for a duck shoot with Yusuf Chandio. The birds were plentiful and weather perfect. I shot extremely well. My bag was 180 in two and a half hours. I must have fired about 500 rounds.

They often take on birds at a long range, so at least two shots are required to bring a bird down. And the big birds do not come down unless you break their neck. Returned to Karachi in the evening.

27 | TUESDAY

📖 As usual some visitors came to see me. One of them, a Muslim Leaguer, talked about the local problems and general spate of rumours which are being spread amongst our people. They seem to believe almost any rumour however absurd it may be. I do not know what it is due to, ignorance or lack of political sense or inability to apply their minds in a rational manner. The opposition, of course, take full advantage of it and use this as a weapon against the government. Most of the absurd rumours are manufactured by them, then spread and circulated. The approach of the lifting date of EBDO has given them just a fillip. He made an interesting statement. Good deal of the activities of the opposition against me are directed to keep me engaged.

📖 Gohar Ayub,[57] my son, told me that Mr Daultana[58] and his wife had been anxious to keep contact with him. They invited him and his wife to tea one day and though wanting to talk politics only mentioned trivialities. Today they came over to his place and repeated the same performance. This shows that either he is too foxy or cannot come down to brass tacks. However, to Gohar's inquiry as to what were his plans on the lifting of EBDO, Daultana replied that the country is being faced with major problems and he would like to remain out of active politics.

📖 The Americans have offered us an additional half a million tons of food grain after a long delay. This is not enough. So we shall have to make additional purchases out of our own cash.

28 | WEDNESDAY

📖 Qazi Isa[59] came to see me and offered his services on lifting of EBDO. He has some political sense and use, but the trouble is that his integrity cannot be relied upon. However, it may be necessary to make use of him in some fashion. Flew in to Pindi. In one way or the other I have been away from home for seven weeks or so.

29 | THURSDAY

📖 Saw my orchards near Khanpur, they are well kept and look in good form. Ripened oranges on the trees look so pleasing to the eye. I have also sown high yield varieties of wheat and mustard. They are doing very well.

30 | FRIDAY

📖 Amir Azam[60] and Qazi Fazlullah,[61] both EBDOed politicians, came to see me. The EBDO by law will be lifted on 1st January. I was given some indication of what they were going to talk about.

Amir Azam has political sense and is a balanced man. He talked for about three quarters of an hour or so and I let him do so. He eulogized for the country but according to him it was not fully explained nor brought home to the people, which only experienced politicians could do. They talked about the problems facing the country: Indian menace, East Pakistan attitude, stand of opposition politicians in West Pakistan. Suggested that I needed support of all. The answer was to concede direct adult franchise for elections to the assemblies by 1975 and in order to ensure that the majority in the Central Assembly and the president were of the same party, let the president be elected by the assembly.

I told him that to start with I am opposed to intimidation and bargaining in the sense of compromising on essentials. Honest and patriotic people even EBDOed should join the Muslim League party and then come forward with any constructive suggestions they have and be prepared to convince or be convinced by others. After all, we have already carried out seven amendments in the constitution and more could be carried out if they were in the interest of the country.

As to a specific proposal, the president will have to buy all the voters he needs in the assembly and the price will be a ministry. Look at the compulsion and demoralization and bargaining it would lead to. Only a dishonest and thoroughly unscrupulous man could then become a president. Does he want this? He said no.

Now look at the consequences of the election to the assemblies on the basis of direct adult franchise. The slogans to the ignorant voter would be parochial and disruptive. The effect will be that the separation demand in East Pakistan and dismemberment of West Pakistan will gain momentum. Central Government will get weakened and rendered helpless. Does he demand that? He agreed that would not be right. I think he left me a chastened man.

Qazi Fazlullah also spoke in the same strain but he also went back satisfied after I explained the hard realities to him.

📖 Recorded my first of the month speech. Emphasized the need for austerity, food conservation and family planning. Told people that ostentatious and wasteful customs must go. I, at least, would not attend any function that was not austere.

DIARY 1967

1 | SUNDAY

📖 Went to see my house in the village. My wife is very fond of this place and keeps on having odd changes made. It is now looking in good shape and the location is so attractive with the beautiful view for scores of miles around. I sometimes wish to go there for rest and some peace but it is impossible to get it as on hearing of my arrival people from dozen or more villages around gather at our place. It is impossible to shake them off and to do so would not look nice as they have connections with our family for generations. On return I came back via the new road which my son Akhtar Ayub got made. It goes along the foothills over beautiful countryside commanding extensive view of the plain of Hazara all the way.

Akhtar is a member of the provincial assembly, lives in the village and does a lot for the people. For instance, he has got this road made, there is a small hospital and a post office in our village. Several villages around have been electrified and now he is busy getting a high school made. He also takes a lot of trouble in finding jobs etc. for the people. All this relieves me of a number of obligations.

2 | MONDAY

📖 Kirmani[1] came to see me from Lahore. He is a provincial minister as well as the secretary general of the Muslim League. Recently they held a meeting at Lahore which did not go off too well. It was mainly due to lack of proper preparations. I told him that they should have known better. After all, a ruling party cannot take things for granted and a setback to the efforts is greatly magnified.

He gave me an assessment of the leading EBDOed politicians' intentions. Daultana is not a mass man so he would like to operate from behind cover. Qayyum[2] might well be looking for a job. On the other hand, he knows what I think of him so he would be forced to remain in the opposition to be the head of Council Muslim League. But he is afraid of being harassed by Daultana's men who are bound to dominate the council. So he is on the horns of a dilemma.

📖 News came in that the EBDOed politicians are gathering in Karachi and the other opposition leaders have decided to get together on the demand for democracy. Under the leadership of Brohi,[3] Bhutto has offered to go to Dacca to sound out the East Pakistani opposition members. My feeling is to wait and see; some coming and going is inevitable after lifting of EBDO and I would like them to do so. This will tie them up because most of them are ambitious men and individual snipers. Everyone is looking for leadership. Their getting together is not going to be easy. Meanwhile, we have to keep the door open for any one of them who cares to join the Muslim League.

📖 My brother Sardar Bahadur Khan[4] came to see me. He talked about several administrative and political matters. His trouble is that he is too dogmatic and bases his judgement on preconceived ideas. It is not easy to carry on an intellectual conversation with him.

3 | TUESDAY

📖 Daultana keeps on meeting Gohar in Karachi. His latest statement is that he has no intention of taking part in active politics but he will see that Qayyum does not capture his party. He has a very poor opinion about Bhutto. He thinks that the man has no character and substance in him. He has unbounded political ambitions but has no standing even in his home district. He keeps on criticizing the foreign policy. If the man had any character why did he not stay on as a minister. He should have resigned instead of being pushed out.

📖 The Indian High Commissioner has been agitating for a meeting on the ministerial level while his government representatives keep on harping that Kashmir is an unbreakable part of India and that Pakistan is their eternal enemy. What good can a ministerial meeting do under such circumstances? However, I have agreed to see him since he keeps on insisting.

4 | WEDNESDAY

📖 Khawaja Shahabuddin[5] came and gave his assessment about the political situation as a result of lifting of EBDO. His view was that these people would not go very far so long as we keep the food problem and the prices of essential commodities under control. A cabinet meeting was held. A number of important problems were discussed and decisions given.

📖 Mr Ghulam Faruque has been trying very hard to increase exports but I told him that we should have a suitable organization that handles exports and also imports of major items which we buy from abroad. Today the onus of export is put on the industrial producer. How can we expect them to find markets on their own. Similarly, we would do well to buy major items of import in bulk and distribute them to the dealers. To do all this, the need is to set up an Export and Import Corporation consisting of the private sector with government participation. This is in any case necessary, now that we have so much better trade with the socialist countries. We could even go further and attach all government export agencies to them. We might even head all this with a minister calling him minister of production and foreign trade. This idea sounded too revolutionary to him and others but I told him to give it a trial. I have no doubt that it will be a big improvement on the present system for utter lack of it.

5 | THURSDAY

📖 The Nawab of Bahawalpur[6] came to see me together with his stepmother, an English lady. She has got into a mess because in the instrument of accession, the late Nawab got the whole of his property defined as personal. In consequence, all the heirs are entitled to a share in accordance with the *Shariah*. This will leave nothing that goes with the office of nawab and the whole institution will break up. All the relics and family heirlooms will get distributed and wasted. One way of thinking is to let this happen but this will be the end of his family and an open pity. Besides this is sure to cause resentment in Bahawalpur. People have a lot of feeling for this house. So I have decided to set up a commission to go into this and other matters and sort things out. My view is that certain essentials should be set aside as the complements of the office holder, and the rest treated as the private property to which all the heirs would be entitled.

📖 Mr Ghulam Faruque came to see me again. He is very worried about the foreign exchange position. Some fifty crores worth of commodity aid is not coming in quickly. As usual the donor countries are putting all sorts of delaying obstacles. Then there has been a heavy outgo on food imports and defence purchases. The debt servicing liability has gone up to 58 crores. All this is very worrying. I told him to hold discussions with the deputy chairman, Planning Commission and the finance minister and let me know the outcome.

Then the food situation is causing anxiety. Although enough food through aid and cash purchases is lined up till the end of June, its transportation into the interior is proving a major obstacle. The railway in West Pakistan can only handle 5000 tons of grain a day. This is causing dislocation of movement of other essential goods like petroleum products etc. The breakdown of power generation in Multan and switch over to oil instead of gas means a train and a half load of oil a day. The prospects for the next crop do not look too good either. There has been no water in the river since sowing of wheat.

With all these things on my mind, on top of it, my wife chose to pick up a quarrel with me over something trivial. So I let her have a bit of my spleen. She does that once in two or three years.

Unless the food situation improves and the economy becomes buoyant again we are in for hard times ahead with inevitable serious political consequences and there are enough mischief makers in our country to take advantage of such a situation.

📖 A German parliamentary delegation came to see me. They showed interest in and appreciated the economic development in Pakistan. Also asked me very pertinent questions. The genesis of the Red Guard movement in China, state of Russo–Chinese relations, Chinese intentions about the sub-continent, possible moves of Russia, lining up with the West against China, chances of countries like India and even Pakistan going communist due to population explosion and food shortage and so on. It just shows how well prepared these people come with the problems of an area. I wish our parliamentarians had the sense to do the same when going abroad. But their trouble is that they are either uneducated or merely literate and are ignorant of the knowledge of the current world problems. I often wonder what do they know of the internal problems. Yet they claim to have an absolute power to rule this country.

6 | FRIDAY

📖 Being a holiday stayed at home. The law minister came to see me and brought a letter of resignation from Justice Murshed,[7] the chief justice of East Pakistan. It will become effective from 16th November. Justice Murshed has a brilliant, intelligent, literary bent of mind and aptitude for languages, but he is impulsive and unstable. From the very beginning I was doubtful of his making a success as a chief justice in East Pakistan.

7 | SATURDAY

The American ambassador came to see me and handed over several bound volumes of cuttings from the Pakistani press. He said that, whereas the press had been considerate to him, they had been very critical of President Johnson and the American policy in Vietnam and elsewhere. Washington was very disturbed. I asked him if he had any complaint against me, the government ministers or officials. He replied in the negative. I told him that it was inconceivable that we should not have an opinion on a burning question like Vietnam, yet we had kept our mouths shut for American susceptibilities. As regards the press, we keep appealing to them, but how can we muzzle them? It is surprising that they don't say worse as people actually feel bad about what is happening in Vietnam. Besides, all these news emanate from American sources. However, I have told him to discuss it with Mr Altaf Gauhar and see where he can help. Then he brought up the question of anti-American propaganda done by the Chinese in Pakistan through literature and cultural troupes. I found there was a good deal of truth in that. So I have told the foreign secretary that this should be looked into. The answer is to tell the diplomatic corps that they must not use Pakistan as a propaganda base against other powers.

Then he complained that our people had stopped their bi-weekly air service supplying Badaber air base from transiting through Karachi. I thought this was an uncalled for pinprick and must be reversed maintaining status quo.

I know that our people are hurt against the Americans, but they must also realise the need for maintaining normal relations with them because of our economic dependence, our interest will be hurt badly if we fall out with them.

The plane flight was put right as it would have proven an unnecessary irritation to the Americans. I expressed my helplessness against the attitude of the press, especially over Vietnam, which was such an emotional question, but told him to get in touch with our information ministry and see what influence they could exercise. Also advised him not to be too touchy. But there is no doubt about it that Vietnam is just like an open nerve with the Americans. Besides, any attack on the person of the President of the United States must be in bad taste. The trouble is that our press is not very mature; people's feelings are hurt over the American attitude during the Indian aggression, which is not easy to forget. Besides, most of the adverse information over Vietnam comes to our press through the American sources. However, there is no gainsaying that our national interest will in no manner be advanced by going on like this. Similarly, we must stop foreign powers from carrying on hostile propaganda against each other in Pakistan.

8 | SUNDAY

Called Shahab, secretary education, and Altaf Gauhar, secretary information, to discuss what we could do to get the textbooks right. At present the provincial textbook committees control this matter. They made an utter mess of it. The whole object of educational reforms has been defeated by teaching wrong things. After some discussions the following conclusions were arrived at:

a. A directive should go from me to the governors that in the interest of uniformity and national integration, the question of textbooks in future will be under the control of the central education secretary. The provincial committees can advise but they should not have the power of authorization.

b. Meanwhile, the following books should be prepared for B.A. courses under central direction:
    1. History of Muslims in India, why and wherefore of Pakistan.
    2. History of Muslims of Bengal.
    3. Analysis of the constitution of Pakistan.
    4. Our foreign policy.
    5. Economic developments and policies.
        Abridged editions of these should be prepared for lower classes down to wherever they apply. Their translation into Urdu and Bengali should also be prepared. These textbooks should become universal in Pakistan.
c. The establishment of the Central Government Publishing House for production of textbooks should be examined.
d. In order to prepare youngsters for occupations, all middle and high schools should have an agricultural plot allotted to them. There should also be facilities provided for teaching masonry, blacksmithing, carpentry, bricklaying, sewing etc.

9 | MONDAY

📖 The Khan of Kalat[8] came to dinner. He apologized for not having called on me for a long time. His reason was that Governor Malik Amir Mohammad Khan had admonished him after the last time he saw me. He told him that he was responsible for removal of restrictions against the Khan and his reinstatement against my wishes. He also told the Khan that I was engaged in the dangerous game of winning over Afghanistan. If that happened Pathans would be the bosses everywhere and where will the Baloch, the Rajputs et cetera be? If that be true then I am surprised at the man's pettiness and short-sightedness. And yet it is people from the Punjab like Feroz Khan Noon and Amjad Ali who keep on emphasizing to me the need of making up with Afghanistan.

The governor is supposed to have told the Khan further that all that is happening to the Balochis is due to the president. He also encouraged Bizenjo to fight the elections against Habibullah Paracha in Karachi.

God knows how far this is true because the Khan is no angel either. But there was a general feeling amongst the people that anyone who came near me was suspected and disliked by the governor.

📖 The American ambassador came to see me in the morning. He brought up the following points:

a. The grant of 70 million dollars commodity loan.
b. Trouble over the flight of their planes from Karachi to Peshawar to service Badaber.
c. Hostile attitude of our press.
d. China using Pakistan as a propaganda base against America.
e. Dissemination of Chinese Communist literature in Pakistan.

12 | THURSDAY

The central Ruet-e-Hilal committee headed by the minister of interior announced last evening that in view of the fact that the new moon had been sighted in Mardan, Malakand and Peshawar, the Eid will be observed throughout the country. This was repeated on the radio several times and also the information that Eid had been celebrated in several Middle Eastern countries and Afghanistan on the 11th should have satisfied anyone with any sense but the mischievous elements amongst our ulema looked for trouble. Starting with Ehtisham-ul-Haq and Maududi from Karachi they rang each other up all over the country that Eid should not be observed on the 12th as they were not satisfied with the government's declaration. I was rung up by the Pir Sahib of Dewal[9] in the middle of the night and told this. In places, they sent men around on vehicles at night telling people on the loud-speakers not to observe Eid on the 12th.

You might say why these wretched people behave in such a manner and create mischief and division amongst people. The answer is simple, they want to run a parallel government in the country and exploit ignorance and innocence for political ends.

I am trying my best to bring about a situation where Islam, instead of being confined to rituals, rites, ceremonies, in other words 'mullahism', becomes a living philosophy of life. But it is quite clear that the ignorant and mischievous elements amongst the mullahs is not going to allow this to happen. The result will be the same as happened with Christianity and with Islam in Turkey and several other countries. In disgust with the mullah, people will give up Islam in its true meaning and this will be a terrible tragedy.

It might well be said that it is my duty to bring home to the people the dangers of which this type of mullah is exposing us to. I would gladly do it but the trouble is that, though our masses are good and God-fearing, they are uneducated and ignorant. They are not yet ready to understand and accept a rational approach. They are, therefore, the perfect audience for the religious and political exploiters.

13 | FRIDAY

Went to see my orchard. Shahid Hamid, Doha and Aslam [secretary general of the Muslim League] accompanied me. My real objective was to see the cultivation of crops in the countryside. Though there has been very little rain during the last several months the crops are still alive. If the rains come within the next week or so they might be saved, otherwise in the *barani* and riverine areas there would be hardly any crop left. We shall then be faced with an enormous food deficit again. The sufferings of the people will be great and our economy will receive a major setback. The mere thought of it makes my heart bleed. But what can one one do other than pray to God and steel ourselves to face the situation as best we can?

14 | SATURDAY

Dr Glen Seaborg, who is the head of the Atomic Energy Commission of the USA, came to see me accompanied by some of his scientists with Dr Salam and Usmani. He was happy with the way our atomic energy stations were developing. He said that in the future the world will have to rely more and more on atomic energy for power and other peaceful uses. When questioned, he said that India was making some plutonium. It was in limited quantities and they could make a limited number of crude atomic devices and she would not have the materials to have a chain of them. In any case, the Americans are insisting on very stringent conditions on the reactor to be supplied by them to ensure that the atomic fuel was not used for military purposes. He said the same thing about the Canadians. Let us hope he is right. Because if India was to acquire atomic military capability, we shall have to follow suit and it will just ruin us both.

I asked him how close we were to using hydrogen for direct fusion without the need for fission. He thought that it will come one day but it will take some twenty years or so, and when that happens, the world will have unlimited fuel at its disposal.

15 | SUNDAY

📖 I attended the opening ceremony of the central training institute in Chaklala. A large number of people including Professor Schmidt and a German minister were also present. Khawaja Shahabuddin, Schmidt and I spoke on the occasion. Schmidt spoke with feeling. She is obviously a great scholar. Gist of my speech is attached on reverse.[10]

📖 Musa came to lunch. We discussed several problems: mullahs, mischief on the occasion of Eid, food problem, our policy with the Balochis in Kalat, Quetta etc.

The fight with the mullahs is political. It started from the time of Sir Syed. The mullah regards the educated Muslim as his deadliest enemy and the rival for power. That is why several of them opposed Pakistan and sided with the Congress. They felt that with the help of Hindus they will be able to keep the educated Muslims out of power. So we have got to take on all those who are political mischief-makers. This battle, though unpleasant, is unavoidable. It has to be waged sometime or the other in the interest of a strong and progressive Pakistan.

With the Balochis we have to be generous and let them run in the manner they understand, provided the *sardars* behave themselves and remain loyal.

I am very glad to hear that the Baloch possess some admirable qualities. Kindness can, but money cannot buy him and also he has an acute head instinct and is devoted to the leader of the clan. I suppose nomadic life forces this on him.

📖 It is quite obvious that food is going to be a major problem with us for a long time. We shall have to import large quantities of food and fertilizers whilst maintaining normal movement of other goods for increasing economic activity. So I have told the principal secretary to form a committee of experts to draw up working papers on the strategy of procurement of food and fertilizer, a plan for their distribution to the consumer and the individual farmer. A plan for movement and transportation. These committees should include provincial representatives and should constantly review the situation. We should also call a governors' conference soon to set the machineries on the ground and moving.

16 | MONDAY

📖 Flew into Karachi. Landed at Drigh Road and inspected Pakistan Air Force jet workshop. I was extremely pleased to see what goes on there. They are now making large number of spare parts in the country and carrying out a number of conversions and modifications on different aircrafts in order to increase the range, firepower and effectiveness. With the stoppage of American military aid and sale of spare parts, the Air Force was in a pathetic state but with great effort on procurement through all sorts of sources and internal production, they have regained their health. We were also lucky to get seventy-five MIG-19s from China and ninety 86-Es from Germany. These are both first class aircraft capable of clashing with any intrusion.

17 | TUESDAY

📖 Flew to Hyderabad and went out to Hala for a partridge shoot with the Makhdoom of Hala.[11] We shot very few partridge, we had collected a large number of Sindhi friends and they entertained us to lunch. The Makhdoom is a nice fellow but ineffective.

📖 Moved down to Hyderabad for the night. Jam Sadiq Ali[12] invited me to dinner and made most elaborate illuminations and preparations and invited a large number of guests. I was very embarrassed and told him so. This sort of thing happens in spite of my telling them to the contrary.

18 | WEDNESDAY

📖 Flew to Badin and shot duck with Ijaz Ali Talpur at Tando Bagho lake. Then flew back to Karachi.

19 | THURSDAY

📖 Spent the day at Karachi. A large number of visitors came to see me. The trouble is that whenever I go to a place, the same people want to see me again and again.

20 | FRIDAY

📖 Flew to Mohenjodaro for the opening of the museum which has been recently built and then moved on to Drigh Road for a duck shoot. It was a fine and warm day and the ducks were lying very high. My bag was 106.

📖 I was very sorry to hear that my old friend Hussain Ali Isran who owned Lung Lake and had entertained me to duck shoots on several occasions had died the previous day. He killed himself by over-drinking. But apart from that he was an interesting, warm hearted, affectionate and hospitable person. May God bless his soul.

📖 Flew into Rawalpindi in the evening. When in Hyderabad several people talked about high prices of commodities. I think the people had never had it so good during the last eight years. Now that these successive crops have failed the prices of commodities have inevitably gone up. They are, therefore, feeling the pinch. However, they have to learn to put up with hardships too.

21 | SATURDAY

📖 Peshawar: Flew to Risalpur and inspected a Pakistan Air Force passing out parade. In strength it was the largest parade they ever had. There were twenty-one Iranian cadets amongst them too. The standard of parade was very high, turnout first class and faultless, arms drill and the march past excellent.

After last year's war, our Air Force had a major setback in consequence of stoppage of American military equipment but through ceaseless efforts of all concerned they have much larger number of aircraft and have attained a high standard of efficiency.

📖 Came down to Peshawar and entertained a large number of Muslim League workers from all parts of the division. Talked to them on the need for reorganizing the League on sound lines and also spoke to them on the food situation and the cause for rising prices. Told them that the government was doing its best to help the rising price and the difficulties being faced by the people.

The people from the irrigated areas of Peshawar and Mardan are concerned about the prices of sugarcane. The mill owners are not prepared to pay the fixed price of rupees two per maund as the sucrose content of the cane has gone down through heavy and sustained frost. This is a perennial problem in this area where sugar cane is cultivated extensively in adverse climatic conditions.

The governor told me that they have decided to expel certain *maulanas* from their districts; these are the ones who took part in creating confusion on the occasion of last Eid. I hope this proves to be beneficial for their mental health.

22 | SUNDAY

📖 A representation of *ulema*, *mashaikhs* and the Muslim League came and protested strongly against the activities of political and disruptive *maulanas*. They were especially incensed at Maududi's statement that in respect of the sighting of the moon the people from Frontier areas are not to be believed and demanded that action should be taken against him.

📖 An interesting letter was handed over to me by Fazal Elahi Chaudhary.[13] It was written by an old Muslim Leaguer who is now practicing law. He said that, whereas the outside world highly appreciated what I have done in the socio-economic and political fields, our own people had very little realization of it. The answer, he thought, was to introduce socialism affecting the needs of the common man and also have a party that carries the message right down. This sounds attractive on paper but socialism to work at all has to have communist dictatorship. Do we want it?

The real trouble is historical and psychological. The people living in the areas of Pakistan have always been ruled by outsiders. They have never been the masters of their own destiny. The result is that they are instinctively suspicious of their rulers and this tendency subsists even today. But one must do whatever good one can and help people develop healthy and constructive outlook.

I was in Aligarh in the early [19]20s. The talk of a Muslim homeland had started. Allama Iqbal's name was associated with the idea. Someone is supposed to have asked him as to where from he will get the men to run such a state. His answer was, such a man will have to come from the north. If this be true then his meaning was quite clear. It is only the people with fighting and conquering history that produce leaders of high grade and states cannot be run without them.

📖 Returned to Rawalpindi and called a meeting of representatives of central ministries connected with food, finance, commerce, transportation etc. I wanted working papers to be prepared on the following:

a. Requirement of additional food during the next year.
b. Strategy of procurement.
c. Adjustments of import policy and the annual development programme.
d. Utilization of transportation of food, fertilizer, exports, imports of other commodities.
e. Distribution of fertilizer, seed etc.
f. Handling of labour and utilization of cooperatives.

I then intended to hold a governors' conference to approve the final plan. I also wanted to set up a watchdog committee to see that all these operations are properly supervised.

23 | MONDAY

📖 I had been having second thoughts on the title of my book, the initial title was *Friends Not Masters*. This was the expression I used when Johnson stopped economic aid to Pakistan in 1964. Later it was changed to *Endure and Prosper* on the suggestion of the publishers. This again was an expression I used on an occasion. I thought of several other alternatives, but none of them quite appealed to me. So I have decided to go back to the original title, *Friends Not Masters*.

📖 Meeting of Quaid-e-Azam's mausoleum committee was held. I was in the chair. We took several decisions to expedite completion and also make arrangements whereby there is enough income created to maintain the place. Some six to seven lakh a year would be required. Ms Jinnah[14] keeps on complaining that the work is not progressing fast enough. I wish she knew what the problems are. But she is only playing politics. If I had not removed the refugees from that area and started construction, nothing would have happened. In fact, I had offered to hand over the whole [project] to her but she refused to accept the responsibility. I suppose she wanted to remain on the touchline to be free to indulge in criticism.

24 | TUESDAY

The chairman, Election Commission, accompanied by the two members of the law ministry, came to present their report on the last elections. G. Moinuddin [Chairman Election Commission] also presented a social work programme which he has been working on for a long time. I have my doubts if a task of this magnitude can be undertaken. However, I have told him to discuss it with Altaf Gauhar and then come to me for the decision. Moinuddin is an old friend of my mine, so I know him. He has some good qualities, but he has a tendency to be unrealistic and impractical so any proposal by him needs a hard look.

Chaudhary Ghulam Abbas[15] came to see me. He had an operation on his stomach so he is looking very pulled down. He is a man of good intentions but highly emotional and unpredictable. His role in Pakistan has not been very commendable. Whenever an occasion arose he has been instrumental in creating problems for the government of Pakistan, just as others of his type have done. He also called Kashmiri leaders in Pakistan 'proved exploiters' and 'problem children'. I do not think any of them have any credit with the people in the occupied territory.

In my election, Chaudhary Sahib sent me a telegram saying that I was the most unsuitable candidate for presidency and that in the interest of the country I must make way for Ms Jinnah. He told me today that he had done that in an emotional bit and had made a fool of himself. How could a woman of Ms Jinnah's temperament and age run the country? These are the type of people one has to deal with. I told him that as far as I am concerned it has been forgotten and forgiven. What is the good of arguing with unbalanced people?

The finance minister, Mr Uqaili, came to see me to discuss certain problems. We are going through a difficult economic situation, so these consultations are necessary. I asked him how he was liking his job. He said it was thrilling. It bucked me up no end. I told him that there were three jobs I would never like to do. To be a bearer, cook or a finance minister, because whatever you do, you can never satisfy your master.

25 | WEDNESDAY

A food and agricultural organization team headed by an ex-president of Switzerland came to see me after a visit to India. Their object was to find out the extent of distress in the two countries as a result of the food shortage. I told him that there were three reasons for our food shortage. Continued drought for three seasons, cut back in American food supplies under PL 480 and the increase in population. We are taking several measures to increase production, but results are going to take time.

When I asked what the condition was like in India, they said that they had visited Bihar and Uttar Pradesh. Apart from food scarcity there was acute shortage of drinking water in the hilly areas. This happened because of absence of rain for a long time. I feel sorry for the poor people. Their suffering must be terrible.

📖 I had sent Sardar Aslam [secretary general, Muslim League] and Kirmani [provincial minister] to Jhelum to make inquiries as to who is the most suitable candidate for the award of the Muslim League ticket for the vacant seat for the central assembly. I thought the opposition will make it a test case and all combine against us, but surprisingly no opposition candidate is contesting the election. So now it is a matter of selection from amongst our own people which makes the task simpler. After the lifting of EBDO this is the first by-election in West Pakistan. We naturally cannot afford to take a chance on it.

26 | THURSDAY

📖 Held a cabinet meeting. Several important decisions were taken, for instance the need for production of textbooks on the history of Muslims in India, history of Muslims in Bengal, book on our foreign policy, economic and development policies and the genesis of the Constitution. These and their abridgment should be produced in the government printing press and distributed by the government. Also, a decision was taken to set up powerful trading bodies for import and export of major items. I have been demanding this for a long time, but the commerce ministry and Mr Ghulam Faruque either did not understand what I am saying or has no faith in it. The trouble is that unless a man has a flexible and receptive mind, he finds it difficult to understand or work on new ideas. And without new ideas no progress is possible.

I was shaken to hear from Ghulam Faruque that he wanted a change of portfolio and would like to become the head of the Planning Commission. I told him that for several reasons this proposal was totally unacceptable. Apart from temperamental unsuitability of Ghulam Faruque for such work requiring a flexible mind and capacity for sustained and logical thinking, the Planning Commission was presently headed by Mr M.M. Ahmed, the best amongst the civil servants, with wide experience of finance and development, besides being temperamentally suited to negotiations with aid givers.

Saw in the press that Ghulam Faruque had removed A.K. Sumar from the Press Trust and engaged Aziz Ahmad instead. I was stunned as Sumar was going so well. Aziz Ahmad is a civil servant of high grade, but temperamentally least suited to such a job. Ghulam Faruque is getting very tiresome.

27 | FRIDAY

📖 I seem to have a touch of flu. The doctor has told me to remain in bed. It is not easy to remain inactive like this. I have heard that Brig. Ahmad, who served as my private secretary when I was commander-in-chief of the Pakistan Army, is suffering from some mental depression. I feel sorry for the poor man and especially for his wife and children. I have told Major General [Mohammad] Rafi [Khan] to check up if there is anything I can do for him.

With President John F. Kennedy and Vice President Lyndon B. Johnson.

With Dwight D. Eisenhower and President Kennedy.

With First Lady Jacqueline Kennedy.

In a discussion with President Lyndon B. Johnson in the oval office.

Horse-riding with President Johnson on his ranch.

President Johnson at the helm of his speedboat, with Ayub Khan on the left.

Giving a friendly pat to President Johnson.

Signing the Tashkent agreement while Zulfiqar Ali Bhutto claps.

Relaxing at the Ziarat residency.

Meeting Chairman Anastas Mikoyan of the Presidium of the Supreme Soviet of the USSR.

With Russian Premier Alexsei Kosygin in Moscow.

Holding talks with the Russian leadership.

Visiting the tank academy in Moscow.

Looking at a Russian tank in Moscow.

Accepting a copy of the Holy Quran written by Hazrat Usman (RA) from the Grand Mufti of Central Asia and Kazakhstan in Tashkent.

Hunting pheasants outside Moscow.

Addressing the nation on the outbreak of the 1965 war as Zulfiqar Ali Bhutto looks on.

Having tea with Lieutenant General Habibullah Khan.

Fishing near Naran.

With the Shah of Iran in Tehran.

Recuperating after a major heart attack.

Photographed with a Mughal painting in the background.

Relaxing at Hawkes Bay, Karachi.

With Field Marshal Sir Claude Auchinleck.

Riding a camel in the Thar desert.

Begum Ayub Khan laying the foundation stone of their house in Islamabad.

With President Tito of Yugoslavia.

At the foundation laying ceremony of Tarbela Dam.

Blasts being conducted to start the construction of Tarbela Dam.

With King Faisal of Saudi Arabia.

With President Charles de Gaulle in Paris.

With the Deputy Defence Minister of Russia, Marshal A.A. Grechko, at the state guest house, Rawalpindi, 10 March 1969.

Accepting a gift from Marshal Grechko after a lunch held at the President's House, Rawalpindi, 13 March 1969.

With opposition leaders at the Round Table Conference held at the state guest house, Rawalpindi.

Meeting with opposition leaders, President's House, Rawalpindi.

Riding in a motorcade with Prime Minister Chou En-lai.

With Chairman Mao Tse-tung.

At the banquet hosted by Chou En-lai.

Watching military demonstrations with Chou En-lai.

King Hussein of Jordan and his young son Prince Abdullah meeting Ayub Khan. Prince Abdullah is presently the King of Jordan.

King Hussein, HRH Princess Muna el-Hussein, Ayub Khan and Naseem Aurangzeb [Ayub Khan's daughter].

With Sheikh Abdullah.

With Governor Amir Mohammad Khan and Zulfiqar Ali Bhutto.

Receiving the President of Indonesia, Dr Achmad Soekarno.

The Holy Quran being presented to Dr Achmad Soekarno by a Pakistani who had served in the Indonesian army during the War of Independence.

With Dr Achmad Soekarno.

Taking a salute at Kabul airport with King Zahir Shah of Afghanistan.

Talking with King Zahir Shah of Afghanistan.

Addressing the first cabinet meeting after the martial law.

With President Camille Chamoun of Lebanon.

Embracing President Celal Bayar of Turkey.

Conversing with Prince Karim Aga Khan.

Laying the foundation stone of Quaid-i-Azam's mausoleum.

Inaugurating the Bab-e-Khyber.

Inspecting a new hostel for the MNAs in Dhaka.

Examining high yield paddy in Bheramara, East Pakistan.

With President Gamal Abdel Nasser in Cairo.

With President Gamal Abdel Nasser and Anwar Sadat in Cairo.

With Prince Philip and Queen Elizabeth. Inspecting the guard of honour presented by the Scots Guards.

Meeting Prime Minister Harold Wilson at 10 Downing Street.

Commonwealth Heads of State and Government with the Queen.

Riding in the state carriage with Queen Elizabeth on the way to Buckingham Palace.

The last ticker tape parade in New York for Ayub Khan.

Enjoying a polo match with President Dwight D. Eisenhower, 1959.

Being received by President John F. Kennedy and First Lady Jacqueline Kennedy on arrival at Andrews Air Force Base, Washington, 1961.

Ayub Khan's motorcade moving up 14th Street, Washington.

Travelling in an open car with President Kennedy.

At a dinner hosted by Secretary General Dag Hammarskjold in New York.

Indian cadets at the Royal Military College, Sandhurst, 1927. Ayub Khan is seen sitting in the front row on right. J.N. Chaudhuri stands in the middle in the last row. J.N. Chaudhuri was in the same No. 5 Company, Platoon and Course as Ayub Khan. He was the Indian Army Chief during the 1965 war. Both were commissioned on 2 February 1928.

Lieutenant Colonel Commanding 15/16 Punjab Regiment, Landi Kotal, Khyber Pass, 1946.

During a physical training course at Kasauli, December 1933.

Walking with the Quaid towards the saluting base on his arrival at Dhaka airport, end of March 1948.

In Dhaka cantonment with the Quaid and Miss Fatima Jinnah.

With family at the Army House. Sons Akhtar and Gohar are not in the picture as they were at Kakul and Sandhurst respectively.

Partying at the Officers Mess, Abbottabad.

Conversing with the new Indian High Commissioner after the credentials ceremony at Karachi.

Gohar Ayub Khan, ADC to the President.

Paying homage at Mustafa Kemal Ataturk's mausoleum. Major General Iskander Mirza is on the left.

Relaxing in an aircraft.

Witnessing Turkish army manoeuvres.

With President Cemal Gursel of Turkey.

President Heinrich Lubke of Germany, his wife Madame Lubke, Ayub Khan, Zeb and Gohar Ayub in Karachi.

At the opening of Warsak Dam.

Addressing guests at the opening of Rawal Dam.

Inspecting Kaptai Dam in East Pakistan.

Inaugurating Ayub Bridge at Sukkur.

Ayub Bridge, Sukkur.

Inaugurating Taunsa Barrage.

Addressing a meeting held to lay the foundation stone for the new capital Islamabad on Shakarparian Hill.

Looking at the site for the future capital Islamabad.

Being received by Mrs Sirimavo Bandranaika, the Prime
Minister of Sri Lanka, at Colombo.

With Emperor Hirohito and Empress Nagako (aka
Empress Kojun) in Tokyo, Japan.

Speaking at the banquet hosted by Emperor Hirohito.

Being received by King Saud of Saudi Arabia.

Touching the Hajra-e-Aswad.

Coming out of the Holy Kaaba.

Witnessing a drill by the Saudi cadets with King Saud.

Prime Minister of India Jawaharlal Nehru, Ayub Khan and a World Bank representative signing the Indus Basin Treaty at Karachi.

Jawaharlal Nehru laying a wreath on the grave of the Quaid-i-Azam.

Pandit Nehru being shown the material to be used for the construction of the new capital, Islamabad.

Presenting a rose to Pandit Nehru.

The foundation stone of Mangla Dam (with Bengali, English and Urdu engravings) laid by Ayub Khan.

Travelling in the royal carriage with King Mahendra of Nepal.

With King Mahendra in the royal palace.

With the President of Ireland, Eamon DeValera.

With the Prime Minister of Canada, John Diefenbaker.

Planting a maple tree in Quebec.

Havildar Abdul Salam who served Ayub Khan as his batman from 16 May 1946 to 20 April 1974.

Despite failing health, Ayub Khan posed for a photograph with his wife a few days before his death.

Painting of Ayub Khan decorates the back of a truck. Other truck art specimens include the inscription 'We remember you since you have gone' in the picture.

28 | SATURDAY

📖 I remained confined to bed with flu. It is an annoying disease. My nose and eyes are continuously running.

📖 It is heartening news that the USSR and UK have signed a treaty not to use the celestial bodies for military purposes and in any case not to use them as a base for nuclear weapons. It is a big step forward and I hope that non-proliferation treaty would come soon. But meanwhile, the beginning of another ruinous nuclear armament race is in sight between America and Russia. The Russians are supposed to have placed anti-missile missiles around Moscow and Leningrad. This has naturally caused a great alarm in America. The pressure is mounting on the American government to have similar capability. The cost would be about 40 billion dollars to them alone. This would be a terrible waste as this expenditure or portion of it spent in the needy world could change the history of mankind. I put the American expenditure of 20 billion a year or more on Vietnam in the same category. Wasteful and purposeless.

Nuclear power has put a terrible power of destruction in the hands of mankind. Its military use might well cause utter ruination of human civilization. These weapons are today in the hands of a few countries. Efforts, which I do not think will succeed, are being made to prevent their spread. Time will come when their production might well become simpler and cheaper and even the small countries might have them. In that case the world will be a very, very dangerous place to live in. On the other hand, the world government may well come into being through terror felt by the countries big and small. It is quite possible that the fear of being hit by smaller powers may well cause the big powers to shed a portion of their sovereignty in favour of world government. Who knows that God's will is not working for such an eventuality because nuclear weapons and territorial nationalism are incompatible and deadly danger to the survival of the human race.

It is a common belief amongst the Muslims that doomsday will come in the fourteenth century—that is of the Hijra. Well, does not the development of nuclear weapons make this a distinct possibility?

Another sombre thought that faces the world and especially the poor world of Asia, Africa and South America is the shortage of food and the population explosion. No amount of application of science to land is going to fill the food gap because of so many limitations and insurmountable difficulties, especially human ignorance. The answer, therefore, lies in control of population. How is it possible until science produces practicable treatment of mass scale remedy? The answer may well lie in sterilization by radiation.

That leads me to another thought. Time is coming when the resources of the earth will not be available just for anyone or everyone. Only those who contribute something will be entitled to them. This may well lead to selective breeding of the human race through artificial insemination. This sounds like a sacrilege but it is not something that can be brushed aside.

But the world will take to these sensible things after a lot of trial and tribulations, because traditionalism is a part of human nature. New ideas make them feel insecure. That is why there is pain attached to the birth of new ideas like the birth of any thing in life, but far greater pain is attached to the acceptance and implementation of a new idea. The sufferings of pioneers, seers, philosophers and prophets emanates from this human trait.

29 | SUNDAY

📖 I understand that the core of the leading mullahs who created mischief during Eid have been externed by the West Pakistan government and are being [...] in outlying places. I hope this will do their mental health some good, and serve as a lesson to others.

30 | MONDAY

📖 Monem Khan, Governor of East Pakistan, came to see me and discussed several problems concerning East Pakistan.

📖 Recorded the first of the month speech explaining the background of current settlement in Balochistan and the food position. Told people that though a difficult situation lies ahead through failure of three crops the future is not bleak and they must not lose heart.

2 | THURSDAY

📖 My principal secretary was rung up by the governor of West Pakistan that a large scale strike had taken place on part of the railway system and it was threatening to become general. Railway men are led by some unscrupulous labour leaders who had chosen this difficult time to put pressure and testing demands forward. These unscrupulous people know that by stoppage of movement of grain and oil at this critical juncture they could paralyse the country. The negotiations are going on for settlement. But if there is none forthcoming then the government will have no course left open to it but to resort to tough action.

3 | FRIDAY

📖 Governor Musa with his senior officials came to discuss with us the railway strike situation which has now become universal. Apparently they have three unions. The leaders of two are communists. There is evidence to show that the National Awami Party, communists, is actively behind the railway men. Two of these leaders are willing to call off the strike but now the rank and file have gone out of control and are not listening to them. Their original demand was for the provision of *atta* [flour] at the control rate but now they are asking for a subsidy increase of pay by Rs 850 and dozens of other demands. Besides, they have declared this strike without going through due process of law. In other words, it is an illegal strike. After discussion, it was decided that the strike should first be treated as a law and order problem and the strikers dealt with firmly. Meanwhile, emergency railway movement plans should be put in operation to ensure that essential goods keep moving.

It was also brought out during the discussion that there is a danger of labour strikes spreading to many fields causing great dislocation and loss in production. Our only chance of dealing with the problem lies in firmness. Any weakness at this stage will only encourage them further.

📖 Sad news came in last night that the Indian Air Force shot down a single engine aircraft belonging to the Lahore Air Club. A young student pilot apparently lost his way and wandered into the Ferozepur area. This is nothing but murder and a most cowardly act and has to be avenged at an opportune moment.

4 | SATURDAY

📖 The American ambassador, who had been on a visit to Washington, came to see me and told me the following:

a. The decision on giving us facilities for purchase of spare parts for lethal military equipment will take about a month to come. He is doing all he can to make things move.
b. Their administration is happy with the attitude of the Government of Pakistan towards them.
c. Our food requirements, he was non-committal on.
d. Tarbela Dam—why the administration could not assure advanced support, World Bank are trying to be helpful but they are short of funds and have their difficulties.
e. Their offer for assistance for the steel mill stands.

f.   Could I help in resolution of Saudi–UAR differences over Yemen? I told him that I have tried already without success. However, we are anxious that this unfortunate squabble should finish and if there is an opportunity, I shall certainly try again.

6 | MONDAY

📖 Bhutto had a long run in talking a lot of nonsense. Time has come when his pretensions should be exposed. The Muslim League party should take the lead similarly to the pretensions of Qayyum. These have also to be exposed.

7 | TUESDAY

📖 The King of Afghanistan with his wife and son and daughter arrived for a seven-day visit to Pakistan. He would like to call it an official visit. No speeches and no joint communiqués. This indicates that they have no intention of moving forward in having closer relationship with us in the political and economic field.

I took him to my orchards near Khanpur and later to Islamabad. Whilst travelling with him in the car, he talked about the need for peaceful relations in the region, gradually opening up to warn us to create peaceful conditions with India before Kashmir could be settled. He said the Indians too felt that something might be done after the elections are over. It is quite possible that he was carrying this brief from the Russians, and in fact, his coming here might well have been motivated by that consideration more than improving relations with Pakistan.

I gave a banquet at night. A toast had to be proposed. He did not want any speech to be made nor radio Pakistan mike to be put on the table. His excuse was, he did not want people in Afghanistan to find any excuse to criticise his visit.

I sat next to the Queen. She is a lady with some grace and an intelligent mind with warm social contact. I inquired from the King, how he wanted the talks to be held the next day. He said he would like to speak to me alone whilst the ministers could talk separately.

8 | WEDNESDAY

📖 The King came to talk with me at 9 a.m. He started off by thanking us for the warm reception and hospitality. Spoke again of improving relations with India. I told him that we shall be glad to do so if India showed any willingness. About our own problems, he harped on Pakhtunistan stunt. He said that they were not making any territorial claim on Pakistan, nor do they wish to hurt our interests. All they wanted was satisfaction for the people of the Pakhtun areas, meaning thereby, that these areas should be given autonomy. I told him the dangers inherent in such a situation for Pakistan and for the people of these areas. We just could not and would not do anything that divides the country. We are engaged in unifying the people and improving their lot. Any thought to the contrary was just not acceptable. I said why not talk of collaboration in non-controversial spheres like trade and commerce and cultural relationships. He said any talk like that would only raise people's expectations for the resolution of political problem, meaning Pakhtunistan. So we closed on that.

Afghanistan is a weak country. It has always lived by its wits; using one power against the other, besides the Kabuli is proverbially suspicious, smooth but treacherous and untrustworthy.

The King did not have any good impression of India. There was food shortage, great economic stresses and strains, political turmoil, squabbles within the Congress Party, lack of leadership. People were bewildered and drifting. They had almost lost hope.

I posed a question to him. Could we have an agreement, however tacit, not to aggress against each other. He said they had no fear from Pakistan and it was unthinkable that Afghanistan should attack Pakistan. There are, of course, chances of border clashes; we should see that they do not occur.

The King kept on mentioning the need for regional collaboration of the type that included India, Pakistan and Afghanistan. He said that religion should not be the basis of political ties. It should be culture, race and common history. He refused to bite at the idea of any tie up that included Iran.

As I have noticed in many so-called Muslim countries, they are very shy of regarding Islam as the binding force. It makes one wonder why it is so. The only reason I can think of is that where there is an extreme form of nationalism, i.e. my country above everything else, secularism has to be the ruling doctrine. The collective aspects of Islam, that is, the feeling for the Muslim *ummah* go overboard and Islam gets confined to rites and rituals and is reduced to mere matter of relationship between the individual and his God.

But that does not mean that the healthy form of nationalism is incompatible with the spirit of Islam. It is perfectly legitimate to think in terms of one's people and the country. In fact, it would be unnatural not to do so, provided the feeling for the Muslim *ummah* is also kept in mind. This is the form of nationalism I am attempting to develop in Pakistan. Build Pakistan, take pride in it, but also be prepared to do whatever you can for the Muslim brethren elsewhere. We could have strong Muslim nations with ability to form Muslim federation/confederation or call it what you like if this philosophy is followed.

9 | THURSDAY

📖 Sahibzada Faizul Hasan came to see me. He made a demand for obtaining sufficient resources to enable him to look after his family but also be able to mount an offence against Maududi. It boiled down to a demand for new route permits for buses and a small industry. He told me how Maududi and some of the other mullahs were. I told him a story which is not without interest. On one occasion, I had appealed to the ulema to lend a hand in unifying and building the nation. Sometime later, I received a letter from Maulvi Ishaq, who is the *khateeb* of Jamia Masjid in Abbottabad, telling me that I was sadly mistaken in believing that people of his profession were capable of doing anything constructive. He emphasized that a cursory study of history should make it apparent that mullahs have always played a divisive and a disruptive role. I must be under no illusion that any good could come from his class. This opinion, though startling and sweeping, cannot be brushed aside lightly coming as it did from an insider.

Talking about the furore that some of the mullahs had created on the sighting of the last Eid moon, he said those people would like us to disbelieve the radio, television, telephone or material mathematical calculations and believe their eyes for the sighting of the moon. I told him that having been fed on *zakat* for so long their eyes should be least reliable. He roared with laughter. I can talk freely with Faizul Hasan as he is an educated man with liberal views and sense of humour.

📖 Flew into Karachi to receive the King and Queen of Afghanistan who arrived half an hour later from Lahore.

10 | FRIDAY

📖 Took the King of Afghanistan for a duck shoot on Mirpur Sakro Lake. The shooting conditions were good and there were lots of birds, mostly mallards. The King bagged 106 birds. He shot well, but I discovered that some birds were put in his bag. This apparently is a usual practice in Sindh.

On the way back, I propounded to the King my theory of why it was necessary for the emergent Muslim countries to get together in the economic, commercial and cultural field leaving out politics and military matters to begin with. He reluctantly agreed. Then went on to talk about our mutual relationship and the question of Pakhtunistan. Suggested that we should hold talks about it from time to time. I told him that my effort was to improve relations between the two countries, but if that was not possible, then don't let us do anything that will aggravate the situation. He said, but Pakhtunistan was a problem for Pakistan and not Afghanistan and they wanted to be helpful. I told him that precisely for this reason, I want them to keep out of it, as it was our internal problem and we are the best judge as how it should be dealt with. I said, what if we started the question that there are few Pakhtuns in Pakistan so they should join us, would not that be as absurd a proposal as theirs, and is that the way of creating friendly relations?

Pakhtunistan has become a fixation with these people. They are not open to reason on it. My suggestion to the King was that the best way of containing Pakhtunistan was to talk about amalgamating Pakistan and Afghanistan. To this he gave no answer.

11 | SATURDAY

📖 The King asked me as to what were the weapons and equipment like, that the Chinese promised us. I told him that they were excellent. Basically, the Chinese weapons were the same as the Russian, but the Chinese had carried out modifications wherever possible for ease of handling and increase of mobility.

I asked the King if they were satisfied with the weapons and the equipment which the Russians had provided them. He said that these were received in three instalments. The first were not so good, mostly old and reconditioned equipment, but the other two were very good. There was great difficulty in acquiring spare parts, but that has been sorted out. All these deals are on easy payment basis. Thirty-year repayment loan with 2.5 per cent interest. Maybe most of these loans are paid for in gas found in the northern areas of Afghanistan.

I asked him if the water resources of Oxus River were being exploited for irrigation and power generation. He said that a giant survey was being carried out with the Russians for this purpose. It will take another couple of years.

I spoke to him on the possibility of us storing water for hydro-generation on the River Kunar. This river starts from Trichmir and flows through Chitral, enters Afghanistan joining River Kabul below Jalalabad. By damming it in Chitral, we could ensure assured water supply to all the generators in Warsak throughout the year. This would also help irrigation and hydro-generation projects in Afghanistan. He said that we might consider this jointly.

12 | SUNDAY

I called the Foreign Minister and the Foreign Secretary and told them the gist of what transpired between me and the King. I told them that we should try to do all we can to maintain existing relations with Afghanistan, but for any improvement, let the initiative come from Afghanistan. Any attempt on our part to push things will only make them suspicious and get back into their shell. As I said before, normal norms of international relationship do not work with the Afghans.

13 | MONDAY

I came to know that during the period I had a touch of flu and had to be confined to bed, that there was a wild rumour afloat that I had had a stroke and that my left side was paralysed. Later, when I attended a cricket match in Rawalpindi and shook hands with the players, it was said that I was only using my right hand because my left hand was rendered ineffective. This and several other instances of wild and mysterious rumours that gain currency amongst our people so readily, shows that either they are totally immature or are cynics and perverts who gloat in sadism. I hope this is a temporary phase, legacy of colonial rule, and our people will get over it soon and regain faith because people who suffer from unfaithfulness can never make good. Another such instance that came to my knowledge was that a foreign correspondent, who recently visited Pakistan, interviewed a certain number of our people and later held discussions with the information secretary. Told him that he was completely baffled. What the other people told him was completely different to what he had told him. He could believe either one or the other. He could not believe both. These incidences should be enough to prove how difficult it is to serve people who will not see a straight thing in a straight way. Perhaps, most developing countries suffer from this malady. But luckily, this scepticism is confined to urban areas. Large majority of people living in the rural areas are free from it.

Stayed at Gharo rest house for the night. It is a delightful place within easy reach of Karachi. Qazi Fazlullah came to see me and stayed to dinner. He spoke about the mischief that Bhutto is indulging in.

14 | TUESDAY

Went for a partridge shoot at Day Khiplo. This place is about 20 miles south of Mirpur Sakro and is owned by Haji Khan who comes from Larkana. This man is hardly literate, but a real pioneer. Making a start from a humble beginning he is now rolling in wealth. He bought this land at a time when there was hardly any life around and no irrigation facilities. He levelled the land and provided water by pumping from River Indus which flows close by. He was the first man to experiment with growing bananas in West Pakistan and now has hundreds of acres of them. He is known as the banana king. He takes a lot of trouble in rearing partridges for me. They were mostly black and the shoot was very good. I shot about 130 birds.

15 | WEDNESDAY

📖 Went across the Indus to where a new bridge is being built. The bridge is a monumental piece of engineering and will be a magnificent bridge. The cost will be about five crores. It will bring a lot of economic benefits to Sajawal area and the area south of it which is now getting irrigated. This will now be directly linked with Karachi.

📖 The duck shoot was good. I shot 101 birds and my son Tahir 75. He is turning out to be a very good shot. After the shoot, went to my farm at Kulab. It is being looked after by Colonel Sadiq, a retired army officer. About 50 acres of a new variety of wheat has been sown. It is doing very well. I told Sadiq to sow it again in March. It is quite possible that it may work in this climate. Reached Hyderabad and stayed at the rest house. It is a very comfortable place.

16 | THURSDAY

📖 Flew to Badin and went to a place called Dhey for a duck shoot with Ijaz Ali Talpur. Returned to Karachi in the evening.

📖 People all over Ghulam Muhammad Barrage are complaining that their rice crop has been a total right off for the last several years. I advised them that salvation lies in growing *bajra* and *jawar* during *kharif* season when the water is plentiful.

17 | FRIDAY

📖 Flew to Lahore and attended the West Pakistan High Court Centenary followed by a reception by the High Court Bar Association. In my address, I then emphasized the following:

a. A true judiciary was *sine quo non* offered to democratic society and I am determined to uphold it.
b. Why can't our courts become the courts of justice instead of courts of law.
c. Can something be done to make justice cheaper and speedier.
d. Are we sure that our laws and the ways they are operated are in consonance with our historical, ideological, cultural background and do people have faith in them. I believe they don't. They regard the system as alien, which has corrupted us and we have corrupted it to make it work at all. It is up to the lawyers to come forward and bring the law in line with the needs and circumstances.
e. To the lawyers I said that mere knowledge of the mechanics of law is not enough. What you have to do is to understand the rationale of a law so that you can interpret and apply it properly, and if need be, change it in accordance with the circumstances.

In the evening, there was a large banquet given by the judges of the High Court. A large number of people attended including some foreign legal dignitaries. Several speeches were made on legal matters.

📖 A friend came to see me and on inquiry he told me that he had been meeting the student community. Some of them made inquiries about the mullahs who had been recently detained. He told that mullahs can do them no good other than marrying and burying them. I think this is not an inappropriate description of the mullah utility.

18 | SATURDAY

📖 Opened the Saigol Chemical Complex[16] near Kalashah Kaku. They will be making rayon, caustic soda, DDT, pesticides, edible oil and several other chemicals. It is an enormous complex, very tidy and neat. What I was particularly struck with was that Pakistani operators, though young, looked alert and sure of themselves. Saigols are good and enterprising businessmen. The trouble is that they do not give adequate dividends to their shareholders and do not pay government taxes properly. However, I like Rafique Saigol. He is an MNA and treasurer of the Pakistan Muslim League. He is a young man of considerable promise.

📖 Several people came to see me in the morning. A representative of the *New York Times*, Chaudhary Zafarullah and Mr Bucha.

📖 Attended a cultural show given by a troupe of Uzbek artistes. The show was colourful, cheerful and close to life. Instead of indulging in high faluting classical stuff they depicted the life of people as they lived. In other words, folklore. Everybody enjoyed it as the Central Asian culture is so close to ours. I told the organizers of the Arts Council to learn a lesson from them and send artists who are closest to the life of the people so that they can really enjoy it.

📖 Held discussions with the West Pakistan cabinet on the problems created by Jamaat-e-Islami and the political mullahs. Certain tentative decisions were taken. I told them that the real trouble was that having attained Pakistan, we shouted so much of running it on Islamic lines without defining what it was that we foolishly passed the initiative on to the mullahs who had always been opposed to Pakistan and the educated Muslim. He, the mullah, got the opportunity of his life to dictate how this state should be run which in the final analysis means that it should be handed over to him as he is the rightful custodian and interpreter of Islam.

19 | SUNDAY

📖 Attended a dinner party given by Chaudhary Mohammed Hussein, vice chairman, Lahore Corporation. A large number of people were invited, but there was only one main course. This was the case in other similar functions too. After all, people are beginning to listen to me. Chaudhary Mohammed Hussein, though uneducated and simple, is a man of integrity and thoroughly dependable.

I have always held him in great regard. The only trouble is that he speaks so indistinctly that others cannot understand what he is saying.

📖 Called on Malik Feroz Noon[17] in the afternoon. Though not in very good health, he looks cheerful.

📖 I was sitting next to Chief Justice Inamullah[18] at the luncheon given by the judges to their guests in the Lahore Fort. The setting was beautiful and inspiring. We started discussing certain personalities in the judiciary and the bar. Justice Inamullah turned around and said that he was frightened and shaken. How is it that I could assess men and their character on casual association and contact? I told him that it has been my lifelong profession. The basic raw material of soldiering is our human material and weapons. A successful commander has got to know them both.

📖 I had asked Mr Kosygin on one occasion as to the cause of their rift with China. He said that Mao Tse-tung wants to be regarded as the Buddha of Communism and expects us to take orders from him of what we do within our country. Besides, he is jealous of our progress. And look at what they have done in Indonesia. They have played right into the American hands. They are not responsible people. They act recklessly. On the other hand, Mr Chou En-lai had a different story to tell when asked a similar question. He gave several well known reasons but rounded up by saying that the Russians are thoroughly unreliable people. You just cannot trust their word. He said the Chinese did not believe us (Pakistanis), when we said that Indians were unreliable but events have proved that we Pakistanis were right. Similarly, Pakistanis will soon find out that the Chinese are right when they say that the Russians are unreliable.

📖 Received Mr Kosygin and party at Chaklala airport. It was the first time I had appeared in public after my illness. The public cheered me lustily. Kosygin is in a good mood. Seems that he may have good news to offer in the supply of military equipment, apart from the generous offer in the economic field.

📖 Entertained the premier to a banquet. He gave a warm speech. Several of our people spoke to him inclusive of the law minister. He said they don't have many lawyers in their country and they don't miss them. When told of the intricacies of our legal system, he said that it should be done away with and simplified like theirs. I told him that I agreed but there are difficulties in the way. He said that private property was probably the cause of many cases. I told him the cause of much of the litigation often is '*zar, zun, zamin*' (gold, woman, land).

20 | MONDAY

📖 Attended the opening ceremony of All-Pakistan Women's Association[19] educational buildings in Lahore. These ladies had done a tremendous job and have a number of educational institutions on self-help basis. I announced the donation of Rs 200,000. Several people came to see me thereafter. *Inter alia*, ex-Major General Akbar Khan[20] and Maulana Kausar Niazi.[21] General Akbar Khan was all apologies for his past misconduct and offered complete loyalty. I wish he meant it. In spite of his past,

I have done a lot for him. He is an unfortunate man. If he had only exercised self-control and waited a bit, he would have gone a long way in the army in any case. He was one of the distinguished officers and totally fearless. He got a first class DSO in Burma in the last war. Kausar Niazi is a mullah with a forward outlook totally opposed to Maududi because of his devious philosophy and conduct. Promised to give me a note on how to counter Maududi and hence what Muslim League should do.

📖 Attended a reception at the Shalimar Gardens given by the citizens of Lahore in honour of the judges of the High Court and their guests. Just as I was about to leave my residence, it poured with rain which came after four months. I thank God and His mercy. I hope the crops would now be saved. There was a large and colourful gathering at the Shalimar in spite of rain. People went mad when they saw me and cheered indefinitely. It did my heart a lot of good to see them in a cheerful mood. An Iranian lady came and told me that I was very democratic and close to people. They regard me as one of them. I told her that there was no other way of infusing them with my philosophy.

📖 I had a quiet evening and dinner in my room. I did a lot of reading and studied briefs from the governors' conference which is going to start in Pindi on the 23rd. The main topics for discussion are going to be food production, transportation, control of mullahs and rationalization of education curriculum and textbooks.

📖 Rang up my wife at Rawalpindi late at night. I have been on the move during this period and inquired how she and the children were. She occasionally suffers from palpitation of heart. As usual, she said that everything was all right. If there was anything wrong she would probably tell six months later. Here is a woman with hardly any formal education but a perfect and an ideal companion, full of commonsense, compassion and insight. Anyone who comes in association with her goes back relieved of worldly worries. She has a word of comfort for everyone. I don't know what I would have done without her. I certainly would not have been able to do what I have done. God bless her.

📖 Later, Pervez came to see me. He had written a very enlightening article on communism and the philosophy of Mao Tse-tung. We discussed that and told him that Islam's only hope of survival as a living philosophy was if the deep rust of corrosion of mullahism could be removed from it and the Muslim *millat* be allowed to make its principles in the light of current requirements and circumstances. I don't see that happening in a hurry but let alone our masses who are dumb and deaf, our intelligentsia even don't have that realization. Talking about our intelligentsia, I have never come across a more spineless lot than them. I don't know whether they have any convictions. Their main preoccupation is a criticism of the government. Standing out for any rightful cause is not part of their makeup.

📖 Flew into Rawalpindi, rested a bit after lunch and worked till 10:30 p.m. at night. I am now feeling sleepy.

22 | WEDNESDAY

📖 Held a cabinet meeting. A number of important discussions took place and decisions were taken. News came in that Khan Bahadur Muhammad Zaman of Khalabut had died. I went to attend his funeral.

📖 The governors' conference commenced. We started with the consideration of the educational problems. The proposal was to set up an organization at the centre that supervised the production of textbooks in conjunction with the provincial committees. We discussed that all sorts of wrong things were being taught, especially in East Pakistan. East Pakistanis, though agreeing with the need for having textbooks that included national outlook, were not in favour of central supervision. Apart from parochial outlook being a natural reflex with them, they thought that financial and commercial publishing interests would be adversely affected. They were assured that their fears were unfounded. Monem Khan looked worried because of relations of his who run a big publishing house.

24 | FRIDAY

📖 Discussed the food situation in the country, likely deficit in the financial year 1967-1968, our programme for attaining self-sufficiency in food, arrangements for inter-wing transportation within the provinces and our food procurement programme. The agricultural development aims were fixed as follows: Attain food self-sufficiency in the shortest possible time and export as much agriculture products either in raw or finished form. Told people to talk less about the food shortage as that is an assured way of scaring people and induce hoarding. We should instead talk of what we are doing to procure food and attain self-sufficiency.

📖 The commerce, industry and finance ministers came to see me together with the director, Planning Commission to discuss the future of a steel mill in West Pakistan. It was decided that having a mill based on the scrap was no solution. There were several snags in it. The answer was to plan to have an integrated mill based on iron ore.

25 | SATURDAY

📖 Continuing the governors' conference, discussed labour situation and measures that could be taken to ameliorate any hardship. It was decided that organized labour in the public sector should be given food and cooking medium [cooking oil, ghee etc.] and sugar on controlled prices, also all efforts should be made to improve management and welfare work.

Whilst talking about self-sufficiency in food, I don't only mean wheat, rice and maize, I also mean vegetables, edible oil, poultry and fish. Special efforts should be made to grow potatoes on a large scale and provide necessary cold storages. This is the one item which can give large yields and these crops in a year in the same field can fill the food gap in the shortest possible time.

The menace of Jamaat-e-Islami and the general attitude of ulema came under discussion. It was decided to appoint a committee with the following items of reference:

a. How can the ulema and the mosques be made the vehicle of national policy and promotion of national objectives?

b. How to neutralize those who are not prepared to help and are bent upon creating disruption?

c. Jamaat-e-Islami is a political party in religious garb. It is propagating that the present government is un-Islamic and should not be obeyed.

d. How should it be dealt with?

A new Trident aircraft has been procured for the president. I have given instructions that it should be used by the PIA to the full to earn its way. I cannot allow such a huge investment to sit idle.

Discussion was taken to set up a committee of all the ministries concerned, under the chairmanship of the secretary information, to help guide and finance the film industry and get them to help attain national objectives.

A committee was also set up to consider students' problems, prevent agitational activity and prevent exploitation by the political opportunist.

26 | SUNDAY

I gave points to the principal secretary and the information secretary for the first of the month broadcast. Called certain number of ministers and secretaries to consider the situation arising out of the Indian general elections. The information so far at hand shows that the Congress will have a bare majority at the centre. Congress has been defeated in three provinces and is in minority in five others. So even if she [Indira Gandhi] can make coalition in them, they will be weak and unstable. The overall position of this central government has been weakened. Its writ in eight provinces is not going to run. It is quite likely that a rightist like [Morarji] Desai will become the prime minister. The portents of that anti-Pakistan feelings will grow and some adventurism may be indulged in. So coming times are going to be more difficult for us and the Muslim League minority in India. As regards the big powers, the Americans should be happy with the rightist rather than a weak central government. The Russians, on the other hand, will have cause for concern. In such a situation takeover by the army cannot be ruled out, but in India straightforward takeover is not possible or likely for several reasons. Lack of requisite personality that commands respect, 17 provincial and one central capital and so on, besides the Indian army is not homogenous. But a takeover by a politician backed by the army is quite within the pale of possibility or even probability. It looks like India has started moving on the path that we and several other emergent countries took almost on inception. The basic reason is perfidy of the politicians and the political uncertainty of the people, apart from political, social and economic strains and stresses. But above all, the Indian election results are due to the ravages of the direct adult franchise and election to the assemblies. How can people whose orbit of interest is confined to a few miles from their village, produce balanced judgements on matters of national implications. Their reaches can only be based on personal grievances, trials and tribulations as exploited by demagogues, fanatics and parochialism. True that the Indian people have come to complain against the Congress for mismanagement and misgovernment, but look at what they have brought instead. Can these people they have elected resolve their problems? Surely not. So the Indian vote and election results have been negative. I have my doubts if the country will ever recover from the shock. That is why I keep on telling our people not to play with the fire of direct adult voting for elections to assemblies. They will only burn their fingers and themselves in the process too.

📖 I believe that the greatest harm to democracy in the emergent countries has been done by the British and Americans in the name of democracy. They would not let us evolve our own system to suit our conditions. The only explanation I can think of is that they want us to remain unstable and weak and at their mercy. I believe their approach is political and thoroughly dishonest.

The escalation in the Vietnam War is most significant and awesome. The rift between the Chinese and Russians paved the way for the Americans to take an active part in the Vietnam War and the recent internal turmoil within China made them decide to seek military decisions in Vietnam. Anything less does not seem to be acceptable. American assessment seems to be that Vietnam, because of the Chinese internal troubles, is now isolated as it has lost the Chinese secure bases and sanctuaries and so the way is now open to bring them to their knees. So from now on, this war would assume awesome proportions, whilst Russia and China are paralysed by this senseless struggle.

But the events all over the world have favoured American fortunes. Starting with the collapse of the Afro-Asian Conference, elimination of Ben Bella and then Nkrumah, recession of Chinese and to a certain extent Russian influence in Africa, collapse of Indonesia, Russo–Chinese rift, turmoil within China and now the Indian election results have paved the way for America to do whatever it likes and whenever it likes with impunity. This would be welcome if America had a philosophy and a message for mankind. Unfortunately, it has not. But for that matter nor have the communists. Their internal strife has exposed them too. The whole world is now aware of the fact that the big powers are only interested in promoting their narrow national interests. And their interests are naked force, subversion or money.

📖 Flew to Sukkur and went onto Khangarh to spend couple of days with my friend Ghulam Mohammad Mahar and do some partridge shooting.

27 | MONDAY

📖 Ghulam Mohammad [Mahar] is a worthy successor of late Ali Gohar. He has first-class home establishment, runs his estate well, has maintained it and is very sensible, shrewd and balanced. He has come on very well indeed. Did morning and afternoon shoots. I shot 137 partridges.

28 | TUESDAY

📖 Did a morning partridge shoot, motored to Sukkur and flew back to Rawalpindi. Met Muslim Leaguers at Sukkur and gave them some instructions on the coming elections.

📖 Today marks the end of the shooting season for the year. This is not a happy thought. Recorded the first of the month speech, in this I tried to bring about what we are doing on the food and the educational front and told them that disinformation of politicians should be resisted and meddling within the student community and using them for political hands should end. Otherwise they will be dealt with. Also cautioned labourers to behave responsibly.

1 | WEDNESDAY

📖 Approved the final draft of my book, saw a string of visitors and dealt with masses of files. My trouble is I feel very uneasy until I finish my work.

2 | THURSDAY

📖 I am not satisfied with the performance of the director of the Intelligence Bureau. I intend setting up a committee under the chairmanship of General Yahya to look into its working and suggest improvements.

3 | FRIDAY

📖 Ex-minister Habibullah Khan[22] came to see me and narrated many complaints of victimization against Mr Sarwar Khan [who had been a minister under the Nawab of Kalabagh]. It is quite possible that there is an element of truth in them. But Mr Habibullah Khan is also unduly touchy and fussy by nature. However, he has been a loyal friend and supporter and we have to take care of his interests.

📖 Certain documents from India came into my hands, stating that Mr Bhutto had been, till 1958, claiming that he was an Indian citizen and that he was staying in Karachi only temporarily. I have asked for further confirmation. It just shows how unscrupulous and soulless this man is.

📖 Khizr Hayat [Tiwana][23] came to see me. I congratulated him on looking well and also his new marriage. He laughed and said that he wished he had not married. In fact, he is having a lot of trouble with his previous wife whom he divorced. Khizr was followed by Muzaffar Qizilbash.[24] I gave Muzaffar a license for a textile mill, which is now running. He seemed contented and happy. In any case, he is a balanced and sensible man with a lot of sense and realism. Both stayed on for lunch. [Qazi] Essa[25] and [Major General] Shahid Hamid also joined us.

📖 I have been concerned about the organization and performance of the directorate of the Intelligence Bureau. I called a meeting of the defence minister and several others and explained the need for a thorough approach into the affairs of the directorate of the Intelligence Bureau and director of intelligence. Finally decided to appoint the C-in-C Army to be the chairman of a committee to go into the matters and submit a report. I think that directorate of Intelligence Bureau is still working on the old lines. Whilst the texture of our society is fast changing, new pressure groups like the political parties, communists, students, lawyers, mullahs, press etc. and labour are developing. Thus, we need to have connections amongst all of them or guidance and early warning.

4 | SATURDAY

📖 Finance Minister Uqaili came in the evening and discussed several economic and financial problems. He is not brilliant but has a lot of industrial banking experience and has sound commonsense and is down to earth. Like all good bankers, he is a pastmaster in saying no without giving offence. Even otherwise, he is a pleasant man to meet and work with. He is, of course, assisted by a brilliant secretary [Ghulam] Ishaq [Khan][26] who, I am glad, is a great stickler for financial discipline. He is fearless in expressing his views.

5 | SUNDAY

📖 Spent a quiet day at home it being a Sunday.

7 | TUESDAY

📖 The Shah had always been very anxious to see the Karakoram mountains. So we took a trip over these areas in a trident jet lasting for about an hour and a half.

The Shah received a roaring reception in Peshawar. An honorary degree was conferred on him by the Peshawar University in a colourful ceremony. It was gratifying to see that about one-fourth of the student community consisted of females. After this ceremony, he was taken around the campus which has now become enormous and impressive.

The Shah and I took a walk around the gardens in the Government House compound. We talked about the Arab problems. Especially the Iranian relationship with Iraq. I emphasised the need for caution on the part of Iran. There is political instability in Iraq. If they are driven too hard, they will only go to extreme Arabism. Iran's best bet lies in avoiding combined Arab hostility, going slow and disarming Iraq of its fears. The Shah kept on harping on the danger to Iran of Arab nationalism and imperialism. I told him that if that was regarded as a bomb, then its fuse was Iraq and I will repeat that Iran could diffuse it by going slow with Iraq and not precipitating matters. Asking for adjustment of boundaries is no way of inspiring or gaining confidence. There is such a thing as a law of 'territorial imperative.' Human beings react irresponsibly and irrationally when their territorial position is threatened or questioned. He said that for adjustment in the Shatal Arab, they could make concessions elsewhere. I said even then this is no time to make such overtures to Iraq. A weak and unstable government cannot entertain such proposals, let alone consider them.

The Shah said that he was very happy that we were assisting Saudi Arabia and Jordan in building up their military strength and our going there is better since we don't recognise Israel. But Iran has to [...]due to Nasser and Arab attitude. Here too I believe that if Iran was to give up its connections with Israel, good deal of bitterness between Nasser and the Shah would disappear. But I doubt whether the Shah is in a mood to listen to such a proposal.

We then discussed King Zahir Shah's visit to Pakistan. I told him what transpired between the two of us and that our policy towards Afghanistan was that of seeking friendship in a manner that does not make them suspicious. In other words, move in this direction at the pace they wished to do. Their joining the RCD is out of the question at present. The Shah agreed and said they are also following the same course. I told him that the real difficulty was that our friends were very suspicious of each other. The Turks and the Iranians distrust each other. The Afghans, though having a quarrel with us, would rather deal with us than the Iranians. The Shah said the trouble with the Turks was that they would like to regard themselves as Europeans and not Orientals. And in any case, what did the Turks and the Afghans do when Iran was invaded in 1941. They did not lift a finger, in spite of being members of the Saadabad pact.

The question of joint ventures, especially in the defence fields, was also discussed. The Shah said they are thinking of starting a telephone factory. I told him why not join us. We could similarly have joint production in electronics, television, tanks, bombs etc. Separately, we shall only be non-competitive.

8 | WEDNESDAY

📖 Took the Shah and the Queen to Torkham, the Pak–Afghan border. They were given a roaring reception by the tribesmen en route.

9 | THURSDAY

📖 Saw the fire power demonstration of the Pakistan Air Force on field firing range. Large number of people from all over Pakistan had come to witness the show.

The demonstration consisted of strafing with machine guns, cannons, and rocketing and bombing by conventional bombs. The napalm firing was most accurate. Ninety per cent results were attained. The F104, F86 and MIG19 and B57 bomber aircraft were used. Sometimes the aircraft came down as low as 20–30 feet. It was the most spectacular show I have ever seen. Our boys showed a very high degree of training, skill and spirit. It was a precision performance of rare excellence and most heart warming, in spite of the cut in American military aid, we can rest assured that the Air Force is in a high state of training and capable of defending the air space of the country and dealing with any enemy.

During the air demonstration, told the Shah how MIG19s were obtained from China. On one occasion, I flew over the Karakorams in the middle of the night, got to Peking in the morning, negotiated and arms deal with the Chinese leaders, and flew back to Pakistan the next night. Elaborate precautions had to be taken to keep the operation secret. Even my household people did not know that I was not in the house. Faruque and Bhutto accompanied me on this occasion.

Spoke to the Air Force officers after the Air Show. They were full of the performance of MIG19s and swore by the F86s, even though it had become obsolescent. The superiority of this aircraft lay in manoeuvrability. The MIGs, of course, have very high performance and versatility.

📖 Heartening news came from M.M. Ahmed from Washington that the World Bank was prepared to underwrite Tarbela and that we could call for tenders on 23rd March. This is due entirely to George Woods, the American administration continued to remain squeamish. Their trouble is that they have lost or do not know the art of doing things with grace.

10 | FRIDAY

📖 Saw the Horse Show together with the Shah and the Queen. A large number of people were present and greeted us. The show, as usual, started off with the mass band display, tent pegging etc. It was magnificent. A cavalcade of prize animals of different descriptions went around. They were beautiful specimens. This show has done a lot for the improvement of animal production breeding in the country.

A discussion took place with the Shah about the happenings in China and their future intentions. The present population of 700 million will grow and the danger is that they will want to expand. I inquired from the Shah whether that would be a bigger crime or the one perpetrated by the White races by usurping all the empty spaces of the world. Look at Australia, Canada and the whole of South America. Vast continents are occupied by a limited number of whites, where the Asian people can't even have a look in. The truth is that the focus of power is gradually shifting from the West to the East. And that means China. She is bound to strive for and attain super power status with America and the Soviets. As regards the Red Guard Movement, it is essentially an internal problem. Mao does not want his people to lose revolutionary fervour and get soft until their dangers are eliminated or reduced. It is true that certain things in this movement are childish and senseless, but such are the ways of human beings. They become infantile and ridiculous in their fervour and bigotry.

11 | SATURDAY

Held discussions with the Shah on our mutual and world problems. Agreed that the experts of the two countries should now be given green light to examine in detail proposals for collaboration in the political and military fields, especially in respect of production materials, ammunition, clothing etc. On joint oil exploration in Iran, the Shah was very generous and said that in order not to make us risk our money on unproven areas, he offered us participation in an area where oil has been found in confirmation with a big oil firm. He said that this matter has not to be viewed as a business deal, but as a gesture to a brotherly country. Saw demonstration of polo in the afternoon. It was a good game. Padja Effendi put up a magnificent show. He scored five goals, all penalty hits. Saw an exhibition of cheap homes. It was organised by Begum Qaramat and very well indeed.

13 | MONDAY

Flew to Lyallpur and laid the foundation stone of the Agriculture University Campus. This place is coming over very well indeed. There are already 2500 students and 300 teachers of very high quality and qualification. They are also doing first class research work. The vice chancellor, Mr Hashmi, is a very eloquent man with progressive ideas. The university later conferred an honorary degree on me.

Before these functions, I went around the Saigol Agricultural Farm where new type of wheat and maize is being sown. It is a very well run farm indeed.

Addressed the farmers, basic democrats and Muslim League workers in the afternoon at the Agriculture Research Centre. It was arranged that these people be taken round the station to show them what sort of work was going on. I believe they were deeply impressed.

The Agriculture University has started a programme of getting volunteers from the rural areas and training them in rudiments of agriculture and in veterinary science. They are then supposed to go back and teach the villagers. The idea struck me that why should we not adopt this on a nationwide basis. It should be obligatory for every matriculate to do this before getting his certificate. I have told the West Pakistan education ministry to prepare a scheme and let me have a look at it.

I am not very happy at the lack of coordination between the Agriculture Research Centre and the Agriculture University. Parallel work seems to be going on in the research field. This seems a waste nor am I happy with the mechanics and utilization of results of research. We erect science councils and so on, but they seem to be doing nothing. In fact, they should be a channel through which ideas are passed on to government for implementation. I am going to have all this looked into.

Flew back to Rawalpindi in the evening. Heard on the radio that poor Soekarno has been removed from the presidency. I had seen this coming a long time ago and kept on telling him to look after the administration and the economics of his country. He did not pay much attention as his heart was not in these things. Now perhaps he understood them. He has been a very good friend of mine and of Pakistan and I cannot help feeling sorry for him, but our relationship has to be with the people of Indonesia. It is up to them to decide how their internal affairs are to be run. We must avoid taking sides on these matters.

15 | WEDNESDAY

A trident aircraft has been obtained for my use. Since I need it only rarely I have told the defence ministry to hand it over to PIA for commercial use and I could hire it whenever necessary. It would have hurt me to see this expensive aircraft just tied up for my sake.

16 | THURSDAY

Left for Multan by air but had to return to Rawalpindi because of inability to land through bad weather. The flight was bumpy. Apparently a strong crosswind was blowing. I am told a large number of people had assembled in Multan and were disappointed at not being able to see me. Similarly, people in Bahawalpur were disappointed that I should not be able to get there.

There has been widespread rain in West Pakistan. This will help the crops a lot. East Pakistan also had good rains. The crops there are in good condition.

I had a note from the governor, West Pakistan on Bhutto and his activities. He is using a section of students, lawyers and the leftists to promote his purpose for they are using him as a focus of anti-government feelings. My comment was that he will use anyone and do anything to promote his selfish interest. The only answer was to expose his personal character, unreliability and opportunism.

18 | SATURDAY

Visited the new secretariat blocks in Islamabad. Five ministries are now established there. These are magnificent buildings, well designed and fitted, comfortable and worthwhile. I only saw one floor in each block. I was told that it entailed three miles walk. Other blocks are either in the process of completion or planning. The president's house and parliament house are also in the planning stage. It is reckoned that in another five years or so, the essential work would be completed. This, of course, does not include the private sector which I hope will continue to grow as time goes on. Then went over to the Islamabad University site. It is a magnificent area, commands a beautiful view. This university is my brainchild. The idea is to do only postgraduate teaching in science, maths, economics, geology etc. with the view to producing first class brain power. I was glad to hear that several highly qualified Pakistanis are coming back home from abroad for teaching. It was also essential to provide first class manpower opportunities at home. A start has been made already in faculties that don't require laboratory equipment. I am glad that the Ford Foundation is willing to support this university in a big way.

21 | TUESDAY

📖 Laid the foundation stone of my private house in Islamabad.

22 | WEDNESDAY

📖 Offered Eid prayer at General Headquarters grounds. There was a large congregation. Then received people at home who had come to greet me.

23 | THURSDAY

📖 Took the salute at the Independence Day parade at the Race Course ground in Pindi. There was an unprecedented gathering of people. The parade consisted of marching columns of the army, navy and air force, mechanized columns of armed units and auxiliary troops. There was a fly past of the air force. Some 120 aircraft took part, including a squadron of the Imperial Iranian Air Force. We were very happy to see them amongst us. It was a living demonstration of the closeness of relations that are developing between our two countries. My endeavour is to see that these relations develop still deeper. I am sure it will make for a good deal of stability in these regions.

There was a reception and investiture in my house in the afternoon. 101 serviceman and civilians were decorated. Some 2000 guests attended. It was a colourful ceremony. But such a ceremony is always attended by a tragic touch, when the relatives and especially the widows of the deceased come to receive the insignias. I always give them some money to help them.

25 | SATURDAY

📖 Flew into Lahore in very bad weather. There has been widespread rain in West Pakistan. There was some danger of damage to crops in places but by and large it will prove beneficial.

Attended two functions at the Punjab University hall, science and research exhibitions, and then addressed a large number of teachers, professors and heads of institutions, answered a large number of questions which they had sent in before. Both the functions went off very well. I was particularly impressed with the research effort. A lot of good work is being done. It is heartening to see that our scientist manpower is increasing and they are applying their minds to the problems that the country is faced with.

Attended the valima of Mr Moinuddin's son. He has recently got married to the daughter of the Begum of Bhopal.[27] She is a nice girl, well educated and sensible. She is a type of girl who will make her presence felt in an independent position. Mr Moinuddin gave me impressions of his visit to

India. There he happened to meet R.K. Nehru and Indira Gandhi. They both told him that because of great envy towards Pakistan, there is no hope of making any concessions on Kashmir. We could not even allow quotations to the effect that Kashmir had been discussed. Moinuddin used to come to me and ask for opening a dialogue with India on Kashmir on unofficial basis. My reply that Indians are in no mood to live at peace with us carried no commitment to him. I hope after his visit to India and knowing the Indian view on the subject, he has come back as a wiser and a chastened man. He is a good man with good intentions but his mind does not seem to grip the harsh realities of life.

26 | SUNDAY

📖 Attended Himayat-i-Islam[28] silver jubilee functions. Donated Rs 300,000 and advised them that instead of expanding unnecessarily, they should construct and consolidate and improve the standard of the existing institutions.

In the afternoon went to see model farms in the union councils. I was very impressed with the quality of dwarf variety of wheat grown. At this pace, we should soon be able to overcome our food difficulty. Spoke to certain members of village and villagers and it was a pain to hear that their holdings had become so small that out of about 70 pairs of bullocks only about 20 pairs can be usefully employed. This change is caused by excessive growth of population. We are doomed if we don't arrest this growth, and quickly. I was told that there was a great level of hunger in the Punjab now.

27 | MONDAY

📖 A number of people came to see me starting with 20 ulema led by Sahibzada Faizul Hasan. They showed resentment against Maududi's activities, calling him a disruptionist and politically motivated. They expressed the desire to counter him in every possible way. They expressed faith in my constitution, which gave the country a strong centre and was nearest to the Islamic concept. Also promised to propagate the issues to the rest and best of their ability. I told him that in order to prove effective, they should organize themselves and appoint representatives who could meet our ministers from time to time to seek guidance. Faizul Hasan then took me aside and told me that he would prefer to deal with officials of the central government. He assured me of the quality work these people could produce, but he could give no guarantee of their integrity where money was involved.

📖 Mohammad Khan Junejo[29] offered to work in Sindh and expose Bhutto on local issues. I told him to go ahead.

📖 Justice Cornelius[30] also came, he tried to explain away laudatory remarks he made on Bhutto in Hyderabad. He was only producing lame excuses. His trouble is that he lacks practical common sense and is a poor judge of men.

📖 A meeting of the central ministers took place with the governor to fix prices for different agricultural commodities in order to assure the farmers a good return for the next three years. I think they have come to a satisfactory provision. Took off for East Pakistan.

28 | TUESDAY

Laid the foundation stone of the telephone factory at Tongi [East Pakistan] and thereafter went to a village where IRRI rice is grown on an organized basis. The plants look very healthy and large, number of tilling far greater than the local varieties. The farmers are enthusiastic and want to take the new seed and the method of cultivation.

I still see the old type of plough used in East Pakistan. It hardly scratches the ground. True, their bullocks are very weak and small, but they could use modern ploughs made to suit their conditions. I told the governor to get samples from West Pakistan.

Discussed the future of Manik Mian,[31] who is under custody. He owned a paper called *Ittefaq*, which turned into a major instrument of disruption. It was decided to let him off.

I am seeing Mohan Mian[32] in a day or two. He is cunning and unreliable. But can be used politically.

29 | WEDNESDAY

Went to Mymensingh by train and addressed three public meetings en route, the fourth meeting was held in Mymensingh. It was a mammoth gathering. Over half a million people attended. Also gave an address at the reception that was held in the evening. Then went to dine at Monem Khan's residence. This was followed by a film on my visit to UK, on birth control and grow more food. So in one way or the other it was a busy day.

I heard that the speaker of the National Assembly, Abdul Jabbar Khan,[33] went to dine with Fazlul Qader Chaudhary[34] at Chittagong and took with him all MNAs and MPs and the officials of local administration. Yet Fazlul Qader was removed from the speakership for the sake of Jabbar and later removed from the Muslim League party for abusing Jabbar in the assembly for which Fazlul Qader has never forgiven me. It just shows how gutless and character less these people are. To put any reliance on such people is the height of folly.

30 | THURSDAY

Saw winter rice cultivation by pump water in a village close to Mymensingh, it was the first time such a thing had happened. The villagers were thrilled. If this practice becomes universal, East Pakistan can add greatly to its food production. What they need badly is winter irrigation.

Then addressed Muslim League workers. They showed great spirit. The Muslim League volunteers especially did good work. I gave them a reward of rupees 500.

Returned to Dacca by train. During the journey talk started on the treatment that was meted out by the Hindus to the Muslims in Bengal in the British period. The Muslims were treated worse than slaves and pariahs. A Hindu would not hesitate to eat food touched by a dog, but not by a Muslim. At that time there was a good deal of resistance amongst the Muslims to use Sanskritised Bengali and yet today they are very anxious to eliminate all Persian and Arabic words from their language.

I told them why do they not write a true history of their past, so that future generations know how their forefathers felt. There is a large refugee element in Dacca. They mostly come from West Bengal and Bihar, their mother tongue is Urdu[35] and so they are naturally demanding Urdu medium schools, I doubt very much if the Bengalis would give them that. They will at once turn it into a political question and victimize these poor people. My advice to them would be to learn in Bengali and ask for Urdu to be taught as a second language.

31 | FRIDAY

Visited Jessore. Addressed a public meeting. Jessore is supposed to be the stronghold of the NAP, that is, the National Awami Party. At one time it was the stronghold of extremist Hindus. The commissioner was not in favour of my going there, but the Muslim Leaguers insisted and I demanded to go there. The meeting went off well. There was a large gathering.

Returned to Dacca in the evening. Begum [of] Dacca[36] came to see me in the morning. She demanded that I should cover the expenses of her son's marriage. I was embarrassed, but I suppose I shall have to assist.

1 | SATURDAY

📖 Attended a meeting of the Muslim League workers and office bearers who are affecting enrolment and holding elections. They came from all over the province. It was a good gathering. I stressed the need for formation of different bodies to meet amicably. Deserving cases must be given due consideration. Later there was a reception by Muslim League parliamentarians at Hotel Shahbagh. Large number of people attended.

📖 Dined at the divisional headquarters mess at Tejgaon. Met a number of officers I knew. They are fast growing and maturing. Amongst them was Brig. Jamshaid who is MC [Military Cross] with a bar and was Sitara-e-Jurat at Chawinda in the 1965 war. He was commanding a battalion that was struck by the Indian armoured division. He, together with Ali Nisaar and others held them for three days until 6 Armoured Division came on the scene and counter attacked. He looked so calm and cool and unassuming. I understand he comes from Domale in the Salt Range. Some of the outstanding junior commissioned officers, and men in my battalion came from that village. They are mostly Awans.

2 | SUNDAY

📖 Addressed some 4000 teachers and guardians drawn from all over the province. They seemed pleased. Attended a dinner party by the government. The governor had invited some 300 people.

3 | MONDAY

📖 Addressed senior professors and heads of institutions of East Pakistan University. They sent me a long list of questions which I answered. I think a lot of their doubts were removed. This trip to East Pakistan has been very crowded and busy, but I saw a large cross section of people and, on occasion, had the chance to speak to them. I am very grateful to Monem Khan for arranging this. In spite of his advanced age he has infinite energy and stamina, also he is doing his utmost to administer the province. He is unpopular with some people, but which strong administrator would not be in East Pakistan? As far as I am concerned, he is loyal, patriotic, and an indefatigable worker. Flew in to Lahore and stayed at the government house.

📖 An international delegation of Muslim countries led by Mr Amjad Ali[37] came to see me in connection with the construction of an Islamic Centre in New York. They are looking for subscriptions.

4 | TUESDAY

📖 Addressed a conference of commissioners and DIGs at the government house. All the ministers were present. A record of my talk should be available in private papers. Recently the elections of Council Muslim League have taken place. Shaukat Hayat[38] and Daultana were contestants for the presidency. Ms Jinnah supported Shaukat and so did Qayyum, though reluctantly. After a lot of dogfight and wrangling, Daultana won. A bitter feud has arisen amongst them and the defeated faction is accusing the other side of tampering with the ballot box and pushing in bogus votes, and yet these are the people who talk so loudly of parliamentary democracy and direct vote. I believe Ms Jinnah is furious that her candidate has lost.

A booklet written in Arabic was brought to my notice. It paints Pakistan and me in a very bad light. Its main burden is that mullahism is not allowed in the country and that my policies are anti-Islamic. This, after what I have done for Islam. I guess there is no indication of the author or the place and origin, but it is suspected of having been the product of Maududi, who is ill. The booklet is supposed to be distributed on a large scale in the Arab world. This is what Pakistan gets out of giving asylum to this traitor and true enemy of Islam. In any other Muslim country, he would have been lynched like a dog, but in Pakistan we have rule of law of which the traitors take full advantage and protection.

8 | SATURDAY

Returned to Rawalpindi and had a quiet day.

9 | SUNDAY

Sunday, played a game of golf in the morning, did badly, spent the rest of the day in reading.

11 | TUESDAY

Monem Khan, Governor, East Pakistan, came to see me along with his finance minister. I also asked our finance minister and the secretary to attend as the governor was to bring up certain problems with financial implications. They were asking for certain concessions, which were not possible to concede.

Discussed with the foreign minister[39] the effects of leftist government in West Bengal on East Pakistan. Chances were that the disruptive elements in East Pakistan will get a fillip. On the other hand, they might get frightened of Hindu domination. The foreign minister did not agree with the latter. He said that East Pakistanis are incapable of seeing beyond their nose. In their hatred for West Pakistan, and especially the Punjabis, they were capable of doing anything stupid. They got an empire as a result of partition of Bengal in 1905 with Assam included. They lost it through sheer stupidity. Instead of fighting for retention of partition, they sided with the Hindus that their language and culture will be jeopardized. Today, they were on a similar turning point of history. One false step and they will go back to serfdom under the Hindus for another couple of centuries.

12 | WEDNESDAY

Long cabinet meeting held in the morning and the afternoon. A large number of subjects were discussed and some important decisions taken.

13 | THURSDAY

📖 The Canadian Minister of Development and Industries called on me. He is on a visit to Pakistan in connection with the opening of the thermal power station in Sukkur, which is a Canadian aided project. We talked at length about the future of the Commonwealth. I said what brought it about was the cover of British military and economic power, which has now gone. Its continuation will depend on replacing the economic cover if not the military cover by two affluent countries like Canada and Australia. If they did not do that the Commonwealth will soon whither away. He has also had lengthy talks with our economic affairs people. They have made out a very good case why Pakistan should get greater assistance.

The Canadians are currently giving us 36 millions dollars[40] worth of aid a year. Most of it is soft terms. Their present aid level stands at 6 per cent of GNP. They have decided to raise it by 1 per cent. Pakistan could make a better showing by added aid.

14 | FRIDAY

📖 Collected foreign affairs, defence, finance and the planning people and gave them my assessment of the new American policy on arms supply to us and their insistence that we get into talks with the Indians on reduction of arms. One look at the budgetary figures will show who is arming and who showed disarmament. Our pre-war budget was about 150 crores exclusive of the American aid. It now stands at 225 crores. The extra 75 crores is a marginal increase on the void left by the withdrawal of the American military aid whereas the Indian budget has risen from 150 to 350 to 800 and now nearly 1100 crores. This is all directed against us and any decrease on our part will tantamount to suicide. Since our equipment is mostly American, we shall be hurt more by this policy.

I told these people to prepare an aide memoir on our views of this new policy and American attitude and conduct on economic aid, food, supply and financing of the Tarbela Dam project. I want to give this paper to the American ambassador for delivery to President Johnson. Whether they mean it or not this had an adverse effect on our economy. Is it their intention to cripple us.

📖 Saw a film on the three Chinese nuclear blasts and the guerrilla warfare they fought during the Japanese occupation. This was shown at my house at the request of the Chinese embassy. They seemed to have made considerable progress in the nuclear field.

15 | SATURDAY

📖 Entertained Eugene Locke, who is now leaving Pakistan,[41] to lunch. He came with his wife and two sons. [G.] Moin[uddin] and his wife and his son with new bride also came. I handed over the aide memoir to him for transmission to President Johnson. He promised to do that. He tried to prove that if worked properly, the new American arms policies should work in our favour. He then told me that feelings in the countryside were favourable to me and that I should do more for them.

Locke asked for my suggestions on Vietnam. I told him that the only sensible course was for the Americans to pull back into a few secure areas and allow the Vietnamese to scout out their own affairs as they liked. The other course would mean prolonged war, great demoralization and tremendous material sacrifices and loss of prestige on the part of the Americans. The aim should be to give the Vietnamese nationalism free play, given that they will not want the Russians or the Chinese to have a foothold there, just as they do not want the Americans to have it. He said that their concern was to have a separate, friendly, South Vietnam. I said that, too, was more likely to be achieved if both Vietnams were recognized as separate entities. If the South Vietnamese can maintain their separate identity, they will do so. It is their right. American pressure is less likely to make them feel that way. He said that one thing was certain. They are not going to pull out of Vietnam and that in the near future pressure against North Vietnam and the Viet Cong was going to increase in an effort to bring them to the conference table. This sounded ominous. It is obvious that they are seeking surrender of North Vietnam and the Viet Cong.

📖 Spoke to Altaf Gauhar of the need to familiarize people at large, the masses, of projects that have been completed or are under construction. This could be done through show of films and by taking people of surrounding areas to projects. It will be a good eye opener for them and educative. Similarly, our effort at developing new strains of grain should be familiarized.

📖 It is understandable that there should be a wave of disappointment on the American military equipment supply policy in the country and it is a good thing to express it, but we cannot totally alienate the Americans completely. It would be against our interests. Meanwhile, we must make a greater effort to tap alternative sources of supply and we are doing so. The snag is the Russian attitude. They have agreed in principle to supply military equipment, but are not yet prepared to go further. We are making inquiries in France, Czechoslovakia, Poland, Romania, and China. Let us see what luck we meet.

17 | MONDAY

📖 Neville Maxwell of the London *Times* came to see me and asked some questions on US–Pak relations, Pak–India relations, Pak–China relations, and our internal problem of food, development and politics. He asked what I considered to be our major problems. I told him menacing Indian military build up and exploding population. If we could have stabilized our population at around 80 million, we could have given our people a living standard equivalent to some of the European countries, but with the increase of nearly 3 per cent per annum, God alone knows what would be the outcome.

18 | TUESDAY

📖 Gave a talk to GHQ officers and the general officers who have come to attend divisional commanders conference. A copy of the points follow.

1. Purpose: giving you a bird's eye view of some of the major problems of the country. This may help in getting correct perspective and reasons for certain decisions.

2. Problems.
   a. Sociopolitical.
   b. Security and defence.
   c. Development and reconstruction.
   d. Food.
   e. Population explosion.

3. Social, political, spread of education, and industrial and consequent urbanization changing social structure. The following pressure groups developing.
   a. Student community-lawlessness.
   b. Teachers.
   c. Lawyers.
   d. Labour.
   e. Religious leaders.
   f. Press.
   g. Provincial and regional pulls.
   h. Opposition parties.
   i. Vast masses of uneducated people, task of governing the country not easy.

4. Security.
   a. Menacing Indian build-up military budget 1100 crores.
   b. The attitude of super powers. Coincidence of Russian policy in building and supporting India to our disadvantage.
   c. Change of American policy since 1962.
   d. Circumstantial and geographic compulsion is to normalize relations with the Soviet Union and China. Just as well that this was done in time. This infuriated Johnson, but we have to keep our appearances with America as well because of our dependence on them. This foreign policy is not easy to conduct. The best way of doing it is to do it silently.
   e. 1965 war fought heroically against tremendous odds. India increased their strength and obtained a lot more equipment from Russia. We, too, had to increase our strength.
   f. The war demonstrated how much pressure the superpowers, and especially America, can exert.
   g. Grateful for what the Chinese and other friends did for us, but in the final analysis we fought our war single-handed and have to do so in future.

What of the future.
   a. Have to watch India more carefully with constant readiness. A weak government in a big country, a source of danger.
   b. Procurement of arms and equipment.
      1. Dependence on our own resources.
      2. So far we have not done so too readily, but have to find alternative sources of supply: France, China, Russia.

3. Create indigenous capacity for production.

c. I am aware of the problems you are facing, lack of accommodation—bear it cheerfully.

5. Development.
   a. Second plan went off very well: Planned targets achieved. Exports increased. Third plan made a start in difficult circumstances, but we are not doing too badly.
      Resources obtained from:
      1. Consortium countries, American attitude not helpful.
      2. Our own resources.
      3. Socialist countries.
   b. Creation of Planning Commission, several autonomous executive and financial authorities, cut red tapism and accelerate development. I saw this clearly a long time ago. Recently, similar financial autonomy given to service chiefs. I hope it will help.
   c. In the third plan, emphasis will be on food, more fertilizer, better irrigation, better seeds and implements. Task is how to awaken our people.

6. Food, shortage due to drought, flood, cyclone and growing population.
   a. Gap about two and a half million tons, American tardiness and change of policy. Last purchases by own resources this year. Next year will also be difficult and put strain on our foreign exchange resources. Great strain on transportation.
   b. But hopeful of the future. Better seeds have greater promise. Provincial governments, too, are conscious and doing their best. People beginning to awaken.

7. Population explosion.
   a. 1951 census 75 million, 1961 census 94½ million. What is it now, God alone knows, how can we better the lot of people like this.
   b. Our efforts on family planning encouraging. I hope we succeed, otherwise man will eat man. The army should give a lead on this.
   c. Given 70 to 80 million people we could have the living standards of some of the European countries.

8. So the coming time is going to be hard and challenging, but very interesting. Lot has to be done in every sphere. So let every one go to it in his own sphere. Miracles are made by sound planning, hard work and courage.

📖 Secretary General United Nations, U Thant, came to see me and stayed on for lunch. He spoke about Indo–Pak relations. I told him that they have no intention of solving the basic problem of Kashmir and reduction of armament. In fact, they are arming furiously. Our hazards are increasing. Meanwhile, they would like to see us disarmed. That is the meaning of the artificial cry over the American decision to sell us spares under certain conditions. They do not want us even to have American obsolete equipment in serviceable condition. They are doing so in the hope that Americans will get disinterested and will not do even this much for us. They have Chester Bowles and several other soft headed Americans who form a fifth group or lobby them. Americans are intelligent people, but it is curious how easily they can be influenced by childish things. Little thought is required to know that India is a lame duck.

U Thant also spoke of his visit to Afghanistan and their statement that they would like to live at peace with Pakistan except for the Pakhtunistan question. I told him this was nothing but interference in our internal affairs. But if they must insist on Pakhtunistan, the answer lies in federating or confederating with Pakistan.

19 | WEDNESDAY

A certain number of *mashaiks* led by Pir Dewal came to see me. They offered their full support for maintenance of political stability and made certain demands. Better running of *Auqaf*, collection of *Zakat*, etc. I told them that we already have them under consideration. This type of people are more relaxed and broad-minded, unlike the mullahs whose minds are grooved and narrowed. One can talk philosophy with them at the same time. They have great verbal facility. That is why innocent and ignorant people come under their influence so easily. Glib talk is like a narcotic. Few people can see through it and remain uninfluenced.

20 | THURSDAY

King Mahendra and the Queen of Nepal arrived on a two-day visit. They have recently been to East Pakistan for a week's visit. I think he has used his closeness to us and China to good advantage. He has been able to resolve most of his problems with India.

Our foreign office in Bhutto's and Aziz Ahmad's time were bending backwards to establish close relations with Nepal and even Sikkim and Bhutan. They thought that these countries could prove a counter to India, little realizing that geography favoured them and was against us. The Indians could cut off these connections at a moment's notice. Besides ,the economic dependence and religious affinity of these countries with India is so great that they dare not offend India. And this proved to be right. India obtained from the king all the statements they wanted on Kashmir etc.

Mr Nixon, former Vice President of United States came to see me and stayed on for lunch. He is on a whirlwind tour of 34 countries in Europe, Asia, Africa and South America on a fact-finding mission. He must have a lot of energy and zeal to do all that. He asked me questions on Indo–Pak, Sino–Soviet, US–Pak and Pak–Soviet relations, and also on Vietnam. He is a relaxed man so one could talk to him freely. The transcript of the talk should be available in my private papers in the office. He was particularly anxious that US–Pak relations should improve.

On Vietnam, Mr Nixon is a hard liner. He did not expect peace to come to Vietnam before 1968 presidential elections. But after that whichever party came into power, war would be intensified. So the prospects are menacing.

Mr Nixon laid great emphasis on political stability in the emergent countries under whatever form of system that suits their condition. He thought it was foolish of anyone to expect transplantation of American type of democracy to flourish everywhere. Look at the mess that the Philippines is in through this folly.

22 | SATURDAY

📖 Held talks with the King [Mahendra] and his staff. They agree to allow us the facilities for installing microwave relay stations in Nepal. These are required for communication with East Pakistan. Also talked of maintaining good relations with US, saying openly that they want to get out of India's clutches as much as possible. They are getting considerable assistance from Russia, China, and even India. There is some US assistance too.

A number of countries are opening embassies in Nepal. There seems to be widespread interest in that area, perhaps due to closeness to Tibet and now that the Chinese road from Lhasa goes through to Kathmandu.

The King praised the Chinese very much for keeping their promise and being very prompt and thorough. He said that the others when told this do not believe it. I told him that our experience was the same with the Chinese. He regarded the Americans as being good people, but childish. Talking about India, he said that the relations were good on surface, but he could never be sure of what is in their mind. But there is one redeeming factor; that they are now far too busy in the internal squabbles. I agreed that the Indians would prepare to have a stooge in his place. He was thought too independent for their liking.

The King and his party departed in the afternoon for Karachi en route to Paris.

📖 Held discussions with Altaf Gauhar on matters concerning the ulema. Maududi and his party should be treated and exposed as they are: pure and simple politicians using the garb of religion. The curriculum in the Abbasia Darul Uloom[42] should be looked into by the Islamic Research Institute and the staff there and in other institutions run by the West Pakistan Auqaf should be screened. Anyone who has political inclinations should be got rid of. In the villages, a *baitul maal* should be established with all charities pooled and spent on the *Pesh Imam* and other needy people in an organized manner.

25 | TUESDAY

📖 Gave a talk to the central government secretariat officers on the problems facing the country. Points for the talk follow:

1. These monthly meetings were given up because of the war interruption. They serve a useful purpose. That is why they were resuscitated and I promised to give the first talk. In future, the cabinet secretary will nominate a representative of a ministry or a department to talk on matters that they are dealing with. What are the problems facing them and what are their thoughts for the future? I expect all concerned to attend.

2. I thought this meeting could begin with questions which I would try to answer, but they happen to be few. So I have decided to give you a quick review of the major problems facing the country. At the end, if your questions remain unanswered, please do not hesitate to ask them.

3. Problems.
   a. Sociopolitical.
   b. Security and defence of the country.
   c. Relations with major powers.
   d. Development and reconstruction.
   e. Food situation.
   f. Population explosion.
   g. A look into the governmental organization and the quality of work output.

4. Sociopolitical. Our intention is to set up an Islamic state. Lack of consensus among the Muslims of the subcontinent led them to create a separate homeland for themselves, emergence of parochialism and regionalism, major increase in the education facilities and industrialization resulting in large-scale urbanization have created the following political pressure groups.
   a. Political mullahism.
   b. Student lawlessness and politicizing teachers.
   c. Disgruntled lawyer community.
   d. Provincial and regional pulls.
   e. Negative, and in most cases anti-Pakistan, attitude of opposition political parties.

All exploiting, God-fearing but uneducated ignorant and gullible masses and even the educated people who show very little sign of knowledge of historical perspective and the dangers that surround them. In other words all those who unfortunately cannot see beyond their noses and think in terms of personal interests, often in the guise of regionalism. Continuous task of building up the resistance of masses. Strengthening Muslim League is the answer, but historically our people have either followed individuals or supported movements. So you can see that to help such a society better itself and lead it is not easy. However, I am not without hope that things will improve and sense of collective consciousness, responsibility and discipline will emerge as time goes on.

The present time is a pioneering time and life of pioneers is never a bed of roses. The answer is to have unfaltering faith, courage, sense of purpose and perseverance. The reward is bound to come.

5. Security and Defence.
   a. Menacing Indian military build-up, especially after 1965 war. Military budget of India rising from 150 to 350 million and now 1100 crores. Ours stands at 225 crores. The increase fills the gap left by the withdrawal of American aid.
   b. Heroic defence put up by our armed forces and the people in 1965 war. This was foreseen and arranged for.
   c. Soviet and American policies towards India and their support.
   d. Termination of American military aid and the recent announcement of their policy on sale of spares.
   e. Meanwhile, we have not done too badly in procurement of armaments. The armed forces are in very good shape. Our efforts are to find alternatives sources of supply. We are hopeful of success. It will take another six months or so before the situation clarifies.

f.   Idea of a citizens' army is fallacious.

6.   Relations with the major powers.
   a.   Have to have good relations with China and Russia for:
      i.   Geographic compulsions
      ii. Economic and military reasons.
   b.   For economic and other reasons, we cannot afford to turn our faces away from USA.
        Emotional approach, no answer. Cold war receding. Our value not so much as it used to be.
        Reasons why we are not getting out of SEATO and CENTO. We shall be quite happy if we
        are told to leave. Even France is not walking out of SEATO. Our presence has a steadying
        effect.
   c.   Relationship with India: I do not see any chances of settlement on Kashmir. A weak
        government in India with powerful armed forces, a source of danger. We have to live much
        more cautiously. Under such a situation, what do we do? Keep leaning against the enemy and
        await our chance. Wisdom and patience is the key to the problem.

7.   Development and Reconstruction.
   a.   Successful implementation of second plan.
   b.   Third plan has made a bad start under adverse circumstances. Communications might well
        prove to be bothersome.
   c.   Source of resources.
      i.   Our saving is considerable because of enhanced foreign exchange earnings and increase
           in internal revenues though they are under great strain through extra military and food
           cost.
      ii. Contribution by consortium.
      iii. Loans and credits from socialist countries. The future is hopeful.

8.   Food situation.
   a.   Why deteriorating.
   b.   Food gap, how made.
   c.   Our plan for self sufficiency.
      i.   The plan reoriented.
      ii. Greater production, fertilizers and pesticides, better seed, more irrigation.
           But the task is now to awaken the man behind the plough. Here, too, the future is full
           of hope.

9.   Population Explosion.
   a.   1951 census 75 million, 1961 census 95 million and now God alone knows.
   b.   Our crusade on birth control. Our solution lies in its success.
   c.   Sensible people must practice and lend a hand in its propagation.

10. Governmental Organizations.

    a.   We are quoted as a model of development. Why? This is due to having a sound Planning Commission and a large number of autonomous financing and autonomous bodies. Normal secretariat red tapism would never have allowed such rate of progress. I have predicted this in 1954. Read my book.

    b.   Recently the three services have been given financial autonomy. I have no doubt that the results will be beneficial.

    c.   But can we say that the executive ministries and departments are working to maximum efficiency. I believe they should be given similar autonomy. Why don't we trust our useful manpower, which is limited.

    d.   Then inordinate delays in disposal of cases, especially pays, pensions, gratuities and accounting. Why not introduce computers and use banks instead of treasuries? All this needs careful look.

11. Any questions?

26 | WEDNESDAY

📖 Today was the first occasion that the cabinet meeting was held in the central secretariat in Islamabad. For me it was a matter of great satisfaction. A mere dream of the new capital had taken practical shape and is now a living thing pulsating with life. The setting, too, with the background of the green Margalla Hills is fascinating and inspiring. We discussed several important problems *inter alia*: decentralization, financial control system and introduction of computers and other mechanical means. Several committees were setup to go into these problems.

📖 Mr Pirzada came to see me in the evening and explained what was going on in Dacca amongst the leaders of opposition parties. They are trying desperately hard to form a common front but at the same time they are suspicious of each other. Being thoroughly selfish, every one of them is trying to score over the other. It is quite possible that they may succeed in having a façade of unity but chances are that it is not going to last long. They also express the fears that if there is a change of regime, the successors may not be as merciful as I have been. One revealing thing that came to light was that Mujibur Rahman[43] had been telling his followers that once they raise the flag of rebellion in East Pakistan, the Americans will rush to their assistance. According to him, there were several American submarines waiting in the Bay of Bengal. I don't believe for a moment that there can be anything in this, but such short-sightedness with the ignorant and gullible people. There is now circulating a story amongst his followers that there will be a revolution in May and that they should be ready for the explosion. It is quite obvious that this man is a menace and will continue to mislead the Bengalis as long as he lives.

27 | THURSDAY

📖 The Turkish Prime Minister, Suleiman Demirel, with his wife, and the foreign minister with a large entourage arrived on a week's visit. I gave a banquet in his honour. He seems to have matured a lot and gained considerable self-confidence since I last saw him. Being an engineer by profession, he has considerable insight into economic and developmental matters. Turkey should move fast under his wise leadership.

28 | FRIDAY

📖 Held a discussion with the [Turkish] prime minister separately on US-Pak relations, our attitude towards CENTO and the RCD. I told him that we have lost faith in CENTO as it failed us as a critical time, but for the sake of our friends, Iran and Turkey, we do not want to break away from it. Also, the circumstances have changed. There is less tension between the US and the Soviets. The relationship between Turkey, Iran, and Pakistan with Russia is also improving. So the need for CENTO as a military pact has receded. In any case, the Americans have no intention of putting military life into it. If it has to continue, it should be called what it is: an economic arrangement of a limited type.

About Pak–US relations, I told him that the Americans have told us plainly that in future its scope will be limited. They have stopped military aid and are giving economic aid in a reduced form and halting fashion. Meanwhile, immense resources are being given to India, who, in turn, is turning their resources into military hardware. I gave him a copy of the aide-memoir which I had given to Locke for delivering to Johnson.

Later we met in another room with our staff and discussed Cyprus, Kashmir, Vietnam and Mr Kosygin's visit to Turkey, etc.

The prime minister told me that there were 200,000 Turks employed in Germany and that the Germans were giving them aid to the extent of 20 million Deutsche marks. Bit in actual fact, what they gave is worth several times more. If an article is worth is worth $100, they price it $10. Asked him if the Turks could buy things for us through Germany as the Germans were reluctant to sell us military equipment direct against America's wishes. He said they would gladly do so. He promised to manufacture things for us in Turkey. I told him that was of no use because they get arms and ammunition as from America and elsewhere, their armament factories are running idle. If they are reactivated for a limited production, the costs are bound to be high which we can't afford. He agreed.

Before leaving, the prime minister spoke about King Faisal's proposal for a World Muslim Conference. He did not think it was a good idea. If the world were to split up on religious basis, it would lead to several serious problems. Then the Brahmans, Christians, Buddhists would have to hold their own conferences. I told him that I can only partially agree with his views. If this conference were to cover political and military matters, then in this age of nationalism and mutual rivalries, it would not be attended by all the members and as such will give a setback back to the Muslim cause. On the other hand, if it was confined to consideration of economic, development and social matters, it could do an immense amount of good. As to calling it a Muslim conference, where is the harm. After all, the Communists have their conferences, the Hindus have them, and even the Western alliances. What are they but the meeting of white people professing the Christian faith. He said, why not attain the aim by calling it a Conference of Middle Eastern and North African countries. It will arouse lesser heat and suspicion. I said be it could be considered.

29 | SATURDAY

 How to teach your mind to think.

1. Run over all the factors affecting the problem until a pattern emerges that covers them all.
2. Suspend judgement i.e. don't jump to conclusions before comprehending all alternatives open to you. It is curious but true that hastily formed judgements require much greater effort to change than to establish a correct conclusion.
3. Rearrange the statements of your problems. Frequently, the solution to a difficult problem appears after a slight physical rearrangement.
4. If you are getting nowhere, try a new approach.
5. Take a break when you are stuck.
6. Discuss your problem with others. It forces you to think more profoundly. In other words, look before you jump. Then, if you find yourself bogged down, try another approach.

30 | SUNDAY

Dr Fazlur Rahman[44] of the Islamic Research Institute came to see me. He was engaged in writing a book on the ideology of Islam. I read his first chapter. It is fascinating, but the language he has used is scholarly and difficult. It has been arranged to attach a couple of knowledgeable people with him so as to discuss the theme of each chapter and then put it in simple language. The doctor can then review it to ensure that his theme has been properly brought out. I am sure that this book, when written, will be a real contribution in the service of Islam. The requirement of simplicity of language is necessary to make it easily intelligible even to the man of limited education.

The opposition party leaders have been meeting in Dacca for the last several days to draw out a common programme, in order to get all the heterogeneous people talking of greater provincial autonomy, undoing of West Pakistan, parliamentary form of government, direct election to the assemblies and a weakened centre. In other words, undoing everything that has been achieved so far. It is quite obvious that these people are bent upon mischief and are looking for trouble. The government has got to get ready to deal with them and cut their nefarious activities.

1 | MONDAY

📖 I had a bit of stomach trouble so was told to stay at home.

📖 Prince Sadruddin,[45] the son of the late Aga Khan, and who is now in the United Nations Secretariat as the head of the organization that looks after the interests of refugees in different parts of the world, came to see me and stayed on for lunch. He is very intelligent and polished and speaks beautiful English. Promised to assist us in rehabilitating about 80,000 refugees who have been driven out from the Mahinder sector of Indian-held Kashmir. He talked about his family affairs, the present Aga Khan, and was appreciative of the way he was conducting himself.

📖 Called the finance minister, the finance secretary and Altaf Gauhar and told them to do the following:

a. Prepare talking points on the recent discussions taken between opposition parties.
b. Prepare a format at a glance as to what the economic position would be in East Pakistan if East Pakistan decides to be too difficult and decides to separate. This is not an immediate possibility but there is no harm in having the score and preparing for the future or the worst. After all, many nations have before now been faced with such unpleasant situations.

2 | TUESDAY

📖 Flew into Peshawar. Inspected the Ternab Research Institute with charts and statistics showing the developmental work that was going on in the two divisions of the *Barani* region. The results are impressive.

📖 Addressed the representative *jirga* of tribal areas of Peshawar and D.I. Khan Division. I was delighted to see them. They are such colourful people. I was especially interested in seeing the Waziris and Masoods from Waziristan and recognized several whom I saw during the days when I served in that area in the army. They shot at me and I shot back at them on many occasions. But it was all in the game and regarded as a fair sport. A great metamorphosis has come over the thinking of these people. At one time they would not allow a primary school to be established in that area. Today, they are demanding schools and colleges even for the girls, hospitals and roads, etc. A lot has been done for them but a lot more has to be done.

📖 I told General Musa that Lahore, as the seat of provincial government, is too close to the border. Besides, the government is bound to be influenced unduly by the local politics. Wisdom dictates that the provincial capital should be shifted to a more suitable place. The government's real estate assets in Lahore could well pay for the new place. However, it is a delicate matter especially with the people of Punjab, and has to be tackled cautiously.

📖 Held a meeting with the governor, commissioner and the IG Frontier Constabulary about the future of Dir State.[46] The place is in an utter mess. The state and the ruler and his brothers' property are not defined. Some tribes don't pay any taxes at all. There is constant struggle between the tenants and the landlords, and above all, the ruler is incapable of bearing any responsibility. So, sometime back his powers were taken away and the political agent told to run the place. On this the ruler was quite happy to begin with but lately, when the question of delimitation of state property and of his and his family arose, he and his brothers got apprehensive. His younger brother is supposed to have instigated the Meshwani tribe who besieged a place called Berwah, took the local *tehsildar* as a prisoner and looted the armoury, taking away some 800 rifles and ammunition. The *nawab* was, meanwhile, sitting in Rawalpindi. A strong detachment of Frontier Scouts had to be sent to recapture Berwah and recover arms. The operation is in progress. Meanwhile, it transpired that to take away the powers of the ruler, a regulation has to be issued. This is being looked into. Also, a brigade group is being moved to Chakdarra to be ready to support the Scouts and the political authorities in Dir.

3 | WEDNESDAY

📖 Held a meeting with the provincial WAPDA and the central finance authority to determine the question of compensation and resettlement of the people who have to be evacuated from the Tarbela Dam area. A meeting of ECNEC had considered this problem and had taken some very cock-eyed decisions. After considerable discussions, I gave the following ruling:

1. A notification will be issued for the acquisition of land and the rates offered will be the average of last twelve months' sales.
2. People owning a half acre of irrigated land and two acres of *barani* land, will be offered land in the colony and the barrage areas on payment basis.
3. The government will bear the transportation charges for those moving to new lands.
4. Areas for building villages will be developed around the lake for those who don't want to leave for other places so they can build their houses.
5. Also advised the finance minister to prepare a scheme whereby the people taking large compensation could invest their money. They could invest in government securities, defence bonds, banks, NIT or even start new industries.
6. I think this scheme should give affected people considerable satisfaction and make evacuation easier.

We then discussed the future of the newspaper *Kohistan* which is a paper now owned by the West Pakistan Muslim League. Mr Bucha is responsible for its running and is finding it difficult in coping with the problem. After some discussion, it was decided to sell majority shares to a reliable businessman who would be prepared to carry out Muslim League policy. It was thought that Ahmad Dawood might be a good choice.

📖 Motored to Saidu Sharif, Swat, for a week's stay.

4 | THURSDAY

📖 Played a game of golf at [Miangul] Aurangzeb's course. It is a beautiful course in non-developed [natural] settings, surrounded by high mountains.

📖 Wrote a letter to the prime ministers of UK, Australia, New Zealand and Canada on the future of commonwealth, which follows:

President's House
Rawalpindi,
Pakistan
4th May

From
Field Marshal Mohammad Ayub Khan
Nishan-e-Pakistan, Hilal-e-Jurat.

My Dear Prime Minister,
Mr Arnold Smith, Commonwealth Secretary General, called on me sometime ago and asked my opinion as to how the interest in the Commonwealth could be maintained and enhanced. I gave him my views which in brief were as follows.

Historically, the Commonwealth started first of all between the white dominions and the mother country, the United Kingdom. Apart from the racial affinity, the fact that Great Britain could give military protection and economic assistance to the dominions was a major motive for the emergence of this unique organization. The situation today, unfortunately, has changed and Great Britain is not at present able to give both military and economic cover, nor is any single country or combination of them capable of giving military cover, but countries like Canada and Australia, which have reached a very advanced stage of affluence, could fill the economic gap especially now when the less affluent countries in the Commonwealth are struggling to attain economic viability. Some assistance in the shape of scholarships, professional and technical handouts to the recipient members has no doubt been given under the Colombo Plan, but it could hardly be expected to make any real impact on the economy of these countries. If, therefore, assistance is given in large hearted manner there is no reason why the Commonwealth should not continue to remain a living organization. If this does not happen I fear that it would just be reduced to the status of an international club, and in due course, wither away which will be a great tragedy for mankind. Mr Arnold Smith asked me if I could communicate these views to the heads of different commonwealth countries and I told him that I would. Accordingly I am sending these views to you for what they are worth.

With kind regards,
Yours sincerely,
Mohammad Ayub Khan.

7 | SUNDAY

📖 Daultana is supposed to have told someone that the presidency of the Pakistan Democratic Movement (PDM)[47] will go to him or Nurul Amin.[48] This would be settled on the 21st when they meet in Lahore. Therefore, they will visit different places, address gatherings to convert people to their way of thinking. When people are so conditioned, the student community will be brought into the picture and direct action launched. I would like to see him do that so that we get the opportunity to deal with him and his likes once and for all. These wreckers can only think of disruption. Stability, progress and welfare of the people is no concern of theirs.

10 | WEDNESDAY

📖 Returned to Rawalpindi from Swat after a week's stay which was a nice break and I was able to relax and think a bit. On the way back from Swat looked up the Punjab Regimental Training Centre at Mardan and then attended the Muslim League workers meeting at Col. Abdul Ghafoor Khan's[49] place in Hoti, Mardan. It was a large meeting and respectably attended. I addressed on the need to organize a strong party and keep it on the right path and counter the moves of the disruptionists.

After the meeting, Col. Ghafoor Khan Hoti and Amir Khan Hoti[50] took me to a room. Amir Khan first tried to clarify that any rumours that he has not been a well-wisher are not correct. Then they complained bitterly against the appointment of Mohammad Ali Hoti,[51] who is their cousin, as a minister. Col. Ghafoor said that he is favouring hostile elements who will never support a Muslim Leaguer, and besides, Mohammad Ali Hoti's father was younger to his father and he is younger to him. How can he bear him to go around in a flagged car. Could I, therefore, not remove him from the ministership and appoint someone from Hazara or elsewhere? It is not necessary that a minister should be appointed from their family. My reply was that a minister who is doing quite well could not be removed in cold blood. This did not convince him. Though not surprisingly as it is typically of our people who are very jealous of each other. I come across this problem wherever I go.

📖 George Woods[52] with his wife and staff came to dinner. George Woods spoke to me separately about financing of Tarbela and the efforts he is making to line up resources. He was optimistic of the outcome. As a matter of fact, additional resources required are not a great deal, about 185 million dollars spread over three years or so and that too after 1970. However, he is a good friend and is doing his best for us.

Then he went on to say that though he was asked to act as a mediator by a couple of powers he would not like to name in Indo–Pakistan disputes, he has decided as a banker to keep off them. However, he cannot help saying that the capital exporting countries are getting disenchanted with the Indo-Pakistan subcontinent because of the great countries' mutual power. Cannot something be done to break the deadlock? I told him that it has been my consistent policy to settle all disputes with India but the Indian leaders are not prepared to budge an inch. Instead, they are piling up arms furiously. In that case what is one to do? However, if we see any change in India's attitude, we shall not be lacking in reciprocity.

George is going to see the Tarbela site tomorrow. He said he would like to be seen there to establish association with the project in the eyes of everybody. I was touched by his sentiments.

Talked about Indira Gandhi. George said that she is an intelligent and charming lady, very conscious of being Nehru's daughter, but she is more like a social worker than an administrator. Besides her mind does not grip with serious things of life. She expresses vague ideas like social justice etc. Morarji Desai, on the other hand, struck him as having mellowed considerably. I told him that he has pathological aversion to Pakistan. When talking about the enormous budget, the Indians told him that Pakistan, in collusion with China, has ambitions of re-establishing Mughal rule over India. There could be nothing more absurd than this, but the Americans do get impressed by such arguments. The Indians know it and lose no opportunity in befooling them or maybe the Americans like being befooled in promotion of their policy in these regions.

11 | THURSDAY

📖 Governors' conference commenced. A number of important problems were discussed and decisions taken.

12 | FRIDAY

📖 George Woods came for breakfast. He flew over Mangla and saw Tarbela and was deeply impressed. He said that one can see that Pakistan is on the march. Then went on to say that whilst India and Pakistan are the leaders in development, what a great pity that they had not learnt to live at peace with each other. So much good could follow if this were to happen. I told him that it was possible if India were to change her policy. After a lot of discussion, he agreed with me that unless there was a change of heart on the part of India nothing much can come out of meetings on the highest level.

📖 The governors' conference continued. The great Mufti and his associates came to see me. A good man but not very practical.

13 | SATURDAY

📖 National Economic Council took place. The annual developmental programme, amongst other things, was discussed. Resources in excess of Rs 51 crores were offered to East Pakistan over West Pakistan. This is in pursuance of my policy to help East Pakistan level up with West Pakistan. Whether this object will be achieved is dependent on how good use the East Pakistanis make of these resources which are mostly generated in West Pakistan.

15 | MONDAY

📖 The deputy foreign minister of Yugoslavia came to see me. This country is giving us considerable economic assistance. We spoke about Vietnam. Said in his view, the Chinese were preventing the Vietnamese from coming to a settlement with the USA. The Vietnamese stance was too uncompromising. In consequence the people of that unfortunate country were undergoing terrible sufferings. The impression he got in Japan and elsewhere was that the war is unlikely to escalate into

a Chinese–USA conflict. I told him that war has its own unpredictable laws. In a situation as this anything can spark a configuration.

📖 Attended the national publicity conference. Addressed members of national and provincial information ministries.

📖 I saw an article in the *New York Times* about Chiang Ching, the wife of Mao Tse-tung. This lady, after leading an anonymous life, is now taking a leading part in the cultural revolution. According to this article, she has intense dislike for the wife of Chairman Liu Shao-chi, and has therefore, acted as a catalyst to oust them with the help of the Red Guards. I can quite believe this because Madam Liu Shao-chi is one of the most remarkable persons I have ever come across. She is remarkable looking in spite of her middle age, full of charm and human sympathy inside, being an intellectual. Any woman in her position would be jealous of her. It reminded me of the tussle between Fatima Jinnah and Begum Liaquat Ali Khan[53] which I believe soured relations between Liaquat Ali Khan and the Quaid.

17 | WEDNESDAY

📖 Presided over a cabinet meeting. Large number of items were disposed of and decisions given. One of the items related to the expansion of the capital issue of the National Bank. It was stated that most of these shares will be taken up by the present shareholders. The bank has deposits over 200 crores, a major portion of which are of the government. In other words, a few people were making large profits with government money. My reaction was that why should not the expanded capital be taken up by the government, so as to qualify for larger shares in the bank's income.

My belief is that instead of continuing to burden people with more taxes, the government should go in for trading in major items of exports and imports so as to generate more resources. Today the middle man was making enormous profits by utilization of cheap foreign exchange provided by the government and hardly paying any taxes. If the jute, cotton, rice etc. exports and imports of iron and steel and edible oils were run on this basis, I have no doubt the government would earn a large amount of money.

My belief is that nationalized industries hardly pay, but nationalization of imports and exports of major items can be a great success. This will upset the traders but it just cannot be helped. The interest of the country must come first. In any case, we have to have import–export corporations to handle trade with the socialist countries, which is fast expanding.

📖 Invited the members of the Muslim League assembly party to tea and gave them a talk on their duties and obligations and reviewed the problems of foreign policy. There is going to be a debate on foreign policy in the house. I told them that we may dislike the American attitude, but national interest deems that we should exercise restraint in expressing our opinions. I also identified the problems facing the country: defence, food, birth rate and the machinations of the opposition parties. The Eight Point programme was nothing new. The original 21 points, then 9 points, 6 points and now 8 points have as the basis only one point. Should the country have three governments as per new trend or one in East and one in West Pakistan. A number of the opposition would like to have only two but they do not want to state that openly in case people, and especially in East Pakistan, get alarmed prematurely. The West Pakistan opposition, having no following, have concentrated on the parochial susceptibilities of East Pakistan and are encouraging them in their perfidy to dig their own grave by giving a fillip to separatist tendencies. It shows how far these people are prepared to go to achieve their selfish ends.

21 | SUNDAY

📖 Returned to Rawalpindi after two days stay in Abbottabad. Briefed Admiral A.R. Khan[54] and the foreign secretary on their visit to China. The Chinese seem to be apprehensive that the Russians will attempt to put us against them. They need have no fear on that score. We do not forget our friends in a hurry, especially the Chinese who stood by us in our hour of trial.

📖 [Major] General Rafi, my military secretary, came over to the house and wanted to see me in a hurry. Said the governor, General Musa, rang him up on the secraphone and told him in a garbled fashion that the DIG police Karachi had brought the information that a certain number of young naval officers were plotting to assassinate me. His advice was that I should not proceed to Karachi tomorrow. I got him to ring up that he should come over and see me tomorrow at 7 a.m., together with his informants and whatever information he had. Meanwhile, I called General Yahya and Brig. Akbar, the director of intelligence and put them in the picture. Told Yahya to get in touch with General Musa and the DIG CID in Lahore and find out more particulars.

The governor's telephone line was out of order but General Yahya got in touch with him. His brother, the DIG CID, confirmed that it was a fact that certain young naval officers had conspired together and that their talk was tape recorded through the assistance of a plant. We shall know tomorrow what is the tenor of this talk and then decide on the course of action. Meanwhile told Yahya and Akbar to standby to proceed to Karachi with me tomorrow.

📖 My son, Gohar Ayub, and his wife returned from China after a week's visit. He went there on the invitation of Chou En-lai and Chen-yi. They were very kind to him and looked after him very well.

The Chinese were concerned about our foreign minister's visits to Indonesia, Russia and Japan in quick succession. They were particularly apprehensive of the Russians who they thought would try to use us against the Chinese. Gohar told them that the foreign minister had to complete his visits hurriedly so as to be back for the National Assembly session in time. As regards our contacts with the Russians, they were necessary to soften their attitude on Kashmir in the Security Council and also dissuade them from building up India against us.

Gohar told me that the Cultural Revolution will go on till the Chinese weed out what they call counter revolutionaries. He said that their production in agriculture and industry has gone up. Their support to Vietnam will continue and was on the increase and they expected the Vietnamese to go on fighting for a long time. Talking about the Chinese, Chou En-lai told Gohar that you must take Kashmir, we have troops on the Northern border and if you want them you will have to give it to us in writing to provide troops, but make sure that you don't and must not fire the first shot.

📖 Musa, together with DIG Tareen, arrived early in the morning. Tareen gave me a report on the conspiracy in the navy and also played the tapes of their discussion.

The story is logically flawless. A man called Sardar Tekali Mughal from Hyderabad got in touch with Tareen and told him that a petty officer called Faiz Hussain of the Pakistan Navy, and who comes from Gujrat, was conspiring to get hold of me and get me under duress to declare martial law, dismiss the governors and the C-in-C and hand over the power to him and his associates. He would appoint Azam[55] as Governor East Pakistan, Maulvi Farid as Governor West Pakistan and Maududi as the law minister.

They way the above details were gathered is rather interesting. Tareen, on hearing this, was anxious to get under Faiz Hussain's skin. So he was on the lookout for a man who was on intimate terms with this man. He found out that a police constable called Habib Khan was such a man. Habib was taken into confidence and ostensibly suspended on some pretext so that he too could complain about the regime with justification. Habib in due course got the details of the conspiracy as mentioned above.

Tareen was not satisfied with this. He discovered through Habib that Faiz was on the lookout for a businessman who would finance him. He wanted three to four lakhs of rupees for buying transport, etc. He contacted a businessman, Munnoo, and appealed for funds. Munnoo got scared and refused to have anything to do with them. Tareen then arranged that a police officer will act as a businessman who was prepared to help. Habib conveyed this to Faiz and took him and a petty officer called Rehmani to the *Seth's* house. They were accompanied by one or two others. These people, on entering the house, were very suspicious and made a thorough search of the house in case it was bugged. Luckily, they could not locate a couple of microphones that were placed in the meeting room and connected with the tape recorders elsewhere. The discussion went on a long time. So there are several reels of the tape.

In this discussion, Faiz revealed that he had plans to bump me off when I was to go, but did not, on a deep sea fishing trip some months ago, and again with the king of Afghanistan. This trip was cancelled. He made all sorts of boasts that he will kill all senior officers and do this and that. Also said that he had a large support in the navy and the other services.

Rehmani appeared to be a desperado in that he once wanted to cut Mountbatten's throat but was dissuaded by his friends from doing so.

Musa and others advised me not to go to Karachi where I had a couple of important functions to perform. I decided against that and came over to Karachi, bringing General Yahya, the director of Intelligence Bureau, with me. I told them to go into a huddle with Admiral Khan, the Naval C-in-C and advised them the course of action. Though I was quite clear in my mind what was to be done.

These people met me in the evening, and the following course of action was agreed upon. The leading six conspirators were to be arrested tonight by the police, they would then be interrogated by joint teams of ISI and the Director, Intelligence Bureau, and further course will be decided upon the results of the interrogation. Depending on the evidence, all the services personnel will be tried by a court martial. Decision about any civilians involved would be taken later.

The viciousness of this man and his associates is obvious but the plan seems amateurish, lacking comprehension, thoroughness and skill involved in such a task.

However, DIG Tareen and his associates have done an excellent job whilst the naval intelligence and ISI were fast asleep. It just shows that we are babes in intelligence work. This is why I have set up a committee under General Yahya to consider the problem and suggest methods of revamping the system.

📖 The foreign minister of Romania called on me. He showed great warmth and friendship and asked me to visit their country as soon as possible. He gave me the impression that, whilst wanting to go along with the Soviets, they would not like to be dominated by them. That is why they have great admiration for the Chinese policy towards the Soviets. In that they see the opportunity for having elbowroom. He talked about the troubled history of his people extending over several centuries. Being Latin people wedged in a mass of Slavs and Hungarians they feel apprehensive and insecure.

📖 Foreign Minister Pirzada came to report on his visit to Indonesia, Russia and Japan. He found them all friendly. The Indonesians expressed affection and regard for Pakistan. The Soviets were also appreciative of our position and promised to give us arms. Only they wanted to discuss details with me.

23 | TUESDAY

📖 There was an investiture ceremony in the afternoon, I decorated 58 people.

📖 Dined with Said Hassan.[56] He told me that when he was our representative at the UN, Bhutto came as the head of our delegation to the General Assembly. He asked to see Christian Herter, the US Secretary of State, and Macmillan, who happened to be attending the session. To Said Hassan's amazement, when seeing Herter, he volunteered to spy for the USA on all UN delegations. When asked for an explanation he said that because of our dependence on the USA it was a good thing to oblige them. Khrushchev, of course, abused Bhutto and said that if Pakistan should look towards India or Afghanistan, Soviets would take our eyes out. He told Khrushchev not to get angry. Pakistan was ready to quit the pacts. Meeting with Macmillan could not be arranged. Instead, the British representative, Lord Gore, invited Bhutto to lunch on which he gave a speech extolling the role of the Commonwealth and said that Pakistan had no use for the Soviets or the USA. Said Hassan said that he felt ashamed and came to the conclusion that the man was completely unreliable, double-faced and lacking in integrity and character.

24 | WEDNESDAY

📖 The Muslim League election organizers in Karachi came to see me. I think the work is going on well. Nine city Leagues are going to be established, elections to the primary Leagues have been held everywhere. There is unanimity on the presidentship of all Leagues except one where Bagh Ali and one more person are involved. It looks like there will have to be an election in that place.

📖 Heard the sad news that when practicing low and flying a B57 bomber, Group Captain Masood hit a bird, crashed and died. He was a very fine officer indeed who was in command of Sargodha during the 1965 war and defended it valiantly.

Mohsin Ali of the *Morning News* came to see me. He originally comes from West Bengal. Asked me how I saw the situation in East Pakistan. I told him I was doing my best but I wonder if they were doing their part. I am giving them all the resources possible for development, but they are making no conscious effort to make a nation, in fact, both the provincialists and the secessionists have combined to blackmail the centre and sow discord between East and West Pakistan. They are consciously Hinduizing the language and culture. Tagore has become their god. Everything has been Bengalized, even the plate numbers on vehicles are in Bengali. A man from West Pakistan feels a foreigner in Dacca. Consciously or unconsciously, they are moving towards separation and exposing themselves to absorption by Hinduism. He agreed with me and said that something should be done to arrest this trend. I told him that only a Bengali could shake them to realism but I don't see any one capable of doing so. Monem Khan is doing his best but he has his limitations. So the prospect is not very cheerful.

25 | THURSDAY

Discovered that it was Air Commodore Masroor Hussain and not Masood who was killed in the air accident yesterday. He too was a distinguished officer. The Air Force has suffered a big loss in him.

I hear that the businessmen who used to make big money without paying any taxes on import of major commodities like steel and edible oil are agitating over our new policy and probably trying to subvert the members of the Assembly which is now in session. I have to tell the commerce minister not to falter but to stand firm.

Mohan Mian from East Pakistan came to see me. He is in the National Democratic Front. He is supposed to have taken an active part in formation of the Eight Point programme of the opposition. Told me that they only wanted democracy and the Eight Point programme was designed to frustrate Mujibur Rahman's Six Points.[57] I told him since when have he and his associates become the volunteers of democracy. Look how Nurul Amin, Daultana, Mohammad Ali killed democracy when they were in power and see how democratic Maududi is in his party. And who is he trying to fool when he says that their Eight Points are designed to undercut the Six Points. In fact, the Eight Points are the first phase; second phase may be the Six Points, pointing the way for complete separation of East Pakistan. I told him that I am aware of their efforts and their moves. They are all traitors, every one of them, and the country and I shall face them if no one else did.

Called the cabinet meeting to my house and reviewed the internal situation. The opposition leaders from West Pakistan, having no roots here, had concentrated in East Pakistan to encourage them on their suicidal tendencies. By evolving the Eight Point programme they have even agreed to let the East Pakistanis dig their grave a little quicker. Time has come when the truth must be faced and a remedy provided. The only way it can be done is by patriotic East Pakistanis to tell their people plainly that the aim of the opposition is separation, but they don't want to say so in case people take offence. That is why the Eight Points and Six Points programme are couched in a language that will attract the East Pakistanis. And if this trend continues then the point of no return would be reached and East Pakistan will go under Hinduism and be separated forever. Manik Mian's newspaper, *Ittefaq*, supported the Awami League. Most of the ministers agreed with me. The following line of action was agreed upon:

a. We should address the members of our party in the assemblies.
b. Our party men should air these views in the assemblies.
c. Our ministers should address people, especially in big cities.
d. Similarly our ministers and party should address gatherings wherever possible.

28 | SUNDAY

📖 Went to Bahawalpur to see how the threshing of wheat was going on. Some 1600 maunds of wheat has been recovered. There should be another 1000 maunds. Our average recovery is 57½ maunds per acre. This is a fantastic yield. With these seeds we can break our food shortages to attaining self-sufficiency in food in the near future.

If it were not for mechanical threshers which the Agriculture Department has developed, it would be impossible to thresh a lot of this size with bullocks. I believe there is a great demand for them all over the country. So I am asking Gohar to consider their fabrication in their workshop.

📖 Saw a report today about the thinking of the Russian diplomatic staff. One of them is supposed to have said, 'in formulation of internal and external policies I am under nobody's influence'. I am surprised how correctly they have assessed the situation.

31 | WEDNESDAY

📖 Just as I was going to bed at night, my wife told me that she did not want to bother me, but a very unfortunate thing had happened which she felt should be brought to my notice. A son of Mohammed Akram, my younger brother, called Ahmad, has killed one man by a pistol shot and wounded four more, two are in a precarious condition. Apparently, what happened was that this lad, who is only about 16 years of age, was going to Murree with a friend on a bus. When the bus stopped at a place called Company Bagh, a boy brought a bucket full of water to clean the bus, some of the water splashed against the side of the bus and sprayed Ahmad's friend. On this, Ahmad abused the boy, who abused him back, and on this Ahmad slapped the boy, whereupon a man from a shop attacked Ahmad with a stick. Ahmad then drew his pistol and shot the man. I suppose some people closed on him and he fired more shots hitting four more people. I was very disturbed to hear this and wish to God that this lad had been killed on the spot. It is a great misfortune when useless relatives add to one's troubles. It is as if I have not enough on my plate already. However, as far as I am concerned the law of the land must take its course and this lad must be made to pay for his misdeeds.

1 | THURSDAY

📖 Addressed the Muslim League assembly party on the internal situation in the country. The burden of my talk was that suicidal tendencies are developing in East Pakistan. Acute Bengali nationalist feelings were emerging and they were drifting further and further away from West. If this trend goes on, as it looks like doing, they will have cause to regret.

2 | FRIDAY

📖 Discussed with foreign minister the programme of my visit abroad, it was decided to go to Romania and the Soviet Union in July. The Soviets are very anxious to see me in Moscow. Later in October, to go to France, Spain, and Turkey.

4 | SUNDAY

📖 Went to Badalpur where my farm is near Khanpur. Uqaili, Sobur, and Sardar Aslam, the Secretary General, accompanied me. I wanted to show them how the new threshers work. It is an extraordinary, efficient machine. Takes about 25 maunds of wheat an hour.

📖 A.R. Khan and Mr Yousaf returned from China and explained what went on there. The result of their visit has been very encouraging. The Chinese have reiterated their faith and friendship with Pakistan and have promised to supply our requirements of equipment and ammunition spread over four years. As regards payment, they left the matter to be discussed later. I am overwhelmed with their kindness. I am going to send a suitable message to them.

📖 I am very anxious to contact Suharto, the former president of Indonesia, and establish personal equation with him. I am, therefore, going to send him a personal message to come to Pakistan as soon as he can. My going there would create complications. Soekarno is a friend of mine and if I go to Djakarta it is inconceivable that I should not go and see him. This might well be misunderstood by the present rulers.

5 | MONDAY

📖 President Nasser's emissary came to thank me for the support we had given to the Arab cause and offered to answer any questions I asked, which I did. My concerns were two:

a. How firm were the Egyptians in denying the right of passage to Israel through the Strait of Tiran. He said they were firm on this.
b. What sort of support had the Russians offered to the Egyptians in the event of war. He did not know much about it.

My hunch is that outbreak of hostilities is inevitable. President Nasser has taken an extreme position on the right of passage through the Tiran Strait. Israel will never accept this and use it as an excuse to go to war. The Americans and British too will be happy about this as it will save them the odium of opening hostilities with Egypt.

An hour later, news came that the Israelis had opened an offensive in the Sinai and the southern sector and heavy fighting was taking place on land and in the air. The time of start was 09:00 hours, which was surprising because such things are done either at noon or late at night so as to occupy initial positions before daylight. Later, it struck me that the determining factor probably was the rising sun which was adverse to the defenders (Egyptians). Anyway, this news was a great shock. I hoped and prayed that the Arabs would be able to deal with this menace now that they have such good equipment. Any major reverse would be a great blow to Arab and Muslim prestige.

6 | TUESDAY

📖 Called a hurried meeting of connected people and caused a message to be sent to the Arab heads of state. All the heads of administration involved in war should do all they could to occupy as much of Israeli territory as possible. Also let us know what could we do to help materially. We would do all we can to give whatever assistance is possible. It should be the cardinal principle of our policy to support rightful Muslim causes, wherever they may happen to be.

📖 Flew into Quetta for a four day stay. Large number of people came to see me, shook hands with hundreds.

📖 Arab sources are complaining that the American and British Air Forces are supporting the Israelis. The American and British are denying this. I doubt very much if this could be true. They would be very foolish in such a participation without knowing the Russian reaction. Suez Canal has been closed to shipping. This is going to affect our food supplies and developmental projects.

📖 Had dinner at the Staff College. They run two courses, staff and war, the latter for senior officers. As such they have a large population. It is a seat of military learning with great reputation. I was reminded of my stay here about 27 years ago.

7 | WEDNESDAY

📖 Addressed the senior officers course at the Staff College on problems facing the country on the lines I addressed the GHQ officers.

📖 *Morning News* indicated that the Security Council had unanimously passed a resolution calling upon the belligerents in the Middle East to ceasefire. Afternoon news from BBC indicated that the Jordanian portion of Jerusalem had been occupied by the Israelis and that the Jordanians had asked for a ceasefire. Also, Israelis were making considerable progress on all fronts in the Sinai and there are some indications that the Egyptians were retreating, even from Sharmal Sheikh. It is sad but true that unless a miracle happens, the Arabs have been licked and have had it. The Israelis will now dictate terms to their heart's content. The Anglo–Americans must also feel satisfied that President Nasser has been cut to size and Russia exposed as an unreliable ally. These are big gains for them.

📖 I was told at lunch that the Voice of America broadcast gave out that two Pakistani pilots have been shot down and captured by the Israelis. These are probably the two officers lent to Jordan.

8 | THURSDAY

📖 Visited the geological institute in Quetta. They are very well staffed, well equipped with model gadgets and doing excellent work. They need greater attention, support and patronage.

📖 A flicker of hope arose when news came in that the Egyptians had gone on to the counter offensive in the Sinai. I hope and pray that they would be able to redeem their honour. But the evening news indicated that the Israelis had broken through Egyptian positions and were heading to the Suez Canal. The Egyptians had evacuated Sharmal Sheikh, of which the Israelis were in full control. The Israeli plan is obvious. They want to cut off the Egyptian forces in the Sinai, not let them cross the canal, and destroy them. Their territorial objectives seem to be the occupation of Jordanian territory west of the River Jordan, in other words, the whole of Jerusalem and the area upon the Jordan River.

9 | FRIDAY

📖 This morning's news indicated that the Egyptians too had accepted the Security Council's call for a ceasefire. This resolution just calls for the ceasefire. No question of going back to the positions held before the war and the Russians went along with it. It just shows how helpless or unwilling the Russians are to help the Arabs. King Hussein, in a broadcast, explained the cause of the war and the weight of Israeli strength and their firepower that they had to bear. He ended up by complaining that their friends, that means the Arabs, failed to render them help which was promised. It looks like the usual chain of accusations and counter accusations has started amongst the Arabs. I understand that President Nasser has addressed his nation this afternoon. Let us see what he has to say. Western propaganda and Israeli diplomacy will probably work for his removal. Seen today in telegrams from our ambassadors abroad, they repeat that the Arab countries and their representatives everywhere are very appreciative of the support given by Pakistan. The telegram from Amman was pathetic, when our ambassador met the king and prime minister and conveyed my messages that we shall gladly send some pilots to fight for them, they almost cried and said that the game is up. Their air force has been destroyed and their troops driven to the east bank of Jordan. Nasser has driven them to this by starting this war, unfortunately. Meanwhile, his troops were running in front of the Israelis as fast as they could. They said that in this tragic episode the only redeeming feature was the fidelity shown by Pakistan.

The Arab accusation that the Anglo–Americans helped the Israelis by air is looked upon by everyone as an excuse to cover up Arab failings. Reports from Cairo and Damascus indicate that the best part of the air force was destroyed on the ground. This is the height of inefficiency and lack of skill. The Israeli attack was predictable. Besides, a minimal radar warning system could have given them the necessary warning to take off and meet the enemy in the air. I was rung up by [Major] General Rafi, my military secretary, that President Nasser has resigned and Mohyuddin has taken over from him. Zakaria was at one time the prime minister, but later removed by Nasser. I had the occasion to meet him, though soft spoken, he is reputed to be a tough man.

10 | SATURDAY

📖 The latest news is that President Nasser has decided to stay on, this is supposed to be in response to the legislature and public appeal. It looks like the Arab defeat is complete. The UAR air, armour, heavy equipment has either been destroyed or captured and so is the best part of their trained manpower. The Jordanian air force has been destroyed and so is their heavy army equipment. The same fate has befallen the Syrians. Israel occupies all strategic advantages including control of the Tiran Strait and the Suez Canal and has the complete backing of the Anglo–Americans. The Russian backing to the Arabs has proved feeble. Therefore, the Arabs are completely at the mercy of Israel which is backed by the Anglo–Americans. The Israelis are, therefore, going to dictate terms and demand their pound of flesh. They will demand freedom of navigation through the Tiran Strait and the Suez Canal and occupation of Sinai and the area west of the Jordan River.

What are the chances of an Arab revival is very difficult to say. The present indications are that they are very dim. Having fallen out with the West and having lost faith in Russia, where else can they go to gain support. Chances are that in the mood of frustration they will fall into despair and indulge in mutual recrimination and become still weaker. So one feels actually very frustrated in their future and misfortune. But one cannot defy the laws of God. The Arabs are paying the price of disunity.

📖 M.M. Ahmed, on return from the consortium meeting, submitted a report. By all accounts the meeting has gone off well and two-thirds of the required amount has been pre-pledged. The Americans have also promised, first instalment of one million tons of food. Apparently, Johnson gave a decision within a couple of hours after receipt of the files. This has created quite a stir in the official circles in Washington as being unprecedented and it may well be due to the letter I wrote to him at the time of Ambassador Locke's departure.

📖 The budget for the year 1967–1968 was discussed in the cabinet meeting before presentation to the assembly. It was a good budget, no fresh taxation, but a certain amount of rationalization. However, we have to think seriously of dealing with those managing agents who do not declare dividends and embezzle money. Similarly, we have to consider taking such measures as will make the stock exchange more vibrant.

📖 The news came in from Amman that our two pilots who had been posted to the Jordan Air Force are quite safe and have done very well. One of them shot down an enemy aircraft and damaged another. The other is supposed to have rocketed the Israeli president's house after King Hussein's palace was bombed.

📖 We sent several more pilots to Jordan. They got held up in Jeddah through lack of travel facilities. The Jordanians have now sent word that they do not need them anymore. They have no aircraft left to fly.

📖 BBC news gave out that six Egyptian generals, with a number of prisoners, were captured by the Israelis. The Egyptians also lost six to seven hundred tanks destroyed, surrendered or captured, large number of heavy guns and ammunitions, aircraft and other equipment. This is tragic, but shows that the Egyptians had no will to fight and that it will take them a long, long time and vast amount of expenditure to make good these losses. News from Turkey is that, barring the religious people, others are happy that Nasser has taken a beating. The contempt for the Arabs has deepened. Nasser happened to have met the Chinese ambassador and gave him the reasons why he accepted ceasefire. His air force was destroyed and his army destroyed or captured in the Sinai. Russia sent no real assistance. In fact, he was afraid that even Cairo might be captured. There was nothing to prevent the Israelis from doing so.

12 | MONDAY

📖 The Iranian Ambassador brought me a message from the Shah. He was worried that the emotional outburst of support to Arabs in Pakistan was not realistic and is liable to get out of hand and might well react on me. In any case, the Shah could feel like that because of Nasser's designs in the Persian Gulf and his attitude towards the Shah, and the attempt made by him and the Syrians to foment trouble among the Arab minority in Khuzestan. I told him that whilst feeling deeply for the Arabs, I am myself concerned about any excessive outburst of emotions on the part of our people. That is one of the reasons why I and the Foreign Minister gave a statement in support of the Arabs and condemnation of Israel. The object was to channelize the emotions instead of being pushed by them. But the fact was that our people do feel for Muslims all over the world. They would feel more so if something happened in Iran or Turkey.

I told him that the Shah and the Iranians too had better make a show of sympathy, because after cutting Nasser to size and exposing the Russians, the Americans had complete freedom of action to move against any country that is pursuing an independent foreign policy. The Shah and especially me might well become the target of their attack. He felt gravely concerned and said that did I really feel so. I said I do, and the ambassador had better go to Tehran and tell the Shah so. All that needs to be done is to condemn aggression, show sympathy for the Arabs as a whole and ask for vacation of Arab territories, specially the holy places occupied by Israel.

The ambassador then asked me how I saw things developing in the Middle East. I told him I didn't see the Israelis giving up key places and areas and I [neither] foresee the Arabs recovering in a hurry. Both the West and the Russians are going to be extremely chary of giving them military hardware. He complained that some of our people have started calling the Persian Gulf the Arab Gulf. I said it was wrong and I shall certainly look into it.

📖 Latest information from Amman is that one of our pilots, Azam, destroyed three Israeli planes and damaged one. His bravery needs recognition. I am told that in 1965 he had destroyed two Indian planes and won the Sitara-i-Jurat.

13 | TUESDAY

📖 Gave a long talk to a large number of editors and pressmen who had come to Pindi for the budget. It was a question and answer meeting relating mostly to internal political and economic problems. Then went on to listen to the assembly debate on the budget. Shah Aziz-ur-Rahman[58] of the opposition was speaking. Good deal of it was nonsense, but he also made some sensible points. Mr Soomro[59] got up to answer him and completely demolished his arguments.

14 | WEDNESDAY

📖 A Muslim summit meeting at this stage could give the Arabs enormous moral support in their adversity, but Nasser is not interested. He is still harping on Arab summit. So it is no good us sponsoring a thing like that, especially when several countries are lukewarm towards Nasser and the Arabs. But still we have to do something. So I have today sent a message to Johnson, Wilson, De Gaulle and Kosygin not to push the Arabs too far and allow the Israelis to grab their territory and especially the holy places. If they did, the bitterness in the Arab minds will deepen the conflict which will recur and the credit of the big powers will go still further down, not only amongst the Arabs but the whole of the Muslim world. Let us hope something comes out of it.

📖 A number of professors of civics and social sciences came to see me this afternoon. They are going to write a textbook on civics for the degree standard. I gave them a long talk. They all seem keen and well motivated. I hope they will produce something worthwhile.

16 | FRIDAY

📖 Arab diplomats representing ten countries came to thank me for support to their cause. I told them that we shall do our best, but their salvation lies in hanging together. Any division amongst them will be exploited by the enemy.

17 | SATURDAY

📖 Foreign Minister Pirzada left for New York to attend the special session of the General Assembly called to discuss the Middle East situation. This meeting has been called on the Soviet initiative. Mr Kosygin has also reached there. The Russians have expressed a desire that I should attend. I have decided not to go as it will unnecessarily involve me in the big powers tussle. Wherever and whatever we can do for the Arabs can be done best by me remaining out.

The foreign minister gave me the assessment of the impact of my speech made on East Pakistan members of the party. The general consensus is that what I said about them was true. They did not know whether the country will remain united or East Pakistan will break away later. In either event, they regard my presence necessary and they think that I shall be generous to them in either case. They will not get the same constitution and deal from any other West Pakistani.

📖 Monem Khan, who is on a short visit here, asked me not to despair of East Pakistan as people who think of separation are few. I told him that I do not see anybody converting them. Generally East Pakistanis have a negative attitude. He is making no conscious effort at making an issue. This is my honest assessment and I would be less than honest and be failing in my duty if I did not warn people of the consequences of a suicidal outlook.

18 | SUNDAY

📖 News came in that China had exploded a hydrogen bomb yesterday. This is a remarkable achievement and a tremendous occasion. From now onwards an Asian country would be competent for world stature much to the dislike of America including the whole of the western world and the Soviets. The focus so far is gradually, but perceptibly shifting to the east, i.e., China.

19 | MONDAY

📖 President Kenneth Kaunda, the President of Zambia, with his wife arrived for a three day stay. Later we held talks. He was very concerned about the British attitude towards Rhodesia.[60] He felt that by renouncing use of force the British had encouraged UDI. He also suspects that British oil companies are providing petroleum, oil and lubricant to Rhodesia. He was worried about his country's future. He suspects that the whites would attempt to take it over.

The president asked for our assistance in building his army, planning irrigation scheme and agriculture, advice on the running of railways and loan of accounts officers etc. I have agreed to assist in principle and have asked our officials to discuss details with theirs.

The president showed concern about Indo–Pakistan relations. He said that the natural leader of Africa was this subcontinent, if only the two components were at peace with each other. I appraised him of my efforts to find peace with India and how India has been trying to avoid it. He asked how could he help? I said the only thing he could do was to convey to Mrs Indira Gandhi our sincere desire to find peace with her country on an honourable basis. The present wasteful military build up was ruining both our countries. He said though he had been in India and Pakistan for a short time, he was deeply impressed by the contrast between the two. In India people were haggard and starved. The rightist and fanatics were in the ascendancy. They were bothered more about saving the cow and ensuring that some 350 million of them do not eat them up. He said the greatest statesmen in India would be the ones who would bring about peace with Pakistan and settle the cow problem. If they did not eat them why do they not export them and earn foreign exchange. I told him that they will have to do the same with the monkeys, too, as they are no less in number and no less destructive.

20 | TUESDAY

📖 The Russian Ambassador came to deliver Mr Kosygin's reply to my message on the Middle East situation. I have received a reply from Mr Johnson, too. Mr Kosygin has spoken in the General Assembly demanding vacation of aggression by Israel and branding her as an aggressor. When the Israeli foreign minister got up to speak, Kosygin, with his party, left the assembly. He is also reported to have refused Johnson's invitation to see him. Johnson also spoke and proposed a five point programme for dealing with the situation in the Middle East. So the position of the super powers is conflicting and opposed. What will come out of it is difficult to foresee.

📖 Description of Israeli attack commencing on 5th June 1967. It is almost a repetition of the 1956 plan.

21 | WEDNESDAY

📖 President Kaunda, with his party, left for Peking. He gave the impression of being very impressed with his visit to Pakistan, wanted us to give them aid in wide ranging fields. I told him to let us have their requirements for examination.

23 | FRIDAY

📖 The ambassador of Iraq came to deliver a letter from President Abdul Rahman Arif. Arif asked me to give talks taking lead in mobilizing support for the Arab cause. I told him what we were doing within our capacity and under the circumstances.

24 | SATURDAY

📖 A representative of the North Korean Government came to see me and explained their struggle for unification of their country. Said that the stumbling block was the US Government, the American forces and a few traitors in South Korea. The UN Commission for Unification of Korea, of which we are a member, is serving no useful purpose. Chile had asked to resign. I told him that we too want to get out of it, but whilst we are there we should see that nothing unjust is done to them. I told him their struggle was long and hard. The odds against them were heavy. He said they recognize this and while building the country they were also building their military potential. Whilst they have regular armed forces they were also giving military training to all able-bodied people in their country. Their relations with China and Russia were good in spite of their difficulties.

I am told that North Korea has made a spectacular advance in modernization and industrialization. For instance 90 per cent of their machinery requirement is built in the country. This is a very creditable performance considering that the country was completely devastated by war only a few years ago.

📖 Air Marshal Nur Khan came to discuss the problem of training Iranian cadets. Their demand is enormous. They want us to take 30 cadets every six months. I told him that we have to do whatever we can to help them.

📖 The Iranian Ambassador, who had gone to Tehran on my behest to see the Shah, came to report the results of the meeting. Basically, the Shah's and my views are similar on the Middle East situation. Whilst recognizing that Arabs, especially Nasser, had made several grave mistakes, it does not mean that the Israelis should be free to expand at will. Therefore, our aim now is to help the Arabs extricate themselves from their present predicament to their best advantage.

📖 Soviet President Podgorny accompanied by their chief of staff has visited Nasser in Cairo. Reports indicate that the Russians are trying to re-equip the Egyptian armed forces with aircraft, tanks and guns etc. The extent is not yet known. Be that as it may, the harsh reality is that it will take the Arabs another generation or more before they can raise their heads.

25 | SUNDAY

📖 Mr Ghulam Faruque, the commerce minister, sent in a letter to say that because of his old age he was feeling the strain of the job and needs a long rest. He would, therefore, like to be relieved of his position. I sent for him and had a long discussion. Eventually I agreed that he could go. There are all sorts of rumours about his integrity, but I have found no evidence to substantiate them. The trouble is that people can be very unkind sometimes and indulge in character assassination.

The question of finding a relief for Ghulam Faruque is naturally exercising my mind. The man has to come from the Frontier. The point is, should he be a serviceman or a politician. If the former, then Ghulam Ishaq is the ideal man. If latter, Col. Ghafoor Khan Hoti might do. He is not a flier but has political sense, family background and means and could also be expected to run about. On the balance it looks that Col. Ghafoor Khan Hoti might be the man.

📖 There is a need to find a suitable secretary general of the Muslim League. Sardar Aslam is a good man but he is lightweight. I will need a man who can get cooperation from the governors and others. Someone suggested Gurmani's[61] name. I was taken aback, but on reconsideration I feel that he might well be the right man, but I do not know whether he would accept. Similarly I feel that Qazi Fazlullah should be employed as a provincial minister. I think there is a need to get men around me who could be useful in the political field and take on so many rascals in the opposition.

26 | MONDAY

📖 Addressed a gathering of local lawyers on the situation in the Middle East and the object of the Law Commission. Also apprised them of the trends in East Pakistan. Asked them why they allowed their bar association to be used as a political platform for the opposition and why they passed judgement on current affairs without finding out facts. It was in their interest to use these institutions for advancement of their profession and for promoting their welfare.

27 | TUESDAY

📖 Received three letters from the foreign minister from New York giving the gist of his talks with Mr Kosygin, and the Egyptian and the Syrian representatives giving their information of the situation in the Middle East and the cause of the war. Kosygin is apprehensive of our role and would like to meet me soon in Moscow. Said that he was willing to consider our demand for arms.

📖 Egyptians say the Israeli air attack came at a time when their pilots were having breakfast. The radar was rendered ineffective through alleged jamming backed by the American communication ship Liberty and that the Israelis brought in thrice the number of aircraft against them than anticipated. The Syrians, on the other hand, are very critical of the Egyptian performance. They regard the Egyptians soft and un-soldiery.

📖 Begum Zari Sarfraz,[62] MNA, came to see me after a visit to Chile, Austria, Czechoslovakia and Morocco. Said that wherever she went she found great regard for Pakistan amongst people. In

Morocco, a man kissed the Pakistan flag on seeing it. When questioned why, he replied for Pakistan being such a good friend of his country. She was struck by the material progress made by Austria and shabby conditions of people in adjoining communist Slovakia. She said that it would do a lot of good to our pseudo-communists to visit these countries. They will then learn what communism means.

📖 Another friend who had been to England recently, said that he visited an MP's house. There he was surprised to see my photograph. After a time he turned around and said that may I ask you a question. What will France do without De Gaulle and what will Pakistan do without Ayub Khan?

28 | WEDNESDAY

📖 Held a meeting with the ministers from West Pakistan and Governor Musa on how East Pakistan could be checked from blackmailing West Pakistan by pressure tactics. It was agreed that both West Pakistan and the centre must get tough administratively and East Pakistani disloyalty must be exposed in the assemblies, in the administration and in the press. It is quite possible that when told that they can walk out of Pakistan if they wish, they may come to their senses.

📖 Report from Cairo indicates that the leaders of Egypt are in the mood for self-criticism. They admit that they have been beaten thoroughly and grave mistakes have been made. Their social and military structure has been shattered and has to be rebuilt afresh. However, they think time is on their side. The western powers were saying that this war was a crusade, nevertheless because of the insincerity of Saudi Arabia, Iran, Tunisia and Morocco, any form of Muslim alliance at this stage was not a practical proposition.

30 | FRIDAY

📖 Recorded my first of the month speech, highlighted our sympathy for Arabs and the black man under white domination in Africa. Gave a *shabash* to the farmers in doing well with the new wheat and rice seeds and exhorted them to grow more summer cereals like maize, *jawar* and *bajra* when the water is more plentiful.

I also expressed my surprise at the war hysteria being created in India against Pakistan. It was nonsense to say that we want to start a war against India. What for? On the contrary, we want to live in peace with that country. However, we seek solution of Kashmir, which has been wrongfully usurped by India.

📖 An awkward question was asked in the National Assembly. Up to the time he became a minister in 1958, Bhutto had been declaring before the Indian courts that he was an Indian citizen residing in Karachi. The object was to get some compensation for the property left by his parents in India. In fact, he was selling his soul for about one lakh fifty thousand rupees. All this was not known to us till recently when the matter was discussed in the Indian parliament and came out in that press.

1 | SATURDAY

📖 The C-in-C Navy came and told me that the naval court martial had announced its judgment in the conspiracy case. Sentences ranging from 3 to 14 years had been awarded. Some are being dealt with summarily. The discipline in the service is being tightened and welfare work stepped up.

📖 We are now in full possession of Indian plans of attack against East and West Pakistan.[63] Our military intelligence has done an excellent job. The C-in-C Army came and reported certain Indian troop movements and reconnaissance being carried out which confirms the Indian plans that have fallen in our hands are genuine. I have told him to plot out all this information on the map and let me have a look at it. The other information is that the Indians are convinced that we are determined to open hostilities this month with a view to liberating Kashmir. What has made them come to this conclusion God alone knows, but there could be nothing more absurd than this. It would be madness on our part to do this. Every factor is against us.

2 | SUNDAY

📖 Our foreign office is of the view that because of the tragic events in the Middle East and the fact that members of CENTO had divergent views and policies, it will do no good to hold the ministerial meeting in the near future. It was, therefore, decided to send the foreign secretary to Tehran and Ankara to explain our views. Meanwhile, they had their reactions to our proposal. The Iranians think that giving so much consideration to the Arabs is not justified, in fact, it will impress the Arabs that the Americans and British are our friends. This is a bit of wishful thinking; our experience of being let down by America and Britain when attacked by India is too recent and fresh to be forgotten.

Beside the Arabs, we have to take note of the Soviet feelings. Any CENTO council meeting at this juncture would be regarded by the Soviets as an unfriendly act, a bad prelude to my impeding visit to Moscow where I intend asking for military and economic assistance.

📖 Called Qazi Fazlullah and offered him a ministership in the West Pakistan cabinet. He should prove a political asset, besides being useful administratively. In return, I asked for three things, belief in my political philosophy and loyalty, and countering the disruptionists in Sindh, and helping the governor in running a sound administration.

Certain people in Sindh are in the habit of talking against one unit. I told some of them that if it was not for one unit, Punjab would have taken away all the waters of the rivers left to us, leaving Sindh high and dry. So they had better be careful of what they say.

5 | WEDNESDAY

📖 The C-in-C Air Force, Air Marshal Nur Khan, came to see me. He is very dissatisfied with his budget allocations, especially the foreign exchange. I have had a long discussion with the finance minister. His trouble is that because of food bills etc. he is very short of foreign exchange. However, I have told Nur Khan to have further discussions with the finance secretary and C-in-C Army to see whether some adjustments could be made.

📖 Nawabzada Col. Abdul Ghafoor Khan of Hoti was sworn in as a minister at the centre in place of Ghulam Faruque. I think he should do well. He is keen, hospitable and humble. I am going to use him more for political work.

📖 I have been shown a report on air battles in Jordan and Iraq written by one of our pilots who took part in them. The Arab pilots were ill trained, casual, squabbling amongst each other often and did not like even rudimentary precautions or preparedness. Whereas the Israelis were very skilful, accurate and daring. However, our lad shot down two Israeli aircraft in Israel.

📖 Received several dispatches from our foreign minister from New York, giving me the gist of his discussions with several foreign dignitaries. I think he is learning the art of diplomacy fast.

6 | THURSDAY

📖 Called the defence minister and told him that the essential requirements of the air force have to be met. Our air force is small and to be effective in war must not suffer from lack of essential equipment. That is the only way we can get on top of the much larger Indian Air Force. He told me that he has managed to offer another 4½ crore rupees worth of foreign exchange to them by cutting down others. This still leaves a gap of 3 crores but we shall see if in six months time what the form is.

📖 A couple of Pakistanis who have visited India recently had reported responsible Indians talking of settling accounts with Pakistan in a decade or so. This seems to be the general mood and we have to keep a careful watch on these sadists.

📖 The High Commissioner of Nigeria called and delivered a letter from their head of administration who has asked us not to recognize the breakaway eastern province.[64] I have told him that we have no intention of doing so. To us this is an internal affair of their country.

📖 I am beginning to think that it might be a good thing if we induct Mr Gurmani as a minister. True, he is an ex-EBDOed man and an arch intriguer but he is a clever man, most of all well informed and an excellent speaker and a writer with a lot of political sense. He could prove useful in the political field and in running the affairs of the Muslim League. So I have asked Khawaja Shahabuddin to sound him out.

📖 Now that all the resolutions before the United Nations Assembly on the Middle East have failed to get two-thirds majority other than Pakistan's resolution forbidding Israel from annexing Jerusalem, it is quite clear that the status quo and the stalemate will continue with Israeli forces staying where they are. The point is, what should the Arabs be doing in that case. My view is that the Arabs should not be in an undue hurry unless they get a satisfactory settlement, which is not in sight. Let the Israelis maintain a large occupation army in distant places. It will put a fearful burden on their economy, which is already in bad shape. True that the world is making large contributions but there is a limit to what they can do. I can foresee Israel pulling out *suo moto* of occupied areas other than those which they consider vital to their security and navigation through the Bay of Aqaba. Having access both to the Mediterranean and the Red Sea, I do not think they are much worried about passage through the Suez Canal.

7 | FRIDAY

A large number of MNAs come to see me daily. Their contention, I understand, is that people around me do not keep me well-informed. But what happens when they come. They start out by eulogizing my services, some genuinely and some not so genuinely, then speak about their rivals and detractors, then often end up by some personal request. In rare cases are national problems touched. The trouble is that most of them have limited education and those that have, do not take the trouble of keeping themselves informed. The truth is that politically we are immature and primitive. Personal and local problems loom large in our eyes. How can direct elections have any meaning under such conditions?

8 | SATURDAY

The cabinet meeting was held in the morning. Import policy and many other problems were discussed. The picture emerging is gloomy. Because of heavy food bills, defence requirements and large debt servicing liabilities, there is small amount left for cash licensing. However, there is a large amount available in commodity aid and under barter arrangements that will be available to us to import certain essential items.

The jute policy was discussed in the afternoon. It has become fashionable for East Pakistan to ask for support prices for jute genuinely higher than the prices warranted by the market forces. The idea is good but huge losses are suffered which have to be borne by the Central Government. However, after a lot of haggling, 12, 26, 27 and 28 rupees were fixed for the superior varieties.

The real answer to jute production and trade is that I have been advocating a jute corporation which deals with the business from the farmer to the exporter.

9 | SUNDAY

News came in the room that Miss Jinnah had died of heart failure. As usual the mischief mongers are always ready to take advantage of such an opportunity to make political capital out of it. Their demand is that she should be buried alongside the Quaid-e-Azam. This will only ruin the symmetry of the mausoleum which is a national monument costing about a crore of rupees. I have told the administration that if it becomes unavoidable then the consultant engineer should be consulted about the exact site. It was decided to give due solemnity to this occasion. Flags be half-masted and the day of burial will be a public holiday. I would be represented by my military secretary and the government by a minister at the burial.

10 | MONDAY

My wife had a recurrence of heart palpitation. It lasted for a short time, but left her weak. She was to come with me to Murree for a week's stay, but the doctor told her to rest for a couple of days. I, too, decided to stay on but she insisted that I should proceed with my programme and have the change I needed so badly and she could follow later. Even in adversity she is concerned more with the problems of others than her own.

11 | TUESDAY

The British High Commissioner[65] called on me prior to his departure on leave to the UK. He asked my views on anti-Chinese riots in Burma, Nepal and India and also their pressure on Hong Kong. I said that I am myself puzzled about the riots in Burma and demonstrations in Nepal. Though both Burma and Nepal are as apprehensive of the Chinese as Nepal is of India, the Chinese have always been solicitous of the feelings of both of them. Besides, Burma cannot afford to go all out, with China being so close to them and also having large communist elements within their country who are in open rebellion against the government in Rangoon. The Nepalese, too, need China's support to hold off India.

As regards Hong Kong, I doubt if the Chinese would carry out a physical invasion but they will most likely continue to create problems for the administration hoping that it would eventually fall into their lap like the way Macao did. But the belief that the Chinese regard British pressure in Hong Kong as a useful outlet for doing business with the outside world, is mistaken. We have it on the authority of Chen-yi that it is not so.

He then came to the situation in the Middle East and what the British wanted was peace. That is why when Egypt blocked passage through the straits of Tirana, they tried their best to bring pressure when it opened and they were certain that it would become a cause for battle with Israel. I told him that I could understand British support to Israel to the extent they are giving. How is it going to further their interest in the Middle East? Judging from the British press there seems to be an irrational and primitive delight that the Arabs have been beaten.

I was glad to see the Security Council had passed a resolution that the Secretary General should appoint a person with observers to supervise the ceasefire between Israel and Egypt. I hope they would go further and ask the two sides to separate at least 10 to 15 miles as a start to facilitate opening of the shipping through the canal. He thought it was a good idea and said he would pass it on to his government. He asked if there was any change in the situation between India and Pakistan. I told him there was none, nor is there any hope in the near future. Indians are in no mood to compromise. So my effort was not to allow the situation to deteriorate.

He then pleaded that we should continue to keep dialogue open with each other as that can be very helpful in international relationships. I agreed.

[Major] General Rafi, my military secretary, returned from Karachi. He had gone there to represent me at Miss Jinnah's funeral. He said that sensible people were happy that the government had given her so much recognition, but generally the people behaved very badly. There was an initial *Namaz-e-Janaza* at her residence in Mohatta Palace in accordance, presumably, with Shia rites. Then there was to be *Namaz-e-Janaza* for the public in the polo ground. There an argument developed whether this should be led by a Shia or a Sunni, eventually Badayuni was put forward to lead the prayer. As soon as he uttered the first sentence the crowd broke in the rear. Thereupon, he and the rest ran leaving the coffin high and dry. It was with some difficulty that the coffin was put on a vehicle and taken to the compound of the Quaid's *Mazar*, where she was to be buried. There a large crowd had gathered and demanded to converge on the place of burial. This obviously could not be allowed for lack of space. Thereupon, the students and the *goonda* element started pelting stones on the police. They had to resort to *lathi* charge and tear gas attack. The compound of the *Mazar* was apparently littered with stones. Look at the bestiality and irresponsibility of the people. Even a place like this could not be free from their vandalism.

12 | WEDNESDAY

📖 12 Division is responsible for the defence of Azad Kashmir. The general has a sizeable force of eight brigades under his command. He came over to explain his plan of deployment. He is well disposed, capable and confident of dealing with the enemy. In the last war, his major handicap was communications, especially in Vatori Bulge and the Neelam Valley. Vatori Bulge is now well served with roads and strongly held. Neelam Valley is still a problem as it is overlooked by the enemy.

📖 The Russian Charge d'Affairs came to deliver a message from his government to the effect that they would like me to come in the first week of September. They have suggested this as presently they are heavily engaged in the Middle Eastern affairs. This is embarrassing as I have already informed the Romanians that I would be coming towards the end of this month. The idea was to go to Moscow after Romania.

📖 Visited Ayubia, the new township being developed in the gullies across Murree. These were old military cantonments which I have persuaded the defence ministry to release for civil use. An improvement trust has been established which looks after the project. There are some 400 old buildings and plots to offer, out of which over 200 have been disposed of. An ambitious rope-way is being established to encourage skiing in winter and for joyrides in summer. I have suggested that a similar township should be established on the hills north of Abbottabad along Nowsherwan Road. There are possibilities of making lovely colonies commanding magnificent views. The height would be about 5000 feet and liveable throughout the year. It would be an ideal place for old and retired people.

📖 Justice Munir,[66] who is an old friend of mine, came to dinner. He said that he was under the impression that I had advised General Iskander Mirza to abrogate the constitution in October 1958. So when on a visit to London he checked up with General Iskander Mirza[67] whether that was true. General Iskander Mirza said definitely not. The decision was his own and at no time had I been consulted on its drafting or issue. I told Munir that was correct. But on the contrary I was always under the impression that he was responsible for that. Munir said no, on the contrary he had advised General Iskander Mirza to allow the elections to take place and the inevitable chaos to develop. Then he would be in a better position and on a better wicket to declare an emergency. I told him that

General Iskander Mirza could not wait that long. He knew that the matter would be out of his hands then as he had no chance of being re-elected as president. In fact, I had asked him on one occasion as to what were the chances of his re-election. He said about 5 per cent.

I asked Munir what was the basis of his advice when Col. Qazi, the then Assistant Judge Advocate General, raised the point. It was the basis of his advice when Col. Qazi raised the point in the presence of General Iskander Mirza that after having declared martial law and appointed a chief martial law administrator, the president had ceased to have a legal position. Munir had then disagreed with Qazi and I was relieved that an awkward situation had been averted. Munir said that he remembered the occasion and how bravely I had told Qazi to keep his mouth shut. But he knew all along that Qazi was right. In any case, the arrangement of having a president and a chief martial law administrator could not work. Iskander Mirza had to go. In fact, he admitted to Munir in London that after declaring martial law, Iskander was conscious of the anomaly of his position.

14 | FRIDAY

The additional foreign secretary came to discuss the question of visits to Romania and the Soviet Union in view of the latest Soviet communication toward giving an impression of over anxiety to the Soviets. It was decided to tell them that the suggestion was under consideration. Meanwhile, the Romanians should be approached to retard the date into the first week of September. If they agreed, then I could visit the Soviet Union after Romania. Otherwise I shall have to go to Moscow direct, which I want to avoid as it has certain international implications.

I have told the additional foreign secretary that so far we have taken the lead at the United Nations in advocating the cause of the Arabs. We took the lead in sponsoring the Yugoslav resolution, then we took forward a resolution, which was passed by two-thirds majority, that Israel undo any action they may have taken in absorbing Jerusalem, and since they are refusing to do so, we are now asking for their condemnation. This is good as far as it goes, but we should be careful that in doing so we do not hurt our own interests by frustrating countries like the USA. Besides, by pushing the Arab cause too hard we may well be embarrassing the Arabs. They might think that we are trying to gain popularity at the cost of their misfortune. And any thought that by doing so we are weaning the Arabs away from the Indians, would be a mistaken belief because the Arabs know the Indian government's susceptibilities. So taking all this into consideration there is need for us to exercise caution while supporting the Arabs. Our real object, is of, course to bring all the Muslims on one platform to defend their interest against hostile elements. Immediately the circumstances are not good but we hope we have put the germ of the idea in people's mind, which may mature and expand in course of time. Let us hope and pray that it does so.

Dined at 12 Division headquarters and met most of the senior officers. They are a fine lot, had gone through fire during [19]65 war and know their job. While talking to them certain ideas came to my mind which I want to discuss with Yahya:

1. Most of our formations are committed to defending certain areas, they all have wide fronts to cover. The terrain they have to defend varies from formation to formation. Take 12 Division for instance. They have 350 miles to defend in a very difficult mountainous terrain. So they have

very wisely divided themselves into eight brigades, six in the front line and two in reserve comprising of their artillery and elements of other supplements and auxiliary arms and troops. This is necessitated by the lateral distances between brigade areas. This will not permit use of supporting arms on divisional basis. Can't this idea be applied to the other formations, and in fact, the whole army? We should then have divisions composed of brigade groups complete with their supporting arms, powerful and flexible, capable of fighting on their own, at the same time admitting of divisional control, concentrated use of artillery where they happen to be deployed closer together.

2. Similarly, the complement of arms and holding of transport in each division or even a brigade group should be correlated to its role. This will need a lot of realistic thinking and planning. For transport we could rely largely on civilian vehicles, the population of which is expanding fast. This will save the army money to put to better use in the teeth of armed struggle.

3. What about training? Because of the expansion of the army and the [...] induction of young officers and raw men, and accelerated promotions especially amongst junior officers, the need for individual training and training in minor tactics is obvious. But any collective training from company and squadron upwards should, as far as possible, be held on-the-job and when the job is close to the Indian border the deployment of troops may lead to jittery Indian reactions. Then the collective training may be held elsewhere but repeated test exercises without troops should be held on-the-job for familiarization of all concerned with what they are expected to do in the event of war. I think this will pay big dividends.

4. And that leads me to the organization of armour. Last war has proved two things, armour on divisional scale will never be used because of the terrain and lack of roads, water obstacles with limited number of bridges etc. An armour formation without infantry can win ground but cannot hold it. It has to pull back to rear for security. In the light of this, I believe that organization of armour in the Pakistan Army is defective. The answer may well lie in the following:

    a.   Armour division should consist of only two brigades, each consisting of two armour regiments and two infantry battalions, strong and antitank weapons and holding adequate quantities of antitank and anti-personnel mines. The artillery should be integral to them.

    b.   For an infantry division, the ideal would be to have an armour regiment integral to each brigade group, but since we have not got that number of tanks, let two brigades and a division have a regiment each. In that case, these brigade groups will have a strong counter-attack element within them when used at a distance from each other and two powerful counter-offensive elements when brigade groups are used in a division setting. This, of course, would not apply to the formations used in the Sindh desert, hilly areas and in the Sulemanki-Bhawalnagar front. Their requirement is for a much larger mobile antitank complement, which perhaps can be provided from other regions.

5. In order to use the minimum number of troops in defence and release maximum number for counter-attack and counter-offensive, concentrated defences in depth should be built on all likely lines of approach from India. These should be simple structures providing cover against artillery and [...] fire positions for automatic and antitank weapons. These should be integrated with antitank and anti-personnel minefield plans. In addition, antitank ditches about a couple of miles long should be dug across the major lines of approach and filled with water wherever possible.

Care, of course, will have to be taken that they do not obstruct our likely lines of counter-attack or counter-offensive.

6. Reverting to collective training, greater emphasis should be kept on night work and even tanks should be called up to do outflanking sweeps at night. It is the only way we can gain surprise and operate even when air situation is not favourable. Much greater proportion of infantry should be trained as guerrillas and commandos, encouraged to employ unconventional methods in attack and defence. Offensive patrols and tank hunting parties should be the rule. In fact, there should be a separate paragraph in operation orders reminding commanders of this need. Better still, before launching an operation the commander should ask his subordinates and even troops to make suggestions on unconventional methods and ways and means of gaining surprise and doing the maximum damage to the enemy with minimum cost. Apart from tactical gain this will get all those taking part in the operations emotionally involved. The result will be electrifying. When you encourage men to think, it is surprising what they can do. Before every operation remind men of fire control and economy in use of ammunition.

7. When employing tanks in offensive, make certain they are all accompanied by infantry, for infantry marries up with them with the objective to keep consolidation, beating back any counter-attack and protecting tanks in retaining ground gained. Tanks must nowhere have to fall back.

8. Our troops, by nature, are not good at digging in. It should be automatic to dig in when coming to a halt for however short a period. A lot of causalities can be avoided in this way.

9. Our troops should be trained to undergo sustained strain and make full use of its ammunition. If the situation permits, they should be battle inoculated. Officers should be encouraged to live and eat with the men in the field.

10. We are trying our utmost to create capability for manufacturing arms and ammunition within the country. There is also a talk of building tanks. My concept of tanks that will suit our conditions is different. A big tank carrying an enormous gun is no solution to our problem; in any case, in the face of modern cheap infantry, antitank weapons the size of tanks do not ensure its invulnerability. In fact, the greater a tank stands out, the more vulnerable it becomes. Why not have a tank that carries these weapons, recoilless guns or guided missiles and you can then have a much smaller tank that sits well on the ground, has a powerful engine for speed and wide tracks for cross country mobility? Such a tank will be a real fighter and play havoc with the enemy. Our heavy bridging requirements will also be cut down considerably.

11. Radio and radar jamming by the enemy has become a well-developed science. Whenever possible alternative means of communications must always be provided. Not to do so would be a criminal neglect.

12. Civil armed forces should be suitably equipped and trained to act tactically even at the cost of the army. They proved their worth in the last war and can be a powerful element to the army in future. Organized and trained *Mujahids* for protection of vital installations, airfields and bridges and rear areas. Also be ready to deal with enemy parachute drops. We must avoid using regular troops for such tasks.

15 | SATURDAY

The Mufti-e-Azam of Syria came to see me. It is his second visit to Pakistan. He is a man of wide vision and broad religious outlook, so different from the average mullah. I invited him to go around Pakistan and talk to our bigots. It might do them some good. He promised to do so in the cold weather. In recognition of his services to Islam and as a friend of Pakistan, he has been given an award.

The general belief is and it is, true that as a result of the recent war in the Middle East, the Arabs have suffered terribly and they would be unable to raise their heads for a long time. But what is not realized is that the British and the West suffer. Through all the shortages and closure of the Suez Canal their economy is going to be hurt very badly. The Westerners and especially the Americans are happy that as the result of the Arab defeat the Russians have suffered a great political and moral defeat. On the surface and on a short term basis, it is true, but in the long term the Russians should be happy that the Arabs, and especially the Egyptians and the Syrians, are now completely at their mercy and in their hands. I think the Russians have a God-given opportunity to establish themselves permanently in the vital strategic areas of the Middle East. This they have been wanting to do for ages.

17 | MONDAY

Had a busy day today, went to Pindi and back again. Held a meeting with the information minister and secretary about the future of *Kohistan* newspaper. Attended a conference on the food situation in West Pakistan. Called the defence minister and the senior army officers and gave them my views on the type of tank we should aim to build. Conferred with the foreign minister on his visit to the UN General Assembly and the Middle East situation and the foreign secretary's visit to Tehran and Turkey. Conferred with the representatives of the health ministry and the chairman, CDA on the location of the hospital in Islamabad and finally opened the central health laboratories in Islamabad. All these required a lot of listening and conflicting views and telling people where they get off, and giving decisions. I was told that all of them went back satisfied even if the decisions were against their preconceived ideas. Human nature is curious. People will squabble with each other until someone takes the responsibility and gives a decision. Then they feel relieved and go back more or less satisfied. And the man who has to give decisions does not have to be an expert in the subject under discussion. He should be a good listener, give all concerned the chance to say their piece, be capable of weighing all acts and have the strength of character to make up his mind and come to a decision and announce it with firmness. Any attempt to resort to arbitrary and hasty decisions, thrusting them down people's throats, is bound to be counter productive. People will then not cooperate willingly. I am a great believer in consultation prior to coming to a decision.

I was astounded to hear from the foreign minister that a number of Egyptian officers worked for the defeat of their country to oust President Nasser. Can there be anything more ghastly than this? What hope of survival has a country which gives birth to such people?

During the food discussion I impressed on the provincial governor and his colleagues that they have to get their people, especially the urban people, used to eating cereals we can produce. The question of likes and dislikes does not arise. All that the government can attempt to do is to prevent people from starvation.

18 | TUESDAY

Certain people like Mr Khuhro,[68] Alamdar Gillani, Pir Mehooz, Hassan Mahmood[69] came to see me and stayed on for lunch. Mr Khuhro was worried that Qazi Fazlullah had become a minister and stolen a march on him. Why could he not be accommodated at the centre or in the Muslim League hierarchy? I told him there was no place vacant at the centre but I should certainly do my best to get a suitable place for him in the Muslim League. I was impressed by Alamdar Gillani, though fat and flabby, he has a lot of common sense and is shrewd and intelligent. He also has a lot of influence in his area. He struck me as a man with promise. Hassan Mahmood's trouble is that he is heavily in debt and expects all sorts of concessions. Therefore, he is an expensive friend.

News from Indonesia is not too encouraging. It seems that Suharto is not firmly in the saddle. There are differences between him and Adam Malik who is a snake and an American stooge. He and Sitiam do not seem to be getting on well with each other, either. Under such circumstances it is only natural that the only organized party, the Communist Party, will eventually prevail provided they are not in a hurry and do not trigger off premature takeover as last time. This will be tragic for Muslim Indonesia and friends like us.

News from the Suez Canal area is not too good either. It seems the Israelis are building up to a showdown with Egypt in forcing the canal open. This may well be welcome by the canal users. Presently the Egyptians have not the military means to prevent this.

19 | WEDNESDAY

A report came in today that Bhutto, at his request, met Ghulam Faruque. Ghulam Faruque told him the following:

a. There will be a financial crisis in Pakistan in six months time.
b. That I am a dictator.
c. The decision to make vehicles and tractors within the country, we should at least start with the manufacture of engines which will go into as many vehicles as possible, was forced by me to favour Gandhara Industries where my son works. This, in fact, was the recommendation of a high committee setup to examine this problem. Ghulam Faruque knew it.
d. That I have given him my book, *Friends Not Masters*, which he returned later. He found nothing worthwhile in it.
e. I have inducted Fazlullah in the provincial cabinet and I am after Gurmani now.

These are the words of a man who went out willingly, wanted me to regard him as my friend and even now is protected against universal accusations that he is corrupt to the core.

I have heard someone say that late Mr Ghulam Ahmed used to describe Mr Ghulam Faruque as a 'brinjal' in a plate capable of turning in any direction. I had the misfortune of employing Mr Ghulam Faruque four times. He has certain outstanding qualities like dynamism, initiative and drive but is devoid of convictions, has doubtful scruples, refuses to make a team, is not open to argument and is very expensive, especially with public funds. Above all he is superficial, lacking depth of thought.

21 | FRIDAY

A very revealing document came into my hands. Mr Khalil of Daily *Jang* received a photocopy of a dispatch order written by McConnaughy, US ambassador in Pakistan, to Chester Bowles, US ambassador to India, approving of his proposal to encourage the BANGSAM movement to promote US interests. BANGSAM stands for a country that will be made by the amalgamation of the two Bengals and Assam. Mr Khalil, instead of publishing it, sent it on to his brother in Pindi to be passed on to my military secretary. There are also attached minutes of the meeting that took place amongst Americans on the subject. As it is in illegible script, an attempt is being made to decipher and type it up. McConnaughy had gone on to say that this proposal has the blessing of Dean Rusk and it should be pushed at all costs. He has also gone on to say that the history of Bengal has always been defiance of Delhi and the present demand by East Pakistanis for autonomy is, in fact, a demand for self-determination. It is necessary to remain in touch with the leaders of this movement and give them all encouragement regardless of the susceptibilities of Pakistan and India. The letter also hints that a start should be made with joint projects in the Eastern region to get the people of the two Bengals used to working together.

Now if this is not subversion of the highest order, what else is it? The Americans are in the habit of saying that it is the communists who indulge in subversion in other countries but the truth is that the American subversion is now universal and surpasses all others.

From this it can be seen how difficult the task of emergent countries is. They have the enormous problem of attaining political and economic stability internally, and saving themselves from subversion and subversive attempts by big powers from without, who do not like to see sound and stable governments emerge in these countries. Basically it is the economic and in some cases military dependence of emergent countries that makes them so vulnerable.

Another document that came with the letter, obviously written by a CIA man, disclosed that 40 per cent of Peace Corps people are engaged in espionage work and the apprehension was that the Indians might get to know this.

22 | SATURDAY

I have asked for the director of intelligence to come and see me about these papers. My guess is that these papers have been procured by Indian intelligence, then copied and sent to Pakistan by hand, and under an unknown signature posted to the editor of a paper not reputed for his sense of

responsibility in the hope that they would be published thus souring Indo–US relationship and exposing the US without hurting Indian interests. If this be so then the Indian intelligence are very smart indeed. I, however, suspected this as soon as I saw these documents.

📖 The Soviet Chargè d'Affairs called and explained what transpired in the meeting of socialist countries held recently to consider the Middle East situation. They decided to give the Arabs all the support possible, but expected that the Arabs would also be realistic. They also expected that I would use my influence with the Arabs to be reasonable and with others to support their cause. I asked to be informed of what the Soviet regard as realism on the part of Arabs. My personal guess is that they want the Arabs to recognize Israel in return for evacuation of their aggression. I wonder if the Arabs are in a mood to do so. Jordan may consider this, but others would not.

📖 I think this visit to the Shah or Shahinshah as he now likes to be called, has been worthwhile. I hope I have been able to clear any doubts about us in his mind, make him take a more rational view towards the Arabs in the Gulf area and warn him of Indian designs.

23 | SUNDAY

📖 Went to Nathiagali and spent a day at the government house. It is a beautiful place in charming surroundings. The lawns are well-kept and the flowers are beautiful with vivid colours. It is the effect of height 7,500 feet above sea level. The deputy commissioner Hazara came to see me. I inquired how my two sons Akhtar and Shaukat, who live in their home area, are conducting themselves. He said that people are full of praise on how well brought up and well behaved my children were. They were also the source of great assistance to the administration and did a lot of useful social work.

📖 Altaf Gauhar stayed on for dinner. We discussed American designs on East Pakistan, their hatred of West Pakistan and suspicion of the central government, attempts to go back to Hinduism and conscious effort to deploy Bengali nationalism. We agreed that they are a willing target for American and Hindu designs. He asked me how long will they remain with Pakistan? I said till India was ready to swallow them. Nonetheless we must make all attempts to save them against themselves. As a start the answer was to have the problems psychologically examined. To do that we should set up a working party preferably of sensible East Pakistanis. We must also get East Pakistan ministers to examine if there is any practical solution. I doubt if this will bear any fruit as the Bengalis have no stomach for self-criticism nor for listening to the truth about themselves. People who do not have these qualities cannot recognize their malady, let alone cure them. Our difficulty is that we cannot break through their mental barrier. Altaf Gauhar asked me whether the Bengalis would be reconciled and satisfied if there was a Bengali president. I told him not unless he was out and out parochial. If he had nationalistic or Pakistani outlook he would be repudiated at once.

24 | MONDAY

Sent for the director of intelligence, the foreign minister, the foreign secretary and Altaf Gauhar and discussed American interests in East Pakistan. They all said that the letter that has come into our hands confirms what we suspected the Americans were doing. There had been enough indications to that effect. However, prudence demands that we make certain thorough and expert examination that the signature on the letter was in fact that of the former American ambassador in Pakistan. We must also ascertain how the letter landed from Delhi to Pakistan. If brought from India by hand and then posted in Pakistan, then who could have done it. Khalil [...] shall have to be interrogated. So the director of intelligence was told to undertake this task in conjunction with the director of the intelligence bureau.

We also discussed a telegram sent by our high commissioner in Delhi. He said that it is wildly rumoured in Delhi and commented upon by the diplomats that Indian antagonists believe that Pakistan is going to open hostilities in Kashmir in August or September. He thought that it is being done with the connivance of the Indian government and especially Chavan. The fact is that there is no substance in these rumours. We have no intention of doing any such thing. All factors are against us. So I caused a message to be sent to the Indian prime minister not to be misled by these things. We do not want war. We want peaceful settlement of Kashmir on an honourable basis. Our high commissioner also thinks that the Americans are working for the replacement of Indira by Chavan who they think would suit them better.

It is not clear what the Americans mean when talking about amalgamation of West Bengal, East Pakistan and Assam. If it is to be done under the Indian hegemony then the physical process might be easier because of the presence of renegades in East Pakistan like the Awami Leaguers headed by Mujibur Rahman and perhaps some elements amongst the National Awami Party, specially the communists and Hindus who, as a first step, would like to take over East Pakistan before communalising it. But then it is not certain that there will be peace and calm in East Pakistan as the Muslims by then might well realize the folly of the step they have taken, besides India may not welcome an American military presence in the area even though it may ostensibly be directed against China. The other alternative is the amalgamation of these territories as an independent state outside the Indian and Pakistan constitutions. This can be brought about by force which means the American [...] force willing rebellion against India and Pakistan. I doubt if this latter can succeed because both India and Pakistan are strong enough to deal with it. Besides, the Hindus and Muslims in Bengal, in their heart of hearts loathe the sight of each other just as the Assamese loathe the guts of the Indian Bengali who is a bully and domineering. Then in Assam, the hill men have the greatest suspicion of the people in the plains. Hence the Naga and Mizo rebellions and demands by other hill tribes like Khasis and the others for separation and autonomy.

The Americans are probably banking on East Pakistan's dissatisfaction with West Pakistan. That may be true but I do not doubt if they would want to or be happy under Indian Hindu hegemony. However, it can be argued that East Pakistanis will not have much choice. India is strong enough to overrun and hold them down. My belief is that the American plan is amateurish as such it will bring nothing but instability in these regions. The only good it would have done would be that it would have harmed the interest of Muslims and Pakistan. It is inconceivable these areas can be brought and held together without a common ideology and that ideology cannot be Hinduism or Islam, that can only be communism. How will that help the Americans? Besides, the Americans do not realize that the Bengali temperament is mercurial and highly unstable. He does not like discipline and does not like making a team. Leadership is difficult to produce. This is because of the nature and climate in which he lives. Both are against them in many ways.

25 | TUESDAY

📖 Mahmud Haroon came to see me. He was really after getting the Muslim League ticket for the by-election in Karachi, but also spoke about Bhutto. Said that Bhutto met and complained to him that *Dawn* had written a leading article against him after the central assembly debate on his conduct and that was not right. And went on to suggest that Bhutto will complain in writing and all he expected Mahmud to do was to apologize. Mahmud refused to comply, on which Bhutto threatened to take the matter to the court. Mahmud accepted the challenge and hoped that Bhutto would go to court. In fact, if he did go to court, the evidence against him is so overwhelming that he would be completely exposed.

Mahmud said that Sindhis are by nature disloyal and unstable. When there was a separate Sindh province the members of the legislature used to vote against a chief minister they supported, without even giving any prior notice. A conspiracy used to be hatched at the last minute and government overturned, simply because someone else offered them a few more jobs or concessions. Governments used to change at the drop of a pin. I told him that my experience of the individual Sindhi is that they are very good friends, hospitable and generous. Politically, too, they have behaved themselves well under the new dispensation. But that may be due to the fact that I am well known in Sindh, and secondly, a presidential system does not admit of so much political mischief as the parliamentary form of government does.

📖 Moved down to Rawalpindi. Heard in the evening that there had been over 11 inches of rain in Karachi in the course of 36 hours and more was expected. A large-scale flood has taken place and has done them tremendous amount of damage, especially amongst the poor parts of the community living in *jhugis*. I have announced a donation of five lakh rupees. I hope this will be of some assistance to the poor people.

26 | WEDNESDAY

📖 Discussed the future of *Kohistan* newspaper. It is Col. Abdul Ghafoor Hoti who should be entrusted with the task. He will supervise its operation and also collect contributions for its running and also himself make a contribution. He readily agreed and will, I am sure, do well. He has political sense and right ideas. Under him will be Manzar-e-Alam to supervise the contents of the paper. It has to become an aggressive mouth-piece of the Muslim League. Then there will be another one or two functionaries who will supervise the business side.

I told the Muslim League people that it is the first time that they have their own paper. They should thank me for it and not let it go out of their hands.

📖 The director, intelligence bureau came and reported that the Americans are engaged in extensive espionage work, especially on PIA's Chinese flights. Several Pakistanis have been subverted and caught. Investigations are progressing.

He also said that, according to his experts, the letter purported to have been written by McConnaughy to Chester Bowles in connection with East Pakistan, is a forgery. Indians or most probably Russians are responsible or it. However, they are making further checks.

News came in that the Shah wants us to land in Tehran at 4 p.m. Then the intention is to fly to Ramsar on the Caspian Sea where the conference will take place.

Heard in the evening news that there had been another severe earthquake in the eastern regions of Turkey causing considerable loss to life and property. This may cause Turkish leaders to change their plan of coming to Tehran on the 28th. We shall know the situation tomorrow.

28 | FRIDAY

We proposed taking off from Rawalpindi at 1450 hours. I was told that the Turkish prime minister has postponed his visit because of the earthquake. Presumably the rest of the Turkish team is coming to Tehran.

29 | SATURDAY

Ramsar: Gathered for the talks at a palace next door to the hotel. The Shahinshah and his team, the Prime Minister of Turkey and his team and I were present. After the opening welcome by the Shah, I was called upon to speak. The gist of my talk is as follows:

a. All three countries expressed sympathy for the Arabs and asked for vacation of the aggression by Israel at the UN General Assembly. However, Pakistan went further and condemned Israel as an aggressor. We did not condemn the USA or the West nor did we support the Cuban or the Albanian resolution. Sensible Americans understand the consistency of our stand, though the strong Jewish or pro-Jewish elements in the administration are incensed with us.

b. Pakistan support to the Arab cause is nothing new. We have been supporting their stand on Palestine since 1948. In fact, we have always supported Muslim causes, wherever they may happen to be. We supported the Turks from the Balkan war onwards, we condemned Russian occupation of Azerbaijan, and we supported the struggle of the Maghreb people for freedom and so on. We are an ideological state; support for the Muslim cause is a part of our faith. But this has not been one-way traffic. When India attacked us in 1965, Iran, Turkey, Saudi Arabia and Indonesia gave us considerable support for which we are grateful.

c. We never condemned the USA or the West. Though there was strong feeling within the country, we tried to channelize it. It is against our interests to antagonize the USA.

d. Identity of views between USSR and us were coincidental. The motives of the two were different.

e. It is not right to run counter to Afro-Asian sentiments. We are part of that world. We are not lovers of Nasser. We have as much cause to complain against him as anybody else, but we have to look beyond him, we must not eliminate the Arab people.

f. The lesson for the small powers in this war is that you cannot put reliance on big powers. Their global aims and interpretations and commitments change from time to time.

What of the future:

a. Soviet foothold permanent in the Middle East. Arabs incensed against USA and the West. USA will be committing a grave error if she continues to alienate the Arabs. USA must insist on vacation of Arab lands. This is the first step towards peace in the region.

b. The existence of Israel is a fact of life. It cannot be wished away. But the tacit recognition of Israel should be left to the Soviets or the Arabs.

c. Closure of Suez Canal is hitting us all. Is it not possible to work for its opening?

Such meetings have a great value. They should be held at least once a year.

31 | MONDAY

📖 Stayed for a short while in Tehran airport and then took off for Karachi by PIA Trident and on approaching Karachi saw menacing banks of clouds. It was still raining on landing and went on for another 48 hours. There had been a total of 25 inches of rain in less than a week. Low-lying areas in Karachi were flooded.

📖 Held a meeting with Governor Musa and members of the local administration on the state of displaced persons on account of floods. They told me that so far 126 camps had been established where free rations and medical facilities were being provided under the supervision of magistrates. The three services and other volunteer bodies were also rendering assistance.

1 | TUESDAY

📖 Offered *fateha* at the grave of Miss Jinnah and then visited a couple of refugee camps. I think they are being well cared for.

📖 Khaliquzzaman[70] came to see me in the evening, thanked me for having come to Karachi to console the flood victims. He then went on to talk about my book. He was looking forward to reading it, but he hoped that I have expressed myself in a forthright manner without mincing words. I assured him that that was so. He said my abiding contribution was the establishment of the system of basic democracy. He said this system can save many a country if their people have the vision to see its virtues and political courage to adopt it. He then marvelled at my large heartedness in going to Miss Jinnah's grave after what she had been saying and doing to me. I told him that I do not believe in matching pettiness with pettiness.

2 | WEDNESDAY

📖 Flew to Rawalpindi. Discussed with Altaf Gauhar my interview with two TV experts on the 20th anniversary of Pakistan which falls due on 14th August. Our cricket team headed by Hanif had done very well in the first test match against MCC at Lords. From a hopeless position in the first innings, they recovered remarkably well to a position where England looked like losing the match. However, it ended up in a draw. Hanif scored 187 not out. It caused a message of congratulation to be sent to him.

📖 Received a message from M.M. Ahmed from Washington that there is every possibility of getting foreign exchange resources for Tarbela lined up. The Americans are relaxing in their rigidity and others are also forthcoming. George Woods is working very hard for us. If all goes well, we should be able to settle tenders and start work at the beginning of next year.

3 | THURSDAY

📖 The defence minister came to discuss the defence expectation of getting spares and ammunition from the Americans. It looks like they are loosening up a bit. It may well be the result of what I said in Ramsar. The Iranians and the Turks must have passed all that on to the Americans.

📖 Called the law minister to set up a committee to consider the following:

a. Increase of members in the assemblies from 150 to 200 each. This is necessitated by the increase in population and evolution of weightage for minority areas in West Pakistan. By virtue of this their representation will decrease and they will have tremendous cause to complain.
b. Restoration of seats for minorities, especially in the provincial assemblies. The provincial assemblies would act as an electoral college.
c. Increase in the members of Basic Democrats, say, from 80,000 to 120,000.

The law minister has just come back from Geneva after attending a conference on the rule of law in the region. I said, is this not a bit incongruous in the sort of world we see around? He said it is true but it was surprising how largely attended this meeting was. America sent some 100 delegates. Australia sent 80. Most of the law ministers, chief justices, attorney generals etc. were present. I wished to God it were possible to teach humanity to live by law. But the trouble is that though man has been able to conquer nature and acquire great power, he has not yet been able to conquer his own nature. The science of social behaviour has still to develop and be practiced. Until then, man's behaviour will continue to be selfish, and struggle and wars will remain with us.

4 | FRIDAY

Recorded an interview on TV for the 20th Anniversary of Pakistan. Mr Bukhari, Aslam Azhar and Suleri[71] questioned me on matters of national and historical importance.

5 | SATURDAY

One hears so much of the cultural revolution and the activities of the Red Guards in China these days. Recently there had been indications of a split in the Chinese army and clashes between people holding opposite views leading to bloodshed. It will be some time before the full story is known. At present much of it is shrouded in mystery, exaggeration and secrecy. But one thing is certain, there is a large element of personal clash between Mao Tse-tung and Liu Shao-chi.

When I went to China, I met the Chinese leaders. I marvelled at the manner in which these people had hung together through thick and thin for so long. However, one thing I noticed at that time was that whereas, when talking, Mao Tse-tung gesticulated to others but never to Liu Shao-chi. In fact, they never looked at each other face to face. I attributed this to probably shyness on the part of Liu Shao-chi but later events showed that this aloofness was based on much deeper causes.

A message has come in from the Soviets that they want me to arrive in Moscow on the 25th September whereas earlier on they had asked me to come in the first week of September. They apologized for this change on their part due to preoccupation, which I am sure is right. However, it is no good we taking umbrage on the change of date. It is in Pakistan's interest that I meet them soon and settle the problems of arms supply. So I have accepted the invitation.

6 | SUNDAY

Some of our papers have contracted with the publishers to publish extracts from my book. The first instalment has come out today. I think they made good reading. I am told that the daily *Jang*, which is also serializing it, was selling it at rupees one a paper.

I have caused a message to be sent to Nasser explaining what I told the American ambassador about the Middle East and the suggestion I made to Johnson. I have asked to see the Russian ambassador for the same purpose and also put them on their guard in respect of the propaganda that the Indians are mounting against my visit to the Soviet Union. The Indians are telling all sorts of lies to put the Russians off.

7 | MONDAY

📖 I was listening to a very interesting programme on the BBC early in the morning. The programme related to the lives of famous men like Gandhi, Churchill, Schmidt and Roosevelt. Recording of their voices and addresses were also transmitted. The most amazing was that of Roosevelt. He said the Republicans continue to criticize and hurl abuse at him, make baseless insinuations against his wife and slander his son. He has been treating all these with the contempt it deserves. But lately his patience is coming to an end. The Republicans have now started criticizing his dog Fala. It is sad that public funds amounting to 1 to 8 or 20 million dollars had been squandered on her. It hurts him no end as it hurts Fala no end. She, being Scottish, cannot bear being accused of extravagance. Loud laughter lasting for several minutes was heard from the audience. It is obvious that Roosevelt was no ordinary wit, apart from being a great leader and a statesman.

📖 Went on to see my lands in the village, which is being levelled by hired government bulldozers. They have done a fine job. Now more land has been levelled and will come under the plough. I hope the other farmers around too will copy this example. I can see that if this process goes on, the agriculture production should increase manifold in the country.

10 | THURSDAY

📖 My book is on sale in Pakistan as from today. I believe its release was anxiously awaited.

📖 Opened the RCD 7th Ministerial meeting at Islamabad. The foreign ministers of Iran and Turkey followed by the Secretary General, also spoke. All the speeches were in warm terms. I emphasized that in order to increase the areas of mutualism our planers should meet to identify them. Let us see how seriously Iran and Turkey take this. This will be the yardstick for mutual collaboration. After the speeches were over, we went to another room for refreshments. The Turkish Foreign Minister Ahsan Sabri said that after return from Ramsar the Russian ambassador came to call on him and inquired what had transpired during the meetings and had any decision been arrived at in respect of the Middle East situation? He told him that how could any decision be arrived at when we did not know the Soviet mind or US policy, and when the Arabs could not speak with one voice. The only thing we could do under the circumstances was to wait and see how the situation developed. Then Sabri asked him why Russia was not being more friendly to Pakistan and why India was being armed to the teeth. The Russian ambassador promised to communicate this to his government. Soon after, the American ambassador came to him and inquired how the talks went and what was decided about CENTO. Sabri told him that he found the President of Pakistan very upset this time. The ambassador inquired why. Sabri said because of you, the Americans. After some discussion the ambassador said that he intends recommending to his government to invite Mr Pirzada for discussion.

Sabri then turned around and said why was public opinion in Pakistan so hostile to America. He should know the reasons but I repeated them and told him that I am doing my best to control the situation but people's feelings are hurt. Besides, the Americans have to do something visible to inspire confidence in people's minds. I also told him of the lurking fear in people's minds that the Americans regard stable governments in a new country as something against their interest. He said that was the Russian policy. I told him that the Russians were now cooling off, certainly in this respect.

📖 A lady called Mrs Kulsoom Sehwani from Bombay came to see me. She is a Muslim, a social worker, and belongs to a society in India whose aim is to bring about friendship between India and Pakistan.

Kulsoom told me how she tried very hard with Nehru to see reason. He kept on expressing his anxiety to settle with Pakistan without meaning to do anything concrete. Then later he expressed his total inability to be able to do anything at all. She then described feelings in the valley of Kashmir. Their cry is to be let alone by India and Pakistan. I suppose they cannot express openly the desire to join Pakistan for fear of reprisals. She asked for a message for India. She was likely to meet Indira Gandhi. I told her to tell Indira that we have no intentions of starting a war with India though we shall react violently against any aggression by them. At the same time, we shall continue to seek a solution for Kashmir, which I believe is in the interest of India as in that of Pakistan. Why is India impoverishing herself and us by the senseless arms race? She mentioned something about confederation. I said it is the last thing she should think of.

📖 Saw an article in an American paper indicating India is quietly sounding countries in South East Asia around China for forming some sort of economic union. Ostensibly to prevent infiltration of Chinese economic influence, but in reality to get a grip over these countries. The Americans are watching this with keen interest, hoping that it will come about, developing into a military tie-up. Hindus, of course, are far too crafty for the Americans. Whilst gaining economic advantages, they will not fall into the military trap. Besides, I doubt very much if these countries will allow themselves to be exploited.

11 | FRIDAY

📖 Gave a reception to the RCD delegates. Later spoke to Sabri and [Ardeshir] Zahedi, the Turkish and the Iranian Foreign Ministers, and impressed the need for the heads of our planning commissions to meet and draw up a plan of joint development. This will enable us to make rapid progress. They expressed wholehearted agreement and promised to consult their masters and let us know.

I asked Sabri, the Turkish Foreign Minister, what was the future of Cyprus. Did you see any solution in sight? He said the matter has become very complicated. The British had made an offer on the bases in Cyprus to Turkey but that does not provide a solution. When asked what was the strength of the Turkish garrison on the island, he said 800 on paper but 14,000 in reality. So the Turks have the means to deal with any awkward situation which may arise. However, he was very bitter that earlier, if Ismat Inonu had disregarded the American warning and acted militarily he would have got away with it like the Israelis did in June 1967. When saying this he probably ignores the fact that the Turkish dependence on America is much greater than that of Israel and the Americans would not have hesitated to cut all aid off from them.

12 | SATURDAY

News came in from Cairo that the Egyptians are contacting the Americans through the Turkish ambassador and without the knowledge of the Soviets and other Arab countries that they have two options, one, go completely neutral or go to the Iron Curtain. They are obviously trying to seek American assistance against Israel. This has caused some concern in the Russian camp.

There is information to the effect that my gesture in the first of month broadcast that we wish to live in peace with India has had the opposite effect in the Congress Parliamentary Party. They had impressed on the government not to be taken in by this and prepare to meet joint Pakistan–China threat. If true, I cannot think of a more perverse view than this. How can such people do anything useful? They have no sense of statesmanship.

When thinking of problems of East Pakistan one cannot help feeling that their urge to isolate themselves from West Pakistan and revert to Hindu language and culture is close to the fact that they have no culture and language of their own nor have they been able to assimilate the culture of the Muslims of the subcontinent by turning their back on Urdu. Further, by doing so, they have forced two state languages on Pakistan. This has been a great tragedy for them and for the rest of Pakistan. They especially lack literature on the philosophy of Islam, so, I have been told, people have to translate into Bengali relevant portions and extracts from Iqbal's writings and distribute them on a large scale. But such a venture has no chance of success unless the Bengalis themselves have the urge to promote it.

13 | SUNDAY

Dr Salam,[72] my scientific advisor, came to see me. He pleaded that now we were setting up a nuclear power plant, we must also invest in a plutonium separation plant. It will help us to produce our own nuclear fuel and also give us a nuclear option. Secondly, he brought a proposal from Dr Revelle[73] of USA on how India and Pakistan could benefit from planned utilization of the waters of the eastern rivers and then, if we are agreeable, he could contact India too and then come out here to discuss details. I personally see no harm in this. In fact, a lot of good could follow like in the case of the Indus basin water settlement, but the trouble is that people begin to read all sorts of sinister motives into a move like this. My own belief is that, when dealing with India, we should keep economics separate from politics. However, I have arranged for him to meet M.M. Ahmed, Ishaq, Fida Hassan[74] and Jaffery[75] and discuss these things with them and then come to me.

Dr Salam said something which is profound and true. There are no moral values left in international relationships and the law of the jungle prevails. Look at what is happening in Vietnam, the Middle East and other places. Any nation that is not capable of looking after itself has no future. So we must be prepared to meet all eventualities. I assured him that I am doing my best to see that the country is well prepared to meet such a situation. An idea which the Finance Minister Uqaili put forward and struck me as being very sound, that we buy large amount of earth moving machinery and utilize it for levelling millions of acres of eroded, but fertile, land on the Potohar plateau and around. But to be effective it should be compulsory and not left to the option of individual owners.

The cost of such an operation could be recovered gradually as part of the land revenue. In fact I had thought of a similar idea when I was C-in-C. My scheme was that if we could have some sort of peace with India we could then turn a couple of army divisions into bulldozer formations and get to work as Minister Uqaili has suggested. Unfortunately, that peace has not come so far. However, it is not too late even now. If these lands could be levelled to retain moisture, we could bring unprecedented prosperity to these people.

📖 A South Vietnamese diplomat in Manila, Philippines, is reported to have said that they face two enemies, the Vietcong and the Americans. Both are killing them mercilessly. The Americans for instance, carpet bomb dozens of square miles of area suspected of containing Vietcong, killing hundreds of people including women and children. Their fate is death and it is immaterial who kills them.

📖 Someone asked me whether my book was the sum total of my experiences. I said no. I could write a lot more, especially on personalities. I think I am one of those lucky people who have met a large proportion of people in the world that are worth knowing. I have admired good qualities wherever found but I have also recognized weaknesses wherever they existed. I have never been enamoured of anyone's personality. This could be called cynicism but in fact it is realism. Human beings are never made perfect.

📖 Dr Salam came to report the result of meetings with different people on Revelle's proposal and the demand for installing a plutonium plant. He was rather disappointed as some people saw sinister motives in Revelles' proposal. As regards the plutonium plant, there was also considerable scepticism. With some emotion, he burst out and said 'I wish to God these wretched people had your vision. They are far too narrow in their outlook.' I told him not to get disheartened and to continue to press his points. I shall assist wherever possible.

14 | MONDAY

📖 This is an auspicious day. Today is the 20th anniversary of Pakistan.

15 | TUESDAY

📖 Held a meeting of the defence committee of the cabinet to review the military situation around us. The director of intelligence gave a review of the Indian and Afghan military build up. These are the two countries that have hostile intentions against us. The foreign secretary gave a political appreciation and the finance secretary indicated what resources could be made available for defence preparations.

The Indian military build up is fantastic. They are increasing their armed forces at a furious rate and filling up their arsenals. The Afghans, too, have built up considerable military strength with sophisticated weapon supplied from Russia. The consensus was that although India had no immediate intention of attacking Pakistan in spite of occasional war hysteria, they will be in a position to do so in a couple of years. Then they will be in a position to attack East and West Pakistan simultaneously.

The Afghans will wait and see how the war goes for us. If we suffer losses in West Pakistan they will not hesitate to stab us in the back and try to gain territory up to the Indus. The excuse will be that they are only trying to save their Pakhtoon brethren from Hindu domination.

Our own preparations to deter aggression have made some progress but there are considerable gaps. Our preparedness suffers for two reasons. Our limited foreign exchange resources and inability to buy military hardware from the traditional American sources. They are even stopping us from buying equipment of their origin from Germany and other countries. However, there are signs of some relaxation.

As far as resources are concerned, the difficulty arises in provision of foreign exchange. The terms of trade are moving against us. We have to pay for large food imports. The debt servicing charges are mounting and the closure of the Suez Canal has resulted in enhanced freight charges. The military requirements are also enormous. It is obvious that the country cannot bear these burdens simultaneously. So we shall have to cut down somewhere. It is quite possible that our development pace may have to be curtailed. So a committee of experts has been set up to give us the answer. What the service chiefs want to know is the maximum that can be made available over a period of five years or so, so that they can plan ahead and procure things on a planned basis. Meanwhile, we shall see what the Russians propose doing. I am hoping they will play the game and carry out their promise given us previously. The Chinese source is valuable but only for small quantities. They have their limitations and difficulties.

---

16 | WEDNESDAY

The new American ambassador[76] presented his credentials, brought good wishes from President Johnson and a couple of his books and an assurance that he will work for betterment of relations between the two countries. He seems an intelligent and open man, presentable.

The Nawab of Kalabagh came to stay for a night. He had a long chat with me saying people say that I am angry with him for this, that and other reasons. I assured him that it was sad that he had betrayed me but all that was over. I bear no grudge towards him. He need have no fear on that account. I told him that I had no option but to ask him to leave service as it had become a common talk among people that the president and the governor do not see eye to eye with each other. In consequence, the administration of the province was suffering and there was a source of suspicion, insecurity and dismay among people. Some of my friends in Lahore and elsewhere are apprehensive that I may be influenced by Kalabagh against their interest. They do not realize that I know something about human beings. I have been dealing with them for the past 42 years.

Very sombre news has come in from our ambassador in Peking. The internal situation in China is getting serious. There is conflict in several provinces especially Canton and Shanghai. Ships are piling up in several ports and railway stations, communications and health services are disrupted. There is a state of tension in Peking and prices are rising. This does not auger well for China when she is faced with so many internal and external problems.

18 | FRIDAY

📖 The head of mission of Morrison Knudson, an American construction firm, Jack Bonny, came to see me. They have some contracts in Indus replacement works and he is now after getting the contract for Tarbela. They also have large construction contracts in Vietnam. He told me they were all labour intensive. They hardly bring any profits. In fact, they will be very happy to pull out of Vietnam as soon as possible. Asked him how he saw the future in Vietnam. He told me that in his view it was a mistake to have got committed there but having done so they have no option but to see it through. He felt that invasion of North Vietnam was inescapable. I asked him how President Johnson was. He told me that he is faced with tremendous problems, mostly inherited, and the most distressing portion was internal strife.

📖 General Mohammadi, the head of defence production came to see me and explained what is happening in his sphere. It seems that things are moving on satisfactorily. The production base is expanding. I think Mohammadi is a good choice. He is quiet but an efficient and persistent worker. He has been promoted to major general recently. His cross swords were wrong way around. So I told him how to wear them correctly. He said smilingly that I keep a watch on everything they do. I told him that is what I am here for.

19 | SATURDAY

📖 Travelled by road to Lahore and stopped in Kharian Cantonment en route. This cantonment is coming on very well indeed. The place is getting covered with trees which are planted in a careful and scientific manner. The corps commander General Hamid explained his plan of operation and defence preparedness, which consists of water obstacles on the major lines of advance from the Indian territory, concrete defences and anti-tank and anti-personnel mines placement. As regards concrete defences they have prepared PSC revetments. There are only two that are portable and can be combined in any commutation and permutation. The plan is to prepare and dump them in forward areas for easy use. They require two days notice to prepare concrete defences and seven days notice to lay the antitank minefields.

I saw the crops en route, especially the basmati rice, in the areas which had got out of use through waterlogging and salinity and were now reclaimed. The rice crop was first class. I was told that 350,000 acres of superior rice has been sown this year and some 1,100,000 acres of coarse rice. If all goes well we should get a bumper crop.

📖 Held a long meeting with the governor and discussed several administrative problems. Whilst in the midst news came that the Indian Air Force was going to carry out a large scale air exercise close to the borders from 21st to 24th August. Large quantities of camouflage nets and sandbags were going to be carried into the forward areas. I eventually got in touch with General Yahya and told him to alert his people as well as our air force in case the Indians meant any mischief. His view was that it may just be a training exercise, but mentioned they shall standby in case it turned out to be something sinister.

I have to fly to Dacca on the 21st. Most of our people want me to cancel my trip as I might be wanted here. I told them that I shall take a decision tomorrow.

20 | SUNDAY

Saw Hakeem Ahmad Shuja,[77] who reviewed my book. He is a revered old man, very talented and an historian and writer of distinction. He asked my permission to use portions of my book for writing short articles and for two editions for the common man and young people. He spoke very highly of the book and said that by writing it I had rendered a great service to the nation. He recommended that the book should be abridged for the younger generation and it should also be made a textbook for the degree and the postgraduate classes.

Talking about democracy, and especially parliamentary democracy, he said it was totally unsuited to our genius. He based this opinion on a long experience of it as the secretary to the speaker of the Punjab Assembly since 1921. He said the system was based on corruption. The member bribed the voters, the minister gave double bribe, once to the voters and then to the members of assemblies and the chief minister or the prime minister bribed thrice. How can you expect any good from a system like this? He said Iqbal, who once had some praise for the system, condemned it outright after he got practical experience of its working.

Addressed a gathering of lawyers. It is the first time I have seen a perceptible change in their outlook. I think they have been hypnotized by my book.

The two divisional commanders in Lahore came over to explain the operational plan. I was very pleased to see that they have buttoned up things to the minutest detail and the troops are constantly exercising on the job.

Attended a luncheon party at Qazi Fazlullah's place. He is very anxious to be promoted as a senior minister. I told him that this will only cause widespread furore without doing any good. But he does not see the point and keeps on returning to his demand.

Addressed the office bearers of city leagues. They have been recently elected and appear to be a fine lot. By and large Muslim League elections are going on very well indeed. I have every hope of their emerging a strong party. Discussed problems of the Muslim League paper, *Kohistan*.

21 | MONDAY

Read a report by the military intelligence on the situation in East Pakistan. The assessment is 95 per cent of the people living in the villages are devoted to Islam and are pro-Pakistan. Amongst the urban population, especially the student community, the teachers and the intelligentsia, majority are either NAP or Awami League, one is left or communist and therefore have no affinity with Pakistan. The Awami League is believer in Bengali nationalism. They would like to have nothing to do with West Pakistan, and in fact, would like to separate their province so that they can run the place at will. The paper made several remedial suggestions. Some are being tried or will be tried but it is doubtful if it is going to change the Bengali outlook. Not unless they themselves lend a hand. At present there is no indication that they would do so.

📖 Saw some of the leading Muslim Leaguers from Lahore, they brought up certain points of local importance which I discussed with them.

📖 Flew to Dacca on a few days tour. Large number of people had gathered at the airport to welcome me. I gave a short address, extorting people to grow more food and attain self-sufficiency as fast as possible. We cannot afford to continue to bear a heavy food bill.

📖 The military intelligence has submitted a paper on the situation in East Pakistan. It is well written and offers constructive suggestions. It was discussed with Monem Khan, Sobur[78] and Shahabuddin. I told them to form a committee to consider the problems in all its aspects and than come up with concrete suggestions.

22 | TUESDAY

📖 Went to Narayanganj by road and then to Chandpur by a river craft to open a marine terminal. Was given a royal welcome at that place. Hundreds of thousands of people including women and children came to greet me. There was great happiness and joy everywhere which gladdened my heart. We got back to Dacca in the evening.

📖 The American press is apt to criticize any democratic system in new countries which is not the exact prototype of their own. By so doing they think they are promoting the cause of democracy. On the contrary, the result is just the opposite. They forget that the conditions, circumstances and prevailing economic and other conditions have a lot to do with the system that will work in a country. They forget also that after their civil war, the north, though familiar with the ballot box, had to suspend the writ of habeas corpus, exiled opponents of the administration, had military in certain areas and closed down a number of papers. The South, torn between the needs of war and the doctrine of states rights, had even greater difficulties.

23 | WEDNESDAY

📖 Addressed a cross section of intellectuals on a subject which tends to be emotional and delicate with the East Pakistanis. I told them that one sometimes hears that Bengalis both Hindus and Muslims have a common culture. How is this miracle achieved, because elsewhere on the subcontinent even after one thousand years of proximity the two communities lived strictly apart with very little in common. This was so because our philosophy of life was totally opposed and so our culture too had to be different. Our contact is perfunctory and shallow. I told them that through emotional upsurge the East Pakistani had cut himself off from Urdu, the vehicle in which Muslim thought and philosophy is expressed. In consequence, he was now totally at sea, drifting. This will prove very dangerous for their future. If not careful they will have no choice but to drift back to Hinduism and be engulfed by it. So it was incumbent on them to produce literature in Bengali on the philosophy and culture of Islam. Failing which they should translate relevant literature from Urdu. Iqbal's poetry is a rich source. I was glad that they saw the point and felt the need for accepting my advice. However, their problem is formidable. They are under heavy cultural dominance of the Hindus. The real escape lies in adopting Urdu as the vehicle of thought but I doubt very much if they would do so. Without meaning any unkindness, the fact of the matter is that a large majority of the Muslims in East Pakistan have an animist base which is a thick layer of Hinduism and top crust of Islam which is pierced by Hinduism from time to time.

24 | THURSDAY

☐ Flew to Chittagong and did the opening ceremony of the steel mill which is the first of its kind in Pakistan. So it was a red letter day in the industrial history of Pakistan. The ceremony over, I went to see a *thana* agricultural demonstration estate. I was struck by the enthusiasm of all concerned. The local MPA told me that every inch of cultivable land was brought under plough and they were growing three crops a year. They were conversant with modern seeds, use of fertilizer and plant protection. The people looked well fed, clean and had smiles on their faces which gladdened my heart. We then went to circuit house for lunch. Wherever I went people greeted me in the hundreds of thousands. The roadsides were jam-packed by people, including women and children, and they stood there for hours in torrential rains. I was deeply moved by this demonstration of affection.

☐ Addressed an assorted gathering in the afternoon and flew back to Dacca.

☐ The GOC 14 Division briefed me on their defence of East Pakistan. The general spoke about sudden eruption of war with India. I told them that sudden eruptions of war is an unknown phenomena, just as a pot does not boil over suddenly—there is always an incubation period.

25 | FRIDAY

☐ Did the opening ceremony of an agricultural scheme close to Dacca. The scheme is novel in its concept. It pumps water out of an area which goes under ten feet of water in summer, and in the winter when the land goes dry, pumps water back into a canal which irrigates it, thus enabling some ten thousand acres to have three assured crops a year. I saw some of the people of the area. They cannot believe their eyes on the blessing that has come to them.

☐ I met an old man called Sufi Zulfikar Haider.[79] He is a scholar of repute, a poet and a writer, deeply religious and practical. I read some of his poems with great gusto. Though 76 years of age he feels as young as a man of 22. I arranged with the governor and Radio Pakistan to make use of his talent.

☐ Flew to Rawalpindi with a half hour stop in Lahore where I met the governor and his cabinet ministers. I told the governor to have a properly prepared scheme for the utilization of lands in the riverbeds that will go dry as a result of construction of dams upstream. Similar lands go dry as do the riverbeds through recession of water in winter. I believe that millions of acres of fertile land could thus be reclaimed and made to yield considerable wealth.

While the foreign press comments about present day Arab politics, everyone once again shouts his belief in Arab unity and practices the opposite, and yet I feel there is a latent urge at least amongst the masses to gain unity.

26 | SATURDAY

Finished reading a book on the recent Middle East conflict written by an American pressman who happened to be in Israel during the war. He is absolutely prejudiced against the Arabs, like most westerners and especially the Americans, but the fact remains that the Arab's misfortunes are their own making. They lack unity, morale, military preparedness and the ability to put their enormous amount of modern equipment to effective use. Their officers lack toughness of mind and body and provide poor leadership to their troops. According to this book, though the Arab army suffered heavy casualties there were very few officers amongst them. Whereas the Israeli casualties, though relatively high, contained large proportion of officers as casualties. And that is how it should be in a good army. That is what happened with us in 1965 war. The officers were in the forefront of the battle.

28 | MONDAY

Addressed the conference of inspectors general of police, emphasized the following points:

1. Their conference should take place once a year so that the working of the police force is brought on the same grade in both the provinces.
2. All policemen from top to bottom should be familiarized with the social and economic situation of the society and its laws and the method of enforcement. Refresher courses should be obligatory for all ranks to bring them up-to-date.
3. All promotions should be dependent on efficiency examinations and tests.
4. As the structure of the society is changing, so are the types of crime and methods of dealing with them. To examine these problems and to keep up-to-date in methods, a research and development section should be set up in both the provinces. Their recommendations should be considered with an open mind and adopted when considered useful.
5. Cases, especially under preventive laws, should be prepared with much greater care and stand judicial scrutiny.
6. Consideration should be given to creation of a separate cadre of the intelligence services.
7. Police force is not getting the right type of young men for their officer corps. This is why I have suggested a new method of selection. This should be given a trial.
8. There is a lot of talk of corruption. We have to devise ways and means of combating it. However, the following actions seem necessary:
    a. An officer living beyond his means should be automatically questioned.
    b. If an officer has a bad reputation he should be questioned but so must his superior whose duty it is to watch these things.

c. There should be inspection item teams right down to district level.
d. No house building or acquisition of property without the permission of the superior officers.

📖 Came across some interesting statements and sayings in my readings:

a. One of the greatest benefits of free speech is that it gives the opportunist the false and misguided chance to talk so much that they talk themselves out of any position of leadership.
b. Certain people were oppressively and restlessly polite for English taste. There was none of the repose and inclusiveness which constitutes good breeding to the British mind. Bertrand Russell.
c. Extravagant admiration.
d. No good thinking can be developed without passion. Can't think hard from mere sense of duty.
e. Success is needed as a source of energy.
f. Human monster—a rational man.
g. Self-regulating society.
h. Moral pretensions.
i. Wise are those who hold their tongue.
j. Very busy people are those who find most time for everything somehow.
k. Only in thought, is man a god. In action and desire we are the slaves of circumstances.

29 | TUESDAY

📖 Attended a briefing at GHQ on the defence of Pakistan. C-in-C Air Force was also present. I was glad to see that GHQ had given considerable thought to their problems and produced sound plans. Everybody seems to be alert, down to formation and unit commanders, and have their noses down to the ground. My belief is that if India attacked Pakistan they would never be able to achieve what they failed to do last time. I emphasized the need for very close cooperation between the army and the air force in planning as well as in training.

📖 The cabinet secretary, who has attended conferences in Europe and America connected with government administration, came and reported results of his experiences. He said that there was general respect and regard for Pakistan for the manner in which political stability and development momentum was maintained. Pakistan was regarded as a model for the developing countries. The system of local governments, basic democracy system was beginning to be appreciated. This system is regarded as the most logical and profitable for the developing countries. My comment was that this may be true, but I doubt if the professional politicians, who are only interested in promotion of their self-interest, would allow the system to be adopted and given a chance to work. This system organizes a society into self-regulating small units and creates discipline and stability. This is the last thing an average politician wants. He revels in '*Chaudrahats*,' that saviour of lawlessness and free for all. He instinctively believes that something good may come out for him. His impression was that the intellectuals in USA were very distressed with the present policy of their government in Vietnam. Their feeling was that by pursuing this policy, America stands exposed in the eyes of the world, as a brutal and immoral power. This is the stigma which will take a long time to live down.

30 | WEDNESDAY

📖 The Chinese first and then the British have been busy lately in beating up each others' diplomatic staff. The trouble has arisen over the riots that have taken place in Hong Kong recently and the British decision to close down three Chinese communist papers and arrest their staff. The Chinese have retaliated by curtailing water and food supplies to Hong Kong. The tension is mounting and it looks like the Chinese are making for British surrender, as the Portuguese did in Macao.

The British made an appeal to us to help evacuation of their personnel, especially women and children. We did not see anything wrong with it so we told our ambassador to contact the Chinese authorities. We did and found them unsympathetic. They said that the British representative himself should have made the approach. Why are they trying to exploit China–Pakistan friendship? In fact, they are working to strain relations between us too. Also, British must know how to deal with the Chinese in changed circumstances. They must shed their erstwhile colonial arrogance. It is quite obvious that the Chinese are in no listening mood.

📖 The Chinese Chargè d'Affairs came to our foreign office and said that the map in my book shows Taiwan in different colours than mainland China. NEA is not included in China, and besides, the provinces of Tibet, Sinkiang and Mongolia are mentioned and not others. Our own people have also a cause to complain that Junagarh,[80] Manavadar,[81] etc., are not shown as a part of Pakistan. It looks like people think that this map is going to determine the future of their territories. It just shows how childish people can be. The fact is that this map is meant to show in a diagrammatical form the geopolitical location of Pakistan. It pretends to do no more. However, I am not going to waste my time in arguing with these people. So I have caused a message to be sent to the publishers that this map might as well be removed in future editions. They wanted its removal in any case for entry into India, as Kashmir was not shown as a part of that country.

The other objection that the Chinese raised was that there is one photograph in the book in which I am seen sitting next to Mao Tse-tung and Liu Shao-chi is also sitting close by. This, they think, will hurt the Chinese feelings. How I am responsible for that I don't know. However, I don't want to cause our Chinese friends any embarrassment so here too I have asked the publishers to either blank Liu Shao-chi, remove the picture or replace it with the one in which Mao Tse-tung, Chou En-lai and I are seen sitting together.

These and many other such incidences which I have not mentioned here would show the complexity of the life one leads. In fact, these are daily occurrences. The art lies in steering through them without losing perspective and getting irritated from time to time.

31 | THURSDAY

📖 A cabinet meeting was held today. The two governors were also invited to attend. I emphasized that whilst the Fida Hussain committee on prevention of corruption will submit its recommendations in due course there are certain actions we should take straightaway. Any government official living beyond his means should be identified and questioned. The corrupt officials should be questioned but also their superiors should be made to explain their conduct and if they have taken no action against them. All officials, including military-built houses or acquired properties should be called upon to explain where they obtained resources. The tentacles of provincial inspection teams should be extended down to divisions and districts.

The provincial governors were told to formulate plans and let me have a copy. Also they should add a heading in the monthly situation report showing what anti-corruption measures had been taken. These measures resolutely enforced should have a salutary effect.

📖 I am getting concerned about Mr Pirzada, our foreign minister. He has not proved much of a success. He is on the run in foreign countries most of the time and often purposelessly. Very suspicious by nature. Has hardly any communication with the staff. Chases small things most of the time and is frightened of taking a definite stand on any issue. There is also some suspicion that he is not above telling a lie. So I am in a fix as to what to do with him.

1 | FRIDAY

📖 M.M. Ahmed, deputy chairman, Planning Commission, came to see me. He discussed several things *inter alia* the rate of development in East Pakistan. He said that despite giving greater resources to East Pakistan, the disparity between the two provinces was increasing. And this has happened since they got greater autonomy. The trouble is that they waste money on buildings and prestigious things instead of spending it on agriculture and such projects which yield greater and quicker production and quicker relief to the common man. This is not the fault of the governor. In any case, he does not understand economics and developmental problems much. He is served by young Bengalis who are not reckoned for their sense of realism. However, the next time I go to East Pakistan I am going to tell them some whole truths. Then in the private sector they have created a situation that no one is prepared to risk his money in that province.

2 | SATURDAY

📖 An intelligence report came in to say that a number of low level clerks and peons in the air force from around Peshawar who are suspected to have Red Shirt[82] leanings, had been acting as agents for the Afghan and Indian intelligence and passing on information of a sensitive nature to them. The intelligence people made a plan and caught them red-handed. The leader amongst those traitors was at one time in the service of the Afghan Consul in Peshawar. He was made to go across to Jalalabad for a briefing by Abdul Ghaffar Khan and then by the Indian Consul General. These people were apparently paid by the Indians and information gathered was shared between them and the Afghans.

📖 I was reading an article on President Johnson in *Newsweek*. He is accused of being a liar, devious, untrustworthy and a political manipulator who tries to keep the centre of the political stage to himself. Now these allegations may be true or otherwise but the point is what good could such criticism of the head of the government of a mighty country be to it. He is, after all, a human being and a sensitive man. His reactions could be either positive and thereby becoming ineffective or defiance in going to the other extreme. Both attitudes are destructive for the country.

3 | SUNDAY

📖 Being a Sunday went to Murree and spent the day at government house. It was most relaxing sitting in the nice sun looking at the beautiful scenery, lovely flowers and green lawns. Read Fuller's[83] book on the genius of Alexander the Great. Fuller, of course, is a superb military thinker and an historian of renown. He explains graphically Alexander's background but specially his character. He obviously was a great genius and with great personal qualities. Apart from having a sharp intellect, imagination, calculating mind and marked personal courage, he was extremely good looking with attractive build, capacity for enduring hardships and possessing a kind and generous heart. He was one of those rare human beings who was completely devoted to his mission in life in total disregard of personal human desires. The maturity of mind and character he showed at the age of 20 is something which is unnatural and unbelievable. Such gifts of God are rare in life. But one thing is certain, that it is only such gifted and rare people who do great things.

📖 The news of the results of the Arab summit conference, if true, is promising. King Faisal and President Nasser have agreed to lay off Yemen and leave that troublesome country alone. The Egyptian forces are to be withdrawn and that is how it should be. Actually, they are needed much more elsewhere. Faisal, on his part, has agreed to give no more support to the royalists. It remains to be seen what Yemenis would do with each other. They are quite capable of tearing each other to pieces unless the other friendly Arab countries provide troops to maintain internal security, which is no mean task in an extremely difficult terrain inhabited by unruly and armed tribesmen. The decision by the rich Arab countries to give substantial economic aid to the UAR and Jordan, who have suffered most, is also welcome news. One only hopes that they will keep their promise. The decision to start supply of oil to Western countries is a clear victory for good sense which the Arabs need so badly. Without this they would have been destroying their economies and their ability to help other Arab countries which need this assistance.

5 | TUESDAY

📖 Mr Pirzada returned from his foreign tour and reported the results. One very curious thing he stated was that the Russians had started issue of military equipment to the UAR and Syria with great speed but soon tapered off. The conclusion is obvious. The Americans must have prevailed on them not to start an arms race in the Middle East as that will aggravate relations between the super powers. The Russians also have a suspicion that the Egyptians are negotiating with the Americans behind their back. This is not true. The King of Jordan has complained bitterly against the attitude and conduct of King Faisal and the Kuwaitis. They have shown no real sympathy for the Jordanian plight, and in fact, the Saudis asked for the payment of debt right in the middle of the war.

📖 Visited Pakistan Ordnance Factory, Wah. I was delighted with the progress they have made since my last visit. They are now manufacturing a larger variety of weapons and ammunition and have plans to expand this further.

📖 I told Mr Pirzada what I expect of him as foreign minister. He is a sensitive man and will probably take it to heart, but it was my duty to point out his failings in time so that he can correct himself. I don't want him to go to the other point of no return as Bhutto did. The trouble with these people is that they begin to run personal foreign policy. This cannot be allowed. What we have to do is to run the foreign policy of Pakistan.

6 | WEDNESDAY

📖 I have caused a message to be sent to Nasser explaining what I told the American ambassador about the Middle East and the suggestion I have made to Johnson. I have asked to see the Russian ambassador for the same purpose and also put them on their guard in respect of the propaganda that the Indians are mounting against my visit to the Soviet Union. The Indians are telling all sorts of lies to put the Russians off.

   📖 Today is a very solemn day, the day India opened a full scale war against us two years ago and the way our people reacted and the armed forces stood like a rock against tremendous odds and beat the Indians to a halt in a matter of hours. There are thanksgiving services and celebrations all over country on the exploits of our heroes.

   📖 I was very happy to receive from Dr I.H. Qureshi the book entitled *A Short History of Pakistan*. It is four volumes relating to the pre-Muslim period, Muslim rule under the sultans, the Mughal Empire, and the alien rule and the rise of Muslim nationalism. It has been written under my instructions by several historians under the supervision of Dr Qureshi. I have no doubt that this book will fill the void which existed in the minds of our people and especially the younger generation and will give them proper perspective of the past and correct perspective for the future. The reason why Pakistan should be clear to all.

7 | THURSDAY

   📖 Khawaja Shahabuddin came to see me after an extensive tour of East Pakistan. He said whilst pro-Hindu and anti-West Pakistan feelings were on the increase amongst the educated classes, the masses were still undoubtedly clear on the concept of a united Pakistan. We should, therefore, do all we can to maintain their loyalty. We discussed these problems at length and considered what concrete actions could be taken to guide East Pakistanis on the right path and prevent them from going back to the serfdom of Hinduism. In the end, I told the Khawaja that let us try all these things, but as I see it these are for all parliamentarians. How to save people who do not want to be saved. I asked him how he saw the future. With tears in his eyes he said the future was bleak. In fact, he feels so depressed at times that he wants to sell his property in Dacca and come over to West Pakistan before the worst happens. There are two things that concern my mind continuously (1) Hindu India's intentions against Pakistan are suicidal, and (2) frustrating tendencies of behaviour of East Pakistanis. God has been very unkind to us in giving the sort of neighbours and compatriots we have. We could not think of a worst combination. Hindus and Bengalis. I told the Khawaja not to lose heart. If worse comes to the worst, we shall not hesitate to fight a relentless battle against the disruptionists in East Pakistan. Rivers of blood will flow if need be, unhappily. We will arise to save our crores Muslims from Hindu slavery.

8 | FRIDAY

   📖 Dr Berg, the head of a German TV organization, came to interview me on the internal and external problems of Pakistan. He has been based in Delhi for a long time and was reputed to have Indian leanings, but lately he has been disenchanted. After two interviews I invited him to a cup of coffee and asked him how he saw the future in India. He said the prospects were sombre, there is utter lack of leadership, political confusion and bickering is rampant. The people have lost hope and the younger generation has turned cynical, believing in nothing. The economic situation is worse still. India's enmity towards her two neighbours, Pakistan and China, is costing it dearly. He foresees years and years of instability. The provinces are getting stronger and at the cost of the centre. It did not mean that India will break up but the power of the centre will become marginal. The real trouble is that India has no ideology (curious), this is exactly what I told Nehru when he came to Pakistan in 1962, to act as a force for integration and cohesion. Gandhi's philosophy of non-violence was supplemented by Nehru's secularism and nonalignment. Both have met their doom because how can Hindu society be turned secular and non-belligerent. It is, in any case, in a shambles because of the changed world circumstances. It is now an empty slogan with no relevance to realities. He said Nehru is largely to blame for India's misfortune. He ruled India as a private property, history will never forgive him for not coming to terms with Pakistan and even China. Any chance of revival for India is out of the question. Similarly, he said they have not got an Ayub Khan and besides centrifugal forces are too strong.

A dispatch has been received from our high commissioner giving an assessment of the political situation in India. The rightists and Hindu bigots, all parties, are getting together. Chances are that they will throw out Indira and put a man like Chavan in her place. The anti-Pakistan and anti-Muslim feelings will grow. They will seek to undo Pakistan and settle Kashmir by military means. So security problems will assume much more serious dimensions as turmoil and instability increases in India and bigoted and narrow-minded Hindus assume power.

9 | SATURDAY

Performed the opening ceremony of Inter Continental Hotel in Rawalpindi. It is the fourth in the chain of such hotels being constructed in Pakistan. These four alone will cater for 40,000 more tourists. In addition, there are plans to build a dozen of so suitable hotels in different places and also convert some of the rest houses in the country for tourist use. All this should give a great fillip to tourism.

10 | SUNDAY

Motored to Saidu, Swat, for ten days' stay. A large number of people came to greet me en route.

I inquired from a man as how was the appointment of Ghafoor Khan Hoti as the central minister taken in the Frontier. He said the Pathan was a peculiar bird. If a Pathan was not appointed the whole area would have complained bitterly, but now that one has been appointed, they are sour with jealousy. Some say he would become my rival in the next elections. Some are so ungenerous as to say that he bribed his way up. Actually, Ghafoor Khan Hoti has made a good start. He is intelligent, shrewd, tidy and quick and is not afraid of taking responsibility and making decisions.

General Hamid,[84] with a small staff, was sent to Jordan on the request of the king. He has sent back a message that the king wants us to reorganize, retrain and if need be, command his army. We are calling Hamid back for consultations before the king's visit to Pakistan. My own feeling is that we should do all that is within our means, barring command of their units. With nationalist feelings on the rise, people do not like being commanded by others. In fact, such an arrangement does more harm than good.

📖 Saw an article in an American paper indicating that India is quickly sounding countries in South East Asia around China for forming some sort of economic union, ostensibly to prevent infiltration of Chinese economic influence, but in reality to get a grip over those countries. The Americans are watching this with keen interest, hoping that it will come about and developing into a military tie up. Hindus, of course, are far too crafty for the Americans. Once gaining economic advantage, they will not fall into a military trap. Besides, I doubt very much if these countries will anyhow allow themselves to be exploited.

13 | WEDNESDAY

📖 For the last couple of days, the radio broadcasts have been announcing breakout of border clashes between China and India in Sikkim of a serious nature in which artillery and mortar fire was used freely. Such incidents are inevitable on an undemarcated border extending over 2000 miles. Any overly enthusiastic platoon commander can precipitate them. However, the Indians will make a mountain out of this to jitter the western powers and even the Soviet Union to extract more aid.

📖 I have just finished reading the fourth volume of the history of Pakistan by Dr I.H. Qureshi and a few other historians. Apart from the fact that its style and language is so absorbing, anyone who reads it cannot help coming to the conclusion that without Pakistan we would have been the serfs of Hindus as the Indian Muslims are. I wish such a book had been written at the very inception of Pakistan so as to eliminate any loose and confused thinking minds of the people, especially in East Pakistan. It is often said that we separated from the Hindus for economic and this and that and the other reasons. The fact is we separated for our very survival. With such competing ideologies how could the Hindus and Muslims have lived as equal citizens of the same country after the British left? In fact, it was inevitable that one or the other should dominate in a common country and the dominated to become third rate citizens, which would have been us being a technical minority even though we were a 100 million or so at the time of partition.

There are people in the old Frontier Province and Sindh who still think that they would have been better off if they had their own provincial administration. Prejudices die hard but if they were to study the past history they would realize that all this area would have been one province if it was not for certain accidents of history. Napier[85] conquered Sindh six years before Punjab was annexed by the British. If the sequence were reversed, Sindh would have had to be amalgamated with the Punjab as it was too small and poor to be run as a separate province. Because of these actors, Sindh had to be amalgamated with the province of Bombay even though this was unnatural. Communication, religion and culture of people were against it. Frontier province was in any case part of the Punjab until 1901 when Curzon ordered its separation for better control of the tribal belt and Afghanistan, poor communications being the decisive factor. Punjab, in those days, was twice the size of the portion that fell to the share of Pakistan, extending well south of Delhi. So the creation of one unit in West Pakistan is fully justified on historical grounds apart from other mighty considerations. The trouble is that after winning freedom from the British and Hindus and attaining Pakistan as a conscious effort, people soon forgot the next step that had to be taken, unification, reconstruction and consolidation, and soon slipped into a parochial and selfish frame of mind. Local prejudices and linguistic differences began to be exploited, specially by the unscrupulous politicians to promote their selfish ends at the cost of the higher loyalty. Sensible and patriotic ideas must remain on continual watch to keep parochialism under check.

14 | THURSDAY

📖 Mr Farooqi, the chairman of the Capital Development Authority,[86] together with a couple of American representatives of Edgar Stone's firm, came to explain the plan of demarcation and furnishing the new presidential palace to be built in Islamabad. The material and colour schemes were skilfully explained on beautifully drawn sketches. I think they have given a lot of thought to the matter and produced an excellent scheme. The tapestry and the materials will be mainly Pakistani and the furniture will also be made in Pakistan. A newer idea was noted, facing the walls with hand woven cotton coarse cloth which is stated to last for 20 to 25 years. I was told it costs three rupees a yard in Pakistan whereas the cost in New York is 7 dollars. The object is to save yearly painting of the walls which is a messy affair, besides requiring considerable skill, which is not easily available.

📖 Read an article in the *Pakistan Times* written by Mr Suleri on the language question in East Pakistan. He wrote this after a visit to Dacca. He believes that the answer is to retain English as the link language for the present until Bengali and Urdu became well known in both the provinces. He advocates teaching of both the languages all over Pakistan. This is nothing but a concession to Bengali obstinacy and short-sightedness and is easier said than done. This will be an added burden on West Pakistan. A child has to learn his local language, smattering of Arabic and perhaps Persian, English and Urdu. The trouble is that the genesis of this mixed problem is not fully understood. The West Pakistanis have their local languages but had adopted Urdu as the link language, not because it is indigenous to any part, but because it was the lingua franca of the Muslims of this subcontinent and which contains the bulk of Muslim thought and philosophy. The Bengalis, on the other hand, decided to have nothing to do with it for short-sighted political reasons. The necessity of finding a link language with West Pakistan seems to be no concern of theirs. They regard this as an expression of their independence and service to the Bengali language. The result is that the onus of finding a solution has been put on West Pakistan, like in many other spheres. Since Urdu, which is the only national link language, is not acceptable to Bengalis, other solutions are sought in desperation which can be nothing but forced and therefore artificial. The most sensible answer is to continue with English as the link language until sense prevails. English is also necessary for international use.

15 | FRIDAY

A Pakistani correspondent employed in the *Asiatic Review* in Bangkok came to interview me. He asked me questions on the situation in South East Asia, our foreign policy and the internal problems. He comes from Sylhet and struck me as very level headed. He had read my book and referred to the portion where I defined parity as parity of opportunity and parity of endeavour. He remarked that much larger resources are being given to East Pakistan, the onus of putting them to good use lies on them.

We even talked to a representative gathering of Swati notables, BD chairmen, educationalists and students. Emphasized need for adoption of modern methods of agriculture and family planning. They were a fine looking lot, dignified, tall and handsome. They asked me some very sensitive questions.

16 | SATURDAY

📖 The Chinese Charge d'Affaires protested to our foreign secretary that our press is turning increasingly hostile to China by publishing articles against the Great Cultural Revolution. For instance, Brezhnev's anti-Chinese speech was reproduced and the *Pakistan Observer* criticized Mao Tse-tung and his Cultural Revolution, and soon the foreign secretary replied that our press and the public were overwhelmingly friendly towards China and in a country where there is a free press such odd lapses, often by a section of the papers; which are even in opposition to the government, should be disregarded did not satisfy him. His reply was that the conduct of the press in all countries was the responsibility of their government. The Chinese are in an extremely touchy and sensitive frame of mind but our interests will be served best by giving them least cause for complaint. It also shows how difficult it is to conduct a relationship with big powers and how careful the press has to be. Taking shelter behind freedom of the press in respect of foreign countries is no excuse. It will do Pakistan no good. We have to be similarly watchful of the Soviet and American susceptibilities.

19 | TUESDAY

📖 Addressed a meeting of notables and Muslim League workers at Ghafoor Khan Hoti's house, who acted as a host. A very elaborate tea party was arranged by Ghafoor Khan after the function. I exalted Ghafoor's work as a minister and told him to assume leadership of the people in the frontier areas and undercut Ghaffar Khan's Red Shirt influence.

📖 The [former] foreign minister of the UAR, Mahmoud Fawzi, came to see me and stayed on to dinner. We discussed several problems, particularly the situation in the Middle East. He did not think that prospects of immediate peace were good as the gap between Israel's demands and the UAR's minimum position was growing. However, UAR wanted a settlement desperately and were prepared to make some concessions. When asked how long could they hold out economically, he said that with loss of Suez and tourism revenues, they could not last more than six months, but with the subsidies now offered by the oil rich countries they could also go on indefinitely. He liked to believe that the promise of substantive aid was genuine and trustworthy. Mr Fawzi is one of the shrewdest men known, but he spoke with great candour and realism. The military defeat seems to have transformed the Egyptian outlook. They are now much more chastened. He then started quoting out of my book and expressed a sincere desire that small countries in Asia and Africa, meaning the Muslim countries, should quickly create a common platform otherwise they will be eaten up by the big powers one after the other. I was startled at this proposal as when I made this proposal in Cairo some years ago, Mr Fawzi was the first man to oppose it. I told him that if they were sincere then they must make up with the Shah of Iran quickly, as without his support and cooperation, no progress can be made. Similarly, King Faisal's wholehearted participation is necessary. He agreed and promised to do his best. He said for the time being we shall live on our wits. I told him not to worry as they have enough of it. My sincere hope and prayer is that this project succeeds. If it does then the age old dream of Muslim unification and renaissance would have come true.

20 | WEDNESDAY

📖 General Hamid, who had been to Jordan on an advisory mission, came to report. The picture given by him about the armed forces of Jordan is very gloomy. The senior officers from brigadier upwards are a poor lot. They have very little conception of the profession. Nor have they much interest in it. The men have no faith in them. The C-in-C knows this, but is helpless as his deputy, who is the king's uncle, would not allow any reforms to be carried out. His main interest lies in smuggling. Apparently, he is the king smuggler in the country. Some officers are also contaminated by him. General Hamid had drawn up a reorganization and deployment plan before the June war. No action has been taken on it.

The total number of casualties suffered by the Jordanian army was apparently 150 officers plus 190 other ranks killed and 1000 missing. The latter are mostly West Jordanians who probably disappeared to their villages.

The army fought badly. Two brigades were engaged in fighting. The rest, instead of going to their assistance or even holding their ground, ran, discarding their uniform and disappearing amongst the civilian population.

The king now expects our people to identify the causes or failure, suggest remedial measures, reorganize, train, and indeed, command the army. This is a tall order and not feasible in the circumstances prevailing there. Vested interests are going to be hurt and we shall not be liked. I am going to talk to the king tomorrow and try to see the need for doing all this with his own people. We would, of course, assist to the extent possible.

The King of Jordan arrived in the afternoon. He looked tired and pulled down. The poor man has gone through a very trying time. I feel sorry for him and his people for their misfortunes.

21 | THURSDAY

📖 In a private meeting told General Hamid to explain to the king his impression of what he saw and heard of the Jordanian forces. In a brief report he brought out the salient points, including the attitude of the Deputy C-in-C, and said that it would be difficult to carry out the task the king had given him in such an atmosphere. The king admitted the weakness of the senior officers and said they had got rapid promotions on departure of the British and that some of them were, in any casel, unsuitable. He was also aware of the attitude of the Deputy C-in-C. Despite that he was adamant that Hamid should carry out his charter and give him the benefit of his findings however unpleasant they may be. General Hamid was directed to continue with his work and produced two reports, one for the king and the other for the consumption of the government and the staff.

In the general meeting, the king explained how they foresaw the Israeli attack was coming and had told President Nasser. Meanwhile, he was very apprehensive of Syrian intentions. There were indications that they were even preparing to attack Jordan. With Nasser he had no contact; in fact he was dealing against him, until he met him a few days before the war. So there was no understanding or coordination between the countries.

Egypt was attacked on the morning of 6th June. President Nasser sent the king a report that they were doing well, that they had downed over 300 Israeli aircrafts (all contrary to the truth) and it was an opportune moment for Jordan to start hostilities against the enemy. It soon transpired that the

Egyptian aircraft had been knocked out and the ground troops were on the run. Any hope of getting assistance from Egypt had evaporated. It was under these circumstances that his troops had to fight, and he admitted that they did not do too well. In fact, their senior officers failed them. He thanked Pakistan for all their assistance and then went on to explain what transpired at the summit meeting in Khartoum. Nasser was surprisingly realistic and reasonable. He thought the decision taken was good.

The king was extremely worried about the future. The Israelis had found a Muslim to form a provisional government west of Jordan and they were attempting to destroy an oil refinery near Suez and also occupy Port Fuad in the north to humiliate Nasser. In fact, they were after his ouster. The big powers were showing no great concern. I told him that they had to be realistic and face facts. Nothing would be gained without winning the support of the USA and the Soviets. To that, the answer was to accept the joint resolution which the two powers agreed to put before the General Assembly and which the Arabs rejected.

He agreed that that was the most suitable answer. But I told him to check it up with President Nasser first before I take it up with the Americans and the Russians. He promised to do so. I have received a signal from Washington that the Americans are interested in my proposal of seeking a solution by phases, but the snag is that they do not accept the partners of Israel on the 4th of June as something they had agreed to. And about the old Jerusalem 1948 UN Resolution […] had only accepted internationalisation. These two problems are going to present a big hurdle in finding a solution.

My advice to the king was that, whilst facing realities and exercising moderation, they should be firm with the extremist Arabs and tell them where to get off.

22 | FRIDAY

📖 Took the king to the Wah Ordinance Factory. He saw some of the shops and was deeply impressed with what was going on. The king and his entourage departed.

23 | SATURDAY

📖 The American ambassador came and delivered two messages. One, on my request to President Johnson to assist in the problems of erosion and reclamation of eroded lands, and the other, on his government's reaction to my proposal for a solution to the Middle East problem. On the Middle East, whilst appreciating my effort, repeated his government's misgivings and demands. However, he assured me that they will continue to give my proposal serious consideration and try to see if they could carry the Soviets with them. I then asked him what if the Arabs (Jordan and UAR) [although Syria seceded from the United Arab Republic in 1961, Egypt continued to use that name officially until the name was changed to the Arab Republic of Egypt] were prepared to accept the abortive joint resolution by US and USSR. Would they be prepared to revive it? He felt very relieved and said he would communicate with his government immediately. I told him that I have been working on the Arabs and will also sound out the Soviets. He thanked me for this and requested if they could be kept informed of the developments. I can see the reason for American enthusiasm. If they can be doing something in conjunction with the Soviets, their political morale gets a tremendous boost which they are looking for.

25 | MONDAY

📖 After usual ceremonies were over, travelled with Kosygin and Podgorny in the same car to the Kremlin and came to the same set of rooms as I was placed in last time. The Kremlin, of course, has been renovated a good deal since. En route, both these gentlemen spoke pleasantly and even affectionately. Podgorny, of course, is a warm-hearted man. Personally I know Kosygin better and I can talk to him more freely. But he conceals a hard interior under a pleasant exterior. Never for a moment does he take leave of his head.

Soon after arrival, talks commenced with Mr Kosygin and Podgorny. Kosygin welcomed us and asked me to speak. I naturally spoke about our burning problem: Relationship with India. I brought them up to date on the events after Tashkent and explained how India had shown no desire to settle the basic problem of Kashmir and reduction of armaments. Meanwhile, they were piling up arms furiously; first from western sources and now from the Soviet Union. They were also whipping up war hysteria against Pakistan. In fact, they were going about even mentioning a date on which Pakistan was to launch an attack, when there was absolutely no basis for this. Why do they do such things, God only knows.

Politically, India was moving fast in the direction of pre-historic Hinduism and becoming more and more bigoted and intolerant. With the military power now existing in India, such people were capable of embarking on any expansionist venture in which case, are not the Soviet interests going to be jeopardized in our Subcontinent? Therefore, does it not behove the Soviets to curtail arms delivery to India, restrain them and also help Pakistan to be able to defend itself. All we want is the right of self defence. We have no intention of entering into an arms race with India, nor can we afford it. In return, we are prepared to give any guarantee that we shall use the arms only for the purpose of self defence.

Mr Kosygin appreciated my assessment, and said that in all fairness, he can't help agreeing with it. However, India, too, had the threat of China and this arms build up is necessary for her. I told him that the weapons they have given to India can't be used in the Himalayas, and in fact, two-thirds of the Indian army is ear marked for use against Pakistan. We have conclusive proof of it and so on. In the end he said that we shall discuss these matters further tomorrow on the hunting ground where Mr Brezhnev will also be present. For the president, all he can say is that they understand our case and would like to help in a manner that does not lead to escalation and confrontation with India. About China, they were not sure who was in control. To them, it looked as if Mao Tse-tung was the master. They had decided to give him all possible help to Vietnam-anything they wanted. The bottleneck was communications through China.

This time the Russians were more openly bitter about China. They said they did not mind being called enemies but why tell lies about them.

26 | TUESDAY

📖 Travelled with Mr Kosygin to the hunting ground some 100 miles from Moscow on the Leningrad Road. He talked all the way about their achievements, pointing out buildings and townships designed to do specific purposes. He said that the aim should be to produce more and more technicians, scientists and mathematicians. Production of lawyers, historians etc. could well wait. He also pointed out the sites of major battles with the Germans in that sector. They had apparently got to within 16 miles of Moscow on this road. The Russians fought desperately to drive them back.

I asked him about what transpired on his meeting at Glassboro with President Johnson. He described how the meeting was arranged: When invited to meet the President, he refused to go to the White House or Washington or anywhere near it. So long as the Vietnam war was on, he could not do it. Then a military cantonment and one or two other places were suggested. He refused those too, and New York. Eventually, Glassboro was suggested and accepted. The topics discussed were mainly four.

The talk then reverted to Indo-Pak relations. I told him that when I said that the writers may have an upper hand in India, what I meant was that only a bigoted and narrow-minded type of Hindu had a chance of ruling India. Such people have only to be lived with to be believed. How insufferable they were. He said, who had better chance, Desai or Chavan. I said latter. I said that things were going to be difficult in India. On arms aid to us, I told him that I had great hopes in him. He said that he had supported our case in their meetings.

We were taken to a wooded hunting lodge. All sorts of animals like the great elk, pigs etc. are bound here and are properly protected. Mr Podgorny and Mr Brezhnev joined us a little late. They were all full of '*gup*' and warmth. Seemed to go out of their way to be nice. Brezhnev kept on embracing me from time to time.

On Kashmir, Mr Kosygin said, let us be realistic: Carving out new frontiers is an impossible job. Look at the trouble we are experiencing in Europe on this account: I told him that our case was different. However, we were not laying down the settlement of Kashmir as a pre-condition for settling of other outstanding problems with India. He was relieved to hear that.

27 | WEDNESDAY

📖 Foregathered for the conference at 10 a.m. All these Soviet leaders were present. Mr Kosygin spoke; the gist of it was that they sought real friendship with Pakistan. They proposed to enlarge economic, cultural and educational assistance to Pakistan and have an agreement extending up to 1975. The experts can work out the details as regards arms supply; they had decided to give arms and they are available for delivery, but there is a delicate point of India's susceptibility involved. They need time to pacify India. I told them that they were virtually giving a power of veto to India. India will never agree. She wants to see Pakistan defenceless. He said no, all they want to do is to tell them nicely that this is necessary. I spoke strongly against it, but they kept on going back to their plea. I then said that why not lay down a time limit. Mr Brezhnev said, six months. I said, this is far too much, we have already waited for two years, a fortnight or a month should be more than enough. Then they said we shall discuss this in the evening. We then departed for Moscow. I accompanied Mr Kosygin.

On the way Mr Kosygin said they had to be careful with India. They are waging a grim struggle against China and the Americans are trying hard to get the Indians in their ambit. I told him that they are already in the American ambit. If they were anxious to control India, they should strengthen Pakistan.

On enquiry as to what were the chances of rapprochement with China, he said NONE. The reason was that there was a basic difference in their thinking. The Chinese, or more correctly Mao Tse-tung, advocated war as a solution to world problems. They were against it as that would mean the end of the world. They and the Americans had the power to destroy the world.

Met again at a football game in the evening. The ground was floodlit. The audience must have been over a hundred thousand. Both teams played with great spirit and skill. During the course of the game, Kosygin told me that Indira Gandhi was arriving.

I asked Kosygin about the story of use of hot line to President Johnson. As soon as the war stared in the Middle East, the Russians knew that the Arabs were in for trouble. This was soon confirmed by events. So he rang up President Johnson, apologising for waking him up in the middle of the night and exerting pressure for cessation of hostilities. If it was not for us and other actions that the Russians took, the Israelis would have captured Cairo and Damascus.

28 | THURSDAY

📖 Gave a return banquet. Mr Podgorny, Kosygin and several Russian dignitaries were present. Mr Kosygin told me that they had decided to give us all the ammunition and radar we wanted. But this must remain absolutely secret. For other things, could we leave a list with them? He also promised to assist with the expansion of our television network. So I have left General Mohammadi, our armament expert, and Mr Altaf Gauhar, the Secretary Information, to work out details. Kosygin then turned around and said, 'You see how far we have travelled in two years.' I said, 'Did we need two years to do this.' He laughed. But it is true that it takes time to develop confidence. We were very foolish not to have developed a relationship with a big and powerful neighbour like Russia earlier. A number of our problems with India got aggravated through this mistake or lapse.

I was shown a telegram from our High Commissioner in Delhi just before the banquet, that it was learned from a usually reliable source that Russia had decided to equip ten Indian divisions. I confronted Kosygin with that. He said, 'there was no truth in that. They had delivered them with certain armaments, but that was in compliance with an agreement arrived at a long time ago.' I said, 'what about these SU 7 Fighter Bombers that were delivered recently?' He said, 'these were meant against China.' I said, 'so were the 130 mm heavy guns and T 55 tanks? As if they could be used over the Himalayas.'

Thinking over US-Soviet relations, I was wondering to what extent they could co-exist. My view is that though they don't want war with each other, complete identification is also impossible. Both are super powers and would be continuously competing for world influence. But identification on specific points of mutual interest is possible. For instance, on non-proliferation or possibly against China. These agreements would be similar to the German-Russian non-aggression pact made before the Second World War and the Russian alliance with the west later when attacked by Germany. Both were opportunist ventures or marriage of connivance and fell apart as soon as the need was over. The

Bitter Cold War, which is still raging, followed when the need for this alliance ceased. This sort of cycle is likely to follow.

30 | SATURDAY

📖 Took off for Simferpol in Crimea. Mr Nikolayevich, Deputy Prime Minister, accompanied me. He is a very pleasant man, easy to talk to. Later, started talking about economic development in the Soviet Union. He said that Stalin was the life and soul of it all. He was a man with wisdom and vision. Wrote profusely. Mao Tse-tung is regarded as a god but Stalin was held in no lesser esteem. But in early the 1930s, things began to go wrong. Some peasants resisted collectivisation; there were instances of sabotage in industry. Some top echelon Communists showed resistance to his ideas and even military men showed signs of defiance. All this made Stalin very suspicious. He felt that counter-revolution was being hashed so he became bitter and vindictive and became very aloof. He had very little contact with others except with [Lavrenty] Beria, who was the Head of Intelligence and kept poisoning Stalin's mind further. Large scale suppression and oppression followed and continued. Many innocent people were executed and imprisoned for long terms.

Then I asked him what went wrong with Khrushchev. He started talking after some hesitation. He said he was a crude and uncouth man. More bluff and bluster than wisdom. He had peculiar ideas about economic matters and agriculture. Also, he used to get carried away with his emotions. Any foreign representative could pump him a bit and get out all the secret information he wanted. With Kosygin and Brezhnev, the situation was different. They were enlightened and reasonable men. All this was very interesting and informative, especially when it came out of the mouth of the top Communist leader. Normally they are very reticent and non-communicative on any serious matters.

1 | SUNDAY

News came in from General Mohammadi in Moscow that the Russians were prepared to offer him only the ammunition for 122 mm gun and the radar sets. They said they had no instructions to give tank gun ammunition. They could not check up as their leaders had gone on tour. Apparently, they were attending big manoeuvres that were being held in the Kiev region. I am going to leave a word with the deputy prime minister accompanying me for Mr Kosygin. He had definitely promised to give this type of ammunition too.

2 | MONDAY

The deputy prime minister of the USSR accompanied me. He asked me if our people were vegetarians. I told him not, except the Hindus. He talked about Mr Desai of India as being a strict vegetarian and a difficult guest to cater for. He then went to say that there are over 30 million monkeys in India and they are regarded sacred. I said, so are millions of snakes and 350 million cows plus so many other things. In fact, everything is regarded sacred in India barring human beings. It is with them that Brahmanic hypocrisy and tyranny knows no bounds.

Received a message from our ambassador in Tehran saying that the shah sent for him and complained bitterly that our radio and the press keeps on quoting the Persian Gulf as the Arabian Gulf and that Pakistan continues to flirt with the Arabs. If we are not careful, he too would also change his mind and have closer relations with India etc. I am going to find out the instances of this complaint but I am surprised that he has taken umbrage over a petty thing like this. He must have been under some stress or worked up by some underling.

3 | TUESDAY

In the evening the deputy prime minister entertained us to a parting dinner. Spoke very warmly and affectionately and said that the Soviet Union would do all that is possible to help us economically. He also told me that Mr Kosygin rang up every day to find out how I was doing.

4 | WEDNESDAY

Took off in a Soviet plane, put at my disposal, for Rawalpindi. My impression of this visit is that it has gone off very well indeed. The Soviet leaders went out of their way to be kind, hospitable and gave me all the time I wanted with them. Made an open offer of economic aid and promised to consider giving military aid. It was quite clear that apart from Vietnam, China is their major concern and they will do all that is possible to contain China. Hence their interest in the subcontinent and now Pakistan. I don't think they are much worried about China–Pakistan friendship, but they would not like to see Chinese influence grow. At the same time, they would not like to see Pak–India relations deteriorate if they can't improve. On Kashmir, their position remains unchanged. They would like to see the issue frozen which is in conformity with the policy they are pursuing in Europe in respect of disputed territories and divided Germany. Internally, the country is prospering and gaining strength.

Progress since my last visit two and a half years ago was marked. People looked well clad and well fed. I saw a lot more transport and especially private cars on roads. The condition of roads has improved and they are building furiously. The economy is booming and wages increasing. People have a lot more money to spend. But the Soviet Union is not a country, it is a world. It will take them another 100 years to develop this vast and almost limitless empire.

The Russians are thoroughly disillusioned with the Arabs. They are disgusted with their military performance and feel the Arabs have not only disgraced themselves but have also given a great setback to their prestige. But despite that, the Russians will continue to give the Arabs military, moral support.

📖 Reached Rawalpindi after six hours flight. Our flight route was Yalta-Sochi-Caucasus-Lake Aral-Samarkand-Kabul-Peshawar to Rawalpindi. The area between the Aral Sea and Samarkand is frightening. It looks heavily pitted, dazzling and completely devoid of any habitation or life. I was given a rousing reception at Rawalpindi.

📖 In Volgograd I was given a set of maps showing the general plan of attack, the Russians counter offensive. This made me think over the whole spectrum of the last war: was it waged with imagination and foresight or not?

6 | FRIDAY

📖 I saw a large number of people today, five ambassadors, several people from the defence ministry and some others. One of them was the ambassador of the United States. He made three points: A much higher level of aid to Pakistan from USA when compared to socialist countries, a definite anti-US trend in our press and could we buy with cash some of the US wheat in addition to PL 480 allocations?

I agreed with him that our press unfortunately has an anti-American slant and I have more cause to complain against it than anybody else, as this conduct is harmful to the interest of Pakistan, apart from being against our declared policy aim of keeping normal relations with the three big powers. So I called the secretary information, Altaf Gauhar, and Aziz Ahmad, chairman, Press Trust and told them to tell the editors and proprietors in very firm terms that before indulging in such mischief they better assure me that we can do without American aid or they have an alternative to it. Failing which they must stop this nonsense. If not, then they had better get ready for what comes to them and what they deserve. The trouble with these people is that they are bitter, either naïve or immature. They do not even know how to safeguard the interest of the country.

📖 Several ideas came to my mind, which I dictated and dispatched to those concerned:

India carries on constant propaganda against Pakistan, it is natural for us to retaliate. Unfortunately, this retaliation often takes the form of sweeping and general criticism of Hinduism and Hindus. This kind of retaliation unifies all classes of Hindus to defend their position. Now India is a country which contains people of many nationalities. The majority of Indian people are followers of Hinduism and in that sense the edifice of the Indian society stands on a foundation of a rigid caste system and class distinctions. The dominant classes in this society are the Brahmans and the Banias. These are the classes which have exploited the people of the subcontinent for centuries. It was to escape their domination and exploitation that we secured a homeland of our own. The fact that we found our salvation in Pakistan does not mean that the domination and exploitation of the people in India by the Brahmans and the Banias has ceased. This is a point which gets lost in general criticism of Hinduism and Hindu society. There are deep schisms in Indian society. These schisms, differences and distinctions should be made use of in our approach to India. We must make the broad masses of India conscious of their Brahman-Bania axis and of the manner in which this axis is operating to their disadvantage. This will need to be done with great imagination, skill and subtlety. And we must avoid general criticism of Hinduism and Hindus.

I would like to discuss this matter at the next governors' conference. Would you in the meantime consider this problem and devise ways and means of implementing the ideas through whatever means may be available to you in the province or in the centre.

Signed.
Field Marshal Mohammad Ayub Khan
October 6,

Copies sent to the Governor East Pakistan and Governor West Pakistan
Ministry for Information and Broadcasting.
Minister for Defence.
Minister for Foreign Affairs.

📖 Then another one. President's House, Rawalpindi.

I would like to discuss the following ideas in the next governors' conference. I am putting them down as points for discussion and would like you to examine them and come up with your suggestions in the conference:

1. Our autonomous bodies such as the Pakistan Industrial Development Corporation, the Water and Power Development Authority and the Agricultural Development Corporation, which started from humble beginnings, are fast becoming unwieldy and cumbersome. These bodies were created to accelerate development works in specific fields. The idea is that official red tapism and interference should be reduced to the minimum and people responsible for specific development activities should have sufficient means and administrative authority to get on with the job. The result of the growth of the size of these bodies has been that internal procedures are becoming complicated and the red tapism has reappeared within these bodies. Some of our autonomous bodies deal with a large number of heterogeneous subjects. As they cannot master and supervise every subject, their efficiency and performance is suffering. This is reflected in their balance sheet and in the cost benefit ratio applicable for most of the enterprises entrusted to them. Most of them are losing concerns. In other words, they are living on public money. This is not a healthy state of affairs and cannot be allowed to go on. I feel a stage has been reached when we should

take a close and critical look at the managerial and administrative arrangements under which various undertakings are progressing.

Take, for instance, the case of EPIDC. This organization is running a sugar mill and will soon be handling several major fertilizer plants. All this is in addition to a very expensive paper mill in Khulna and a steel mill in Chittagong. The same applies to PIDC in West Pakistan. Would it not be proper to create autonomous boards of management for each major item of production? The coordination and general supervision of their performance could become the responsibility of a development ministry, which might be created for the purpose.

These are just first thoughts. You may be able to think of some other approach to the problem, but one thing is clear: We have to find a more efficient and workable system of running the different enterprises of production.

2. I saw a large hydrofoil carrying up to 300 passengers operating in the rivers and seas of the USSR. Some of them travel at speeds of anything up to 60 miles per hour. I felt we could with advantage adopt this kind of craft for use in the waterways of East Pakistan. It might be a good idea for East Pakistan to nominate one or two persons to go to the USSR and study the performance and structure of these crafts. This is for the governor of East Pakistan only.

3. We have a number of research institutions which are conducting a certain amount of research in the field of medicine, agriculture, science etc. These institutions are governed by councils most of whose members are, to my knowledge, men who retired from different services and professions years ago. The councils have first to get their ideas accepted by the government, after which these ideas are presumably transmitted to heads of different implementing agencies for adoption. Not infrequently the ideas either wither away under departmental consideration or get lost under the resistance of implementing agencies. This is obviously not a satisfactory state of affairs. Would it not be better for the minister concerned in the centre or in the province to head these councils, and key positions for the council could be given to heads of the implementing ministries/departments dealing with the subject. Let me illustrate. The medical council would be replaced under the chairmanship of the central health minister. The provisional health ministers would be vice chairmen of the council and heads of medical departments in the provincial governments. In the defence forces and in the railways, officials could be nominated as members of the council. Some suitable retired people from the profession could also be put on the council. Constituted in this manner, the council will be able to take decisions and ensure implementation of these decisions.

4. There are a number of agricultural research institutions in the province. I understand that they come under the agriculture ministry whereas the agriculture universities come under the education ministry. The inevitable result is lack of coordination between the research institutes and the agricultural universities. We should give serious thought to bringing the agriculture research institutes, as well as the agricultural universities under the ministry/department.

5. We continue to have disciplinary problems with the student community, our political background and our present social and legal system is conducive to lack of discipline among the younger generation. We can either learn to live with this situation or try bringing about some improvement in it. I suggest we give a trial to the second alternative. There are two things which might be done.

a. Introduction of mass physical training in every school and college. I have been emphasizing this for a long time. I hope something has been done to implement this idea. Also hope that the implementation is being done on imaginary lines and not in a manner which would irritate the students. The educational authorities should fix proper timings for physical training and it should be insured that the training is imparted during normal hours and students do not have to come twice to their schools and colleges, once for receiving physical training and again for their classes.

b. Simultaneously, we should work out a scheme whereby the student community is required to engage itself in development and social work, shall we say, in union councils and town committees, before they are promoted from one class to another and given their certificates or degrees. Good work in this field should carry extra marks to determine divisions and for entrance to government service. The best form of work would appear to be agricultural extension work. This would, of course, require some prior training in agriculture, but I think the agricultural universities should be able to assist in this.

Unless such a scheme is worked out, we will not be able to get the younger generation involved in productive and rewarding field of work. It is through such practical work that they will come to recognize the nature of the problems which people are facing and the extent to which they can make a contribution towards their solution.

6. Those of us whose staple diet is wheat use it in the form of chapattis. The average housewife does not realize how much fuel is wasted in the preparation of chapattis. We have limited quantities of fuel which we must conserve. This idea of everyone cooking separately for himself is really a relic of Brahman/Bania emphasis of class distinction and social prejudice. Must we continue with that? I think serious thought should be given to the installation of large scale bakeries all over the country and especially in towns and cities. To begin with, we should require every existing or projected flour mill to have a bakery of a certain size attached to the mill. This should be made compulsory.

Will you please examine all the points before we meet in the governors' conference in November 1967.

Signed
Mohammad Ayub Khan
Field Marshal
June 10, 1966[87]
Copies sent to the Governor East Pakistan,
Governor West Pakistan,
Central Ministers,
Deputy Chairman, Planning Commission and
Cabinet secretary.

📖 Another such note has been sent from the President's House, Rawalpindi.

Here are some more points, which I would like to discuss at the next governors' conference in November 1967.

It is necessary to educate our young people in the ideology of Islam, similarly, it is necessary to acquaint them with Islamic history and Islamic traditions. At high levels of education there should be adequate opportunities for students to specialize in theology. However, all this has to be done in the context of present day realities and contemporary requirements. The object should be to enable the people to imbibe the spirit of Islam and to move with the times in the full consciousness of Islamic values.

I have said more than once that Islam should serve as a vehicle of progress and as an instrument of advancement. It is only thus that we will be able to move rapidly into the age of science and technology without isolating ourselves from our ideological base. There is today a sharp division in our educational system. We have on one side our schools, colleges, and universities where modern education is imparted to the younger generation, on the other side we have the religious institutions which style themselves as *Dar-ul-Ulooms*. We have to ask ourselves whether this division helps to integrate the community or puts them in two different camps, which do not have much in common with each other. We have to face this problem in duality in our educational set up. We can either leave both kinds of institutions as they are, but they will only perpetuate a schism and may alienate those educated in modern schools and colleges from the ideology of Islam. This we cannot allow to happen.

I realize that there is no easy solution to the problem. Any suggestion either to disband the *Dar-ul-Ulooms* or alter their orientation would be resisted by the more conservative elements in our society. It may be possible to provide for sustained education in Islam in our colleges and schools at all levels. Education in Islam should be compulsory up to a set level and beyond that people of requisite talent and ability could take up theology for specialization.

I would like this matter to be considered dispassionately so that we are able to find some means of resolving it and also taking the people with us. Perhaps we could have a general discussion on the subject in some appropriate forum so that people may be able to express their views publicly. There is, I am afraid, little consciousness of the importance of the subject. The general attitude is not to touch this problem because it will provoke controversy.

In the meantime, we could at least have a rule that no one should be able to start a new *Dar-ul-Uloom* without government permission. In respect of the existing religious institutions, […] should be related to the type of courses prescribed in these institutions. This would be one way of encouraging institutions which adopt modern courses. The institutions under the Auqaf Department should seriously take up modern courses of education and show the way to other institutions.

I do not want to force my ideas, but I have no doubt in my mind that it is our responsibility to face this problem in the interest of unity of our people.

1. The desirability of utilizing the service of *Pesh-Imams* to educate the people in the areas of influence. How would it do if we were to give a course of training to selected *Pesh-Imams* on the same lines as is done for Basic Democrats? Those who successfully complete the course could be associated with their respective union councils or town committees to advise on matters of social

interest. They could form a panel of advisors for the BDs. This would elevate the social status of *Pesh-Imams* and give them a sense of participation.

They could also be acquainted with problems of social and economic development and provided with suitable literature, which they could use for explaining different social and economic problems to their audience. They could advise the people about hygiene, civic responsibilities, new agricultural methods, use of fertilizer, etc. Those who are found useful and effective should be rewarded by the grant of awards and given some honorarium. They could advise on specific matters, particularly those affecting family relations.

2. A number of officials and other senior people in different professions find it difficult to occupy themselves profitably after retirement. They quickly lose touch with the community and abandon themselves to laziness and frustration. At the level of district councils some of these people could, with advantage, be put on advisory panels. For example, the district council may have an advisory panel for health, and selected, retired physicians or surgeons may be requested to serve on the panel. Similarly, panels for education, religious affairs, family affairs could be set up.

We will have to devise a proper mode of selecting retired people to serve on these panels. Perhaps the Thana Council and the Tehsil Council could serve as an electoral college for the selection of advisors from amongst retired professionals and civil servants. These people will not be members of the district councils and will be required to serve only in an advisory capacity.

3. I have been emphasizing for quite some time the need to delegate more authority and functions to basic democrats. I would like to know what precisely has been added to their sphere of responsibility and authority. There is a natural disinclination on the part of government departments to hand over any operation or function to basic democrats. I am told that in West Pakistan, primary education, which used to be the responsibility of local bodies, is now handled by the provincial education department. In East Pakistan, the *thana* irrigation scheme which was originally supposed to be implemented by the basic democrats, has perhaps been taken over by the Agricultural Development Corporation. Unless responsibilities are entrusted to BDs they will not grow. And if their growth is retarded we will lose the only base for creating leadership in social and political affairs of the country. I will be grateful if the governors could personally see to this matter and advise me how best to ensure transfer of adequate responsibilities to basic democrats.

4. Too much money is still being wasted on educational institutions providing general education. These institutions produce people who are interested in clerical and white collar jobs. What the country needs is manpower trained in scientific subjects and specific professions. I feel coordination at the central level in respect of technical and scientific education and higher education is absolutely necessary. We should, I think, set up a board to coordinate planning and implementation in the field of technical and scientific education and higher education. The day-to-day responsibilities and administrative authority will continue to vest in the provincial governments but this board should be made responsible for ensuring coordination and uniformity. The provinces should be represented on this board and the central education secretary should act as a convener and chairman of the board.

5. Officials seldom take leave. One reason may be that they feel uncertain whether they will come back to the same job on the expiry of leave. Another reason may be that they just do not know what to do during the leave. The result is that efficiency suffers and people end up in a groove.

In other advanced countries government servants are required to go on leave for a reasonable long spell, once a year. We should, I feel, introduce a roster in every ministry, department and organization according to which every government servant should take leave once a year. Normally an official should get away from his job for at least 14 days in a year. But government should encourage people to take leave for three to four weeks.

I suggest that you consider all these matters before the governors' conference. I hope the cabinet secretary will have self-contained summaries prepared on each one of the points that I have mentioned in this note and in my previous notes so that we can discuss them in the conference and take final decisions.

Signed
Mohammed Ayub Khan,
Field Marshal
11th October, 1967

cc: Governor East Pakistan
    Governor West Pakistan
    All Central Ministers
    Cabinet Secretary

7 | SATURDAY

📖 Carried out the opening ceremony of a small dam at a place called Dungi near Gujar Khan. This is the 12th dam of this type that has been completed in the area around Rawalpindi and will irrigate about 1200 acres of land. Such water storages will prove a boon to these areas and bring prosperity and happiness to them. Simultaneously, a land reclamation scheme is in operation, which would have made 140,000 acres of land available for cultivation by the end of the year. The hope is that some millions of acres of land will be so treated in due course and when that is done the life of the people of these arid areas would be transformed.

📖 Moved onto Lahore by road. A large number of people, especially women and children, came out to greet me en route.

8 | SUNDAY

📖 Spent a quiet day and performed the opening ceremony of a Regional Cooperation for Development course at the Administrative Staff College in the evening. This course consists of ten Pakistanis, six Turks and five Iranians. I think it is an excellent idea, bringing the senior administrators of these countries together.

9 | MONDAY

📖 Travelled by road from Lahore to Lyallpur. Saw several plots of IRRI rice and GA-1 maize, which looked very good and so did similar crops elsewhere. This means that the farmer's interest in agriculture has been fired and this is seen in the benefits of new methods of cultivation and utilization of better seeds etc. This is a very healthy sign. I think we are on the threshold of an agricultural revolution in the country.

Another thing that pleased me most was that all land in Sheikhupura District and the adjoining *tehsils* that had gone out of use through waterlogging and salinity, has been brought back to health by 2000 odd tubewells that have been installed in that area. The countryside is covered with flourishing crops. A new life and hope has come to the people. They were very thankful to me for having originated this scheme.

📖 I performed the opening ceremony of maize festival being held at Lyallpur. Experts from 17 different countries are attending this function.

11 | WEDNESDAY

📖 The director of intelligence brought me certain documents indicating that the Indians had become suspicious that we had some inkling of their plan of attack on West Pakistan. They had, therefore, changed their plan, but told their commanders to continue simulating the original plan for the purpose of deception.

📖 A French lady correspondent came to interview me in view of my impeding visit to that country. Also, a French TV team interviewed me.

12 | THURSDAY

📖 A cabinet meeting was held. Several important questions were discussed, including the continued anti-Pakistan propaganda by Afghanistan. It was decided that our continued passivity on this subject is being misunderstood. We shall have to rebut their distortions subtly.

13 | FRIDAY

📖 General Cariappa[88] and Mr Desai from India came and called on me. They said they have come in a private capacity, exploring possibilities of improving relations between India and Pakistan. Their formula was recognition of Kashmir as the basic problem, devising machinery for its settlement and meanwhile settling other problems like air services, telecommunications, issue of visas etc. The aim should be to lower the heat before Kashmir could be tackled. I told them that we are willing and indeed have openly expressed our willingness to settle other problems through diplomatic channels but the solution of these problems without Kashmir is not going to bring about amity and understanding between the two countries. Kashmir, according to us, was the outward manifestation of Indian hostility towards Pakistan. If India wanted peace with us then they must first demonstrate change of heart by educating public opinion suitably and then show genuine willingness to settle Kashmir with us on the basis of justice and fair play. We know Kashmir can't be settled in a day but they must be seen moving in that direction. Along with that, scaling down of forces to a level which inspires confidence must be attempted. They agreed and suggested that a joint machinery might be set up to process the problem. Mr Desai offered to act as a moderator as he knew the private secretary to Indira Gandhi. This man happens to be sensible and might well be able to influence Indira.

General Cariappa asked me as to what could be the basis of settlement. I said as far as we are concerned, our interest lies in the catchment areas of Chenab, Jhelum and Indus and in the Muslim population. We had no intention of taking over Hindu majority areas. I asked him why were they victimizing poor Muslims in India when they had ceased to have any influence or standing and have indeed become third-rate citizens. Also, why don't they stop atrocities on the poor Kashmiri's and release Abdullah[89] and Afzal Baig. They should also take back 120,000 Muslim refugees that had been driven out from the Naushera area at the point of a bayonet. He felt ashamed of all this and promised to do whatever he could. He insisted on visits by parliamentarians and students as that would generate a lot of goodwill and understanding. I told him this was not yet possible as people's minds are too inflamed to accept such moves at this stage.

I am not over optimistic about the outcome of this visit but these people represent saner elements in India and it is in our interest to encourage them in their efforts.

Mr Desai was openly critical of the economic and other policies of India and sounded gloomy about the state of internal affairs. It was embarrassing to hear that I was the master of this subcontinent and could prove its saviour.

General Cariappa told me that whenever he comes to Pakistan, the communist press accuses him of seeking counsel from me as to how to bring about a military takeover of the government in India. The fools don't realize that even if he was inclined that way, he being a retired man, has no power or influence to do such a thing, besides India was too big a country. I told him that even if the circumstances warranted, takeover of 17 provincial governments and a central government was not a feasible proposition. However, what is possible is that someone like Chavan may take over with the backing of the army.

He felt that declaration of martial law in certain Indian states might well become necessary.

14 | SATURDAY

📖 Flew to Karachi in the evening. Saw General Yahya who has just returned from his tour of Iran. He happened to meet the Shah too who repeated his complaints against us. According to him, how is it possible for us to maintain friendly relations with China, Soviet Union and USA simultaneously, and similarly, how could we be his friends whilst wanting to be the friends of Nasser. I briefed General Musa who is visiting Iran to tell the Shah that he is right in thinking the way he does in respect of our relations with the superpowers. It is not an easy matter to keep this balance but we have no other choice. We are the victims of our geopolitical situation. As regards President Nasser, all we are trying to do is to normalize relations. It is extremely doubtful if he would seek our friendship. He is far too committed to India. I think the Shah has got mentally tied up unnecessarily and is suspecting our motives for no rhyme or reason. He thinks that we are seeking the leadership of the Muslim world and are operating against his interest behind his back. Nothing could be further from the truth.

15 | SUNDAY

📖 Received the Prime Minister of Albania, Mr Mehmet Shehu and his party, who arrived from Peking. They flew direct, Peking to Karachi, over Sinkiang, in ten hours. He is a nice man and warm hearted. During the talks in the evening, he explained the security problems facing Albania, the hostile attitude of USA, their fallout with the Soviets after Stalin's death, the USA–USSR collaboration to dominate the world and their close ties with China. Said that Indian attack on Pakistan was US–Soviet inspired and phase one of aggression against China. He spoke in terms and usual communist jargon based more on emotion than reason.

There was to be a banquet in the evening followed by speeches. I took the precaution of having the speech looked into by our foreign secretary. It was full of hard words against America and Soviets. As the prime minister was not prepared to change his speech, and we could not allow our soil to be used as a platform for propaganda, it was decided that the speeches should be done away with and a simple toast proposed. I am glad I took the precaution of his speech being looked into and finally dispensed with otherwise it would have been delivered causing an awful furore.

16 | MONDAY

📖 Took off for Nice en route to Paris on a four day state visit to France. I understand the French take the precaution of greeting state guests a day earlier in an intermediary place in their country so as to ensure that we get to Paris in time the next day to start the tour on schedule. We were suitably received on arrival and then taken to a very nice hotel overlooking the sea. Nice is a summer resort where a large number of tourists come from all over Europe. The Germans, apparently, are their largest customers. This place apparently was developed by the British prior to World War I. Queen Victoria used to spend her winters here because the climate remains mild throughout the year. Nice has a background of a range of hills. There are several old castles built on top of cliffs in most inaccessible places. This was a measure of defence against the Arab raiders in the Middle Ages and later the Turks.

📖 Had dinner with Karim Aga Khan in his father's house on the seashore in Cannes. Several important guests were invited like the Prince of Monaco and his American actress wife. She is charming and sensible but he is a goof and peculiar, riddled with complexes. There was an old French lady who apparently got very fond of Mr Fida Hassan, my private secretary. She thought he was the most handsome man she had ever met and wanted him to come to stay with her on his next visit. Zeenat, Fida's wife, was not listening in. She was on another table. It just shows how peculiar women can be. Soekarno's youngest wife was also present amongst the guests. She had come down from Paris where she stayed for the occasion.

I and my daughter Naseem inquired about Soekarno and his affairs. She burst into tears and told us that she knew very little about him as no communication was possible. All she knew was that he is at Bogor under surveillance. She did not think he would leave the country. He had been struggling for Indonesia since 14 years of age so he would rather die than leave it. I felt so sad because Soekarno was such a good friend of mine and Pakistan. I used to warn him that he should pay more attention to economic reconstruction than politics. He never listened. That is the trouble with most of those who fought for the freedom of their country. Having attained it, they did not know what to do with it.

The Aga Khan[90] then took me out in the compound where his father, Ali Khan, is buried temporarily. Ali was such a charming man and such a dear friend of mine. May God bless his soul.

Karim is faced with a problem of where to find Ali's final resting place. Ali had left a will to be buried in Syria where there is a large Aga Khan community. They are willing to have his body but the Syrian government, which is Sunni, is demanding 100,000 pounds as a ransom. This is dirty tricks and nothing but blackmail. I offered him burial facilities in Pakistan. We shall be very happy to assist.

Finally we got back to the hotel, it was 4:00 a.m. by Pakistan time. So I had to take a pill to get some sleep but my room was very stuffy and hot, besides the din of traffic from a major road closeby kept on coming the whole night long. Hotels in Europe are no places to live in for rest or peace.

17 | TUESDAY

📖 Left for Paris, Orly airfield where we were met by General de Gaulle, his cabinet ministers, senators etc. The general drove with me and we entered the main Paris city. The hood of the car was removed. Large crowds were waiting for us on both sides of the road. They welcomed us warmly. I and my entourage were put up in the portion of the Foreign Office reserved for VIPs, the Napoleon the Third suite. Apparently he was very keen on town planning and building. In my bathroom, the washbasin, the bathtub and other facilities are gilded.

I met President de Gaulle at 5 p.m. at the Elysee palace. The meeting lasted for an hour and a half. In the meeting there were President de Gaulle, myself, and an interpreter. We talked mostly about problems facing Pakistan like relationship with USA, Soviets and China and its delicacy and continued arms build up and hostility of India. De Gaulle listened with patience and understanding. Said that Pakistan has a right to exist, to be able to defend itself. Promised economic and military assistance. I asked for softening of loans items plus 200 M-47 tanks which they are replacing with their own tank AMX-30. He promised to look into that. About the Middle East, he felt the Americans will take no initiative until the presidential elections are over. Jewish influence is too strong in that country. This is a sombre thought. It means that the poor Arabs will remain under pressure and strain for a long time.

There was a banquet at the Elysee palace followed by a reception. There were only Pakistani and French guests. No foreigners. The cream of French brainpower were present in large numbers. It took us over an hour to shake hands with them. So one does get some exercise on these trips in one way or another. When introducing me, the president had a word of comfort and praise for every guest. The old man can be really warm when he wishes to. I asked him how he was in parliament. He said, don't believe the press; I can command a majority. Meanwhile, a commentator on the BBC was discussing how ill de Gaulle was.

19 | THURSDAY

📖 Had an exclusive meeting with President De Gaulle. Monsieur Pompidou also joined in. We spoke about the Middle East situation. De Gaulle's view was that both Jordan and Egypt were in a reasonable mood. Israelis were, however, in an uncompromising mood. The US could not pressure them due to Jewish influence in America and a heavy commitment in Vietnam. In fact, Vietnam had robbed USA of all initiatives. If it were not for Vietnam, the Soviets and they would have come closer in many fields. This was followed by a full scale meeting by the French and the Pakistani representatives. De Gaulle and I were present. Here our bilateral problems were discussed. The French promised to consider our problems sympathetically. I took the opportunity to invite the president and his cabinet colleagues to Pakistan. They promised to visit at an appropriate time.

20 | FRIDAY

Called at the Elysee Palace with my party to take leave of the president and the members of his government. My impressions of the visit to France are as follows:

The French are interested in developing a closer relationship with Pakistan. On attitude toward international affairs, we consider our position closer to them. They regard us as honest and reliable people. I believe de Gaulle told his colleagues so and I advised them to help us. In the economic field, they may well decide to soften terms of credit with us. Contrasting Indians with us, they regard them as frauds. On world problems, de Gaulle thinks the Israelis are in no mood to give up their gains. They wish to hang on to everything they have occupied. Towards US, he showed no rancour or animosity. His health, which has become the subject of speculation in American and British circles, appeared to me to be good. Amongst his cabinet ministers who impressed me most was his defence minister. Madame de Gaulle is a most gracious lady, simple and unassuming, yet full of common sense and wisdom. She must have been a a tower of strength to the old man in his difficult life.

Mr Pirzada has returned from the UN assembly session. There he met President Johnson, General Eisenhower, Dean Rusk and Robert McNamara. He said they now understand Pakistan and its posture. Rusk said that they were primitive in treating Pakistan shabbily but they were irritated by Bhutto's criticism in conjunction with Subandrio and Chen-yi. However, that is all over and in any case President Johnson regards President Ayub Khan as a personal friend. General Eisenhower was much more forthright. He said the State Department is a poor judge of friends. They had no justification for giving precedence to India over a loyal friend like Pakistan.

We took off from Orly airfield at 11 p.m., being seen off by the prime minister, and landed at Constanza airport in Romania on the Black Sea coast. A Romanian aircraft was laid on to bring us to Bucharest where we were met by the president and other dignitaries of the Romanian government. The diplomatic corps and a large number of spectators were present. We were given a rousing welcome. A little later I called on the president and later attended a banquet at a palace which was used by the former kings. The dinner was a pleasant function. The president and the prime minister, amongst others, were present. Light Romanian music added to the colour. The Romanians are open, gay, musical but tough and hard working people.

21 | SATURDAY

📖 Went out for a shoot some 40 miles outside Bucharest. The president reached there a little before me. We shot till 1:00 p.m. Though there was not much to shoot, the shoot was well organized and conducted. Lunched in the field. President Stoica is a very pleasant man. An excellent and assertive person and a good talker. He told me all about economic, agricultural and industrial problems of Romania. He has been the minister for industries so knows all the facts and figures by heart. Apparently he has no formal education and spent a lot of time in prison in his early life for his political beliefs, but he is passionately dedicated. By all accounts, Romania, though still an underdeveloped country, has made phenomenal progress in every field and the people are much better off than they ever had been before.

📖 Rested in the afternoon and had a dinner in the bedroom. It was the first free evening I have had for a long time.

📖 I call Romanian progress phenomenal. The following few facts will illustrate. They produce their tractors and trucks, there are over one lakh tractors working on land, and farming the plains is completely mechanized. Other industries like machine making and petrochemicals etc. are also coming up. Fifty-seven per cent of the population is working on the land, the rest in industry. They also are trying to reduce the population by family planning methods. Their production figures are interesting. 8 million tons maize, 7 million tons of wheat, large scale sunflower, soybeans, potatoes, tobacco etc. production. High scale of dairy production and poultry and wine production, most of the things are exported. I was told that the maize production is more profitable than gold mining in that it would cost far more to produce gold worth that much. Their rain is periodic and uncertain so they are thinking of going in for large scale irrigation, which is possible. They expressed a desire to study our system. The phenomenal progress in agriculture has been made possible by pooling of land, large scale mechanization, passing on to the farmers the necessary know how, and making them work modern agriculture not possible without large scale investment which only big farmers and corporations can afford. The above descriptions will sound like pleading for a communist system. That is not so. All I am trying to describe is what I saw and observed and what they have achieved. Surely not without tremendous cost and human suffering, loss of individual liberty and regimentation but one thing is certain, that these achievements have been made possible under hard work and hard work of this magnitude is not possible without regimentation and discipline. But life is like that, you cannot have something for nothing. In backward countries with limited resources, human needs cannot be met with unbridled personal liberty. One or the other has to give way. I think the solution may well lie in adopting Islamic concept, personal liberty to the extent that is good for the society. If this is accepted then our social, economic, legal system will have to be suitably adopted.

26 | THURSDAY

📖 Received a summary of his talks with the Shah from General Musa. The Shah is levelling more and more trumped up charges against us. He is, in fact, becoming very tiresome and cantankerous for no rhyme or reason. Other than this he thinks he has the right to lead us by the nose. Let us see what transpires when I meet him in Tehran. I rang up the Shah and congratulated him and the queen on their coronation.

27 | FRIDAY

📖 Mr Pirzada, our foreign minister, submitted a written report on his meeting with Dean Rusk in Washington. He met Rusk twice. On the first meeting Rusk promised to look into the problems of spare parts etc. for us and said that in spite of what has happened President Johnson had a great regard for me. On the second meeting he opened up and said that Pakistan failed them in Korea and Vietnam. Also, we were responsible for starting the war with India. The Chinese ultimatum to India during our war was a real challenge to the United States. From that time on, Pakistan had lost the United States. As such, US special relations with us have ceased to exist. Our relations now can only be termed as normal and friendly like with any other country. Further, we must understand clearly that the US is a superpower. It will be as brutal, premeditative and as ruthless as possible where its interests are involved, whatever the cost. This may sound brutal and strange but basically the behaviour of all big powers towards smaller countries is the same and shows how cautious we have to be when dealing with them. However, most of Dean Rusk's allegations are based on half truths. Our side of the story is either not known or is ignored. So I have caused Pirzada to write to Rusk and tell him what the truth is.

30 | MONDAY

📖 Prime Minister Demirel accompanied me to the airport. I told him why we could not be too enthusiastic about participation in CENTO activities. Now that the Americans have openly told us not to expect any protection from them against India, it is incumbent on us to resist from doing anything that will antagonize the Soviets. Positively, we want arms assistance from them and negatively, we want to inhibit any tendency on their part to encourage India against us. He understood my point and showed sympathy with it. He said he would be talking to the Americans about this.

31 | TUESDAY

📖 In Turkey some intellectuals and pressmen who came to see me question the wisdom of continuing with CENTO and even remaining in NATO. I told them we should not break up CENTO as that would be resented by the USA on whom we have considerable dependence. Turkey also had a lot to gain militarily and economically by remaining with NATO. True that Britain and France, backed by the USA, had destroyed the Turkish Empire, but Russia too had been the traditional enemy for centuries. Turkey is in possession of one of the world's most sensitive waterways. It was a source of strength as well as weakness. Therefore, Turkey needs the protection of a world power.

In any case, the rest of the world will not forget that the Muslims are Muslims. Look at the amount of fuss the Christian world made when the question of Turkish entry into NATO was mooted. They all protested against the entry of a Muslim country.

📖 When Prime Minister Demirel drove with me to the airport, I had congratulated him on the success he is making of his job. I think he has come on a lot and has grown in stature. He is head and shoulders above anybody else in Turkey. I had heard that the bodies of Adnan Menderes and other ministers, who were hanged a few years ago, are buried in the jail compound and were to be transferred and buried in a compound of a mosque in Istanbul. It reminded me of my efforts to save them because I knew that it would inflict a lasting wound on the Turkish body politic. Demirel called it a great crime. I understand that people from all over the country are going to come to attend the burial. I hope the occasion does not turn into a law and order problem.

📖 Landed at Tehran where I had a lengthy discussion with the Shah on the baseless accusations he is levelling against us. I can think of only two reasons for this outburst. Either he is over-obsessed with fear of the Arabs in the Persian Gulf area and is taking unwarranted umbrage on our sympathy for the Arab cause or he is using this as camouflage to have a tie-up with Israel on one side and the Indians on the other. If he does that, he will stand isolated in the Middle East. I made this clear to him in no uncertain terms.

📖 The notes written during the flight on PIA on PIA letterhead:

Tehran, 31st October 1967—points for talks with the Shah:

1. Congratulate on coronation.
2. Assure him of my genuine desire to see him remain strong. Without him I can see nothing but chaos in Iran.
3. Be genuinely thankful for the demonstration of his support during the war with India. I, too, made an open declaration that we shall stand by you thick and thin. We have also acted always as friends. Lately a series of complaints made against us. What the real reason is, I can't say. But I assured His Majesty that these allegations have no substance nor is there any change in our attitudes towards Iran and you. Any such thing is unthinkable.

List of complaints:
1. Pakistan press and radio described Persian Gulf as the Arabian Gulf. Show Altaf Gauhar's paper on this. Also remind Shah how much our press writes in favour of him and Iran.
2. Pakistani press involvement with the Arabs. This is nothing new. I explained the reason so many times. They would be more sympathetic should Iran unhappily get involved in serious difficulties.
3. Recent movements of our foreign minister in Arab countries. Reasons:
   a. Gauge the future of Arab requirements.
   b. Are they going to be realistic in settlement with Israel?
   c. Any chance of early Suez reopening. We are all suffering economic loses.

Nasser no friend of ours. We not seeking his friendship as it is doubtful.

Precautions:
a. Dispatch of Pakterwan.
b. Dispatch of a foreign secretary.
c. Calling for Ramsar meeting.

Has anybody else taken so much trouble to keep us informed?

4. My autobiography:
a. Praises Nasser.
b. Decries monarchy.
c. Does not bring out special relationship with Iran.
d. Does not mention Shah's effort in normalizing relations with Afghanistan.
e. No mention of the support Iran gave us during 1965 war.

Show how baseless these allegations are.

5. India is making increasing overtures to Iran. That is a sure way of isolating Iran.
6. Pakistan seeking Muslim leadership. We have no desire to seek anybody's leadership.
7. Pakistan's relationship with the Soviets and China disturbing. Why?

Appeal to the Shah to understand our point of view and not misunderstand unnecessarily.

2 | THURSDAY

Dr I.H. Qureshi, who was a member of the board which was set up to sort out Miss Jinnah's belongings came to report the outcome. He was interested in the future of Quaid-e-Azam's personal effects and papers, which have been separated. The suggestion was that his personal effects should be placed in the relics room in the museum area and the papers handed over to him who is also sorting out the old Muslim League papers. We shall have to take permission of the heirs for any such disposal.

Carried out the opening ceremony of the Karachi Television Station. This will be a great boon to the people of Karachi and the surrounding areas. I am told that TV sets in large numbers have been bought by the people.

The Russian ambassador showed great anxiety to see me. He came over in the evening and gave out that the Soviet government will give us certain type of ammunition and radar equipment on a phased programme. They were also prepared to send out a team of experts to try the same ammunition of these types to test it in our guns. But they want all this to remain strictly secret. He also asked me to go to Moscow for a short participation in the 50th anniversary of their revolution. How can I do that at such a short notice when I have been away from the country for so long and there is so much to do at home? Besides, what will I look like in the company of communists from all over the world? I would certainly look odd.

3 | FRIDAY

Dr [Amir Hassan] Siddiqui,[91] a former historian, came with a bundle of books he has written on Islamic history, constitution, political institutions etc. Advocated that the only way to save Islam is to finish the mullah. I have asked for him to be used by the education and the information ministry and also to be put on the advisory board with the West Pakistan Auqaf department.

A deputation of followers of Bahaullah[92] came to see me and gave me a book on his writings. They seemed cultured people.

Visited the biological laboratories of Karachi University. There are some very competent scientists who are doing excellent work. The university campus, which is new, is filling up and already looks a big sprawling city. I also saw the sorting out of Muslim League papers which Dr Qureshi is supervising. These papers, though jumbled up, are in very large quantities and constitute a complete record of Muslim political activity commencing from 1905.

Amir Bhai, a nephew of the Quaid-e-Azam, who is an Indian citizen, called on me with his wife. He struck me as a very intelligent, sober and balanced man. He is a leading lawyer in Bombay. He has come here to assist Miss Jinnah's heirs to settle the inheritance problem amicably. They were followed by Chaudhary Khaliquzzaman. He proposed to move a resolution in the forthcoming Muslim

League working committee to confer a title in recognition of my services to the country. I told him that it would be embarrassing and difficult to accept, but he kept on insisting.

4 | SATURDAY

Visited the Hub river dam site. The work is progressing satisfactorily. When completed it will irrigate about 60,000 acres of land and should prove a great boon to the people of Karachi. Through it should be possible to produce all the vegetables, milk products and poultry required for the city.

5 | SUNDAY

Flew into Rawalpindi. The Pindites and the Muslim Leaguers gave me a grand reception.

I got a telephone call from Mr Kosygin from Moscow. Podgorny and Brezhnev were present with him. I congratulated them on the 50th anniversary of their revolution, the progress they made during it and wished them a happy and more successful future. They sounded to be in a very happy mood.

7 | TUESDAY

Heard this morning that we had been elected unanimously to a seat in the Security Council vacated by Japan entirely on our own efforts without the assistance of big powers. This rebounds to the skill and the effort of our people. I have sent them a letter of congratulations and also warned them of the responsibilities that would devolve on us. We shall have to take stands on international problems with attendant hazards. Our representative will have to be cautions and pragmatic and will have to have quick means of communications with us. I have told the foreign secretary to set up a working party to work out general directions to our representatives.

Foreign minister came to see me, very excited, as I was having lunch and told me that according to the Russian ambassador we have struck oil at a place called Toot near Fatehjang. The oil was gushing out and the drillers were finding it difficult to control it. This is a most welcome need. I do hope it is in large quantities.

8 | WEDNESDAY

Flew to Peshawar and attended Jashn-i-Khyber function in the evening. A troupe of PIA, who performed for the queen during the state visit to England, gave a fine exhibition of dance and drama.

9 | THURSDAY

Went to Kohat and addressed a meeting of Muslim League workers and then performed the opening ceremony of Tanda Dam. This is relatively small, but a fine project of side storage of water and will irrigate 32,000 acres of parched land in Kohat district. It will be a great boon to the poor people. It was on my insistence that this project was started. The experts said that it was uneconomic. Purely in monetary terms it may be, but in human terms it will pay hands down.

📖 Aftab Kazi,[93] the chairman of WAPDA, told me something of immense interest. After completion of Tarbela, the Indus would have got left 22 million acre feet of water to store. They have discussed a storage place in the Thal desert which can absorb all this water. The project in the form of dams and dikes would cost about the same as Tarbela, but would be constructed on dry land, therefore, we can take our own time over it. After that all that can be done to Indus is to build a series of hydel power plants on its uplands, above Tarbela. The other thing he told me was that the capacity of Khanpur Dam can be doubled if the village of Khanpur is allowed to be submerged. I told him why not. Such sacrifices have to be made in the national interest.

13 | MONDAY

📖 The governors' conference commenced. A large number of items will be discussed today, and we covered considerable ground mainly on the points raised by me. Some important decisions were taken. They should have far reaching effect in the social, economic, and educational fields.

14 | TUESDAY

📖 The governors' conference continued. We discussed and took decisions on several more important problems.

15 | THURSDAY

📖 The meeting of the National Economic Council took place. Two major items were discussed. The causes of growing economic disparity between East and West Pakistan and the size of the annual budget plan for the two last years of the third plan.

📖 It is baffling but true that in spite of much larger development allocations to East Pakistan in recent years, the disparity has risen from 28 to 39 per cent. The Planning Commission has identified the causes: a weak administration, neglect of agriculture, wrong priorities of projects and hostile attitude towards private sector, especially investment from West Pakistan. The constitution requires that the state of parity will be reported in the assembly every year. I have no doubt that there will be a furore when this state of affairs is divulged. But this is the direct result of excessive autonomy and Bengalization of civil services. They do not have the necessary drive to push through a highly sophisticated developmental programme. However, we have decided to set up a working group to suggest what corrective action can be taken.

On the size of annual development programme, there was a difference of opinion between the Planning Commission demand and the finance, who felt that the resources of the magnitude required could not be mobilized for several good reasons. I told them to work in close collaboration and do the best they could.

17 | FRIDAY

📖 Herr Volkow, a German military scientist, came to see me in conjunction with the defence minister. He is interested in Pakistan and seems genuinely willing to help. A team from his firm came to inspect our manufacturing capability. In their view a good base exists in indigenous manufacture of different weapons and explosives. It seems we can make a good start with rockets for close and medium range. Also, light anti-tank and anti-personnel mines that can be sown from the air and from the ground with great ease in front of advancing enemy tanks and infantry. It is full fragmenting in the sense that it will go off if touched. In other words, such a minefield does not have to be protected with fire. We also discussed the possibility of manufacturing a really light tank with low silhouette, good cross country mobility and carrying anti-tank rockets or missiles and a 105mm gun. I was intrigued to hear that he had developed such a vehicle and had shown it to the German general staff. They are not yet interested in it. I told him that we are. It is only such an armoured fighting vehicle that we can afford. So we would go ahead with its manufacture, if we were satisfied with its performance. It was decided that we should send General Mohammadi to Germany and have a look at these things and submit a report.

📖 A meeting of the Muslim League Working Committee was held. After the review of the internal situation and our foreign relations and the state of the economy, the committee decided to increase the basic membership of assemblies from 150 to 200 and induct 10 members in the central and five each in the provincial assemblies based on merit using the assembly as the electoral college. Certain organizational matters were also discussed and decisions taken.

📖 The finance minister sought an interview with me at short notice and repeated that he had received a signal from our high commissioner in London, that the devaluation of the pound was eminent. This is very disturbing news as it has come to us at a stage when our cash revenues are low. With devaluation, they will be reduced still further. However, sometime back I had taken precautions to send the governor of the State Bank to the Bank of England to see what we could convert into dollars. The position today is that 17 crores are held in dollars and 30 crore in sterling, the figure that will be affected if devaluation takes place. I have directed the finance minister to set up a committee to examine what consequential action we may have to take in respect of our currency because it is quite certain that with devaluation of sterling several other countries will also have to follow suit.

18 | SATURDAY

📖 The editors and senior journalists of the Press Trust papers were brought to me for a pep talk. They are by and large doing a good job, but they are not aggressive enough in exposing disruptive tendencies of the opposition. I explained to them the background and the reasons for which the trust was created. Its duty is to develop healthy journalism that promotes unity and solidarity, coupled with progress in other spheres. Negatively, they have to expose those who are playing dirty politics, confusing and misleading people. I think they are generally dedicated people barring some, who are to be weeded out. Another topic they have to keep off is hostile criticism of the big powers. These are mere pinpricks and do no good to our interests.

📖 Governor Monem Khan came and harangued me for nearly three hours. He is an excellent man and a loyal friend, but very long-winded. Takes a long time to come to a point. I have not the heart to tell him that.

19 | SUNDAY

📖 Our economic experts are still considering what action we should take on devaluation of sterling. The alternatives are being considered. No one action other than streamlining of the bonus voucher to devalue to the same extent that the British have done. Devalue to open market value level of rupee, that is 26 per cent. They have asked for more time to consider the consequences of each.

📖 Went to Abbottabad for a few hours and returned in the evening.

20 | MONDAY

📖 Held a cabinet meeting in the evening to decide the issue of devaluation. It emerged from the discussion that unless we devalue to the extent of about 70 per cent or do away with bonus arrangement, more devaluation would be nothing but appeasement of IMF, World Bank and aid givers. Since this is an improbable factor why devalue unless we were driven to it. So we decided that there shall be no devaluation, with prayers that it proves to be the right decision. My own feeling is that we should be able to pull it off.

21 | TUESDAY

📖 The Americans seem to be taking an interest in the information we gave them that there is a possibility of fruitful negotiations with Hanoi provided the bombing stops. Harriman, who is coming here for the opening of Mangla celebrations, is also visiting Bucharest to sound their prime minister as to the prospects. They have asked us if we would act as a channel of communication with Hanoi, through our ambassador in Peking. We have decided to keep out at this stage as we cannot run the risk of being misunderstood by the Chinese. We are also doubtful whether Chinese would like negotiations to start at this stage.

22 | WEDNESDAY

📖 A cabinet meeting was held. A number of important items came up for discussion and decisions taken. We also decided to instruct provincial governments to consider amending the law to introduce whipping for those who indulge in adulteration of food and for crime against women and children. These vices are increasing and need to be drastically reduced.

📖 The director of intelligence has managed to obtain a copy of Indian strike corps plan of attack against West Pakistan. This should be of great help to our defence planners. In fact, the Indians now have three plans, one for the wet and one for the dry season in case we open hostilities, and a separate one in case they decide to aggress against Pakistan.

23 | THURSDAY

📖 Today was a red-letter day for Pakistan. The opening of Mangla dam[94] and the commissioning of power generators took place in a very colourful ceremony in the Mangla fort. Guests came from all over Pakistan and also largish contingents from the countries who had helped us with resources, and RCD countries. They read out warm messages from their governments.

Mangla is a gigantic project, which will have live storage of 5.2 million acre feet of water and generate over 2600 k.w. of electricity. It will give us a sure water supply in winter and will change the agriculture, economy, habits and way of life of people.

Along with Mangla, several link canals and barrages have been completed, which will enable the water to be taken to the Bahawalpur area and below. The earthwork of these canals is several times bigger than the Suez and Panama canals. Some 500 crores have been spent on them. A similar amount will be spent on Tarbela dam and Chashma Barrage on the Indus. These are truly monumental works and the harbinger of agrarian revolution in Pakistan and are the fruits of a stable, progressive and reliable government.

24 | FRIDAY

📖 I had a busy day today. The delegations of Australia, New Zealand, UK, Germany and US came to see me. I also received the ambassadors of Malaysia and Cambodia. This was followed by a lunch I gave in honour of all the foreign delegations that came to attend the inauguration of Mangla Dam. Then I addressed a public meeting in Liaquat[95] Garden arranged by the Muslim League. It was a mammoth meeting where I mounted a full-scale attack on the opposition leaders who are busy misleading and confusing the people. I exposed their pretensions and rebutted their allegations that we were incurring debts and wasting the money.

Mr Harriman heads the US delegation. He saw me separately and spoke about Vietnam and the possibility of getting negotiations going with Hanoi. I told him that the Romanian prime minister had spoken to me on the thinking of Hanoi and advised him to get the prime minister of Romania to act as a medium of communication. I gained the information that the Americans would like to get talks started if possible on their terms.

I told Mr Harriman and the American delegation that it seems incongruous that on one side America is spending 30 billion dollars a year on the war in Vietnam to maintain their presence in that part and on the other side they were beating a general retreat in the developing world by curtailing and mutilating the aid bill and reducing it to insignificance and inefficiency and ineffectiveness. He agreed with me that this was disastrous.

25 | SATURDAY

📖 The ambassador of Cambodia called on me. He is based in Cairo and accredited to Pakistan. I questioned him on the internal problems, prospects of war in Vietnam and how they are affected by it and their relationship with Thailand. He was not clear what would be the end of the war in Vietnam but one thing was certain that America could not stay in the area for long and that the South Vietnamese government could not be saved without American support.

📖 I went to Khunda, a place 20 miles beyond Fatehjang on the Kohat road, to attend Allah Yar's brother's *Valima* lunch. A large number of dignitaries from this region were present and what a fine lot of people they were in looks, fidelity, courage and patriotism. I noticed that power lines have been driven into their area. This will help them to dig tube wells and pump water for storage or irrigation proposes, which will bring them immense benefits. Their land is very fertile. The only trouble is that the rainfall is uncertain. The Khanpur dam water will also benefit this area a lot. In fact, most of this water will irrigate areas in Campbellpur district.

26 | SUNDAY

📖 I was rung up by General Musa around midday and told that he had heard that the Nawab of Kalabagh had been shot and killed by his son Asad. Apparently, Asad went to see his father in the morning to report something. During the course of the talk, hot words were exchanged between the two over the running of the family estate. The Nawab accused Asad of mismanagement and he in turn accused Noor Mohammed, a trusted servant of the Nawab. On that the Nawab is alleged to have whipped out his pistol and fired two shots at Asad slightly grazing him on the arm. Asad in return fired five shots hitting the Nawab in the neck, chest and stomach. He died on the spot. I told the governor to send the IG police to see that no one was unnecessarily implicated. IG on return reported to me and repeated the above story. It is an obvious case of self-defence, but all the same, tragic. The Nawab deserved a better ending but by his feudal background he was prone to dictation and intolerance.

📖 Chancellor [Kurt Georg] Kiesinger of Germany with his wife and a large entourage arrived on a three day visit.

27 | MONDAY

📖 Talks were held with Kiesinger, first in privacy, and then in the presence of our representative teams. I gave him a view of Vietnam, situation in the Middle East, Sino–Soviet relations, our relations with big powers and India. I then asked for technical assistance on arms supply, more aid, technical assistance, removal of trade imbalance etc. He was very sympathetic in respect of our demands except on supply of 200 American tanks. He said this was against their policy to supply offensive weapons to areas of tension but he will go back and have it examined. He was very forthcoming in aid for Tarbela. The German worry is reunification, ensuring American presence in Europe and closer political ties with France. He was sympathetic to British entry in the Common Market but did not see any future in pressurizing De Gaulle and also was not certain of British motives. He thought they want to come for more economic than political reasons. My own view is that the British would not be able to get into the Common Market. De Gaulle would not have them. In the end they will have to fall back on America. They may even have to have some sort of political union with them to escape their chronic economic difficulties. I told Kiesinger that they, combined with France, could play a major role as moderators amongst superpowers and thereby enhance the chances of German reunification. He felt deeply interested in this thought.

I was deeply impressed with Kiesinger. He is a man of stature and wisdom with a warm heart and glowing sincerity and straightforwardness. In fact, most of the leading Germans I have met are men of considerable human virtue.

28 | TUESDAY

📖 During my discussion with Kiesinger on economic matters I made two points. First, the extent of our deficit trade should be converted into rupees and the Germans buy goods from us with them. These goods will have to be outside our traditional foreign exchange earnings. Secondly, why should we be charged interest on loans when we run a deficit trade balance with their country? He and his associates promised to consider these proposals. Let us see what comes out of it. Chancellor Kiesinger and his party took off by a jet plane first to fly over the Karakoram, see the Mangla and Tarbela Dam sites and then go on to Lahore. Since Lahore was under fog they returned to Pindi and decided to go to Karachi and then on to Germany.

📖 Carried out the inauguration ceremony of the Lahore Museum, which has been renovated and tidied up. Mr Bashir,[96] the additional chief secretary, is mainly responsible for it. He has taken a lot of pain over it.

29 | WEDNESDAY

📖 Left by train for Sindh area. Reached Ghotki in the morning and went to Khangarh to shoot partridge with Ghulam Mohammed Mahar, an old friend of mine. I shot quite well. I bagged 108 birds.

📖 Reached Khairpur in the evening to stay with His Highness the Mir. Was told by the commissioner that acute form of Sindhism was raising its head in certain cities. It was being fanned by members of the NAP, almost a communist party, with the help of labour and the student community. I told him to deal with these rascals under the maintenance of law and order. That he was suspicious that Qazi Fazlullah also lends a hand in these matters. Qazi also interferes with the administration, the usual past time of the old and discredited politicians. I am going to take the first opportunity to bring him to earth.

30 | THURSDAY

📖 Went to shoot partridge on the Mir's reserve. The place was stiff with birds, shot 207 birds beating my previous records of 137 partridge. During the shoot an unfortunate accident occurred. Nawab Col. Abdul Ghafoor Hoti shooting low, wounded six beaters. Two of them had lost an eye each. I was very upset on hearing this and told him to compensate these people adequately.

1 | FRIDAY

📖 The Sheikh of Abu Dhabi is on a visit to Pakistan sponsored by the United Bank of Pakistan which has a branch there. He is fond of hawking and hunts bustard in the desert. He keeps about 75 falcons which are murderous birds. He is about to go back home and expressed a desire to see me before departure. So I invited him to fly to Sukkur where I entertained him to lunch. I was deeply impressed by his rustic wisdom, sagacity and warmth of heart. He spoke very highly of Pakistan and expressed the desire to acquire property here and live here from time to time. These desert Arabs are delightful people, hospitable and generous.

2 | SATURDAY

📖 I am delighted on two counts. One, there has been rain in several places in West Pakistan and more is expected. Raining in November and early December is rare in these areas but it is God-sent, if it comes. It will do an immense amount of good to the wheat crop. Secondly, the tender for Tarbela Dam has been opened. The lowest bid of 259 crores had been made by a German firm. Other bids were 384 crores, 366 crores and 296 crores. The lowest bid is far below our expectation and it may well be possible to find the foreign exchange component from our own funds and the balance left over from the Indus basin replacement funds.

📖 From the official press reports it is said that Mr Bhutto has held a two-day convention in Lahore to launch his so-called People's Party. Reports further said that it was a tame and childish affair. His major attempt is to misuse the student community, a dangerous game. But we are watching his activities. He will be dealt with in no uncertain fashion if he crosses the limit.

4 | MONDAY

📖 Took a night train and reached Karachi in the morning.

5 | TUESDAY

📖 Air Marshal Nur Khan returned from China and reported on the outcome of his visit. He was received by the senior military officials, Vice Premier Chen-yi and Premier Chou En-lai, and given a patient hearing in all consideration. He discussed with them the problems connected with the maintenance and repair of the MIG-19 aircraft, weapons, and ammunition, radar and ground control systems. The Chinese were most helpful and forthcoming. The premier said that in two years time their production will gain full momentum and they would be able to supply our needs to the full, provided we stand firm on the matter of self determination in Kashmir and resist Indian expansionism. He also offered to build the Karakoram highway from Khunjerab to Passu. The premier also spoke to him about the cultural revolution. He admitted that large scale disturbances have taken place in the country resulting in enormous casualties; even the army suffered a lot as they were told to control the situation without use of violence or weapons. The struggle often took place between over enthusiastics and others. The Cultural Revolution, which seems to be a passion with them, is dying down in the cities where things are under control and the idea now is to extend it to the rural areas. How are they going to keep it under control, there god alone knows. Nur Khan's impression is that Chou En-lai is holding the country together, but his health is failing through over work.

📖 The air force mission sent to UAR, Iraq and Kuwait came to report the outcome. About UAR the impression is that they have a large number of good aircraft, ground and radar equipment but their air force is demoralized and have little idea how to put this equipment to good use. They expect Pakistan to provide volunteers to manage their air force and fight for them. This we obviously can't do, as we have to be continuously watchful of India. Instead, we have decided to send half a dozen experienced pilots under a senior officer to train their leaders in the art of air combat who in turn should be able to train the rest. The same applies to the Iraqi Air Force. Kuwait's demands are modest. They want some technicians to be trained here, which we can easily do. There is some risk in hurting Iran's interest in doing this, but I have already spoken to the Shah. Besides, our presence and influence in these countries should be of assistance to Iran.

7 | THURSDAY

📖 Flew into Dacca and was received by a large number of people, members of assemblies and other notables. In the address of welcome delivered, I told people to remain united and work whole-heartedly for the advancement of the country and their own betterment.

📖 The Central Assembly is in session. A few days ago some of the opposition members created a scene and misbehaved in the house. The speaker ordered their removal. Since then they have been staying out. This caused some of our ministers concern and they foolishly started bargaining with the opposition for production of a face-saving device and their return. I told them this would make the opposition more irresponsible. The matter lies with the speaker and the opposition. He only told them to go out for the day. Now that they wish to stay out permanently, what is it that he can do?

There are some constitutional amendments before the assembly. One of them relates to increase of membership in the three assemblies from basic 150 to 200. The need has arisen because the weightage given to the smaller provinces in West Pakistan vis-à-vis the Punjab is coming to an end. If the membership is not increased, the representation of smaller provinces will be reduced by one third. From this some members of smaller provinces have developed an argument that just as there is parity between East and West Pakistan in spite of disparity in population, the same formula should apply to representation from different areas in West Pakistan. This is a fallacious argument and I would not be a bit surprised if some East Pakistanis have sown this idea. Their attempt, unfortunately, always is to keep West Pakistan divided. They don't realize the historical factors that apply to parity between East and West Pakistan. The object was federation of units of equal size, otherwise federation does not work whereas in West Pakistan the object is unification hence representation on the basis of population.

8 | FRIDAY

📖 I heard that this demand is gaining momentum, so called in Ghafoor Khan Hoti and told him to caution people of the dangers of raising such an issue. I think he was able to sober them down.

📖 I have drafted a paper on the problem of agriculture cooperatives. It is more in the form of a questionnaire. A number of problems will need detailed examination. A copy is below. I wonder how far the idea will succeed, but if accepted, it may well change the whole social pattern of society. However, we shall have to proceed with caution so that people don't get scared by misunderstanding the object.

President's House, Dacca
08 December 1967.

Land utilization system in Pakistan.

1. Natural calamities in East Pakistan coupled with sustained drought conditions in West Pakistan created an unprecedented food shortage in the country. This coincided with the time when American policy on PL-480 hardened, making it difficult to fill in the food gap on easy terms. Therefore, a large amount of cash resources had to be spent to buy food. This was a blow but had the effect of alarming both the government and the people. Everybody became conscious of the fact that unless we modernize agriculture, fill in the food gap, and indeed, produce more to export, we are sunk. So the search for better seeds, utilization of more fertilizers and pesticides and introduction of agricultural machineries started. Meanwhile, dissemination of information on these matters through all mass media commenced with the view to awaken the farmer to new opportunities and necessity. In consequence, we are by God's grace on the threshold of agricultural revolution in the country and the hope is that we shall very soon be self sufficient in food and may even have enough to export. This optimism is welcome but can we say that we have found an optimum final solution. I say no.
2. Maximizing of yields is possible only if agriculture is fully modernized and mechanized. Both these requirements demand large fields. This is not possible in our social and inheritance system where fragmentation of land holdings is inevitable and when the holdings themselves are so small. Consolidation of holdings is one solution, but it breaks down every time fresh inheritance opens. Cooperative farming is another alternative, provided it is compulsory. Voluntary cooperatives in our country have been abysmal failures.
3. When I talk about agriculture cooperatives I don't mean collectives. In the latter the right of private property is extinguished. This we must not do but at the same time this right should be established in a manner that the land does not get subdivided and that means giving the claimant's share rather like a cooperative society.
4. If this proposal be accepted then the following are some of the problems that will have to be resolved:
    a. What should be the size of a cooperative in irrigated and non-irrigated areas and then in East and West Pakistan?

b. How should the shareholding be determined on land revenue or the current market price of land contributed?

c. Where will the tenant fit in? Will he be entitled to any share, if so what would be the basis?

d. What should be the organization of the management and how should it be constituted, supervised and replaced in case of need?

e. Since agriculture cooperatives will be universal in the country, what higher hierarchy of the basic cooperative would be needed and what would be their function.

NOTE: For satisfaction of internal needs, fulfillment of export quotas, and requirements of agriculture-oriented industries, it would be necessary to lay down targets for each basic cooperative unit, *thana*, *tehsil*, district, division and province. Hence the need for an organization to each administrative tier. These tiers are also needed to lay down cropping pattern of taxation, arrange finance and material support and supervise marketing etc. Later they can be helpful for introducing more sophistication like processing of produce, cottage and small-scale industries etc.

f. How will the wages for the labourers and functionaries in the cooperatives be determined and how will the needy and indigent be taken care of?

g. How will the cooperatives be financed and what will be the marketing arrangements?

h. How will the profits be distributed?

i. Provision of machinery. Should it be owned by the cooperative or should the government provide this on hire? In either case, the chain of machinery pool and repair shops will have to be established.

j. What type of technical and professional manpower would be required in the basic cooperatives and above? A close liaison with the educational department would be needed to produce them

k. Because of paucity of funds, technical manpower and time required in motivation, introduction of machinery will have to be a slow process. But as time goes on, some manpower will be displaced from the land. What arrangements can be made for their gainful employment?

5. This scheme will have to be launched with great care and due preparation. Otherwise it will be dubbed as communistic and the landowners will feel that it amounts to expropriation and will get scared. Therefore, the following will need consideration:

a. Preparation of scheme.

b. Preparation of the atmosphere for launching.

c. Time of launching.

6. Finally, I would like to emphasize that in the process of modernization and industrialization, we must recognize the fact that land is our best and quickest return giving asset, besides we are a two-crop country. We must, therefore, make the most scientific and effective use of this asset. If we do that we shall bring satisfaction, happiness and contentment to people and keep social turmoil at bay, besides conforming to the concept of social justice of Islam. Also, we would have organized our society on a self regulating basis founded on mutualisms and active participation of large majority of people. This will inevitably release new ideas and dormant qualities of people. A great upsurge in thought and action would occur leading to greater material prosperity, political awakening and stability. The identical step of introducing cooperatives would be revolutionary

but the consequences that will follow would bring a far greater, healthy and peaceful social and economic revolution for the good of all. So the task is worth embarking upon in a scientific and well considered manner before it is thrust on us by circumstances over which we have no control.

Signed
Mohammad Ayub Khan
Field Marshal

📖 Mr Sultan,[97] our ambassador in Peking came to see me. He is normally a balanced, calm and cool and collected man. But he seemed shaken and perturbed over affairs in China. He did not think that the Chinese were in a complete mess and in a state of civil war, but there had been large scale disturbances and dislocations in the country through the Cultural Revolution. Why they brought it on themselves when they were doing so well in every walk of life was beyond comprehension. Now a curious phenomenon is occurring. Mere urchins are in control of everything and are in a position to command and question anybody and anything. Men with vast experience and tremendous background of sacrifices have been humiliated and demoralized. Chen-yi was treated like that. In fact, when he refused to bow his head in some confession, a youngster forcibly bent his neck. Chou En-lai's turn was coming next, but he escaped. Life in Peking is hell. From 7 a.m. to 11 a.m. loudspeakers blare out mass thoughts. Every day processions do the same. There is no source of entertainment, command performances in theatres are all propaganda on Mao's thoughts. It looks like the cities are getting a bit quieter, but there is a wave to shift these activities to the countryside. What will be the effect and how these urchins will behave is anybody's guess. The teachers have deserted schools and colleges, because the students show no respect to them and question their integrity at every step. I can't imagine any other country living under such conditions. Once these youngsters taste power and find an excuse to escape their work of study and learning, it would be impossible to bring them to heel again. Look at what we are suffering from, especially in Dacca, Karachi and Lahore, through use of students for political purposes during the independence struggle and later by the politicians.

10 | SUNDAY

📖 Flew to Kaptai dam on an amphibian plane. Later carried out the inauguration of the Dawood Rayon and Cellophane factories. A large number of people attended the ceremony. This project is gigantic and original in concept, costing 13 crores. It is based on bamboo which is produced in that area. Ahmed Dawood, though an uneducated man, has original ideas and is a very sound businessman. He, with his brother, now owns a vast industrial empire.

📖 On the way out to Kaptai and back I told Monem Khan how several streams and rivers in the area can be used for the purpose of low irrigation. The trouble is that the administration and engineers in East Pakistan are not conscious of such great opportunities that are crying for exploitation. Great wealth is being lost through ignorance.

11 | MONDAY

Returned to Dacca.

12 | TUESDAY

Flew to Mongla by an amphibian plane and landed amongst a large number of cargo ships that were boarding and unloading. This is going to be an inland port, well protected from weather hazards and capable of accommodating a large number of ships. Already it is handling 1.5 million tons of cargo a year. The anchorage has a water depth of 90 feet and so can accommodate any size ship, but there is a large sand bar near the sea that limits the size of the ships that can enter the river. This will have to be dredged some day. An expensive, but necessary operation.

Addressed a large public meeting arranged by the Khulna Muslim League. I spoke for about an hour and exposed the pretensions of the opposition thoroughly. I warned the people that all opposition leaders have been tried and found wanting. Their sole aim is promoting of selfish interests at the cost of the people. Their attitude is that they have nothing constructive to offer to the people. The people should be particularly wary of them and especially the proposals of 21-points, 6-points and 8-points and other points. Their real aim, which they don't want to disclose in case the people get alarmed, is to weaken the central government, separate East Pakistan and accept the over-lordship of India. In other words, they want to take the people back to slavery. I hit them hard in other respects, too. I believe the opposition is smarting under my words. Their trouble is they cannot answer what I say and they also know that they are being thoroughly exposed. After the meeting, flew to Tiger Point at the end of the Sunderbans and spent the night in the governor's launch, *Mary Anderson*.

13 | WEDNESDAY

Boarded a small launch for a crocodile shoot. We cruised around for about four hours but saw only one young croc, who jumped into the water as soon as he got scent of us. Sunderbans is a beautiful marshy forest, crisscrossed by many streams and rivulets. It is infested with tigers, deer and wild boars, but negotiation of the forest is very difficult because of the tide water that goes over it. Besides the surface is covered with spikes and *sunderi* roots which stick out nearly two feet, varying from three inches to three feet. These are, in fact, the roots of certain trees that come up for breathing and the tree is called *sunderi*, a phenomenon unheard of elsewhere. That is the reason why these tigers are not easy to get at. Hardly three or four are shot in a year. I believe they are small in size because of the climatic conditions, but clad with shining fur. This is because of plentiful and easy feeding. They live on hogs and deer.

Returned to Dacca in the afternoon. There is an indication in the Dacca press that there are indications even otherwise that Bengalis are disappointed that they were not able to split the West Pakistanis in the National Assembly over the 8th constitutional amendment. They were hoping to, even perhaps working, that the Sindhis and the Pathans would rebel again the Punjabis once the question of representation in the assemblies came up. Luckily, I was here to smoothen this mischief in time.

14 | THURSDAY

The meeting of the Economic Council was held. The Planning Commission's paper on growing disparity in GNP between East and West Pakistan in spite of higher allocations to East Pakistan, was discussed. The Planning Commission view is that this is due to the fact that their projects are not wisely chosen, a lot of waste takes place. Money is spent on the public sector which just provides the infrastructure for the private sector which they do not encourage, and through neglect of the agriculture sector. The East Pakistanis are reluctantly admitting this, and demand that more should be spent here in the public sector and that even money spent on defence and the central government organs should be equally divided. How do you deploy defence forces and split the central government to meet their needs of parity is not understood, and how will spending more money on the public sector do any good when the private sector, which produces goods and services, is not allowed to grow. The central government and the West Pakistan Government exposed the fallacies and complained bitterly that East Pakistan is a bottomless pit. Both the centre and West Pakistan are suffering through trying to fill it. My sum up was that the causes of this malady were the following:

a. I fulfilled my promise of giving more resources to East Pakistan but they have proved unworthy of this sacrifice.
b. Their main aim is to get resources from the centre and use them without any regard to the welfare of the people.
c. The centre–province relations were wrong.
d. The centre raises resources with great difficulty and the provinces spend. As the liability for repayment and debts lies at the centre, the provinces have no compulsion to show financial discipline. This has to be corrected.

The real trouble is that Governor Monem Khan, though a very good man, knows nothing about economics, development or higher administration. All these things are in the hands of Dr Huda,[98] a Bengali civil servant. These are limited, bigoted, provincialist and have never been famed for a balanced outlook or sense of responsibility. Besides, I don't think they are up to these tasks. They are little men with narrow vision. Coaxing may help, but only up to a limited point. So it does not require a prophet to predict the future of East Pakistan. It can only be in level of men running it, who themselves suffer from grave limitations.

The Indian high commissioner called. He had been wanting to see me for some time. He said the feeling in India was growing that the enmity with Pakistan was brazen and an expensive hobby and that India would like to find ways and means of normalizing relations with Pakistan, but the trouble is that Pakistan lays down preconditions of settlement of Kashmir. Could not some progress be made in other spheres? I told him that there had been two wars on Kashmir. This fight had been going on for 20 years in other spheres. So how could there be any measure of trust without its settlement and reduction of armed forces. He proposed that nothing much could happen without a joint declaration of intent by me and Mrs Indira Gandhi as a start. I told him that my intentions should be clear. I want settlement of all outstanding problems with India including Kashmir on an honourable and just basis. If Mrs Indira Gandhi is prepared to make such a declaration, I shall gladly join her. He said he will go and put this proposal before her. I don't know how genuine Indians are, but there is no harm in keeping the doors of negotiations open and testing their faith.

15 | FRIDAY

📖 Qazi Qadir,[99] our minister in East Pakistan, came to see me. He has been a good Muslim League worker but feels neglected by Monem who also has reasons to distrust him. However, we must not frustrate him too much. He made a startling statement. Bengalis are by nature treacherous and unreliable, but they have faith in me. Even the opposition seems to think that their personal safety is due to me. What would have happened in the last war if I were not at the helm of the affairs?

📖 I am told the people are asking that why my Bengali ministers do not speak out about the opposition the way I do. The reason is simple. They have no guts even if they have convictions, which is doubtful.

📖 We discussed the redrafted report to be put before the House on interregional parity and passed it with slight amendments. It was repeated that the answer lay in East Pakistan on taking its finger out and getting down to managing its economic affairs in a sensible way.

16 | SATURDAY

📖 Visited army units in Tejgaon. They are in the process of doing individual training, which I thought was very realistic, earnest and imaginative. Everybody seemed keen, alert and conscious of his responsibilities. A great awakening has come to this army after the 1965 war. The gunners have started training young Bengali Mujahids in simple gunnery. They are coming on well indeed. They have also evolved a simple but effective method of towing guns on country roads by bullocks. This will add to their cross country mobility.

17 | SUNDAY

📖 Even talked to the senior civil officers in East Pakistan, central and provincial ministers and the central secretaries, the précis of the talk is attached below.

Dacca
17th December 1967

Points for talks to the senior officers in Dacca:

1. Happy to see you and have the opportunity to address you. Also be available to answer any question you may wish to ask. Please don't hesitate to do so.

2. On taking over in 1958, I found the country in the following state:
   a. Failure of politicians. Why?
   b. People unaware of dangers to their very existence.
   c. An unworkable political structure and mess.
   d. Demoralized administration lacking purpose or the will.
   e. State lacking any coherent policy.
   f. Economic mess.
   g. Society riddled with parochialism.
   h. A sense of grievance in East Pakistan that it is economically neglected and that it is not getting the opportunity to run itself and that it is being colonized by West Pakistan.

   A very depressing state of affairs indeed, but it was not without hope. I felt that Pakistan could still be saved and given purpose in life.

   I have no superhuman power. All I could offer was sincerity of purpose and spirit of dedication, in other words, my best. I hope that the solution I offered would be regarded as conducive to the promotion of people's self interest.

   I could only offer solutions. Implementation depended on the people. If they played their part, I felt they should find their salvation. This was true then and it is true today. So what I have tried to do in the past nine years was in accordance with the set purpose and a definite aim. At no time was there any groping in the dark.

3. Unify this nation based on the ideology of enlightened Islam. Give it purpose in life and set it on the task of reconstruction and development to enable it to enter this age of science and technology as fast as possible. It depended on its progress and salvation.

4. Steps taken and still being taken:
   a. Make people aware of these harsh realities. To what extent I have succeeded, I don't know. I don't expect total conformity, but do hope for some conversions.
   b. Revive civil administration to enable it to perform its new task with confidence and courage. That is why:
      i. Screening
      ii. Sensible disciplinary court, but protection of the presidential system.
      iii. Providing opportunities for refresher courses and reorientation.
      iv. Creation of autonomous bodies and their reasons.
      v. Toning up the district and divisional administration.
      vi. Assuring East Pakistan to run the administration by East Pakistanis. Some people don't like this, but there is no other way to giving self confidence to people. However, you are on trial. You will be judged by the results you achieve.
   c. In the economic field:
      i. Giving East Pakistan much larger allocation. Attainment of parity made a state policy. Meaning parity, parity of opportunities and is also parity of endeavour. Dead parity can be obtained in a very short time by stopping West Pakistan from doing anything. But, I want East Pakistan to pull in level with West Pakistan. Don't think that West Pakistan is all developed.
      ii. Reorganizing and making effective planning arrangements in the centre and provinces.

iii. Doing utmost to gain confidence in the minds of donors and aid givers. Pakistan now cited as an example.

iv. Second plan a thumping success. Third plan going well in spite of difficulties, note of caution about loans.

v. East Pakistan will do well if it observes the following:
  a) Labour intensive and high yielding projects.
  b) Avoidance of waste.
  c) Less emphasis on public sector and more and more emphasize on private sector. There is a need to get over mental inhibitions and suspicions of outside capital.
  d) Emphasis on agriculture.

d. Organize the society in self regulating units in the form of BD and giving the country a presidential form of government to ensure stability. Our system being closely watched by the rest of the world.

5. Harmonizing life throughout the country by giving common system of education, law and administration. Introduction of religious institutions and production of new books.

6. Carrying out reform in every walk of life. The amount of scientific examinations carried out of problems are simply enormous.

7. I believe these measures have served the country well. Given this rate of progress for the next 15–20 years, the face of the country should change. It is in everybody's interest to see that this process is not interrupted. Remember this process can be sustained only if political and economic stability is maintained.

What of the future?
  a. Let us get over parochialism and narrow mindedness. These things are out of date and self defeating.
  b. Country's future depends on working this constitution. If essentials are touched, the country would be lost.
  c. Internal peace and harmony should be maintained so that all energies concentrated on the attainment of our aim.
  d. Future of autonomous bodies, some advice:
    a) Watch smuggling.
    b) Have faith in the constitution.
    c) Support stability and support those who support it.

Signed
Mohammed Ayub Khan
Field Marshal

📖 Invited a number of jute industrialists and the finance and commerce ministers with their secretaries to dinner and let them talk about economic matters and adjustments required to be carried out after the devaluation of the pound sterling. They are all going to meet tomorrow to thrash out details, but it is obvious that by and large the measures we have taken are sound. The talk was all about high economics but I was able to take a useful part in it as I am now quite familiar with their language.

18 | MONDAY

📖 Had consultations with East Pakistan's secretariat, WAPDA, and ADC officers on extension of irrigation and promotion of agriculture. They seem to be taking interest in the problem, especially the young lot.

📖 Left Dacca and reached Karachi in the evening. The 12 day visit to East Pakistan was quite fruitful. It helped me to see how things were going. I was also able to goad the administration to do better. They need this continuously.

19 | TUESDAY

📖 I had asked President Johnson's assistance to send us experts to help formulate a plan for watershed management to prolong the life of Mangla and Tarbela and to reclaim eroded lands on Potohar plateau. He very kindly sent an advance party of four experts. It stayed in Pakistan for a week or so and had a preliminary look. They came to report their findings. In their view both these problems are manageable, though involving considerable labour and cost. They promised to send out a bigger team to go into the problems in detail and submit a comprehensive report. I hope this will be ready by the end of the year, when we can get going in right earnest.

📖 Chaudhary Khaliquzzaman came to see me in the evening. He gave me a book which he has recently written. It is all about the struggle for Pakistan and the part he played in it. He also spoke about the Muslim League matters. He is very a earnest and dedicated old man but now getting fussy about small matters due to old age.

20 | WEDNESDAY

📖 Flew to Nawabshah and did partridge shooting in the Pai full of birds mostly black partridges. The bag was 244 amongst three guns. I shot 139.

📖 Flew into Rawalpindi in the evening. A number of my children and grandchildren were present. I had a very relaxing hour or so with them.

21 | THURSDAY

📖 Took a day off and worked at home. I am in the process of reading a book called *Revolutions or Dictatorship* written by R.E. Kapoor,[100] an ex ICS officer. It is a book about Indian development efforts, politics, and foreign policy, and is fascinating to read. It is the first time I have come across an Indian writing with such candour and sense of realism. His view is that Indian pretensions of bigness, grandeur, tall talk and her bad relations with her neighbour, her weak political and social structure will spell her ruination.

22 | FRIDAY

📖 The American ambassador saw my principal secretary at short notice. He said that President Johnson was on a visit to Australia, seeks permission to fly over Pakistan air space, land at Karachi for refuelling and see me if possible, but all this must be kept strictly secret and that all measures should be taken for the president's security. I told him that I shall go down to see him and that other requirements will also be taken care of.

📖 The DIB submitted a report of the investigations of a conspiracy to bring about independent Bengal by force of arms, unearthed in East Pakistan. The leader of the movement is alleged to be a young Bengali naval officer. He, with the connivance of the Indian mission in Dacca and assistance of a few others, approached a large number of junior army people, civil servants and politicians in an attempt to sell the idea. Many showed sympathy including a minister in the central government. Some like Manibur Rehman gave active encouragement, but the only two who refused to have anything to do with it were Mashiur Rehman[101] and Mohan Mian, both in the opposition. They said they will have nothing to do with unconstitutional means. The decision to how to deal with these people will be taken after the inquiry is complete.

23 | SATURDAY

📖 Malik Muzaffar, Nawab of Kalabagh's son, came to see me and narrated the events that led to the Nawab's murder. It appears that Asad, his son, killed him in self-defence but there was no love lost between the father and his sons in that they are not all that sorry that he has gone. Muzaffar blamed the close associates of Nawab who poisoned his mind against the sons. They kept his mind disturbed and in any case since his departure from governorship, he had become unduly irritable.

📖 Flew down to Karachi some two hours before Johnson's arrival to see that all arrangements were laid on. I had sent my foreign minister and the principal secretary in advance to attend to them. President Johnson arrived at 2:00 p.m. On getting down from the aircraft he shook my hand warmly and embraced me, an unusual practice with the westerners. We then both went into a separate room and held private talks on international problems, but more so on our mutual problems. On Vietnam, he is anxious to terminate fighting, but on his own terms. He seemed well satisfied with the performance of the commanders and the troops in the field and showed no anxiety about the outcome. He said he had no intention of escalating the war in North Vietnam, nor getting involved with Russia and China. He had refused to allow bombing of Haiphong, which is often full of Russian and Chinese ships. After Pearl Harbour, he knew what bombing of shipping can lead to. About our mutual problem, he promised to look into the following:

a. Permission to buy second hand American type of tanks in Europe or America.
b. Give another half a million tons of wheat under PL 480.
c. See that our aid cut is the minimum.

He congratulated me on our economic performance and I thanked him for the several things he had done for us lately. He inquired about the relationship with India. I told him that the Indian leaders had shown no anxiety to patch up with us. On the future presidential elections, he was not sure he would stand. The Johnsons drive hard, and die young. He has already had a heart attack and does not want to die on the country like Woodrow Wilson. My own belief is that Johnson will contest if he saw a good chance. At present, he is not certain. Vietnam has given his image and prestige a great setback. Health will be the cover should he decide not to contest.

24 | SUNDAY

Flew to Mohenjodaro and went to Larkana for a duck shoot with Hussain Ali at Lung. It is a small lake but a great sanctuary. I saw an awful lot of birds there, but it happened to be a cold, cloudy day, so the birds either departed after a few shots or flew very high. I bagged 55 birds.

25 | MONDAY

Had a briefing by the engineer in charge of the Larkana drainage scheme. This district is severely affected by waterlogging and salinity. Besides, their rice crop has been destroyed by the stem-borer pest for several successive years. In consequence, people show visible signs of impoverishment. Once the drains are complete, a large proportion of their lands will be reclaimed, but the problem of the stem-borer will still remain, the real answer to which lies in uprooting the rice stubs in the whole district and burning them, but the people are too ignorant or lazy to do so. I suggest changing the crop pattern. If sugar mills are installed, they could switch over to sugarcane, which is a lucrative cash crop.

Inspected the rice research station at Dhorki, some 18 miles from Larkana. This station is run by an agricultural scientist called Abbasi, who is extremely knowledgeable and is doing excellent work. I am going to recommend that he should be suitably awarded.

Met the local Muslim Leaguers and other notables and entertained them to dinner. They looked a keen lot.

26 | TUESDAY

Was to shoot at Drigh Lake, but had to give up the idea because of inclement weather and instead flew to Rawalpindi. The flight was hectic. Flew through the clouds most of the time, and later had to do very low level flying to land at Pindi where it was pouring with rain.

27 | WEDNESDAY

The Germans have made the lowest bid for the Tarbela Dam. Their bid has been examined and found to be all right except that they have raised certain conditions which are contrary to terms and conditions as laid down by WAPDA. It looks like they are trying to be difficult either to extract something more from us or back out of the contract. So I have directed Aftab Kazi to proceed to Washington where the German representatives are and tell them not to make asses of themselves. Meanwhile, I have directed him to put the German ambassador in the picture and tell him that if his people do not behave, we shall be obliged to go to the next lowest bidder. Aftab Kazi told me that the water storage in Khanpur Dam can be doubled by spending an extra four and a half crores rupees. All the water discharge of the river can then be impounded and utilized, but it does mean submerging of an extra seven thousand acres and the whole of Khanpur village. I told him to go ahead with it. He also explained to me the plan of storing all the extra water of the Indus after Tarbela in the Thal desert. This will bring immense benefit to the country.

28 | THURSDAY

📖 We have had a very wet spell in West Pakistan for the past week or so. This should do an immense amount of good to the wheat crop. Mr Fida Hassan, my principal secretary, has been retired from service and appointed as my advisor with the rank of a minister. He was itching to see this happen, but I am happy to retain him. He has served me very well indeed. He is sober and sensible and commands trust.

📖 I met the law minister, who is in Lahore, and told him that he should arrange for the present attorney general to make way for Mr Pirzada, our foreign minister. I think he will do better in that capacity. Meanwhile, I shall take over the foreign ministry myself and make Fida Hassan do the running around when needed.

📖 I have decided to replace three East Pakistani ministers, if I can find suitable replacements. These people are dead weight to me. They contribute nothing administratively or politically. I had placed considerable hope on Altaf Hussain. As the editor of *Dawn*, he used to criticize and admonish the whole world, but since he has become the minister, he has turned into a dead mouse. He just does not open his mouth in public.

📖 The Russian ambassador brought me mounted heads of stags I shot in Russia. They are beautifully done. One of them has six points. He also brought films of my visit to the Soviet Union. He later read out a report indicating what his government was doing to induce India to settle some problems with Pakistan. That is the reason why the Indian High Commissioner has lately been making faint approaches to us to negotiate peripheral things. We have decided to discuss resumption of air services, we have also asked the Indians to discuss the diversion of the waters of the Ganges after the construction of Farakka Barrage.[102] The Indians are only willing to do so on the technical level. In other words, they want to drag their feet.

30 | SATURDAY

📖 Reports from Kabul indicate that the Afghan government's attitude towards us is hardening and they are going to freeze the relations as they are. The excuse is that remarks in my book about Kabul's intention towards Pakistan. The reality is that the king having found during his recent visit that we were not going to allow them right of interference in our internal affairs, a demand palpably unreasonable, surrendered to the hard liners like Etamadi[103] who is now the prime minister and a protégée of Daud.[104] So we are in for intensified cold war with that country again. This is nothing new, we know how to deal with it.

📖 Reports from Delhi indicate that the Indians want to trap Abdullah and Afzal Baig by offering them re-elections in occupied Kashmir. They seem to be tempted to accept this in the hope that they will be able to gain majority and form a government. Once they do that, they would have accepted the Indian constitution and all talks of freedom of choice to the Kashmiris through a plebiscite would die a natural death.

31 | SUNDAY

📖 Went to inspect my orchards in Badalpur. The citrus is now ripe and looks beautiful. The Mexi-Pak wheat which is cultivated is also coming out well.

DIARY 1968

1 | MONDAY

📖 Nawab of Kalabagh's servant Noor Mohammad came to see me and told me his tale of woe. He complained that the Nawab's sons are persecuting him because of his loyalty and fidelity to their father. The district administration had to be told to give him due protection.

📖 The Eid-ul-Fitr moon was sighted tonight and announced by the radio. There was no fuss by the political mullahs. They have probably come to realize that their demand for running a parallel government is not going to work.

2 | TUESDAY

📖 Eid prayers were held all over the country with great enthusiasm. The weather, too, was fine. A large number of people came to my house to offer greetings.

3 | WEDNESDAY

📖 I went to my village in the afternoon where I had invited people of my family from several villages to tea. Many turned up and it was a very fine gathering. My wife had also gone to the village and a large number of women from surrounding villages also came to see her. In fact, this happens whenever she goes there. She gets little peace, but she is so fond of her house that she goes there often to get a bit of change.

5 | FRIDAY

📖 The defence minister, the C-in-C army, and the defence and foreign secretaries came to see me in connection with making up the deficiency of tank population in the army. There is a need to replace the old Shermans and make good the war losses, although some 230 tanks have been received from China and 270 more are expected during the next five years. Their proposal was to buy 250 new German or French tanks and the rest from the second-hand American service stocks in Europe. The Americans have agreed to release 100 now and consider release of another 100 later. These we could retrofit and upgrade within the country. I told them that buying new tanks from Germany was out of the question. For political reasons, the Germans just won't sell them. The French AMX 30 is very expensive, and would probably take just as long in getting as the Chinese tanks. The answer was going on buying as many second-hand American tanks in Europe as possible and put new diesel engines in them and keep on agitating with the Russians for advance T series tanks. Don't underrate the Chinese promise, and finally, put new diesel engines in as many old Shermans as possible. All these measures should give us all the tank population we need. Meanwhile, in conjunction with Balkow, the possibility of manufacturing light tanks within the country.

They told me that the Russians are being mangy. They are demanding advance payment for a small consignment of gun ammunition they are sending us for testing. I told the foreign office to take this matter up with them.

📖 The press has reported the North Vietnamese foreign minister said that they would come to the conference table if the Americans stopped bombing and other war-like activities. This is a confirmation of what I had gathered from the Romanian prime minister sometime back. I hope the Americans take advantage of this offer and get out of this muck into which they have bogged down, though their enemies would like to see them wasting themselves for as long as possible.

📖 I have been reading some literature on Indian internal and foreign policy and its military and economic efforts. Thoughtful Indians are of the view that they are very faulty and have cost India dearly. India is bleeding white and the people are undergoing unbearable sufferings. Two things have unbalanced India completely: the 1962 clash with China and the 1965 war with Pakistan. The military budget has gone up inordinately high. So, whilst wanting a Kashmir solution, we should show no undue anxiety. Let India bleed till she can no longer bear the burden of big power chauvinism. She may then come to her senses and realize the value of peaceful neighbourly relations with Pakistan. In any case forcing the pace by us won't help as it did not do in the past.

Sheikh Abdullah has been released by India lately. This is no particular indication of India's peaceful intentions towards us. I think they want him to accept the inevitable of a settlement within the Indian constitution. There are some doubts if he would fall prey to these temptations. His people won't accept it even if he wishes to. However, whilst wishing him well we should avoid building him up too much. He is not all that trustworthy a character. Our best bet is Afzal Baig, who is a much more solid and dependable man.

📖 The DIB [Director Intelligence Bureau], reported that a spate of rumours are afloat regarding the conspiracy case in East Pakistan and the consequent arrests. Therefore, there is a need to take the public into confidence and issue a press statement. Other ministers were not in favour, but I have forced the pace and caused the whole story to be published. I think it should have a good effect. However, the complicity of Indian diplomatic staff in Dacca indeed had to be divulged and one of their representatives named. A demand had to be made for his withdrawal. They, in retaliation, have expelled one of our diplomatic staff. This is nothing new and was expected.

📖 I was discussing the conspiracy case with Khawaja Shahabuddin and the maladies from which East Pakistan suffers. His view was that my staying there longer would help. I told him that for one I am a busy man and I can only function from the base, and secondly, such a solution cannot have a lasting effect and change by changing the psychology of people.

---

6 | SATURDAY

📖 A spate of religious leaders came to see me on Tuesday. Pir Dewal followed by Kausar Niazi and then Pir Zakori.[1] All had their plans for moulding public opinion, but basically all are antagonistic to each other. The explanation of these plans was, of course, followed by a series of personal requests and favours. I asked a friend as to what attitude should I take towards them. His answer was that this class of people is only good for creating mischief and causing confusion. They have never done any good to Muslim society and have always been a headache for the Muslim state. To divert their attention from antagonism to the state, the answer was to let them neutralize each other by infighting, which is, in any case, their main preoccupation. If this analysis be true then it is a sad commentary on the conduct of our priesthood.

📖 People not in touch with realties often wonder why it is not possible to make solid and well disciplined political parties in the country. I, too, used to think the same until it dawned on me that historically, Muslims, for that matter oriental people, have supported causes but have not sustained party programmes. It has never been our historical experience. That is why building up the Muslim League party has been such a slow process.

7 | SUNDAY

📖 After a long discussion with Khawaja Shahabuddin and Altaf Gauhar decided to make collections of private libraries and Muslim League records and put them in the national library, otherwise they would all be wasted and destroyed. We also decided to have the following books written on behalf of the Muslim League:

a. Biography of the Quaid-e-Azam.
b. History of the Muslim League and its struggle for attaining Pakistan.
c. The perfidious role played by certain Muslim dignitaries and organizations.

8 | MONDAY

📖 General Aryana, the chairman of the joint chief of staff of the Iranian Armed Forces came to call on me. He was accompanied by General Tuania, the officer who made a lot of purchases for us during the 1965 war. They broached the subject of joint production of tanks and other heavier weapons and asked for our support in inducing Kuwait and Saudi Arabia to participate. I told them that the tank I was interested in is different, but there may be other spheres in which collaboration would be possible. But the trouble was that in spite of a lot of sweet talk, nothing much happens. If we are serious then we must start doing something concrete. It is only then that others would be interested in collaborating with us. They agreed and promised to speak to the Shah.

9 | TUESDAY

📖 Abdul Jabbar Khan, the Speaker, came to see me and spoke with great feeling about the East Pakistan conspiracy case. He condemned the conspirators and the opposition parties vehemently. He may have other limitations, but he certainly does not lack patriotism. His misfortune is that he has several sons who are particularly political agitators who keep on going in and out of jail for their misdeeds. This must be a source of great worry to him.

📖 I sent for Abdus Sobur Khan and questioned him on the part he is alleged to have played in the conspiracy. He denied all knowledge and tried to show that the people in East Pakistan are greatly shocked by the incident. They think that whatever reputation they had built during the war has been demolished and that they have been put back by 20 years or more.

Anyhow, one good thing has come out of the publication of full details of the conspiracy. The whole spate of wild rumours and speculations have come to an end. One of the things that was being talked about in Dacca was that all this was trumped up by West Pakistan to malign and discredit East Pakistani civil servants. I knew that such like stories would be made up. That is why I told the reluctant officials to come out with the whole truth.

10 | WEDNESDAY

📖 Marshal Tito of Yugoslavia and his wife arrived on a week's visit.

11 | THURSDAY

📖 Official talks started with Marshal Tito. We first talked separately. He inquired about the relationship with India and the fate of the Tashkent Declaration.[2] I told him that India had killed it as she had no intention of settling Kashmir with us. After a good deal of discussion, he told me that he will do his best to impress on the Indian leadership the necessity of normalizing relations with Pakistan. In that case, a great strength could come to this subcontinent. I thanked him for this, knowing full well that any such talk will make no impression on the Indian leaders. This meeting was followed by a full-scale discussion on the world and economic problems in the presence of our representative teams. The tone was very high. About the Middle East, we agreed that nothing much will come out. The Arabs were divided, Israelis were getting more obstinate and the American administration was in full support of them. His foreign minister gave a hopeful picture of Europe. He expressed no strong feeling on Vietnam.

📖 Arshad Hussain, our High Commissioner to Delhi, came to see me and reported on his meeting with Afzal Baig and Abdullah. His impression was that whereas Abdullah looked well and unnerved in his stand, surprisingly, Afzal Baig was softening. Baig was being converted to the idea of taking part in fresh elections if held with the hope of forming a government. He does not realize that it was a trap whereby the Indians wanted to kill the plebiscite demand once and for all. I told Arshad Hussain to warn Afzal Baig and Abdullah. Their background was agitation. They should maintain that. Once they came into the administrative field they would be finished. As to coming to Pakistan, Abdullah should refrain from doing so unless the Indian leaders had shown genuine desire of settlement with Pakistan, otherwise he will only get discredited.

12 | FRIDAY

📖 Saw Tito off at the Chaklala airfield. He left for a night's stay in Lahore.

13 | SATURDAY

📖 Left for Karachi in the evening. Received Tito and his party at the airport, later took him for a round of inspection of the Karachi shipyard where Yugoslavs are collaborating with us in building ships. We also took a trip round Karachi Port, which was full of ships.

📖 Khawaja Shahabuddin sent me a note on the East Pakistan conspiracy. A copy, together with my reply, is affixed below. I am afraid my reply is caustic, but it had to be so. I have very little patience with unreliable people. The accused in the East Pakistan conspiracy have been taken into custody under DPR [Defence of Pakistan Rules] where the intention is to try them by a court martial. I rang up Yahya and warned him that the DPR has been destroyed by the Supreme Court on behest of Cornelius. If he is not careful, all these people will soon be let off by the High Court and the whole case will get into a mess. The opposition will take full advantage of it to malign the government and mislead the people. He must, therefore, take them into military custody and charge them under the Army Act.

These are noble thoughts and one would like to think that the recent conspiratorial activities were confined to a few misguided people in East Pakistan. But the world knows the truth and no amount of whitewashing is going to hide it. The truth is that a hymn of hate against the central government, West Pakistan in general, and Punjabis in particular has been assiduously chanted, by practically every shade of East Pakistani politician, from the inception of Pakistan. The motives have varied and I don't have to narrate them here except that the unification and solidarity of Pakistan has never been one of them. So what has come to light now is neither surprising nor unexpected. You can only expect to reap what you sow. That is the law of nature. So to say that East Pakistani politicians, and particularly the opposition, have no hand in it and do not subscribe to it, belies the truth. Mr Jabbar Khan, the speaker, has a sense of honesty and has told the truth, however, unvarnished it may have been.

What sort of statements our central ministers from East Pakistan should give on the conspiracy is up to them to decide. They would probably prefer not to be called upon to put themselves in an embarrassing situation. Barring one or two, the rest have so far diligently refrained from guiding their people on any sensible lines. Those who used to lecture to the world have ceased talking even in their sleep through a morbid fear of becoming unpopular. They seem to think that they are the darlings of the people in East Pakistan and will remain so by keeping their mouths shut. Let them continue to do so.

Signed
Mohammed Ayub Khan
Field Marshal.

📖 Letter written earlier by Khawaja Shahabuddin dated 10/01/68.

Submitted for President's perusal.

We have given a great deal of thought to the question of the issue of statements by political leaders, especially from East Pakistan, but ultimately came to the conclusion that it will be wise not to do so particularly as this might be used by the defence as prejudicing the trial court. However, I would like one thing to be kept in mind and whenever an opportunity occurs it should be emphasized that the names of the culprits conclusively prove that the East Pakistanis as a people have not the slightest idea or inclination of secession. As a matter of fact they are in no way less loyal and staunch Pakistanis than any other citizen of Pakistan. Otherwise, the prevalent feeling amongst certain sections of West Pakistanis that the East Pakistanis are generally unpatriotic and pro-West Bengal will gain confirmation.

I would like to urge humbly, but firmly, that the following may also be kept in view while dealing with this very delicate matter:

1. So far there is no indication of any political party being involved. Therefore, it will be unfortunate if government leaders or pro-government spokesmen were to cast reflection on them. Otherwise, the impression may gain ground that the government is trying to take advantage of the ill-conceived activities of a handful of disgruntled people to suppress their political rivals. Statements like the one made by the speaker are likely to be misinterpreted or misrepresented.

2. It may, on the other hand, give the impression that it was all cooked up by the government in order to beat down the opposition.

3. The political leaders themselves have been guilty of such tactics in the past and so people would readily believe it with the result that main culprit, India, will be exonerated. It may also give the impression here and abroad that there is substantial support for such an idea.

4. There is another danger in accusing the entire opposition or any particular political party. The supporters and sympathizers of the opposition will become resentful and frustrated because an aspersion was being cast on their patriotism and people may come to look upon them with suspicion. In such an atmosphere, they would become easy prey for anti-state activities or activities against the government.

5. It is, therefore, essential that this matter should be treated on a national and not partisan basis by all concerned. If the president agrees with this I would suggest that:
   a. A directive should go to all ministers and government spokesmen to keep the above points in mind.
   b. Similar instructions should be issued by the party to all its important leaders.

Signed
Khawaja Shahabudin

📖 Took President Tito to inspect the Karachi shipyard where Yugoslavs are cooperating with us in shipbuilding. I was glad to note that this shipyard has already got going and is manufacturing several types of machinery. I then took him around the harbour which is now handling over 9 millions tons of cargo but in view of the expanding economy of the province either the capacity of this port will have to be expanded or another one will have to be built.

📖 We are getting more protests from Arabs countries on Tayyab Hussain's statement on the name for the Persian Gulf and the Straits of Bahrain. This wretched man has created an unnecessary problem for us.

📖 News came in that Cambodia has smashed a plot to blow up Marshal Tito when on a visit to that country. Tito was not much perturbed but thought that it was unnecessary for Prince Sihanouk to dramatize the event or broadcast it to the world. The assassins are alleged to be of Chinese origin. Tito could not make out why they wanted to kill him when he was doing so much for Vietnam.

📖 Met Agha Raza at a party. He started talking about the changed attitude of the Shah of Iran. He though that Zahedi, their foreign minister, was the villain of the piece. He was responsible for misleading the Shah and so long as he was there, relations between the two countries will remain strained. It was he who was responsible for persuading the Shah to make up with India after Chagla's visit to Tehran.

📖 Asked Tito if he would be willing to sell us arms and ammunition. He agreed willingly. He promised to let our ambassador have a list of what they were manufacturing so that we could choose what we need.

14 | SUNDAY

📖 Took Marshal Tito to Mirpur Sakro for a duck shoot. Normally the lake is full of birds this time of the year. Unfortunately, there were very few birds today. Besides there was a strong breeze. The birds were, therefore, flying very high. Tito shot five birds and I shot 27. However, he seemed to have enjoyed the day. On the way back, he expressed the desire that relationship between the two countries should permanently grow and there should be greater economic collaboration. I have welcomed this suggestion provided the items of terms of credit were made more acceptable. He promised to look into it when he got back home.

Marshal Tito is 75 years of age but he is vivacious, alert, full of life and well preserved. He likes the good things of life and leads a luxurious life. Somebody said that he has the coldest pair of eyes he has ever seen. If true, he needs and deserves them as otherwise how could Tito have gone through what he has, survived and built his nation. He may be a demagogue but he is a builder with an acute economic sense. That, I believe, is his strongest point. He is extremely shrewd, has good judgement of men and is a man of few words, but every word he utters has meaning. He also has a sense of humour and a humane approach. As the Queen of England once told me, for a brigand he has done remarkably well. Madam Tito, of course, is a lady with great charm and attraction. You cannot help admiring her.

15 | MONDAY

📖 Saw Marshal Tito and his party off in the morning and then went to inspect the naval installations, especially the assembly of midget submarines. These are two types, one carrying a crew of nine and has a range of 1200 miles, the other carries only two people, frogmen. The latter one is a curious contraption. It is open from top and bottom. When it dives, the crew also submerges into water. Both types are designed to get close to enemy ships and fix timed charges and then get away. The bigger ones can also carry a couple of torpedoes that can fire from a range of 3000 yards. These midgets, together with the full sized submarines we are getting from France, should give our navy a pretty good punch and the ability to hit the enemy at the surface.

16 | TUESDAY

📖 Attended a dinner party at the naval mess at Karsaz. Met a large number of naval officers. Moved by road to Chandio's lake in Sajawal area, crossing the river Indus at the new bridge. It is going to be a long and expensive bridge but will link lower Sindh area east of the river with Karachi thus facilitating quick movement of men and material to the Karachi market.

17 | WEDNESDAY

📖 I told the commerce minister on the phone that his ministry should consider levying surcharge on goods imported on commodity aid and our own foreign exchange to level up with the international value of our rupee. We have to mop up surplus money and public finances to also ensure that goods don't become too cheap in the country. They will only be consumed beyond need.

The industries ministry has called for bids for supply of crude for the eastern refinery. I believe some bids are really low. I told the minister that the decision should be taken in the ECNEC.[3] Such a matter cannot be left to one man to decide.

25 | THURSDAY

📖 Streams of people came to see me. The air chief painted a gloomy picture due to non-availability of extra foreign exchange. The defence minister explained the position and said that the very best had been done. The Russian ambassador came to deliver a message from Kosygin who was visiting Delhi. I wished him a good trip and hoped that he will not further arm India and make them more irresponsible. Shahab came to explain what was being done on the educational front. A lot of good work is being done to produce updated textbooks and rationalize the syllabus.

📖 The American ambassador came early in the morning and delivered a message from President Johnson on the capture of a spy ship by North Korea. This was intolerable and against international law. He had, therefore, taken certain military precautions but as a preliminary he was warning the Security Council and needed our support as our representative is the chairman for this month. The ambassador pleaded that our response be passive. Our answer was that irrespective of the merit we are for peace and we shall certainly support such a consensus. I told the ambassador that they had better move with caution in this case. Both Russia and China were close. They are not going to remain passive spectators if a shooting war starts. My personal belief is that the Americans have got hooked and they would like to be taken out of it somehow, as any rash move on their part will lead to serious repercussions.

📖 A cabinet meeting was held in which a large number of questions came under discussion. I particularly went for the Bengali ministers and expressed my disappointment at not pulling their weight and guiding East Pakistan on the right lines. The present conspiracy was the direct outcome of the perfidy of hideous elements and their silence. Mr Altaf Hussain was particularly vehement in denouncing the conspiracy. He called it suicide, not secession, and promised to write and speak in Bengali. Shahabuddin also made a similar promise.

📖 Received the King of Jordan and his entourage. He has come on a one-week state visit. Poor man looks very pulled down and anxious. His country has suffered most in the recent war and I do not see how his losses can be made good. All actors are against him. The Israelis are arrogant and intransigent and have the fullest backing of the USA, whereas the Arabs are disunited and working at cross-purposes. So the future of Jordan, like of UAR, is bleak.

27 | SATURDAY

📖 Had talks with the King of Jordan. He seems frustrated; all his efforts at making the Arabs keep a united front are not succeeding. His efforts at another Arab summit have failed. King Faisal is unwilling to come through fear that he may be called upon to make greater financial contributions. Faisal was wanting to be excused. He said that he would go along with any decision that was taken at the summit. Meanwhile, Faisal is concerned with the situation in Yemen. Russia, Syria and even Iran are meddling. So he feels free to assist the royalist. South Yemen is also an uncertain actor. It is not known yet what different elements they would pull together. In the Persian Gulf the oil sheikhs who have their mutual rivalries, are feeling uneasy. They feel that after withdrawal of the British in 1971 either Saudi Arabia or Iran will swallow them up. Iraq is expecting trouble in the Kurdish area, being backed by Israel and Iran. They have, therefore, already withdrawn some units from Jordan. There is one Saudi unit in Iraq that has very good equipment but no intention to be trained to use it. Nasser is a real disappointment. He is in bad state of health and on the verge of a breakdown. Egypt's loss of equipment has been made good by the Russians who have placed their men in every unit to train the Egyptians. The morale of his own army is reviving but he needs equipment. The Americans have been making promises and counter promises. His chief of staff is currently on a visit to Washington to get the final answer. Meanwhile, the Russians have promised to give him equipment, if driven to war he will have to accept it. Only, he is afraid of Faisal's reaction who contributes so much money to his budget. Complete identification of USA with Israel has alienated the Arabs and the Russians have got a wonderful chance to consolidate in the Mediterranean region. They have got the chance which they had been longing for, for centuries. This is largely due to American short-sightedness. In fact, he is very depressed at this but I told him not to lose heart. He should concentrate on putting his own house in order and hope for greater cohesion to come amongst the Arab leaders at some time or another. The recent misfortune should have opened their eyes, but they have not. But one thing is certain: The Arab people are not going to remain passive forever. One day they will get rid of the government they have, get together and face the common enemy. This struggle is going to be long and bitter, after all, the Crusades went on for 400 years or more.

As far as we are concerned we shall continue to stand by them and give them whatever support is within our power. He was visibly moved and showed appreciation. Also, I told him that though the Russians are pouring arms in the Middle East, they have very little respect for the fighting qualities of recipients nor do the Russians want the war to restart. In fact, it suits their purpose for the US to identify more with Israel and get more and more exposed and isolated. I also advised him that he will find better political acceptance in the Middle East, and security, by accepting Russian arms.

28 | SUNDAY

📖 Governor Monem Khan came and discussed the problems of East Pakistan and especially the consequences of the recent conspiracy case. He gave me some indication of the opposition's intentions and doings of the Indians through radio and press. We chalked out a certain line of action and told him to rebut Indian disinformation and keep in touch with the intelligence agency. He has a hard task ahead of him but he is a brave and patriotic man. He will face the situation without any fear. I have complete faith in his loyalty.

JANUARY–MARCH

This has been a period of trial and tribulations for my person. I have suffered a series of serious illnesses rendering me ineffective for a long time. King Hussein gave a banquet at the Intercontinental Hotel in the evening. An hour or so before dressing up, I started feeling pain in my arm and congestion in my chest. These pains were more severe than I had been getting for some time and I felt that I may not be able to attend the function. However, by sheer will power I got ready and luckily the pain too subsided and I sat in the car. The function over, I came back home and as I lay down in my bed the pain came back again. I telephoned my physician Col. Mohiuddin who gave me some sedatives and a couple of injections. I slept comfortably, and the next couple of days the pain was mild but my stomach gave me trouble and I had the urge to go to the toilet every now and then. This was followed by blockage of urine. What had happened was that my prostate gland got inflamed, causing these maladies. For getting the urine out they had to put in a catheter which had to be drained every now and then. One night the clip blocking the mouth of the catheter got displaced and my body got covered with urine. I dreamt that I had got caught in a thunderstorm and felt that I was soaking wet. However, when I woke up, I realized what had happened so I called the doctor who was sleeping next door. He put the damn thing right. I had to have this thing in for several days which was most irksome.

On the fourth day I felt acute congestion in my chest and burning sensation in a portion of the heart. I felt as if a red-hot iron lance had been driven through it. However, this sensation lasted for a few hours. Meanwhile, I had developed fever which lasted for several days. I had very little sleep during this period, yet I felt quite cheerful despite immobilization in bed. Several top physicians like Professor Goodwin from London, who is a top cardiologist in the UK, Shaukat Sayed from Karachi and others gathered and took very good care of me. I am most grateful to them. Col. Mohiuddin, of course worked day and night and I lost 7 pounds in weight in the bargain.

I thought I was well on the way to normal convalescence. Suddenly, on the night of 16 February I felt pain on the right side of my back which increased in intensity as time went on and became almost unbearable. The doctors, after some discussion, came to the conclusion that I had an attack of pulmonary embolism. In plain words, blockage of blood vessels in the lungs caused by a couple of small clots of blood. They sent for Professor Goodwin who very kindly came back again and confirmed the diagnosis. Meanwhile, they started treatment which consisted of giving me injections every few hours and pricking my fingers to test blood. I did not mind the injections but these pricks were most distasteful. So the treatment was no less unpleasant than the disease itself, but it had to be done. Of course, with this malady, I developed preliminary and recurring fever and pain. It gradually subsided.

On hearing of my illness, my children and relations gathered. A large number of guests kept on coming. I was worried about my wife who is not in very good state of health but she told everybody not to show any concern in my presence and, in fact, there was no need to. I had not the slightest worry at any moment, I had a firm belief that I would pull through, and even if I did not, why be afraid of death? It had to come one day. All one hopes is that so long as one lives, one leads a healthy, honourable and useful life.

My children and wife put up a bold front. They remained cheerful in my presence though in private they were deeply worried. They worked day and night looking after the guests and making other arrangements especially Gohar and Naseem. All of them gave all they could in charity. It is God's blessing to have a family like that.

📖 The news of an unprecedented Indian military build up on land, air and now in the Indian Ocean with large Russian assistance is disturbing. Their intention seems to be to take the place of the British in these seas on British withdrawal and be in a position to intimidate and dominate all the countries washed by the waters of the Arabian Sea and Gulf. Pakistan will be their main target of intimidation.

📖 A long letter was received from Kosygin during my illness explaining how our relations were improving in many fields but there was a need to hold further talks on our demands for military supplies, and so, could I come over to Moscow? I sent back a reply that it was time he visited us. In fact, there were some indications that he would welcome an invitation. So he has expressed his desire to visit Pakistan from 17 to 21 April, subject to exigencies of circumstances. If he comes we shall naturally express our deep concern on the attempt to create military imbalance on this subcontinent. Expectations are that he will be more forthcoming in the economic field but tardy in the military field.

📖 We are facing a delicate situation with the Americans. The time has come for deciding the future of their installation at Badaber.[4] We have decided to give them notice for closure of this place as we cannot afford to continue to incur the displeasure of the Soviets and now the Chinese. The Americans, though expecting this, are bound to make some fuss and may even retaliate but we have no other choice.

📖 The second pound devaluation, the British failure to enter the Common Market, its economic and military dependence on the USA and shrinkages of influence in the world and especially the withdrawal from the East of Suez, all point to one thing, its position and even existence, depends on the USA. If realism were to prevail, she should become part of the USA and bargain to be counted not just as the 51st state but perhaps fourth or fifth.

📖 I have seen an interesting article by Nirad Chaudhuri,[5] a famous Bengali writer in English. He analyses the causes of the constitutional breakdown in West Bengal and comes to the conclusion that Bengalis, and for that matter all the Hindus, are not capable of governing themselves nor exercising political power. They are narrow minded and fractious and suffer from crises of character.

📖 The United States seems to be in a mess. Johnson has refused to seek a re-election. Gold revenues have been depleted, the Vietnam War is proving a distractive pastime, and internally, the community is torn apart through racial strife. They have offered to curtail the bombing in North Vietnam and open negotiations with them. How far these measures will succeed remains to be seen but most of these maladies are the outcome of an ineffective policy in Vietnam and the superb fighting qualities and staying power of those people. The racial problem, of course, is due mainly to the narrow mindedness of the white people. They are behaving in the same manner towards the Negroes as the Hindus are behaving with the Muslims in India.

📖 Our National Assembly had set up a house committee comprising primarily of Bengalis to find out why the private sector was lagging behind in East Pakistan. Mr Sobur Khan was appointed as the chairman. The outcome was as expected. The recommendations were fantastic. They enumerated economic strangulation of West Pakistan, diverting all resources to East Pakistan, and as many other absurdities as you can think of. I was astounded to hear of its unbalanced composition. Why was West Pakistan not suitably represented and why did the finance ministry not take an active interest in its composition? The recommendations, of course, failed to mention the real cause. Antipathy and abhorrence of the government and people of East Pakistan to the intervention of West Pakistan and foreign capital, and also through poor work performance and poor discipline. I believe the cabinet decided that this summary should be shelved and an official committee be appointed to go into the matter. They pose an absurd problem and put the onus of providing a sensible answer on the central government and with that done they try to erode it. The whole object is to get whatever they can by blackmail. Meanwhile, they are doing nothing to consolidate the nationhood. In fact, they continually try to behave and act as different to West Pakistan as possible. How long will this partnership last, I do not know.

I am surprised at the Bengali outlook. It does not conform to any rational yardstick. They were exploited by the caste Hindus, the Muslim rulers and even the British. It was at the advent of Pakistan that they got the blessing of freedom and equality of status and a real voice in running of their government. Something which was unknown in their history. Any normal people should have recognized and rejoiced at this blessing, but they and their politicians and so-called intelligentsia show no realization of this. Instead, they urge to fall back on their Bengali past. This can only result in their complete absorption by Hindu West Bengal influence. In addition, they have cut themselves off from Muslim culture and thought through abhorrence of the Urdu language in which it is expressed, thus making themselves vulnerable to Hindu culture.

11 | THURSDAY

📖 We have been getting disturbing news about the frame of mind in which the Shah of Iran is at present. He regards all Arabs as Iran's deadly enemies. He has fallen out with [King] Faisal and has expressed open hostility towards the federation of crucial Arab sheikhdoms. He has even expressed his intention to take Bahrain by force if need be. The basis of this claim is that Bahrain was under Persian occupation for 40 years or so in the 18th century. In other words, he is doing all he can to unify all the Arabs against him. Even if he regards them a danger he would be wiser to keep them divided by remaining on friendly terms with the monarchs and the traditionalists because they are as much afraid of revolutionary Arabs as he is. One theory is that he is encouraged in this attitude by Hoveida, the prime minister, but especially by his young Foreign Minister Zahedi, who, I am sure, fancies himself as a successor to the Shah. Our trouble is that if this federation asked for recognition we cannot deny it as that would give other Arabs cause for complaint and also absolutely affect our nationals who are working in the oil fields. Another danger is that India will fill the vacuum if we fall out with the Arabs. I know that the Iranians would not like it but the Shah has to inform them of our difficulties.

On departure of the British in 1971, there would undoubtedly be a power vacuum in the Persian Gulf. The Americans have shown no interest in filling it, and what the Russians would do remains to be seen now that they have good relations with revolutionary Arabs as well as Iran. The Indians, too, must be watching the situation with avid interest. They are longing to become masters of the seas in South Asia.

12 | FRIDAY

📖 The director of military intelligence came to see me and showed me a copy of the latest Indian plan of attack on West Pakistan. The plan is well made and is designed to bring overwhelming force to bear against us in several places. We shall have a hard task in meeting the challenge but, by God's grace, meet it we shall. I am going to discuss its implication with General Yahya. It is obvious that our defence preparedness has to be stepped up. I discussed this with General Yahya. He is fully in the picture and confirmed that if gaps in equipment are made up, they shall be able to meet this challenge.

17 | WEDNESDAY

📖 I received Mr Kosygin and party at Chaklala airport. It was the first time I had appeared in public after my illness. Public cheered me lustily. Kosygin was in a good mood. It seems that he may have good news to offer in supply of military equipment field apart from their generous offer in the economic field.

Entertained the premier to a banquet. He gave a warm speech, several of our people spoke to him, including the law minister. He said they do not have many lawyers in their country and they do not miss them. When told of the intricacies of our legal system, he said that it should be done away with and simplified like theirs. I told him that I agree but there are difficulties in the way. He said that private property was probably the cause of many cases. I told him the cause of most of the litigation often is *Zar, Zameen* and *Zan*, that is on gold, land and womenfolk.

18 | THURSDAY

📖 Held a private talk with Mr Kosygin. The précis of my talk is attached below.

Rawalpindi, 18 April 1968

Points for talks with Mr Kosygin:

1. Welcome. Our attempt to normalize relations—downgrading CENTO, closing Badaber.
2. (a) Indian arms build-up with Soviet assistance. Some of the things promised recently. Our people disturbed.
    (b) Indian build-up directed against us. We have positive proof.
    (c) Weak central government liable to embark on adventure.
    (d) Any thought that India will go socialist is against their religion.
    (e) If peace disturbed, all big powers will be affected.
    (f) We are only concerned about our security so need arms to guard it. In doing so we do not want to depend on one source in this part of the world.
    (g) Indian navy ambitions in the Indian Ocean imperialistic and very disturbing.
    (h) Our requirements:
        1. T55 or 54 tanks with 100 mm guns. 200.
        2. 130 mm guns. 130.
        3. Missiles for ships.
        4. 57 mm antiaircraft guns.
        5. Bombers 20 with all necessary ammunition for all the above.
        Deal depends on terms and conditions and our budgetary position.
    (i) Solemn assurance that we shall not provoke India. Continue seeking peaceful solution of Kashmir.
    (j) Soviet military mission. Defence minister, can our people visit their establishments?
    (k) Show appreciation for collaboration and assistance in the economic field. Following are under consideration:
        a. Aid dollar 175 million.
        b. Promise 60 million.
        c. Steel plant—Russia, want feasibility study.
        d. Oil exploration.
        e. Cooperation in television, radio and telecommunication.
        f. Assistance in agriculture, fisheries, and other fields.
        g. Barter deals.
        h. Increase in trade.
        i. Basmati rice barter.

3. State of relations with India.
   a. Implementation Kutch agreement.
   b. Opening of telecommunications.
   c. Talks on opening air services.
   d. Farraka barrage.
   e. But no advancement on Kashmir. Indian leaders continue to issue provocative statements.
4. Find out their views on
   a. Vietnam.
   b. Middle East.
   c. Persian Gulf.
5. Our views on
   a. Non-proliferation.
   b. UN.
6. Extend invitation to their leaders to come more often.

Kosygin gave a resumé of the industrial development and political situation within USSR. They are proud of the progress being made. Spoke of the difficulties with China and complained that President Johnson was dragging his feet on talks on Vietnam. He was not being true to his word. The USSR, though having a different public posture, was anxious that the talks should start. That war was costing them a lot. He showed concern about the successor to Johnson. Said that Nixon would be very dangerous as he had a dictatorial outlook. Said that though USA called itself a democracy, its president had more powers than a dictator. Finally, he came to Indo–Pakistan problems, and expressed strong desire that our relations should improve. Though not giving up India, he expressed his government's policy to give military hardware to Pakistan of a limited nature. Hundred tanks, sixty 130 mm guns, eighteen SU-7 fighter aircraft and some AN-12 transport aircraft with ammunition etc. were promised. I told him what our requirements were. He promised these would be considered by his colleagues. In addition, Kalabagh Steel Mill, if feasible, was promised and so was a nuclear power plant in East Pakistan in 1975. Amongst other sombre things I think this is a big step forward since we first had contact three years ago. The talks over, Mr Kosygin told me that on Indira Gandhi's request, he had decided to fly to Delhi for an hour after leaving Karachi and then fly direct to Moscow. She has to be strengthened against the rightist elements. I wished him luck.

Talking about birth control, Kosygin said that the Soviets were dead against it. In fact, they were encouraging growth of population as they had so much empty space to fill. Besides, they did not want to see Asians spread all over the world and the white men become a zoo specimen. The latter account was revealing.

19 | FRIDAY

We had another session of talks in the morning in which the problems with India and Afghanistan were discussed. Though pleading with us to normalize relations with India, he did not show any inclination to give a helping hand in resolution of the Kashmir dispute.

Mr Kosygin and party left for Lahore in the morning, where he was given a rousing reception. Whilst we were in the course of discussion, a message came from Mr Johnson asking me to sound

Mr Kosygin out if he would use his influence with the North Vietnamese and accept Pakistan as the venue of talks. Kosygin reacted rather sharply and asked why Johnson is not accepting Moscow as the venue after having declared that he would be prepared to talk anywhere and in anyplace. What is wrong with that place? They have an embassy there and sure means of communication with Washington. In any case this is a matter for the comrades in Vietnam to decide and they could not interfere. I sent a reply to that effect to Johnson adding that whilst the Soviets are anxious for the talks to commence and fighting to stop, they will not change their public posture. Johnson sent a reply thanking me for promptly sounding Kosygin out and though his reaction was not in the affirmative it is quite possible that my approach will influence his future thinking.

On a relaxed occasion, Mr Kosygin started talking about Stalin. Stalin was a giant of a man, a profound thinker and very hardworking, very hospitable and amenable to reason. He used to write his own speeches. Never allowed officials to record talks with foreigners. He used to record them personally or get one of the party members to take notes. He had a fantastic memory. In personality and calibre people like Churchill and Roosevelt looked pale in his presence. He was also very hospitable. The only trouble was that his dinner parties went on till early hours of the morning. I was about to ask him why he was denounced and vilified after his death, but we had to move on to the dinner table. The present Soviet custom is to disperse as soon as a meal is over, which I think is very sensible. Long drawn out meals can be very boring, at least for a man like me.

20 | SATURDAY

The Soviet ambassador verbally delivered a message from Mr Kosygin, thanking us for the warm reception he was given in Pakistan and giving the gist of his talks with Mrs Gandhi in Delhi. He emphasized to her the need for progressive resolution of outstanding problems between India and Pakistan and emphasized that things like Bhagirathi division of waters of the eastern rivers, return of boats captured by Indians in the Rann of Kutch and evacuation of the area allotted to Pakistan in the Rann should be settled quickly. She did not comment on these matters but said that some people in India were against making any more concessions to Pakistan. She was also apprised of Soviet intentions to sell some arms and ammunition to Pakistan. She showed concern and asked if she could divulge this in Parliament if questioned. She was told to refrain from doing so as she was given information which was confidential. Kosygin also conveyed to me the good wishes of Mr Brezhnev, Podgorny and other Soviet leaders and repeated his invitation to me to visit the Soviet Union again whenever suitable.

I thanked the ambassador and through him Mr Kosygin and other Soviet leaders for taking so much interest in our affairs and for taking me into confidence. It was our policy to settle all disputes with India and we shall continue to seek opportunities in future too, but I was not aware that India had made any concession to us at any time. However, I am grateful to Mrs Gandhi. If she insists [...] I also expressed my thanks for the kind invitation and told the ambassador that I shall be delighted to visit the Soviet Union at an appropriate time.

With the change in the world situation in general, and growth of economic and military strength within the Soviet Union, its leaders are fast changing their international image and behaviour. From the boorishness and crudity of the past, they had become sane and matter of fact like the British, acting more like the agents of a superpower than world revolutionaries. This change may also be due to the fact that power in the Soviet Union is not now centred in one person. It is held by a Troika who had to act in the spirit of consensus and therefore restraint. But such is the history of revolutions. First, intellectuals produce the idea and then fanatics put it through in practice accompanied by great fervour and cruelty and pragmatics bring it to earth. Conservative reaction is ultimate fate and perhaps aim of all revolutionaries. The Soviet Union, I believe, has entered this last phase while China is in the second phase of revolution, phase of fervour and fanaticism. That is what Mao Tse-tung stands for but it is inconceivable that this phase will last forever. It, too, will taper into the last phase in course of time. The French word for the last phase of revolution, I believe, is *Thermidor*. I suppose it means cooling of or returning to normal.

25 | THURSDAY

I saw in the press a statement made by one of our economists on the Planning Commission. He made the following points amongst others:

a. A commission should be set up to plan the education and training of manpower required in the country within the foreseeable future. I have been thinking of this for a long time. We must get on with it and gear our educational system accordingly.
b. Our present industrial policy has created accumulation of inordinate wealth in the hands of 20 families.[6] This is no news. We are aware of the problem and have been trying hard to effect diversification without much success. The identifications of a known problem is not much use, a lot of people indulge in this past time, which is futile. They would be helpful if they took the trouble to offer sensible solutions.

Mr Uqaili, the finance minister, came to tell me that my idea of imposing capacity tax on industries is operational and is going to be applied to the textile industry from 1st May. This will bring ten extra crores in revenue. The good and efficient industrialists should be happy because any production after a stage will be free of all taxes. However, those who fudge and there are many unhappy, have threatened to see Uqaili out of his job. I told him to take no notice of it.

26 | FRIDAY

Appointment of Mr Arshad Hussain as Foreign Minister in place of Mr Pirzada was announced today. Mr Pirzada will go back as the Attorney General for which he is more suited. I have great hopes in Arshad Hussain. I hope he makes a success. He has the family background, education and experience to do so. At any rate he was very effective as our high commissioner in Delhi under difficult circumstances.

A Chinese mission under the leadership of a four star general has come to inspect and discuss with us problems of Karakoram Highway. The Chinese seem to be very anxious for its early completion and don't quite realize how stupendous, difficult and time absorbing the task is. We have arranged for them to see the whole length of the road alignment by a helicopter right up to the Khunjerab Pass then come back and discuss the problem with us. Then there is the question of expense. Our requirement is a one-way natural service road with occasional bypasses up to Gilgit. Such a road would have to cost about 15 crores, but the type of road they require up to Khunjerab would cost anything up to 70 crores or more, which will put a great burden on our resources and affect our development programmes. So I have told the defence minister to bring this home to the leader of the Chinese team and talk him into sharing this burden with us. His assessment is that they might well be willing to do so.

28 | SUNDAY

📖 I have just finished reading a book by Sudhir Ghosh[7] called *Gandhi's Emissary*. It is divided into two parts. Part I deals with period preceding the partition of the subcontinent and Part II deals with the affairs of independent India. In Part I the author played an important role, first as a messenger of Gandhi to the cabinet commission under Mr Cripps and later almost as an advisor to the commission on Indian affairs or more correctly as a promoter of Congress or Hindu desires. The British were anxious that in order to maintain India as one entity, the Congress and the Muslim League should come to some sort of mutually agreed settlement. The Congress was not prepared to accept this. Gandhi and Nehru amongst others demanded that power should be handed over to the majority, that is, the Congress. That is the Hindu, who would bring the Muslims to heel as best as they could even by use of force. Some even expected assistance from the British in supplying force. So the exact extent of Hindu perfidy was unbounded. They wanted the British to help them in complete subjugation of Muslims. In Part II, the author discusses his activities as the employee of the Indian government. The different capacities, his relationship with Nehru, his assessment of the Indian politicians and the civil servants and his complete disenchantment and frustration. This book is worth reading, especially the chapter on the Indian experiment with socialism. I have asked for this chapter to be reproduced in large numbers and distributed amongst our officials as a good deal of it applies to us too and has lessons for us.

1 | WEDNESDAY

📖 Heard on the BBC that the USA and North Vietnam have after all decided to open talks in Paris commencing 10th May. This is very good news. Let us hope that in due course the talks will lead to cessation of hostilities and some sort of peace. Real peace can only come if China and the USA come to some understanding and leave the small countries in South-east Asia alone. In other words, allow them to become neutral and have governments of their own choice, communist or otherwise.

📖 I have just finished reading Senator Fulbright's[8] *Arrogance of Power*. He has shown great depth of thought and insight and has gone on to prove that America is misusing its tremendous economic and military power to its detriment, in pursuit of wrong purposes and policies. America should support nationalism even if it is combined with communism, instead of attempting to destroy communism which in any case is turning nationalist. First, communism is, in his view, an essence of humanitarian faith and is not in itself reprehensible.

📖 Sad news came in that one of our transport aircraft on a flight to Gilgit crashed in the Kaghan valley killing 22 passengers consisting of several air force officers and men. Asad, the political agent of Gilgit, who came from Ghazi, was also killed.

4 | SATURDAY

📖 The National Economic Council considered the annual development programme. Its size was nearly 1000 crores inclusive of the private sector. The public sector consisted of 570 crores. East Pakistan was given the major share. The growth rate of 1967 and 1968 was estimated to be over 7 per cent. Major gains are expected in the agricultural sector. The increase in cereals is expected to be 3.4 million tons. Yields in cotton, jute, sugarcane etc. have also made spectacular gains.

7 | TUESDAY

📖 Arshad Hussain was sworn in as the new foreign minister in place of Pirzada.

📖 Held a Muslim League Party meeting in the evening and gave them a talk. Notes of the talks are below:

Rawalpindi
7th May '68

Points for Muslim League Assembly party.

1. Happy to see you again. You are going to have a long session as a large number of bills are due for consideration. Hope you will have a pleasant stay. Please don't run away without permission and do not break the quorum.

2. My health, grateful for the sympathies of people. I am now all right except that I have to take things quietly. Anyone who wishes to see me can see Mr Fida Hassan. The problems will be attended to.

3. You know that our major concern is the safety and security of the country and reconstruction and development of the country. I would like to touch on both. Security, is India building a strong military machine with the help of the USA and now the Soviet Union. They are giving this help to build India as eventually to pose a threat to China, but India has different designs. Meanwhile, central government weakening, future rulers of India are going to be bigoted Hindus, a weak and bigoted government of a big neighbour can be a source of great danger.

4. So coming times going to be difficult for India's neighbours and especially Muslims in India and Pakistan. We have to be more on guard. No time for selfish and petty politics. We are doing our best to create a deterrent but there are great limits to ours. Besides, it is difficult to get materials. However, we are not doing too badly. I am confident that we shall Inshah Allah hold India as we did last time

5. Mr Kosygin's visit went off better than expected. They are not going to give up India, but nor are they going to ignore us. This is a big move forward compared to what it was three years ago. Meanwhile, we hope to have a friendly relationship with the USA and China. Our relationship with everyone not at the cost of another.

6. Economic field, our growth 8.3 per cent, big strides in the agricultural field but good deal more to be done. We have to increase exports.

7. Family planning.

8 | WEDNESDAY

Had the defence minister and the finance minister come to my office to discuss the armed forces' new pension code. At present, there is a great divergence of views between what the armed forces want and what the finance is prepared to give. So a cabinet subcommittee has been appointed to go into the problem. I told these two ministers that the cabinet subcommittee can bring to bear no particular wisdom on the problem. After all, what particular experience have they got on these intricate matters? It seems to me that the best course is that the matter should be reverted to the two ministers concerned and they should settle it on some sensible basis. The defence minister suggested that if the finance ministry could suggest a figure they could give extra, then the rest could be settled. I said this would be too arbitrary. The answer was to either increase the pensions in relation to increase in pay or accept the Indian Pension Code whose circumstances are similar to ours. I hope this will bring the argument down to earth.

10 | FRIDAY

Carried out the selection of three judges for the West Pakistan High Court in conjunction with the governor and the law minister. There were eleven candidates, some practicing lawyers and some session judges. I was pleasantly surprised to see some very promising candidates amongst the lawyers. They were impressive personalities, with sound character and knowledge, and good background. I hope they would all be absorbed in the judiciary in due course. The session judges, on the other, hand were a poor lot.

I am given to understand the judiciary resents such interviews. They expect me to sign on the dotted line on the recommendations of the chief justice of the high court and the supreme court and the governor, conveyed when often their recommendations differ. I am damned if I am going to do that and be led by the nose. In point of fact these interviews do a lot of good. It gives the president the opportunity to discharge his duty consistently and gives satisfaction to the candidates that every effort was made to do justice.

I am delighted to hear on the radio that a violent storm that had developed in the Bay of Bengal and was heading for East Pakistan turned east south of Cox's Bazaar and petered out. These storms known as cyclones have become frequent and have played havoc with life and property in East Pakistan. The experts think that they are due to special hot spots in the sun which seems to focus on the bay and that they will continue to do so for another decade or so. Meanwhile, poor East Pakistanis are in for a bad time.

I have been talking about splitting the autonomous bodies like IDC, WAPDA, ADC etc. as they are becoming far too big and as such getting clogged with their own red tape. Besides, we have reached a state of development where specialization is required in major items of production. Mr Uqaili is the head of the committee which is going to go into this, but meanwhile, I have told him and Governor Musa to consider setting up separate boards for procurement, storage and disposal of food grains and for supervising, executing and distributing pest control and fertilizers. West Pakistan could set up a cement board controlling IDC, factories at Hyderabad and Dawood Khel and ADC factories at Rohri and Wah straight away. Later, when the steel project comes up, I hope it will be under a separate board. Similarly, the heavy machinery and the electrical complex should have their own boards. I believe such an arrangement will make for a good deal of efficiency, better expertise and lowering of cost.

11 | SATURDAY

The appointed foreign minister, Arshad Hussain, came to call on me. He thanked me for his elevation. I told him that he was appointed for his professional efficiency as our foreign policy was too complicated to be handled by the amateurs who tend to become extremists, forgetting the interest of the country. He said, talking about extremism, that he wanted to seek my guidance on the type of things our representative is saying on behalf of the Arabs at the Security Council. I told him that I, too, was surprised. How does this stand on behalf of the Arabs help the interest of Pakistan? Why does not the foreign office control him? He said control and monitoring was needed. The Arabs, he said, had peculiar emotions about the *ajami* Muslims.[9] They expect all out support without wanting to do anything themselves in return. On inquiring, he gave me his assessment of the situation in India. Economically, because of the bumper crop, things have improved. The prices of food stuffs were still high, but the purchasing power of the farmers has improved giving a fillip to the sale of consumer goods. The public sector, which was doing badly, has had a shot in the arm because of the promise of large scale purchases by the Soviets. Their anxiety is to keep leftist India floating and

prevent the takeover by rightists. The Americans, too, are helping. They want to see India become a rallying point for the small countries in South Asia and act as a counterpoise to China. Further, they do not want to see India go communist and go under Russian influence. Politically, the situation is bad. Caste system, lingualism, regionalism and Hinduism are gaining ground leading to divisive trends and a continual dogfight. But there are also people who are trying desperately hard to keep the unity of the country. It is very difficult to tell what is the strength of each sector. The central government is very weak, Indira's position is precarious, Chavan and his supporters on one side and Morarji Desai on the other, are looking for opportunities to topple her. However, she has been lucky so far and has survived by making some wise decisions, but she is in no position to take any major initiatives. Meanwhile, they are building their own strength furiously. And that is where the danger lies.

📖 Kosygin's recent visit to Delhi brought no cheer to the Indians. They were definitely disappointed on his shift of position on Pakistan and Kashmir. He apparently told them that Ayub Khan was a moderate and wanted peace with India. He was in good health and fully in control irrespective of what the Indians may have heard to the contrary. In Kosygin's view the Indian military budget was backbreaking. Their economy was weak and could not sustain a war. In any case, the Soviets would not like to see another war on the subcontinent. It would be fraught with grave danger so his advice was that, apart from settling peripheral problems, some progress is necessary on the substantive dispute of Kashmir. What that progress could be is left to them to decide. The Indians put forward the supposed threat of China. Kosygin did not think that China would attack India, but even if she did, much less force than the Indians have would do. He also told them their decision to issue some arms and ammunition to Pakistan.

📖 Sent for the defence minister, told him that the only way we could have an effective armoured element in our army was by renovating our existing tank population by diesel engines. We are a poor country and purchase of new tanks was beyond our means but the trouble is that an average officer in the army does not understand this. So I told the defence minister to make a plan and let me have a look at it.

12 | SUNDAY

📖 Had occasion to discuss with General Yahya and General Hamid the organizational training, defence preparations and the weapons problem. They are beginning to understand and implement my ideas. Training is focused on the task each formation is assigned. Concrete defences and antitank obstacles are being constructed in all sensitive areas. The object of these defences is to attain economy of force, that is, deploying as few people as possible on the holding task so as to release the manpower for the counteroffensive. They are also beginning to be convinced about my theory that a tank can never get old so long as it has a working engine and tracks. Those are the two things that have to be changed on a tank from time to time. They told me that Bolkov, the armament expert from Germany, had sent in blueprints of the type of armoured vehicle I have been thinking of. I am going to have a look at it. If the idea works, he would have revolutionized tank war. Bolkov, I am told, is very pleased.

15 | WEDNESDAY

📖 A very interesting report written by Chester Bowles, the American Ambassador in Delhi, has come to hand. He talks about political trends in India and their future direction. His assessment is as follows:

a. Congress is breaking up. It may well be a minority in the next elections, even at the centre.
b. Regional tribal and linguistic trends are gaining momentum. At the bottom are the lower caste Hindus attempting to throw away the yoke of the Brahman and the Bania.
c. This trend may well cause division of India into 50-60 states rather like the United States with coalition governments in the provinces and even at the centre.
d. The process may well be accompanied by bloodshed. Gandhi's gospel of non-violence is dead. Violence is regarded as a normal act.
e. The extremist parties like RSS,[10] Hindu Mahasabha[11] and Jana Sangh[12] will use anti-Muslim feelings to gain support.
f. Muslims will suffer because of the strong feeling against them and because they are divided.
g. He thinks that these trends, however regrettable, may bring health to the Indian polity.
h. India is safe for the present as there is no one to replace Indira Gandhi.

During the British period, Churchill is supposed to have remarked that India was an administrative unit enforced by the British and not a political unit. That is coming true.

17 | FRIDAY

📖 Four newly appointed ambassadors came to present their credentials from Libya, Ceylon, Austria and Hungary.

18 | SATURDAY

📖 I had been very anxious to seek a suitable opportunity to publicly express my views on the future of agriculture, the agricultural community and the need for launching cooperative farming. Such an opportunity came today when agricultural machinery had to be demonstrated on a piece of land where I had sown Mexi–Pak wheat in my compound, that is the President's House compound. I had invited the MNAs and the representatives of local gentry and entertained them to tea. Thereafter, I gave a talk. It was reported in the press. Let us see what reaction it provokes amongst the people. The following yields of Mexi–Pak wheat were obtained on my lands in Badalpur near Khanpur, Hazara and also in Sindh. In Kulab farm, this is near Tando Muhammad Khan, average of 35 maunds per acre in an area well over 200 acres. In Badalpur, near Khanpur in Hazara, 114 maunds in an area of one and a half acre. It works out at 91.8 maunds per acre which is a fantastically high yield. In Chitri, a village next to Rehana in Hazara, 90.32 maunds an acre sown in line and 86.30 maunds in an area sown by broadcast methods. These lands are *barani*.

20 | MONDAY

📖 Reports from our delegation to Delhi on the question of division of waters of the eastern rivers indicate that India has no intention of being either reasonable or playing it straight. So it would be a long drawn out argument, like the way Indians have behaved with us over so many other times, but that is the way they are built, devious, thoroughly unscrupulous.

📖 An envoy of North Vietnam came to see me and explained how they were facing up to intense bombing and how the fighting was going on in South Vietnam. He said this was a war of liberation. They were fighting for freedom and would go on doing so irrespective of the odds until it was achieved. They were manufacturing their own arms and ammunition but were also getting supplies from the socialist countries on a liberal scale. He admitted the presence of North Vietnamese troops in the south. Their tactics were to attack in small numbers so as to escape the effect of American bombing. Then he gave me a souvenir. It consisted of a piece of metal taken out of one of the 2800 American aircraft they had destroyed. One cannot help admiring the courage and tenacity of these people. How can such people be denied freedom which belongs to them. They will get it in the end and with a vengeance.

📖 Since the commencement of the year the decade of reforms is being celebrated in the country. I was not in favour of this originally, as I thought that it might turn into my eulogy, a sort of thing I do not like. However, the results have shown that this campaign through the press and the radio is doing a lot of good. It is making people aware of the progress that has been made in every field. In other words, it is proving to be a highly educative programme. All credit goes to Mr Altaf Gauhar, who originated the idea and is responsible for running it.

21 | TUESDAY

📖 Brigadier Akbar, the head of military intelligence, came to see me and showed me the Indian administrative instructions for an attack on East Pakistan. It goes into great detail, inclusive of the civil administrative arrangements for the areas overrun. I wish the Bengalis, who think and talk in terms of greater Bengal, could be shown what future is being planned for them by those whom they regard as their friends.

📖 I am intrigued by a light tank produced by the French. I was shown a brochure on it. It weighs 9.5 tons and carries a 90 mm gun, which fires a hollow charge projectile at muzzle velocity of 800 meters and has an effective range of 1200 meters. The price of the hull without the gun is supposed to be 70,000 rupees, which is not easy to believe. However, I have told Major General Mohammadi to proceed to France at once and get one or two of these vehicles for trial and then consult Bolkov in Germany with a view to its manufacture in Pakistan. He is also going to Belgium to strike a deal for the 200 M47 or M48 tanks they have. I have told him to buy them in whatever condition they are. We can think of renewing of engines later.

22 | WEDNESDAY

📖 Information has come to hand giving the details of socialist countries credits and loans given to India for procurement of military hardware, Russia topping the list. These amount to about 600 crore, repayable in Indian goods in ten years at two and a half per cent interest. The credit will be used for establishment of jet aircraft MIG 19 and MIG 21 factories and purchase of other aircraft, submarines, long range guns, tanks, air to air and ground to air missiles etc. A demand has also been made to the Russians for the supply of TU-16 jet bombers. Meanwhile, Indian ordnance factories are working round the clock producing most of the requirements for weapons, ammunition, electronics, and clothing etc. With the imported and indigenously produced equipment the Indian armed forces are being modernized at a rapid pace. Their effectiveness due to the enhanced firepower and mobility is progressing at a fast pace and will continue to improve as time goes on. The meaning of all that should be clear to us. This fantastic military build-up is directed against us. The Indian chauvinism will grow and the coming times are going to be hard for us.

23 | THURSDAY

📖 Held a cabinet meeting. Some of the important subjects discussed were:

a. The future constitution of Azad Kashmir.
b. Acquisition of land in Islamabad for capital development.
c. Institution of benevolent fund and a group insurance fund for civil servants.

The foreign minister and the foreign secretary showed me a copy of the letter written to our representative at the Security Council to exercise moderation in presentation of the Arab case. While supporting the Arabs, we should avoid confronting the United States. In other words, do not lose sight of the interest of Pakistan. We also discussed our reply to the American ambassador, who is coming to see me, should he raise the question of extension of the agreement on Badaber base. The decision was that we must resist this as the presence of this base in Pakistan has become a major provocation to those countries against whom it is directed and they have threatened us with dire consequences should this be allowed to stay.

25 | SATURDAY

📖 I am no believer in observing my birthday. For one, it is an unnecessary custom, and secondly, where is the occasion for rejoicing when one has lost one more year of life. However, some people have started making a lot of fuss on my birthday, which is 14th of May.[13] This year, for instance, they made a lot of fuss in Karachi. Held symposiums and discussions on my life. It is also customary to receive messages on such occasions from different heads of states. There is one from President Johnson, too, it reads as follows:

'Mr President,

Ladybird and I send warmest personal regards to you on your birthday. Your recovery from illness is ample reason for celebration not only in Pakistan, but wherever are men of honour, courage and statesmanship. We join millions of friends around the world in wishing you many happy returns. You always have a special place in American hearts.'

This is the story on the date of my birth: Whereas I was born in November 1905, my recorded date of birth is 14 May 1907. This apparently was the date given to the headmaster of the primary school which I joined, by an old servant of ours who used to accompany me.

📖 It is very heartening to know that during my sickness the organs of government worked very well indeed. Perhaps accepted responsibilities and took decisions. There was no letup in the tempo of work. The meaning of this is that the institutions have taken root. And people are beginning to have faith in them. This augurs well for stability.

📖 There was a question put by an opposition member in the Assembly on the future over Badaber Base. Naturally, the government had to disclose that a notice has been served on the Americans as provided for in the agreement for its evacuation. This has caused a stir in American circles. Our ambassador from Washington reports extensive discussions have been held in the American administration which considers its retention a necessity. It is obvious that the Americans will exert all sorts of pressure on us for its continuance, a situation we cannot countenance in the face of Soviet and Chinese protests and threats. We are already on the Soviet atomic target list because of the existence of this base and the fact that the U2 aircraft used to take off from Peshawar. Meanwhile, the Americans have withdrawn military aid and betrayed us on the bilateral agreement in accordance to which they had pledged to come to our assistance in the event of aggression. So the truth is that we are bearing an intolerable liability to our security on account of the Americans. Our ambassador tells us that the Pentagon is blaming the State Department for sacrificing relationship with Pakistan for the sake of India and not recognising the strategic importance of Pakistan.

We are facing a delicate situation with the Americans. The time has come for deciding the future of this installation at Badaber. We have decided to give the Americans notice for closure of this installation as we cannot afford to continue to incur the displeasure of the Soviets and the Chinese. The Americans, though expecting this, are bound to make some fuss and may even retaliate, but we have no other choice.

27 | MONDAY

📖 The Russian ambassador came to inform me today that they would be willing to receive our military purchase mission anytime in June and that mission could also discuss with the Soviet authorities the question of a visit of a Soviet military mission to Pakistan. This was good news. The idea is to send General Yahya as the head of the mission. Contact with the Soviet top military brass would then be possible.

29 | WEDNESDAY

📖 Read an interesting article by an Indian economist on the state of the Indian economy, the sum total of which is that the economy is suffering from price inflation, deficit financing, perverse income transfers and erosion of savings. It is from these ills that balance of payments difficulties, capital market decay, closure of production units and unemployment arises. Over investment and over spending can be highly dangerous. We, too, have to be watchful of these ills. Good deal of over spending in India is perhaps due to the fantastic military budget, which in the main is a non-productive expenditure.

30 | THURSDAY

📖 Mr Jaffery, Secretary Industries, reported the gist of his talks in New Delhi on the decision of the eastern rivers' waters and their effect on the Farraka barrage on the Ganges, and Kobadak and projected irrigation schemes on the right bank of the Ganges in East Pakistan. He saw the irrigation minister and commerce minister, Ganesh Singh, who happens to be particularly friendly to the foreign secretary, and held forthright discussions with the Indians. Whereas they were socially nice, they showed no inclination to discuss substantive matters. All they wanted to do was to talk about exchange of data, which has been done so often. In other words, they were forestalling for time, one of them frankly said that what would people think if they gave us the Ganges water. In the final communiqué it was announced on the insistence of Jaffery that the matter be upgraded to the governmental level for decision on the policy matter: that is, the determination of Pakistan's share of water before further technical discussions can proceed.

My own feeling is that whilst agitating with the Indians, we should assume the worst, that is refusal by India to guarantee any flow of waters from Farraka and work out how much water will, in effect, escape from Farraka in the dry season and how much regeneration will take place at the points of utilization by us. We may well find that regeneration in that porous soil gives us all the water we need for irrigation in the lean period, which is the month of April and May. For the rest of the year the volume of water in the river is so great that the Indians cannot stop the downstream flow whatever they may do. However, Farraka is bound to affect navigation. The extent of this should also be worked out. So, whilst there is no doubt about the Indian meanness, the situation is not hopeless and we do not have to be at their mercy as we were in West Pakistan.

📖 Read an interesting article by Quintin Hogg.[14] Telling passages are:

Eight years in the economic policy committee of the cabinet left me with a profound distrust of economists, treasury officials and so called economic experts and theories. Genuinely it has always puzzled me why in all the economic jargon one question never seems to be asked, let alone answered and discussed. The question is, what is the actuating mechanism that creates new wealth.

He goes on to answer:

Freedom is a great creation of creative force. Freedom is the engine missing from Mr Jenkins motorcar, freedom of enterprise operating for profit is the forgotten actor in the economy. The failure of successive governments to encourage this actor is what renders almost everything they have done in this country for years infructuous.

Some more interesting passages in the paper were:

The public is notoriously fickle. It lives in a love-hate relationship with its leaders and hatred can follow love as rapidly as a cloud's shadows fly across ploughed fields....

And then, democracy is the most acceptable political system that man has devised, but it is appallingly clumsy, unfair and wasteful. It knows only one method of swapping horses and that is to drown the beast that is superseded.

2 | SUNDAY

📖 Sent for Kirmani, President, Provincial Muslim League and gave him the following tasks:

1. Complete elections to the provincial council and hold election of office bearers as soon as possible.
2. Set up a liaison-cum-advisory body of a few chosen individuals, preferably outside the government. Their task should be to supervise League bodies at different levels, see that the wards or BDs have been formed suitably, smoothen all local squabbles amongst the Leaguers and later help in the conduct of the election process.
3. Form Women's Leagues in every city and town. For supervision form a body at the provincial level.
4. Create a supervisory League cell in Karachi; Gohar Ayub could head this.

These measures will generate a lot of enthusiasm and put life into the League organization.

📖 The monument at the site in Lahore where Pakistan resolution was passed under the chairmanship of the Quaid on 23 March 1940 is ready. We discussed its opening and decided that it should synchronize with the session of the Pakistan Muslim League Council meeting sometime in November.

3 | MONDAY

📖 Held a cabinet meeting and took decisions on several important economic matters. One proposal related to encouraging participation of workers in the enterprises in which they were employed.

4 | TUESDAY

📖 Mr Justice Fazl-e-Akbar[15] was sworn in as the Chief Justice of the Supreme Court in place of Justice Rehman, who has retired. Justice Fazl-e-Akbar is the first Chief Justice of the Supreme Court from East Pakistan, but he will be retiring in November this year on attaining 65 years of age to be followed by another East Pakistani, Hamood-ur-Rahman. They are both good and sensible people. I believe they are both refugees from West Bengal. After the swearing in ceremony, I entertained him and the rest of the members of the Supreme Court and the other guests to lunch. They all enjoyed themselves and the conversation was most interesting.

📖 Governor Musa entertained the National Assembly members to a dinner party at the Hotel Intercontinental in Rawalpindi. I also attended. The members and especially East Pakistanis turned out in their best. When commented upon, some said that after all there was a vacancy in the cabinet.

5 | WEDNESDAY

📖 Governor Monem Khan came to report on his tour impressions of Turkey, England, Egypt and Iraq. He came back deeply impressed with Turkey and its people, thought well of Egypt, but was disturbed with the state of affairs in Iraq, where he found insecurity and instability. He also showed me some documents indicating that some of the MPs of Awamis headed by a few Hindus, perhaps inspired by Calcutta, were planning to launch a terrorist movement in East Pakistan. Their aim was to unify the two Bengals, in other words, bring about Hindu rule in that area under the guise of Bengali nationalism. It just shows how stupid some of our people are. They want to deliver themselves to the Hindus on their own accord.

📖 Just heard that Senator Bobby Kennedy was shot at and critically wounded when he was coming out of a hotel in Los Angeles after a Democratic Party primary convention. This is shocking news and an abominable act in a country which has pretensions to being the leading democracy in the world. It seems that some people are after the blood of the Kennedy family.

6 | THURSDAY

📖 The Khan of Kalat, whose state has been merged into West Pakistan and gets an allowance of rupees 6.5 lakhs annually from the government, is a colourful talker. He comes to me sometimes and tells me that Prophet Muhammad [PBUH] comes to him in his dreams and gives him messages for me as he is extremely interested in my welfare. I mentioned this to someone whose explanation was that the Khan probably takes narcotics of some sort and perhaps sees things. On the other hand, being highly intelligent he gets into trances. Along with these messages, he used to ask for his restitution as the ruler or be made a deputy governor. His object of calls was to regain his position in Balochistan, which, apart from being out of the question, was fraught with danger, considering his past and his capacity for intrigue. However, we have decided to give him the status of an advisor to the governor for Baloch affairs. This was announced today. He was mighty pleased and said that it coincided with his 68th birthday. Handled properly, he should prove useful when administration is dealing with disruptionist elements in Balochistan and for guiding people on the right path.

📖 Heard the tragic news of Robert Kennedy's death. He succumbed to his injuries sustained in the head in spite of a brain operation.

📖 Arranged a demonstration of agricultural implements and machinery for MNAs and the local notables. I pointed out whereas we have done well in wheat, rice and maize production, the production of cotton and sugarcane had not been given the same attention. One of the things that can augment food enormously is potato. We should be producing this on a large scale, but this cannot happen unless the farmer is offered a reasonable floor price, which again is dependent on provision of cold storages for preservation. The answer seems to be to set up a potato board in each province which should pursue the matter in all aspects. Also, our cattle wealth is being eaten up fast and there has not been enough meat in the country. This deficiency can only be made good by poultry and fish, which can be produced quickly. So enterprising people should take to this profitable and much needed line. The most effective method of utilizing fodder, especially dry wheat and rice straw, is to mix it with molasses and put 3 per cent urea in it. It is surprising how well the cattle do on it. I have tried it on my own cattle with amazing affect. They will not eat anything else. Mr Khuda Bakhsh Bucha, Minister of Agriculture in West Pakistan, told me that some people were getting rattled at the talk of agricultural cooperatives. For instance, Mr Gurmani anxiously inquired what was the plot and could he be told something of it in advance. Gurmani has turned a keen farmer. He owns a lot of land. I told Bucha that there is no cause for anxiety, whatever happens, the right of owning private property would be retained. Then I showed him my paper on the subject. The thing probably is that Bucha himself has got rattled. He, too, owns a considerable amount of land.

8 | SATURDAY

The budget for the year 1968–1969 was discussed at the cabinet meeting and presented to the House by the finance minister. Estimated revenue receipt 688.93 crores, expenditure 557.21 crores including 121.01 crores as share of provinces, surplus 131.72 crores. Capital expenditure 539.67 crores and receipt 545.65 crores, deficit 5.98 crores. This was made good by extra taxation. The defence budget was increased by 22 crores from 223 crores to 245 crores. Many small remissions were given. I believe the budget was very well received. However, we are concerned about the ADP and the import policy. These are to some extent dependent on foreign aid, which has not yet been pledged, because the Americans are not willing to commit themselves. Consequently, the other members of the consortium have also decided to drag their feet. Nonetheless, the overall picture gives cause for satisfaction. Rise in revenue receipt, development expenditure and foreign exchange is fantastic. When compared to 1958 figures, the country, by God's grace, is well on the way to finding economic salvation.

9 | SUNDAY

Today was the Prophet's birthday. It was celebrated with great enthusiasm throughout the country. Seminars, *milad*, meetings were held all over. Press and Radio Pakistan did a great job in propagating the Prophet's message and teachings.

11 | TUESDAY

I have caused a letter to be written to the Governor, West Pakistan on the following subjects:

1. How far has the extermination of goats got? It is imperative that they be finished. What little vegetation one sees in the country is due to reduction of goats and camels and stoppage of *pawinda* migration from Afghanistan. They used to bring a large number of animals, which devastated the countryside.
2. Concentrated effort should be made through the agricultural department, radio, television, and the press to teach people how to feed and look after cattle. We export oil cakes and molasses when they could be used for feeding and fattening cattle mixed with wheat and rice straws and sprinkling of urea.

3. Irrigation water in the PAT feeder is not being used as the land covered by it has not yet been settled and there are major disputes amongst the claimants there. What can be done to overcome this as we cannot allow half a million acres of land to remain unused and investment of seven crores on the canal to remain dormant?

4. The consultant's report on the working of the Multan power station is heart breaking. They have identified major flaws in its running and unprecedented inefficiency. One thing that stands out is that the engineers in charge were not trained by the manufacturers of machinery. Are we taking precautions that these things do not happen again elsewhere?

I am quite clear in my mind that in order to ensure speedy installation and correct functioning of enterprises, we should engage consultants as supervisors. This will add to the cost, but it will pay in the long run and unfortunate experience of the Multan power plant will not be repeated.

A report was received from Hakim Ahsan, our new Ambassador to Afghanistan to the effect that their foreign office officials, the prime minister and the king, during his interview with them, kept on harping on the so-called outstanding problems with Pakistan, i.e. Pakhtunistan, with this difference that the king was a little more suave. Ahsan told them that the interest of both the countries would be served better if we talked more about collaboration in the areas of agreement. There was considerable scope for collaboration in the economic field. Why not explore those areas instead of treading the barren path of conflict. In his earlier report, Ahsan had said that the Afghans see to it that something derogatory is said daily about Pakistan in their press and radio. I am not surprised by the Afghan attitude. I have been of the view that they will always maintain a posture of quiescence and hostility towards us and will not hesitate to stab us in the back whenever the opportunity arises. Our defence arrangements must cater for this. Any wishful expectation that the people of Afghanistan will not go against us has no relevance. People can always be mislead and worked up by an unscrupulous government in a time of crisis.

The Iranian ambassador came to call and conveyed the Shah's greetings. Said that the Shah was very happy to hear that I had completely recovered. He regarded me as a friend in whom he had great faith. I told him that I was not only the Shah's friend but his sincere well wisher and that of Iran. He then came to the problems of the Persian Gulf. Said that the Shah knew that he could not take Bahrain but he could not give up the claim to it until his demands were met. These related to a couple of islands at the entrance of the narrows to the Hormuz Strait. He also felt that the sheikhs of crucial states were too weak and backward to run a federation. There was bound to be turmoil after the British left and he did not want another power to take their place. The future of the Gulf should be left to the countries around it. The Shah was happy that Kosygin, during his visit to Iran, did not even mention this problem. I said, does it mean that he was not even thinking about it?

13 | WEDNESDAY

A dispatch was received from our ambassador in Washington giving an account of the conversation that took place between M.M. Ahmed, who hosted a dinner party, and an American senior official. Mr McNamara. The President of the World Bank was also present. The gist was as follows:

a. United States Congress is very angry with Pakistan because of the 1965 war with India. They maintain that it was the volume of American aid that enabled the two countries to divert their own resources to building up their armed forces.

b. The Congress was very critical of the arms race started by Pakistan against India.

c. Pakistan will soon realise its folly of cultivating friendship with China. When the Chinese over-run Thailand, Burma and India, they will also over-run Pakistan. Then Pakistan will feel the need of a common defence with India.

d. There is corruption in Pakistan.

e. For these reasons, Congress may put a moratorium on aid to Pakistan or may even cut it drastically.

Mr M.M. Ahmed and our ambassador tried to answer these charges, but it seems, not very effectively. The answer was that this type of reasoning on the part of the Americans was a classic example of ignorance of facts and subjective reasoning, not only relating to our affairs but also to world problems like Vietnam etc. In fact, most of the American predicaments arise out of this mentality. They set for themselves wrong aims based on ill-digested facts and are surprised when they don't get results. In our case, was it not India that crossed the international boundary and attacked Lahore and Sialkot sector and did we not have the right to defend ourselves and fight for out survival? As to an arms race, who can say that we started it? A mere look at the budgetary figures will prove this. Pakistan's military budget of 225 crores against India's 1100 crores. What sort of race is this? Has Pakistan not got the right to have some sort of deterrence? How can our relationship with China be regarded as a danger to this region? In fact, this may well deter them from doing anything untoward. And have we not offered joint defence to India, which she spurned and have we not said time and time again that we want peace with India on an honourable basis. No one wants to deny the existence of corruption in Pakistan but no respectable person takes any pride in it or is not anxious to eradicate it. The trouble is our legal system and social habits. At any rate, corruption in Pakistan is far less than in many developing countries and even the advanced countries. The real trouble is that the American administration and the Congress expect us to sacrifice even our national security for the promotion of their ill-conceived global interests. They want us to buy the enmity of China and the Soviet Union and accept the hegemony of India. This may sound nonsensical, but unfortunately, it is true.

14 | FRIDAY

The National Assembly debate on the budget is continuing. The opposition, being negative and destructive, naturally cannot see anything right with anything, but even some of our party members have spoken with malice. Abdul Hameed Jatoi and Wasan attacked officialdom, all and sundry, and made baseless accusations against the regime. I had to call the officials of the Muslim League Parliamentary Party and tell them that the government was honour bound to defend the good civil servants. After all, they cannot all be bad. So therefore, these two legislators, with Khar, who spoke in the same way in the assembly, should be served with a notice to explain their conduct. If the explanation is not satisfactory, they should be expelled. We can easily afford to lose a few of them.

15 | SATURDAY

I have set up a working party to examine how best we can give the student community and the labour a greater opportunity and feeling of participation. With labour, reasonable pay and working conditions are necessary, but these by themselves do not satisfy the human ego, so we are trying to create a fund consisting of 2.5 per cent of net income of each concern to be set aside for dispersal amongst the labourers on retirement. But above all, I would like to see them consulted frequently on methods and conditions of working. We should give them psychological satisfaction, as well as improved production and establish a better human relationship between labour and management. With the student community, a similar arrangement or a dialogue with the teaching staff should be established whereby every aspect of their life should be discussed. In addition, more attention should be paid to their living conditions and welfare. Mass physical training should become a regular future of student life. These measures, I believe, would go a long way in removing misunderstandings and frustration, which lead to irresponsibility and indiscipline.

17 | MONDAY

We have recently introduced a benevolent fund and a group insurance scheme for government servants of all descriptions at the centre and have instructed the provinces to do the same. I believe it will do a lot of good if these schemes are extended to the working classes, even in the private sector. Once an employee or the worker has an assurance that his family will be taken care of if something happens to him, he will work with confidence and self-assurance. By God's grace we have had a very good rice, cotton and wheat crop. As such, farmers would be making large cash incomes. I have told the provincial governors and the finance minister to give it a thought as to how surpluses can be turned into savings before they are squandered away on futile ceremonials.

20 | THURSDAY

General Yahya is proceeding to Moscow to negotiate an arms deal. I have told him to look into the following if the Russians are willing:

1. Offensive use of helicopters.
2. Ground to ground tactical missiles and anti-tank missiles.
3. Procurement of 57mm anti-aircraft guns. They are obsolete with the Russians.
4. Emphasize with the Russians that though they were responsible for arranging the Tashkent agreement yet they broke its spirit by arming India to the teeth and creating an explosive situation on the subcontinent.

It has come out in the Indian and US press that an American team headed by a State Department official is going to visit New Delhi in the near future to hold political economic and military discussions. India will obviously use this occasion to get more economic and military aid by raising the Chinese bogey, but in effect to build up against us. I have told the foreign minister to check on what mischief they are up to. I have also told him to put protest to the British that the sale of an aircraft carrier to India will amount to a hostile act against Pakistan. Any such transaction will further tilt the military imbalance against us heavily.

📖 The Sheikh of Abu Dhabi has asked us to provide some naval personnel to man his crafts and also train his infantry detachment for one year. I have decided to send someone to Abu Dhabi to examine his problem and advise what needs to be done. I am also thinking of sending someone to induce him to invest in Pakistan and lend us some money. He is bursting with riches. This year his oil royalty is expected to be 168 million dollars.

📖 The idea of equality is much more powerful than we suppose and you cannot kill ideas with cops, that is, policemen. Revolutions feed on themselves and are not satisfied with progress. Whilst thinking of these problems, it struck me that Naseem Hussain,[16] who represents *Dawn* in London, might be the right person to make a start. He is honest, sincere, intelligent, knowledgeable and patriotic with warm social contacts. He could fill the role of an unofficial emissary with distinction. So he was sent for and told to consider this proposal. He came up with a very sensible solution. To influence policy makers in any country you have to speak from a platform that is of interest to them, such a platform could be a Society for Promotion of Peace in Asia. This would be of immense interest to the American policy makers. This society could be organized in London and then extended to America. Naseem could head it. Once the society gains attention and credence, Naseem would be welcome in any literary or administrative circle and he will be in a position to put forward Pakistan's point of view. I told him to go ahead with full speed without loss of time.

📖 President's House, Rawalpindi

1. I have come to the painful conclusion that our public sector and especially the production units in it are a big liability and in most cases running at a loss. There is enough evidence to show that they are badly planned, over capitalized and over staffed with people inadequately trained, inefficiently and uneconomically run and not even kept reasonably clean. This can only be due to careless planning, neglect of training of staff, poor supervision and general lack of sense of responsibility. Then there is a craze on the part of the people concerned that money should be sunk in projects. Whether the investment gives any return or not is no concern of theirs. This is, to say the least, a shameful state of affairs, especially when a considerable portion of the investment is based on foreign loans and credits which have to be paid for and are being paid for by our hard earned and scarce foreign exchange.

2. This ruinous state of affairs cannot be allowed to continue. I would, therefore, ask you as the chairman of the committee which was setup to examine the future structure of autonomous bodies to consider and make recommendations on this problem too. To me the answer seems to be to engage a set of consultants as inspectors of these installations under the president. I would go further and recommend that they should be used to inspect private enterprises as well. It is only by adopting a method such as this that we can have a hope of making our investments pay.

3. Another matter you might consider is the advisability of creating,

a. An economic coordinating ministry at the centre to direct and supervise the activities of the ministries of finance, commerce, industry, and also the Planning Commission and their affiliated bodies.

b. A similar department in the provinces with similar task covering the activities of the autonomous bodies and the secretariat of the department of industries, finance and perhaps agriculture.

Signed.
Mohammad Ayub Khan
Field Marshal
20th June 1968

25 | TUESDAY

The repeated breakdowns in our powerhouses and uneconomical production in the industrial concerns in the public sector and even in the private sector is causing me great concern. The country, which is being developed on borrowed resources with heavy rate of interest, cannot afford this luxury. Something has to be done and quickly to reverse this trend. So I have written a note to the provinces and the central ministries and have suggested remedies for their consideration.

[A copy is given above. This note was produced earlier by the president, dated 20 June 1968].

26 | WEDNESDAY

Several people came to see me in the morning, amongst them was Nawabzada Asghar Ali, MPA of Gujrat; Sardar Muhammad Iqbal, MNA of Khunda; and Sardar Khizar Hayat, MNA of Chakwal. You could not come across more nice people than these. Men of great integrity and reliability and thorough gentlemen. Such people are the salt of this sacred earth.

I was talking to one of the ministers of the affairs of the National Assembly. I asked him how would he sum up the Bengali attitude. He said they were riddled with complexes, logic and reason has no meaning for them. All of them, inclusive of government party members, want to grab whatever they can from West Pakistan. The majority of them want to remain in different to West Pakistan and the Muslim culture. A good few would like to have as little link with the centre and West Pakistan as possible. Some would even secede and join with West Bengal. There are very few who think in terms of all Pakistan.

Heard of poor Ayub's death in Washington. He died of heart failure. He was our representative at the World Bank. A valuable and highly experienced administrator has been lost.

Naseem of *Dawn* had recently interviewed the Shah in Tehran. He noted the following:

a. The coming year is going to be the Indian year in Iran. Desai is visiting Iran in the near future. Several other Indian missions are also scheduled to go. There is going to be exchange of visits by the two navies. The Indians have offered training facilities to Iran.

b. The Shah is getting closer to India to dominate the Persian Gulf with their assistance. The Russians and the Americans may well be behind this move for their own reasons.

c. The Shah said that he had recognised Israel because it was a fact of life. When told that China, with a population of 700 million people, is also a fact of life, the Shah kept quiet.

d. When told that India had built up tremendous arms strength, the Shah saw no harm in it provided it was not used against Pakistan. This is the height of naivety.

27 | THURSDAY

Held a cabinet meeting today, some important decisions were taken. The central Ministry of Health will run the Jinnah Hospital and Postgraduate Training Centre at Karachi. Also they will run the Institute of Tropical Diseases in East Pakistan in conjunction with Ayub Hospital. This is in Peshawar. These institutions will cater for the higher medical training of doctors from both the wings. Apparently this problem has been the subject of discussion between the finance and the health ministry for several years. They could not come to any agreement. To me the answer was obvious as soon as I read the summary.

The printing press in the central government in different places is run inefficiently, a committee was set up to examine this problem. The decision was that we should form a textbook and printing corporation, which is to be run on commercial lines for the ministries and departments of the central government. This should make for economy and efficiency.

I ordered that, like the public servants, a scheme of benevolent fund and group insurance be introduced for the private sector too. We give a number of honours to deserving people, but this does not help the lower grade officers and staff. I propose that such people be given cash awards. A few *lakhs* spent like this would go a long way in building up the morale of public servants.

28 | FRIDAY

Received a long communication from our ambassador in Washington on the American communication centre in Badaber. The American administration seems to have decided that the maintenance of this centre is vital to their security and so they are thinking of using 'carrot and stick method' with us to ensure its continuance in Pakistan. The alternatives they are going to try on us are as follows:

a. Continue to stay on in disregard of the termination notice without renewal of the agreement.

b. Get extension for every six months.

c. Offer the manning of the operation of the installation by our personnel.

d. Keep some facilities here and some elsewhere, possibly in Iran.

Whilst these negotiations are in progress, they will intimidate us by threatening to withhold economic aid which, in any case, is under fire in the Congress, or offer us inducements in the form of military hardware etc. Our problem is that we cannot afford to antagonise the Soviet Union and China, which the Americans would very much like us to do. If we relent, the Americans may even expose us to the Soviets and the Chinese to queer our relations. In any case, there is no secrecy in the United States on such matters and we cannot risk being exposed. So the coming months with the Americans are going to be difficult.

1 | SATURDAY

📖 Addressed the press editors on national and international problems. The minutes follow.

Points for the editors. Thanked them for the sympathy they showed during my illness.

1. Agriculture breakthrough needed for larger fields and mechanization, pooling of land (get Altaf Gauhar to read my paper; this will have to wait for elections).
2. Dialogue with students and labour, give them the feeling of participation.
3. Educational system to be brought in line with our requirements. Need for a prospective manpower plan, a commission being set up to go into the problems.
4. Future of autonomous bodies have done a lot of good, splitting of them and forming more boards, public committee set up, public sector, how to make it pay.
5. Introduction of group insurance and benevolent fund for all employees of government at the centre and the provinces, ask the private sector to adopt it too, the press might adopt these with advantage
6. Workers identification and interest in production, workers fund two and a half per cent, income of a concern to be put into this.
7. My visit to UK.
8. The plight of Muslims in India causing us great concern.
9. My worry about corruption, violence and adulteration.

Our trouble is that our life pattern and institutions are based on materialism and individualism.

📖 Discussed with Musa, Kirmani and others the details of the West Pakistan Muslim League council meeting on the 14th of July in Lahore. A committee was set up to recommend the names of the office bearers that will be put up for elections.

2 | SUNDAY

📖 An idea struck me that it will do a lot of good politically and socially to embroil the women in Muslim League work. In fact, they are most anxious to lend a helping hand. So a central committee consisting of Begum G.A. Khan,[17] Begum Zeenat Fida Hassan[18] and a lady from East Pakistan was set up, they will be assisted by provincial committees and their task will be to organize women's committees in as many cities and towns as possible and also lay down their tasks. If this movement gains momentum, and I don't see why it should not, it may well prove to be a major actor in women's emancipation apart from proving a powerful political pressure.

3 | MONDAY

📖 M.M. Ahmed reported on the proceedings of the Aid to Pakistan consortium meeting on return from Washington. Apparently they were deeply impressed by our performance and progress and endorsed our requirement for the coming year, which amounts to 550 million dollars. However, this does not mean that they have pledged the money. In fact, we are completely in the dark as to what the Americans would do. Their Congress is in a cantankerous mood and is itching to slash this aid bill, if not reject it in toto. So the future is uncertain.

M.M. Ahmed also visited Paris at the behest of the French government even though they were experiencing internal turmoil. In spite of their difficulties the French showed magnanimity. They increased the annual aid by five million dollars and softened their terms.

I am very happy that De Gaulle's party had such a thundering success in the recent elections and his stand has been vindicated. But whether this will dampen the style of disruptionists, remains to be seen. All one can say at present is that the French nation has recovered itself just short of the precipice of ruination and disaster. So I am causing a message of congratulations to be sent to De Gaulle.

📖 Begum G.A. Khan spoke to me about Gohar Ayub in glowing terms. She got to know him on a mission to China and was deeply impressed by his manners and conduct. She told me to take care of him and give him the opportunity for higher training with delegations etc. abroad. She thought one day he should lead Pakistan. Now this may sound like flattery, but it is not. This has been my assessment of him. May God help him to attain his ceiling and have the opportunity of serving his country.

4 | TUESDAY

📖 Invited the local Muslim League Women's Committee to tea and took the opportunity to emphasize the important nature of their task. They have to lend a hand in awakening people to a sense of civic responsibilities, friendliness, better care of children, thrift and shunning sectarianism and wasteful customs. The texture of our society is changing through spread of education, industrialization and urbanization. It is imminent, therefore, that our norms will also change. In doing so let us take care that we retain the good points of our culture whilst there is no hesitation in adopting the good points of others. The other extreme of blocking the influence of western and industrial culture is futile. It just won't work, the world is shrinking too fast communication-wise, and ideas travel fast. In any case, why should we deny ourselves the blessing of other people's knowledge?

6 | WEDNESDAY

📖 Mr Amjad Ali Chaudhry of Sylhet[19] was sworn in as a minister of the central government, in place of late Altaf Hussain. In coming to this decision I had to consult a number of people. The trouble is that in East Pakistan there is such a dearth of men of calibre. It reminds me of the talk I had some years ago with Akhtar Hameed Khan[20] who runs the Comilla Academy. I asked him if he could suggest some people from East Pakistan who could be considered for employment as ministers. He is a man of few words and often curt. He said in East Pakistan you should be content with four anna man. Expecting anything more is futile and a waste of time. I do hope Amjad Ali proves a bit better than that. He certainly has a good background, thinks in terms of Pakistan and is not a bigot like others from that province. He also shows no hesitation in expressing his views openly.

📖 I had to give a decision today on the vexed question of pensions for the armed forces personnel. A long and bitter argument had been going on between the services and the finance ministry.

Naturally, the services were asking for the moon whereas finance offered two alternatives, increase in pensions proportionate to increase in pay which took place sometime ago or accept the formula that applies to the civilians. As the latter happened to be more favourable, I accepted it, with some increase for the ranks of colonel and above. This will increase the pension of all ranks by 30 to 40 per cent though even our existing pension code is higher than that of the Indians.

8 | SATURDAY

A military mission headed by General Yahya Khan which was on a ten day visit to the Soviet Union reached Karachi this morning. A message was received from General Yahya that he received an extraordinary reception from the Russians and they went out of their way to make his visit fruitful. As regards our military requirements they met practically all our demands barring the bombers, which they refused to supply. They promised to give 200 T54 and T55 tanks, 112, 130 mm guns, 500 rocket launchers and convert our ships to take ship to ship missiles. As regard the aircraft, they offered to let us have as many MIG-21 and SU-7 as we wanted. For the first three items, the contract has been signed, the terms are easy, 10 years loan with 2 per cent interest repayable in rupees.

The interior minister told me that he had heard on the BBC that Bhutto, who is on a visit to England, has been indulging in fulmination. He said that Pakistan was under naked dictatorship and so on. Later, news came in that Pakistani students in London had raided the high commissioner's office and he had to call in the police for help. It is quite possible that they were instigated by Bhutto, perhaps in support of Mujibur Rahman, an accused in the Agartala conspiracy case. Details are awaited.

9 | SUNDAY

I spent a sleepless night because of an attack of fibrillation of my heart. It is nothing new but has become more frequent during the last couple of years. Despite this, I had to attend the office because several important people had been scheduled to see me. Mr James McCormack, Chairman, Board of Directors of Communication Satellite Corporation, followed by the US ambassador, followed by the ambassador of Iraq and followed by the ambassador of Russia. All had important messages to deliver and important points to discuss.

Our Foreign Minister, Mr Arshad Hussain returned from a visit to Turkey. He came back very impressed and said the Turks now understand our stand on CENTO. How can we take enthusiastic part in the pact, which the Americans call purely anti-USSR, at a stage when the USA has withdrawn its support from us leaving us no alternative but to go to the Soviets for help and assistance? Talking about the Shah of Iran, the Turkish impression is that he has started behaving like a jealous old woman taking offence on anything you tell him, especially about the Persian Gulf and the relationship with the Arabs. There is no hope of curing him, so the only alternative is to just listen to whatever he says. We cannot afford to offend him. The stakes are much too high. The Turkish foreign minister, who was about to visit the USSR, asked Arshad Hussain as to what should he tell the Soviets about Pakistan. This was a kind gesture.

📖 There have been extensive and devastating floods in East Pakistan due to rise of water level in the river Brahmaputra and unprecedented rains in several districts. Several lives have been lost and extensive damage has been caused to property and standing crops. The Governor, East Pakistan is coming here in a day or two and will tell us more about it, but meanwhile the rains are still continuing. I feel so bad for the poor people who have suffered so much.

11 | TUESDAY

📖 The Indians have started an organized howl in their press, radio and elsewhere against the suspected promise of sale of military equipment to us by Russia. A protest has been sent to the Russian government through their president who happens to be in Moscow now. It is being made out that we shall use these arms for aggressive purposes and thereby bring instability to the Indian subcontinent. What in effect the Indians want is that Pakistan should remain defenceless so that they are free to swallow it at will. So any attempt to build any defensive capacity on our part is resented.

12 | WEDNESDAY

📖 General Yahya reported on return from his visit of Russia. The gist of his talk is already recorded. He was given a great reception and shown great consideration. Kosygin also gave him an interview. This has never been done with any other military mission. The Russians offered him far more than we asked for. For instance, missile cutters or missile boats OSSA, SAM missile with 1200 mile range. The price asked for equipment contracted also is very reasonable. The cost of a tank comes to 6 *lakhs* and the 130mm guns 1.5 *lakhs*. These prices are one-third of the prices quoted by the western countries.

13 | THURSDAY

📖 Went by train to Lahore to attend the West Pakistan Muslim League Council meeting. Thousands and thousands of people came to greet me en route and seemed happy to see me at Lahore railway station. There was a vast crowd even though darkness had fallen. The railway station and the route to the governor's house where I stayed, was tastefully illuminated. I noticed amongst the crowd a large number of labour representatives with banners.

📖 In the morning the uncle of the King of Jordan had come to see me with a letter from him. It contained the proposal for the king's youngest brother to get married to Begum Shaista[21] Ikramullah's youngest daughter, and seeking my blessings. I readily agreed, praying that it will be a happy marriage. I don't know the girl but the boy is well-educated, intelligent and a sensible lad.

14 | FRIDAY

📖 Due to incessant rain on the previous night, it was not possible to hold the Muslim League Council meeting in an open secluded place. So the venue had to be shifted to the old Punjab University hall. This was done at short notice, which speaks volumes for the efficiency of the organizers. The audience consisted of the councillors, about 500 elected from all over the province, a number of old Muslim Leaguers who fought the battle of Pakistan with the Quaid-e-Azam, party members of the provincial and central assemblies, and the ministers. It was a fine gathering and an historic occasion. The cream of the province was present. The proceedings of the meeting started with election of the office bearers. Mr Kirmani, the president-elect gave a speech followed by an economic review by Mr Uqaili and a talk by Chaudhary Khaliquzzaman. I spoke last and covered a large canvas.

In the evening, I held a reception. Some 2000 people turned up. Large numbers of women from all over Pakistan were also present. They were very enthusiastic in a forming Muslim League Ladies Wing all over the country. I believe that this movement will bring about a real awakening amongst the women of the country.

News from East Pakistan is bad. Chittagong district had received 49 inches of rain in five days. 30 inches fell in 24-hours. The whole countryside is flooded out, some 8 *lakh* people are affected. River Karnaphuli is discharging 290,000 cusec of water, the highest recorded in its history and is flowing at 20 knots. No ship can enter or leave the harbour. Some select portions of Rangpur and other places are similarly affected. It is too early to say what is the extent of the loss. It must be colossal. Relief work is going on. The provincial government has sanctioned rupees 45 lakhs. I have sanctioned rupees 50 lakhs from the central government plus rupees 10 lakhs from my welfare fund. With these regular floods and cyclones devastating life, property and crops, it is obvious that as far as food is concerned, East Pakistan's salvation lies in the winter crop and artificial irrigation, but East Pakistanis don't seem to realize this and insist on wasting resources on things like steel mills and machine tool plants, little regarding that first things must come first.

15 | SATURDAY

Returned to Rawalpindi by train.

16 | SUNDAY

The director intelligence, General Akbar, came to report on his impression of the visit to Russia. He was impressed with their attitude and candour. He thought that they react very much like us, are people with wide sympathy and understanding and felt that unless Pakistan was strong, stability could not be maintained on the subcontinent. They were also getting to know the deviousness of the Indians. They kept on talking about me in words of high regard. Akbar also showed me a copy of the offensive plan of the 1st Indian Corps against West Pakistan. It has been marked out in great detail, right down to the battalion, especially the crossings and bridges over the Ravi. To exploit success, an Infantry Division and an Armoured Brigade has been earmarked as reserve to this Corps. I congratulated him for this very great achievement. Getting to know the enemy's plan in advance is rare good fortune and can be a great contributory factor to success. As regards our plans, I have given instructions that there should be as little paperwork as possible. Orders and instructions should be issued by word of mouth to the extent possible.

Akbar also showed me the Indian road plan. It is a colossal effort, for instance, they are building a major highway connecting Bareilly in Uttar Pradesh to Tejpur and beyond in Assam, a length of some 1500 miles. This is an American supported project. Another road has been built connecting Simla with Leh through Mandi. This road goes over a pass of 15,000 feet. Yet another road system starts from Ferozpur and goes right to Kutch running along the West Pakistan border. This is 70 tons specification.

17 | MONDAY

The American Ambassador came to see me at short notice with a message from President Johnson, the burden of which was that in spite of the fact that America had given us aid worth 3.5 billion dollars, we were insisting on winding up Badaber Base and that we had allowed discussion to take place on this in the Parliament. He went on to say that if we could not rescind the decision, we should at least agree to a programme of winding up that would enable them to make alternative arrangements. In saying all this, he forgets that our security hazards and political liabilities have increased to a dangerous level due to this installation. We knew this and yet kept our part of the contract whilst the Americans betrayed us at every turn. They built up India against us, failed to come to our assistance in 1965, despite bilateral defence agreement, and finally stopped military aid. Now even spares are not given to us easily. Yet they expect us to expose ourselves to the enmity of India and China. They think that we exist for their convenience and that our freedom is negotiable. I have told the foreign minister to prepare a reply on the above basis but couched in polite language. However, there would be no harm in making some concessions over the duration of winding up.

18 | TUESDAY

Flew into Karachi midday. This was my first visit to Karachi after my illness. A large number of people turned up to receive me on the airfield. Similarly, there was a large collection of people en route, which was tastefully decorated.

19 | WEDNESDAY

Governor Musa came in to see me. I had sent him to Quetta to find out the causes of trouble that had taken place between the Pathan and non-Pathan students in a local college leading to firing between them and the police. He told me that the Afghan consul stationed in Quetta was behind the trouble. He instigated the Pathan boys through some Pushtoonistanis to create trouble. Later, Minister Sarwar Khan had been sent there to look into the matter. He too misbehaved, admonished the police in public and gave succour to the mischief makers. I told the governor to obtain his explanation and also let us have a complete report on the Afghan consul's conduct. He must have been acting under the instructions of his government. Yet we may have to take up the matter with them.

20 | MONDAY

📖 The Shah and his ministers stayed to lunch with us. In the afternoons we foregathered for talks. I wanted to talk to him alone. He agreed. I started by asking the awkward question of our mutual relationship. There are indications that there has been some erosion in it. Iran seems to have some grievances against us. I would like to know what they are as their continuance would only do harm to both the countries. The Shah started off by saying that our attitude towards the Arabs had caused them anxiety. After all, what could the Arabs do for us? I told him that our support to the Arabs was dictated by these considerations, religious affinity, and an effort to under-cut India's mischief in these countries and be in a position to act as a cushion between Iran and the Arabs. So he must not misunderstand our motives. We then moved on to the shape of things to come in the Gulf after the British withdrawal in 1971. I told the Shah that unless the countries of [...]—big and small—get together to have common defence arrangements, other naval powers like India or Russia will get sucked in. The effect will be disastrous for all of them. He agreed and said that he was willing to enter into any form of agreement with these countries but he could not give up his claim to Bahrain or the small islands in the Hormuz Straits at the entrance to the Gulf. I asked him what he would be satisfied with. He said some sort of face saving device, like a referendum on Bahrain. As to the islands, I told him why not work for a joint militarization of them in conjunction with the Arabs? He did not disapprove of the idea. I told him time was of the essence. He must make quick moves to bring about a joint plan. He agreed. I have also sent a signal to King Faisal who wanted me to intercede on his behalf with the Shah to act quickly. If these efforts bear fruit, a lot of good should come to this part of the world.

We then discussed our relationship with China, Russia and the United States. Our resolve is to maintain good relationships with all of them on a bilateral basis.

I told the Shah about Indian military preparations against us, their victimisation of the Muslim minority, their ambitions in the Indian Ocean and Persian Gulf and told him to be careful in dealing with them.

23 | SUNDAY

📖 Went to the Hammersmith Hospital for a medical check up. Professor Goodwin and another cardiologist went over me. They are very satisfied with what they have seen so far. But they have to carry out more tests tomorrow and the day after. They do a thorough job of these things.

📖 Naseem Hussain, *Dawn*'s correspondent in London, whom I have charged with the mission of forming the 'Peace in Asia Society' brought Mr Noel-Baker[22] to lunch. Noel-Baker is a member of the Parliament and chairman of the foreign relations committee and a Nobel prize winner, and has agreed to be the chairman of the committee. He is a very kind man though getting on in age. When this society gets going I hope an effective platform would have been formed to expose India's perfidy in Asia.

25 | TUESDAY

📖 Abdur Rehman Khan, our ambassador in Germany, came to see me. He raised certain points of importance concerning our relationship with Germany. They are very good friends, our relationship with them must remain warm. They had been asking me to spend some time at one of their spas. I had to decline the invitation, as there was not enough time to spare.

26 | WEDNESDAY

📖 Professor Dr Salam, one of our famous mathematicians, came to see me and brought several good books and reading material. He was worried that Islamabad University had not included biology as one of the subjects. This he considered essential for developing the art of plant genetics for agriculture. He also thought that duplication of certain subjects that are taught at the Pakistan Institute of Nuclear Sciences was not necessary. In fact, this institute should be a part of the university. I told him to come over to Pakistan and discuss things with us. But his suggestion makes me think that perhaps all institutions imparting higher education research organizations should come under this university. It would then be possible to obtain further coordination amongst them. Perhaps we might go even further and establish a ministry of science and technology.

📖 I thanked Duncan Sandys, an MP, for the trouble he had taken in 1962 to arrange a meeting between Nehru and me to settle the Kashmir issue. He said that the Americans sabotaged that meeting. Kennedy at Nassau, and later, Grove would not see the logic of British pleading that there should be no arms delivery to India until Kashmir was settled, as how else could India face China. Kennedy rejected this argument saying that their priorities were made up. China was on the top; they could not get involved in Kashmir. Also, his embassy in Delhi kept on telling him that no pressure should be brought to bear on Nehru at this stage as otherwise his government would collapse.

📖 Had a long discussion with the high commissioner on the affairs of the Pakistan community in Britain. They are by and large uneducated and driven with parochial differences—Bengali against West Pakistani—then there are differences amongst West Pakistanis, they wouldn't get together. Bengalis are not all disloyal. There is a small minority that indulges in disruption but the rest are not prepared to disown them. In other words, they have inner sympathy for them. Meanwhile, the West Pakistanis are getting tired of the activities of this element. They may well beat them up in future and this would not be an inappropriate answer. But one thing is certain there is not much communication between the high commissioner and the community. The answer would be to find a suitable replacement from the Punjab, as the bulk of Pakistanis here are Punjabi-speaking. Then this mission is grossly over staffed; everybody says so. This is a legacy of the past when we had a lot more to do in Britain. I must get this looked into when I get back home.

📖 Moved to Selsden Park hotel. It is a beautiful place in the wooded country at the edge of London. Very peaceful and quite lovely walks and golf course close by.

29 | SATURDAY

📖 The long awaited decision by the Pope[23] on birth control was announced. He stood for complete rejection of birth control by artificial methods basically on two grounds, one, that women could be misused by men, and two, that some dictatorial governments may well use it as an instrument of advancing their political ambitions. Nothing could be more absurd and baseless as these arguments are about a matter of great importance to mankind. Facing population explosion and its attendant consequences, only a priest obsessed with dogma and hide bound with tradition could have such an impractical approach. That is why any form of rule by the priest [hood] is so reprehensible and irrational in an educated society. The reaction, of course, to this order in Europe and America even amongst the priests has been sharp and vicious. There is every chance that Catholic society may well get split on this issue.

8 | THURSDAY

📖 Justice Munir came to see me. He suffered a heart attack sometime back and now suffers from depression and insomnia. He has come over here for treatment but he is a completely broken man, and has lost all faith in himself and life. I was very sorry to see him in that state and gave him all encouragement.

📖 The news of Richard Nixon's nomination as the Republican Party candidate came in yesterday. He gained a clear majority on the first ballot which is rare. Nixon is a friend of mine. I have known him for a long time. How will he do as president if elected is difficult to say, but as far as Pakistan is concerned American policy can't be much different whoever is the president. Their obsession with communism, especially in China, makes their sight very jaundiced.

11 | SUNDAY

📖 Spent a quiet day making up for lost sleep, had a chat with the governor of West Pakistan who put me in the picture on the problems of the province.

📖 Rang up Governor Monem Khan to ascertain the flood situation in East Pakistan. I was told that things are getting back to normal.

📖 Exchanged views with Kirmani, Khizr, Aslam and Gohar Ayub about the affairs of the Muslim League. The movement is gaining momentum and order is emerging

12 | MONDAY

📖 Reached Rawalpindi in the morning. People had arranged a grand reception at the airport; a large number of ladies had turned up which is a happy sign. It is the outcome of initiation of the Muslim League women's organization. I believe this movement in due course will deliver a death blow to the culture of purdah provided we don't talk about it and don't force the pace.

13 | TUESDAY

📖 Called several ministers and secretaries and gave them the following points to examine:

a. Our high commission in London is bloated and overstaffed, a large number of people are redundant; judicious planning could lead to a saving of 25 to 30 lakhs a year all in foreign exchange. A committee under Fida Hassan was set up to examine proposals to this effect which I have brought from London.

b. The leading bankers in the country should be asked to institute mobile banks based on wheels to visit major villages on a fixed schedule to accept deposits and cash cheques. Large amount of money is going into the farmer's pockets as a consequence of enhanced agriculture yields. This will be wasted if not suitably mopped up.

c. PINSTECH[24] should form part of Islamabad University and subjects taught here should not be duplicated in Islamabad. Consideration should also be given to setting up an organization to control and direct all research and scientific activities in the country.

d. A non-official like Ibrahim Rehmatullah should be appointed as the head of TCP [Trading Corporation of Pakistan]. He will manage it better and be able to answer hostile propaganda by the traders more effectively.

e. A suitable non-official should be considered for appointment as high commissioner in London. The bulk of the work there is consular and political because of the presence of a large Pakistani community and a gang of disruptionist elements from East Pakistan.

f. Instead of giving bonus as at present, the industrialists should be called upon to give a portion of their profit to the workers. This will stimulate greater production and also make the industrialists keep their accounts straight; then he shouldn't be able to fudge his accounts easily and dodge taxation.

g. The new pension code for the armed forces should be published quickly.

h. In future all public funds including local bodies should be deposited in the state bank or the national bank. Their deposit in other banks is not safe. Lately a couple of banks have been declared bankrupt and have succeeded in embezzling over five crores of local bodies money.

📖 Mr Arshad Hussain, the Foreign Minister, reported on his visit to China. He was given a rousing reception wherever he went and it was demonstrably being shown. The object, I suppose, was to show to the Russians, Indians and the Americans that they had not lost Pakistan. He was met by Chen-yi, Chou En-lai and even Mao Tse-tung who spoke to him for a long time. They showed friendship and support to Pakistan. They are convinced that the Vietnam War is not going to terminate and that America, in connivance with Russia, will in desperation attack China in collaboration with India and Japan. They are preparing for such a contingency. It will be at that stage that India may attack Pakistan with the blessing of America. Personally, I can't see events taking such a course. America would be very foolish to embark on a continental conquest. Already their people are sick and tired of Vietnam. As regards further military aid to Pakistan, they hesitated to commit themselves but felt they may be able to help in a year's time when they hope their production will go up. The Cultural Revolution has apparently given some setback to their production. Meanwhile, they encouraged us to get whatever assistance we could from Russia and America. The meaning of that is clear; they are not able to bear our liabilities.

16 | FRIDAY

📖 Told Governor West Pakistan that as the Khan of Kalat has been made advisor for the Baloch, a prominent Pathan should be made advisor for the Pathan tribes in Balochistan to keep them safe from Achakzai's[25] influence and exploitations by the disruptionist Baloch. Nazar Mohammed would probably be a suitable choice.

17 | SATURDAY

📖 Mr Kosygin, once describing his talks with Mr Johnson in America to me, asked the president what they were fighting for in Vietnam? When told, for the freedom of the South Vietnam, Kosygin said, freedom from whom? This just describes the situation in Asia. These countries must be left alone to evolve their own salvation. Any thought that China will in due course swallow them up is utter nonsense. Such things are not possible in this age of nationalism. All that can happen is that China will attract more attention if she is in a position to give these countries economic and military support.

📖 Just heard that the C-in-Cs of the three services in Turkey have tendered their resignations. I hope this does not lead to another turmoil. It will put Turkey back by years. The cause of tension may well be the attitude of people in government towards the United States. Some people consider America is becoming unreliable and would like to see some measure of disengagement with them, and an easing up with Russia. The cutback in American aid maybe an emotional factor.

19 | MONDAY

📖 Points for talk with the Manpower Commission:

1. Very happy that this commission has come into being and also with its composition; so much talent and experience is represented.
2. The need for such a commission was overdue. I have been deeply concerned with the lack of coordination between our manpower requirement in the coming future and the educational system. How can such an educational system be purposeful or prove fruitful. The educational system, to be purposeful, has to meet the manpower requirements of the country and also be so designed that it brings happiness and success to the individual.

Our educational system must be purposeful for two reasons:

a. We have not the means to waste on an uncoordinated and purposeless educational system.
b. We can not afford to produce educated manpower that is unproductive, therefore, unemployable and frustrated. The social hazards are too great. Quote Mr Kosygin's remark on this subject.

We not only have to educate our people purposefully but we also have to instruct them in the techniques of modern life from which there is no escape. The world has shrunk communication-wise. Ideas travel fast.

Your terms of reference are all laid down. They are comprehensive but should you feel the need enlargement of the scope, don't hesitate to do so. As to the shortcomings of the educational m and the problems we are facing, they are indicated in the extracts of Mr Mahbubul Haq's[26] They conform to my views which I have been expressing from time to time.

expect from you a report based on heavenly wisdom. All I expect is a well considered d workable scheme. It can be corrected in the light of experience.

'ng such a scheme you should study what the countries like us faced. Also see how ountries resolved their problems. Your scheme must also be within our means. In other words, you have to work backwards, have the resources that can be made available for education.

5. As I see it, the problem of education is something like this.
   a. Need for universal literacy. How can we speed it up? Lot of wastage in child education. No adult education. How can this be put right?
   b. Sorting out of people for higher education and at what stage. The numbers will be relatively small. The bulk will consist of those who will have to be diverted to professions, crafts and skills. They pose the more difficult problem.
   c. Can we introduce abridged courses as a temporary measure in subjects that lend themselves to such a treatment?
   d. The role that the private philanthropist, individuals and private industry will have to play.
   e. Review of curricula and arrangements for training teachers.
6. The future of Islamabad University. Putting atomic energy institutes under it and even the Islamic Research Institute. Creation of a coordinating body to control and coordinate the activities of different science councils and research bodies.
7. Finally, I would like to say that we can only better our lives if we enter this highly competitive age of science and technology in the right spirit. This spirit demands rational and scientific attitude and intellect. Intellect is the basis of all progress. This is what you have to help us to create.

21 | WEDNESDAY

News came in this morning that Czechoslovakia was invaded by the Russian, East German, Polish, Hungarian and Bulgarian forces. The Czechs did not offer any resistance but there are indications that shooting has taken place in a number of places and casualties inflicted. The Russian statement is that this intervention has taken place at the invitation of the Czech government and the troops will be withdrawn when no longer necessary. BBC news is that this move of the Russians has met with large scale condemnation by some communist countries as well as communist parties in the western world. President Tito and the president of Romania are particularly vocal.

The Russian Chargè d'Affairs came in the evening and delivered a message from his government explaining why they had taken such a step. The object was to save socialism, frustrate designs of the regime that was in coalition with the imperialists, and to protect Soviet vital interests. The real reason probably is that the Russians did not want to see erosion in their satellite world endangering their security, and liberalization spreading to their country. But be that as it may, this step of theirs is going to have far reaching consequences. Disenchantment with communism will spread, inner contradictions within the communist block will grow, East–West détente will get a setback, the cold war will recommence and peace in Vietnam will be put off for a long time as the hawks in America will get greater support after this precedent. All this is very sad for peace in the world and for mankind.

22 | THURSDAY

📖 Held a cabinet meeting. The major problem discussed was the future of wheat sale price from government godowns and rationing. There is enough wheat in West Pakistan. The decision was that we should do away with rationing and wheat control except that the millers will have to buy half of their requirements from government godowns at rupees eighteen and fifty paisa per maund. The government has large stocks, some lying in the open. If they are not disposed of quickly there is a danger of them rotting in the rain. At this rate the government is going to suffer some loss but that can't be helped.

The other decision we took was to set up a committee to go into the problem of introduction of mechanization in farming in West Pakistan, and later in East Pakistan. This has now become a burning question.

The effect of the Agartala conspiracy case on public opinion in East Pakistan was discussed. Everybody agreed that the political advantage of warning people of such people's designs of selling out to India was not taken. Altaf Gauhar was detailed to proceed to East Pakistan and tell the governor this aspect should be taken care of.

Lately, we have taken the following decisions which will have far reaching effects on the future of the country:

a. Giving $2^1/_2$ per cent share of profit of industry to the workers. I hope we shall be able to raise this whilst doing away with bonus.
b. Setting up of manpower commission with a view to coordinating education with manpower requirement.
c. Mobile rural banks.
d. Introduction of agriculture cooperatives.

Discussed with the foreign minister and the foreign secretary the attitude we should take with the Czechoslovakian crisis. The foreign minister was of the view that as several countries and important people had condemned the Russian action we should show some identification. I was against it as such an action will be of no assistance to the Czechs and will only antagonize the Russians against us. The decision was that we should issue no statement as none was called for. After all how many countries issued statements supporting us when we were attacked, and that our role should be that of a moderator both inside and outside the Security Council. Apparently, the Indian Lok Sabha has strongly condemned the Russian action. I hope the Russians will react suitably and realize what sort of people they have armed to the teeth and are supporting.

23 | FRIDAY

📖 A resolution was moved by ten nations in the Security Council condemning the Soviet Union for aggressing against Czechoslovakia and demanding immediate withdrawal of troops. Very hot words were exchanged between the Soviets and the American representative. It was vetoed by the Soviets. In the previous voting as to whether this should be discussed, eleven members were for it, two against and three abstained including Pakistan. India, though showing regret on Soviet action, also abstained. Meanwhile, the Soviets are finding it difficult to set up an alternative government in Prague.

28 | WEDNESDAY

📖 Held political talks with King Hussein. I was surprised to hear that all these guerrilla raids in Israel were by the Palestinian refugees and carried out without his permission or even knowledge, and were launched from Syria and other countries, whereas he and his people became the victims of Israeli reprisals to which he has no answer as the enemy is superior on land and air.

29 | THURSDAY

📖 Mr Altaf Gauhar, who was sent to East Pakistan to assess the situation, reported as follows:
a. The damage to the crops due to floods is not as great as made out to be.
b. The reaction to Mujibur Rahman's activities and his associates in the Agartala conspiracy[27] case is not such as would make people consider them as traitors. There may be people who think them so but there is no one who is prepared to come in the open and condemn them. His supporters are collecting money for defence and for use by themselves and people are contributing. One young Bengali, however, told Altaf Gauhar it seems we are set on a course of self-destruction. This remark sums up the situation.
c. Manzur Qadir,[28] the prosecution lawyer, considers that there are 50:50 chances of Mujibur Rahman's conviction. The three CSP officers are sure to be convicted and also some minor fry.
d. The governor agrees that our party members should expose the perfidy of the conspirators by whatever means possible.

30 | FRIDAY

📖 Regarding the future of Badaber, we have to act quickly in a preventive action before pressure builds up against us. This pressure will come when the American ambassador returns to Pakistan from his visit armed with his government's instructions. The plan is to send for the American representative and tell him that the people against whom Badaber is directed have come to know the American intention. They've warned us that the use of these facilities in any form or shape will be regarded as a hostile act. This should leave no room in the American mind for doubt about our position.

📖 Gave a talk to the bankers on the extension of the banking system to the rural areas through mobile banks, based on vehicles, boats or a railway carriage. It is simple and cheap but a system that can bring about a major revolution in the social habits and economic outlook of the broad masses of people. In any case, there is an immediate need to mop up vast amounts of money that is going in the pockets of farmers through enhanced agricultural production to prevent undue inflation, pressure being put on the prices of other commodities, and stop or curtail wasteful expenditure. But the bankers must also do their duty by the farmers by ploughing back this money in the agricultural economy, relieve them of some of their burdens, and help them modernize. The bankers could also start industries or commerce based on agriculture produce. I also emphasized the need for setting up modern bakeries in all cities and towns to save the housewife the trouble of making *chapattis* day in and day out. This, in fact, is Hindu custom and we must do away with it.

📖 The meeting of Quaid-e-Azam's *mazar* committee was held. The progress up to date was reviewed and future programme discussed. From the consultants and architect's proposal it looked like a lot of unnecessary things were being added making the expenditure go up exorbitantly high. A committee was, therefore, set up to go into these proposals and approve only those that were absolutely necessary. It was impressed on the committee that the emphasis should be laid on the mausoleum and its completion as soon as possible. Other things could be constructed later, if needed.

31 | SATURDAY

📖 Recorded my first of the month speech.

📖 Members of Rabita-e-Islami, who came from Saudi Arabia, met me in conjunction with Justice Cheema and Maulana Hussaini, who run the Islamic centre in Geneva. We discussed the trials and tribulations of the Muslim world and the problems we were facing in this age of science and technology. Our salvation lies in unity, at least on the cultural and economic field, and making the Quran a vehicle of progress. Its principles and teachings have to be pursued in the language of reason so that it appeals to the modern man.

📖 Flew into Rawalpindi.

1 | SUNDAY

📖 A very interesting article by Z.A. Suleri on the perfidous policy of the Kabul government towards Pakistan. No Pakistani should be under any illusion that they will not stab us in the back whenever they get an opportunity. I am saying this because our people are apt to be sloppy and emotional when talking about them. Even some of our ambassadors have tried to mislead us about them from time to time. I know of one ambassador who used to deliberately conceal their misdeeds and ill intentions towards us.

5 | THURSDAY

Dr Fazlur Rahman, director of the Islamic Research Institute, came under countrywide adverse criticism fanned by the ignorant and politically motivated mullahs. The allegations, which were totally false, were made against some remarks made in his book, *Islam*, which he wrote some years ago and which was later published by the Oxford University Press. This book is a highly scholarly work written for an European audience and an attempt to remove some false impressions about Islam. When the criticism gained momentum he held two press conferences refuting all the allegations. These clarifications would have satisfied any honest critic, but the mullah, who regards any original and objective thinking on Islam as his deadly enemy, was not going to be pacified. This sort of argument is just the grist he wants for his mill. Meanwhile, the administrators at the centre and the provinces got cold feet. Some of them persuaded the doctor to resign. He must have also got frightened. After all, it is not easy to stand up to criticism based on ignorance and prejudice. So I had to accept his resignation with great reluctance in the belief that he will be freer to attack the citadel of ignorance and fanaticism from outside the governmental sphere. Meanwhile, it is quite clear that any form of research on Islam which inevitably leads to new interpretations has no chance of acceptance in this priest ridden and ignorant society. These people will not allow Islam to become a vehicle of progress. What will be the future of such an Islam in the age of reason and science is not difficult to predict.

📖 News of a devastating series of earthquakes from eastern Iran have been coming in. A large number of villages in the affected area have been destroyed and dozens of thousands of people have been killed, wounded or rendered homeless. We have sent a large medical contingent, medicines and tents on two aircraft to Mashhad. I am sure they will be able to render much needed service.

6 | FRIDAY

📖 Two more plane loads of relief stores were sent to Mashhad today. There is further news of earthquake devastation from that area.

📖 Today is Defence of Pakistan Day, the day on which the Indian army crossed the international border three years ago and attacked Pakistan in overwhelming strength. They were, however, brought to a halt in a matter of hours on all fronts and heavy casualties were inflicted. This war was short but entailed heavy and vicious fighting. Our armed forces, much smaller in strength, fought with great valour and defeated the enemy on every front. On each occasion over a thousand tanks clashed with each other. Those were glorious days for Pakistan and will always be remembered in the annals of history. So naturally the people are celebrating the occasion with great fervour.

7 | SATURDAY

I presented the national flag to the Pakistan Air Force at the Chaklala air base. The drill and the turnout of the air force was first class. A lot of people, inclusive of the diplomatic corps, attended the ceremony. I congratulated Air Marshal Nur Khan, his officers and men on this fine performance.

I was told by the defence minister that our planes carrying relief personnel and material for the earthquake victims in eastern Iran were made to land at Kandahar by the Afghans and held up for several hours. It made me furious. I have felt that we were dealing with brutes. I asked for a full report from the defence ministry.

Rang up the Shahinshah and inquired about the situation in the earthquake affected areas. He said that he had visited the area, everything was under control, and he also thanked me for the assistance we had rendered.

8 | SUNDAY

In the development field we have done well in the agricultural sector and there is room for further improvement. We are also moving on rapidly with the creation of industries supporting agriculture. But what good will all this do unless the devastating rate of population growth is checked. So family planning is the other side of this coin. The two must go hand in hand, the meaning of that is that we must enlarge our family planning programme in a big way. I have told M.M. Ahmed to keep this in view when formulating next year's development plan.

M.M. Ahmed told me that the World Bank, under Mr Robert McNamara, is thinking of giving really soft loans on long term basis. He is also setting up a commission under Mr Lester Pearson of Canada to study the problems of aid and make recommendations in the hope, perhaps, to induce affluent countries like the USA to have a rational attitude towards this problem. I wonder if Pearson's exhortations will have much effect, but a real good dose of cold war might well have. Ahmed said that he was trying to get representation on this commission for Pakistan. I think our experience of planning and development will be helpful for the commission. We should undoubtedly agitate for resumption of aid on a much larger scale and softer terms but we should also work for conversion of the existing loans to softer terms and longer repayment period.

Mr Qamar-ul-Islam stated that a larger population need not be a liability. It could be turned into an economic asset. I told him that in our social system this was an erroneous notion. During the twenty-five years of existence of Pakistan, could he quote one instance in which this has proved true? In this age of science and medicine when things can be done so much quicker by them, reliance on manual labour is totally uneconomical and wasteful of time.

10 | TUESDAY

📖 Attended a briefing at GHQ operations room on the building of concrete defences I had ordered on the likelihood of invasion from India. The object is to hold the enemy firmly with as few troops as possible, releasing the balance for the counteroffensive. I think they have made a good start and I have begun to believe in the efficiency of this arrangement.

We then saw a M-47 tank fitted by a 12 cylinder GM diesel engine. An Italian firm has done the job and made a very good show of it. This conversion together with certain internal modifications makes the tank brand new with far greater engine power and range operation making 300 miles. This is a great step forward.

📖 Held a meeting with the cabinet ministers and Governor Monem Khan on the affairs of the Muslim League in East Pakistan. The Provincial League Council meeting will be held in Dacca on the 22nd of this month to elect its office bearers. The governor was told to prepare a panel of names which can be considered on my arrival in Dacca on the 19th. These people have to be such that can command the confidence of the governor and be able to work with him.

13 | FRIDAY

📖 Bhutto, since leaving the cabinet, has been indulging in every form of mischief and disruption, directed at me of course, but not even sparing the vital interests of the country. Lately he has given a talk in Hyderabad talking about bloodshed and disclosing state secrets, which he came to know of as minister, embarrassing friendly countries that had given us military assistance during the 1965 war. The law ministry is examining the speech with a view to taking legal action.

16 | MONDAY

📖 General Yahya came to complain that the information ministry had circulated in its weekly press digest an article written by someone in Glasgow that General Yahya was aspiring to succeed me. Such rumours keep on floating in the country about the governor, ministers, and of course, about me. For instance, it was said that I had gone to England to stay there permanently. How and where these things start, God alone knows. Either these are the concoctions of the opposition or loafer type of people who frequent restaurants. One has learnt to ignore them but the point is that our people are so gullible no one has the courage to question or bring to the notice of the authority people who indulge in such a nefarious activity.

📖 Held a meeting with the fruit experts and the officers of the agriculture department, West Pakistan and discussed with them the need to propagate Khorasan-type fruits in the areas like Chitral, Gilgit, Baltistan, Skardu, Waziristan etc. These areas are cool and free from summer rains so they should be ideal for producing melons, grapes, figs, apricots etc. I told them to prepare a plan and let me have a look at it. I am glad that these people are very keen, with a little bit of encouragement from me they have made great advancements in the culture of fruit in West Pakistan. Our fruit now is of a very high quality.

📖 Referring to tank demonstrations I saw the other day, I told General Yahya to teach his people that the tank must move at the fastest possible pace in the face of the enemy. The best protection for the tank is mobility, it is not possible to hit a moving tank easily. Secondly, to hit a moving tank you have to aim your gun and that does not come easily to every soldier just as it is not easy to hit a flying bird with a shot gun. So it is necessary to provide every anti-tank gun with an aiming gadget. In a tank battle the delivery of the first shot is crucial. You must score a hit otherwise the enemy will get you.

18 | WEDNESDAY

📖 A writer from America called. Mrs P.T. Lenine[29] is writing a book called *The Anatomy of Greatness*. She asked me who had the greatest influence on my thought and action.

In the course of my life I have come in contact with many leading personalities in different walks of life. These contacts grew as my own responsibilities increased. In my meetings with statesmen, politicians, administrators and scholars I had occasion to study and observe them from close quarters. I learnt a great deal from them. Two persons, however, had very considerable influence on my mind. One was my father and the other was the late His Highness the Aga Khan.[30]

My father was a kind and humble man, God-fearing and steeped in piety. He had a most impressive appearance and tremendous physical strength. His education was limited but he had a great awareness. He was sagacious and possessed a penetrating mind.

The Aga Khan, when I met him was at the ebb of his life when he was crippled by heart trouble, though he was still mentally very alert. I deeply admired the extent of his knowledge of world affairs, men and events and his foresight. He gave me some very sound advice.

Whilst not falling under the spell of any one individual I have been attracted by qualities such as intellect, bravery, strength of character, sympathy, humility and talent whenever I found it. These are qualities which I have always respected even amongst my bitterest critics.

I do as much reading as is possible for me and some writing has captivated my mind. I have always been deeply influenced by the profoundity of the Holy Quran and the guidance one derives from it. The life of Prophet Muhammad, the last of the prophets, may peace be upon him, based as it was in its practical application on the Holy Quran, is a great source of inspiration for me.

Among the scholars from this part of the world and persons whose writings have inspired me most is the late Dr Iqbal who is aptly given the epitaph of 'The Poet Philosopher of the East'.

In the military phase, I have always enjoyed reading the works of Captain Liddle Hart, Major General Fuller of England and General Heinz Guderian of Germany. I have great admiration for General Douglas MacArthur of the United States of America. In organizing, training and equipping the Pakistan army as its commander-in-chief, I made considerable use of the ideas of these people. I have found General MacArthur's approach to military problems extremely fascinating, though he was not free from vanity. But given his looks, personality and intellect this failing is perhaps excusable.

📖 There is a plan to set up several rice husking mills in West Pakistan. Our rice production is increasing fast. I believe the rice husk has appreciable oil content. So I have ordered that oil extractions mills should also be set up alongside.

19 | THURSDAY

📖 Flew to Lahore en route to Dacca. On arrival at Dacca was given a rousing reception by a large number of people who had come from all over East Pakistan. I suppose they were anxious to see what I looked like after the recent sickness. I had to shake hands with over 300 people.

📖 The elections of Muslim League office bearers looked like developing into a storm. I was told that Mr Sobur, backed by Qazi Qadir and a few others who are hostile to Governor Monem Khan, declared himself as a candidate for the presidency. This was an obvious mischief and it was the first time Sobur had shown any such intentions. My talk with Sobur confirmed this. Sobur was complaining that Monem Khan was building Amjad Hussain from Khulna against him. Whereas Monem Khan feared that Sobur was acting for his ouster and replacement. I got them both together and told them that any open rift at this stage would be most damaging to the party. There must be an agreed solution. A lot of haggling, argument and counter argument took place between the two. Though I had told Sobur previously that if he insisted on his candidature he would have to resign from the central ministry. This shook him and he realized that I meant business. I was at wits end and both were being stubborn, however, in the end I told Sobur that he should be satisfied if Amjad Hussain was not appointed as president or the secretary general and that others were nominated by the governor in consultation with party members.

He agreed and on that we parted. But before that I told them that they had not changed much since 1905 when Nawab Sir Salimullah[31] called a meeting in Dacca of the leading Muslims from all over India to lay the foundations of the Muslim League. Nawab Salimullah took the chair in the meeting in which there were a large number of Bengali delegates. After a stage he left for a rest and Nawab Mohsin-ul Mulk took his place. The Bengalis started misbehaving. Mohsin-ul Mulk got fed up and dragged Salimullah out of bed and said that he should come back and control his people and tell them how to behave themselves. Salimullah came back and settled the Bengalis whereupon they settled down. I told them to take their fingers out and learn to behave as responsible people. I also sent a word to Qazi Qadir to keep out of mischief. Let us see how they behave themselves.

20 | FRIDAY

📖 Addressed a convention of Basic Democrats. It was a large gathering, some 15,000 people were present. The *pandal* was very well arranged and the audience remained very orderly throughout the proceedings. At the end a resolution was moved calling upon me to contest the next elections. It was unanimously passed with great applause.

21 | SATURDAY

📖 Visited Chittagong and addressed a cross section of people. They had suffered terribly during the floods but the administration has done a lot for them and they too have braved the calamity with great fortitude.

📖 Sent for Qazi Qadir and Wahiduzzaman[32] and asked them why they were making mischief. They complained bitterly against Governor Monem Khan, his highhandedness and vindictiveness etc. I told them that it may be so, but is this the time to make trouble? The Muslim League will die forever in East Pakistan if it is not formed at this stage. They agreed to keep quiet but asked to be allowed to talk in the League. So I sent word through Sardar Aslam to Monem Khan that when preparing a list of office bearers he should consult these people too.

---

22 | SUNDAY

📖 Sardar Aslam, the secretary general of Muslim League, reported the next morning that he had conveyed my message to the governor who got very excited and agitated. Fought with all his staff and everyone around him. However, Wahiduzzaman and Qazi Qadir did turn up and submitted some names for consideration as office bearers in the Muslim League. That excited the governor still further. In other words, no agreed list of office bearers had emerged thus far and the League council meeting was to take place in 15 minutes time. It looked like there was bound to be turmoil in the meeting so I had to do something quick to avert the crisis. I decided and told people around me that we shall only elect the president and the secretary general that morning on which there was an agreement and seek the consent of the council to declare the names of other office bearers later. This went through the council without any hitch. Nawab Askari and Fakhur-ud-Din were elected as the president and secretary general, about the rest I shall have to set up a committee to propose names. In that we shall have to give representation to dissident groups. The governor may not like it but he should have to swallow it. We can't wreck the organization for the sake of the governor.

During this argument and turmoil, Fakir Abdul Mannan,[33] the outgoing president of the Muslim League, confessed to Sardar Aslam that Bengalis are crooks that is why they respond to the leadership of a crook. This reminded me of my meeting with the old man known as Baba-e-Urdu [Maulvi Abdul Haq] who had come to Dacca in 1948 to promote the cause of Urdu. He advocated that most of our ills can be cured if we take to Urdu. In Dacca, he was not meeting much response. I told him why does he not elicit the support of Maulana Akram Khan[34] who ran a paper and was an Urdu scholar. The old man said that he knew Akram well and regarded him as the biggest hypocrite and a crook. I was astounded and shocked and surprised. I used to think that Akram Khan was patriotic and nationalistic.

---

24 | TUESDAY

📖 Carried out the opening ceremony of the new High Court building in Dacca. It is a fine building, combining functioning needs with Muslim architectural beauty and was much needed. Monem Khan and his administration have done a fine job in getting it built. The Chief Justice delivered the opening address to which I replied. The burden of my talk was that repeated slogans on the rule of law and supremacy of judiciary were not the problem. Everybody believed that the problem was the suffering of the common man through the manner in which this legal system was applied. In consequence it is slow, expensive and riddled with abuses. It also, puts the common man at a tremendous disadvantage against the man with means who can buy justice. Also our legal education was inadequate and allowed ill-suited people to enter the profession. Unless the people in the profession attended to these problems they will lose whatever prestige they have; however little they have in the eyes of the people.

After the ceremony the Chief Justice of the Supreme Court, who sat beside me for a cup of tea, confessed that the legal profession had become sordid. Lawyers employed touts who sucked the blood of the litigants, especially those from the rural areas. They make these poor innocent people sell their property and mortgage their future by playing on their fears and ignorance. The solution, he thought, was to appoint a legal advisor in each union council for guiding litigants. I told him to write me a note on this subject. I know if such a system is introduced the lawyers will get still further alienated from me.

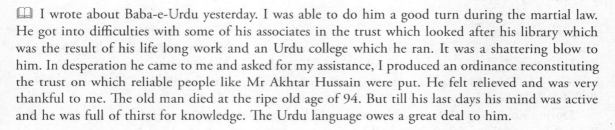 I wrote about Baba-e-Urdu yesterday. I was able to do him a good turn during the martial law. He got into difficulties with some of his associates in the trust which looked after his library which was the result of his life long work and an Urdu college which he ran. It was a shattering blow to him. In desperation he came to me and asked for my assistance, I produced an ordinance reconstituting the trust on which reliable people like Mr Akhtar Hussain were put. He felt relieved and was very thankful to me. The old man died at the ripe old age of 94. But till his last days his mind was active and he was full of thirst for knowledge. The Urdu language owes a great deal to him.

📖 It takes a long time to get anything sunk in Monem Khan's mind. I got him to see the need for giving representation in the Muslim League to every section. I told him to include representations of Wahiduzzaman, Qadir and Hashimuddin[35] as the office bearers and give me a complete list for announcement before I leave as I do not want this question to remain open and become a sore.

📖 Mr Aftab Ahmad of the information ministry located in Dacca, came to see me and delivered a paper on the situation in East Pakistan. It makes depressing and dismal reading. How is it possible to help people whose minds are totally shut to reason, and full of suspicion and scepticism. Geography, history, climate, natural hazards and racial traits might well be responsible for this malady. On the contrary, there might be much deeper reasons.

Aftab Ahmad was followed by Mr Siddiqui,[36] the Chief Justice of the East Pakistan High Court. He had a similar dismal story to tell. Most of the lawyers, led by Hindus, were anti-government and oppositionists for no obvious reasons other than negativity. Those that were loyal, and there are some, have not the courage to come out in the open. During the coming elections the opposition was going to fight on two fronts, in the field and in the courts. He foresees the High Court being inundated with writ petitions. So he wants his full complement of judges, a couple of candidates that were passed over in the last selection, should be appointed. I told him to see the law minister. He was particularly sore about the people here for not condemning the Agartala conspirators. He said he told the lawyers on one occasion that they had their choice of rule by a Pathan or a Hindu.

📖 Report on the situation in East Pakistan given by Mr Aftab Ahmad of the information ministry.

Ministry of Information and Broadcasting.
A report on East Pakistan.

I record below a brief summary of the impressions that I have formed during my eight month stay in East Pakistan. These impressions have been categorized under the following:
1. East–West relations.
2. Political situation.
3. Economic situation.
4. Cultural situation.
5. Student problem.

East–West relations.

The East–West relationship is perhaps the most important problem in our national life. There is, I think, a psychological aspect of the problem which needs to be kept in view.

As a rule, East Pakistanis are a very sensitive people. They react sharply when they have a feeling that they have been left out or that they have not been given their due.

During Kosygin's visit for instance one could hear people complaining in Dacca that it was all a West Pakistan affair and that East Pakistan was not considered good enough for a big power representative. One tried in vain to explain the tight schedule of Mr Kosygin's visit but what one could not explain was as to why even the Governor of East Pakistan and the Speaker of the National Assembly could not be invited to attend some of the functions at Rawalpindi, Lahore and Karachi.

Another frequently mentioned grievance is that Dacca is supposed to be the second capital of the country but there are very few central government offices here. The genuine demand is that the headquarters of some of the central government autonomous bodies, now located in Karachi, should be shifted to Dacca.

The points that I have mentioned above are perhaps not very important in their own way but they add to the already existing feeling of suspicion and mistrust.

One would not like to generalize but one feels that East Pakistan has a strong craving for attention. At the same time they have a tendency to be exclusive and suspicious of all those who do not belong to their soil. This attitude of mind has been expressed in its extreme form in Mr Qammar-ud-Din Ahmad's[37] book, *A Social History of East Pakistan*. He has referred to almost all the well known families of Muslim Bengal as outsiders. It is a revealing book in many ways, coming as it does from a fairly prominent East Pakistani who incidentally was the ambassador to Burma during the prime ministership of Mr Suhrawardy.

I do not think most East Pakistanis would subscribe to Mr Qammar-ud-Din Ahmad's point of view. I know a good many of them who contest it vigorously. But it does indicate a noticeable trend.

Political Situation.

The opposition in general is quite active and vocal in East Pakistan. Apart from the regular political parties, pockets of opposition exist among the unaffiliated intelligentsia. Unlike the political demagogues, members of the intelligentsia do not normally use the press as their platform. But their musings and whisperings tend to build up a negative and sarcastic attitude which contributes to the general mistrust and bitterness against the government. More often than not, this attitude reveals the narrow provincial point of view. One frequently hears complaints about what has not been done, but rarely any acknowledgment of what has been done.

Agartala conspiracy case.

By far the most important political event of the period under review is the Agartala conspiracy case. The alleged obviously derived inspiration and strength from the prevailing mistrust and bitterness. The general reaction to the case can be summed up as follows:

a. Those who are pro-Sheikh Mujibur Rahman do not believe that he was involved in it at all.

b. Those who are anti-Sheikh Mujibur Rahman say that the government has made him a hero by giving him a trial like this.

c. According to the sane and sober section of opinion, the alleged conspiracy was the mad dream of a few low placed individuals. The government had a good legal case but it should not have been given so much importance.

d. This section of people also think that by giving the case so much importance the government has made secession a talking point amongst the people.

Surprisingly, the alleged Indian involvement in the case has not aroused any sharp public reaction. As a matter of fact, there has been no strong public condemnation or even private expression of indignation in any section of the people, official or non-official. Officials just do not talk about it.

This is not to say, however, that there is any widespread sympathy for the accused or for their alleged nefarious designs. The people in general do not really want secession. The demand for parity and autonomy, however, is fairly widespread and incessant. It may also be mentioned that the president is held in high esteem by the people. This feeling transcends any hostility towards the government, provincial or central. He is accepted as a friend of East Pakistan and his word carries conviction.

Economic Situation.

The economic disparity between the two wings is perhaps the most talked about thing in East Pakistan. Figures which show the existence of disparity are overemphasized. The fact that the gap is being gradually narrowed down is generally ignored. But nobody pauses to consider the historical and economic causes of disparity.

The slogan of disparity is linked up with the slogan of regional autonomy. The opposition uses disparity as a stick to beat the government because parity has been accepted as a constitutional obligation. It is difficult to build up an equally plausible case for regional autonomy.

Flood Control.

The 'grow more food' campaign of the provincial government has been seriously affected by the recent heavy floods. The governor called a conference of the commissioners, deputy commissioners and other senior officers to discuss the ways and means of accelerating the 'grow more food' campaign. I was the only central government officer whom the governor was kind enough to invite to attend the conference as an observer. The conference decided to adopt certain measures to achieve the target of self sufficiency in food, one year in advance of the original date 1970.

The food problem, however, needs to be resolved on a permanent basis. The East Pakistan flood commission has recently presented a top priority flood protection plan. It has recommended implementing the programme outside the regular annual development programme and the five year plan.

Flood control is a serious problem demanding urgent solution. It is often said here that if the problem of salinity and waterlogging in West Pakistan could be attended to under special arrangements, why can not the central government make special arrangements for solving the problem of flood control in East Pakistan.

Farraka Barrage.

It is also said that if Pakistan could arrive at a settlement on the Indus Basin problem in India despite the Kashmir dispute, why can't we settle the Farraka barrage problem by adopting a similar approach. What is conveniently forgotten is the fact that Pakistan is ready and it is for India to agree to enlist the good offices of an international agency like the World Bank before we can proceed further.

In recent months, however, statements from high officials and ministers of the central government on the Farraka barrage have had a good effect. The President's own reference to the problem in one of his statements was particularly well received. It created confidence amongst the public that the president is mindful of the fact that the problem poses a serious threat to the economic life of East Pakistan.

Cultural Situation.

Culture is a sensitive area. In East Pakistan it has become even more so because there is a definite tendency amongst East Pakistanis to assert their separate cultural entity. My study of the post-independence history of the province shows that this feeling of cultural separateness, Bengali culture, gathered momentum with the language movement. The language movement was itself an attempt to assert a separate entity.

The language issue is no more alive. But February 21st is still observed with great enthusiasm. It has been turned into a sort of a demand's day. This year as many as 35 pamphlets were issued on the day which I sent to the ministry with my note for further scrutiny. This incidentally is also the day when smashing of non-Bengali sign boards of shops and offices, even government offices is carried on as a matter of routine.

February 21st is not the only day when politics puts on the garb of culture. There are some other days too. For instance, the 1st of Beesakh and the birth of Tagore.

The 1st of Beesakh, I gather, was celebrated in the old days by both Hindus and Muslims. It has now assumed a new political colour under the influence of the movement for Bengali culture. Some aspects of the 1st Beesakh celebrations do indeed show Hindu influence.

Cultural diversity is a fact of life in Pakistan. Various regions in Pakistan have distinct cultural features, not all of them deriving from purely Islamic traditions. We have to accept these cultural diversities because they form part of a larger and broader entity, the overall cultural unity of Pakistan.

At any rate, I do not think it is advisable to take a very strong position in such matters. Why make them into issues? We already have enough issues on our hands.

I may perhaps also add that the best way to fight the reactionary forces of orthodoxy and obscurantism is to encourage and promote cultural activity. These activities, by their very nature, inculcate a liberal outlook and it is only through a liberal outlook that we can make progress in the modern world of science and technology.

Student Problem.

There has been some student trouble during the period under review but it never assumed any serious proportions. There are certain days when you can expect trouble. I have already cited three of these days, February 21st, 1st of Beesakh and Tagore's birthday. Another one is September 17th which they observe to commemorate the demonstrations they held against the Hamood-ur-Rahman report[38] when a couple of students were killed by police firing.

Practically all the opposition parties have their student organizations. The National Students Federation, the Muslim League's students organization, gained considerable strength in this year's election. Unfortunately, however, there are wild stories of the vandalism of the National Students Federation students on and off the university campus. One hears these stories from all sources, private individuals as well as government officials. It is unfortunate that the student's organization which is known as a pro-government party should have such a bad name in the public. During one of Mr Bhutto's visits to East Pakistan, it was a faction of the National Students Federation who organized the two public meetings he had at Dacca.

Signed
Aftab Ahmad
Joint Secretary
September 22nd, 1968.

📖 In East Pakistan they talk about Bengali culture common to both Muslims and Hindus. How can this be true when sources of inspiration are diametrically opposed. The philosophy of Islam and Hinduism are poles apart, we too had Hindus in our part of the world. There was nothing common between them and the Muslims. Our customs, dress, method of cooking, beliefs were totally different. Even the language was spoken differently by the two communities. This same must apply in Bengal. Hinduism does not seek integration.

25 | WEDNESDAY

📖 Addressed the press editors from all over Pakistan on internal and foreign affairs. The talk lasted for two hours. Told them that though the country had made tremendous progress in many fields, internally it was beset by two serious maladies.
1. Divisive call by the opposition, and
2. Reaction by the bigots.

Both dangerous to a society struggling to unify, integrate and enter the age of science and technology demanding enlightened and rational approach. The press must join the fight against them.

📖 Laid the foundation stone of the Dacca television station. This media is making rapid progress in our country. Within a few years best part of the population would be able to see television. Used properly it can be of great educative and informative value. The credit of this goes to Altaf Gauhar who has worked tirelessly and imaginatively for this and other national building projects.

📖 Justice Fazal-e-Akbar came to discuss the Supreme Court's problems in Dacca. They visit here twice a year for about two months and need living and court accommodation. I considered the problem and gave my decision as follows:

The judges will use the residential accommodation to be provided for ministers in the new capital. The ministers will occupy that accommodation only for a couple of months in a year during the winter assembly session in Dacca and use the two court rooms in the new high court building. He was satisfied but Governor Monem Khan had other ideas. He wanted the Supreme Court to take over the present High Court building and convert it for use as the court as well as for accommodating the judges. The object being to lay the foundation of eventually splitting of the court into two benches, one for East Pakistan and one for West Pakistan. I was not having that nor was I going to allow wasteful expenditure on this old and dilapidated building.

Later, Fazal-e-Akbar met me at a dinner party and said how quickly I was able to give the decision. He recalled an occasion when he took some problem to Khwaja Nazimuddin who was then the chief minister of this province. After explanation for an hour or so, Khwaja Sahib asked him to come again some other time. Second time Khwaja Sahib asked him to have a walk with him in the lawn and to do the talking which he did, at the end of it Khwaja Sahib pointed out a duck and said, do you think it would be good eating it roast or fried. The discussion went on for some time and when he reminded him of the problem Khwaja Sahib said quite frankly, I was not able to take in what you said, I was thinking of the duck. I told him that was the reason why he proved such a poor administrator.

Decision making does not come easily to everybody, it is a rare man who can make up his mind, give a decision and take the consequences.

Fazal-e-Akbar asked for administrative powers to be given to the chief justice of the Supreme Court over the high courts. At present judges hear cases and do not give decisions for months and months. They give stay orders automatically even on false allegations regarding work on projects etc. People complained to him and he can do nothing. I told him to talk it over with Mahmood-ur-Rehman, he could incorporate in his recommendations. Mahmood is the chairman of Law Reforms Commission. I also told him that this is exactly what I wanted to do at the time of framing the constitution but was opposed by the legal pundits on the grounds that it will impinge on the independence of judiciary. As an alternative I provided for the supreme judicial body to deal with disciplinary cases and which the judges are so reluctant to use. They have no compunction in imprisoning and even hanging other people but against each other they would not lift a finger.

26 | THURSDAY

📖 Went to Narayanganj by road, boarded the *Mary Anderson*, the governor's launch and went up the river for a cruise, disembarking at Dharma, returned to Dacca for lunch. It was an enjoyable morning, cool, hundreds and thousands of people had turned up to greet me. They were in a festive mood in their Sunday best, it was good to see them happy. Attended a banquet given by the governor.

27 | FRIDAY

📖 Gave the governor the following points to consider:

a. Appoint a minister from amongst the refugees.

b. Now that Askari[39] has become the president of the Muslim League he should be made a minister to become effective.

c. Nurseries for fruit trees should be provided in each union council. I would like to see fruit trees being planted around every village and household.

d. Institutions connected with Bengali language and culture should be brought on patriotic management. The best method of redeeming Bengali Muslim is through culture and ideology.

e. Nazar-ul-Islam's[40] patriotic poetry and drama should be projected through the medium of TV, mobile cinemas and radio.

f. Emphasize pump irrigation.

g. The education minister and his staff should keep the student community embroiled in cultural and ideological activities.

h. Women leagues should be set up quickly.

📖 Left for Lahore reaching there in the afternoon. Mr Haq, the acting governor, discussed several administrative problems.

28 | SATURDAY

📖 Visited the rice experimental farm at Kalashah Kaku, some 10 miles outside Lahore. Here the agricultural scientists are doing excellent work and developing quick growing dwarf varieties of basmati rice. They had met with considerable success. Later, addressed a big gathering of farmers from all over the rice growing areas of the Punjab. Found them in a receptive and happy mood.

The breakthrough in agriculture in West Pakistan is undoubtedly due to the awakening on the part of the farmers and the assistance the government is giving. But it is also due to the efforts made by our scientists, agricultural university and institutes. The agriculture department, which has some outstanding dedicated people like Malik Khuda Bakhsh Bucha, the support given by the governor and constant drive by me. Unfortunately, these things do not exist in East Pakistan. The people in top echelons know very little about agriculture and show little enthusiasm. Modern agriculture is not a new way of life there, yet the scope of improvement there is immense.

📖 Left Lahore by train reaching Rawalpindi in the evening. My object was to see the condition of the crops en route. I saw nothing but rice fields for dozens and dozens of miles an outstanding change within a year or two. No more crude Persian wheels for drawing water. There are tubewells all over. This gives the farmer more water for irrigation and also helps to combat waterlogging and salinity. That is the reason why a large amount of land that had gone out of use has come to life again and the price of land has appreciated considerably, but the contrast is striking when you enter the arid areas from Gujrat. The condition of crops is poor through failure of the monsoon. Most of them have dried up prematurely. So the life of people between the river Jhelum and Dhamial line is hard except where there is some irrigation. Besides the lands are badly eroded. That is why I am having a thorough examination carried out of this area with a view to levelling land and preserving moisture. But it is surprising that this is the area that produces the finest soldiers for the Pakistan army. I suppose they are toughened by nature. Those that can survive under these conditions can survive under any condition. Time and again it has been proved that our soldier is capable of enduring unbelievable hardships. May God bless him. He is the cream of the soil and [soldiering is] a proud profession.

📖 I am told that Bhutto, in a meeting held at Hyderabad, used strong language and even abused me. I am awaiting a copy of this report. It appears that he is looking for trouble which he will get without doubt. Only I don't want to see anything unlawful happen. For such people, you don't have to lay a trap. They lay it themselves and fall into it so all one has to do is to be patient and wait. The opportunity will surely come.

29 | SUNDAY

📖 Went to see my newborn grandson, Akhtar's son, in the CMH. He looks a nice little *chokra*. I am required to name him. I suggested to his mother that Hamid Ayub might be a good name. I inquired about his sister just senior to him. Apparently, she likes the boy but refuses to come near her mother. I suppose she blames the mother for the new arrival.

📖 When in Lahore I was told that people are anxious that I pay a visit to the Mazar of Data Ganj Baksh as thanksgiving for my recovery. I told them that whereas I have the greatest of respect for the Data and his teachings as given, my trouble is that I am not a grave or pir worshiper.

1 | TUESDAY

📖 Caused a letter to be sent to the governors that apart from good education and good management for the student community there is need for taking care of their physical and mental health. For physical health, mass PT should be introduced in schools and colleges, for mental health free discussions should be held on the principles of Islam, the need for Pakistan, a strong centre, the unity of culture amongst the Muslims throughout the subcontinent because of the common source of inspiration, and how can Islam be made a vehicle of progress. These discussions should be held on the teachings of Shah Waliullah,[41] Sir Syed, Iqbal, Quaid-e-Azam and Nazar-ul-Islam. We may even go further and produce a book on these subjects based on the teachings of these great men. I believe that this will be a source of education for the younger generation and a number of misconceptions could be removed. Such an education is necessary throughout the country but more so in East Pakistan. There the immigrants feel for Muslim unity but the Shudhra converts, who are indigenous, composing the bulk of the population, and especially those who have got a smattering of education, have a great urge to revert to Hinduism by the language and customs if not the temple. Saving them from a reversion to serfdom and domination of Hinduism is the supreme task in East Pakistan especially so when they themselves are proving such willing tools. I can't make out why Hinduism with its abominable social systems holds such fascination for people. I suppose that whilst being hated by a class above when you can hate the class below satisfies human perversions.

📖 There is to be a summit meeting of the RCD in Dacca in December. In order that it is purposeful, I intend suggesting an agenda relating to our mutual problems otherwise the talks end up in generalities without coming to grips with concrete problems. Similarly, I want the area of mutual collaboration defined and restricted to tangibles. This is necessary in order to demonstrate to people that something worthwhile is happening.

2 | WEDNESDAY

📖 There are too many people in the government who prefer to serve the country from outside. Ministers, secretaries and others push off to foreign countries on the slightest pretext. For instance, currently the foreign minister and the foreign secretary are out. The finance minister and the finance secretary are out and education minister and his secretary have threatened to do the same. I have told them that if the country can be run without these people why not get rid of them and do without them. So I am getting sick and tired of this and made it clear that under no circumstances will the secretary and the minister go out together. Then lately our governors have been invited by some friendly countries for goodwill visits. This is all right but they have got into the habit of carting every single member of their family with them. It does not occur to them that this is undignified behaviour. So I am left with no alternative but to sit on them and hard.

3 | THURSDAY

📖 Flew to Risalpur and then motored to Saidu Sharif. Saw large numbers of the people en route who had come to greet me. I intended staying in Swat for a week as a break and be with my grandchildren. Two of my daughters are married here. The Wali is also very kind and hospitable. He attends to his own work and leaves me alone, so I can do a good deal of reading apart from sightseeing. The drives into the valleys around here are fascinating.

4 | FRIDAY

Professor Tucci,[42] the famous Italian archaeologist, who is a great authority on Buddhism and works in Pakistan, Afghanistan, Nepal and Tibet etc. came to lunch with his wife. He is 75 and she is about 36. He is a very interesting man to talk to. He wanted permission to translate my book into the Italian language. I readily agreed. Talking about his own country, he said it was in a mess, the students are out of control, the teachers play politics through the students, there is no discipline amongst labour, strikes are the order of the day, there is a large communist party in the country, the government is weak and incapable of dealing with any crises. The future seemed dark to him. He felt that democracy had failed to provide the answer. Something drastic has to happen to put things right. What that could be, is difficult to tell. Even communism has lost its charisma since the Russo–Chinese rift and the Soviet actions in Eastern European countries. I told him that whatever binding force religion had, even that is lost especially after the senseless encyclical that the Pope issued on birth control. If he had offered a reason, he might well have been able to establish respect for religion. But the foolish man lost a great opportunity.

5 | SATURDAY

In my first of the month speech and even in Dacca, I had spoken of the common theme of Muslim culture throughout the subcontinent as the source of inspiration, i.e. the teachings of the Qur'an, were the same. After all, the culture of the people flows from the philosophy in which they believe. Further, although our regional languages are the medium in which the culture was expressed and sound different in reality the basis of all of them is the same or similar. This encourages one to hope that one day the synthesis of these languages may emerge as one language. This happened to coincide with the statement made by a judge in Lahore that the only sensible thing to do was to accept Urdu as the lingua franca of the country.

The spirit of those whose experience […] expressions are different […] but the disruptionists in East Pakistan have banded them together and described them as an attempt to undermine Bengali as a state language. Mr Nurul Amin has chosen to […] but so was a man called Maulana Abdul Rashid Tarkabagish,[43] now the president of the Awami League. What Tarkabagish stands for God alone knows. I have not met this man but I have heard that he was a close associate of Mr Suhrawardy and one of the major disruptive actors in East Pakistan. He opposed Pakistan and wanted to establish a separate kingdom with Mymensingh as the capital. This is the type of well wishers East Pakistan has.

Visited the orphanage for girls my daughter Naseem has established in Saidu, it is meant to cater for about 50 girls. The place looks nice and clean and well run. She has received a lot of donations from different people and she keeps on collecting more. I have donated Rs 15,000 and have promised another Rs 50,000.

6 | SUNDAY

📖 It is curious how the hands of God work. Take for instance the case of Tarbela dam, which will cost about 500 crores and will be the biggest of its kind, or my personal relationship with George Woods, the late president of the World Bank, and this friendship developed because of the close relationship between my daughter Naseem and Mrs George Woods. How it came about was like this, I went to the USA on a state visit on the invitation of President Kennedy. Naseem accompanied me. We later went to New York where Mrs Woods met Naseem and took her sight seeing. They developed fast friendship which has continued since. So people in Pakistan do not know how much they owe to my daughter. She and her husband are going to USA in the near future and will stay with the Woods. When the Woods come to Pakistan they stay with them.

7 | MONDAY

📖 I had occasion to send a note to the Commander-in-Chief of the army on tank-infantry cooperation and a letter to Hilaly.[44] As these would be of interest to the reader, I am attaching them.

Saidu Sharif
7th October 1968
From Field Marshal Mohammed Ayub Khan
Nishan-e-Pakistan, Hilal-e-Jurat

I am beginning to have serious doubts about the manner in which infantry tank cooperation is achieved in attack. At present tanks crawl with infantry in a leisurely fashion. These tactics are based on conditions prevailing in the First World War and even in the Second World War when antitank weapons were limited and the infantry had certainly no such weapons. This rate of advance in present day conditions when infantry is equipped with effective antitank weapons would be suicidal. In any case, infantry marching in the clouds of dust raised by the tanks would be rendered half-mad by the time it reaches the objective, if at all.

The answer would then lie in making the tanks move as fast as possible to gain the objective irrespective of losses we suffer. My brief in this is that in that case losses may be very few and the infantry moving fast to marry up with the tanks for mopping up the enemy in consolidation. Some infantry may even be mounted on rear tanks if not leading tanks so that the tanks have close protection when objective is gained. In order to avoid and reduce casualties such operations might well be carried out in darkness or before daylight.

When the enemy is well dug in and has covered his position with antitank mines, frontal attack would undoubtedly be costly. In that case, if the infantry has been launched frontally the tank should attack the enemy at full speed from the flanks in order to help capture the objective or beat off the enemy tank counterattack, now that the enemy has a tank unit as an integral part of an infantry division.

Please consider these proposals and discuss them with me when you meet me next.

Addressed to:
General A. M. Yahya Khan,
Hilal-e-Pakistan, Hilal-e-Jurat
Commander-in-Chief. General Headquarters, Rawalpindi.

Signed
Mohammed Ayub Khan
Field Marshal.

[Then he again writes]

President's Camp Saidu Sharif
7th October 1968
From Field Marshal Mohammed Ayub Khan
Nishan-e-Pakistan, Hilal-e-Jurat

My dear Hilaly,
Thank you very much for your letter of 27th September enclosing a copy of the views which Mr Nixon professes to hold on the presidency of the United States. In fact, I had read in the *New York Times* the fuller account, which is also attached with your letter. These precepts are good as far as they go, but the crux lies in the demand that the president must have the time to do concentrated thinking before taking great decisions. The value of such thinking rests on the sort of philosophy that the president believes in. Today, I don't see America possessing any philosophy that attracts mankind. The only thing that they can sell is their undoubted superior technology and use of their wealth to gain influence. But the factor of wealth is not being used very sensibly, either. On one side 3 million dollars an hour are wasted in a futile war in Vietnam, on the other side every effort is being made to do away with the aid to developing countries when aid is not charity, but good business creating markets and bringing profits. Nevertheless, I wish Mr Nixon all the best as he happens to be a friend of mine and hope that he will live up to his profession.

With best wishes,
Yours sincerely
Mohammed Ayub Khan

Addressed to
His Excellency Mr A. Hilaly,
Ambassador of Pakistan,
Massachusetts Avenue, Washington DC

10 | THURSDAY

Left Saidu Sharif for Mardan where I visited the Punjab Regimental Centre and then addressed a public meeting at Col. Ghafoor Khan Hoti's place in Hoti. En route a large number of people turned up to greet me, so many decorative gates were made on the road costing a lot of money and labour. These things embarrass me but it seems difficult to stop them. The public meeting went off very well indeed. Col. Ghafoor Khan Hoti had made elaborate arrangements. In my address, I told the Muslim Leaguers to work with zeal and attack Khan Abdul Ghaffar Khan for his anti-Pakistan activities and perfidies. That traitor instead of playing politics within the country was acting as a willing tool in the hands of enemies of Pakistan merely because they were feeding him. Ghaffar Khan has been the major disruptive actor for the Pathans.

📖 Took a plane from Risalpur and reached Pindi. Mr Fida Hassan, my advisor who attended the Chinese National Day celebrations in Peking, met me on the airport and reported the result of his visit. Apparently, the Chinese and especially Mao Tse-tung made a lot of fuss of him and his party. Mao gave Fida Hassan a long talk on how to defend Pakistan and specially the cities of Lahore and Sialkot which are bound to be attacked by the Indians in the event of war. Mao's solution is tunnel warfare. The Chinese communists did a lot of that during the Japanese occupation. I told Fida Hassan that our aim is to destroy the enemy before he reaches these places. So we are constructing large scale antitank obstacles and concrete emplacements for outsmarting and antitank weapons along the border. The object is to economize in manpower and weapons in defence so as to be able to spare as much force as possible for offensive operations. The Chinese keep on talking to us in terms of guerrilla warfare because that is their experience, besides they have the space for this. Unfortunately, we lack depth in our country and besides some of our centres of population, communication links, headworks and canals lie near the border so we have to be ready to defeat the enemy as soon as he enters our territory. This is what we did last time and we have every hope of success should he aggress again.

12 | SATURDAY

📖 The Kabul radio and press keep on carrying out virulent abuse and propaganda against us. In fact, they never stopped it even after resumption of normal relations. We remained silent in the hope that they may learn to behave themselves. But time has come when we must retaliate. This we have started doing through our powerful transmitter in Rawalpindi. The aim is to expose Kabul government lies, Ghaffar Khan's perfidy and show friendship and sympathy for the plight of the Afghan people. Some political officers on the frontier and our ambassador in Kabul have been alarmed, but they are now convinced that the steps we are taking are a minimum necessity.

📖 The Indians have offered to open talks on Farraka barrage at the secretary level. We are accepting this offer and must, as otherwise India will feel free to deny us the Ganges water altogether. Mr Jaffery, the secretary concerned, has sounded out the East Pakistanis. It seems that they are approaching the problem politically and are asking for the moon and are not being realistic. This is exactly what the Indians would like us to do to prove how unreasonable we are. So I have got to get these people together to bring them to earth like the way I did in West Pakistan on the eve of the Indus Basin Water Treaty settlement. Otherwise we shall lose everything. Realistic assessment is that if we are assured of 20,000 cusec of water in the dry season we should not be doing too badly.

📖 Successive devastating floods in East Pakistan are making people think of solutions which are quite impractical and totally beyond our reach. For instance, they are talking of outlay of 1,600 cores for embankments and dredging. The real object is to make the project double the size of the Indus basin water replacement works. Now how can you dredge 1000 miles of river lines carrying millions of cusec of water half of which is silt. Even if the dredging were possible the channels will get filled up with silt in a matter of days. East Pakistan's problem are great, but I wonder if they don't make them worse by treating everything on political and unreliable levels. Now when this problem comes up for discussion a lot of heat and unnecessary unpleasantness will be generated, but what else is the answer. Efforts will have to be made to bring them down to reason.

13 | SUNDAY

📖 General Musa, Governor West Pakistan, came to see me. He had been on a visit to the Soviet Union and Iran. Both visits went of satisfactorily. Musa had taken a large contingent of his family members with him. I told him this should be avoided in future as it is embarrassing to the host and is undignified. I also gave him the following points for consideration and action.

a. Beirut University had developed a high yielding variety of wheat for arid cultivation and Spain developed a special type of jawar. Their seeds should be obtained and tried in Pakistan.

b. He should take care of Amir Ahmed Khan, Secretary Agriculture, he is a very useful man.

c. A scheme for combating water logging and salinity in Mardan and Peshawar districts should be prepared.

d. Certain Muslim Leaguers should be detailed to mark certain members of oppositions and expose them whenever possible.

e. Minister Sarwar and Qazi Fazlullah are liabilities. The answer would be to sack them, but because of the nearness of elections we can't take this risk so they should be given a stern warning.

f. The affairs of private institutions are in a bad shape, they should be dealt with properly.

14 | MONDAY

📖 The foreign secretary and our ambassador in Kabul came to see me and discussed the attitude of the Kabul government towards us. It is down right hostile. They have even attacked us in the General Assembly to the joy of the Indians. I suppose they wanted to please their paymasters. The decision is that we should give them as good as we receive in future. The ambassador complained that there are a large number of people on his staff who have been there for 12 to 15 years. They have developed a vested interest and advocate peace with the Afghans at any cost. He asked for their transfer. The foreign secretary is looking into it. Talking about the king, the ambassador said that he was an absolute crook. I told him that was well known.

📖 There is a great scare spread in Lahore that the authorities are going to inoculate school students against [smallpox] as a measure of birth control. It started with Karachi and then to Hyderabad and is the handiwork of the Jamaat-e-Islam. Our people are so gullible that they take leave of their senses and believe every damn nonsense. I hope the provincial government can catch hold of the mischief makers and twist their necks.

15 | TUESDAY

📖 The law minister held a seminar in Lahore on the constitution of Pakistan. It was attended by all the judges and leading lawyers and some first class papers were read. They all agreed that the constitution was an effective umbrella under which the country could progress.

16 | WEDNESDAY

📖 Military intelligence sent me a file containing a cutting from an Iranian paper attacking the Turks, very strongly calling them barbarous and arrogant people who do not know how to live with their neighbours in peace. The whole thing started with the alleged Turkish cultural attaché in Tehran who attempted to contact Iranian Turks. Apparently there are 14 million of them. The Iranians asked for his removal. This came out in a Turkish paper which caused this retaliation prompted obviously by the Iranian Foreign Minister Zahedi. Zahedi is a bad character, but seems to have a lot of influence over the Shah in spite of the fact that he divorced the Shah's daughter. Perhaps these things are not taken seriously in Iran; in our society such a relationship would be untenable. However, this is a sad development and I hope the Turks will show a spirit of generosity and not allow future relationship to deteriorate. In fact, Zahedi agitated the Shah in the same manner against us over trivialities and then caused a nasty article to be written in a paper. One has to be very careful of this man. He can be up to any mischief and the Shah's trouble is that he can be very petty.

📖 The price of sugar is going inordinately high in the country in spite of importation on bonus. What is happening is that some of the big business houses, who have large holding power, are importing sugar and letting it out in bits to keep up the price, making anything of up to 80 per cent profit. This is scandalous and can't be allow to go on, so I have told the commerce minister to examine requisitioning all sugar stocks in the country and handing it over to the Trading Corporation of Pakistan for sale. Similarly, all future importation of sugar on bonus will be restricted to Trading Corporation of Pakistan.

📖 I don't know about the businessmen elsewhere, but ours are damn rascals. He will not hesitate to suck people's blood if he gets half a chance. I wonder how long we would be able to protect him and the private sector against the people. One day people will take their revenge on him.

18 | FRIDAY

📖 A team of agronomists, who under the auspices of Ford Foundation and Rockefeller Foundation developed high yielding wheat, rice, maize, etc. seeds, came to see me. They had been around in East and West Pakistan and were tremendously impressed by the progress that has been made, especially in West Pakistan. Complemented us on the achievements made in agriculture in such a short time. They regarded Pakistan as a model for the rest of the world, but also pointed out some of the problems created by plenty. Those we have to attend to, rapidly. I told them to reduce their ideas in writing so that we can process them systematically.

📖 The American Ambassador came to see me on my initiative. He had been to Srinagar recently on a holiday and wanted to tell me how the people felt. He started off by saying that he had never seen such a large concentration of troops as there are around Srinagar. But you hardly see any troops on the streets. Similarly, large convoys move to Ladakh daily. Freedom of worship is allowed. Big congregations are seen in the mosques during prayer time. But people look bewildered and unhappy. If the choice was between India and Pakistan, they would choose Pakistan. But if the alternative choice of independence was offered, they would prefer that. He saw photographs of Sheikh Abdullah and myself prominently displayed everywhere. He suggested that if we agitate the question once again at the Security Council, why not offer the alternative of independence as well. That would appeal to the world opinion. I told him at length the snags involved.

Then the ambassador came back to the question of Badaber Base. He said he was terribly disappointed that our people are not agreeing to functioning of portions that will be dismantled within a stipulated time frame of the deadline. I told him that the Russians are bound to get to know this and will accuse us of bad faith. He said his hands will be strengthened with the State Department if some concession was shown. I promised to get this looked into but foresaw many difficulties.

19 | SATURDAY

One keeps getting evidence on the reaction by the Iranian and especially their foreign minister on trivial matters. Recently they have protested on allowing an Iraqi officer at our staff college to call the gulf the Arabian Gulf. He was called upon to give a talk on the situation in the Middle East in the course of which he used this expression. There was an Iranian officer attending the talk, who reported the matter to his people. Another instance occurred in the case of a man from Bahrain, who turned out to be the head of the intelligence and also has something to do with their finance ministry. He came here on the invitation of Habib Bank people who have a branch in Bahrain. The man who looked after him here is called Rizvi, the same name as our DIB. Neither the foreign office nor the DIB knew anything about the presence of this man in Pakistan until a protest was received from Zahedi by our foreign minister inquiring why was this man invited by us and entertained. Zahedi went on to say that the head of the intelligence who was to visit Pakistan on the invitation of our DIB will not be allowed to come. Dealing with such petty minded people is so frustrating. Another news is that the Americans are going to train Israeli pilots on Phantom jets in Iran. This is tragic.

Had a meeting with the foreign minister and foreign secretary, defence minister and a representative from the ISI to discuss the American ambassador's request about Badaber. It was decided to be a little flexible and show some spirit of accommodation. We cannot alienate the Americans completely. Our economic dependence on them is large. Accordingly, the foreign secretary was directed to send for the ambassador and tell him the following:

a) The period for dismantling all the electronic equipment will be one year commencing 1st January 1969.
b) A programme shall be drawn up to show which portion of the installation will be dismantled from month to month.
c) The equipment will be allowed to remain operative till the time of stipulated dismantling.
d) He should be told that in making this concession, we are taking a big risk with the Russians.

When told this, the ambassador offered gratitude on behalf of himself and the government. I also spoke to him on the telephone on the same subject and reminded him that President Johnson when passing through Karachi had offered to let us have two hundred M47 Patton tanks. He assured me that the matter is well taken care of.

Air Marshal Nur Khan C-in-C PAF visited the USA on an official visit. Our ambassador reported that he met with most of the senior officials at the Pentagon, the State Department and some of the senators, and members of the Foreign Arms Aid Committee. By all accounts he has put forward Pakistan's case for supply of arms with great skill. In consequence, all those who were opposed to such a move are thoroughly convinced that by denying arms to Pakistan, they have done their cause no good. He told them very plainly that we are not without options. The Soviet Union is willing to sell us all we want, but in that case our influence over the moderate elements in the Middle East will be reduced to nothing and this will have far reaching consequences for the West. When the British withdraw from the Persian Gulf, the Soviets will naturally come in to fill the gap with the assistance of Iraq, Egypt and India. This is a telling argument. Let us see what will be its affect on the new administration. At the moment, the Americans are in a state of flux in view of the presidential election fever.

---

22 | TUESDAY

📖 Mohammed Al-Arabi, special representative of the Algerian president came to deliver a letter from him inviting me to visit their country. He spoke in very warm terms and said that apart from the president and the government, the people of Algeria would be delighted to see me. I, too, have a fascination for these people and would like to visit them and the other countries of the Maghreb. I might be able to do something next year.

Politically, of course, the Algerians are firebrand. They would like the Middle Eastern Arabs to fight it out with Israel. I believe they still have some units stationed in Egypt. I was astounded to hear from him that they have a serious language problem in the country. Apparently, during the French rule only French was allowed to be talked, teaching of Arabic was totally banned. Reading of Qur'an was allowed, but there was total ban on its translation from Arabic. It just shows what a curse foreign rule can be and what inequities can be perpetrated and how subject people are humiliated.

📖 A batch of 21 senior officers headed by General Shari, commandant of Staff College, came to see me. They are undergoing one year course. They appeared a clued up lot and asked me very pertinent and searching questions on the internal and external problems of Pakistan. The meeting lasted an hour.

---

23 | WEDNESDAY

📖 Recorded a television talk for Revolution Day. A copy of the note is attached on reverse [see below].

Rawalpindi
22nd October 1968

My dear countrymen:
Assalam-o-Alaikum

1. Today marks culmination of ten years of revolution, its coming no pleasure, but necessity, save the country, saving important, but more important security and building. This easier said than done. Process involves identification of problems, realistic planning, mounting of resources and resolute execution. Above all, total involvement of people.

2. Let us take stock.
   - Ten years have been hectic, lots of planned activity, trials and tribulations and successes. A sound foundation for advancement and development laid. Lot achieved, but a lot more needs to be done.
   - One thing we can be certain of not having and that is boredom. There is no limit to the amount of work that lies ahead.
   - Indeed our salvation lies in unity and hard work.

3. In the field of security India's attitude is crucial. She has shown no desire to live at peace with us.
   - Calling us enemy number one, building enormous military machine, going back on solemn promises on Kashmir, taking irrational attitude on every dispute. Take for instance case of Farraka Barrage the best offer has been no war pact, but without a pact defining how mutual disputes will be settled.
   - We perforce had to build deterrent force, an expensive business.
   - Apart that it had to be organized, equipped and trained to meet an adversary several times in strength because we foresaw events clearly and catered for them in a realistic manner.
   - 1965 war proved the soundness of our concept and approach. An army several times our strength was brought to a halt in matter of days if not hours and crippling losses inflicted. In places we pushed him right back into his territory.
   - Our men fought with burning fire in them on land, sea and air and displayed great skill and courage on the battlefield, often going without sleep or food for days fortified in the belief that their cause was just and the whole nation was behind them like a rock.
   - Such instances are rare to meet in annals of war.
   - I was never in doubt of the outcome.
   - Several friendly countries assisted during that period, we are grateful.

4. Since then India doubled her forces, feverish military build up going on, we can not be oblivious of this so prudent precautions are incumbent on us, those responsible for defence of the country fully alive to the situation and ready to meet it, you can rest assured of that.
   - But basically we want peace with India first, then with anybody else, but on a just and honourable basis. Whenever India is ready we are ready. Until then we have to remain on guard.

5. Foreign policy. It is essential and its rationale should be well known by now.
   - A small power must recognize its limitations based on bilateralism, not using one against the other, keep out of major power politics as we cannot influence issues. We cannot expect unlimited help as we cannot give unlimited help.
   - Such a foreign policy can only be run by honesty, sincerity and straight forwardness.
   - It can be run by sobriety, dignity and quietly, demagogy, chauvinism and tall talk have no place in it. It is word of honest man that finally counts.

– It was a difficult task to get these foreign policies understood, but it is now understood and I believe, respected.

– RCD another landmark in our foreign policy, outcome of statesmanship of His Majesty the Shahinshah and Turkish leaders.

– Has great potential for stability and peace in the region.

– One thing should be closely understood, the limit of closeness to big powers determined and dependent on their policy. It is not something that a small power can get by wishing.

6. Now let us turn to affairs at home. We can take a lot of credit for what has been achieved. The following are the nature of infrastructure.

– Land reform in West Pakistan, scientific and realistic strengthening of middle class.

– In East Pakistan, middle class destroyed by politicians, scope for correction limited but some effort made to correct devastation.

– Evolution of system of basic democracies apart from anything else, society organized into self regulated units, its potential for good unlimited.

– A workable scheme of constitution is contribution towards stability and progress apparent.

7. Resettlement of refugees and their contribution towards building this country significant.

– Settlement of Indus basin water dispute and building of replacement work of gigantic nature in record time

– Gratitude due to friendly countries and two presidents of the World Bank.

– Revamping of administration and setting up large numbers of autonomous bodies to expedite development.

– Educational reforms, we are still at it.

– And host of other innovations not easy to remember.

– In the economic field results impressive, GNP increased by 55 per cent, agriculture production by 40 per cent, industrial production by 160 per cent, per capita income increased from Rupees 318 to 515.

– Most of the consumer goods now produced in the country.

– Exports doubled, but we have to do more.

– Objections to debt spurious and malicious. Every hundred dollars invested have given 33 dollars annual return.

– We are trying hard to do away with the need to take loans, but it is going to take time, loans and credits necessity, not pleasure.

8. Our economic policy is pragmatic, we allow free play to the public and private sector—let the one who can do a thing best do it. This policy has paid. However, in East Pakistan the private sector needs much more free rein.

– Aware of the objections to concentration of wealth in few hands. We are trying to diversify prior holdings.

– This vexed problem, but large proportion of profits being reinvested. However, better treatment of labour, provision of better working conditions, better utilization of capacity and producing quality goods, taking care of the interest of the consumer and prompt and correct payment of taxes imperative.

– Recent hoarding of imported sugar and such incidences to push up prices leave a bad taste in the mouth, such exploitation intolerable.

– Society expects businessmen to show much higher level of social awareness and response.

9. A real breakthrough and indeed revolution achieved in agriculture in West Pakistan. East Pakistan too moving in that direction.

– We shall be reaching soon stage of self sufficiency and indeed exportable surpluses of vast magnitude.

– This will create and has created new problems, which have to be faced.

– How this happened.

– Provision of scientific imports and modernizing agriculture, hard and dedicated work by our scientists and officials, awakening of the farmer a great blessing, private initiative, 61,000 tube wells sunk in West Pakistan.

– Sky is the limit in agriculture if we use irrigation machinery and pool land for cooperative farming.

– Farming community coming into big money. Need to turn some of it into savings, hence mobile banks hope these savings will fill credit gap for the farmer who in turn will utilize it for improvement of farming.

– Works programmes especially in East Pakistan have done a lot of good to the rural community and landless labour, this must continue as a part of ADP, annual developmental plan.

10. Sum up of these gains impressive by any standard, prosperity coming, but it has given rise to certain problems that need a change of outlook and approach of old measures don't do.

– Spread of education and urbanization through industrialization.

– Need for modernization to be competitive in the industrial and especially the agriculture field.

– Checking population explosion, the need apparent, I don't have to go into details.

– Then due to prosperity and material opportunities, certain social evils have emerged or got accentuated. Every sane and patriotic person would like to see them eliminated. Government has done its best to produce laws and rules that will help, but there are serious limitations under our legal system that must be recognized, however, the government will continue to do its best to seek whatever remedies are possible meanwhile. The society too must show moral courage and not allow prevalence of social evil.

11. Object of celebration of decades of reform.

– Self praise not intended though those that have done good work and there are many worthy of highest praise.

– The object was to make people aware of the problems of the country, how they were identified, how some resolved, some in the process of resolution and under what circumstances and limitations. This exercise has not been chicken feed. It has been an uphill task against tremendous odds. So don't let any one in the country take them for granted or believe that such things can happen automatically without sound thinking, sound planning, discipline, hard and yet harder work. Miracles in mundane life don't happen without these efforts.

– One good thing that has emerged through these celebrations is that a lot of useful ideas and information has become available on every conceivable subject. I hope it will be compiled and used by the people for research or self edification.

12. In solving our problems, I talked of difficulties we encountered, of course there have been many, but no less formidable has the attitude of those amongst us who opposed Pakistan and don't want

to see it consolidate and flourish and those who oppose for the sake of opposition. Instead of offering solutions to the problem we face they continued to plead for resurrection of their discredited myth and beliefs in the hope of misleading the people. The current of life trend in Pakistan has gone past them, I don't have to remind you to be aware of them whatever else they may have as their aim they have no intention of promoting your interest or that of the country.

13. Now that of the future fourth five year plan being formulated, I would like to see it debated by the people in a purposeful and constructive manner.

   – The outline of the socio-economic objectives of the plan will be given out by the Deputy Chairman, Planning Commission, shortly and also the method of conducting discussion on it. Hope all knowledgeable people will contribute with their ideas.

   – The tasks before us are that whilst maintaining the tempo of economic growth and creating an effective deterrent force, we must have:

   a. Creative measure of social justice and income distribution.
   b. Correct regional imbalances to the extent possible.
   c. Replace foreign assistance gradually.

14. In doing all this we should derive guidance and succour from our ideology.

   – We owe our national and cultural identity to Islam. Our whole pattern of thinking and conduct is governed by the fundamentals of Islam, which are unity of God, equality of man and social justice.

   – These fundamentals contain those profound truths which completely transformed society and gave a new orientation to human and civilization.

   – These fundamentals have exercised an overwhelming grip over humanity because they gave man a new conciseness of his existence. His unique and supreme position among God's creations was established through these fundamentals.

   – The awe inspiring concept of oneness of God, the consciousness of the equality of man and the upsurge for establishing a just and humane society based on the principle of social justice deeply stirred the thought and emotions of people to whom the message of Islam was conveyed in is most lucid and direct fashion.

   – Why Muslim society degenerated because of ignorance of these fundamentals and because the directness and meanings of these fundamentals were lost in practice.

   – Through ignorance, misinterpretation, and misapplication the Muslims were diverted from their main point of life.

   – Instead of following these principles we allowed ourselves to be surrounded by a host of rituals, legends and superstitions.

   – Progress demands that we should restore the fundamentals of Islam to their original position. Islam has to be communicated to moderate society in the terms and language we can understand. The purpose of Islam is to help mankind to progress and it is in this sense that we must make Islam an instrument of progress.

📖 Had a busy day in meeting people. Called Syed Hassan and Nawab Junagarh[45] to lunch. Attended a reception by the municipal corporation. The vice chairman Ziaullah had been after me for a long time. I was very happy to see people attending the reception looking cheerful and relaxed. In my address, I praised the refugees for their sacrifices and their contributions in consolidating Pakistan.

The television address on the eve of Revolution Day was shown in the evening. The talk lasted for 35 minutes and came out very well.

24 | THURSDAY

Pir of Dewal came to see me. After usual pleasantries, which is the normal technique of softening a person, he made several requests: Some mullahs operating against his leadership should be dealt with. I should provide the money for an institute that he wants to run and that I should build a mosque in his village. The Auqaf Department of West Pakistan, Mr Masood, should be removed from his job and he is not helping his party people. There is no dearth of my 'well wishers'. The only trouble is that they happen to be very expensive.

27 | SUNDAY

Held an investiture in the afternoon. Some 103 people were decorated including children who had shown spontaneous bravery and had excelled in art. It was a colourful ceremony followed by a reception.

28 | MONDAY

Mr Pirzada, the Attorney General and Mr Akhund, the Law Minister, West Pakistan came to see me in connection with the allegations against Bhutto. They discussed his speech in a public meeting at Hyderabad in which he divulged several state secrets and also the case relating to misuse by him of government earthmoving machinery.

29 | TUESDAY

Attended a dinner party at Ahmed Dawood's place. His house was lit up with elaborate lighting. The naval band was in attendance and several professional singers were present. An obvious case of conspicuous consumption which arouses the jealousy of an average man. I keep on hinting at the dangers involved in this, but these people who have become rich quickly, don't take heed although Dawood normally is very humble and so are his brothers and their offspring. In the party Dawood's American partners in the fertilizer factory were also present including the head of their firm. He had come out on a quick three day visit to Pakistan after spending some time in India. He showed great appreciation of what is going on in Pakistan. Felt people here were proud, self confident and full of urge to advance whereas in India they were listless and drifting. Coming here from India was like coming into light from darkness. About the presidential elections in his own country he felt that the people were not thrilled by either of the two candidates though Nixon would perhaps be better. America needed a conservative president who would cut expenditure and balance the budget.

30 | WEDNESDAY

Flew from Karachi to Rawalpindi.

31 | THURSDAY

📖 The governors' conference started, several important matters were discussed and decisions taken.

📖 During the course of the conference Governor Monem Khan complained bitterly of Hindu influence being introduced by the educationists and so called intelligentsia in the language and culture of East Pakistan as a calculated policy. All Muslim influence was gradually being eliminated. He meant to imply that Education Minister Anwar-ul-Haq[46] from East Pakistan was instrumental and party to that trend. Anwar-ul-Haq's explanation was that the present generation in East Pakistan having been educated by the Hindus could only express themselves in the language they had learned. Shahabuddin's comment was that all this is an expression of Bengali nationalism, which I think is nearer the mark.

📖 Governor Monem Khan came to see me and explained several things in his own meandering way. Finally he came to the matter of flood control in East Pakistan. The demand is for an outlay of sixteen hundred and sixty-three crores of rupees spread over 10 to 15 years. A body to be set up at the centre that will supervise work and arrange finances that should be in the form of grants. Where these finances let alone grants will come from is not considered relevant. The object is to show acceptance of a plan twice the size of Indus basin water treaty settlement and throw the whole responsibility on the centre. True, flood control is a problem in East Pakistan but it is not going to be approached in a practical and economic way like anything else in East Pakistan. This problem, too, is going to be approached on a political level. As such, more and more unpleasantness will be generated.

📖 Bhutto is in the process of touring Frontier areas and indulging in all sort of irresponsible utterances. He may lack several other things, but he does know how to use his tongue.

📖 News came in that President Johnson had ordered cease fire of bombing on North Vietnam. This is welcome news, let us hope that it leads to some sort of peace.

1 | FRIDAY

A meeting of the National Economic Council was held in which the socio-economic objectives of the fourth five-year plan were discussed and adopted.

4 | MONDAY

Attended the groundbreaking ceremony of Tarbela Dam. The ceremony consisted of speeches by the central minister of industries, chairman WAPDA West Pakistan and followed by me. The gathering consisted of ministers and secretaries of the central and provincial governments, diplomatic corps and other notables. Mr Cargil of the World Bank was also represented. The flags of all donor countries to the Tarbela project were flying.

On the termination of speeches I was called upon to pull a lever which set in motion three sirens one after the other warning people to take cover. Then three charges were set off on the far side of the river making a loud bang rather like an artillery barrage. It was an impressive sight, a great day for Pakistan. I had worked very hard for this day and so did many of my associates. I pray to God for His blessings for the project and for the country.

Governor Monem Khan of East Pakistan was also present on the occasion. He looked rather pensive. They have the tremendous problem of devastating floods, cyclones and creating facilities for artificial irrigation. Luckily, I was able to persuade Cargil, that is the World Bank representative, to help us resolve whatever is possible. He had promised to go across and look at things. What is needed is preparation of a workable scheme by experts first.

7 | THURSDAY

It is now confirmed by the radio news that Richard Nixon is the winner in the American presidential election by a narrow majority of 50 thousand in the 70 million popular vote cast. And yet he gets 287 electoral votes, 17 more than required and about a 100 more than his next competitor Hubert Humphrey. Meanwhile, both the houses of Congress have gained Democratic majorities. This is going to make things difficult for the president with the Congress in passage of laws. However, in the American system it has been possible for a minority president to work with the opposition party, majority Congress.

11 | MONDAY

Last week or 10 days have been hectic. Bhutto has been spreading a lot of poison in the Frontier area and inciting the student community in particular and the political malcontents in general, especially the Red Shirts. He went first to Kohat where he addressed the usual bar meeting. The lawyers as a class are prepared to listen to any nonsense. He also addressed a public meeting indulging in all sort of fabrications and lies. In DIK [Dera Ismail Khan] he forcibly climbed the roof of a private house to address the crowd. I believe the owner has registered a case of criminal trespass.

☷ A batch of Gordon College students who had gone to Landi Kotal and brought some contraband materials were apprehended by the custom officials and their goods confiscated.

☷ This morning there was a meeting arranged by the Muslim League in Peshawar. Nawabzada Abdul Ghafoor [Khan Hoti] spoke first; he was followed by Mukarram Khan. Before he finished two shots were fired by a young man in the crowd. They were aimed at me, but went very high. There was a pensioner *subedar* sitting next to this young man who overpowered him and brought him to the dais where he was taken over by the police. Meanwhile, confusion started amongst the crowd. I at once got up and began speaking. This steadied the people and they listened to my speech in pin drop silence. I did not see this man firing. I only heard the shots, but my sons Akhtar and Tahir both saw him get up with a pistol in his hand and at once fell on me to protect me.

Later, others also surrounded me, throwing a protective screen around. During this episode I was not in the least concerned. I know by experience that even under ideal conditions it is not easy to shoot with a pistol accurately beyond 20 yards. My only worry was that no one kills the man.

The police soon reported the young man's name: Hashim, son of a hide dealer who came from village Umarzai near Charsadda. He is a student of polytechnic and failed his recent exams. He is reported of good character and yet when arrested he was [under the] influence of drugs. So far he has not come out with much except that he wanted to kill me so that Bhutto could take over.

13 | WEDNESDAY

☷ Bhutto and Wali with their henchmen were arrested under the Defence of Pakistan Rules last night for causing confusion and inciting violence in the country. They have been taken to jail and I hope they will stay for a long time. They have been responsible for a good deal of mischief. Khawaja Shahabuddin, Admiral Khan and people from the secret agencies came to me with recommendations that whilst on the one side strong action against the mischief makers was justified, on the other hand we should initiate certain actions in respect of the student community, labour, class III and IV government servants and do something about curbing corruption. I told them in no uncertain terms that they were demoralized and wanted to demoralize me too. They were sadly mistaken if they think they will demoralize me. Any weak action or appeasement at this stage will be misunderstood and unappreciated, and in fact, will boomerang on the government, leading to much bigger and impossible demands encouraging gangsterism to become the pattern of life. Am I going to be a party to it?

The current thing to do was that before the names of the detainees were announced on the radio and in the press, the governor of West Pakistan should go on the air explaining that this action was necessitated by the grave situation that these people had created and in the interest of law-abiding citizens, who have nothing to fear. True, there are certain things that are hurting the average citizen, but the government was doing its best within its means to ameliorate them. Similarly, government would consider removing any irritant and inconsistence to the student community, but only in an atmosphere of peace and calm. This was done. Meanwhile, we should set up a committee identifying these irritants and inconsistencies and announce them removed at an appropriate stage.

16 | SATURDAY

📖 Mr McNamara, the President of the World Bank, has a great reputation for efficiency but besides that he is the one American I have met who is capable of saying yes or no on the spot. He is dead honest. I asked him how he viewed the election of Richard Nixon. He said it all depended on what his foreign policy was like and that would be judged by the type of person he has as his secretary of state, treasury and defence. Any withdrawal from friendly world contact would be fatal for America. He would also be judged on how he rallies the nation and makes them raise their sights. The potential for rising to great heights is there.

17 | SUNDAY

📖 Asghar Khan, former commander-in-chief of the Pakistan Air Force, who belonged to the Bhutto group for a long time, today held a press conference in Lahore and launched a scathing attack on the government and to [his intention to] join politics in opposition. I made the following note when I heard this: Asghar Khan has seen fit to make a vile attack on the government and its policies based on half-truths and downright falsehoods. This neurotic and unreasoned person may surprise strangers but those who know him well are well aware that it is nothing but fulminations of a shallow, frustrated and shut in introvert not above cunning and deceit. In fact, we knew full well that even in service he used to keep odd company and his associates have been working on him since his retirement to come out with such a statement. In doing so he has disgraced his uniform apart from setting a poor example for his service. Be that as it may be, he has to be countered and met.

📖 I have been told by several knowledgeable people that in my talks our people will react better if I appeal to their emotions as are they are so emotional. Things like Kashmir and Islam appeal to them immensely. Facts and figures about development and their future well being don't have the same pull. I am not surprised but I do feel sad.

📖 Lots of leaders have tried this and landed their country and their people and themselves in an awful mess. Take Soekarno, Nasser, Nkrumah, etc. They have ruined their people for not attending to concrete problems. It is not realised that the secret of survival lies in hard work and economic strength. This too is the message of the Quran: Read, write, think and act. The very first that was revealed to the Prophet is 'READ.'

18 | MONDAY

📖 The information minister and the defence minister have been examining what should be our reaction to Asghar Khan's[47] speeches and action. The information people are of the opinion that we should let him expose himself more before counter attacking. Chances are that people will soon find out that he is tongue tied, superficial and lacks charisma.

📖 Justice Hamood-ur-Rahman was sworn in as Chief Justice of the Supreme Court. A number of judges, ministers and senior officials attended the function. Prior to that I had separate talks with him over disciplinary problems of the courts and also the broadness of the language of Article 98 of the constitution which gave the courts unlimited powers. I am clear in my mind that the first thing we have to do when the assembly meets next is to amend the relevant sections of the constitution, otherwise there would be utter lawlessness in the country.

📖 The route permit system enforced in West Pakistan for buses etc. is leading to all sorts of malpractices and giving a bad name to the government. I have been able to persuade Musa to do away with it and let people run buses as required on a regulated basis.

📖 On Nixon's prospects, the cardinal fact about the next administration is that its most difficult problems are insolvable within the four short years which it can count upon. In the last analysis the question is whether the new president can convince a predominant majority of the people that they are a nation and that they can have a government that they can trust. Such unity and confidence cannot be brought by promises, but only with demonstration that the government does and can govern.

Along with ending the war and maintaining the rate of economic growth, there will have to be impressive evidence given by the Nixon administration that the country is really moving, though by different methods, to the reform and reconstruction of its social environment. Nor can we shrink from the fact that as against continued disorder the civil authority must be upheld. The country longs for peace and it will support authority against disorder even before all grievances which caused it can be reduced.

19 | TUESDAY

📖 I keep on hearing that there are of a lot of malpractices and corruption of route permits and running of passenger buses in West Pakistan. I have been impressing on the governor that the issue of route permits be done away with and anybody wishing to go into this business should be allowed to do provided the buses confirm to certain stands. This will eliminate corruption, introduce competition and improve the standard of service. So today West Pakistan has declared commencing 1st January 1969 there will be no restriction on the plying of buses.

21 | THURSDAY

📖 One hears lots of complaints that the Muslim League is inactive and is not pulling its weight, as such, a political vacuum is created which the opposition readily fills. I agree that the Muslim League is not as active as it should be for several reasons. One of them is that they feel that in the final analysis I shall bail them out and do something to put things right. The other is that they belong to a government party, and can't be irresponsible and indulge in arousing people's passions and emotions as the opposition does. Nonetheless, they have to be activated and made to take political initiative. I have, therefore, issued the following instructions.

a. The Muslim League in cities and towns should be told to chalk out a regular programme of political and social work and holding of public meetings, they should be given appropriate talking points.

b. Under no circumstances are the opposition meeting to be disturbed, but at the same time we must not allow the opposition to disturb our meetings. This can be ensured by having volunteers ready to deal with any disturbance.

c. The administration down to *tehsil* level should be told to keep contact with the local Muslim League leaders and seek their assistance in spheres where they can be useful.

23 | SATURDAY

Asghar Khan is going around the country addressing bar associations. He is repeating the same arguments against the government and me and drawing attention. He plans to go to East Pakistan too and is trying to persuade General Azam Khan to accompany [him]. There are some indications that he may not be welcome in East Pakistan, as he has pronounced anti-India feelings, which means confrontation against India to which East Pakistanis don't subscribe. There are also reports to the effect that the younger element in the army and air force are impressed with him. There are others who regard his conduct as reprehensible.

26 | TUESDAY

After a lot of discussion the following decisions were taken:

a. A committee was set up to look into the problems of students with a view to removing any irritants or legitimate complaints. Meanwhile, those that were real mischief makers should be dealt with firmly.

b. It should be ensured that the basic consumer goods are available at reasonable prices even at the expense of development and people should be informed of the supply position by the appropriate authority from time to time.

c. The Muslim League should be activated to take its full part in countering disruptions. But to my mind there is urgent need to re-establish the government's authority firmly. I, therefore, had a discussion with the law minister on the admissibility of lifting the emergency from the purview of the courts. He agreed. This will need constitutional change. It is the first thing we must do when the assembly meets in Dacca on 6 December.

27 | WEDNESDAY

The British Foreign Minister, Michael Stewart, came to call on me. We discussed the Persian Gulf problem, Chinese intentions, Russian moves in Eastern Europe, Rhodesia, Nigeria, Vietnam and likely foreign policy adopted by president-elect Nixon. The British are worried about their economic future. Their restrictive measures to tighten the balance of payments are not producing desired results fast enough.

28 | THURSDAY

📖 Today, reports indicate that there have been widespread disturbances by students and hooligans in several towns. They indulged in looting and arson. Muslim Leagues and family planning offices were made a special target. The curious things is that young school children of 10-12 years of age have also taken to violence.

29 | FRIDAY

📖 Recorded a television speech in place of the usual first of the month broadcast. I reviewed the situation of lawlessness in the country and condemned the activities of the disruptionists. Told the students that the acts of vandalism in which they are indulging in no way help solve their demands or hold hope for a better future. They are either misguided or being used by the disruptionists. The students, especially the young ones, spearhead the attacks. We have, therefore strengthened, the police by military units in places. I hope their presence will have a steadying effect. If not, we shall have to move on to the next drastic step to bring people back to sanity. I hope that this step will not be necessary.

30 | SATURDAY

📖 Held a meeting of the defence committee of the cabinet. The question of foreign exchange allocation was discussed. The requirement of the services, of course, is enormous, but the trouble is that we are so short of it besides we are entering a difficult period for foreign exchange. Aid climate is bad, some of our commodities are not selling well and because of the currency crises in the western world we are afraid that even our traditional commodities may not fetch enough. The services, and especially the air force, wanted ten extra crores. It was decided that a review of foreign exchange earnings should be made in the near future to see what more can be done.

I told the services that they should be clear on priorities. In my view the first essential was to maintain whatever we have, that is, acquire necessary spares and then buy anything new with what is left over.

The army was given permission to raise certain numbers of units for which the equipment is available and in sight.

The financial experts think that our armed forces are beyond our capacity. This is known, but what else can we do against the odds. India today has 30 divisions and comparable air force and navy.

1 | SUNDAY

📖 Addressed the Central Secretariat officers and officers of GHQ at the National Assembly hall about the current wave of lawlessness in the country, its causes and the manner in which the opposition politicians exploited the situation on the country. We are doing everything that is possible to remove genuine grievances of the students, ease the life of wage earners and ensure that essential commodities in the country are available to meet the demand. But we are also determined to deal with lawlessness. Under no circumstances can the country be allowed to slip into chaos. If democracy is to work then political activity must remain within bounds of decency. In any case, the duty of the civil service and the armed forces is clear. They must carry out lawful orders and not indulge in partisan politics. Those who wish to are free to leave the service and take to the streets.

2 | MONDAY

📖 Held a meeting of the Pakistan Muslim League. The present political situation in the country was discussed and the organization was given a guideline on meeting the situation. The decision on the formation of Central Muslim League Council was also taken.

4 | WEDNESDAY

📖 Flew to Lahore, discussed the political situation with the governor and others. Also discussed the advisability of amending article 98 sub para 2 of the constitution so as to exclude the jurisdiction of the courts in cases under the Defence of Pakistan Rules (DPR). The West Pakistan administration was insistent that this should be done, but the contrary view prevailed that this is not the opportune time to do so. It will only give the opposition further handle to whip up agitation claiming that the rights of the citizens are being curtailed, though in fact, we would be doing no more than securing the Defence of Pakistan Rules as it was intended to be.

5 | THURSDAY

📖 Flew to Dacca. Monem Khan had arranged an elaborate reception as he always does, but in this instance more for political reasons. He told me that the opposition plans were that the Pakistan Democratic Movement intended to hold a meeting at Suhrawardy's[48] grave and then march through the city carrying antigovernment placards and then later expand the programme to whip up agitation. Bhashani[49] and his communist friends intend to make a start with a public meeting in the Paltan Maidan and then carry out demonstrations and calling for strikes, etc.

Discussed the amendment of Article 98 of the constitution again in the cabinet. Governor Monem Khan and some of his ministers were also present, the consensus was that this was not the opportune time to do so. In any case the object could be achieved by the use of the security act and the provincial detention law. These laws provided for hearing by a tribunal and so are outside the purview of the courts. I, however, suggested that we might secure the DPR by providing a hearing by a tribunal and for that it might be a good thing to make a reference to the Supreme Court. The constitution provides for such a contingency.

6 | FRIDAY

📖 Addressed a large gathering of the educationists, agriculturists and basic democrats. It was a good meeting.

7 | SATURDAY

📖 Addressed a meeting of the presidents and secretaries of the districts and subdivisions of the Muslim League. Told them to get busy on countering the disruptionists. Heard of some disorder in Dacca city. Cars and other vehicles were stoned and in places shops looted. A convoy of East Pakistan Rifles was brick batted. The East Pakistan Rifles opened fire in self-defence. Some people were wounded.

8 | SUNDAY

📖 Bhashani and his followers declared a total *hartal* for two days. Meanwhile, Section 144 was imposed in Dacca and Narayanganj area. However, he decided to defy Section 144 after mid-day prayers. When police entreaties failed to dissuade him, coloured water was sprinkled on him and his crowd, whereupon they beat a hasty retreat and dispersed.

9 | MONDAY

📖 Flew to Thakurgaon and then went on to Dinajpur by road. En route saw the new tubewell scheme. It is now functioning well. Some 60 thousand acres of almost virgin land has been brought under irrigation. The people are learning the art of using water and want extensions of such schemes. They are also getting big yields through use of modern seeds and fertilizers and are getting well off.

    Addressed a large gathering at the airfield and then in Dinajpur. The arrangements were excellent. The deputy commissioner of the district was a live wire and clued up man, very keen and full of ideas. A couple of months back there had been unprecedented floods in this area. It was the first time in known history that such a thing happened in this district. The people suffered a lot but the government also did a lot for them. Monem Khan took personal interest in relief work. People seemed appreciative of all that.

12 | THURSDAY

📖 A grandson of Mahatma Gandhi, who is also the grandson of Rajagopalachari, and runs an MRA institution in Pauabghani near Poona, came to see me to discuss Indo–Pak relations. He started off by saying that in our […] relations India was the main culprit. Her intolerant, bigoted attitude and her going back on solemn promises was the root cause of the Kashmir debacle and bad relations. There were a lot among the educated classes against Pakistan. People like him were doing their best to change this mentality and had made some dent but the odds against them were great. However, they had not given up hope. I told him that was Indians' and our misfortune. Peace between the two countries cold be a great boon for India in many ways. Anyone with a grain of commonsense should realize this.

📖 Asghar Khan arrived yesterday and indulged in his usual fulminations. He will stay in the province for ten days or so addressing bar councils, etc. Qayyum is also coming on the 22nd.

📖 The National Democratic Front and other oppositionists have given a call for a province-wide strike tomorrow. Monem Khan has made a radio broadcast telling people not to fall in the trap. He has also laid on arrangements to deal with the situation. Apparently, the opposition have hired a lot of ruffians to obstruct traffic, etc. In view of the disturbed situation I have decided to postpone my visit to Saudi Arabia and not to attend the Prime Ministers Conference.

13 | FRIDAY

📖 Asghar Khan, accompanied by people like Murshed and Farid, attended *Jumma* prayers at Bait-ul-Mukarram and indulged in political speech-making. Slogans were raised against me and the government to which some people objected. He then tried to defy Section 144, whereupon the party was sprayed with coloured water. Some arrests were made including Lieutenant Colonel Mukhtar who is posing as his secretary. A case has been registered against them.

📖 I had detailed Shahabuddin and Sobur to bring about a rapprochement between Monem Khan and the dissident Muslim Leagues. Shahabuddin reported failure as all the dissidents were riding a high horse. He asked if I could see them tomorrow. I agreed.

14 | SATURDAY

📖 Saw Monem Khan and the dissident Muslim Leaguers in the morning. Before letting them talk I made clear two points.

1. The governor will not be removed irrespective of what anybody says.
2. Muslim League party can only work if people are prepared to cooperate with the governor.

Then they started narrating their complaints, some true and some imagined. However, it was clear that they expected some relaxation on the part of the governor who tends to be rigid. I then met Monem Khan and told him that there were only two alternatives, ignore them or pacify them. Circumstances demanded that the latter course be followed. He agreed and also agreed to see them sometime. Returned to Rawalpindi by a direct flight.

15 | SUNDAY

📖 Yusuf Haroon came to see me. Talking of the agitation in the country, he said that the new entrants to politics like Bhutto and Asghar were trying to whip up people frenzy with the two superseding the old politicians and starting a sort of suicidal movement. This has to be checked at all costs. The opposition plan is to direct all criticism on me in order to demolish my image and the people are so gullible that they are to believe any rumour however fantastic. They are not in a rational mood. How long they remain in this state of madness remains to be seen. But if they don't get their balance back, they will be paving the way to the disintegration of the country. My fight is to save us from this disaster. I get questioned sometimes as to what makes me serve the people. There are two things that made me do that: that I am born in this country, and secondly, I know the dangers to which they are exposed to. My effort has all along been to save them from those dangers.

20 | FRIDAY

📖 Sensible people including the intelligence agencies keep on coming to me and show great concern over the present political situation in the country and the state of mind in which people have got into. Their concern is as follows:

a. I am surrounded by senior officials whose bona fides are not above doubt. Their intentions are not good and they have not kept me well informed, especially about the state of student's affairs. In any case, why have they not taken preventive action in time and removed some of the obvious irritants and grievances?

b. Both the governors names are tarnished and administratively they are ineffective and incapable, especially Musa.

c. The custom of keeping service chiefs for more than three years is reprehensible. This must come to an end.

d. The celebration of a decade of reforms has produced a great irritant to people in any case. Why was it done for so long?

e. Although people have worshiped me in the past, today I am the target of an attack. This trend has to be reversed at all costs.

f. As a measure of appeasement why can't I at least get the assembly to amend the constitution to allow election of legislators by direct adult franchise. This will take the sting out of the opposition.

g. Then there is talk of the economic hardships of the middle class and also accusation of corruption.

h. Most of my ministers are ineffective. Nobody listens to them. Why can't I get better men?

i. Bhutto and Asghar are charlatans and self-seekers. They will ruin the country.

j. The Muslim League is inactive and ineffective.

All these things are true to a certain extent and one is doing one's best to tackle these problems. The real difficulty is finding men of calibre who can bear these responsibilities so one is forced to do with the human material one has.

21 | SATURDAY

📖 Now some of the mullahs under the banner of the Jamiat-ul-Ulema of Pakistan, who are mostly Ahraris, old Congressites, Deobandis, all well-known anti-Pakistan elements, have taken to demonstrating in the streets, curiously enough, in conjunction with the leftists, a curious combination.

An ugly incident took place in a bench of the High Court in Karachi where Justices Shaukat and Bashir were sitting hearing Shorish Kashmiri's writ petition under DPR. During the course of the hearing Shaukat called the advocate general a liar and a bluffer—most unbecoming on the part of a judge. The advocate general protested against this behaviour and accused the court of being biased, whereupon the court decided to not continue with the case and issued a long tirade which was to be issued to the press. The chief justice has appointed a new bench, but was unwilling to give a statement for doing so. However, something was got from him with great difficulty. I think he just lost his nerve. Our judiciary is in a pretty poor state. Having come predominately from the legal profession they have very little discipline. That is why it so essential to get suitable CSP officers in the judiciary.

23 | MONDAY

Mr Jaffery, Secretary, Water and Power, who headed a negotiating team on sharing of the Ganges water with India reported on return from Delhi. He had a hard time bargaining with the Indians who were devious and uncooperative as ever, and it proved very difficult to pin them down to anything reasonable. They are offering us very little water. However, they have agreed to hold the next meeting in Islamabad in March. I told Jaffery that apart from preparations for the next meeting we should go over to Dacca and put as many people as possible in the picture. Apart from anything else, politically this is necessary. The Indians were anxious that the meeting should take place on a technical level. I was anxious that the level be raised to secretary if not a minister to which the Indians were not agreeable, but I forced Jaffery on them.

24 | TUESDAY

Reached Karachi in the morning preparatory to the RCD summit meeting. Both the Shahinshah of Iran and the Prime Minister of Turkey are expected to arrive tomorrow.

25 | WEDNESDAY

Received Prime Minister Demirel in the morning, and whilst driving to the President's House, I mentioned to him the political convulsions we are experiencing within the country. He said they are experiencing similar problems. Some of the student's and other problems are genuine and should be attended within our means, which are limited, but a good deal of agitation is based on political mischief. Little do politicians realise that without political stability and peace within, it is impossible to do any economic development or achieve any progress. Turkey has bitter experience of it. It was through internal squabbles that the Turkish Empire was lost. Again, it was through internal bickering that the tragic happening of 1960 took place, which took the country back by several years. He was amazed that the people of Pakistan don't realise what I had done for them and what external dangers they would be exposed to if internal control was not maintained.

📖 Received the Shahinshah in the afternoon. He looked relaxed and cheerful. He took well deserved pride in the fact that Iran is making tremendous economic progress. This year they expect their growth rate in GNP to be over 11 per cent, which is unprecedented. Apart from growing oil royalties, they are finding more and more minerals and the agriculture is also progressing. Iran is moving fast toward the takeoff stage. Luckily, the Shah is personally interested in development and he has a cabinet that is similarly oriented. The resources are being spent for useful purposes. The Iranians, who had taken their money out, are bringing it back and investing. The middle class is expanding.

📖 RCD summit meeting started in the afternoon. In welcoming the guests, I reminded that the RCD was not a pact or agreement but a movement based on equal partnership and understanding. It was a unique example of goodness and solidarity which the other countries similarly placed could well emulate. We must do everything possible to make it a success for peace in this region and peace in the world.

26 | THURSDAY

📖 Full scale discussion took place in the morning again in an restricted session. Mr Demirel took the floor. Afternoon session was devoted to RCD affairs. A report by the three planners produced earlier was approved. There was a good deal of fellow feeling and warmth by all in their approach. Iran seemed much more forthcoming and there was talk even of closer political collaboration. It seems to be drawing on all that in the present day world, small and separate countries cannot make their voice felt. So it is necessary to create large and viable groupings and that indeed is the intention of RCD.

27 | FRIDAY

📖 The Shahinshah and the Turkish prime minister departed for home. When escorting the Shah to the airport, I expressed the hope that some collaboration in the military field will continue. He responded rather listlessly and complained that a sergeant in one of our air force training schools had mentioned to an Iraqi student in the presence of an Iranian student that why don't the Arabs kick the Iranian bastards out of Bahrain. This matter was reported to the Shah. On check it was found that the sergeant has used the word damned and not bastard. Then in some aviation conference in Manila, our delegate supported the Arabs against Iran. I was grieved to hear this. The Iranians are very touchy people. We must be careful of their susceptibilities. I, therefore, ordered the defence minister to give instructions to all the defence chiefs to ensure the Arabs and Iranians in our institutions are not allowed to mix with each other and that our people must scrupulously avoid commenting on political and controversial matters.

28 | SATURDAY

📖 The cabinet meeting was held and new import policy passed.

29 | SUNDAY

📖 Flew to Lahore, held discussions with Manzur Qadir and the law minister on certain constitutional and legal matters. Also took stock of the political situation in the province with the governor.

30 | MONDAY

📖 Addressed a large gathering of Muslim League presidents and secretaries from districts and municipalities and rebutted various allegations and misleading arguments used by the opposition. Condemned their tactics involving lawlessness and violence and reminded them of their duty to combat all this.

📖 Flew back to Rawalpindi.

DIARY 1969

1 | WEDNESDAY

📖 Now that there is an air of agitation in the country, everyone wants to force himself on me and offer 'advice'. The intention is good but it is getting tiring. No one offers a concrete solution.

6 | MONDAY

📖 Sent Mr Shahabuddin to Dacca to feel the pulse of the saner elements in the opposition. Do they realize the dangerous consequences of their barren, negative and agitational approach? If they are not careful, all this agitation will turn into a battle between haves and have-nots, which will affect them all. So if they are prepared to see things the way I do, I am quite prepared to discuss any healthy changes in the Constitution. Meanwhile, some attempt is being made to caution the *ulema* too.

7 | TUESDAY

📖 The opposition parties have been meeting in Dacca to chalk out their future programme. The PDM have decided not to take part in the polls under the 'Present Wholly Unacceptable Constitution' and called upon the nation for its determined and united support in the struggle to achieve what it called full democracy through direct elections based on adult franchise.

The basis of this decision is obvious. They cannot find a suitable candidate for the presidency: the new entrants to politics like Bhutto and Asghar Khan are unacceptable; and they want to keep the agitation pot boiling against me. The real brain behind such moves has always been Mr Mohammad Ali and Daultana. They also want to discredit the constitution in the eyes of the people. In other words, bring about utter chaos in the country. So the administration has to be on special guard to checkmate them.

📖 Mr Amjad Ali came to lunch. I asked him what he thought were the causes of the present unrest. He listed them as follows.

    a.   Rising prices.
    b.   Lack of participation on the part of the intelligentsia.
    c.   Maladministration, especially on the lower level.

I told him our prices compared favourably with other countries. He said because of increase in the military budget the indirect taxation had increased, which was reflected in higher prices.

📖 The intelligentsia feel that they can only have a feeling of participation if direct vote was introduced for election of the assemblies. Certain amount of maladministration and corruption was always there but with the extension of education it is felt more and voiced loudly.

Then there was the question of succession. The present uncertainty has to be removed. These are all very cogent points and worth consideration, perhaps with the opposition, if only they were prepared to be reasonable.

26 | SUNDAY

📖 Last two weeks have been tumultuous in the country. There have been demonstrations and protests against the government in the main cities. Rawalpindi has been particularly bad, where students and other hooligans have indulged in arson and vandalism directed against government property and public transport. Police in Pindi was short handed, so they were augmented, the other day they got fed up and did some cane-beating.

Three days ago situation in Dacca got out of control. The crowd, mostly students, had attacked the civil secretariat and burnt two Press Trust papers' buildings and machinery and several private houses. The situation got out of hand. The army had to be called in and curfew imposed. Karachi too had a bad day yesterday. Curfew had to be imposed there too.

Mr Shahabuddin had a private meeting with some of the opposition leaders in Lahore to see if some meeting ground could be found and settlement effected. The meeting came to nothing through Ch. Mohammad Ali's mischief.

1 | SATURDAY

📖 Last few days have been very disturbed in East Pakistan and West Pakistan. There have been a spate of demonstrations, looting and arson in several cities. The army had to be called in and curfew imposed in many cities. It had some steadying effect and also the false impression spread by Asghar Khan that the army will not support the government was dispelled. In fact, the army, whilst exercising great restraint, shot wherever curfew was violated. However, this is no cure for the malady that has gripped the people. Improvement of administration and economic conditions seems to be the answer, but the trouble is, where are the resources to come from?

4 | TUESDAY

📖 Khawaja Khairuddin and Mohammad Ali from East Pakistan came to see me along with Khawaja Shahabuddin. They had met different opposition leaders who showed willingness to meet me and my team and offered cooperation on certain terms that seem reasonable. What they are asking is election to the assemblies on direct vote and selection of ministers from the assemblies and creation of the office of the prime minister in the centre and chief minister in the provinces, all under the president and governors. Incidentally, Mohammad Ali is the most sensible East Pakistani I have come across.

5 | WEDNESDAY

📖 Flew to Lahore and sent a letter of invitation to Nawabzada Nasrullah Khan as the convener of the Democratic Action Committee to come and attend a political conference in Rawalpindi on 17th February accompanied by whomsoever he decides. Let us see what comes of it. Just heard that Bhutto has decided to withdraw his writ petition and go on hunger strike to death unless the emergency is withdrawn. My reaction was that he should be taken to Larkana and confined there, where he can fast as long as he likes.

6 | THURSDAY

📖 Reached Dacca. The administration apprehended trouble by the students, but nothing much happened. Was disturbed to hear that several of the national assembly members of our party were playing with the opposition and wanting to defect, led by Wahiduzzaman. He is an ambitious man and a big mischief-maker.

8 | SATURDAY

📖 Met Nurul Amin at Khawaja Shahabuddin's place on his request. He sounded reasonable though asked for certain preconditions to the commencement of talks.

📖 The students held a big meeting in Paltan Maidan and made fiery speeches. It seems that though some may be extracting money from hostile politicians and foreigners. They are under nobody's control.

9 | SUNDAY

The Muslim League Working Committee and Council meeting were held on 8th and 9th. The proceedings went off fairly well.

Heard of the Sindhi MNAs on the warpath. They are asking for dissolution of the one unit on flimsy grounds, though Sindh has come off best in this deal. I told them that such a thing could not be considered, though I was prepared to recommend to the West Pakistan government to set up a committee to go into the grievances of the smaller regions and rectify whatever was possible.

10 | MONDAY

Nawabzada Nasrullah called on me, accompanied by Khawaja Shahabuddin. Spoke in connection with talks. He sounded reasonable.

11 | TUESDAY

Reached Lahore midday by air.

14 | FRIDAY

General *hartal* was declared by DAC [Democratic Action Committee]. It was observed in most cities.

15 | SATURDAY

Since the emergency is to be lifted on the 17th, Bhutto and others detained under DPR [Defence of Pakistan Rules] have been released.

16 | SUNDAY

News from Dacca is depressing. Bhashani held a meeting in Paltan Maidan, ostensibly for holding funeral prayers of an Agartala conspirator prisoner killed when attempting to escape. He then encouraged the students to indulge in large-scale arson, several houses belonging to ministers and the government have been burnt. Apparently, Bhashani pointed out the places himself. The governor rang up to say that he has enough evidence to arrest Bhashani. Justice Rahman, who was president of the Agartala tribune, escaped by a hair's breadth. Manzur Qadir, too, was chased.

The members of DAC have decided to accept my invitation for parleys. They are supposed to be coming tomorrow and the meeting starting on the 19 February.

Governor Musa came to see me in early February and gave me a long note explaining that the situation in the province could be controlled only through imposition of martial law. I was taken aback, but he said what else was the answer when the civil arm was rendered ineffective through the intervention and non-cooperation of the courts. Safety acts etc. had been rendered completely ineffective and so were the emergency laws through broadest interpretation of article 98 sub para 2 of the constitution. Shooting people in large numbers was also no answer. I said even then we had to be patient and try to cope with the situation by constitutional means. However, I will call the C-in-C to see what he has to say. The C-in-C stated that partial martial law at this stage was not the answer.

21 | FRIDAY

The last few days events have been moving fast. Law and order situation deteriorated everywhere. In Dacca and surrounding areas there were sporadic cases of looting and burning of private property of ministers and supporters of government especially in surrounding areas. Today the news was that Sobur's house and Amjad Hussain's house in Khulna was burnt and several shops looted.

I have being going over the events of the last few weeks in my mind. The situation is that whilst the opposition has been whipping up lawlessness, our own party is disintegrating. A start was made by Sobur and Wahiduzzaman in East Pakistan, then the Sindhis and now people from the Frontier areas in the West Pakistan assembly. In other words, the Muslim League party has ceased to exist. The opposition is attacking me day and night. Their object is obvious. Once my image is damaged and terrorism intimidates people, they think they can have a walkover. In these circumstances, the choices before me were as follows:

a. Stick out whatever the cost and fight the battle single-handed. I am all prepared to do that, but would that cool the situation and enable elections to take place? I have my grave doubts. Besides in the present atmosphere my ability to influence peaceful elections would vanish rapidly.
b. Impose martial law—restricted or covering the whole country—in which case all sorts of events will follow: abrogation of the constitution, abolition of the assembly, and my abdication, etc. These steps will have a disastrous effect on the future of the country.
c. Declare I am not a candidate for the next presidential election. This may help to cool the situation, enable the elections to be held and leave me some power to influence the election of a good man if the presidential system is to stay.

So after a good deal of thought I have made a declaration that I shall not contest the next election and that this decision is irrevocable. My hope and prayer is that it turns out for the good of the country and that the pre-[19]58 chaos does not return. When I finished recording my broadcast, Altaf Gauhar said, 'Pakistan has committed suicide'.

23 | SUNDAY

Held a cabinet meeting including the two governors and explained to them the reasons for my decision not to contest the next elections. They were naturally sad, but understood the reason. A lot of concern was shown for the deteriorating law and order situation. I have, therefore, set up a committee including the commander-in-chief to go into this matter and report the results by tomorrow. When the others had left, the C-in-C was definite the time had come for imposition of countrywide martial law to save the country. Partial martial law won't do any good.

📖 A serious political situation is emerging. Bhutto in West Pakistan and Mujib in East Pakistan are gaining ascendancy. Something has to be done to prevent such a dangerous combination.

25 | TUESDAY

📖 Held a meeting of the Muslim League negotiating team in the morning and a cabinet meeting in the evening. It was becoming apparent that the DAC people, though having serious differences amongst each other, were unanimous on two points: Creation of a constitutional assembly on the basis of adult franchise and parliamentary form of government as a start. Other issues could be taken by the assembly later. The demand for a parliamentary form of government emanates from East Pakistan, whose undisputed leader is now Mujib. This will be ruinous and will lead to a change of government every month, but the politicians in their selfish interest are hell bent to insist on it irrespective of what may happen to the country. The question is, can this be staved off? But staving off such a thing at this late stage was out of the question. I was shown a document by Wali Khan drafted by Ch. Mohammad Ali and agreed to by other DAC leaders […] against all that would have been a single handed effort without the support of the people, who had already been beguiled by the opposition […] and the part which was disintegrating and subscribing to these views with an eye to catch popular support. They, in fact, started competing with the opposition in putting forward extremist demands. Incidentally, Wahiduzzaman claims […] breaking the principle of parity and demanding representation for East Pakistan on population basis. This happened some weeks before Mujib became the champion of this demand.

26 | WEDNESDAY

📖 Received a message last night that the DCA leaders want to meet us at 10:30 a.m. to seek permission to disperse for sometime for consultation and meet again on 10th March. I gave a short welcome speech, which was replied to by Nasrullah Khan. It looks like there are serious differences amongst them and some, like Daultana, did not want talks without the presence of Mujib as a free man. His plan seems to be to wreck the conference and make an alliance with Mujib. In other words, let Mujib rule East Pakistan and allow him [Daultana] the mastery of West Pakistan. This has been his thesis since the time of late Mr Suhrawardy: dominance for Awamis in the East and the Muslim League under him in the West.

Incidentally, Mujib came to see me last night. Our talk was cordial. He seemed conciliatory though making no bones that he was the uncrowned king of East Pakistan and he must be recognized as such. There was no give and take in his points. He was greatly under the influence of extremists in his party and the students who were completely out of control.

28 | FRIDAY

📖 When considering the genesis of the present turmoil in the country, I often wonder if the pace of reforms and development I introduced in the country have not been ahead of time, therefore incomprehensible to the people. They have been taken out of their stagnant past, probably too rapidly, and are feeling naked and uncertain. Modernization demolishes old and stagnant socio-economic institutions and new ones are time consuming and difficult to build. Often people are unwilling to accept them. Change is in any case terrifying to human beings. It leaves them confused and frustrated which they develop into the form of lawlessness and violence and defiance.

I am also worried about the future; the parliamentary form of government looks like its coming and East Pakistan will ask for maximum autonomy in the beginning and later secession. Meanwhile, they will encourage dismemberment of West Pakistan. The central government would be weakened. All this could lead to the disintegration of Pakistan—a terrible thought. This has been haunting me ever since Pakistan came into being.

2 | SUNDAY

Held a meeting with MNAs and MPAs of West Pakistan. The object was to boost up their morale and make them stick to the Muslim League. They could then be a decisive factor in the new assemblies. I told them that I will stay as their president as long as I am here. They were insisting I should withdraw my decision not to contest the next elections and stay as the president of the Muslim League even when I retire. I told them that the latter decision will be taken when the times comes. I hope this has given them some satisfaction.

There are several places where processions are being taken out and people are going on hunger strike on my behalf. There are several such people outside my compound who fast for 48 hours and are replaced by others. I am trying to persuade them to desist from such action whilst deeply touched by their feelings.

3 | MONDAY

Several people came to see me to discuss the situation within the country; they are deeply perturbed and uncertain of the future. They think chaos will prevail when I leave. All this is depressing.

4 | TUESDAY

Hartal[1] was observed all over East Pakistan. Several cases of arson and looting were reported. Such incidences also occurred in several places in the Sindh area. In one place a train was stopped and looted.

Mr Daultana came to see me along with Mr Shahabuddin. Talked about the coming DAC conference with me. He is a cunning old fox but very clever. I only wish he had some strength of character. During the round table conference, I was amazed at the wholehearted support he gave to Mujib's Six Points and other demands. The man was obviously talking with his tongue in cheek. He certainly is a master of politicking but is utterly devoid of statesmanship. What a pity. But for this he could have been a statesman of the country.

5 | WEDNESDAY

General Yahya came to see me. He was very pessimistic about the state of affairs in the country, felt that this rot could only be stopped by imposition of martial law. I told him that there is a meeting with the opposition on the 10th and we have to see the developments as to how it progresses.

7 | FRIDAY

The leaders of the parties comprising the Democratic Action Committee [DAC][2] met in Lahore to formulate their demands. I understand that there was a lot of coming and going without much success. However, eventually a consensus is supposed to have evolved on the basis of presenting certain points on which there is an agreement and freedom was given to each party to present its separate demands.

📖 Monem Khan came to see me. He explained the law and order situation in the province, which is very bad indeed. In fact, it does not seem to exist. The civil administration is rendered ineffective. Apart from the mischief makers, gangs of communists and terrorists on the prompting of Bhashani are raiding police stations and the houses and properties of Muslim Leaguers, and asking the chairmen and members of Basic Democracies to resign. Where any opposition is offered, the inmates are killed and their properties looted and burnt. In consequence, most of the civil officers have left their posts and so have the local rent collectors, and their records have been burnt. People are not allowed to bring foodstuff to the market nor are distributors allowed to take food from government godowns or allowed to distribute where modified rationing is enforced. The idea is to create artificial shortages and force people to make hunger marches. In consequence, large scale smuggling of food is taking place to India unchecked as the East Pakistan Rifles who guard the border are employed for the maintenance of law and order.

8 | SATURDAY

📖 Monem Khan is under severe attack and his life and person are in danger. In fact, his unpopularity has been universal for a long time. So I suggested that he might take some leave and quit to which he agreed. My idea is to appoint Dr Huda in his place. Being an intellectual he is regarded in high esteem, though once he becomes a governor, it remains to be seen how he retains his acceptability. Bengal is not a place where a man can remain popular by doing his job.

9 | SUNDAY

📖 Labour trouble in many places, constant demonstrations, etc., have affected production. Investment is drying up. The stock exchange has slumped and money is being taken out of the country. The coming days are going to be hard for Pakistan.

10 | MONDAY

📖 Met the DAC in a conference. Nasrullah Khan gave out the agreed points, which are direct adult franchise, federal parliamentary form of government with full regional autonomy. Then the others started spelling out their separate programmes. Mujib insisted on his points with East Pakistan representation on population basis. The PDM are going to speak tomorrow. After that we shall give our comments. It is obvious that each party in the DAC has its own interpretation of parliamentary form of government.

11–12 | TUESDAY–WEDNESDAY

Talks with the DAC continued. Talking was done mostly by the opposition. The Bengalis are pressing for regional autonomy, control over their economic resources and weakening the centre, and dismemberment of one unit. It was disturbing to sit and hear all this. Finally, I had to give my decision. There was unanimity on two points, viz., direct elections and parliamentary federal government. I promised to take these to the assembly. There should be no difficulty in getting the first point passed, on the second there would be because of East Pakistan's demand on representation of population basis, regional autonomy, etc. These will open up the rest of the questions. Besides, it is not easy to gather together two-thirds majorities under the present circumstances.

Whilst I was preparing for my final answer to the DAC, the point arose whether I should refuse to go beyond the acceptance of two items and offer to accept anything else on which the opposition could come to an agreement. Lot of discussion took place. Manzur Qadir was strongly in favour, whereas Altaf Gauhar and the Law Ministry were strongly opposed. In the end, I decided not to go beyond the two points. I did not want to become a party to the dissolution of Pakistan not did I have the mandate to do so. Thank God I took the stand I did, what would eventually happen is not promising, but at least I would not be a party to it.

13 | THURSDAY

Marshal Grechko, the Defence Minister of USSR, came, together with his team who are on a visit, to lunch. He looks an imposing figure and a fine man with a lot of sense and humour. He wanted to speak to me separately. The burden of his talk was that the Soviet leadership was very concerned about the state of affairs in Pakistan, and especially about me. I, who had put the country together, given it recognition in the eyes of the world, why did I decide not to fight the next elections when the armed forces and a vast majority of the people were behind me. I gave him my reasons. He asked if I could not change my mind. Did I need any help? Mr Kosygin was prepared to meet me anywhere and any time, openly or otherwise, if it would help my position. I thanked him and declined the offer as my mind about the future was made up. He showed disappointment.

14 | FRIDAY

Some of the DAC leaders came to call on me. I told them that the real trouble was that we have no intention of making a nation. There is too much parochialism in our make up. Besides, the outlook of Bengalis was totally different to that of West Pakistan. Here people are influenced to a certain extent by Iqbal's teachings, whereas in East Pakistan, because of the language barrier, they are attracted towards Tagore etc. and the binding force of Islam is tenuous.

Ch. Mohammad Ali came in the evening and spoke at length. He pleaded that all possible measures should be taken to checkmate Mujib and prevent the separation of East Pakistan as then it would not be possible to maintain this army and we may have to demobilise in which case India will at once ask for the surrender of Azad Kashmir. He also talked about getting these constitutional bills through. I apprised him of the difficulties we shall have to face. You may or may not agree with his arguments but he certainly expresses his ideas with persuasion and logic. He frankly admitted he had been working against me for the last ten years. I told him that his prayers have been heard.

15 | SATURDAY

📖 It is sad, but the pressure for removal of the two governors is mounting. So I have conveyed to both with great reluctance that they shall have to leave fairly soon. It break one's heart to see that happen to one's friends, but sometimes political necessities can be compelling.

16 | SUNDAY

📖 Yusuf Haroon has been designated as Governor of West Pakistan.

📖 I am doubtful the two amendments we wish to bring before the assembly will go through. Even the moderates will try to outbid the extremists in demands. I have told some Punjabis to get influential Punjabis to make statements that they would not be averse to undoing West Pakistan [one unit] so as to gain the confidence of people of smaller provinces to prevent them depending too much on East Pakistanis. I have also said that two commissions should be set up to determine the financial and administrative consequences of undoing one unit. I am told the Frontier, Balochistan, and even Sindh would not be viable without substantive support from the centre. I would like a similar commission for East Pakistan. My object is to prevent rush actions being taken. Whatever is done must be scientifically considered.

18 | TUESDAY

📖 General Musa and his wife came to say goodbye yesterday. It was sad parting from a friend who had worked with me for so long. Though he is over 60, I have offered him the ambassadorship to Moscow. The Russians like him.

19 | WEDNESDAY

📖 Carry out my promise to call the assembly for considering two amendments.

📖 Bhutto continues to attack me. I have told some people that if they don't want me to retaliate then they must [...]. So I have also told the home minister that people at large are unaware of the over all law and order situation in the two provinces. It is necessary that they should be put in the picture through press statements.

20 | THURSDAY

📖 Held a cabinet meeting in the evening to discuss the political situation. The home minister gave details followed by the home secretary who had just returned from Lahore and Dacca. The picture painted is sombre. Critical situation had been reached in East Pakistan, whereas in West Pakistan the effort was to cripple the economy. Labour force everywhere was misbehaving, production has gone down and prices are shooting up.

The civilian labour force in Karachi dockyards had struck work. No loading or unloading of ships was being done. In one case a ship went back empty as it could not be loaded with cotton. Bhashani has been in Karachi and elsewhere spreading disaffection. Expectations were that the situation was likely to deteriorate.

The holding of the assembly for effecting the two constitutional amendments was in any case out of the question and even if they get together they will be subjected to terrible pressure by students and others. Besides, it was very doubtful whether a two-third majority could be got together.

Mr Manzur Qadir came and pleaded that I should address the nation appealing for calm and quiet and make a promise that a constitutional commission would be set up to go into all demands with sympathy. He said it would have an electrifying effect. My pleading that time had gone past for appeals had no effect on him. He kept on insisting that it must be done. Manzur is a very good man but rather unpractical.

My brother returned home from Haj. He fell ill and had a rather hard time in Jeddah. [King] Faisal, when told to pray for Pakistan, said he would do so if Ayub Khan was at the head of it.

21 | FRIDAY

Called the Law Minister and Altaf Gauhar to discuss Mr Manzur Qadir's recommendations. They both felt inclined to accept them and call the assembly for carrying out necessary amendments to the Constitution for two items agreed with the opposition, adult franchise and parliamentary form of government. I told them to hold consultations with the defence minister, the commander-in-chief and the home minister, and then come to me, which they did at midday. The commander-in-chief told them that the situation was far worse than they imagined. General Yahya was annoyed and said that the new governors cannot carry out miracles nor can the constitutional changes calm the situation. He will carry out his duty to the country. It was clear as to what Gen. Yahya Khan was heading for.

Monem Khan came to call and stayed on for dinner. He was, of course, under emotional stress on relinquishment the governorship of East Pakistan but described the situation there as very dark. Mr Huda, his successor, came a little later. He felt that through village peace committees, etc. he could bring normalcy to the province. I have grave doubts whether he can succeed. However, such suggestions create doubts in one's mind. So I rang up some people and told them to come and speak to me tomorrow.

22 | SATURDAY

A.R. Khan and Altaf Gauhar came. I also called Monem Khan. The decision was that I hand over to the Commander-in-Chief on the 25th. This is a sad but unavoidable decision under the circumstances when the existence of the country is involved. Desperate measures have to be taken. Let us hope and pray that the outcome will be good for the country.

24 | MONDAY

📖 Prepared the handing over letter, which I will send to Yahya tomorrow. The speech for the nation is being prepared. It will be recorded at 11 a.m. tomorrow.

📖 An opposition leader told me the other day that people had demolished my system which I had built. I told him only that they want to demolish whatever previous regimes had built, i.e., one unit and parity, and even demolish what the Quaid had built, that is Pakistan.

📖 Today I have written a letter [see Appendix 1] to General Yahya explaining how the civil machinery has ceased to be effective and why it is necessary for me to step aside and hand over to him so that normalcy and decency can brought back.

25 | TUESDAY

📖 Recorded my speech [see Appendix 2] to the nation explaining why it was necessary for me to step aside.

26 | WEDNESDAY

📖 Invited the members of cabinet and explained why I had resigned.[3] It was quite obvious that the politicians are hell bent on disrupting the country, and besides, economic life was coming to a halt. Workers and even government officials had said goodbye to discipline. In any case, I could not sit on the dissolution of Pakistan by lawful or unlawful means. As a result of my resignation the governors, ministers etc. stand dismissed. I told someone jokingly that as a real general election had taken place I can see a leader for two governments in Pakistan will change […]. I can't see any politician of national outlook or stature rise for a long time to come. Besides democratic methods are foreign to our people.

27 | THURSDAY

📖 Peace and calm is coming to the country, labourers and officials are going back to work and the schools and colleges are opening. People are behaving as if nothing had happened. It just shows that in spite of so much talk about democracy what our people really need is to be commanded. That has been our history for centuries. That being the case I can't see how democracy can work in Pakistan. Undue freedom is at once taken to the extreme and turned into license. Besides, our laws are so framed as to [be open to] interpretation, which encourages lawlessness and disruption.

28 | FRIDAY

📕 Some discussion has taken place amongst martial law administrators as to what should be done to those politician, like Bhutto, Asghar, Mujib, Bhashani and possibly Daultana, who were responsible for fanning the recent disturbances. They seem to have come to the conclusion that just yet they should not be touched. I wonder if this is correct. These people are sure to raise their heads again as soon as they get an opportunity and repeat the turmoils of the past. This should not be an acceptable risk.

📕 Poor Eisenhower [former President of the USA] died after a prolonged illness. His wife sent me a special message to attend the funeral ceremony, which unfortunately I could not. He was a great gentleman and a very good friend. He underwent prolonged suffering during the latter period of his life.

31 | MONDAY

📕 Foreign Minister Mian Arshad Hussain was concerned that General Yahya had not adopted an internationally recognized designation, which is causing complications.[4]

📕 I remember during the last presidential elections in 1965, the American ambassador told me plainly that they will not operate against me but they will not work for me either. The meaning of that was plain: that they had created the organisation and ability to do either. A frightening thought.

📕 Some people are of the view that the Americans have been instrumental in fanning the present disconent in the country. It is believed that they supported Bhutto to expose the leftists on the pattern of Indonesia so that the rightists could deal with them. Then they switched over support to Asghar as it suited their requirement. Bhashani, on the contrary, had the support of communists in West Bengal. Chinese involvement is doubted. American policy is supposed to be based on their dislike of my policies: they want to see a weak and diminished Pakistan so that India is free to face China more positively and perhaps take military interest in South East Asia against China. Such conjecture cannot be brushed aside. The menace of big power interference in the internal affairs of weaker countries is real and constant. They don't want to see new countries stabilise unless it suits their purpose. Previously, the communists and especially the Russians used to be blamed for such activities but it seems now the Americans have surpassed them in this technique and skill.

1 | TUESDAY

📖 Mr Suleri has written a penetrating article on the root causes of political maladies in Pakistan. I entirely agree with his diagnoses, but I don't agree that the remedy suggested will draw much attention and bind people together. Islam, as propounded by the theologians, has ceased to be a living philosophy. It does not offer socio-economic satisfaction in an institutionalised form. Besides, the pull of parochialism and Bengali nationalism is so great that any remedy for constitution that does not take these actors into consideration is bound to fail.

I can claim this much credit that I succeeded in keeping the country together for the last ten years and made them do constructive thinking. That is no mean achievement. And if they had gone on like this for another ten years or so the country would have reached the takeoff stage and the people would have entered the scientific and technological spirit of the twentieth century. However, they decided to do otherwise, reject my system and run away from the path of progress and self-control. The result is that even the existence of the country is now in jeopardy. I hope and pray that God saves them from extracting due price for their folly.

📖 Started for Swat where I intend staying with Naseem and Aurangzeb [daughter and son-in-law] some time before my house in Islamabad is ready for occupation. I hope to be able to rest, do some reading and have the opportunity of playing with my grandchildren. In any case Swat is a heavenly place to stay in and especially during the spring when the blossoms are out. Before leaving I met all the members of the household staff, thanked them for the service they have rendered me and assured them that my successor will take care of them. Most of them were in tears. It was inevitable. They had spent ten happy years with me and especially my wife took special care of them.

📖 Reached Saidu Sharif midday, had lunch with the Wali, rested in the afternoon and went out for a walk. The Wali too had a spate of troubles starting with the students leading to defiance by some people whom he had nursed for so long. But it is all quiet now and people are coming to him in hoards owing allegiance. But the writing on the wall is clear. Personal rule is no longer fashionable in these times of individuals and agitations. He will be wise in making necessary changes and shedding power gradually before opposition mounts up.

13 | SUNDAY

📖 Since coming here I have had a very quiet and restful life except for a short drive or 2-3 miles walk. I do very little, not even much reading. In other words, I am getting used to a retired and sedate life. It is true that lots of visitors come to see me, but Aurangzeb acts as a good road block. He only brings to me such people that I simply must see. But I receive a large number of letters mostly appreciating what I had done for the country and sorry that I had left, but some asking for all sorts of fantastic things believing that I am still the president. I am warned that I shall be beseeched by visitors on return to Islamabad: I am not quite relishing the prospect.

📖 One or two American friends whom I had known for a long time had written penetrating things. One said that a leader who wishes to remove the miseries of his people and reform them runs the risk of also bringing about acute awareness amongst them that whilst some difficulties and sufferings have been eliminated why can't others be dealt with in the same manner. And as all things in like take time especially when the resources are limited, they burst out in emotional frustration. The other said that it was a marvel that how were a divided people like ours held together by me for ten years and made to progress. How true these observations are. I can see very clearly that after the martial law is lifted and politics allowed and preparation for any form of election made, the turmoil of the past will come back with a vengeance. Large scale looting, arson, murder and rape will be the order of the day. Nobody will be allowed by the political *goondas* to vote freely. East Pakistan will separate and West Pakistan will split up in penny packets. Pakistan will exist only in name. All politicians who are thorough self seekers are thinking on these lines. What a gloomy prospect for this unfortunate country.

📖 General Yahya, in one of his press conferences, has stated that at an appropriate time elections will be held on the basis of direct adult franchise and chosen representatives of the people will be given the task of framing a constitution. This is the height of wishful thinking. I can't see people being allowed to produce something workable even if they had the desire or the capacity to rise above parochialism and think in terms of Pakistan. In any case, the pressure groups from outside will never allow them to do anything sensible even if they wish to.

The most disturbing feature is the quality of politicians in the field. They are either political *goondas* or downright opportunists and self-seekers. God help the country if it goes in their hands.

It is surprising that during the course of history, and especially after the freedom struggle of 1857, intellectual, political and spiritual giants were born amongst the Muslims, yet when Pakistan was born we needed such people most. We are left with nothing but pygmies. We just can't rise above ourselves. If they have the brains they have no character and vice versa. A country of this size with its peculiar and vast problems can't be run by such people. They are just not up to it.

I am reminded of a story, which the Nawab of Kalabagh once told me. In 1946 or so he was staying with his cousin, the Sardar of Kot Fateh Khan, in Delhi, he told him you know what this man Jinnah is doing, he is wanting us to go under the Shudras of Bengal. I was annoyed at this at the time, but now that Bhashani and Mujib are making their intentions clear the danger is becoming real. Asking for 56 per cent representation[5] in the centre is tantamount to asking to rule Pakistan. Meanwhile, the tragedy is that West Pakistan is so badly divided, which the Bengalis will exploit to the hilt, and a number of West Pakistani ambitious politicians will lend a helping hand. The fools in East and West Pakistan do not realize that unequal political partnerships never hold and work. I think this demand may well be a camouflage for separation. If not accepted by West Pakistan, they can well turn around and demand secession.

14 | MONDAY

📖 Colonel Ghafoor Khan Hoti came to see me in connection with the affairs of *Kohistan*, which is a Muslim League paper. They are in a bad way and the paper is losing heavily. The decision was to go into liquidation and cut our losses. Col. Ghafoor Khan Hoti told me that there was talk of removing or retiring so many central secretaries, including some good ones. I hope it is not true as the regime will find it difficult to replace them. Incidentally, all the ministers have been given the goodbye. He also mentioned that Nur Khan is asserting himself a lot. I hope he does not turn out to be a headache for Yahya.

As to the future, Yahya has given out that chosen representatives of the people will frame the constitution at an appropriate time. I wonder how it will go. Unless these fellows are under threat of dissolution for producing a constitution within a year or so, they will go on squabbling for years, and fancy the type of constitution these people will produce who think of nothing but themselves. Col. Ghafoor Khan Hoti's suggestion was that I should guide Yahya. I do not think this will be wise. I will certainly give my advice when asked for but not otherwise. The man in command must have the freedom of making his own decisions.

📖 There is some talk of Air Marshal Nur Khan asserting himself unduly. He is a good worker with ideas, but unboundedly ambitious. It is quite possible that Yahya will have trouble with him later.

25 | FRIDAY

📖 During the last week martial law authorities have made a statement that a special board will be set up to look into complaints of corruption from the president down to joint secretaries. It affects the activities of the officials concerned and each department. The investigation can be started by the board *suo moto* on complaint by the administration or on the complaint of an individual.

We too were contemplating introducing similar measures even including distant relations, but everyone argued that such a provision will be misused and become the greatest instrument of oppression and vilification. It will be used by the opposition as instrument of character assassination, so we decided to find out what, for instance, countries like India with similar circumstances like us do.

The measure now contemplated by the martial law authorities may do some good.[6] But there are two dangers involved in this. One, people down below would not accept responsibility for fear of accusations and everything will get pushed up to the president leading to over-centralization of the administration. Secondly, all sorts of bogus complaints will be lodged even against the president. On investigation they may be found baseless, but meanwhile great damage would have been done to his reputation and prestige. And I have no doubt that the opposition will not hesitate to use this instrument. It is not difficult in our country to buy people for such purposes.

But what steps are they going to take against the lower echelon remains to be seen. It is at the district level that corruption hurts the masses most. Corruption is endemic in some departments like the PWD, the MES, revenue department, police etc. It is there that eradication is most difficult.

26 | SATURDAY

📖 I have never been afraid of retirement. In fact, I always look forward to it as I have no false pride or fondness for pomp and show for remaining in the limelight. I am not exactly an introvert, but I do abhor undue publicity. However, I am used to working very hard and I was wondering how I will adjust myself to retirement. Inactivity was irksome in the beginning, but it is surprising how I have adjusted.

28 | **MONDAY**

📖 This morning's news broadcast announced the resignation of President Charles De Gaulle. This is a sequel to losing the referendum on giving more powers to regions and curtailing the powers of the Senate. De Gaulle had announced that as an honourable man he could not stay if the vote went against him. Looking at it from this distance there was no compulsion for him to stake his future on such an issue.

3 | SATURDAY

📖 A number of senior civilian officers are being retired at short notice and at times unceremoniously. This is causing a lot of concern. If senior people have to be retired, it is incumbent that this is done with some decorum. Besides, I do not know how they are going to be replaced. We are very short of experienced people.

4 | SUNDAY

📖 In a recently written article, Mr Suleri has made certain false allegations against me and my regime for denigrating the Quaid and his philosophy. This is an utter lie. I have, therefore, written the attached letter [see below] to General Peerzada[7] rebutting Suleri's lies.

Saidu Sharif
Swat State
5th May 1969
From
Field Marshal Mohammed Ayub Khan
Nishan-e-Pakistan, Hilal-e-Jurrat,

Dear Major General Peerzada,

Mr Z.A. Suleri has written an article 'Nothing Short of Reconstruction' in the *Pakistan Times*, Rawalpindi edition, of 4th May 1969. He puts down many of our political misfortunes to the dimming of spirit of emotional attachment to the ideology of Muslim nationalism as enumerated by the Quaid-e-Azam. I am sure that every true Muslim and Pakistani feels the same and laments. But then he goes on to say that the death blow was, however, given by the last regime. It did not merely dismiss politics. It brought into dispute and disrepute the ideology. It sought to dethrone the Quaid-e-Azam from his pedestal as the father and founder of the nation. While lakhs of rupees were spent, mind you in foreign exchange from the public exchequer, on the publication of the various editions of *Friends not Masters* not a paisa was budgeted to produce an authentic biography of the Quaid-e-Azam. With his dethronement was swept off the ideas and ideals which were the warp and weft of the movement. Then he goes on to say that it was no accident that 14th August, the Independence Day, to which the emotions of the whole nation were attached, was downgraded. I take serious exception to these statements which are far from the truth. First of all my instructions to the information ministry were that not a penny from the public exchequer will be spent on the publication of my book *Friends not Masters*. In the publication of this book the publishers incurred all the expenses depending on whose liability a certain item happened to be. These matters can be checked up with Mr Altaf Gauhar. And when the royalty started coming in I donated the sum of rupees one lakh fifteen thousand to an educational trust I have created for deserving students in my area.

I believe the circulation of this book in other countries has made some contribution towards familiarization of Pakistan.

Secondly, as regards the production of the Quaid-e-Azam's biography, I made several attempts to get reference papers from the late Miss Jinnah who refused to part with them. However, she agreed to allow Mr G. Allana[8] to write a biography of the Quaid-e-Azam and let him see the papers. But then I believe they fell out with each other and Mr Allana has written a book too on his own. I then asked several distinguished historians headed by Dr I.H. Qureshi to write two books, one, *The History of Muslims of the*

Subcontinent[9] leading to the emergence of Pakistan, this is now in circulation. The other, *History of the Muslims in Bengal* in order that the younger generation there is made aware of the need for adherence to Islamic ideology and necessity for a strong centre. Also to remind them of the sufferings their forefathers underwent under Hindu and British domination and that without Pakistan and adherence to its ideology history might well repeat itself. The production of this book was made the responsibility of certain eminent Bengali historians. I am not certain whether it has been produced yet or not. I also encouraged a book called *Why Pakistan* written by Professor Chaudhary[10] of Dacca University. It is an excellent book and revolves around the Quaid's teaching. In addition the education ministries both at the centre and provinces were given instructions that the aspects of Muslim national outlook as advocated by the Quaid-e-Azam should be disseminated at a wide scale amongst the younger generation besides teaching of Islam. Radio and press media were also constantly reminded to emphasize these aspects.

Further if Mr Suleri's memory is not too short, it was I who started the building of the Quaid-e-Azam mausoleum in the teeth of Miss Jinnah's opposition. The Quaid-e-Azam's birthday and death anniversary are celebrated with all solemnity.

Despite all these things if anybody blames my regime for dethroning the Quaid-e-Azam, to put in civilized language he is either deliberately twisting facts or does not want to tell the truth.

As regards the celebration of the 14th August, the day of emergence of Pakistan, it was done with the same fervour as before. The only difference being that the military parades are held on the 23rd of March, the day Pakistan became a republic, instead of 14 August. This was done on the behest of the defence forces as well as because the 14th August lies during the height of monsoons both in East and West Pakistan when heavy rains are expected, and do occur taking away all the glamour of the military parade apart from producing hazards for the air force and creating traffic problems in mud and slush and a great inconvenience to the spectators.

I am writing this at length in the hope that you will get Mr Suleri and others like him to make sure of the facts before making sweeping and incorrect statements. This is not an unknown trick used to please the newcomers despite the fact that I have been the greatest benefactor of Mr Suleri.

The truth of the matter is that our empathy towards fundamentals is due to much deeper causes, which will need much lengthier explanation.

Yours sincerely,
Mohammed Ayub Khan.

Addressed to Major General S.G.M.M. Peerzada
Sitara-e-Quaid–e-Azam
Headquarters Chief Martial Law Administrator
President's House Rawalpindi.

---

7 | WEDNESDAY

📖 Extracts from writings of De Gaulle:

'There can be no power without mystery. There must be always something which others cannot fathom, which puzzles them, stirs them and rivets their attention. Nothing more enhances authority than silence. It is the crowning virtue of the strong, the refuge of the weak, the modesty of the proud, the pride of the humble, the prudence of the wise and the sense of the fool'.

9 | FRIDAY

📖 Malik Qasim, the secretary general, came to report the outcome of his contact with the Muslim Leaguers both in East and West Pakistan. There is general agreement on appointing vice presidents and a skeleton of central council of the Muslim League. Certain names were suggested which I approved. I think this measure will help the genuine Muslim Leaguers to get steady and not look for refuge elsewhere.

25 | SUNDAY

📖 Moved from Swat to Islamabad on 17th to my new house and the permanent residence. It took a lot of effort to furnish the place, but my wife and my orderly Abdul Salam and others took a lot of trouble to get it into shape. The house is located on a small mound and commands an extensive view all around. The dazzling lights of Islamabad have a fascinating effect at night. But one feels uneasy about the happenings in the country and future political prospects. The martial law people are doing their best, but victimization of the business community and the civil servants is having a demoralizing effect. The future is uncertain, business is sluggish and new investment shy. This is going to affect production and employment opportunities bringing in its wake a lot of dissatisfaction. It is quite possible that some people would like to cast doubt about my future intentions in the minds of the administration and especially General Yahya. I have conveyed to him that though for technical reasons I cannot give up the presidency of the Muslim League, I have no intention of taking active part in politics. It will be the height of absurdity to do so.

2 | MONDAY

📖 A prominent refugee from Kashmir came to deliver greetings from Sheikh Abdullah. The Sheikh is very worried about the happenings in Pakistan and my quitting. Thinks that our people have lost all sense of balance and destroyed any prestige Pakistan had in the eyes of the world. This man himself also looked disgusted, said that people from this part of the world had always welcomed the invaders for minor gains. Their nature is still the same as of old.

3 | TUESDAY

📖 A businessman from Karachi, who had been to Europe to obtain credit for purchase of a couple of ships, said that whereas in the past a Pakistani was sought after, today nobody would look at him. Wherever he went he was cold shouldered so he came back empty handed.

4 | WEDNESDAY

📖 Khuda Bakhsh Bucha paid a call and said the people in the villages feel cheated at the change of government. They feel that they were beginning to benefit by my agricultural policies which the town man did not like. They should have put up a fight against them. Bucha was afraid that there may be further land reforms. It is understood that Yahya had two long meetings with Bhutto, one in the office and one in his house. It is curious that the man mainly responsible for the turmoil in the country should be so encouraged. He is going to make great political capital out of it.

📖 Jalil, of the Pakistan National Oil, came to call in the afternoon. He talked about industrial matters, the effect of martial law regulations, calling for returns etc. from the industrialists and complained about the unsympathetic attitude of the officials. That seems to be accountable because the ministers could not exercise control and the press could not be used etc. He lamented the misfortune of the country in consequence of the recent disturbances and suggested that a probe might be carried out as to why they took place when the country was making so much progress. While leaving, he hinted that I should be careful of my friends. I said which friends. He said the martial law people and even General Yahya. Even he had complained to someone that I had inflicted myself on him for a meal and that I interfere in his work and this is resented by people below.

His suggestion was that I should go abroad for sometime. Actually, there was no question of any infliction on him. I did, however, tell him a few things like the future of Swat state, the need to be cautious in putting a squeeze on the industrialists in a manner that does not retard production etc. This can by no means be regarded as interference.

In fact, a day later when Aurangzeb met him on Swat affairs he mentioned several things about me which indicated that whilst he had all respect for me he would not like to be associated with me. As to my going abroad, it is just out of the question.

9 | MONDAY

📖 Mr Akhund, the ex-law minister in the West Pakistan government, came to see me from Hyderabad. He pleaded that the Muslim League must come out with a suitable manifesto soon. No Sindhi can support a programme which does not promise the disintegration of West Pakistan [one unit]. Now that there are so many jobless educated Sindhis and so many settlers have come from outside and a large number of refugees have settled down there, the anti non-Sindhi feeling has become very acute. They even talk of joining India or Afghanistan, if need be. The feeling of belonging to Pakistan and Muslim brotherhood has worn thin. The Frontier people and the Bengalis talk in the same terms. I shudder to think what would be the outcome of all this.

14 | SATURDAY

📖 The American ambassador came to say goodbye as he is retiring from service. He showed reluctance initially to comment on the political future in Pakistan but eventually opened up, saying that there is no leader of international stature, no national party. There are several people who call themselves leaders, but nobody knows whom they represent. Besides, they are all pulling in different directions. There is some talk of merger of parties. It is doubtful whether anything would come of it. General Yahya is doing his best to get them together but he has a difficult job.

As far as I'm concerned, he commented that I'd done a great deal for my people. Now the time has come for me to do something for myself and my family. He suggested that I might settle down somewhere else. Islamabad is not yet a place for retired people. Besides, it is not good for me to be constantly looking at the Secretariat buildings and the proposed site of the White House. This may be true, but I cannot go elsewhere. I can't live in the village and my house in Abbottabad is too small. In fact, I had built this house as a place for retirement. True, I lead an isolated life here as most people who know me are afraid of the reaction of the new regime in seeing me, but that is inevitable and has to be accepted. I have to get reconciled to the status of a private citizen. I am told Yahya too is not happy in my living here. Why it should be so, I don't know. I am no problem to him.

21 | SATURDAY

📖 A couple of knowledgeable people came to call on me from Lahore. They were both in tears when talking about the state of affairs in the country, and indeed, were apprehensive of the future of Pakistan. The mischief makers had succeeded in ousting me but there was no one in the country to hold it together. They were really in anguish and I had some difficulty in trying to soothe their feelings.

25 | WEDNESDAY

📖 Ayub Khuhro came to lunch. He started off by saying that we are not a nation and united for democracy. Even the Quaid-e-Azam told him in 1947 that freedom had come much too early, before our people were ready to hold it. As to running any democratic system, we were just incapable of doing so. Khuhro said that the Quaid-e-Azam was lucky he died so soon. People were beginning to defy him. He had to be heavily guarded on state and public functions.

Talking about the present situation Khuhro wants the old provinces restored in West Pakistan. He said no one can get elected in Sindh unless he advocated this. Common facilities could be run by a sub-federation or the centre which he wanted to be strong. He was opposed to Mujibur Rahman's formula that will mean the end of Pakistan. When told that his friend Daultana supported Mujib's stand, he said he was going to talk to him and find out more about it.

📖 Ahsan Sabri, the foreign minister of Turkey, who is now on a visit to Pakistan, came to call on me. He spoke to me with great affection and said that I could regard Turkey as my second home and come and stay there anytime I would like. He also brought for me greetings from his president and the prime minister. I said they were going to face elections in October this year and hoped to return with a clear majority, but they had seven opposition parties and the student's community to face. I do hope the students do not cause the same problems for them as they did for us.

26 | THURSDAY

📖 Islamabad has been very hot for the last fortnight or so. Naseem and Aurangzeb had come over to take us to Swat for a change. So we shifted today. Saidu is also hot but much better than Islamabad, day temperature here does not go beyond 100 and the evenings are pleasant.

8 | TUESDAY

📖 Several Muslim Leaguers came to me from different parts of the country and showed great concern for its future. They do not see anyone being able to hold it together and begged me not to disassociate myself from politics. They even asked me to return to active politics. This, of course, is out of the question though I shall not sever my connection with the Muslim League. But one can see that there is general uneasiness and uncertainty in the minds of the people. They can see politicians breaking up this country into pieces.

I was hoping that Yahya would be able to fill the gap after I left. But this does not seem to be happening. The so-called leaders in the opposition and the press are happy as they are often met and consulted and given a free hand to criticize, especially me and anyone connected with me. But the rest of the people are in a state of uneasiness. They either feel harassed or live in a state of fear. No one is certain of the future. Meanwhile, the politicians are offering solutions for getting out of the constitutional tangle, all different to each other. There is no evidence of a national outlook or consensus. Everybody is pandering to the gallery or looking at the problem plainly from a personal angle. The free-for-all pattern of pre-October 1958 period politics is back in full swing.

Someone asked me as to what I considered was my greatest achievements? I said if nothing else I held this country together for ten years. The breakthrough in agriculture production, the new foreign policy, the Indus basin settlement and completion of gigantic works connected therewith and resettlement of refugees, land reforms and consolidation of some 12 million acres of land, establishment of the BD system etc. are no mean achievements by any standard. But what is the good of it all when I have not been able to teach our people to make a nation. A good deal of my effort seems to have been wasted.

13 | SUNDAY

📖 There is a lot of talk in our press about floatation of an idea by the Russian leaders hinting that a conference be held at Kabul consisting of representatives of the Soviet Union, Iran, Afghanistan, Pakistan and India to promote mutual trade over the land routes. Promotion of trade may be an objective but the Russian aim seems to be to create a belt of friendly countries around China and isolate it. The relations between China and the Soviets have steadily deteriorated and a number of serious border clashes have taken place. Our people are naturally concerned that under no circumstances must we do anything which can be construed to be hostile to the Chinese interests and quite rightly so. The Chinese are the only big power that came to our assistance in the time of the [19]65 war and even risked war with other big powers. I do not think any government in Pakistan can be so foolish as to disregard the friendship with China. So I am glad to see that Air Marshal Nur Khan is visiting China, perhaps on Chinese invitation. The only wise course for us to follow in relations to big powers is to maintain bilateralism and not get involved in big power politics. This is not neutralism, it is true nationalism.

20 | SUNDAY

📖 Chaudhary Mohammad Ali[11] has given a long interview to Shorish Kashmiri[12] on constitutional matters, which has also appeared in the *Pakistan Times*. He has blamed me for being overambitious and conspiring with Ghulam Mohammad[13] and Iskander Mirza for dismissing constituent assemblies, abrogation of the constitution etc. This is all nonsense. I have explained the truth in my book *Friends Not Masters* without any reservations.

21 | MONDAY

📖 I was shocked to see in the press that General Musa's eldest son Ibrahim has died. Poor Musa and his wife must be heartbroken. Ibrahim had very good manners but was peculiar, given to debauchery and excessive drinking. He gave a lot of trouble to his father. I have sent them a message of condolence.

📖 Aurangzeb's eldest daughter got married today to Sultan-e-Rome's [younger brother of the Wali of Swat] son. Both are nice persons, I wish them a long and happy life.

📖 I was amazed to hear that the government had issued instructions that family planning activities in the tribal areas should be stopped. This is a retrograde step. The crying need of the country is to control the population explosion.

24 | THURSDAY

📖 Some thoughts on economic development in underdeveloped countries:

Some economists consider economic development as essentially the accumulation of capital. This is important but the real core of the problem is what happens in men's minds, especially in their habits and organization for working together.

Economic development is a whole complex of interdependent changes manifested simultaneously in the physical environment, new roads, building, harbours, machines, implements, chemicals; in the form of association by which men live and work, growth of cities, changes in government, factory organizations, business corporation, banking, readjustment in land tenure, family practices, even religion. To put it briefly we are least likely to go wrong when we think of economic development as a massive problem in human education and social readjustment and only secondly as a problem in equipment.

The human and psychological side of development must go hand in hand with the economic development. Non-compliance with this will result either in failure of the development process to take and become self generating or creation of a menace to freedom. What it amounts to is that people have to develop themselves before they can change their physical environment and this is a slow process. However, what is important for a developing country is to establish an upward trend, [...] for once founded feeling that things are getting better that there is progress. Also, economic gains have to be seriously equitably divided.

People in developing countries need economic progress to overcome hunger, disease, ignorance, lack of creature comforts, but they also yearn for freedom, status and self-respect.

The social restraints to development are tenacious because they are deeply embedded in habits of millions of individuals in the accepted social arrangements we call institutions. And the system of values by which people decide that some things are good and others bad, some important and others less important. Vested interests too if not actively hostile are likely to be operative to many of the measures required for economic modernization. Habits of thought and conduct are the most stubborn obstacles to development. There does seem to be one type of natural resource that is highly connected with the level of development, every modern economically advanced country lies in the temperate zone, though not every country in the temperate zone is advanced. A belt around the equator between the tropics contains not a single, highly developed country. There must be an inherent cause for this. A concerted research on overcoming these causes is called for. There is need for inculcating ideas and ideals for development to take root. Empty minds and souls provide as good a breeding ground for communism as empty stomachs.

Everywhere there is a strong demand for change, for revolution in the sense of deep-going transformation of economic, social and political life, and it is already on. All the communist elite have to do is to capture the revolution. They do not have to create that. Measures of penetration to successful should be directed both at the fundamental conditions that create mass discontent and also at the conditions that make the intelligentsia of these countries susceptible to recruitment as active agents. To the latter especially inspiring ideas are as important as bread.

Hunger alone does not make communists. They are made by belief, dedicated fanatic belief.

In their attempts to influence the people of underdeveloped countries, the communists put great emphasis on appeals not to the material wants of the man, but rather to the human desire for status, equality, freedom from domination or oppression especially domination by foreigners.

27 | SUNDAY

📖 People like Rashidi, who are paid to write against me, fulminate that I have done nothing for East Pakistan in the economic field and that is why they are more estranged against West Pakistan. This is utter nonsense and a blatant lie.

30 | WEDNESDAY

📖 Saw the Wali. Naturally he is upset about the merger though he has been talking it over with the authorities. I think his real grouse was that this announcement was not made without making reasonable arrangements for his safety in case people rose against him. In fact, what happened was that the people took just the opposite view. They felt that their fate was decided without consulting them. Besides they had never been under outside rule since the times of Alexander the Great so there were demonstrations in favour of the Wali. I think it is fear of the unknown that is worrying them. They are used to a certain way of life. They are afraid of changes which may be to their disadvantage.

I warned the Wali against allowing the situation to get out of hand. There is martial law and it would not do any good to the people or the Wali. The thing has to be taken calmly and people's point of view represented to the authorities should they be in a listening mood.

 Mr Bhutto, in one of his meetings with lawyers, stated that amongst his services to the country there was the expression of willingness to fight India for a thousand years and that if he was in power Jerusalem would never have been lost. The audience cheered. This shows how politically immature and gullible people are. Any trickster and joker can befool them. None of them had the sense or the courage to say show us the way to fighting India for a thousand years and how we could save Jerusalem when the Arabs had lost it. And in any case if he is so sure of himself why does he not go and fight with the guerrillas now. What is there to stop him? They are in desperate need of volunteers. Then Bhutto went on to attack me. Asghar and other politicians are doing the same and some elements in the press are relishing it. Not being able to attack the martial law regime and not having any constructive programme to offer, they have nothing else to say except to indulge in negativism knowing that the administration will not lift a finger.

31 | THURSDAY

 Again there was a lot of commotion and demonstrations in Mingora and Saidu. There was news of people coming here from all parts of Swat and Buner to protest against the merger decision. The political agent, meanwhile, turned up and told the Wali that he must do everything possible to stop this as it was against the martial law and the army was put on two hours notice to march if necessary. The Wali sent a warning everywhere that demonstrations must stop, but people could send their petitions if they wish to. I am told some 25,000 petitions have already been sent to General Yahya. Thousands of telegrams have also been sent. The post offices are full of them. However, luckily there is peace and calm and people have steadied. But the trouble is that the Wali does not go and face them. They would feel consoled if he did.

4 | MONDAY[14]

📖 Some people from Charsadda area accompanied by the father and a brother of Hashim who attempted to shoot me, came in with the petition that he should be pardoned. I told them that as far as I was concerned I hold no personal grudge against him.

5 | TUESDAY

📖 A representative of the US Embassy came to deliver Mr Nixon's letter which he wrote from Lahore. It was nice of him to have thought of doing so. I have known Nixon for a long time and we have met on a number of occasions. In fact, close relations between US and Pakistan started as a result of my meeting Nixon when he came for the first time in 1953. I think it was in the Government House Peshawar when Mr Shahabuddin was the governor. I had prepared a paper which Nixon took from me and probably used it as the basis of his report to the government of Pakistan.

15 | FRIDAY

📖 Former MNA Mureed Hussain Shah from Sialkot turned up. He was very upset about the state of affairs in the country and said that there is growing feeling in East and West Pakistan that I should come back to politics. When told to look for someone else as the head of the Muslim League, he said that there was no one in whom people have any faith. People like Sobur, Qayyum, etc. are all played out.

16 | TUESDAY

📖 The commissioner called all the heads of state departments and gave them a briefing that for the present nothing will be changed. The administration, the system of revenue and the services etc. will continue to operate as before. In other words, the status quo will be maintained. This is a wise policy and the people should feel reassured.

20 | WEDNESDAY

📖 Malik Qasim, Secretary General of the Muslim League, came to discuss the problems of the League and especially the problems connected with the civil suit that Wahiduzzaman and others have started against us in a court in East Pakistan. The information is that they intend to launch a similar suit in West Pakistan to prevent the League bodies from functioning and also to freeze our funds. The legal advice is that they will get an injunction unless we take certain remedial actions. We discussed these and took certain steps. Let us hope they prove effective.

21 | THURSDAY

📖 It has come to my notice that in certain institutions my book *Friends Not Masters* was prescribed as a textbook. The government has issued instructions that the book will not be used as a textbook in future. This was to be expected.

22 | FRIDAY

📖 Sultan Chandio, the grandson of the famous Gabby Khan from Larkana district, came to see me to discuss the future of the Muslim League. He said most of the prominent Sindhis have joined one party or the other even those who derived considerable benefit from me. Main consideration is personal benefit: where they can get most from. For instance, Pir Pagaro[15] and his group have joined Mujibur Rahman who stands almost for dissolution of Pakistan in the hope that he will become the prime minister and make Pagaro the governor of Sindh.

He said two disturbing things. One, that the Sindhis are planning to drive all the outside settlers out whenever they get the opportunity. Secondly, the martial law authorities are very apprehensive and shy of touching the politicians even if they break regulations. On one occasion, Bhutto, whilst going to Jacobabad, addressed a public meeting, which is prohibited by martial law. Some arrests were made but they were released within two hours. Bhutto openly goes about saying that he was responsible for ousting Ayub Khan and bringing in Yahya who dare not do anything against him. Bhutto's meeting with the president at his house in the evening presumably for political discussion and bouts of drinking is broadcast in the press. This naturally turns his head, but what is worse is that the common man gets an impression that disruptionists are encouraged and patronized. The administration does not seem to realize that all this is liable to recoil on them whenever politicians like Bhutto get an opportunity. He will not spare even his father for his personal ends.

28 | THURSDAY

📖 Sabir, who is the chief reporter of *Pakistan Times* in Rawalpindi, came to call. Spoke despairingly of the politicians, especially Asghar and Bhutto. He commented on Suleri's perversion and ungratefulness for whom I had done so much. Suleri is now sacked from the *Pakistan Times*. About the future, he felt we are just incapable of running any form of democracy. Press world, he said, was full of opportunists, blackmailers and leftists. All are in the market and can be bought.

Sabir told me that Ghulam Faruque has given a long article in the press accusing me and the late Altaf Hussain for having blocked the steel mills project in Karachi. This is utter nonsense. The decision was given on merit and the merits were that Ghulam Faruque had made himself the head of consultants of big industrialists who were to contribute a certain amount of money and the bulk was to be provided by the government or the financing institutions. The industrialists were unwilling to cooperate with each other, though not saying so in the presence of Ghulam Faruque. The government naturally had to have second thoughts and put the thing in the public sector. Ghulam Faruque was naturally annoyed as he was deprived of big commissions on purchase of machinery, etc. How could the government put a project of a 100 crores or more in the private sector merely to please Ghulam Faruque?

30 | SATURDAY

📖 Nawabzada Col. Abdul Ghafoor Hoti who is a treasurer of the central Muslim League came to discuss party matters. He pointed out that party accounts had not been properly kept and some of the documents were missing. He was going to look for them with Qasim and in the office. I think they are with Qasim.

Col. Ghafoor Khan Hoti, who owns a large amount of landed property, is busy dividing his lands amongst his heirs and selling the balance. He thinks fresh land reforms will come either during the martial law regime or certainly when the civil government comes into power. So he is busy converting as much of his assets into liquid form as possible and has no intention of investing them here because of the uncertainty of the future. He looked demoralized, is even thinking of migrating to another country. Thinks that the pressure against the haves will increase as time goes on, especially during the weak civilian regime when it comes. Told me that several businessmen have surrendered licenses for projects, like fertilizer factories etc. Hyesons and Adamjees,[16] who were so anxious to go into this business, have pulled out. Production and exports are decreasing and prices are rising.

1 | MONDAY

📖 The Wali of Swat had a car accident. Luckily he suffered minor injuries. I went to see him. He is looking a little more relaxed after relinquishing power. Told me that during the agitation against him, he even offered to pressmen to publish his side of the story. But they refused, they said they could write anything against him for nothing, but nothing in his favour for anything. Those were the instructions from the administration. I have heard that similar instructions have been issued about me and my regime.

6 | SATURDAY

📖 Left Swat for Islamabad en route stayed for a reception given by Nawabzada Col. Abdul Ghafoor Hoti at his brother's place near Mardan. A large number of notables from Mardan district turned up for the occasion. When asked about my future programme, I told them that whereas I would maintain my connections with the Muslim League, I have no intention of contesting elections. They were a bit dismayed and kept on insisting otherwise. The place of function is an orchard and belongs to Amir, Col. Ghafoor Khan Hoti's elder brother. It is a veritable fairyland and some four thousand ornamental lights are embedded in the walls alone. This is an obvious case of conspicuous consumption which is so irritating to the common man. Moneyed people should avoid these things at all costs. Col. Ghafoor Khan Hoti's entertainment, as usual, was magnificent although I had told him to lay on a simple arrangement.

📖 I notice that the people look morose. They were uncertain of the future, especially those in industry and business.

📖 The weather in Islamabad is very pleasant, although the rest of the plateau is dry. This area has received a lot of rain and is nice and green.

8 | MONDAY

📖 I understand that Bhashani's and his communist associates' plan is not to take part in the next elections. They want the secessionist element led by Mujibur Rahman to succeed and then be discredited by the people. Once that happens, time will be right for the communists to take over. The idea then is to form up with West Bengal and Assam and form a separate country assisted by China. This is a wild dream. How will India allow its two provinces to secede and how will China support it in the face of Indian, Western and Russian opposition. But it just shows how reckless people can be, especially Bhashani, who has been a major disruptive factor in East Pakistan.

📖 Sent for Malik Qasim and told him that they had better make alternative arrangements to take my place in the League. My association is not in their interest for preparing for the forthcoming elections.

10 | WEDNESDAY

Qasim consulted Qizilbash and Mahmud Haroon,[17] whilst Mahmud was understanding, Qizilbash was curt and suspected my motives in attending Col. Ghafoor Khan Hoti's function in Mardan. He gave the impression as if I was trying to stage a come-back, which is far from the truth. Qasim then saw the president, who seemed more understanding, but the fact remains that any political activity on my part will be looked upon by the administration with the greatest of suspicion.

11 | THURSDAY

An ex-JCO ADC of mine came to see me from Nawabshah. He painted a dark picture of the future of refugees and new settlers in Sindh. The old Sindhis are bitter against the new Sindhis. This feeling has been fanned by the bigoted Sindhi leaders. The present situation is also bleak. Fear of authority has gone and crime is increasing. Justice is difficult and expensive to get. Corruption has increased. Curious thing is that the young officers administring martial law refuse to see even the ex-soldiers from their own regiments.

13 | SATURDAY

Disturbing statements are made even by responsible and knowledgeable people about General Yahya's conduct and lack of adequate attention to state affairs. He goes to the office late in the morning and comes back at 1 p.m. Rest of the time is spent in drinking, womanising and some sleep. Whether in Karachi, Dacca or Rawalpindi, this routine is repeated. A woman called Rani, wife of a sub-inspector who lives in Pindi and is a real bad character, is another supplier. She uses the president's name freely and takes bribes from the people for *safarish*. All this is widely known and is becoming an open scandal. What a pity, like this the value of a good man would be lost. Hamid, too, shares these binges but with some dignity.

18 | THURSDAY

General Pakravan, the Iranian ambassador, came to pay a farewell call. After preliminaries he said that as a friend of Pakistan he was deeply concerned about the state of affairs attaining in the country and the future. What the politicians were saying and doing was disgusting and revolting. No good can be expected of them. People too were not showing sense of responsibility. Don't they realize that I had put a shattered country together and had done so much for it. Pakistan had become a model for developing countries. All that has been put in jeopardy.

The Spanish ambassador also called as a matter of courtesy.

Sobur Khan, accompanied by Hashimuddin from East Pakistan, came to call. Sobur Khan had sent a message earlier that he wanted to see me immediately in connection with the conspiracy that Monem Khan had planned against him in conjunction with Qasim. What he meant was that Monem Khan was promoting the cause of Fazlul Qader Chaudhary against Sobur, but Fazlul Qader, the animal he is, had already cooked his goose by making irresponsible statements in Karachi, which Qasim openly denounced. Qasim was also present who assured Sobur Khan that his fears were completely unfounded. He also reminded Sobur Khan that in spite of his misbehaviour on several occasions, he had kept his mouth shut although they had every reason to challenge him openly. What Sobur Khan is after is to become the president of the Muslim League. That is well and good, if the new council, when formed, elects him. The trouble is that Sobur Khan too is an opportunist and as unprincipled as Wahiduzzaman and Qazi Qadir etc. But perhaps he is the lesser evil than many others.

Sobur Khan and Hashimuddin painted a gloomy picture of East Pakistan. Leftism and communism are on the increase. Hindus are active. Bengali nationalism and anti-West Pakistan feelings are growing. Separation is openly talked about. Students are flexing their muscles and made the martial law authorities yield to them for holding an Education Day meeting on the university campus. Students from all the colleges in Dacca city either came in processions or on trucks carrying red banners and shouting political slogans. They are openly talking about the feebleness of martial law. Labour, too, is restive, despite pay increases. They are not working properly and are demanding fantastic wages. Consequently production has gone down, business is slack and prices of consumer goods are shooting up. Mr Harry Twist, the Deputy High Commissioner of UK and a friend of Aurangzeb who had been on a prolonged visit to East Pakistan and met almost all the political leaders, told him that the province was turning leftist rapidly and separation was talked about openly. They feel that they can live on their own. Besides, martial law holds no fear for them. They, especially the students, think that they can defy it with impunity. Things are getting to a boiling point. He wondered if the people in West Pakistan, and especially the central government, was cognizant of the situation. He estimates Mujib commands 60 per cent, Bhashani 30 per cent and others 10 per cent support. Mujib will lose support gradually if elections are not held quickly. He knows it, hence the hurry. Mujib feels that as an all Pakistan leader, he cannot make much of a mark. Hence, he seeks a dominant role in East Pakistan. He was surprised at the amount of bitterness that exists in the minds of the people like Mujib, Hamidul Haq Chaudhary[18] and others towards West Pakistan. They feel that West Pakistanis only want them for exploitation. No amount of argument to the contrary can dislodge this belief, however irrational.

20 | SATURDAY

📖 Qasim made a press statement yesterday that I do not want to remain the president of the Muslim League. Hence, the ordering of fresh elections to the provincial and central councils, so that fresh office bearers can be elected. What effect the announcement of my relinquishment of presidency will have on the future of the Muslim League remains to be seen. I think most friends would be disheartened and it may even disintegrate, but in the present circumstances there is very little I could do to help them. Besides, I want to be rid of all possible encumbrances.

📖 Sobur Khan, Hashimuddin and Qasim came again this morning. They have come to some sort of an agreement on the composition of a body to be set up in East Pakistan that will supervise elections to the Muslim League councils. Events have shown that Sobur Khan too is an opportunist. In fact, he is the man who initiated disruption in the party by picking up a quarrel with Monem Khan. He suddenly became overambitious and wanted to become the governor and have a free hand in disposal of any property in East Pakistan. Later, he joined hands with Wahiduzzaman and Qazi Qadir and brought about a real breach in the party. It is they who first raised the cry of representation on population basis for East Pakistan and encouraged the Sindhi's and others to ask for dismantling of one unit, besides filing a case against me and challenging the composition of Muslim League bodies.

21 | SUNDAY

📖 Fazal Ellahi Chaudhary, our former deputy speaker, came and talked about the failures of my system. Chaudhary said that this was due mainly to the failures and lapses on the part of provincial governments. After all, it is in the provinces that problems affecting the life of people are administered and if they are not done well, complaints and frustrations build up. Also, we made a mistake in not lifting the emergency soon after the 1965 war was over. It should certainly have been lifted after the judgment of the Supreme Court that the application of even the emergency laws was subject to judicial scrutiny, and the Constitution suitably amended. If that had happened the imposition of martial law would not have been necessary. Emergency laws would have been more than enough to control the situation. This, too, is very valid reasoning. In fact, I did think of these things at the time, but unfortunately my law ministers sought solutions in amending the law rather than the Constitution. The matter went to the Supreme Court and was promptly struck down. Thereafter, the political situation deteriorated and all hopes of amending the Constitution faded away. No member of the party would have dared vote for the amendment for fear of victimization and terrorization by the agitators.

23 | TUESDAY

📖 Mr Daultana and Bhutto, whilst airing their views on the future Constitution and its formulation, have made bold statements and threatened that under no circumstance will they accept enforcement of the Constitution by one man. If this happens they will fight. This is tantamount to an open threat and challenge to Yahya. How will he take it remains to be seen. The mischief, of course, stems from the fact that Yahya started off on the wrong foot. Soon after the promulgation of martial law, he started fraternizing with the politicians and saying that he was here only temporarily. This was sweet music to the ears of politicians and was exactly what they wanted to hear. They have sensed his weakness and will continue to exploit it as time goes on.

24 | WEDNESDAY

📖 Disturbing news has come that India has been admitted as a member of the Muslim Summit Conference in Rabat on the plea that there is a large Muslim population in India. They put pressure on King Faisal of Saudi Arabia, and according to the press, President Yahya supported the move. Why should Pakistan have supported the move at a time, when thousands of Muslims are being butchered and their properties destroyed by the Jana Sangh Hindu *goondas* in Gujarat, passes comprehension. I wonder how well Yahya is informed of the situation in India and feelings at home and how he is advised. Feelings in Pakistan are certainly running high but besides that the Indians are not going there for the love of Islam or feelings for the sacrilege of Masjid-e-Aqsa, they have gone there to ensure that Muslims don't forge a common platform. This is one thought that sends cold shivers down their spine. The irony is that India was represented by their ambassador in Morocco, a Sikh, pending the arrival of their delegation headed by a Muslim minister, a stooge of the Hindus.

25 | THURSDAY

📖 Today news says that the Pakistan delegation has decided to boycott the conference on the plea that the Indian Muslims are not represented by their nominees and are returning home. In other words, the conference is wrecked and all chances of forging cohesion amongst the Muslim countries is lost. India has gained her aim and we are made to look like fools in the eyes of the world. What a great tragedy, a great opportunity has been lost for Pakistan. Other Muslim countries may or may not be in need of such a cohesion but we are in desperate need to counter balance India.

📖 The afternoon news announced that the Indian representatives have been debarred from attending the Muslim Summit Conference on the insistence of Pakistan and that General Yahya was attending the final meeting this afternoon. I am glad the situation has been retrieved after initial bungling. Let us hope some good comes out of it.

29 | MONDAY

📖 Mr Batalvi asked for help in moving the remains of Chaudhary Rehmat Ali[19] to Pakistan. He is buried in Cambridge. He was the man who coined the word Pakistan and worked for it when everybody called him a madman. The poor man died a pauper and had to be buried on charity. I told him that I will give whatever help I could and would ask the Muslim League to help too but at present it was not the right political climate. Politicians are likely to distort the move and sow doubts in people's minds. So the answer was to wait till the political climate improved.

2 | THURSDAY

📖 Student leaders in Dacca University who, in defiance of martial law, held meetings and took out processions a few days ago were being proceeded against. In fact, some of them had been arrested by the army. Sensible people felt relieved in the hope that the administration had, after all, decided to take action against the disruptionists, but today's radio news announced that they had been pardoned by the president *suo moto*. This does not auger well for the future as it will be regarded as a weakness on the part of the government and taken full advantage of. Next time they will do something worse. There is a danger that there will be open and general defiance all around. Meanwhile, Bhashani has called the rally of peasant leaders in Kushtia on the 6th. Scores of thousands of people are expected to attend. This is obviously communist inspired. If his plans fructify, the countryside will also be set ablaze. On the labour front, too, all is not well in East Pakistan. Labour is giving a lot of trouble and production, especially in jute mills, has gone down considerably. So it looks like the situation in East Pakistan is explosive and liable to erupt. The further danger is that all this is bound to affect the situation in West Pakistan too.

3 | FRIDAY

📖 The local Superintendent of Police in Islamabad came to call to discuss the problem of the guard the police is required to provide for me. He looked apprehensive that as a result of the decision in Dacca the student agitators will raise their heads here too. In fact, one of them has given him a warning already. The law and order situation has deteriorated, crime has increased and so has corruption. The main cause was that the police was demoralized. When martial law complaint centres were operative any bad character could lodge a complaint, true or false, and have the local police official held up in the presence of so many people. In consequence, they started taking the least line of resistance. According to another person, corruption has increased because the police, when apprehending a culprit, tell him to settle the matter with them or go before the martial law court where he would be sure to get stiff punishment. He naturally prefers to settle on the spot for a consideration.

The SP told me that though the Convention Muslim League was not popular, people in the village mourn my departure. They say that a golden chapter of Pakistan's history has been closed.

📖 Malik Qasim came to see me in the evening. He went to Dacca in connection with setting up an electoral body for the Muslim League. He came back very disappointed with the conduct of Wahiduzzaman and especially Sobur Khan. Generally he was very depressed on account of the deteriorating situation in East Pakistan. An intelligence officer told him that the Bengalis were openly talking about secession and the spate of cases that have been started against us in connection with the Muslim League. It is the first time I found him like that.

7 | TUESDAY

📖 Pir Ahsan-ud-Din from East Pakistan came to call. He said that the students in Dacca University were getting restive. They are being egged on by Mujibur Rahman and Bhashani. Bhashani's group, though smaller in number, is more aggressive and effective. They are openly asking for separation but this is not the voice of the common man. However, the common man is being duped by the slogan of complete provincial autonomy etc. Secessionists take good care not to put forward their demands openly. They camouflage it in terms of local grievances. Pir's group and PDP are trying to counter this move but they are short of funds. The industrialists don't help as they have been warned off by the administration, though Mujibur Rahman has collected huge sums only recently. So could I help him with some money? I told him that in the present circumstances how could I help? His feeling was that with the surrender of martial law to the students and its general ineffectiveness, the students, labour and the communists will create hell in the country. In addition, Bhashani is busy organizing the peasantry. If they too join hands with the rest, anything can happen, while the Indians are waiting for an opportunity to take police action against East Pakistan and swallow it. The politicians are oblivious of this impeding tragedy. Their main concern is aggrandizement and promotion of selfish interests.

9 | THURSDAY

📖 Inamullah Khan of Motamir-e-Islami came with a message of felicitation from the Grand Mufti of Jerusalem. Inamullah also attended the Rabat Summit Conference and met King Faisal and other dignitaries who were very solicitous about me. They bemoaned the fact that my services were lost to the Muslim world and there was no one to compare with me from Indonesia to Morocco. I was thankful but also felt very humble. I wonder if I deserve all that praise.

11 | SATURDAY

📖 Raja Zafar-ul-Haq and Sheikh Zafar Mahmood, advocates from Rawalpindi, came to call in the evening. They are both practical and clean people. They had come to plead as to why my experience and knowledge could not be utilized for the good of the country without getting unduly involved in party politics. I told them that this would not be possible for the simple reason that those in power would not like it, besides, our people are in no mood to listen or talk reason. They are being fed on emotions and slogans and this has become the staple of their lives, realities they are not prepared to face. Hence, complete confusion about the future. This situation suits the leftists and they are doing everything possible to aggravate it. From their point of view the more confusion the better. They said that polarization between the rightists and the leftists has assumed an acute form. Even in the bar people come to blows over these matters. Bhutto's followers are especially bigoted. There is no doubt about it that Bhutto, in spite of his grave shortcomings, has been able to create a leftist following amongst the student and lawyer community in many places in West Pakistan. Talk of socialism somehow appeals to the people. It is something new, therefore arouses curiosity, whereas Islam they have been hearing of for the last 1400 years. Besides, it is not presented in a form that appeals to the modern young man. What a tragedy.

12 | SUNDAY

📖 Today's papers have published the government's decision to name thoroughfares and streets in Islamabad after personalities and places of feature in Pakistan. One of the thoroughfares has been named after the late Mr Suhrawardy who had at one time announced that whereas Ayub Khan has taken the capital to Islamabad and Pindi by train, I will bring it back to Karachi by plane. My name has been omitted, not that it matters a bit to me, but it shows the extent of meanness of people in authority that they are not even ashamed to falsify history. Who can deny that I am responsible for the concept, naming and development of Islamabad. It is my creation.

13 | MONDAY

📖 Yusuf Haroon[20] and his wife came to lunch. He works in New York in a banking and financing firm and is currently on a short visit to Pakistan. Our intelligence regard him as a CIA man. How far it is true, it is difficult to say. Currently, he is engaged in effecting an oil deal with the Algerian government who have disallowed an American firm from operating. He is trying to buy the American interests on pay-as-you-earn basis. He will run into big money if the deal comes off. He said that Pakistanis are welcomed in Algeria as they don't speak Arabic, as such they don't pose a political problem, whereas the Egyptians and other Arabs are suspect. The Algerians are unhappy over the Egyptian oriented revolution in Libya. They would have liked this to happen under their guidance. The real problem with the Algerians is that they have very few educated and trained people. The French did very little for them in this respect.

About affairs in Pakistan, Yusuf said that our credit abroad has gone down very low. No one is prepared to invest money in Pakistan, as they are uncertain of the future. One of the reasons for this uncertainty is that the present administration has given the impression that it is transitory. He said that the harassment of businessmen and officials has done great harm, whereas the real troublemakers have been allowed to go scot free. He saw very little coherence in what the politicians are talking about and doubted their ability to handle the problems of the country when they came to power.

15 | WEDNESDAY

📖 A couple of people came from Lahore. The gist of their talk was that I am blamed by some people for bringing about two martial laws. How ignorant they are of realities. On the other hand, a feeling is growing that the present martial law and my resignation were forced on me by the army. This is true that the internal situation had so deteriorated that the Commander-in-Chief General Yahya had told me and so did General Akbar, the head of the military intelligence, that unless martial law was imposed quickly a situation of civil war might develop and the task of the army would become more difficult.

📖 Mahmud Haroon came to call in the afternoon. He is on his way to Canada to attend the Colombo Plan Conference. He does not seem to be happy about the state of affairs. Martial law is losing momentum, disruptive elements are getting encouragement and good people are shaken. Politicians are misbehaving and fighting amongst each other. They cannot make up their minds about the shape of the future.

16 | THURSDAY

📖 The Mir of Hunza and his wife came to call. They are on their way to attend the Aga Khan's wedding in Paris. I found them in a state of tension. He told me that the Chinese have done a tremendous job on the Karakoram road.[21] They have built it up to Passu, but on my instance a couple of years ago, they agreed to build down to Baltit. They are now within reach of Baltit. The road is 43 feet wide, this is a tremendous performance. Apparently, they work like beavers.

📖 The Saudi ambassador came to pay a courtesy call and expressed his sorrow and that of his monarch on my departure from government and the misfortunes that have befallen me and my country. I thanked him and asked for my thanks to be passed on to King Faisal too, whom I regard as a great Muslim and statesman. He bemoaned the conduct of disruptionists in the country and hoped that Pakistan's multifarious problems, especially the economic difficulties, would be overcome. He then asked for my assessment of the conclusion of the Rabat Conference.

18 | SATURDAY

📖 Dur Mohammad Usto[22] from Jacobabad came to see me. He said that anti one unit feelings were being fanned by the Sindhi politicians. In fact, it was not the people's cry. It was the cry of politicians whose main interest is to create more jobs for themselves. Bhutto, too, has been able to create a following for himself. A couple of pirs and a few landlords have joined his party. Fancy them doing that. They will be the first victims of his so-called socialism.

19 | SUNDAY

📖 Heard sad news this morning. Poor Nawab of Mamdot[23] had died of heart failure. He was an old diabetic case. He was one of those who was in the vanguard of the struggle for Pakistan and suffered and sacrificed so much for the cause. May God bless his soul. I have sent a message of condolence to his wife and also asked Qasim to represent me at the funeral.

📖 The Turkish ambassador came to deliver a reply from President Sunay and Premier Demirel to my message of congratulations on their recent electoral success. He said please let us know if there is anything we can do, we have a great regard for you and we do not change easily.

📖 Wahiduzzaman is supposed to have told someone that Mujibur Rahman's plans are that on coming to power, he will make East Pakistan secede and declare independence, then negotiate non-aggression pact with India backed by USA and the Soviet Union. At the start, India will soon dominate East Pakistan if not physically occupy it. There are two dominant reasons. She wants East Pakistan's jute and also the use of her waterways and the railway system for through communication to Nepal and Assam where, apart from requirement of vast trade, she needs these facilities for maintenance of the enormous army India keeps on that front. As to the expectations of American guarantees, it is nothing short of living in a fool's paradise.

1 | SATURDAY

📖 Sir Cyril Pickard, the British High Commissioner, came to convey greetings and the good wishes of Mr Wilson and his cabinet. He seemed particularly concerned about conditions in East Pakistan and the irresponsibility of the politicians there; with growing population, food shortages and falling jute prices, the province will face ruination if they do not get down to attending to the essentials. He felt that the future of jute was dark. The synthetic substances were replacing it fast. He thought of going across and talking to Mujib to caution him of the dangers ahead but felt that it can only do marginal good. The curse of the parliamentary system is that politicians compete with each other in making fabulous promises to catch votes and find it difficult to retreat from the positions taken. Talking about my life and that of the Wali of Swat whose powers have been taken away recently, he asked, was it the custom in this part of the world to ostracize those who have gone out of power? It was something new which did not happen in his country. He was sorry about the breakdown of the Basic Democrat system, without them who will distribute fertilizer, seeds etc to the farmers.

📖 Khawaja Shahabuddin and his wife, who are staying with their son-in-law here, came to lunch. He was lately in East Pakistan for a couple of weeks, and came back very apprehensive of the future. Young communists like Sobur's son were talking about a bloodbath and repetition of what happened in Iraq some years ago. He [Shahabuddin] has a large family and a good deal of property which he has distributed amongst them. Most of them have sold out and come over to West Pakistan. Khawaja's son-in-law is secretary of home affairs. I asked him what did he think of the situation. He said as usual the intelligence reports were not so pessimistic. He said very soon the break up of one unit will be announced and what a mess it will be in setting up new provincial administrations. West Pakistan's progress will be put back by a couple of decades. I said that was one way of achieving parity with East Pakistan.

3 | MONDAY

📖 News from East Pakistan is bad, there have been major clashes between Urdu speaking refugees in Dacca with the Bengalis who resented the demand for electoral enrolment forms to be printed in Urdu for them. The army and the East Pakistan Rifles had to be called in, who had to resort to firing. Several people have been killed and wounded. Urdu-speaking refugees have always had a thin time in East Pakistan.

9 | SUNDAY

📖 There are rumours abroad that:
1. There will be no elections as there is no consensus amongst politicians. And if the elections are held the students and labour will create a terrible turmoil in the cities and such people will be returned who have the support of these elements. Communists and leftist elements will gain ground.
2. Realization is dawning on people that anti-Pakistan elements like Mujibur Rahman, G.M. Syed,[24] Baloch *sardars*, Red Shirts and communists are coming up and they will have to be given a fight.

The only organization that can do so this is the army. The Punjabi element especially would not like to see them take over the country. That may be so, but there is no indication that the present administration would be prepared to accept the challenge and seek a head-on clash. It will amount to complete reversal of their present policy. Besides, it will be very costly. Such action at the commencement of martial law would have been different, but now it is too late. The psychological advantage and initiative has been lost.

3. The younger elements in the army may challenge General Yahya. I personally do not agree with this. The structure of the army and its size does not permit it. It will be a great tragedy if it ever happens.

4. General Yahya is going to announce very soon the break up of one unit, higher representation to East Pakistan in the central legislature and the outline of the rest of the constitution. This is all right, but how are so many details flowing from this decision to be thrashed out, obviously in the assembly with a Bengali majority? One shudders to think what chaos it will lead to.

5. Once the unit is broken Nur Khan will be retired as his polices like that on labour, education, etc. have caused major embarrassment to the government. This may well lead to a flare up amongst the students who are looking for trouble and the labour who regard Nur Khan as their benefactor.

6. About 160 officers in the civil [service] are going to be retired for corruption etc. and their properties confiscated.

7. A feeling is growing amongst the thinking people that the administration has leftist leanings and has identified itself with them. Some are thinking of leaving the country.

8. Our exports in commodities are falling, but cotton yarn and cloth is doing very well. Most of the mills, though working short of capacity through labour troubles, are booked up for six months or more.

9. A knowledgeable diplomat is reported to have said that the people have no confidence in the present administration and they have no confidence in themselves.

10. No one is clear about the future. They are confused and perplexed. They are doubtful even about the future of Pakistan.

12 | WEDNESDAY

📖 Col. Mohiuddin, the President's physician, who also looks after me, came to see me on return from an Iranian tour with President Yahya. He said that the tour went off well. Any estrangement that existed with the Shah in my time has been removed. President's Shiaism has helped. The truth, of course, is that the Shah has the president in his pocket. Look at the open support Shah got from Yahya over the question of Shatt-al-Arab,[25] which I would never have given. It has soured Pakistan's relations with the Arabs without doing any good to Iran. He said that Yahya drinks very heavily and is an alcoholic. He was worried about the state of his health, but was rarely allowed to go near him. His military secretary keeps him well isolated. Even his brother Mohammad Ali cannot see him easily. The only people who seem to have access to him are General Peerzada and General Hamid who join him in the evening for drinking and bouts of womanising. In Karachi, 4 to 5 women were brought in every evening for selection. One was kept for the night. This is known all over Karachi. About me though there is still a good deal of criticism. There is also a realization amongst thinking people that services of a great man have been lost to Pakistan.

📖 Bucha, though a civil servant by profession, is famous for his knowledge of agriculture. I used him a great deal to increase food production in West Pakistan. He told me that through mismanagement even West Pakistan is now running short of wheat. They are asking the centre to provide two lakh tons of wheat. This is sad if true. Then the food gap for East and West Pakistan would be in the order of two million tons, a tremendous burden on our meagre foreign exchange resources.

13 | THURSDAY

📖 There is an American lady who is known for her predictions and has even written a book on them. Most of them have come true. Recently she made some prediction about the future of Pakistan. This appeared in the *Time* magazine. Its entry has been banned in Pakistan. There are all sorts of wild rumours about it.

📖 Shahabuddin appreciated my remaining quiet as otherwise all the opposition parties would gang up against me and the Muslim League. It is better to let them snipe at each other.

📖 My son Gohar Ayub was here for a couple of days. While discussing the problems of the country I told him that those that sought solutions in socialism must realize that the only form of socialism that can produce results in our conditions of vast population and limited resources is communism. This system, with all its drawbacks, does organize the society, works and makes them work. It is through discipline and work that material conditions of the people can improve. But such a system can only be brought about by leadership of a very high grade and conditions and dedication. I don't see it emerging in this country. He said it will emerge, and from the army, but it will take one or two more martial laws. I found it difficult to disagree with him as in our army a large number of leaders come from the lower middle or peasant proprietary class. They naturally tend to be agrarian and socialistic. The conduct of the present military regime towards pressure groups of leftist trends is a fair pointer to the future.

14 | FRIDAY

📖 Just heard that former president General Iskander Mirza has died in London. His body is being brought to Tehran for burial. I must send his wife a message of condolence.

27 | THURSDAY

📖 Yusuf Haroon gathered from different sources that Yahya is going to announce the following tomorrow:

1. Adult franchise and parliamentary form of government, which has been accepted.

2. Dismemberment of one unit, accepted in principle. Details to be worked out by the constituent assembly.
3. Representation on basis of population.
4. Constitution drafting unit to be set up to form the Constitution within three months, thereafter it will continue as the normal legislature. This, he said, would spell the ruin of the country. Nur Khan, he said, is a friend of his but he is hasty and unpractical. He is taking major policy decisions on the advice of whiz kids who may have been bright students, but lack practical experience. It looks like experienced people are not being consulted either by the central or provincial governments. They seem to be very self-centred.

Yusuf Haroon explained the reason why General Iskander Mirza's body was given a state funeral with full honours by the Shah of Iran. Apparently, General Iskander Mirza approached the Shah through Zahedi, the foreign minister, to intercede on his behalf with General Yahya to let him visit Pakistan for a month or so to see his children. General Yahya told the Shah that this was not the opportune time. He could come when things settled down a bit. General Yahya was quite right in saying that and the Shah was satisfied. But later, General Iskander Mirza received a letter from General Peerzada repeating that in curt terms. General Iskander Mirza sent this to Zahedi, the foreign minister of Iran, for the information of the Shah adding that General Yahya did not have the courtesy to even sign the letter himself. Apparently, the Shah was incensed and Zahedi, the foreign minister, must have put more fuel on the fire. Zahedi is supposed to be related to Begum Iskander Mirza. A day or two later General Iskander Mirza died. On hearing this, the Shah asked the British government to treat General Iskander Mirza as an Iranian citizen and see that his coffin was ceremoniously brought to the airport accompanied by a representative of the Queen where an Iranian aircraft was awaiting to take the body and mourners to Tehran. In the absence of this episode General Iskander Mirza's body would have been buried in London. I can see the Shah's reaction. He is very sensitive and tends to overreact to the slightest affront. Zahedi, knowing his temperament, plays on his weakness to retain his power.

Yusuf Haroon also told me that when he was here last time he had told Nur Khan to maintain a dialogue with the Baloch leaders and also G.M. Syed. Instead of doing that he went to the extreme, reinstated all the rebel Balochi leaders, embraced and entertained them in the Government House including Bizenjo[26] who is an out and out communist. Now that they have been boosted sky high there is no holding them back. He also treats G.M. Syed as the uncrowned king of Sindh. The effect of such amateurish actions will be far reaching.

Yusuf Haroon said a curious thing is happening in England. Any Pakistani businessman who goes there on a visit is lavishly entertained by those Britishers who have interests in Pakistan. The object is to find out what is going to happen to their investments in Pakistan. They are extremely worried.

📖 Bhutto, I am told, is happy with the present state of affairs. Any form of stability does not suit him. He thinks that there will be another revolution, presumably led by the army, replacing General Yahya. Then there is nothing to stop him from coming to the top. He is a power hungry man with unbound ambitions. If Yahya was to rise to the occasion even now and deal with such people firmly, the situation can still be saved.

📖 Mr Khuhro also came to call and discussed the League affairs. He said that Daultana's collusion with Mujibur Rahman was nothing short of a dangerous intrigue. Daultana has given open support to Mujibur Rahman's Six Points and representation on population basis. Mujibur Rahman is going to demand only one house with East Pakistan majority. How is Daultana going to make West Pakistan accept it?

📖 General Yahya has announced his constitutional plan. Undoing of one unit, representation on population basis, election of the assembly commencing 5th October, assembly to frame constitution within 120 days failing which it would be dissolved. Political meetings will be allowed from 1st January. Let us see what comes out of it. Most people will be pessimistic. I, at least, have one consolation. I am spared the agony of dismembering the country. People would have accused me of undoing something which Quaid-e-Azam had made.

I was looking at the text of Yahya's announcement on constitutional matters again. He is going to give the assembly the right to determine its own system of voting. The Bengalis, being in the majority, would naturally vote for simple majority. They could even persuade some representatives of smaller provinces to go along with them. The object would be to line up against Punjab and to have as weak a centre as possible. This will be disastrous. In other words, the Bengali majority will be the arbiter of the future of this country.

1 | MONDAY

📖 A Pakistan air force officer who was my ADC and is now with the president, came to call with his wife. He is an intelligent, pious, patriotic, but reticent young man. But this time he was bursting to talk, perhaps to let off steam. He said the following:

1. The present administration, not having a clear cut policy, gropes in the dark. They are, therefore, living from day to day. They say they are not interested in staying on and yet they view everything from a political angle. All major decisions are so motivated irrespective of long term effects.

2. Most of the policy decisions are amateurish and have had an adverse affect having gone awry like the labour and education policy, treatment of businessmen and civil servants.

3. Nur Khan and General Peerzada have had a decisive influence in framing these polices, although Nur Khan has fallen out of favour lately. The admiral is not consulted much though he is the soberest of the lot. General Hamid is the only sobering influence with the president.

4. Right or wrong, General Peerzada is blamed universally for acts of omission and commission. In any case, he is shallow, hasty and verbose, besides being petty and vindictive. This, of course, was my assessment of him, when he acted as my military secretary for some time.

5. The recent policy announcement on the constitution was made to head off probable political eruption in East Pakistan. Things there are on the boiling point and even now an eruption is expected after Ramazan. The hope is that this announcement will divert people's attention towards party politics and especially between Bhashani's NAP and Mujibur Rahman's Awamis.

6. The food situation in East Pakistan and the economic situation throughout the country are very bad. Things are crumbling, the president and General Peerzada feel really concerned.

7. Another set of people who are close to the president are the two Alvi brothers, who take credit for appointment of ministers and for removal of officials. The president, in loyalty to old friends, allows them proximity. He did not, of course, mention that his mother-in-law and her sisters are another set of people who openly sell the president's name. They happen to be girl friends though some of them look like pregnant buffalos.

8. Nobody expects the proposed constituent assembly to succeed, although a decision has been given on the future of one unit and representation on population basis, the thorny question of voting system in the assembly, simple majority or 2/3rd majority, the question of a second house and division of power between the centre and the provinces is going to be very difficult to resolve.

9. The president keeps away from me because of objections of people like Asghar and the rumour spread by the opposition that he used to consult me secretly, which of course is utterly untrue.

10. The original list of Class-I officers to be dismissed or prosecuted was 500. The president asked for them to be cut down, it now stands at 271. He is asking for further reductions which does not seem possible. The prosecuted will be tried by summary military courts. Covering martial law regulations are being framed.

11. He talked about the oft repeated intention of East Pakistan to secede.

12. The decision to undo one unit has been announced without working out the mechanisms and details. This will lead to real meddling and chaos.

13. There is talk of appointment of governors to the new provinces in West Pakistan, Rasheed to NFWP, Qizilbash to Punjab, Mahmud Haroon to Sindh and Akbar Bugti[27] to Balochistan. Fancy Bugti becoming a governor. No bigger a scoundrel could be found anywhere. There is no mention of Nur Khan. It looks like he is on his way out. The future of Karachi is not yet known.

14. It is curious but hardly any decision remains secret. The things that are not known to the staff are talked about by the people and which eventually turn out to be true.

15. There are rumours that Major General Gul Hassan,[28] the Chief of the General Staff, has higher ambition. I told him this could hardly be true. Besides, it is difficult to imagine that the army will support such a move.

16. The military secretary to the governor in East Pakistan is a naval officer from West Pakistan. He is feeling so insecure that he is going to send his family back home after Eid. He said all Urdu-speaking Muslims in East Pakistan feel the same.

17. The central ministers don't count for much. They are presented with prepared things by the martial law staff.

In the end the poor lad asked if the country could still be saved. I said I hope and pray so. I am writing this at 10:30 p.m. at night. So you can imagine what sort of sleep I am going to have. But then one hears such depressing things every day.

2 | TUESDAY

📖 Shaukat Ali, son of Imran Khan, who was a friend of mine, came to see me. I had helped him to go to England to do his bar. He belongs to Dacca and was a close lieutenant of Maulana Bhashani. Now he has given him up and joined the Awami League. Talking about Bhashani, he said the old man is now 84. He had a prostrate gland operation sometime back, the doctors told him that he was good for another 20 years. I said that then God help East Pakistan. I am told that at the time of partition Nehru complained to Sir Sa'adullah of Shillong that Sylhet[29] district was being divided and the major portion being handed over to Pakistan. He will see to its destruction. So there was no cause for worry. Bhashani has been the major disruptive actor in East Pakistan. He is an unprecedented rabble-rouser.

📖 I understand that during the recent editor's conference held by Yahya a question was asked why action was not taken against me. He replied that he had found nothing against me but if anybody has any evidence he could go to the court.

📖 I asked my son Akhtar Ayub as to how will it do if Qayyum became the head of the Muslim League. He said that unless I was prepared to take active part in politics, the Muslim League would cease to exist. My supporters, out of consideration for me, will wait for a while, but soon they will

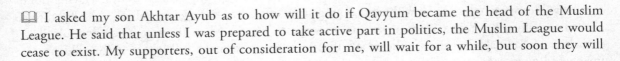

seek alliance with others. Some will go to Daultana, others to Qayyum and so on. Most of them on the Frontier will follow Qayyum as he is the only plausible counter to the Red Shirts. Council League, through the influence of Daultana, would join them and there is a link between Mujib, Daultana and Wali Khan.[30] Though by no means ideal, Qayyum is the lesser evil and the only alternative, so I have told him to sound out Qayyum on whether he is prepared to take the lead in the Muslim League.

3 | WEDNESDAY

Rashidi[31] came to see me this morning. I particularly wanted to see him to give him a bit of my mind on scurrilous articles he had been writing about me. I reminded him of what I had done for him from time to time. I appointed him as an ambassador over the head of foreign office advice to the contrary. They told me that he was a man devoid of any character and utterly lacking in scruples. He was capable of selling the country and this proved right when we heard from several sources that he had been selling our cipher and committing many other irregularities. Later, when he returned to Pakistan, I saw to his maintenance from different sources. In return what do I get, abuse from him. He was ashamed of his conduct and tried to make lame excuses. He said he had taken the courage to call knowing that I will forgive him and so on.

Rashidi told me not to give up the Muslim League. Otherwise the field would be left free for my enemies to take their revenge on me when the assemblies come into being. The answer was to appoint a suitable vice president. He thought that Qayyum would be a liability. Yusuf Haroon, Sardar Bahadur or even Khuhro might do.

About the recent declaration of the president on constitutional matters he said he found an undercurrent of resentment in the Punjab on the break up of one unit. They feel that the cause of Pakistan has been damaged and the process of disintegration started. Whilst they had made so many sacrifices in the national interest they also feel that Bengalis and the smaller provinces are out to do Punjab down. This feeling can assume explosive proportions and there is no leader of any stature in the Punjab to hold it in check.

There is no hope of the constituent assembly succeeding. Rashidi did not see how agreement could be reached on burning issues like the system of voting, division of powers between the provinces and the centre and the second house. He was sure that there will be a breakdown and then what? Politicians will certainly be discredited.

Rashidi said that basically Bhutto is a fascist. He is power hungry and wants to misuse it and victimize people. He did a good deal of that when he was a minister. All this talk of socialism is nonsense. Sindhi Mahaz knows that and will do all in their power to see that he does not get elected from Larkana. He said that Bhutto had no chance in Larkana even if there were more than one seat in the district from the central assembly. I did not agree with that. If Khuhro is untouched in his seat, who else will compete with Bhutto. He said there is a man that is being groomed. Bhutto is asking Ghulam Mustafa Jatoi[32] to vacate his seat for him, which is doubtful. He said the only other way Bhutto can come into power is by becoming a minister by getting around Yahya. Having done that he will turn on Yahya or he will incite young army officers to rise against Yahya. G.M. Syed told all this to Yahya. Yet Yahya sends a personal message to Bhutto when the recent scuffle took place with him in Sadiqabad. This is unheard of. Bhutto is going to make full use of it to build up his image and give credence to believe that the president is in his pocket. He said Bhutto is spending money lavishly. A large number of people are paid upwards of 500 each. Most of the press correspondents are paid. Where is he getting all this money from?

Rashidi, along with G.M. Syed and others, went to General Sher Ali [Pataudi], the minister for information. They complained that in spite of the martial law regulations, anti-Islamic and communist propaganda was being made in the press which is full of communist views. They were going to explain more but Sher Ali cut them short by saying that he has already countered 80 per cent of them, 10 per cent more are on the point of conversion and he is working on the rest. Seeing that the man's mind was shut and he had his own make believe they decided to take leave and came away as it was no use continuing with the talk.

📖 Some people are asking the president to make his position clear vis-à-vis the assembly. They expect him to act purely as a constitutional president. In other words, endorse what the assembly says and become ineffective.

📖 Asghar Khan has announced today that he has decided to retire from active politics now that his limited mission of removing the corrupt and despotic regime has been achieved and a clear guarantee has been given by the president that elections will be held and democracy restored. He will watch its progress with interest.

This announcement may have been caused due to frustration with the politicians who, having used him during the upsurge, are now giving him no place in party hierarchy or it may be a trick to become neutral and be available for an office to any party that comes into power. It may also be due to realization that he has no hope of getting elected from anywhere. I think he has made soundings in many places without much hope of success. He and Bhutto would, of course, have liked to have seen the presidential system stay in which they saw chances of being selected as a candidate by one party or the other.

When Asghar Khan talks about having achieved limited objectives of mission he, in fact, together with Bhutto has done much more than that. They have between them laid the foundation of destruction of this country by playing on the sentiments of the people and misleading them.

4 | THURSDAY

📖 Mr Anwar Bhinder, the ex-Speaker of West Pakistan, came to call. He told me that there are indications that the supporters of Qayyum headed by Kirmani are intending to spring a surprise by installing or recognizing Qayyum as the president of the Muslim League. In this connection they are eliciting the assistance of students and other rowdy elements. I rang up Qasim who confirmed that some such mischief was afoot. I told him to come over tomorrow with some other friends so that we could discuss the situation.

5 | FRIDAY

📖 This morning's papers confirmed Kirmani's intentions. He, without anybody else's permission, announced the dissolution of the present office bearers and the working committee and reinstatement of those bodies that existed under the 1962 constitution which is now defunct, with himself the president. His intention is to clear the ground for handing over the organization to Qayyum, Hassan Mahmood, etc.

📖 As arranged Qasim, Allah Yar and Mohammed Anwar turned up at midday. After a lot of discussion we decided to take action that will secure the provincial league funds. They were to go back to Lahore immediately to discuss with other friends as to what action can be taken to neutralize or remove Kirmani and replace him with someone more suitable. This is not going to be easy. It may well lead to violent conflict.

6 | SATURDAY

📖 Jalil Ahmed, former MNA from Gujranwala, came to call, he is a shrewd political observer. His assessment was as follows:

1. Last agitation in West Pakistan was mishandled because of lack of political acumen on the part of Governor Musa. He did not understand the situation and could not handle it properly besides he was a poor contrast to his predecessor Nawab of Kalabagh who was a shrewd politician and a sound and firm administrator.

2. East Pakistanis initially were not willing to join the agitation. They accused the East Pakistanis of being ungrateful to me who had done so much for the whole country, especially for East Pakistan. Later, when things got out of control in West Pakistan, East Pakistanis perforce had to join.

3. There is a great feeling of apprehension amongst the rural population for me in the Punjab. They feel I had given them a new lease of life. They feel they have never been served so well before nor are they going to see be served like this in future.

4. Since the new assembly is going to be a constituent assembly, the tendency will be for each province, especially East Pakistan, to ask for the maximum they can get; therefore only the extremists will be elected from that province. There is very little chance for the moderates to come in.

5. East Pakistan will demand the following:
   a. Weak centre with no powers of taxation. They also feel that on their own they will be able to improve relations with India as they must for reasons of security and economy. There are some advantages for this in it but there are also dangers of their very survival. If they demand this then it is much better to let them separate, in which case West Pakistan must also change its policy towards India. It is in our interest to ease tension with India and see that moderate elements attain the upper hand there.
   b. Shifting the capital to Dacca. They may not press hard for it if the first demand is met.
   c. Press for similar autonomy for the provinces in West Pakistan, as they are demanding for themselves. The object will be to gain the support of smaller provinces. This will be highly dangerous. He said Asghar is finished and Bhutto has hardly any following. They would both have been forgotten if it was not for the communist elements in the press, especially the press trusts. They are keeping Bhutto alive.

6. Muslim League can only be kept alive if replacement like me could be found. But in the Punjab where it still has a following Kirmani must be replaced. He is incapable of running a team.
7. Our foreign policy is so delicate that only an expert hand could conduct it. Since my departure people are very apprehensive that its conduct has fallen into immature hands. Already some serious mistakes have been made. Our performance at Rabat and our stand on Shatt-al-Arab are glaring examples of ineptitude. We should certainly avoid a situation of conflict with India.

8 | MONDAY

The central working committee of the Muslim League met this morning at my house. I was very glad to see that such a large number of people turned up at such short notice, especially from East Pakistan. The meeting lasted nearly four hours, the following resolutions were passed:

1. Kirmani to be ousted from the party and Mr Yasin Wattoo[33] to replace him as the president of West Pakistan Muslim League. I am sure this will put new life into the party.
2. Fazlul Qader Chaudhary to be appointed as the vice president in the East Pakistan vacancy. This was a demand of East Pakistanis. He would also perform the functions of the president until the new president was elected. Disciplinary action against Wahiduzzaman and Qadir was deferred.
3. Instructions were issued for election of fresh councils. However, the difficulty of holding elections in West Pakistan was realized as a result of the decision to create old provinces.
4. Wattoo was told to consolidate the League in the Punjab and then he and others to go around to the Frontier, Sindh etc. to rally our supporters. They should be told to cooperate with others but not lose their identity. Then they will be in a better bargaining position.
5. We condoled the demise of late Nawab of Mamdot who had sacrificed so much for the cause of Pakistan.

I think it was a timely meeting and some useful decisions were taken.

Heard in the morning that Asad, who was charged with the murder of his father Nawab of Kalabagh, has been acquitted. I am glad to hear this as the family is saved from further disintegration. I am told that he had to spend five to six lakhs in fighting this case. Chaudhary Nazir Ahmed, his defence counsel, robbed him mercilessly.

It came in the press this morning that 303 Class-I civil officials have been suspended and will be proceeded against under martial law. They can be given punishments ranging from dismissal to three years rigorous imprisonment and confiscation of property etc. I am told they represent 10 per cent of total Class-I cadre. Some of them must undoubtedly be corrupt but most of them are very intelligent, efficient and able officers. As it is we are short of able men and the administration is suffering. With the departure of these people efficiency will go down still further. In any case no officer is going to take decisions in a hurry in future knowing that he cannot count on the support of the administration. Bureaucratic inertia will grow and people will suffer. In any case this is not going to eliminate corruption, a good deal of it takes place in the lower echelons and I am told that this has increased considerably since martial law.

This is not to say that corruption should be condoned or ignored. It is a curse and all efforts should be made to curb it if not eliminate it, but the methods used should be such that can work in normal times and under normal law. Occasional draconian actions under martial law is no cure.

📖 A civil servant came to see me in the afternoon. He said that this martial law has come to victimize private enterprise and the civil officials. I wanted to add that it has also license and encouragement to every blackguard to malign me and my relations and associates.

9 | TUESDAY

📖 Hassan Amin, who runs the Sherazad Hotel in Islamabad, came to call. He has contacts with people like General Yahya, Bhutto etc. He told me that Yahya and his junta consider Bhutto as the man to back politically. I told him this will have international repercussions which Pakistan can ill afford to ignore. Bhutto is widely distrusted in the outside world. He is regarded as thoroughly unreliable. In fact, heads of several governments told me so on a number of occasions. The cause of this liking by the junta is obvious. Birds of a feather flock together. These people have similar characteristics, habits and past times.

📖 Yesterday we heard that Kirmani, on sensing that he might be removed from the presidency, locked and sealed the Muslim League office in Lahore. This morning I was rung up by Khizr and Wattoo that they have taken possession of the place without any difficulty. All their supporters gathered there and were jubilant. Kirmani came, made bit of a fuss but went away.

📖 Sobur who has been misbehaving since I left office and had been issuing undignified statements about me, now has come out openly to say that he wants my resignation, etc. It is surprising how the world changes. I always regarded him as a doubtful character who would crack under stress, which he has done now.

10 | WEDNESDAY

📖 Malik Qasim has given a rejoinder to Wahiduzzaman, Qazi Qadir etc., stating that whilst I was in power they were the biggest sycophants, lackeys and beneficiaries. And now that I am out of power they are indulging in the meanest accusation against me and make false and baseless accusations. They go about saying that when they met me the other day I said derogatory things against the people of Pakistan and expressed my disappointment with them. Whereas what I told them was that they had better stop their nefarious role in disrupting the party. If they could not do any good, they might at least stop from making mischief.

📖 There is a feeling amongst some people that Asghar Khan's retirement from politics and remaining available for use by the nation if and when required, is intended to put him in a neutral position and has been done in collaboration with Mujibur Rahman. The idea is that when Mujibur Rahman becomes the prime minister he will support Asghar Khan's candidature for the presidency. Even if it is true, which I have doubt, no politician is going to support a soldier, not even Yahya, for anything.

In fact, after the experience of three martial laws, which even though came about through their own misdeeds, they suspect the army and are going to make every effort to neutralize it. I have heard even my own supporters say that the chances of re-imposition of martial law will be reduced or eliminated if 50 per cent recruitment is done from East Pakistan or if the army is composed of all sections of people or if it becomes a national army as it is not today.

I have told them that contrivances of this nature are of no avail. Civil authority can become supreme only if the politicians run their country well. If not, the army has perforce to step in. This is an inescapable law and is the experience of all the emergent countries. They do not realize that the army, being a disciplined force with national and patriotic outlook and also being responsible for the internal and external defence of the country, cannot remain passive when ill discipline and irresponsibility prevails all around them putting the country in jeopardy. The only answer is for the politicians and the people to run their affairs well. The army will then be more than happy to confine itself to its own job, but looking at the problem from a broader angle, a country is lucky to have a good army and civil service to fall back upon and to save it from disintegration should things go wrong politically. This applies in particular to the new countries. Those countries that do not have these elements have suffered terribly. Congo and even Nigeria and Indonesia are glaring examples. Look at the suffering of those peoples and what they are undergoing.

11 | THURSDAY

📖 Today is Eid-ul-Fitr. I was wondering whether to go to my village for the prayers or go to the local Jamia Mosque. I decided on the latter course and called the local police inspector and informed him so. He turned up this morning to take me to the prayer ground. After the prayer the people mobbed me. Everybody wanted to shake hands with me. So it was with great difficulty I managed to reach my car. Later, all manner of people men, women and children called on me and my wife right till 9:00 p.m. in the evening. So I hardly had any time to see my children and grandchildren who had come to greet us.

12 | FRIDAY

📖 General Khalid Sheikh (retired)[34] met General Hamid, Chief of Staff, and suggested that if at any time his views were required on any matter of which he had any experience he would only be too glad to give them. Hamid, normally a sensible man, took offence to an innocent suggestion like that and said that, 'they were obsolete goofs and would need assistance'. Sheikh was absolutely flabbergasted and taken aback. He realized that power had gone to the man's head and he was no more normal. Sheikh also said that there was a movement afoot to move the Planning Commission to Dacca. How will that help development of East Pakistan was difficult to say, after all, the Planning Commission is not an executive body. That rests with the provincial authorities wherever the plans are formed. I suppose the object is to force the central government's hand to allocate more money to East Pakistan to be spent in the public sector irrespective of the fact whether it gives any return or not.

📖 A man close to the president spoke about his private life. Said that he liked the man as he has so many good qualities but he is not attending enough to the affairs of the state and is not contributing with ideas. Previously he used to drink in the morning too, but now he has three stiff whiskeys after midday. He has no lunch. In the evening drinking starts at about 6:30 and goes on till midnight. Then very often nights are spent with women. But he said in spite of all this the president looks fresh as a daisy the next morning. Then he described the fiasco at Rabat, how the Indian inclusion was taken lightly in the beginning. How our journalists, especially Naseem Hussain of the *Dawn,* fought with the foreign office advisors and made the president take a stiff stand at the end. The situation was saved by a hair's breath. The Indians were smart, but they were not smart enough. If they had sent a purely Muslim delegation our efforts to exclude them from the conference would have proved of no avail. The turmoil in the country when massacre of Muslims in Ahmedabad was going on and the emotions of our people were aroused would have been terrible.

13 | SATURDAY

📖 Saw in the press that Sobur Khan and others are calling a meeting of some defeated Leaguers in Dacca to oust me and Malik Qasim from the party. He has no *locus standi* or authority to do so. All that they can do is cause more confusion. So Malik Qasim has arranged with someone in Sheikhupura to ask for a stay order. Let's hope he gets it.

15 | MONDAY

📖 I had dinner with General Shahid Hamid and his family last night. It was a quiet affair, we three sat alone and talked about things. They were bitter about General Sher Ali, especially about his recent interview with the foreign correspondent in which he said that he objected to Ayub Khan's methods of dealing with others as a commander-in-chief. He used to drive people as donkeys and ponies. That is why, he, Sher Ali, left the army otherwise he was sure to have become the commander-in-chief. The truth was that he was retired because he had reached the end of his usefulness.

Then General Shahid Hamid and his wife came to the real point which they wished to make. Where was the need for holding the meeting of the Working Committee of the Muslim League the other day in my house and why don't I resign from the presidency. This, in fact, is the wish of the president. I told them that the main purpose of the meeting in fact was to find a successor, which is Fazlul Qader, to whom I have delegated all my powers until such time that the new president is elected. This can be done only by a popularly constituted council, which has to be re-formed as a result of the court cases that have been brought against us. If it was not for that, the matter would have been settled long ago. I have personally no interest in politics and I am certainly not a candidate for the Muslim League presidency. Please tell the president, though it has been conveyed to him several times before, which General Shahid Hamid seemed to have been aware of. General Yahya must have informed them of that. They promised to do so. Yahya has a habit of talking to my acquaintances about me. What people who see him say about me and how they object to his having any dealing with me etc. The objective may be to keep me warned and put me on notice just in case.

16 | TUESDAY

📖 Gohar Ayub returned in the evening. He met several people. General impression is that Yahya's policy speech on the constitution matters has made a very favourable impression. There is also appreciation of the fact that only 303 officers are being dealt with for corruption etc. when thousands might have been affected. These things give him acceptability and credibility for another 12 to 18 months.

I discussed with Gohar, Yahya's persistent demand that I should quit the Muslim League. He agreed that it was the right course to take and he had been thinking of asking me to do so for some time. In fact, several people in Karachi were expressing a similar opinion. I told him that there was some merit in his suggestion, but once I lose the party platform, who would feel the obligation to defend us against volatile criticism of the opposition? I see that Yahya's announcement had a very favourable foreign press. Let us now hope that the politicians and others will behave themselves after the 1st of January when free political activity will be allowed and elections to the constituent assembly are held in a reasonably peaceful atmosphere and a working constitution is evolved. On the other hand, there is apprehension in the minds of the people that feelings between the rightists and leftists are becoming accentuated and becoming acute and this tendency is likely to take a violent turn in the heat of election. Students and labour etc. will be used freely in this struggle.

Gohar Ayub's assessment of Asghar's announcement for retirement from politics is as follows:

He jumped into politics at the height of countrywide agitation when Bhutto was arrested creating a vacuum. Asghar filled that. His timing was excellent. People who are fanning the agitation accepted him with open arms. The fact that he was the C-in-C of the air force, which did so well during the war and had a vague reputation of being honest, etc., gave him added impetus. Besides, the politicians were looking for such a man who could split the armed forces, and who would have become a factor in the politics of the country. So he got a very good start and if the presidential form of government had stayed, he should have had very good chances. To his misfortune, this was not to be and the parliamentary democracy looks like coming in, in which he has very little chance of getting elected even as a member of the national assembly. So if he had adjudged the situation more shrewdly, he should have given up politics at the time when you had resigned. His image would have gone up sky high and whenever there was an opportunity people would have longed to have got him back. Instead he lingered on, exposed himself more to public gaze. They soon realized that he was limited and a shallow man. He seems to be a dark horse so to that extent he has harmed himself, meanwhile, the older politicians jilted him after making full use of him. In the end, he got frustrated and left politics in an effort to retain whatever reputation he had got left. His hope is that there will be turmoil in the country again and he will be able to stage a comeback. This does not sound far-fetched.

21 | SUNDAY

📖 Nasrullah Khattak,[35] a former MNA from Nowshera, and Pir Zakori from Dera Ismail Khan came over yesterday. Pir Zakori then asked me as to why don't I remain as the head of the party. My answer was all that is happening in the political field is against my conviction. The country is being fragmented, centre is being weakened, extreme form of provincial autonomy is being talked about and so on. If, in the political field, I can only denounce this, which happens to be against the grain of present thinking, so what good will I be doing to the country and the party. Talking about the break up of one unit, Nasrullah Khattak told me that he and his father have been building contractors for the last 40 years. Most of the time they worked in the Punjab. Never on a single occasion did they come across discrimination because they were non-Punjabis. Zakori, of course, was much more apprehensive of the break up. He felt that the re-creation of the Frontier Province would mean great suffering for the common man. Peshawari leadership would be re-established, most of our officials serving elsewhere will have to come back, mobility of labour and movement of vast number of workers that the Frontier people own will cease, bringing in its wake a gradual and economic suffering. People in D.I. Khan and adjoining tribal areas have already realized this and are very unhappy. That is the reason for the recent strikes against government personnel and kidnapping. When political activity is allowed from 1st January, they are going to protest and agitate against the break up in a big way.

29 | MONDAY

📖 My wife has a house in Abbottabad, which is rented out to the army. Through an oversight, this income was not reported to taxation authorities so it had to be declared under a martial law regulation together with all her other assets. A notice was served on her to appear before the local income tax officers. My private assistant represented her. The income tax officer worked up an enormous sum which had to be paid as tax. This was, in fact, on the agricultural income, so I engaged a lawyer to explain the case. He came to know, that instead of sending her case to the appropriate committee, a special high-powered committee was set up to examine cases of my family members. So I am singled out for special consideration from the administration. They seem to be out to harm me to the extent they can.

📖 Fazlul Qader Chaudhary, Qasim, Wattoo, Allah Yar and Khizar came to dinner last night. They had a very good Muslim League meeting in Lahore, large number of people attended from all over the Punjab and I was told that Chaudhary made a good impression on them. Fazlul Qader Chaudhary had met Yahya in Dacca lately. Yahya is anxious that I must leave the League. He would have liked to see Qayyum take my place. The rebel group now knows this and takes encouragement from it. His concern is to see that I am no more a rival. What a fantastic notion after my declaration to the contrary. What interest can I have now in politics? Fazlul Qader Chaudhary also got the impression that Yahya has some respect for me, but the staff around him is ill disposed. There is constant pressure on Yahya for action against me.

30 | TUESDAY

📖 It is now confirmed that the government instructions have gone out to income tax officers to send the returns of my relatives to Rawalpindi for thorough scrutiny and submission to a special high-powered committee that has been set up for this purpose. The object seems to be to look for loopholes so that some action can be taken against them. In other words, they are being treated as criminals. When looking at Shaukat Ayub, my younger son's returns the officer concerned remarked that people say that Ayub Khan's sons have half of Pakistan, but no such thing seems to be there in these papers.

Shaukat Ayub was represented by a lawyer and his manager. Before entering the ITO's office, his head clerk told them that if they were prepared to give Rs. 2000/- as bribe he could tell what questions they were going to be asked. They refused the offer. This happened on the day that the suspension of the 303 officers was announced for corruption etc. So much for deterrent effect of this action.

31 | WEDNESDAY

📖 Shahabzadi Mehmooda Begum,[36] who is a former member of the provincial assembly, is an old social worker and a member of our party, came to call. She has property in Bahawalpur, but is now settled down in Lahore. She is a sensible and sincere person, showed happiness that the party meeting at Lahore went off very well. People are happy with the appointment of Wattoo and Fazlul Qader Chaudhary, but they are longing to have me back.

DIARY 1970

1 | THURSDAY

📖 The press cuttings about my resignation from the League are attached at the back [see Appendix 3]. I hope that Fazlul Qader Chaudhary would be able to hold the position at the national level and Wattoo in the Punjab. They have already infused some life in the organization and the League workers have regained their morale.

The letter [Appendix 4] was made known to the press by Mr Fazlul Qader Chaudhary on Wednesday in a hurriedly called news conference. He said, 'I have accepted the responsibility with all humility'.

10 | SATURDAY

📖 It is now definitely established that income tax returns of all my family members have been collected by the martial law headquarters by Brig. Rahim and are now in possession of General Peerzada. The object seems to be to find loopholes for starting criminal cases. However, General Peerzada appears to be of the view that such an action cannot be taken in isolation against one family. It will have to be extended to the families of all those who have been in power and that will be an endless job. Besides, it will only amount to gaining cheap popularity. Some people will welcome it, but many others will not be impressed.

18 | SUNDAY

📖 According to this morning's news there has been a battle between the followers of Maulana Maududi and others in Dacca in the Paltan Maidan during a Jamaat-e-Islami public meeting. One person is reported killed and 400 injured. The meeting was dispersed and the dais burnt. The Maulana was chased back home and so were his followers. In Pindi too there have been scuffles between hostile student groups. Road traffic was interrupted for some time. Meanwhile, Bhashani is arranging a big rally of farmers and workers in a place called Santosh.[1] Red-capped delegates are reported to be pouring in from all directions. Bhutto is rioting in Peshawar and areas around, spreading class hatred and disaffection. All this sounds like initial skirmishing before genuine mobilization is complete and full scale battles start. We are having a foretaste of democracy, which the politicians shouted hoarse for and promised that once their form of democracy came everything would be lovely in the garden.

19 | MONDAY

📖 Khawaja Shahabuddin came over for a chat. He said that communists were very active in East Pakistan. Communist intellectuals were producing literature on a large scale and distributing it in the villages.

The impression that Mujibur Rahman was losing ground in East Pakistan was not true. His following was large and was increasing. Incidents like the riots that took place on the Paltan Maidan the other day, in which his followers were engaged, had added to his popularity and dominance. He was able to establish his strength and showed to people that no party could challenge him. However, one thing was certain that unless the administration was able to establish law and order firmly, things were liable to get worse and might even get out of control. If true, it was the last opportunity the administration had in establishing its authority, but would they do it?

Khawaja was happy that Fazlul Qader Chaudhary was appointed as a president of the Muslim League. He was an excellent choice as he could speak the language of his opponents. Wahiduzzaman supported Qayyum for his supposed appeal in East Pakistan. This he thought was a mistaken notion. He wondered where these people were getting the money from to move about the way they were doing in great style and luxury. Perhaps the industrialists were helping.

📖 In protest of riots in Paltan Maidan, the students have declared six hours *hartal* in Dacca city yesterday. Several vehicles were burnt during the *hartal*. It looks that from now on the student community would be on the rampage.

25 | SUNDAY

📖 Malik Qasim said that attempts were being made by the authorities and pressure put on us for submission to Qayyum and sharing party funds with him and his associates. Qizilbash called him especially and proposed that a committee of six people, three from each party should be set up to administer the funds jointly and finished up by saying that he meant what he said. In other words, he held out a threat. Similarly, a senior military intelligence officer was sent to him to say that they had better cooperate with Qayyum Khan to counterbalance Wali Khan. He also gave the impression that there is a tie up between Fazlul Qader Chaudhary and Mujibur Rahman to which the administration is allergic. There is, of course, no truth in that.

Qasim naturally reacted strongly against these proposals and said that he regarded all this as uncalled for pressurization and could give no answer without consulting his associates. Fazlul Qader Chaudhary apparently flared up when told this and had to be dissuaded from issuing a press statement. Instead, he is going down to Karachi to see Yahya.

Malik Qasim seemed to think that all this was happening without Yahya's knowledge. I don't agree with that, in a centralized government ministers cannot take up positions on major issues without the consent of the president. The administration's concern is understandable. In order to get a strong centre, they have to counter Mujibur Rahman and his associates in West Pakistan. But for that Qayyum Khan is no answer. He may do for the Frontier, but against Mujibur Rahman an East Pakistani is the answer and despite his failings, Fazlul Qader Chaudhary is the best choice. So the administration should be doing all it can to strengthen his hands.

26 | MONDAY

📖 Bhutto is on an election tour of the Frontier and the Punjab areas. He talks a lot of nonsense about the 1965 war and my role in it, but at the same time he has been offering catchy slogans of socialism, which appeal to the common man, especially at the present juncture when there is so much economic distress. So he has been attracting big crowds. Under the circumstances, if he had suitable candidates, he would have been able to get several elected. He is no socialist himself, but his aim is gaining power through means fair and foul and soon. He has hit upon the idea of propagating socialism without spelling out what it means. The idea of socialism is beginning to appeal and it is likely to gain momentum as time goes on unless the administration can be made cleaner and more efficient and economic and social conditions improve. These conditions are stubborn and not susceptible to easy solution.

📖 I was told that Fazlul Qader Chaudhary demands that the recruitment of the armed forces should be on a 50:50 basis from the two wings. At present, East Pakistanis feel that the best part of the defence budget is spent on West Pakistan. This, of course, is true, but there is no escape from it. We are up against an enemy five times our size. We can only face and hold him in check with quality manpower, which lies in West Pakistan and there too in a few northern districts. It is they who have so far successfully defended both East and West Pakistan. God help us if the army gets diluted.

This preponderance of West Pakistanis in the armed forces and especially in the army applies to the rank and file and is regulated, but there is no restriction on entry of the commission ranks from anywhere, subject, of course, to suitability. The trouble here is that such quality manpower is not easily available in East Pakistan and those that may manage to get selected to the academy do not find army life comfortable.

The alternative suggestion is that East Pakistan should be compensated by so much extra development there. I wonder if the country can afford that. Extra resources are just not available unless all development is stopped in West Pakistan, which apart from anything else, would be economically preposterous. The position is now that a good deal of development in East Pakistan is financed by resources developed in West Pakistan. But arguments like this keep on cropping up and in the absence of wider outlook it exacerbates feelings of bitterness and encourages separatist tendencies. The logical solution would seem to lie in having a looser form of relationship than federation between the two wings. In fact, even PDP's eight points amount to that, let alone Mujibur Rahman's six points.

28 | WEDNESDAY

📖 Apparently people like Valika[2] were very badly treated by the martial law over some government land he had taken over. They made him appear before them for weeks, made him wait for 12 hours or more at a time and hurled all sorts of abuse at him. He had to leave the country in desperation. It is only recently that he had returned. Other businessmen feel similarly shaken. Investment is very shy as the entrepreneur is not sure of government policy apart from being a target of abuse by labour, consumer and the government.

29 | THURSDAY

📖 Mahmud Haroon and his wife came to call, he made the following points:

1. The rash of disturbances in the country was likely to grow as time went on and political tension mounted. Holding of elections might well become difficult.
2. There is bound to be bloodshed if the elections are held and even when the civil government comes into power they just won't be able to satisfy the demands of the people or carry out their irresponsible promises. Each party is busy promising the moon.

3. The military are anxious to hold elections, but if the law and order situation deteriorates they will have to take strict measures. I doubt that they will bend backwards to appease the political agitators.

4. It is curious that politicians, who agitated against the 1962 constitution as given by one man, now they are asking the president to resolve all major constituent issues for them.

5. There were some senior military officers who were partial to Bhutto. Now they have cooled off after he has started involving the army in politics.

6. Every politician expects the administration to support him on the plea that if his opponent came into power this, that or the other would happen to the country. This means that none of them is sure of himself.

7. Student community is today the most potent political force. All politicians are depending on them for support, but they have realized their power and are dictating terms.

8. Daultana was rapidly gaining ground in the Punjab, but since his statement on the capital, alliance with G. M. Syed's Sindh Mahaz, his secret tie up with Mujibur Rahman and Wali Khan, he is losing it just as rapidly. That is the trouble with the man lacking character.

9. Sole aim of politicians was to get into power irrespective of what happened to the country or the people. Scruples did not enter into consideration.

10. Asghar is going around saying that he is taking soundings before deciding which party to join. In other words, he is looking for the highest bidder. Speculation is that he will join Mujibur Rahman's Awami Party or a purely provincial and a sectarian party.

11. A fifth general, Adam Khan, has joined politics. These fools are making a laughing stock of themselves, even a half wit like Adam can't resist the temptation.

12. Politically we are in the same mental state as the mourners are on the last of Moharram. They cut themselves with knives and almost want to kill themselves. The whole thing is irrational and after all what good this mourning could do the martyrs. Yet if you ask them to desist, they will not hesitate to kill you. When a man turns into an animal he is worse than a beast.

13. A number of politicians are seeking monetary assistance from foreign powers. This, if true, is highly irresponsible, shameful and dangerous. That is how foreign powers get a hand in the internal politics of the country, manipulating things and bringing about political instability.

The fact of the matter is poor and developing countries like ours can hardly be called free. Our economic and other types of dependence is so great that we are always vulnerable to big power manipulation who disapprove of our politics and policies. And enough people within the country can always be bought as foreign agents. I remember during 1965 presidential election the ambassador of a big power told me openly that they would neither support me nor oppose my election. A clear warning that they had the means to interfere should they wish and if I was not careful. Unprecedented affluence in the advanced countries has brought home the fact to them that in order to dominate backward countries struggling to develop, economic imperialism was far more effective than political imperialism. The thawing of the cold war has further reduced the value of the developing countries in the eyes of the advanced countries as their room for manoeuvre has been reduced to next to nothing. It is a humiliating situation to find ourselves in to say the least. But what is the escape? It will be a long way coming.

14. Sindhis, he said, were politically most unreliable. They have been known to have gone back on their signed pledges on the Quran. It happened with Sir Hidayatullah[3] on one occasion. They

pledged support to him one night and went back on it the next day. His government fell. Real reason is that they can't live without power. They will do anything to gain it. Bhutto is no exception, but he will be faced with a tough fight in his home area. There is a man with religious following and is determined to oppose him.

31 | SATURDAY

General Musa's brother has been fined rupees 4 lakh by a military court for allegedly taking advances from a cooperative bank of which he is a director. He was told to produce the money within 24 hours. Later it was extended to one month, poor Musa is in a fix. For one, his brother has been singled out for victimization when so many others have done much worse things to the cooperatives banks, and secondly, he wanted more time to be able to raise the amount. He tried to get in touch with the president's and General Hamid's staff. They refused even to talk to him. Musa was advised by a friend to keep his dignity and put up with the adversity manfully.

A Pakistani returning from abroad after a long stay gathered [...] from foreigners there:

1. Yahya is giving a long rope to the politicians, purposefully. He has promised elections, freedom of political activity and is keeping on the right side of them in the hope that if they manage to frame a constitution they will keep him as a president.
2. If the politicians fail to frame the constitution, he will keep on ruling as a martial law administrator.
3. It is a mistake to bring back democracy. It just won't work. Even repeated elections are no answer, more and more extremist elements will get elected.
4. In a democracy they see no hope for the future of Pakistan unless Mujibur Rahman turns out to be capable of running the country. This, of course, is a misconception. Mujibur Rahman is a pure and simple agitator. He has no brains, no administrative acumen, is unreliable, impulsive and emotional. He is a wrecker not a builder. Besides, his loyalty to Pakistan is extremely doubtful.
5. The foreigners wonder how did my government collapse. I explained the circumstances and difficulties.
6. The Americans had a hand in my downfall. They would like to see a weak Pakistan, run by a weak man. So they spent a lot of money fanning last year's agitation.
7. They were not certain where the power lies. Is it in the hands of General Peerzada, General Hamid or General Gul Hassan, or is it a collective leadership? The president does not seem to be a free agent.

1 | SUNDAY

Heard this morning that Nur Khan had resigned and was replaced by General Attiqur Rehman[4] as governor of West Pakistan. The exact cause of Nur Khan's departure is not known, but there were hot rumours for some time that General Yahya and he did not get on well as they did not see eye to eye on many points. Nur Khan's ability to maintain law and order was doubted. His lax attitude towards labour and students was suspect. It is doubtful whether it is true, but he was regarded as over ambitious and having designs of supplanting General Yahya. Now that he is retired I hope he does not make an ass of himself as some of our retired generals and Asghar have done by joining politics and acting as a politician of lower repute. How they tolerate their association surpasses comprehension.

2 | MONDAY

Today's news indicated that Muslim League meeting in Lahore was disturbed by students and the PDP meeting in Dacca was brick batted and the leaders molested. Nurul Amin had to run for his life. Maulvi Farid Ahmed[5] was beaten up. It seems that this is going to be the pattern of political activity in future, martial law is ignored, respect for law and order has gone, even the so-called leaders have no restraining influence, the student community is particularly out of control, in recent union elections the students in Lahore University beat up the place good and proper, the vice chancellor's house was ransacked and doors, windows and other fittings were smashed in many other buildings. Lawlessness has become the order of the day amongst the so-called educated people. Very soon it will seep downwards. Labour and low grade employees are already infected.

3 | TUESDAY

I am putting down a concise version of Mujib's Six Points:[6]

1. Federal form of government on the basis of Lahore resolution of 1940.
2. Federal government to deal with only defence and foreign affairs.
3. Separate fiscal and monetary policy.
4. Federal government to have no tax levying authority.
5. Separate external trade account for each federal state.
6. States to have constitutional authority to maintain paramilitary or territorial forces.

These terms, if agreed to, can only mean a very loose form of confederation verging on separation. Most Bengalis, including the moderates, feel the same way, though they pretend not to agree whole heartedly but the general approach is to retain what they have and get whatever they can from West Pakistan. This seems to be their definition of provincial autonomy. They will press this hard knowing that West Pakistan is in no position to bargain as it is a house divided against itself, and they might well get away with it to hasten to their doom and then to the doom of West Pakistan. Indian planners must be laughing up their sleeves and waiting gleefully for exploiting many situations that will present themselves. The clever ones amongst them must also be advocating a policy of luring Pakistan into a false sense of security even by making minor concessions here and there so as to hasten the process of disintegration.

📖 The Nawab of Kalabagh, when governor, also said to me that sooner or later Bengal is going to separate, but under no circumstances must this come from you. He was a shrewd and farsighted man, an uncanny judge of events.

4 | WEDNESDAY

📖 I am told that President Yahya at times puts some young women in his car and goes around the city unescorted at night. It is an irony that whilst he does that some officers are being thrown out of service because of alleged loose character.

📖 Mr Daultana is on a tour of the Frontier districts. Yesterday he addressed a public meeting in Dera Ismail Khan in which he was heckled, but besides that he denounced Mujibur Rahman's Six Points. I was amused as the same Mr Daultana supported Mujibur Rahman's Six Points demand vehemently at the round table conference meeting. I pity this man. He has lots of qualities and would have gone a long way in life if only he had some principles, scruples and character. Someone described him once as a man devoid of soul.

8 | SUNDAY

📖 Khawaja Shahabuddin turned up. The official policy, according to him, was to support Bhashani against Mujibur Rahman in East Pakistan, the latter being regarded as more dangerous. This was a mistaken notion. The reality is that Bhashani and his associates are preparing the province for a communist revolution. Through occasional peasant rallies and long marches they are getting the rural population involved. There will be hell to pay if they are launched on countrywide agitation for which they are being prepared.

📖 I understand that Air Marshal Nur Khan's exit from the governorship finally came over his inability to control ill discipline and lawlessness in the Punjab University campus. On the president's remonstration over this, he submitted his resignation complaining that he could no longer work with him. The president apparently was anxiously awaiting such an opportunity. He promptly accepted the resignation. Somebody said it was a cheap riddance. I personally feel sorry for him. Though impetuous, hasty, over ambitious and perhaps immature and unsocial, he was a man of considerable merit in many other ways. He was courageous, full of initiative and a go-getter. His trouble, I think, lay in that, in these troubled times, he was in too much of a haste to make his mark. He in fact tried to go beyond his ceiling. People who do that often come a cropper.

12 | THURSDAY

📖 Qayyum Khan has been romping up and down the country abusing all and sundry. Somebody said that he is an awful coward. He would not do such a thing unless assured of official support. The thinking is that he is being built up by the administration against Daultana and Bhashani and Mujib. Nothing could be a more dangerous thing to do if true. Both these fellows are most unreliable and unscrupulous. They will have no hesitation in turning against their benefactors, if they get half a chance. Qayyum will sell the country down the drain if it brings him any benefit at all. During the 1965 war with India he returned from Europe via Kabul. Someone said that he offered his services to India, heaven forbid, should she be able to over-run Pakistan. It may sound far fetched, but I would not put anything beyond Qayyum.

📖 Sheikh Mujib may be exploiting parochialism but its causes are probably much deeper. The Bengalis have a long, long history of exploitation by outsiders. Their hot and humid climate puts them at a physical disadvantage and the marshy nature of terrain with poor communications make them exclusive, mother-attached and inward looking. No wonder they are secretive, unsocial and unpredictable. It is not easy to tell what is in their minds. So they are not an easy people to get to know. Though there are some exceptions too, time may change all this, but that is a long way away. Meanwhile, we must be realistic and accept things as they are and have a constitution that enables disparate people to live in the same country. In other words, instead of seeking unity we should live content with some measure of unification as a start. While saying this, I don't mean to imply that West Pakistanis are angels; they too are badly divided amongst themselves and local prejudices are acute and they are being fanned day and night by politicians. Being petty and selfish, the politicians are busy cutting the country into pieces of sizes in which they can fit in.

15 | SUNDAY

📖 Mahmud Haroon came over in the evening, he has just returned from East Pakistan. He was concerned about the food situation. Anyway, he was also deeply concerned about the political situation. Said that Mujibur Rahman has become a legend and spearhead of Bengali nationalism. He draws large crowds in his meetings, most of them just come to see him and then go. Not being a good orator, he can't hold the crowd. The answer, he said, lay in good people getting together, especially in West Pakistan to counter him etc. The usual sermon one or the other hears in this country which amounts to nothing but wishful thinking. If good people mean the celebrated political leaders then they will do such things as suit them personally. They are not going to be motivated by the well being of the people or of the country. If they were capable of doing that, why would we have been in such a mess. I said, accept the fact that Mujibur Rahman would come in with big majority and would also be able to buy people in West Pakistan and have a plan ready to meet that situation. His constitutional demands are going to be of the extreme nature as he has to constantly keep in view the following provincial elections, which he must win to keep a hold on the province, his real base. If Mujib succeeds in doing that, Yahya will be in no position to refuse certification of a constitution, however unreasonable or unjust to West Pakistan. He will be forced to hand over power to Mujibur Rahman and the like.

17 | TUESDAY

📖 There is general consensus that officialdom in East Pakistan is fully behind Mujibur Rahman's demands. So there is no question of their remaining neutral in the coming elections. Also, they are not seeking immediate separation. That may come later after the province is well-developed and they have, substantial share in the armed forces. In fact, they would like separation to come through the hands of West Pakistan by driving them to extreme frustration and desperation, by making impossible and unreasonable demands.

20 | FRIDAY

📖 I see Suleri has become the editor of an English daily called the *New Times* freshly started from Rawalpindi. Though an opportunist of the first order and a thoroughly unreliable and ungrateful man, he writes well. He has written a couple of articles about the real intentions of Mujibur Rahman as a result of his recent visit to East Pakistan. It is becoming crystal clear to even East Pakistanis that by emphasizing economic aspects all the time, he is concealing his real intention, which is political, that is separation.

📖 Malik Qasim came to call. He had been on a visit to East Pakistan. Said that Fazlul Qader was quite active and has started holding meetings and taking out processions. He said he was been intimidated by Qizilbash to share power with Qayyum Khan's party in the name of Yahya. Even military intelligence tried to browbeat him to submit to Qayyum Khan. Fazlul Qader Chaudhary reacted strongly and complained to Yahya through General Sher Ali and even threatened to divulge this in the press. Therefore, Yahya reacted and said that he was only interested in amalgamation of the Leagues and nothing else.

24 | TUESDAY

📖 General Khalid Sheikh (retired), who was chairman of Capital Development Authority and is now on leave pending retirement, came over in the evening. He looked dejected, gloomy and pessimistic, made the following points:

1. Fourth Plan—out of allocation of 5,000 crores, the Bengalis demand 3300 crores exclusive of flood control leaving 1800 crores to West Pakistan inclusive of expenditure on Tarbela. All the facts and figures produced from the Bengali angle are passed on to the press and even to Mujibur Rahman, who utilizes them to the full. The West Pakistan point of view gets no publicity. West Pakistani ministers do not work as a team and none of them is a man of any caliber. Justice Cornelius pretends to be holier than the Pope, but is basically a fraud. General Sher Ali is a superficial bombast and talks a lot of nonsense, especially against me. Qizilbash takes great pride in doing the least amount of work. How people like Sher Ali were selected passes comprehension, perhaps for their anti-Ayub feeling.

2. The officials, General Khalid said, were completely demoralized. They were frightened to death of taking decisions for fear of being accused of all sorts of things. A large number of those who

were suspended had not yet received their charge sheets. In fact, framing charges and hunt for material was undertaken after suspensions. Then he gave me a copy of a foreign report by the *Economist* in which there is an article entitled, 'The Pakistan Purge Act I'. This related to the suspension of 303 officers as a measure of cleaning the administration under pressure from young army officers. Phase II, he said, will be action against members of my family, ministers etc. for which the pressure was building up. He said it would be to the credit of Yahya that he has still restricted such pressure, but chances were that he might resort to taking such action as a diversionary measure should the political and economic situation deteriorate in the country.

3. Islamabad. General Khalid Sheikh said that work was coming to a halt. In fact, Bengalis in the secretariat were obstructing everything.

4. Yahya. He said Yahya spent most of his time in orgies and drinking and womanizing. Sometimes openly in places like Karachi beaches. The whole country is beginning to know that as most of the time was spent in recovery from these excesses he had hardly any time to attend to affairs of the state. The burden, therefore, falls on General Peerzada who passed it on to his two brigadier assistants and then to the officers below. For instance all the work connected with the action against the 303 civilians was handled by a lieutenant colonel. Also, it would not be wrong to say that the country was being run by the Standard Bank of the Alvi brothers. The two Alvi brothers had great influence over Yahya and so had these women in Pindi. All this was very disturbing.

5. Foreign policy. People felt that there was undue leaning towards Iran. Turkey was being neglected.

6. The army. General Hamid was a nonentity. He gets soaked every day. None of the generals commands any respect or following. The middling officers do not hesitate to express such views. The talk of take over by colonels was not uncommon.

7. He was depressed and emotionally upset. He was looking for a job in Saudi Arabia. He would like to go out of the country.

8. Constitution. The only answer was West Pakistan to determine the type of centre required and then ask East Pakistan to what extent they would like to go along with that. I told him that I had exactly the same view. The trouble is that such a plan could only be formulated around a Punjabi and unfortunately there was no one of such stature in the Punjab today. Lack of effective leadership in the Punjab is the misfortune of West Pakistan.

📖 I am told that Pir of Dewal, having exploited my name for so long and amassing so much wealth by skillfully duping people, now talks against me in an attempt to rehabilitate himself. For some time past he had been losing ground as people discovered that he was a skillful fraud. His problems also arose out of mixing the profession of *piri* with politics. These people do not realize that *pirism* and politics do not make a good mixture. Politics ruins a good and lucrative profession by making the man controversial.

25 | WEDNESDAY

📖 Dastoor Dara, who is a Parsi and a banker and broker at Karachi Stock Exchange, came to call. He said that West Pakistan shares were appreciating and that of East Pakistan going down. Politics, of course, was bad but then it would always be bad. People were now realizing what a blunder they had made. Politicians were threatening nationalization. They might be able to nationalize insurance, but nothing else. They just won't be able to manage it.

27 | FRIDAY

📖 I have seen in the press that G.M. Syed has gone over to Dacca to meet Mujibur Rahman. On arrival at the airport he said that he supported Sheikh Mujibur Rahman's Six Points wholeheartedly. The meaning of that is clear. He would like Sindh to have same sort of extreme autonomy as the Bengalis want. I am not fully conversant with the Syed's political past, but one thing is clear and certain: he has been a major disruptive and an anti-national actor in Sindh.

28 | SATURDAY

📖 I am told that Bhutto has lost favour with Yahya over shouting too loud against Tashkent, Rann of Kutch fighting etc. in an effort to malign me but also dragging the army's name into it too. That is why Bhutto has started attacking General Sher Ali and even Yahya, lately. He is employing his usual tactics of browbeating the government into silence and submission, knowing that they are not likely to react. I am also told that Bhutto has started getting at the younger elements amongst the army officers. If true, his plan looks ahead five to ten years. He knows that even if the elections are held, which he does not want, the leftists are not going to command a majority, not this time. So the elections are not to his or the leftists' liking nor is the framing of the Constitution. He would like to see more confusion and chaos and eventual takeover by young colonels in collusion with him. But even if the elections are held and a constitution framed, his hope is that there will be early breakdown and another army takeover, this time by the younger element with whom he wants to be on good terms. So his moves, though dangerous, are well calculated. I hope the intelligence people are alive to it.

These tactics of Bhutto are not new. Even when he was a minister he took great pains in cultivating people like Yahya, General Akhtar Malik, General Gul Hassan, General Peerzada etc. in the hope of making use of them when the occasion arose. This effort paid dividends as even now these people have a soft corner for him and have gone out of their way to shield him and indeed helped him build himself up politically.

2 | MONDAY

The plot next to my house in Islamabad belongs to the late Nawab of Kalabagh. His sons are building a house there today. Asad, who had killed his father, came to inspect the place. I called him over for a cup of tea. Naturally, I expressed sorrow over the sad incident and inquired about what had happened because the Nawab was a friend and I am interested in the family. Asad's reply was very perfunctory, without much regret. I was astonished but perhaps he was shy of telling much to me. He was tried by a high court judge and acquitted. The provincial government has now gone in for an appeal to the bench. This, Asad said, was done on the behest of Abdullah Khan Rokhri[7] and connivance of Air Marshal Nur Khan who was then the governor. Asad, of course, blamed Doctor Tusi and Noora, their *kardar*, one of the Nawab's trusted servants, for instigating the old man against his sons and creating bad blood in the family. Rokhri's interest, he said, was political. He wanted to eliminate the family as political rivals in Mianwali district from which they all come. Air Marshal Nur Khan, of course, is related to the Nawab and was brought up by his mother.

3 | TUESDAY

Ashiq Batalvi is on a visit again from London. He came to call. This man said that he wanted my assistance in getting the remains of Chaudhry Rehmat Ali, the man who coined the word Pakistan, transferred from Cambridge where he is presently buried, to Lahore. I gave him a letter for Malik Qasim recommending that it was a fit case for support by the Muslim League. Rupees one lakh fifty thousand would probably cover the cost. I hope the League can help. I believe poor Chaudhry Rehmat Ali died in strained financial circumstances after doing so much for the Muslim cause. I wish I had known when in power. I would certainly have asked for the government to bear the cost of transferring his remains to Pakistan as a matter of national honour. If Jamaluddin Afghani's[8] remains could be brought to Kabul by the Afghan government, why couldn't we do the same for Chaudhry Rehmat Ali?

8 | SUNDAY

I had a curious experience today. Two bearded tribesmen from Miranshah, South Waziristan, turned up. One of them started talking in Pashto. The other cut him short suddenly and told me in perfect English that he had something to say in private on a prayer carpet. I was astonished. However, I took him to another room and sat on a prayer carpet beside him. He told me he was the reader of the political agent in Miranshah and was educated in Islamia College, Peshawar. Apart from his work he was deeply engrossed in religion and he had come with a message from his spiritual leader. The time will come when people will demand your return to power. It is your bounden duty to respond to such a call. You must not refuse it under any circumstances. I thanked him for this but did not tell him why I could not accept such a proposal.

When they were departing I offered them some money to defray their expenses. To my surprise one of them expressed vehement refusal. It was the first time I had known a tribesman to refuse money. But my surprise was soon dispelled when the other told him to pipe down and accept the money. The reader reminded me of an occasion in Waziristan operations when he and I, driving in a jeep, got through a tribal ambush unscratched and wonderedat our luck at the end how we escaped death. I do not remember the occasion but it may well have happened. Life, in Waziristan in those days, was constantly in danger.

During my term of office I took special care to ameliorate the economic conditions of tribal belts as most of the crime and aggression there can be traced to poverty. The British, in a hundred years rule, never had unbroken peace there and had to constantly resort to military expeditions lasting for quite some time. But because of the economic and other measures we took in my time there was never any serious trouble in this highly explosive area except in Bajaur where we had to resort to military action because of the Afghan aggression in collusion with the Nawab of Dir. I made the plan myself which luckily proved effective without any serious military effort or action. A task which the experts in the British period used to reckon would require commitment of two divisions was accomplished with a fraction of that and with the least amount of fallout and bitterness and resentment. Lately, there have been several cases of kidnapping by the tribals from the settled districts. This is a sure sign of deteriorating economic conditions. And these two persons admitted frankly that it was their poverty that drove them to indulge in such despicable actions.

12 | SUNDAY

Sir Morrice James,[9] who spent a number of years in Pakistan, is currently the British High Commissioner in Delhi. He is on a visit to Pakistan and came to call on me. Sir Morrice James is a nice and a relaxed man. Talking about the situation in India he said that the split in the Congress was forced by Mrs Indira Gandhi. She now runs a minority government supported by the Akalis,[10] DMK[11] and the communists. She had made large promises in support of the common man which were not matched by action. This, when it was realized this would cause frustration and opposite reaction. In the next elections the fight would be between her and the communists. I was surprised to hear of the communist ascendancy. I thought the Mahasabha and the Jana Sangh were coming up. He said their strength was confined to Hindi-speaking areas. The non-Hindi speakers were very allergic to them and react very strongly against any move on the Jana Sangh's part. The Muslims too shifted their loyalty to the communists in the belief that they might get better protection from them. The communists, though divided, were dedicated people. Their personal integrity was above reproach. Sir Morrice James said that the situation in West Bengal was bad. The communists were on the rampage. Loot, arson and murder were common and the police were helpless and nobody alone deposed against the communists. If things really got bad and the army took over they would put the thing down in no time.

My belief is that provinces may go communist, but not the whole of India for the simple reason that I do not see leadership of all India-stature arising even amongst the communists. Their divisions into pro-Moscow and pro-Peking groups is another inhibiting actor. Above all is the pull and compulsions of Hinduism. No Hindu can shake out of caste and class restrictions however he may perhaps profess to the contrary. I told Sir Morrice James to tell this to the Indians.

As I see it the basic problem of India and Pakistan is centrifugal tendencies. This subcontinent has not known peace and unity except under the British rule. Now that they have gone the age old tendency is reasserting itself. The solution does not lie in British return but for us to learn to live together in our respective countries as civilized nations with the spirit of give and take.

14 | TUESDAY

📖 It was said that Bhutto had fallen out of favour with Yahya and yet he was given an interview one evening and stayed on till 1:00 p.m. at night partaking in the orgy of drinking, singing and dancing. It is obvious that these two are on the same net. They are birds of the same feather. It is also said that visits to Karachi are pleasure trips not working trips. Call and dancing girls provide company.

16 | THURSDAY

📖 I saw in the press that Wali Khan, the Red Shirt leader, whilst giving an interview to a foreign correspondent said that Ayub Khan had imposed martial law in 1958 to prevent his party from demonstrating their loyalty to the Constitution of Pakistan by taking part in the forthcoming elections. To an outsider this explanation may sound plausible, but those who know the truth are well aware that this is a hoax. For one, Ayub Khan did not impose martial law. It was the President, General Iskander Mirza, who did so. And I never heard or said that the attitude of the Red Shirts was a determining actor in the decision he took. Everybody assumes that Red Shirts were anti-Pakistan and nobody ever bothered much about them. He is now assuming self importance, out of all proportion to reality.

Khan Abdul Ghaffar Khan and Wali Khan met me two or three times during the early period of my office. Ghaffar's theme was that one unit should be broken up and the Frontier Province should be left to him and I should take care of the rest of Pakistan. Talk of democracy, he said, was a waste of time. It would never work amongst our people. He also used to complain of the excesses of Khan Abdul Qayyum Khan. I used to tell him that his ideas were archaic. The days of personal rule had gone. In any case, no Pathan has ever ruled the Pakhtoons. How did he expect that they would allow him to do so now? My impression was that he wanted to create another Afghanistan of which he and his family would be the rulers. One thing I noticed that whenever talking anything serious, Ghaffar used to make Wali Khan go out of the room. He did not want him to hear what went on and to be influenced by what I was saying. Whereas my effort used to be to convert Wali Khan who struck me as being more amenable to reason but completely under the thumb of his father. He does not do anything against the old man's wishes whose tenacity, organizing ability, and the ability to influence people's minds is singular. I wish he pursued a bigger and nobler calling instead of purely parochial linguistic and racial obsession. But his trouble is that he lacks education without which broader vision is not possible.

19 | SUNDAY

📖 I had another welcome visitor Mr M.M. Ahmed, the Deputy Chairman, Planning Commission, whom I have been wanting to see for a long time. He looked morose, unhappy and pulled down, indeed a broken man. He said he had been yearning to see me earlier but the things were so unpleasant that he avoided doing so.

M.M. Ahmed is one of the best officers we have and he has done a great job as the head of the Planning Commission. I had complete confidence in him and gave him the fullest support. Normally, he is reticent but today he was yearning to unburden his mind. So I let him talk. He said it was a pleasure to have worked with me and be inspired by my burning patriotism and desperate effort to develop the country, response was compulsive and they worked without let up and with pleasure. Those days were not known before and would never come again. If the people knew what they had lost, they would never forgive themselves for their folly. He was speaking with such sincerity that all this could not have been put on or said to please me, it came from his heart.

I asked him to what extent he, Ghulam Ishaq Khan and Qazi were consulted on economic and administrative matters. He said very little. The president showed inclination to do so but officers around him seemed too strong and invariably had the last say. The focus of power and decision making seemed to lie unused. It did not seem to lie with the president. He was intelligent and grasped the point quickly but was lethargic and had very little knowledge and besides he was reluctant to assume responsibility and take decisions more from fear of his associates than anything else. For instance, disastrous policies like the treatment of the private sector, labour policy and treatment of civil servants etc. were announced against their advice. In any case, they were given very little time to even consider these matters. The education policy was also going to be forced in the same manner, but luckily they were able to persuade more mature suggestions and might come out in a more practical and a reasonable shape. In these matters, Air Marshal Nur Khan had done major harm by forcing ill considered and hasty measures. The president could not resist him.

The fourth plan was in doldrums. The original idea was to defer it till the civilian government was formed. He warned Yahya of the dangers involved there. The momentum of development would be lost and the aid givers, who in any case were not enthusiastic, would completely cool off. As such, the country would find itself in a great predicament. So Yahya agreed to the formulation of the plan.

The Planning Commission's proposal was that the public sector should be of the size of 4,500 crores: 2,500 crores for East and 2,000 for West Pakistan. These figures are including flood control in East and Tarbela Dam in the West. The Bengalis simply refused to look at that. They wanted 3,200 crores exclusively for flood control. This would have left the rest with nothing to share. So there was no decision, but meanwhile he had to go to the consortium meeting and was not even in a position to say that his government had accepted the plan. What sort of hearing would he have got? So for the purpose of bargaining with the aid givers the president reluctantly agreed that the figure of 4,500 crores might be maintained. The aid givers, including the World Bank, he said, had become very cagey. They were not prepared to commit themselves until they were sure of political stability. That was a matter of great concern. Even on a thing like flood control they were non-committal, especially the Americans. The Bengalis had an illusion that the Americans would bail them out even if they separated. Lately, the head of USAID was on a visit to Pakistan. M.M. Ahmed suggested to him that they might provide five lakh tons of wheat for five years, the proceeds of which could be utilized for flood control projects. The man baulked and said that such projects needed international support and should be handled by the World Bank. As regards the internal resources M.M. Ahmed said that East Pakistan produces 30 per cent and West Pakistan 70 per cent, and 800 crores would have had to be transferred to East Pakistan in the programme of 2500 crores.

One of the possible suggestions the Bengalis made was the land revenue up to a certain level be totally abolished in East Pakistan and made good from bigger holdings in the West. At this stage some of the ministers insisted that development of hardly any significance had taken place during the last ten years. On that he burst out and told them what the truth was. He was going to follow that up with a detailed paper, I asked for a copy which he very kindly agreed to provide.

On the future of one unit M.M. Ahmed said that he, Ghulam Ishaq and Qazi were told by the president to produce a paper considering all aspects but before they were ready with the reply, the president announced the break up of the unit without prior consultation with them. Their study had disclosed that the Frontier Province and Balochistan would be in heavy deficit to the extent of nine and eight crores respectively to just run the administration. This did not include development. I told him that now this fateful decision had been taken, the effort should be concentrated on saving the autonomous bodies which take care of economic development of West Pakistan, which is economically and geographically one, irrespective of what the politicians say, from disintegrating. The only answer was to put these subjects in the centre with West Pakistani legislative control in the care of the Planning Commission. These bodies cannot function without scientific and expert coordination and powerful support, a sub-federation could not provide these requisites. He agreed.

He was worried about the falling exports, internal revenue and the neglect of family planning. He said there was not an occasion that I did not touch on this subject and warned people of the looming danger. Today, hardly anybody mentions that subject. The experts reckon that at the present growth rate of 3 per cent, our population would rise to 250 million by the turn of the century and the danger of man eating man of which I used to warn about to come to pass.

About the prospects of future constitution he said the Bengalis wanted a built in arrangement whereby they could separate at an appropriate time. City people were by and large with Mujibur Rahman and of his way of thinking, but the rural population thought differently. Even now they talk to me with elation from any rural area. I said it may be so but in the end the opinion of civil servants, lawyers, students etc. would prevail.

He said we were all accused of ignoring social justice, little realizing that a cake had to be formed before cutting and distributing it. He quoted my saying that you can't distribute poverty. He recalled that when discussing the strategy of the fourth plan, I told him that stage had come when we should be paying more attention to the social side and we have taken certain measures to give a fairer deal to the workers.

He said lately he had been feeling ill in health and mind. The specialists examined him and told him that physically he was perfectly all right. His problem was mental. He was probably making policies that were distasteful and against his conscience, which he said was true.

I suppose he felt a bit relieved after unburdening himself but passed on his depression to me. It was so painful to hear all that. All that was built so assiduously for the development and progress of the country is being destroyed. Most of the decisions taken so far have been negative and retrograde.

21 | TUESDAY

📖 Mr Fida Hassan, who was my principal secretary and then advisor, came to call. On my retirement, he too was retired. Then Ahmed Dawood offered him a job in his oil company. On which Dawood was warned by the martial law people that they did not look upon the arrangement with favour. He then saw General Yahya and asked for a job like the general managership of the proposed steel mill. Yahya gave him a hopeful reply but he soon gathered that the military people around him are ill disposed to all those who were close to me. They were accused of having misled me. So he is cooling his heels in Lahore doing nothing.

22 | WEDNESDAY

📖 Mahmud Haroon came in the evening and stayed on to dinner. He said he was deliberatively avoiding to see me. As a member of the cabinet he was disillusioned and dejected with what he had seen, heard and experienced and he did not want to pass on his depression to me who had laboured so hard for this country and had its good at heart. I thanked him for that but did not tell him that I already know enough to sink anybody's heart.

Mahmud said that there were intrigues in the cabinet. Yahya and his military advisors' attitude was uncertain and unrealistic. The Bengalis were thoroughly unreasonable in everything, the civil services were demoralized, the economy was sagging, lawlessness, especially amongst the students and labour community was increasing, the politicians were being thoroughly irresponsible and busy confusing the people and offering the moon. There was competition in extremism. Yahya and his associates did not understand politics. They were do-gooders who thought that they would be able to control the politicians by appeasement. They were specially bending backwards to appease East Pakistanis who had found out that they could get more by pressurization than by doing some work which they would loathe. His impression was, barring the generals who were doing well by rapid promotions, the rest of the officer corps was unhappy at the way things were developing. Recent promotions in the higher ranks had also caused a lot of heart burning. Bhutto was busy selling the theory that only the army could save the country provided they use him as the front man.

Fazlul Qader Chaudhary, he said, was doing well and had proved an effective counter to Bhutto. There was a possibility of getting the three factions of the League together but Qayyum has set his mind against it. He was being backed by Qizilbash and Yahya. That was known to the politicians. They had therefore a readymade excuse to attack the establishment openly which was always a popular theme with the people. In fact, that process had already started. General Sher Ali was being attacked openly and General Yahya in an indirect manner, that trend would gain momentum.

27 | MONDAY

📖 A peasants rally was held in Toba Tek Singh under the chairmanship of Bhashani. Representatives from all over West Pakistan and some from the East [Pakistan] attended. Bhashani spoke in his usual strain advocating communism but under the garb of so called Islamic Socialism. He put forward certain demands combined with the threat that if not accepted he would launch guerrilla warfare in the country. Several of his lieutenants also spoke. Amongst them, Mr Mosib-ur-Rehman, who made a frontal attack on the president and called him a traitor alleging that the promise of elections was a hoax meant to make the politicians fight so that he had an excuse to retain power indefinitely. He is also supposed to have said that the president's house was a brothel and the president ran it. In consequence, Mosib-ur-Rehman has been arrested and charged under certain martial law regulations.

28 | TUESDAY

📖 Altaf Gauhar came to see me today and stayed on for lunch. The poor man has gone through terrible mental torture. He was given a charge sheet after 93 days of suspension. They obviously wanted to break his nerves by keeping him in suspense. Apparently the charge sheet was a lengthy one but not one concrete instance was quoted. His reply in defence consisted of 200 pages. But I don't suppose it matters how convincing his reply is. They are determined to do the worst to him. This will be a terrible injustice. An extremely valuable man is being sacrificed to satisfy sadistic, morbid impulse which comes mostly from General Peerzada though I know that many others were also terribly jealous of him. Another man who might well be playing a major role in this sordid affair is Ghiasuddin,[12] the defence secretary. He is a characterless skunk good for nothing but a great intriguer and a confidant of General Yahya. Razvi,[13] the Director Intelligence Bureau, and General Akbar, Director of Intelligence of the army, are also ill-disposed as is General Peerzada towards Altaf Gauhar.

📖 In a broadcast and telecast speech this evening on constitutional and other matters, the president made the following points:

1. The National Assembly to have 313 including 13 for women seats.
2. Provincial polls by 22nd October, in other words, within a fortnight of central polls. Denial of dual membership has not yet been mentioned.
3. Pakistan to be a Federal Islamic Republic.
4. West wing to revert to pre-one unit position by 1st July.
5. Maximum provincial autonomy.
6. Lay down certain guidelines for constitution making.
7. Legal Framework Order[14] for the operation of the assembly to be issued.
8. Also warned the politicians to desist from creating law and order situation.

These are wise steps. I hope and pray they prove fruitful. I am doubtful however after the warning given to the politicians. Having given them long rein for so long and allowed them familiarity it would be very difficult to bring them back to heel. People like Bhutto, Bhashani, Mujibur Rahman etc. are not the sort of people who take broad hints.

30 | THURSDAY

📖 The Legal Framework Order issued today lays down allocation of seats to East and West Pakistan in the National Assembly and the number of seats in the East Provincial Assembly, creates four provinces in West Pakistan, lays down fundamental principles for constitution making and prescribes rules of procedure for the working of the National Assembly. Prohibits double membership and keeps the power of authentication in the hands of the president without which the constitution will not be effected. Presumably, the Constitution will be only agreed to if it lies within four walls of the fundamental principles. This is good as far as it goes provided that it works and the extremists, especially from East Pakistan, cooperate. My fear is that if they find it going against their whims they might well walk out of the assembly. However, there are a couple of major checks against that. Fear of fresh elections after 120 days and pressure from the elected provincial assembly members who would be cooling their heels until the Constitution is framed, are anxious that it should be completed quickly.

31 | FRIDAY

📖 Manzur Qadir had rung me up last night recommending that I might give an interview to Hamid Nizami,[15] editor of a paper called *Nawa-e-Waqt*, which issues from Lahore. Nizami had agreed to publish true facts about so many distorted statements that are made about me from time to time. Normally, I avoid pressmen and I had more reason to avoid Nizami who had always operated against me, but on Manzur's insistence I agreed to see him. He came in the evening. He questioned me mostly on Bhutto's statements. I apprised him on the facts of each case, the Tashkent declaration, fighting in the Rann of Kutch and its limited objective, the reason why I visited Baltistan in 1962 as I had to undertake this journey to see whether the strategic road to Sinkiang border was feasible over the Khunjerab, why an attack on India in 1962 would have been disastrous, how I told Bhutto in February 1966 in his house in Larkana to leave the cabinet sometime in July as I could not carry him anymore. His talk of having resigned so many times is nonsense. His character failings and how he was suspected in every capital and so on. I told Nizami to make use of this information without quoting me as in that case I would have to come out in the open myself. I am told that Bhutto has turned into a real demagogue. He talks of things that appeal to the common man, indulges in dramatics and follows Hitler and Mussolini in their stage behaviour. They, of course, used to spellbind the audience, make the hair stand and blood boil and work them up to a frenzy.

1 | WEDNESDAY

📖 It has been announced today that Major General Rehman Gul, Major General Riaz and Major General Azhar have been promoted to Lieutenant General and appointed as governors to the new provinces of Sindh, Balochistan and Frontier respectively. Lieutenant General Attiqur Rehman will stay in the Punjab.[16]

2 | THURSDAY

📖 Bhashani and Mujibur Rahman of Awami League have commented adversely on the Legal Framework Order issued by the president. The former demands prior settlement of the guarantee of provincial autonomy and representation as the basis of occupation, in other words workers and peasants rule. The latter objects to Section 25 and 27 of the order as being undemocratic and totally unacceptable. One relates to retention of power of authentication of the constitution by the president in his own hands and the other relates to amendments in addition to the rules of procedure for the assembly to be done only by the president. Awami Leaguers have gone on to say that unless those amendments were made, they would find it difficult to take part in the elections. There is also an adverse comment by one of their members on the guiding principle laid down by the president as being undemocratic, impinging the sovereignty of the assembly.

These are opening shots of dissension calculated to maintain an air of agitation alive in the province in support of the Six Points and Eleven Points[17] programmes. So any thought of these people being reasonable or helpful in framing the constitution would be illusionary.

6 | MONDAY

📖 I see that M.M. Ahmed, the Deputy Chairman of the Planning Commission is being criticized in East Pakistan for saying that sluggish growth rate there was due to neglect of agriculture and the private sector, which of course is true and known to all. Similarly, Mujibur Rahman has criticized the finance minister for saying that there must be, reason for the flight of capital from East Pakistan, which would be looked at. Even Governor Ahsan, who is a very sober man, has lamented lack of fresh investment in business, commerce, industry and bad labour-management relationship leading to reduction in employment and production. All those friendly and sound advices are being taken as a slur in East Pakistan and instead of accepting and rectifying the shortcomings, solution is sought to give the whole matter a political turn and indulge in blackmailing tactics. How unfortunate these people are. They do not want to help themselves and would not allow others to help them.

📖 Last night, I had severe burning sensation in my chest on both sides. I sent for the specialist the next morning. On check-up it was found that I had slight coronary disorder, a lack of blood supply as they call it. He told me to take rest which I did. In consequence, I am feeling much better.

8 | WEDNESDAY

I see that Mujib is getting louder and bolder in his protest and demands. He has almost threatened that unless Articles 25 and 27 of the Legal Framework Order issued by the president is suitably amended and the assembly made completely sovereign, his party might boycott the elections and launch a movement in favour of the Six Point programme. This could be due to the fear that he may not get the sort of majority expected in the coming elections and the guiding principles laid down for constitution making may not allow acceptance of the Six Points or that East Pakistan would not be allowed to use its brute majority to impose a constitution of its choice. The basic thing is that he does not want to take a position of reasonableness or otherwise, perhaps through fear of Bhashani who is already outbidding him. So the prospect of holding elections are not bright, much less for constitution making. The politicians are shouting hoarse for restoration of democracy and yet they are doing mighty little to help in framing a constitution. If they were honest, patriotic and sincere why could they not get together and come to some sort of a settlement on the remaining points of the constitution as a number of important issues have already been settled by the president.

10 | FRIDAY

About the president, Col. Mohiuddin said Yahya was putting on a lot of weight through excessive drinking and keeping late hours with women. He certainly knows how to relax. In Karachi and Dacca Commander Saeed was responsible for laying on relaxation arrangements. In those two places every night was a gala night. In consequence, he does very little work and is completely in the hands of General Peerzada who talks to him as an equal. He rarely heard General Peerzada address him as 'Sir' on occasion of binges. Col. Mohiuddin deliberately kept away to retain what little respect he had for the man. He said even otherwise it was morally disagreeable to be near him. It amounted to killing one's conscience but what was one to do, duty was duty and had to be done.

In an attempt to persuade the president to reduce his weight, he had to tactfully question him on his eating, drinking and sleeping habits. He said most of his replies were evasive and false, that was the way with alcoholics. They felt no shame in telling lies. That reminds me of the story often told of Emperor Jehangir that he was in the habit of making fabulous promises to people when under the influence of liquor. When asked for fulfilment later he would tell that what fools they were to rely on the promise of a drunken man.

15 | WEDNESDAY

Last few days have been rotten for me. I am all right otherwise but when the pain comes on in the chest it is excruciating. Even the pills do not have much effect. So they have started giving me pethidine[18] injections. In the beginning they too were temporarily effective but now they do suppress the pain as well as make me relax and induce sleep. The pain, they say, is due to narrowing down of a minor blood vessel around the heart preventing free blood flow causing lack of oxygen and pain. They say so far it has caused no serious damage in the functioning of the heart.

16 | THURSDAY

📖 Fazlul Qader Chaudhary said that Yahya's agents like Razvi, the Director Intelligence Bureau, keep on pestering him on behalf of Qayyum Khan and Yahya's brother, Mohammad Ali, is openly canvassing for Qayyum Khan in Lahore. It was very difficult to fathom Yahya. When you met him he said one thing, whilst in practice he did exactly the opposite.

19 | SUNDAY

📖 Agha Mohammad Ali, Deputy Inspector General IB (Intelligence Bureau), the elder brother of General Yahya came to look me up. He showed concern for my health and prayed for my early recovery. He kissed my hands and feet and said that they would always be well-wishers and admirers. Our masses, he said, were foolish and bad. They did not recognize their well-wishers and were easily misled. I thanked him and wished his brother well in discharging his heavy duties and responsibilities. However, he seemed in a hurry to leave. Mohammad Ali, though a policeman, is a sincere and straight man and probably one of the impeccable characters. He is so much different to his brother.

He was followed by General Hamid who has recently returned from a visit to Algeria and Morocco. Both the countries, he said, were developing and are well-off but Algeria has a great future. It is full of oil, gas and mineral wealth. They are short of trained manpower but it was only a matter of time before they made good that deficiency. They were also following sound political and economic policies.

Hamid was pessimistic about the future of politics of the country. On October 5, elections had to be gone through but he did not see any chance of political stability emerging. Politicians were so divided and showed no inclination to get together, agree on a common programme and reduce the number of parties. In that case, I said, breakdown is inevitable and wisdom dictated that they have a contingency plan ready. In the event of another breakdown it is not inconceivable that so-called colonels may jump the gun over the heads of the generals who would have demonstrated their inability to save the country. I also told him that too much patronization with the political *goondas* would do them no good. Bhutto, for instance, is supposed to have spent five hours with the president the other evening. It is known all over, and does the president have so much time to waste? Why does he not spend some of it in seeing good people? On the type of centre, I told Hamid that requirements of East and West Pakistan were different. They must be careful to see that in appeasing East Pakistan they do not destroy West Pakistan as well. He saw my point, but how much say in these matters he has is not known. Our real problem unfortunately is lack of national aim, national leadership, limited resources, growing population, unemployment and lack of realization of these acts together with absence of social organizations to deal with them. Planning and resolving them requires practical approach not theorization in abstract as we are so prone to indulge in.

20 | MONDAY

📖 I have just finished reading a book called *Through the Crisis* written by S.M. Zafar who was law minister in my cabinet. The first portion relates to sequence of events as known to him. He laments or criticizes my declaration that I would not be a candidate for the next presidential elections. This, he thinks, did a lot of harm. He blissfully considers that if I had not done so, I would have retained my influence on the assembly which would have passed the two concessions later promised, on which there was a consensus, i.e., direct elections and parliamentary form of government. And the constitution would have been saved. For one, none of this would have happened. Knowing that in a parliamentary system, my re-election as president would be uncertain, and in any case what power the president has under that system? Most of our members would have defected and ceased to be answerable to party discipline. And secondly, once these two measures were even tabled and talked about all other hydra-headed motions like the breakup of one unit, doing away with parity, Six Points etc. would have been pushed, as they were, irrespective of what I did. The assembly would have turned into a mad house and the members would have been guided by the mobs in the streets, threatening blue murder and threatening to set the country ablaze. No, the reasons why I made that declaration was that, for one, the agitation was directed against me. I could only stay there by force, which constitutionally was not easy. Secondly, I hope that I might be able to save the presidential system and the constitution with some amendments by getting out of the way of the opposition and allaying their fears that they had not wanted to compete with me. The fact that the plan did not work does not mean that it was devoid of merit. In fact, the events would have been no different even if I had not made that declaration. The opposition would have become more desperate, and law and order would have deteriorated still further.

Then there were other reasons. I have never been an unwilling man and I loathe to stay in a position where I am not wanted. I did not mind the howling of the opposition. After all, it had been going on for the last ten years, but when some people also joined them and rejected my programme for their betterment, I thought they had the right to look for leadership elsewhere. I hope and pray that they find it, though I have my grave doubts.

Then Mr Zafar analyses our people's psychology. He says that collectively they are more for spiritual, moral value and economic and social justice than for material betterment. There is a great deal of truth in that. I have often said that an average man in Pakistan may be the greatest sinner himself yet he expects his leader to be brave, wise and saintly. These are high specifications and do not come by or be found combined in a personality. That is our dilemma and that is why I fear our history will remain chequered. Our people resent injustice whether social, economic and quite rightly too, or by authority. This consciousness has become acute since independence. Previous to that the history of the masses in the subcontinent was nothing but woes of oppression and suppression by one or the other overlord. Masses were never bothered about the change of rulers. Their plight was the same under all of them.

How to satisfy this just demand is a stubborn problem. Certainly under any form of democratic system because the task is to make people work more so as to be able to give them more justly. Also inculcate honesty and integrity. Our fear is that some sort of regimentation would be unavoidable. The point is, will it come by evolution and common consent or by bloody revolution which very few would like?

It is understandable that our people gave no priority to material advancement, yet this is not realistic. May be that through material well-being we may find solution to other maladies. After all we cannot build spiritual and moral values on empty stomachs. A hungry man is an angry man and therefore irrational. True that you do not live on bread alone but you cannot live without it either. Mr S.M. Zafar ends up with the prayer that for the sake of building a secure, happy and prosperous

Pakistan the political leaders should conduct themselves in this, that or the other manner. These prayers have been offered *ad nauseam* in the past without success. I do not see how they are going to bear fruit in the future. The fact is that our politicians have forgotten and learn nothing. This is our great misfortune. To sum up, Mr S.M. Zafar's attempt is laudable but one would like to see much more frankness and critical appraisal of our weak and strong points like the way Nirad Chaudhuri has done about Hindu society in his book, *Land of Circe*. This is refreshing and instructive to read. But why blame Mr S.M. Zafar. Most of Muslim history is the work of commissioned or paid people therefore either an eulogy or a cover up is effected. Even when written by scholars it is either defensive or an apologia. Critical inquiry and statement of unpleasant truths is absent. Even Ibn Khaldun[19] when writing about controversial religious matters hedges and leaves by stating different points of view without giving his own judgement.

I would like to explain why I keep on harping on harder but organized work to enable us to find our salvation. People seem to think that nationalization is the panacea. That is not true unless it can be made to pay and bring greater profit. Under the present social system the experience has been the reverse, certainly in production of consumer goods where comparison is available with the private sector. The latter is far more efficient and productive.

But even if everything is nationalized and the proceeds equitably distributed our problem is not going to be solved for the simple reason that our total GNP is not enough to meet the present daily requirements of our people, and leave something for capital formation and development. The answer therefore lies in more production in every field especially in agriculture and by adoption of modern methods on countrywide scale. That means organizing the society for collective work and making it work because individual and voluntary effort is not going to take us far. That really is a task to which our politicians and thinkers should be bending their minds and to find a methodology that will work and produce results. Along with higher production methods, a system of fair distribution not only to the workers but to the needy and indigent should also be worked out.

This does mean regimentation but then what else is the answer. But that does not mean that by adopting some such method amounts to giving up Islamic values. If we are sensible, it need not be so. In fact, retention of Islamic values would help to gain the support of the masses who are deeply religious. Along with that, our ideas of democracy will also have to undergo a radical change because the two things seem contradictory. If these things are done, communism can be averted, otherwise it is inevitable without any assurance that it will be a success and there is no knowing what the cost will be in human suffering and in other respects. But either of the systems requires men of great calibre to launch and run which are not in sight. So the so-called socialist of today, who is nothing but a political opportunist and votary of Islam who is stuck in the quagmire of the stagnant past, is no answer. They are rabble-rousers but can't do anything constructive.

21 | TUESDAY

📖 I have gone through pretty hard time during last fortnight or so. I used to get excruciating pains in my chest once or twice a day and at night. But thank God I am feeling better since yesterday. I was able to sleep well last night and had a peaceful day today. My ailment is diagnosed as angina but they tell me that fresh channels of blood supply have opened up around the hardened artery, which happens to be a very small one. This shows that I am not as young as I like to feel.

All my sons came to me this morning. I was pleased to see them. It was after a long time that we all have been together alone. It reminded me of an occasion when my father went to visit a friend in a village close to ours. I and my younger brother accompanied him. On seeing us his friend welcomed us and told my father never to go together with his sons to avoid attracting the evil eye.

22 | WEDNESDAY

📖 [Major] General Rafi came to look me up in the CMH where I have been for a number of days in Rawalpindi. He is now commanding a division in Jhelum. The first thing he said on entering my room was that he hoped the place was not bugged. I said it could not be as I came here at short notice, besides with the air conditioner going on a receiver would not able to pick much. [Major] General Rafi who had been my military secretary tried to reassure me not to worry about what was being said in the press. This happens to most people who leave office etc. In fact, the answer was not to read the papers at all. In any case there was nothing but muck in them. He said my misfortune started with the 1965 war and then my illness and so on. I agreed.

He said the common man was not worried about the constitution as much as rising prices. Things were getting out of his reach. There will be a greater mess if and when the civilian government of the parliamentary type comes. They would be unstable and incapable. And how will they satisfy people's demands let alone fulfil their fabulous promises. They would be thrown out in no time.

He lamented General Peerzada's closeness to Yahya. He said in a place like that wisdom is more important than cleverness and intelligence. That man he said was a bad influence on Yahya. He hinted that General Peerzada had not forgotten his removal from being my military secretary because of his illness.

He said at present the policy seems to be appeasing pressure groups irrespective of the cost. This will work for a while but very soon pressure on the economy will become unbearable with the disastrous consequences. Already the prices have rocketed sky high. The price of dollar, he said, had risen from 8 to 11 rupees in the open market. What the president needed was a man of wisdom, knowledge and strength of character, who could tell him where to stop. General Peerzada is not such a man; he is callous, morbid, and reckless and probably encourages unwise decisions.

📖 It came on the radio last night Mr Daultana has announced that he was neither a candidate for the presidency of his party nor would he accept it if offered because his failing health did not permit him to discharge such an onerous responsibility. True that he does not look too well and looks very much pulled down and so he may be genuine in his statement. On the other hand people like Shaukat Hayat, who is blindly ambitious, may have caused difficulties for him. In any case Daultana's fading out will upset the political balance in the Punjab and on the all Pakistan level may help Qayyum who has the backing of Yahya. But Qayyum Khan is no chicken either. He is over 70, suffers from diabetes and blood pressure. Another six months of campaigning is not going to do him any good.

📖 General Wajid Ali Burki[20] has been visiting me in the hospital regularly except for the last couple of days. He said he attended receptions in the president's house and then at the Chief of Staff's House. The guests were mostly generals and he said he never saw so many before. Most of them were youngsters whom he did·not recognize. There have been, of course, a lot of promotions lately and the army too has enlarged. Yahya spoke to him for a while and said that his endeavour was to see that socialists do not come in. If that is so, then what is the meaning of fraternization with Bhutto. He also said that he tried very hard to get all the Leaguers together, but failed.

27 | MONDAY

📖 We talk about democracy and government by the chosen representatives of the people, etc., and that is how it should be, if we had two or the most three solid parties. In our case on the contrary we have dozens of them, over three dozen, possibly or more. The reason is simple; in our case allegiance is predominantly personal—likely winner or the man likely to come into power. Principles are seldom involved and party labels, barring one or two exceptions, are meaningless. Moreover, the politicians themselves shift positions. Tags are interchangeable. Such being the case how can we help to run a stable government under the parliamentary system.

30 | THURSDAY

📖 I am sometimes accused by some of my opponents to have encouraged the communists during my regime. This is a white lie and travesty of truth. What had I to gain by such action? In fact, on the contrary I tried to do all I could to curb and arrest the spread of communism. That was the reason why Progressive Papers Limited,[21] that was the mouth piece of communism and were spreading poison day and night, were taken over and turned into a national trust and I kept on pressing that they be purged of communists, a task which proved stubborn because of the legal inhibitions. In any case, I was much too busy with other pressing problems to attend to this matter. Anyhow, these people were kept under control during my time but now that they have been given free rein they have raised their heads again and are engaged in their nefarious activities with full force. They and the communists throughout the country are keeping themselves in the public eye and awaiting an opportunity when they can exploit a popular complaint. In East Pakistan such an opportunity might well arise from June onwards when shortage of food is felt even in good years, let alone in a year like this when there is shortage of two million tons of food. True, the government is doing its best to make good the deficit but distribution is always a problem there.

📖 Strikes have become a curse in Pakistan. There is no profession in which there has been no strike or has not threatened to go on strike. Even the professions like teaching, medicine and engineering are not free from it. Someone has aptly described Pakistan as 'Strikistan'. These are signs of economic strains and stresses and a general lack of discipline, but above all, loss of prestige by the administration and authority, social changes and economic development etc. on the curves, but they have a long gestation period and politics does not wait for them.

It is a common practice in eastern countries to hound and gun for the man who leaves office. His mail is censored, telephone is tapped, he is followed and watched and such other pleasantries are visited on him in a furious belief that he was bound to be hatching some sort of conspiracy or counter revolution.

2 | SATURDAY

As arranged, General Ayub the Director General, Medical Services, Col. Shaukat Syed from Karachi and Dr Nasir from Peshawar came to examine me in the CMH Rawalpindi. They are both heart specialists of repute. Their finding was that I suffer from a special type of angina which comes on after meals and when resting. Though irritating, it was not dangerous so far, but it would take time to wear off. Meanwhile, the answer was to rest and take it easy.

It is curious but true that my illness in life has been prolonged and chronic. In consequence, I have suffered a lot. As a youngster, I got malaria, which lasted for about nine months. Round about 1922, I got nasal congestion, which is still with me despite several nasal and throat operations. It is probably due to some allergy. Then in 1951, I had an appendix operation, which lasted for nearly three hours as it happened to be deep down near the kidney. This affected my system to such an extent that I used to get slight fever for several years after. My nervous system was also affected, which interfered with my sleep and gave me constant discomfort and headache. I suffer from it even now. Then I had a heart attack from two years back accompanied by blockage of urine and blood clots in the lungs. Recovery took a long time and I have never been free from some sensations in the chest since. The present angina, which the experts say might well be chronic, is the prolongation of it.

In other walks of life too, whenever there has been any serious trouble, by some curious turn of fate, I have found myself in the middle of it. All attempts to avoid such situations prove of no avail. In consequence, I have been praised sky high and at times slandered mercilessly. So somehow my good and misfortunes have been of the extreme though in all conscience my intentions and performance have been no different in either of these circumstances and yet the reaction from the people varied. Therefore, I developed a philosophy from early on in life. I was never unduly elated by praise in fear that the opposite is probably around the corner. It does not take human beings long to change their minds. Fickleness of the human mind is proverbial.

3 | SUNDAY

Mian Bashir, the Inspector General of Police, who is retiring on pension, came to see me in hospital. He is very emotional but an outspoken, patriotic and tough little man. I have known him for a long time and have helped him whenever in trouble, which was quite often. He cried on seeing me, kissed my hands and feet. He said that whatever the people of this country had done they had not harmed me but had harmed the country and themselves. Pakistan's name which I had taken sky high was now in the dust. The world had lost all respect for us since my departure. Foreign dignitaries used to feel flattered to be received by me. Men like Eisenhower used to embrace me. Today our so-called leaders were taken for granted and used as stooges. He was very glad that he was leaving service as he felt disgusted in serving men who were no better than him. How could one have any respect for them?

About law and order, Bashir said it could be put right in no time but this government had no intention of showing its teeth. They were out to appease political *goondas* and remain on the right side. They keep on saying that their objective was limited to holding elections and handing over power. But handing over to whom? For political chaos and disintegration all those men in the political field were known. They were incapable of keeping the country together let alone running it. The answer

was to deal with about 20 political *goondas* and there would be peace and calm in the country and so on. He wanted to talk more but the doctors stopped him from doing so. So he left. His parting words were that under no circumstances must I leave the country. There were people here who would not hesitate to tear up those who meant any harm to me.

9 | SATURDAY

📖 M.M. Ahmed came to look me up after his return from the RCD meeting in Turkey. He said some useful decisions were taken for future collaboration. It remains to be seen whether they would be implemented. He said the Turks, though slow in making up their minds, are unwavering in implementation once they agree on anything. Whereas you could never be sure of the Iranians. Besides, they expect to be pampered and take offence on slightest excuse. He said every Turk he met inquired about me. They still call me the President. To them Pakistan was Ayub Khan.

11 | MONDAY

📖 I was amused to see in the press today Bhashani saying in a public meeting in Chittagong, the *maulana* made a note of appreciation for the administration of former President Ayub Khan, which earned credit from all over the world. He asked President Yahya to emulate the example of his predecessor in the matter of administration. Instead of putting political elements behind bars, the government should try to root out corruption and bribery, he added.

📖 Col. Mohiuddin who went with the president on an official visit to Turkey and looks after me medically, came to look me up on return. He said wherever Yahya went the Turkish crowd raised the cry of Ayub Khan Zindabad. Large number of Turks made inquiries about me, especially Ismet Pasha[22] who is an old friend of mine. General Yahya, he said, conducted himself well and the Turks too were courteous but they did not show the same warmth as they used to me. I think the reason is that the Turk by nature is cautious and cool. It takes time to win his affection.

13 | WEDNESDAY

📖 I spent the day in my house today. It was a good change but I had several mild recurrences of chest pain.

15 | FRIDAY

📖 An eminent man from Lahore, whose name I have now forgotten, came to see me sometime back and said something which made me stagger. He said on oath that the late Qasim Razvi who was regarded a tiger and hero of Hyderabad Deccan, in his later life took to touting and taking bribes from people for putting in a word with magistrates, etc. I could not believe my ears. If true then the man must either have been very hard up or this was the other facet of his character. His power of leadership and organizational ability and personal courage is very much applauded in Hyderabad. But in reality he was responsible for the ruination of Muslims in Hyderabad Deccan. It was through his lack of realism, stubbornness and short-sightedness that rape of Hyderabad Deccan by the Indian army took place.

17 | SUNDAY

📖 Mr Ghulam Ishaq Khan, the finance secretary, came to call. He had been here once or twice before but was not allowed to see me. He was on the committee that worked on the administrative and financial details of break-up of One Unit. I got the idea that he was pleased with the decision. He said smaller and backward provinces would stand to gain by better supervision. I agreed, provided there was political stability. As I saw it there was some chance of stability on the Frontier and Punjab. Sindh and East Pakistan and especially the centre were doubtful.

18 | MONDAY

📖 I had a rotten day today. I was to leave the hospital this evening and go back home but started having pain in the chest at 1:00 a.m., which lasted till 5 p.m. They had to give me a pethidine injection to control the pain. The doctors have decided that I must stay on in the hospital for a couple of days more, which is a damned nuisance but unavoidable.

21 | THURSDAY

📖 I had another bad day today. Pains in the chest after lunch, then again after dinner. Also pain in the gums, some in the teeth and in the throat. But I still went out to my lands to see the wheat thrashing operation going on. Completion is going to take a long time as there is a lot of wheat. For a farmer it is a thrilling experience to see the produce come in. So it was a good change despite my ailments and pains.

A doctor tried to console me by saying that Insha Allah I would be all right, but being in pain therefore not in the best of moods, I said how long is it going to be stretched, I have been hearing this for the last six weeks without much result?

22 | FRIDAY

📖 More people have confirmed the incident of a Begum falling on Yahya's lap in a selected gathering in Karachi. Then she and her husband getting an interview the next day. I said if I had done one hundredth of such a thing there would have been widespread criticism, especially from the politicians. I was told yes, because I stood in the politician's way whereas so far they think Yahya does not. They are quite content with him debauching as much as he likes so long as they are given the freedom to do what they like.

23 | SATURDAY

📖 I had a bad night again, five or six times doses of pain in the chest which I never had before. Even an injection of pethidine gave only temporary relief. Therefore could not sleep for more than a couple of hours.

📖 M.M. Ahmed came to see me last night. He is fed up with the way the personnel of the Planning Commission are being pushed about in the interest of Bengalization. Most of them are leaving and seeking jobs with the World Bank. He is afraid that he would never be able to get suitable replacements. I told him the only way East Pakistan can have satisfaction is to have its own planning commission. That way they may learn and be able to teach others that on borrowed resources sensible priorities are essential otherwise nobody would support prestigious and non-paying projects like the bridge over the Brahmaputra, nuclear power plant, petrochemical etc., when the province should be spending all the resources it can in bridging the food gap. By having a separate planning commission West Pakistan would also be able to get on with its development without making unnecessary comparisons. In any case West Pakistan needs a separate commission now that there are going to be so many provinces in it, for coordination, if not for other reasons.

24 | SUNDAY

📖 Several people came to see me today, amongst them Malik Qasim. He said Yahya is playing a curious game. Amongst his ministers Qizilbash is supporting Qayyum Khan, Rashid is supporting Wali Khan, Mahmud Haroon is supporting us, Governor Ahsan is hobnobbing with Bhashani and he himself with Bhutto. He seems to be afraid of Daultana. His effort was to replace him with Dr Javid Iqbal[23] but he failed in his endeavour. There is also talk that Asghar Khan is acting under Yahya's instructions. He did not know what the object of this game was. I said the object could be to keep them humoured but divided and make use of them as required. Also keep their mouths shut from criticism.

I believe Daultana said on one occasion that he was regarded as the genie of politicking but Yahya seemed to excel him. I do not think he was very far out. Yahya seems to be the master of the art of deception, giving false impression and concealing his intentions. I do not suppose many people know his mind. People like his brother [Agha Mohammad Ali, Deputy Director Intelligence Bureau], Qizilbash and Razvi, the DIB DG, may know a bit but only a bit. He keeps his cards very close to his chest in order to keep everyone guessing. This, I suppose, is a great asset in politics. Talking as little as possible and not hesitating to mix with any political *goonda* and saying the things that please him without touching the essentials. This may not be the way of leadership but it certainly is the way of keeping the opposition dispersed, confused and divided.

📖 Someone told me I was a simpleton when compared to Yahya and I did not know his methods. That, I think has an element of truth in it. I am not crooked as I am not built that way. Beside, rightly or wrongly I was endeavouring to weld the people of this country as a nation and develop the country. My methods had to be different. Tricks would not have worked. For this type of work different qualities are required.

25 | MONDAY

📖 I had a relatively quite night. The doctors have decided to let me go home this evening. I am hoping and praying that my pain will disappear. I have been in the hospital for seven weeks where I was extremely well looked after. Everybody was so kind and went out of their way to be helpful and make my stay comfortable, but even then hospital life can be very boring.

📖 My son Tahir Ayub took me out for a drive. While he was driving he asked me what the doctors thought about my sickness. I gave him their assessment and told him that though they thought I could go on for a long time. I really had no regret even if I did not. I had led a full life equivalent to about ten people. Very few people held responsibilities of the magnitude I was fortunate enough to hold, travelled so much, met so many leading people in the world and saw so much. I am also thankful to God that he blessed me with a noble wife and well-behaved children with merit. So what more do I want. My only regret is that I belong to a country whose people have not learned the art of living together and making a nation, gaining stability and getting on with the task of reconstruction and development, despite my best efforts, and that is the most that a man can offer. The fact that I did not succeed can either be due to inadequacy or ill timing of my efforts or unwillingness or inability of the people or a combination of all these factors. Time alone will tell where the truth lies.

26 | TUESDAY

📖 My doctors told me to see as few people as possible. In any case, they come and tell me about the affairs of the country. Nobody had good news to tell in Pakistan today. How true it is everyone who comes has sorry tales to tell about the politics, economics or other affairs of the country.

28 | THURSDAY

📖 Begum Jabbar, the wife of the former speaker, and her two sons turned up. She asked me for monetary assistance and my help to get her a license for a textile mill in West Pakistan. It took me some time to convince her that I no longer control party funds or have any say either with the present rulers. She was offered a license of East Pakistan which she was not prepared to accept as no one was prepared to invest money there because of highly uncertain conditions and hostile political attitude to private enterprise and disturbed labour conditions. I advised her to accept the license despite these difficulties as someone may pick up the courage to finance her.

Jabbar Khan has several sons, some from his previous wife, who are very intelligent but all communist and leftist. One of them passed his MA when undergoing a jail sentence. So they are a liability to him except one who is in the Civil Service[24] and is doing well. The younger ones from this wife are also very bright, but look to be going the same way as the others. One of them told me that people in East Pakistan hold no grudge against me. In fact, in many schools and colleges my photographs are prominently displayed. They, however, hold Monem Khan responsible for all the troubles. They thought that there would be so much violence and bloodshed that it would be impossible to hold elections.

1 | MONDAY

📖 Altaf Gauhar came over for lunch. He has recently been dismissed after careful consideration of his case by the president. How could the president give careful consideration to his 200 page reply to the charges levelled against him and many others similarly implicated is not easy to understand. The fact is that the president and his advisors were determined to deal harshly even brutally with civil servants of any calibre and they have done so in a vindictive spirit against all canons of justice. If this measure was a cure for bribery, corruption, nepotism or misuse of power than there would be some consolation. On the contrary, these maladies have increased and the country has been deprived of the cumulative experience of hundreds of brilliant officers. To replace them, a generation or more would be required. Meanwhile, the country would be in the hands of inexperienced mediocre bureaucrats, inexperienced soldiers and selfish and thoroughly incompetent politicians. To expect to make any progress under such conditions would be the height of optimism. As for his plans for the future, Altaf Gauhar said that he had to lie low for some time. The government policy was to debar people like him even from earning a livelihood. Industrialists had been told not to engage him. Law colleges had been told not to give them admittance. Those that hold law degrees were not allowed to practice and so on. So there was nothing else for him to do except to await elections for some time. Things might change after that. I felt sorry and disgusted to hear all that. There must be some limit to victimization, vindictiveness and callousness. This is nothing, but gross misuse of power.

2 | TUESDAY

📖 Mr Brohi was here on a visit to Rawalpindi. He wanted to see me. I asked him to come over to lunch, which he did. He is, of course, knowledgeable, learned, and a good talker. He was very depressed about the state of affairs in the country and regretted the fact that people of Pakistan were in a deep coma. Any call to sanity was nowhere. Nor was anyone prepared to talk sense. The worst culprit was the press. But one thing was certain that those that created the turmoil were now regretting it and feeling my absence. I did not remind him that he was one of them in his own way. He was a great protagonist of direct elections, and parliamentary form of government, the two demands which opened the Pandora's box and all sorts of extremist demands cropped up.

He regretted the fact that we had become aimless people and had no binding philosophy left. The binding force of Islam was being seriously questioned, certainly by the younger generation. There seemed to be nothing that could bind East and West Pakistan together. To East Pakistanis the enemy was West Pakistan. People were completely blind to facts and realities. The greatest tragedy was that the younger generation was being fed on these ideas. They live in a spiritual and moral vacuum. The present generation was bad enough, but what good would the younger generation be when it grew up. So what sort of hopes could we hold for the future? The prospect was gloomy. Economics had a good deal to do with it, but then people must learn to live within the means of their country and endeavour to increase them. Our solution lay in putting greater emphasis on agriculture. Then he said what a miracle I brought about in agriculture in West Pakistan. I said the same would have happened in East Pakistan, if only they listened to me and not put emphasis on prestigious projects. He showed concern about deteriorating economic conditions in the country and falling exports. He said the laws of economics, if flouted, extract a heavy toll.

Talking about Mujibur Rahman, I said, you are the man who pleaded his case with me. He admitted his mistake, but said that the man who wrecked the Round Table Conference was Daultana. His objective in building Mujibur Rahman up was to demolish my support in East Pakistan and put him under obligation. It was a deep laid conspiracy.

Mr Brohi said that the problem of evolving a durable relationship with East Pakistan was baffling. They were in no mood to be reasonable or listen to reason. I said it would be a great mistake to force anything on them. They must be free to do things in their own way. Constitutionally, we have to swallow the bitter pill and accept confederation or something even looser. No other form of relationship with them has a chance of acceptance or survival.

Mr Brohi departed by saying that he did not want to depress me anymore. But on some other occasion, he would like to talk to me at length on these matters, especially on the constitution in which there were so many imponderables that it was difficult to tell how they would be resolved.

📖 I am told that the Turks treated Yahya and his entourage coldly and formally during his state visit. There was none of that warmth and affection that used to be shown to me, especially by the common man. In fact, during my visit they used to go wild. Also, some of the Turkish officials were very blunt. They inquired about me and told the Pakistani staff that they were unworthy people and did not deserve my services. Wherever Yahya went slogans of Ayub Khan Zindabad were raised.

3 | WEDNESDAY

📖 The National Economic Council has agreed on the fourth plan. Details follow:

a. Total size of the plan will be 7,500 crores.
b. Public sector expenditure 4,900 crores.
c. Private sector expenditure 2,600 crores.
d. Out of the 7,500 crores, East Pakistan's share will be 3,940 crores and West Pakistan 3,560 crores.
e. Out of the public sector of 4,900 crores, East Pakistan is to get 2,940 crores, West Pakistan is to get 1,960 crores. This is a split of 60:40 per cent.
f. Growth rate of 7.5 per cent aimed in East Pakistan and 5.5 per cent in West Pakistan.
g. Allocation of 4,500 crores made for flood control and Tarbela over and above the plan and so on.

This looks very nice on paper, but where are resources of this magnitude to come from. By further taxation and deficit financing, when people are already groaning under the heavy burden of taxation and inflation is rampant? West Pakistan could guarantee more resources, but can it when its development has been deliberately cut back? On top of it, West Pakistan will have to transfer large resources to make good these promises to East Pakistan.

Expecting the growth rate to rise to 7.5 per cent in East Pakistan seems to be the height of wishful thinking. If past experiences are anything or any guide it required a Herculean effort to raise the growth rate from 1.5 to 4.5 per cent, which fell again to 1 per cent because of neglect of agriculture and low rate of production in the industrial sector through strikes etc., which have become a common occurrence.

11 | THURSDAY

📖 Mahmud Haroon came to call in the evening. He said he very much wanted to see me before but avoided doing so as he had nothing but depressing news to give. Nothing was happening in the country which could give cause for optimism. It was becoming quite clear that East Pakistan was a millstone around our neck. Their main and constant effort was to grab whatever they could. That was apparent during discussions on economic and food matters. In spite of so much extra outlay on imports, they were again demanding two million tons of food. He did not see how the two wings could stay together. The real trouble was that they don't want to work. They seek solution to every problem in politics.

I asked Mahmud Haroon about the background of the issue of the recent order freezing the funds of the Muslim League. He said that was done by martial law headquarters without consultation with the cabinet except Qizilbash. The object was to break up this party in order to find support for Qayyum Khan. It was presumed that Daultana would then be compelled to join Qayyum too. If that happened West Pakistan would be able to face Mujibur Rahman and other extreme demands. I told him that this was wishful thinking. Chances are that those that break away from this party would join Daultana and Mujibur Rahman. He agreed and said that by taking that action the president had made himself a partisan to the most reliable man and made others his enemies. They would all criticize him and a man like Fazlul Qader Chaudhary was not going to keep quite. He said that the president did not realize that taking political decisions on the advice of novices is most dangerous.

20 | SATURDAY

📖 Yahya is going to Russia on a state visit. I see in the press that he will get no fighter escort, no gun salute, will not be put up in the Kremlin, and only Podgorny will come to the airport to receive him. This is so different to what they used to do for me. All the Russian leaders used to come to receive me and made so much fuss. Furthermore, wherever I went most of them used to accompany me. I hope this change in their attitude is not indicative of coolness towards Pakistan.

21 | SUNDAY

📖 The Spanish Charge d'Affairs in Islamabad, who is a friend of Aurangzeb, visited East Pakistan and saw many people including Sheikh Mujibur Rahman, who rubbed his bare foot all the time, almost under his nose. He said it was a sickening experience and felt sorry for Pakistan if such a man became its prime minister. He felt that Mujibur Rahman was not so rabid as the people around him and especially the civil servants who wanted nothing short of separation.

📖 I listen to news from Radio Pakistan for two reasons. One is to find out what further blunders the government is committing, and two, to know what the weather forecast is. The rest of the news is all unconvincing, sham and rubbish repeating empty statements of leaders of some two dozen parties posing as the friends of the people, but in reality hankering after power.

24 | WEDNESDAY

📖 Mr Qayyum, the joint secretary president's secretariat, came to deliver a message from General Peerzada that the president intends giving a statement on the skeleton staff that has been given to me on retirement as there has been a lot of publicity and some criticism about it in the press. He suggested a vague sort of formula that instead of keeping three orderlies might two be returned. The steno could sit in the President's Secretariat and come to me from time to time. The police guard could be shown as a part of the local police force and I need not fly the flag as I have not done so far, and relinquish liaison on an ADC when attending formal functions etc. I said the publicity in the press was given an angle. It was shown that I have been given certain concessions as a field marshal, my rank restored, making me senior to the commander-in-chief. Asghar Khan then fulminated that I was put in a position from which I could stage a comeback and all that sort of nonsense.

Now it was up to the government to defend its decision or not. If not, I shall return all the staff and I have no cause to complain, but if I am allowed to retain them, I would not like my two orderlies to be shunted out now as they are poor people and have grown up children studying in Islamabad. Their education would be dislocated. It is a human problem. Besides, they have been given extension till the end of the year. As to the suggestion that they can show the rest of the staff wherever they like but how will they hide the fact that they are employed at my place. Besides, the president would be inviting more criticism by going into unnecessary details. If he is to give a statement it should be brief to the effect that I am on pension establishment as a field marshal and no concessions are attached to this rank. But I have been given a skeleton staff as a retired president which is customary in all civilized countries.

I think a little criticism has jittered the man and he does not have the moral courage to defend his orders. The main theme of his policy has been to give way to pressure.

26 | FRIDAY

📖 Some thoughts on the emergence of new nations and problems they face:

a. New nations emerge in the name of nationalism and popular sovereignty, but that does not mean that they are either a nation or a democracy. The principles are just norms and slogans and not facts.

b. These principles are spoken of by the westernised elite but they are not accepted by the masses who are still traditionalists. For these the older loyalties to dynasty, religion, tribe, region, localities, still make the principal appeal. These societies are deeply divided by neutral and ethnic pluralism by provincialism, regionalism, and castism. The tiny westernised elite of politicians, bureaucrats, soldiers have a formidable task of establishing national consensus and economic growth in the face of fragmentary political culture and backward rural economy.

c. Hatred of the imperial power is not the same as national self-consciousness and political consciousness. In these circumstances popular sovereignty, provincial particularism, communism, tribalism, flays the westernising elite by the heels. Nationalism and popular sovereignty succeed in discrediting traditional belief systems or at least in displacing them, but not supplementing them. The result is confusion and tension over legitimacy and over what form of rule and which political values are duly worthy. Hence the new leader's quest for synthesis of new and traditional values is not an easy task.

d. Thus, in these societies a political formula is elusive. Legitimacy is still at large. They lack the prerequisite's of political maturity. Consensus on the legitimate locus of sovereignty and consensus on the procedures for establishing morally valid public decisions. Thirdly, they lack civilian organizations willing and capable of defending and sustaining the society's political institutions. And this is directly related to their economic backwardness. The natural preconditions for adequate civilian organizations do not yet exist.

e. Tribal, religious and ethnic organizations, which are the lot of most of them, were more likely to pulverize the new state than to integrate it.

f. The civilian organizations that were likely to integrate like trade unions, business corporations and chambers, voluntary organizations, political parties which are not mutually exclusive and which cross the tribal ethnic and religious boundaries to produce countrywide and functional organizations do not exist. Nor does the belief that the basis of modern politics rests on function and not on a particular territory.

g. Referring to civil functional organizations again, they can only develop if there is a high level of commercial intercourse and individual activity. High level of operational income to provide the necessary social surpluses. Also high level of communications and literacy. These are the conditions, which bring about political awareness, self-consciousness and articulation.

h. In most of these states, the material conditions are not sufficiently advanced to harmonize society, are too developed to leave it in its traditional state, but are just developed enough to exacerbate divisions. The industrial proletariate is too weak to be accepted as a legitimate constituent in the political process, too strong and wretched not to be an extreme and disruptive force.

i. The slogan of popular sovereignty also acts as a dissolvent. It brings about factions and conflicts which work to advantage in homogenous societies, but which, if self-divided, simply accentuate the local tribal, religious and class differences. The feeling grows that it is popular sovereignty for the whole, why not for the sections as well. So there is a tremendous conflict between the real requirement which is unity and strong centralized control, and popular feelings, which have a strong pull for division and disintegration. How can such societies then have political stability and progress? Most of their time is wasted in debate on how to live or not live with each other. Constitution making is thus a farce in these conditions and if it does not get made it cannot hope for acceptance and loyalty from the people. The only way it could run is by enforcement by a few of the westernised elite. And that could not be called a durable arrangement especially when this elite manipulates to serve their purpose as they often do.

j. The new factor of student power, who can and have played havoc with many countries inclusive of Pakistan, is another unsettling actor, the real mischief makers may be few, but the rest get intimidated in supporting them and the politicians, in selfishness and short sightedness, make use of them, and so do the foreign powers who do not hesitate to make mischief wherever it suits them. The Russians used to be accused of such practices, but the Americans have now surpassed them. Their CIA has worldwide tentacles and pursue their dirty work relentlessly. Their efforts are concentrated on keeping the rulers of the country in their pocket. They demand complete submission to their will although the leaders may not be able to carry his people on such policies and geographical situations may not allow it. They do not realize that a leader without the support of his people is worthless. Some people tell me that the Americans financed the agitation against me, that may be so, yet the country's interest demands that we remain on good terms with them. Our economic and other dependence on them are too great.

k. It is a mistake to attribute instability to low standards of living. This is common in traditional societies and compatible with very stable politics. The instability arises out of movement away from traditionalism, it is the introduction of sharp and as yet localized social discontinuities that make for instability. It is accentuated as modernization takes its hold and literacy and communication increases the people's exposure to the possibilities of receiving a more attractive kind of life.

l. The less wealthy, the less industrialized, the less educated and the less urbanized a society, the less politically stable it is likely to be.

m. Population explosion, uncontrolled urbanization, mass education, coupled with lack of employment opportunities, general state of unemployment or under employment for the masses, unwillingness or inability of the traditionalists to change their attitude with the times are all aggravating actors leading to instability, especially in a country like Pakistan where resources are limited and demands are unlimited.

n. The absence of honest, dedicated, and knowledgeable political leaders, lack of political parties with roots amongst the people.

o. Sum total of these factors is the root cause of present unrest and instability in Pakistan. The surprising part is how the country remained quiet for ten and a half years. Some told me that there was wide spread rumour in Karachi that General Yahya had fallen seriously ill in Russia. I did not believe it, as according to the radio, he attended all the scheduled functions there and returned to Karachi this evening and met the press.

📖 A person came to me and said that Yahya's constant fear was that I might stage a comeback as a result of popular upsurge, as he knew that nobody had any real respect for him. So he suffers from Ayub-phobia and was doing everything possible to demolish my image, but that was not proving an easy task. As time went on, people would miss me more and more. At any rate, they could not easily forget what I have done for the country.

One thing that disturbed me most was to hear that there was a growing feeling of revulsion against the army in the minds of the people. The army was being regarded as an occupation force and an instrument of oppression. Instead of bringing relief to the common man, its rule had made his life intolerable. I think this feeling emanates from the army's inability to maintain law and order and rising prices of basic commodities. Loss of prestige in the outside world was another growing factor.

29 | MONDAY

📖 Col. Mohiuddin came to check me up this morning. He had been to Moscow with Yahya and returned from Karachi last night, whereas Yahya and his party returned this morning. Apparently the whole lot was to return last night, but the programme was changed at the last minute. Yahya's girlfriends wanted the pleasure of his company for another night. Mohiuddin said that Moscow visit went off all right, but the reception and treatment was not as warm as they gave me. He said Yahya avoided talking to him. Might be that he did not want to be cautioned against alcoholic and sexual excesses. He also got the impression that he was not welcomed in that crowd. He feared that they might throw him out, so as a precautionary measure he was thinking of extricating himself with some grace. Besides, he said, it was no pleasure to serve a man for whom one had no respect. Apart from anything else, Yahya was given to moods, when relaxed he became unduly familiar, yet when not in a mood he would just look through a man as if he had never seen him in his life. So he said, every time he accompanied the president and saw more of him he returned more depressed.

1 | WEDNESDAY

📖 Today is a fateful day. One Unit has been broken into four provinces. The new governors and their secretariat staff are in position. A great experiment at unification of the people of West Pakistan has come to nothing because of parochial outlook and lack of national perspectives. However, it does not mean that the provinces can live without each other's assistance. The economic life of the whole of the Indus basin has become one. So many common facilities have been created on the correct functioning of which the welfare of the whole region depends. So let us hope that after the first flush of separation the provinces would settle down to attend to their primary task of creating a better life for their people, instead of indulging in inter-provincial bickering. I pray to God that this comes about and mutual distrust and venom disappears.

📖 I am told that the director in charge of the Russian desk at the Foreign Office has said that despite glowing reports in the press on the success of the trip to Moscow by the president, the reality was different. The Russians were most unhappy at the departure of the Field Marshal. In fact, from that day they ceased talking to them and stopped deliveries of military weapons to the army and air force etc. They made plain their unhappiness during the visit. The promise to support the steel mills was all right, but it was hedged by so many ifs and buts and so was the promise to give project aid during the fourth plan. In a banquet address Kosygin laid great emphasis on making use of the Tashkent declaration and attacking those in Pakistan who criticized it. He wondered what they wanted, total destruction of India and Pakistan, ruining their economy and bringing more poverty and suffering to their people? In private, he is alleged to have told Yahya to fly to Delhi instead of Pindi and settle smaller matters; if bigger issues were intractable like the way they were trying to do with the Chinese. He meant well and one knows that they are very anxious to see that communications between India and Pakistan remain open so that recurrence of 1965 conditions are avoided. Their global policy demands that there should be peace on the subcontinent, but settling minor matters does not help to bring about real understanding between India and Pakistan. Unless there is some progress on Kashmir our relations will continue to remain sour. Besides, it suits the Russians and the Indians to talk of settling minor matters as they are in illegal possession of other territories and want to hang on to them, though China does not want an immediate settlement. All they are asking for is the recognition of the fact that some territories are in adverse possession of the Russians, a proposition that the latter are not even prepared to accept.

3 | FRIDAY

📖 For the last three days, I have been having constant fever. It started of with acute pain of the colon. Col. Mohiuddin, my doctor, thinks that it was a touch of typhoid. I must have eaten something that brought it on. The trouble is most of the cooks and servants in our country are carriers. It is problematic why one does not feel prey to these diseases more often. Perhaps being exposed to these hazards for so long one develops some sort of immunity. But the fever has not affected my appetite much. I can still eat a certain amount and keep up my strength.

4 | SATURDAY

📖 It is an open secret now that the administration is behind Qayyum Khan. Freezing of our party funds was done at his behest. I would not be a bit surprised if it did bring some of the other parties together in self-defence, ostensibly against Qayyum Khan, but in reality against Yahya.

Wali Khan has today charged that Qayyum Khan was getting support from the administration and the officials. He has also accused Qayyum Khan of encouraging violence and warned that should he not desist then they too would use the same weapon. He has gone on to say that Qayyum Khan had conveyed to the president that the elections should be held in order to ward off any agitation and expose the inadequacy of politicians to enable him to stay in power. He promised that he would see to it that difficulties were created either from within or without the assembly to ensure that the constitution could not be framed. This need not seem far fetched. I would not put anything beyond Qayyum Khan.

It seems that Yahya is falling more and more into the net of unscrupulous and reckless people like Qayyum Khan, Qizilbash, Hassan Mahmood, Wahiduzzaman etc. He, having compromised himself, seems to be their prisoner now. I think he started this collaboration under an illusion that Qayyum Khan could prove a rallying point for the moderates and produce a counter to the extremists. Qayyum Khan has indeed gathered a following albeit with the help of the administration consisting mostly of the well to do, the class he hates and the class which won't cut much ice with the extremists of the left or right. So he cannot do much good except creating mischief to suit his ends. He will not hesitate to cut even Yahya's throat if it suited his purpose and he found an opening.

Malik Qasim flew over from Lahore. He said that freezing of party funds has given them a setback and was done with malice to build up Qayyum Khan at their expense. But at the same time it had done them some good, otherwise people would have been looking towards the money all the time.

The trouble is that Yahya is backing the wrong horse and working on wrong advice. Qayyum Khan would never be able to foregather, substantial majority. Mujibur Rahman, Daultana and Wali Khan and such like will get together against Qayyum Khan first and then Yahya, if they got an opening. At best Qayyum Khan can collect 25 to 30 votes in the central assembly.

10 | FRIDAY

📖 I have written nothing during the last few days, though my fever went down five days ago. I feel dazed with the amount of antibiotics I have been taking. These are wonder drugs, but they do have side effects. Perhaps they also kill the essential bacteria inside the body, upsetting the natural balance. But I have not lost much weight as I retained my appetite and kept eating my meals, mostly meat.

📖 The freezing of the Muslim League funds in an effort to break-up the party and find support for Qayyum Khan and hand over the funds to him is beginning to have its natural repercussions. Earlier on Fazlul Qader Chaudhary had given out a statement criticizing the action but more recently both Malik Qasim and Yasin Wattoo gave out statements of our accounts refuting the baseless charges of spending funds against public interest.

11 | SATURDAY

📖 Aslam Khattak[25] came over from Peshawar. Apart from other things said about the government which have been repeated by so many, he said there was no political decorum left. Politicians hurled baseless abuses against each other. In a recent function in Mardan in honour of Col. Amir Muhammad Khan Hoti, a poem was read out in which a wild attack was made on the character of Wali Khan's wife (Nasim). They retorted by publishing a scurrilous article on the doings of Amir Muhammad Khan's grandmother and threatened to say a good deal more about other womenfolk of the family. Violence, he said, was very much in the air, political murders might well become common—one heard so much of it.

12 | SUNDAY

📖 Malik Qasim said freezing of funds would have an adverse affect in Bengal. Mujibur Rahman is spending big money and now people are in need of it to counter him. He also said that the plan of the regime was to hand over funds to Qayyum Khan after freezing them. But with all the exposure that had taken place that would not now be possible. Instead the regime was collecting funds for Qayyum Khan from bankers and industrialists and their identification with them was felt all around. Fancy getting identified with despicable people like Qayyum Khan and his associates who are utter frauds.

He was very sarcastic about so many generals taking part in politics and offering themselves for elections. He said they would all fail as none of them had any roots or equation with the people. Getting on a stage and giving a speech was one thing but obtaining votes was another matter. He said why could they not be stopped from exposing themselves and bringing a bad name to the army. I told him in case sermons are no answer, hard facts of life and meeting reverses, after incurring a lot of expenses will soon bring them to their senses.

15 | WEDNESDAY

📖 Yasin Wattoo came to call and stayed for lunch. He, Fazlul Qader Chaudhary and Qasim were summoned here by Zone A Martial Law Administrator General Tikka Khan.[26] He said that in their criticism against the freezing of party funds they had also attacked and doubted the president's neutral position. They told him that was known to everybody. They said nothing new or unusual. However, Tikka Khan was very anxious to get a statement from them that the president was non-aligned, which Fazlul Qader Chaudhary gave out with the hope that the president would be just as fair to them as he was to other parties and release their funds. Tikka said that he could not promise, but he hoped that their funds would be released. I believe a similar statement was obtained from Daultana in the same manner, which came out in the press and is known all over.

Fancy relying on such a false sheet. The whole country knows that Yahya and his intelligence machinery has been working for Qayyum Khan and yet Yahya wants people to say that he is neutral. It is difficult to understand what made him think that Qayyum Khan would be able to command a countrywide following so as to make Yahya stake everything for him.

20 | MONDAY

Qizilbash, the finance minister, is coming more and more under fire for political interference and for providing a very unpopular budget. Many sections of the people are dissatisfied and resentful. Someone said that unless Yahya gets rid of Qizilbash and General Peerzada soon, which he won't, he would become the focus of criticism.

21 | TUESDAY

Some people expect me to take the field again little realizing that the circumstances are not good nor does the state of my health permit that. What is needed is much more younger people, fired with patriotism, possessing moral courage with attractive and workable programme and zeal to somehow weld these disparate people into a nation and set them to work to find their solution. Maybe I am asking for the moon, but then what else is the solution?

22 | WEDNESDAY

I was told that Hassan Amin who ran the Sharazad Hotel on contract for several years was called by the Chairman, CDA, this morning and shown an order signed by the Martial Law Administrator General Tikka Khan that he was to hand over the hotel to the chairman within half an hour of receipt of that order. I was shocked to hear that the rights of a citizen could be trampled upon in such a high-handed manner. This is worse than the Sikh rule, which was notorious for its brutality and disregard for law. I am sure that Tikka Khan could not be the originator. He must have been ordered to do so by General Peerzada under instructions from Yahya.

General Peerzada is a ruthless and callous brute and has been instrumental in getting Yahya to agree to dealing with so many officers and others who don't belong to a pressure group in a very rough and unjust manner. Why Yahya goes along with this sort of conduct, I don't understand. Either he thinks in the same manner as Peerzada or he is too busy in his own pastime to bother about what is going on. Malik Qasim was upset over Aurangzeb joining Qayyum Khan. I told him that he was helpless, the government pressure was so great on his father that he could not resist. So his joining Qayyum Khan was through compulsion and no love. In any case, it should be taken for granted that all the tribal votes are captives of their government and will do as they are told. So it was no good blaming Aurangzeb.

I was astounded to hear that the junta was planning to arrest Malik Qasim and others on the statement they made on confiscation of their party funds. It seems that they had second thoughts and withheld their hands. I must say Malik Qasim and others had gone through very difficult times trying to keep the party alive in the face of heavy odds. A repressive and irresponsible government with unlimited powers is bent upon breaking them up and the party at all cost.

28 | TUESDAY

In a meeting between our representatives and Indian representatives on division of waters of the river Ganges held in New Delhi a few days ago, India agreed in principle that Pakistan was to get some share, to be decided in a later meeting. This is a step forward reached after nine years of protracted negotiations and politicking.

I can't think that this change is due to India's sudden realization of the justice of our case or change of heart. It may well have come about through Russian pressure or India's desire to ask for quid pro quo in the form of transportation facilities over our railway and river systems for appeasement of East Pakistan, in the hope that they will tend to be drawn towards India and away from West Pakistan or a combination of all these factors.

29 | WEDNESDAY

📖 General Yahya made a policy statement yesterday in which he, amongst others things, declared that the elections would be held as scheduled and that law and order would be made and maintained at all cost. The latter is a welcome threat, but it is not going to deter the political *goondas*, who have been given such a long rein. So it had a ring of hollowness. Meanwhile, Bhutto has held out a threat that unless the cabinet was dissolved before elections, all political prisoners, students and labour leaders who had violated the law released, and the assembly made completely sovereign, his party would not take part in the elections nor would he be responsible for the consequences. His objective obviously is to intimidate the administration. He may also be doubting the wisdom of going into the assembly with a small following and in which there is not much chance of framing a constitution, certainly not of his liking. His communist supporters may well have advised him to stay out to build his image as the champion of have-nots and critic of the rightists.

Never for a moment did it enter our minds that we should invade and take over Indian territories, nor have we ever heard any responsible or sensible Pakistani say that. True we wanted an honourable and just solution of Kashmir, but no more.

We are not so mad as to aggress against a country several times our strength, had we the economic or military strength to do so. Even the short and sharp war of 1965 left both the countries exhausted. Its economic repercussions are being felt even now. Besides, it would be the height of madness to take over an unassimilated Hindu population. If 700 years of Muslim rule did not succeed in fusing Muslims and Hindus together how could it be done in three days of burning nationalism? Besides, why have we asked for separation if we had expansionist designs?

No, this is the misfortune of India and us that she just refuses to understand our intentions. All we want is to settle Kashmir and live as good neighbours with her. A lot of miseries of both the countries would be removed if India were to understand and believe this simple truth, but unfortunately they have shut their minds to reality either as a matter of deep prejudice or as an expediency for consolidation of home front or both. They also have not learnt that a little kindness or generosity can disarm a Muslim more easily than anything else. This comes out of their arrogance, narrow mindedness and lack of statesmanship. They are basically commercial people. Long term investment in human values has never been part of their history except for the Rajputs, who today unfortunately don't count for much in Indian politics. Some of Menon's thinking on Pakistan is as follows, this is Krishna Menon,[27] who was once their defence minister.

Krishna Menon's line on Pakistan is as brittle and unyielding as that of the right. India must stand firm on Kashmir and make no concessions whatsoever. She must reject Pakistan's claim of the UN-western block pressure for plebiscite which is no longer relevant and in any event was never pledged in the form assumed by many observers. Pakistan's aggression has never been decried and India's right to the entire former princely state remains unqualified. Full integration of Kashmir State into India is logical and right and should be consummated, talk of independent Kashmir is nonsense and should be quashed. The one point on which he departs from the extreme right is his willingness to accept the ceasefire line of 1949 as a de facto boundary line in the interest of having better harmony between India and Pakistan. The right advocates force to incorporate the occupied territory.

Krishna Menon has urged this policy on countless occasions with the intensity of a true believer. Indeed, he is seen to regard it as a personal mission to educate his people on the truth of Kashmir and to instil the determination not to yield an inch. And to those who talk about concessions or Kashmir's secession, he declares no settlement that would surrender Indian territory to Pakistan is constitutionally possible in India. There are many millions of people who feel this way with supreme assurance in his cause. He added Lal Bahadur Shastri[28] and presumably any future prime minister would not do it. He knows public feelings on this matter. He cannot do it even if he wanted to, though a few hours before his death in Tashkent I had lunch with Shastri. He gave me the impression that he was sick and tired of Kashmir and was anxious to find a way out and without elaboration he cautioned there are graver and most sinister implications in this surrender. All this was said before the 1965 war which confirmed the need this hard-line as the popular policy did. It should have done the opposite. The war took place because of the hard line policy of Krishna Menon and anyone else in India and so on. He ended up by saying that only positive elements in Menon's [...] first is that India will try to establish a relationship of genuine peaceful coexistence based on the status quo.

In another place, Krishna Menon said that why should Pakistan talk about Kashmir now. It was Jinnah who demanded that the state rulers should have the right to determine the future of their states. In the case of Kashmir the ruler acceded to India and so that was the end of the matter.

I have written all this at length so as to make it quite clear what the enemy's intentions are.

3 | MONDAY

📖 Mahmud A. Haroon came in the evening and explained why Qayyum Khan was being supported so blatantly and openly. Qizilbash and Razvi, Director General, Intelligence Bureau, had a good deal to do with it. The thinking was that between Bhashani and Mujibur Rahman in East Pakistan, the latter was a better bet. In West Pakistan, Qayyum Khan was chosen as Daultana was regarded as too tricky, as if Qayyum is an angel, but latest assessment of Razvi was that Qayyum Khan would dominate the Frontier, Daultana in Punjab and Mujibur Rahman in East Pakistan. The situation in Sindh would be confused. So there was a certain amount of disenchantment with Qayyum Khan especially by Qizilbash who was hoping to build up his position in the Punjab through him. Qayyum had not been able to make much headway in East Pakistan either. At best he would get a following of 30 or so members throughout the country.

He said that Qizilbash had foregathered leading businessmen and asked for funds for Qayyum Khan. Some of them came to seek his advice. He told them if they had to oblige why not wait till the president asks them.

I told Mahmud A. Haroon that why not advise Yahya to desist from being vindictive on our party men. True he could harm them but in the process of being partisan he will do himself greater harm. Haroon promised to do that.

He asked me how I saw the situation. I told him I wish I could see a silver lining anywhere. To me the future looked bleak.

4 | TUESDAY

📖 I was delighted to hear Altaf Gauhar has found a job as an economic advisor to some firm. The poor man was down and out and could not even support his children's education.

7 | FRIDAY

📖 News about the floods in East Pakistan is very bad and saddening. Millions of poor people with their crops, dwellings, belongings and cattle have been affected. The floods having affected the northern districts bordering the three river systems of the Ganges, Brahmaputra and Meghna have now moved down to the southern districts of Dacca, Comilla and Faridpur etc. Vast areas have gone under water. I suppose the districts lower down will also be affected until the great volume of water dissipates itself into the sea.

People talk about flood control measures and schemes worth two billion dollars are supposed to have been prepared. I wonder if such a volume of water can ever be controlled. It may be possible to build embankments in the northern districts, but how is this possible in the river and delta almost flush with the sea.

Misfortunes of East Pakistanis are great. Some are due to vagrancies of nature and climate and some man-made. Their solution does not seem to be in sight or even possible. Similarly, much talk about parity with West Pakistan is championed but for some natural and man-made reasons, it would never be attained. I tried very hard, but soon found that it was a much more stubborn problem than imagined, not that West Pakistan is so advanced as to be unreasonable or that there is no poverty here. Apart from few a pockets the rest of the people suffer from dire poverty and deprivation.

I see that Qayyum Khan reached Dacca the same day as Yahya. I suppose the object is to influence people with simulated closeness and collusion with Yahya. He has also been talking about postponement of elections. He could not have done this without prior clearance from Yahya.

📖 A PIA Fokker Friendship plane taking off from Chaklala airport for Lahore last night with 30 passengers onboard crash-landed some miles away. According to preliminary reports, it exploded in the air killing all passengers. There were no survivors. It is tragic and heartbreaking that so many innocent and valuable lives were lost. Some cynics remarked that what a pity that it was not full of those politicians who were the bane of the country's life. The country could well afford to do without them. It would not be much of a price for getting some peace.

10 | MONDAY

📖 Bhutto has done an extensive tour of central Punjab. He has been drawing big crowds, apart from his fraudulent lure of socialism etc. He has been making the most dishonest and highly damaging statements. He said when he came to power Indira Gandhi dare not have a sound sleep. He would see that Jashan-e-Islam processions were held in Delhi and Srinagar instead of cities in Pakistan and that he would repudiate all foreign loans and so on. Now such statements can only be made either by a lunatic, which he is not, or an utter exploiter and scoundrel who does not hesitate to play with the sentiments of people to gain his political goals in spite of the harm caused to the country. And yet untold people clap and cheer him. Now what can you do with people who are politically so immature? Why should the unscrupulous politicians not exploit them as no one amongst the crowd has the sense, knowledge or courage to challenge their absurd claims and promises. The crowds lend themselves to becoming captive audiences.

There is a rumour that Bhutto is also a favourite of the administration and is encouraged, though Qayyum claims that he is given preference. How Bhutto, with socialist pretentious, would be useful to the administration is difficult to tell. There is talk that Mujibur Rahman too is given a glad eye or perhaps feared. How are these heterogeneous elements expected to form a team is incomprehensible. Mujibur Rahman's whole philosophy is based on hatred towards West Pakistan.

12 | WEDNESDAY

📖 Aurangzeb, my son-in-law, returned from Dacca after a ten day visit. He was full of gossip, for instance:

a. When Yahya landed at Dacca, he was dead drunk.
b. He had ostensibly gone there to supervise flood relief work, but in reality was busy relaxing with women and drinking. He was surrounded by women even when going down on river trips on the *Mary Anderson*, the governor's launch.
c. Nobody had any respect for him. Some resent his personal conduct but finish up by saying that after all it was his personal life.

d. Mujibur Rahman had a vast following. He would come in with a big majority. The administration was frightened of him and Daultana. That was why they were making desperate efforts to built-up Qayyum Khan. But however well Qayyum Khan delivers the goods, he may have had some intellectual capacity, but does he have the moral? There was every likelihood of postponement of elections. The administration thinks that Qayyum Khan stands to gain thereby.

e. There was no sign of anti-West Pakistan feelings. People were talking in terms of one country. This, of course, depends on what sort of people he met.

f. Aurangzeb visited Nawab Askari Jute Mills. The workers swarmed around him when told that he was my son-in-law and showed great warmth of feeling.

g. The labour situation has much improved.

All in all this is the best news I have had from East Pakistan about the internal situation. I always pray that they stabilize and settle down to a constructive life. Aurangzeb also told me that when Yahya landed at Dacca and drove into the President's House people en route shouted 'Ayub Khan *zindabad.*' There seems to be an impression that I am still the president of the country. Also the administration is not apprehensive of Nur Khan now that he has joined the Council Muslim League. They think that Daultana has promised him the presidency of the country and they may even get him elected for the National Assembly in place of Pir Saif-ud-Din from Campbellpur District.

Aurangzeb was sounded out by Governor Admiral Ahsan on whether the Field Marshal could not persuade the Fazlul Qader Chaudhary group to merge with Qayyum Khan's party. He told them that, for one, he had given up politics all together. Secondly, he had no leverage left with those people, having left the party. It seems that they are desperately anxious to build up Qayyum Khan. All the inequities perpetrated on our people are motivated by that objective.

13 | THURSDAY

A Bengali talking to a West Pakistani said they were aware of the fact that Mujibur Rahman was a liar, untrustworthy and a braggart, but that was entirely an internal matter. To them his value lay in being the spearhead of attack and symbol of defiance against West Pakistan.

14 | FRIDAY

Asghar Ali Shah from Rawalpindi came to call. He talked about an interview he had with General Yahya some time ago, in which he gave his oft repeated assessment of future politics. The gist of which is that even if the political governments were formed they would not last for more than a few months, then there would be another breakdown etc. He said the administration was anxious to postpone elections, in any case till December, in the hope that Mujibur Rahman might lose ground; they are terrified of his popularity. The floods in East Pakistan had given them a good excuse, but they were very apprehensive of Mujibur Rahman's attitude, who wanted elections held on schedule, otherwise he might well boycott them and create a serious law and order situation. He was also aware of the government's intentions.

Asghar Ali Shah was very apprehensive of the probability of murderous clashes between Wali Khan and Qayyum Khan's party in the Frontier and between Bhutto's party and Jamaat-e-Islami, especially in Pindi. He said Bhutto's party was gaining ground in West Pakistan, especially in the cities. He was spending money lavishly. Where he got it from was a mystery. Most people think that the CIA was financing him to keep the country unbalanced. So any postponement of elections would be to his benefit. He would get more adherents as time went on.

According to him, Bhutto's party men were getting very bold. In a recent public meeting in Pindi a film actor who had recently joined him attacked me, Gohar, Daultana, Maududi and even Yahya. He had the courage to say that when his party comes to power they would have Yahya dragged in the streets and eaten up by dogs. He [Asghar Ali Shah] said unless Bhutto, Mujib and Bhashani were destroyed, the country would never be saved. I said if that was the case, then why was Yahya so partial towards Bhutto. He said because their vices were common, birds of the same feather fly together.

He said Bhutto was an extremely ambitious man and impatient to get into power. He had established contacts in the army. His hope was that in the event of another breakdown, he would head the coup. I would not put it past him, if he was thinking and planning like that. But he is a wishful thinker if he believes that army men would take orders from him or share power with him. Ashgar Ali Shah was very sad that by dragging Islam into politics and using it as an instrument of promotion for political self-interest the religious parties had discredited it, certainly in the eyes of the younger generation.

📖 As I see it the constitution makers will face three formidable hurdles on which people have taken rigid stands without any give and take. In the main they are as follows:

1. The extent of provincial autonomy and the shape of the centre. It is very doubtful if Mujibur Rahman would be allowed by his extremist followers to retreat from his position.
2. The demand by certain sections for socialization of economy, that is, control of production and distribution by the state. An attractive but not easily workable idea in the present circumstances.
3. And above all, Islamization of the constitution which also caters for the requirements of today's life, this harmonization is something many people tried and failed to resolve. Perhaps it cannot be resolved.

Assuming that there is no agreement on these problems in the assembly and it is asking for too much from the sort of people who will get there, and assuming that the administration sticks to its decision to dissolve the assembly after 120 days, it will be faced with giving some sort of a sop to the people without jeopardizing its position. They may well activate the provincial assemblies and allow them to form governments under the tutelage of the appointed governors. They may even induct some politicians in the central cabinet under the cover of martial law. This solution will, however, come up against two snags:

1. The powers of the provincial governments, in other words the extent of provincial autonomy, will have to be defined. This is a thorny problem. East Pakistan is bound to show dissatisfaction and many even will non-cooperate.

2. The administration may not be able to hold down this position for any length of time. Pressure or withdrawal of martial law and handing over power to the politicians will grow.

15 | SATURDAY

📖 Just heard on the radio that the president has announced postponement of general elections to the National Assembly to 7th December and the provincial assemblies to 19th December due to floods in East Pakistan. Even otherwise some politicians were clamouring openly and some like Qayyum Khan in subdued tones for this in order to gain time to improve their chances of greater success. Mujibur Rahman, on the other hand, was against it. He felt that his popularity will be eroded. Let us see what his reaction will be like.

The average candidate would, however, be unhappy and for a very good reason. He will have to work for two more months and spend lot more money and efforts to maintain the interest of his supporters and voters. As it is, direct adult franchise is proving expensive. Two extra months will increase the burden and break the back of many candidates, but this is the luxury people asked for and agitated for, they should not grudge paying for it.

26 | WEDNESDAY

📖 I had an unexpected visitor, Ghulam Jilani Malik,[29] former MNA, who was my bitterest opponent. He turned up at my house and asked to come in. He had some interesting things to tell.

1. At the time of my sickness in 1968, the Speaker was not made to officiate for me as neither Yahya nor A. R. Khan wanted that. They were both competing to replace me should I become a casualty. Yahya may have entertained such ambitions but I doubt if A. R. Khan would. He was too subservient to Yahya. Besides, it was Yahya who had the command of the army.

2. During the troubled period of late 1968, Yahya's son contacted him several times to meet his father. So on one occasion, Yahya travelled with him from Lahore to Rawalpindi. He told him what a mess I was making of the country and also grooming my son, presumably Gohar, to succeed me. Yahya went on to say that something should be done about that. Jilani said that he tried very hard to see and tell me of that and also warned me not to be sure of army support in the event of a real crisis.

3. Jilani was in close touch with Bhutto before the start of the agitation. Bhutto's plan was to start aggressive agitation, which the administration could not cope with. Once law-and-order broke down, declaration of martial law would become inevitable and my removal certain. So he started with a violent attack on the administration and me from Hyderabad, which was answered by Musa, to which Bhutto replied from Dera Ismail Khan. Jilani prepared the reply. Then other events followed in quick succession including the attempt on my life in Peshawar in a public meeting. The agitation became country-wide rapidly.

Soon after Bhutto was arrested and when in Montgomery [Sahiwal] jail he sent for Jilani and told him to get a man called Irani to meet him as soon as possible. This man met Bhutto and came straight to Pindi and stayed at the Intercontinental Hotel. Jilani had sent three men to watch his movements. They reported in due course of time he had visited Yahya's house one night and so had Asghar Khan and Sher Ali who too were in Pindi in those days. He was heard saying that he would also join the movement. Jilani was sure that Yahya wanted Asghar to take on the role of Bhutto and Sher Ali to replace Asghar Khan who should be arrested. He was also sure that Bhutto must have sounded out Yahya on his plan before launching.

I can believe the rest, but I don't know if Yahya took Asghar and Sher Ali into confidence. Asghar probably went to sound out Yahya whether there was any possibility of martial law being imposed should the situation deteriorate.

I am told that Yahya goes around saying that the politicians had no business claiming credit for my removal. It was he who had given me the push.

30 | SUNDAY

Saw in the press this morning that Mr Daultana had resigned from the presidency of Council Muslim League due to ill health. Whether this means withdrawal from politics as well, is not clear. Mr Daultana's quitting should be no cause for regret, but it is going to have several adverse repercussions. There is, of course, going to be a dogfight in his party over succession, but another danger is that members of his party may be tempted to join Bhutto or Qayyum Khan, more likely the former. Both eventualities would be serious. In any case, the Punjab would be left more leaderless than it is today. The consequences of this could be dangerous when the time comes for making a constitution. East Pakistan, and parochial and anti-Pakistan elements in West Pakistan are going to take full advantage of it. A divided and leaderless Punjab will mean a breakthrough for these people.

31 | MONDAY

Bhutto is getting more and more aggressive and attacking the government more frontally everyday. He thinks that he has built up sufficient strength to do so and the government dare not retaliate. Considering this as evidence of weakness on the part of the government, more and more people are likely to join his party. And even if he is arrested, which is highly unlikely, he is bound to gain popularity.

9 | WEDNESDAY

📖 Razvi, the Director General, Intelligence Bureau, asked to see me. He came over in the evening. He asked if I could tell him where was the letter which Bhutto wrote to General Iskander Mirza, when he appointed him as a minister in 1958. I told him I had no knowledge of it. I doubt if Iskander left it in the office. If so it should be available there. Furthermore, it was I who appointed him as a minister and I must have told this to Iskander Mirza, but it is quite possible that Bhutto may have written to thank Iskander Mirza for the letter and win his support. I know that Bhutto had been trying to win Iskander Mirza's confidence in the past.

27 | SUNDAY

📖 There is general belief that Bhutto is gaining ground everywhere, especially in the Punjab, whereas in the past he was thought to win 12 or so seats for the assembly, the present estimate gives him 50 to 60 seats, which of course, would put him in a very strong position. There are also rumours that there is a good deal of bickering in his party over the distribution of tickets. He is favouring landlords and moneyed people in this respect much to the annoyance of his workers and new supporters. What affect this will have on his prospects remains to be seen. I also understand that Bhutto is planning to contest from several areas including Lahore to demonstrate his popularity.

28 | MONDAY

📖 Khawaja Shahabuddin came to call after a long time. He was in Karachi for most of the summer. He made the following points:

1. There was every likelihood of elections being held, perhaps accompanied by some violence.
2. The type of constitution that may be framed depended on what strength the extremists like Mujibur Rahman came in. If he came in with the pre-dominating strength, he would raise the ante and be thoroughly unreasonable. If, on the other hand, he came in with weak support, he would have to compromise and be in a reasonable mood.
3. Army attempts to obstruct the process of constitution-making would strengthen Yahya's hand. He could then justify his counter stance on the inability of the politicians to frame a constitution because if men don't agree on how to rule themselves someone else will rule them.
4. If the constitution is framed and the government is formed, Yahya would most likely be retained as the president.
5. Bhutto was gaining strength, especially in the Punjab. He was likely to get about 15 per cent seats.
6. The Qadianis and even the Shias were supporting Bhutto as a counter to Maududi and Daultana whom they regard as the greatest of enemies.
7. Daultana's resignation was under compulsion from the government and his chances of change of mind was also due to cleavages. They probably realized that Qayyum Khan could not be built-up by destroying Daultana.

8. But none of them in the field were capable of running a government. Breakdowns were inevitable.
9. Nobody looked to the future with confidence, gloom is written large on the faces of the people.
10. Fazlul Qader Chaudhary group would get the least support.
11. Nur Khan had done irreparable damage to the country within a short time.
12. He thought S.M. Zafar's book was very superficial. I told him that Zafar was a good man, but immature. It is surprising how even those that are successful in the legal profession in our country, lack practical common sense. They lived and worked amongst people and yet were so out of touch with realities. In any case, Zafar has written that book to show his innocence and be on the right side of the legal fraternity, who are critical of him.

Khawaja Sahib then talked about the events before and after partition and wondered at the manner in which history was being falsified in a blind crazefor the cult of personality worship. He wondered if any Muslim history was worthy of any credence. Our people dislike facing hard realties and love to live in make believe.

He went on to say that the rightists will lose in the elections through internal divisions and mutual conflicts. The leftists would be the beneficiaries.

30 | WEDNESDAY

📖 Qazi Isa from Quetta also turned up in the evening. He said that the NAP in Balochistan was badly split and extremist Balochis like Bugti, Marri[30] and Mengal[31] were isolated. Besides, they were divided amongst themselves. Qayyum Khan's League was unpopular because of leadership being put in the hands of Zehri[32] who was neo-rich, vulgar and unpopular. In any case, formation of a stable government in a house of 20 members was going to be a difficult proposition.

9 | FRIDAY

📖 A.K. Sumar, former MNA, came to call. According to him, Altaf Gauhar as information secretary was not free from blame for a number of misfortunes that befell. He, being a leftist, encouraged such elements in the press, radio and television. They got together and did a lot of damage at a crucial time. I told him that I had found many people say that, but I can't recollect a single occasion on which I found any cause to doubt his loyalty. Also, his efficiency was beyond expectation and question. He may have had leftist tendencies, but they were not apparent.

The Election Commission allotted symbols to different parties. The number of parties involved was 19. The independent candidates were not included in this number. This hodgepodge is supposed to frame a constitution and then run the country under a parliamentary form of government. What a hope. Khizar, the former MNA, came to call and said as far as he could make out power lay in the hands of three men who are close advisors to Yahya; they were General Peerzada, Razvi and General Umer[33] the head of the National Security Council.

He said that Bhutto, in a public meeting in Lahore, transgressed all limits of attacking Yahya and he was quite expecting to be arrested so he spent the night drinking in Kasuri's place, but nothing much happened although he was tipped by someone in the administration that he was about to be hauled up. Bucha said that he was sure that Bhutto had good contacts in the administration as well as in the army that he said was highly dangerous.

14 | WEDNESDAY

📖 Someone told me that Yahya seems concerned with the present situation and was losing faith in the people around him. He did not have much trust in anyone. Also, people were not too happy about his going to the UN although there is an advantage in his meeting Nixon there. They also seem to be dissatisfied with him because of the present state of chaos in the country. They think he has deliberately created the situation for personal ends by encouraging Bhutto and others. I personally think this to be far fetched though I do feel that he pampered Bhutto and others in the false hope that they will play to his tune.

📖 I see that Mr Brohi is advocating a presidential form of government as being the most suited to our conditions. Yet this man opposed it when I was in that position.

📖 October 15th is the date of filing nomination papers for the Central Assembly elections. Parties have issued the list of nominations of their candidates. By and large they are the same people who were members of the former assembly and of our party. It shows that it makes no difference whether people are elected by direct or indirect vote, not at least for the present. So all the cry for direct elections to find true representatives of the people was mere dust to be thrown in the eyes of the people and a measure of exploitation.

15 | THURSDAY

📖 Begum Liaquat Ali Khan came to call. She has come here in connection with the opening ceremony of the Liaquat Memorial tomorrow, which she had caused to be constructed. She talked about the perfidy of people in politics. How they had got Liaquat assassinated and how they had behaved with me. Then she talked about the plight of the common man. She said that even the bare necessities of life were now out of his reach. The prices had rocketed sky high. She was very fearful that one of these days the masses will burst and rise in desperation. She did not think that any civil government would be able to control the situation. Even the martial law regime was hard put to it without an open revolt.

29 | THURSDAY

📖 A man who accompanied General Yahya on his visit to the United Nations special session of the General Assembly, said that the news media in Pakistan gave the impression as if the special session was held for our benefit, but in reality when the president gave his address the hall was practically empty. Also very few people turned up for the address he was to give to the press corps. This made the president furious with the ambassador who had arranged the meeting. On one occasion he addressed the ambassador as a stooge more in jest than anything else. This was flashed in the New York press causing much embarrassment. His interview with the staff of *Time* was arranged by Hamid Jamal, our press attaché, on a personal basis and went off well.

He said the general impression in America was that Bhutto was coming in with a big majority and that socialism or communism was on the increase. The president tried to dispel this impression.

31 | SATURDAY

📖 Mr Uqaili, who was my finance minister, called last evening and then came to lunch today. He had been engaged by the World Bank for preparation of a development plan for Indonesia. He said that the Indonesian economy was in a bad way before too but real deterioration and galloping inflation by a hundred fold came in as a result of military confrontation with Malaysia.

Coming to home affairs, Uqaili was pessimistic about the future. He feared that East Pakistan will make West Pakistan sick. East Pakistanis should have the so-called autonomy they want, but based on their own resources. Their contribution to the central government was about 25 per cent. That amount together with their foreign exchange earnings should be set aside for central and provincial expenditure in East Pakistan. It was the only way to teach them responsibility. Their food gap was 2.5 million tons this year, most of it in rice. The bill for that would be a hundred and fifty crores, the best part of their foreign exchange earnings. They should also be given permission to negotiate for foreign loans, as Mujibur Rahman demanded. I said this is the only logical solution, but there is no leadership in West Pakistan to put such a thing across. The politicians here are concerned with the promotion of their selfish interests. They will not hesitate to temporise if it suited them.

Uqaili was very critical of Yahya. He said that the man had no time to attend to the serious business of state. He was too busy drinking and womanising. How did he know that? I asked. He said even a child in Pakistan knew that. It was common knowledge in Karachi that throughout the night women come in and go out of the president's house. Then he turned around to me and said that I owed it to the country to give him sound advice before disaster overtook us. Uqaili did not know that it was the last thing Yahya wanted to do, consult me.

1 | SUNDAY

📖 A terrible tragedy occurred yesterday at the Karachi Airport on the occasion of the Polish president's arrival from Lahore. A local catering van plowed through the line of receptionists who were greeting the president killing the Polish deputy foreign minister and three Pakistanis and wounding several others. The president was narrowly missed. He cut short his visit and flew back home carrying the dead body with him. It would be very difficult to live down such a performance and act of disgrace.

10 | TUESDAY

📖 I was shocked and grieved to hear from a member of a news agency that General De Gaulle had died of a heart attack within fifteen minutes [of the attack] in his home village while sitting before the television listening to the news. He would have been 80 years of age on the 22nd of this month. He was a great man who did so much for his country, sometimes in the face of violent opposition from his countrymen. They made several unsuccessful attempts on his life. By all accounts De Gaulle was devoted to the cause of good for his country, but seemed to have a poor opinion of his countrymen. Perhaps they did not come up to his expectations.

De Gaulle's funeral is going to take place in a quite manner in his village without any pomp or show or state ceremony in accordance with his will, which he drew up in 1952 and placed a copy with Pompidou who was his associate and is presently the president of France. A memorial service would, however, take place in Paris, which is going to be attended by some 82 kings, presidents and heads of government.

I am particularly grieved at his death as he showed so much kindness to me from time to time and was a good friend of Pakistan.

14 | SATURDAY

📖 The best part of East Pakistan and especially the coastal belt ranging from Khulna to Cox's Bazaar, has been hit by another devastating cyclone. Winds up to 120 miles per hour and 15 to 20 foot tidal waves have been experienced, flattening and washing away everything that came in their way. The off-shore islands had especially been badly affected. Hundreds and thousands of cattle have been lost. Exact figure of loss of human life is not yet known, but guesses of 50,000 or more is mentioned. This means that the province has suffered three successive major natural calamities this year. This is heartbreaking. One feels so sorry for the people; there is no end to their suffering.

17 | TUESDAY

📖 A couple of people, who came from East Pakistan, had occasion to fly over the cyclone affected area and did not think the damage was as great as it was made out to be. However, from the photographs that have appeared in the press and shown on TV the picture looks pretty grim. Loss of life and property must have been pretty extensive. Meanwhile, there has been a generous response from all over the world. Aid in kind and money is pouring in from many countries and being delivered to the affected people.

📖 A friend who had recently been to China said that in spite of tremendous progress there was no lack of evidence of the existence of poverty. However, they were working very, very hard and in an organized manner whereas we were not. And without work there was scant hope of finding salvation. If we thought that political agitation and slogan mongering was the panacea, then we were sadly mistaken.

Contrast this with what the Japanese do. Taking a holiday is regarded as verging on disloyalty. No wonder that some Americans have predicted that by the turn of the century Japan would be the richest country in the world with a GNP of 4.5 trillion dollars, a staggering figure for a country with hardly any indigenous resources other than industries and technically trained manpower.

20 | FRIDAY

📖 I am told Qayyum Khan and his associates are being cold shouldered by Yahya. They are being denied proximity. In the past, they had almost free entry to him. If so, this change has come about through disillusionment. Qayyum Khan has not been able to muster the following he claimed, and as such has proved a disappointment even though he exploited Yahya's name to the full and compromised with him. There is also talk that Yahya has begun to rely on Mujibur Rahman and his Six Points are regarded with respect. Yahya has been led to think that Mujibur Rahman can be controlled whereas GHQ thinks otherwise.

General belief is that Mujibur Rahman will come in with a following of 110 to 120. In West Pakistan, the likes of Wali Khan, G.M. Syed and particularly Daultana are bound to join him, the last for personal reasons and also for protecting the interests of the Punjab. A feeling is growing in Punjab that their interests can be served best against the hostility of other provinces by joining the government. However, such a powerful combination would pose formidable problems for Yahya. He would be in no position to deny them what they want and they would certainly want the assembly to be sovereign and be able to set up a government pending the formulation of a constitution. As a result they will offer Yahya the presidency with limited powers until such time that martial law is lifted. This will be to the good if stability is achieved, but chances are that the opposition, in particular, will activate the rebels and take their grievances to the streets. What the effect of this will be on the people and in particular the army is anybody's guess.

I am told that the businessmen in Karachi are reluctant to contribute to the East Pakistan relief fund as a measure of protest against the treatment of the Bohra, Khoja and Memon business communities etc. and the treatments they are receiving at the hands of Bengali nationalists in East Pakistan. Inter-provincial rivalries are on the increase even in the West [wing] but they are becoming particularly sharp between the East and West [wing]. The Punjabis are becoming louder in their protest. They feel aggrieved on being exploited and at the same time abused and seem determined to put an end to all this. What has incensed them most are the anti-Punjabi speeches of Mujibur Rahman and his advocacy of a separation-like programme.

21 | SATURDAY

Now that contact is established with the cyclone affected areas, the extent of the damage is beginning to be known. It is staggering. Some three million people have been affected. The estimate of the human death toll ranges from 1.5 lakh to 10 lakhs. A much larger number of cattle must have perished and houses and crops over millions of acres destroyed. This is heart breaking. The only redeeming feature is that the administration is moving vigorously to rehabilitate and the world at large has responded generously with aid, goods and cash worth more than 15 crores offered so far. Some countries have sent helicopters and assault boats for quicker distribution of relief materials in inaccessible islands and outlying places. This should help in distributing food, clothing, medicines and construction material.

22 | SUNDAY

East Pakistan politicians and especially Bhashani and his group are attacking the administration vigorously for not taking adequate steps to take relief to the affected people promptly and adequately. They maintain there is no coordination amongst governments. Relief agencies and materials are moving in a haphazard manner from Dacca whilst the population is suffering and dying. It looks like the government does not exist according to him and in any case the central government is taking hardly any interest. A good deal of this is probably politicking but there must be some element of truth in it too. Several foreign countries that are bringing material to Dacca by air are complaining that they have to wait for hours for unloading. Organizations like UNRRA have got so disgusted with the inefficiency of relief organizations that they have started operating on their own. There is no doubt about it that the communications to these areas are hazardous and non-existent and difficult but it is also clear that relief organizations in the province which is subject to these calamities is ill organized, inefficient and lacking contingency plans. True the ferocity of the cyclone was unprecedented but the relief organizations too had their trousers down. There is also an indication that the initial estimate of the damage by the government was low; hence, an attitude of complacency. And yet the rest of the world made much more realistic assessment; hence, such prompt and generous response.

27 | THURSDAY

Whereas Bhashani is fulminating and accusing the central government and West Pakistan of all sorts of perfidy and holds threats to boycott the election if not postponed, Mujibur Rahman has gone further and carried out blistering attacks against them for lack of sympathy and inadequate relief measures, and given an ultimatum that the failure to hold elections in time would be regarded as a sure indication of reluctance to give autonomy to Bangladesh. The only course open to them then would be to sacrifice another million people in a struggle to win their political rights. The object of the struggle would be to win autonomy and not secession—at least not yet, he maintained. I had heard a similar statement made by a man like Sobur Khan in a cabinet meeting though he is regarded as a moderate.

It is obvious that Bengali thinking on autonomy and eventual separation is common to politicians of most shades and it is not surprising. The bond of common religion is not as strong and enough today as we would like it to be. Besides, there are powerful forces that work against it. For one, the process of development through which we are passing is by itself disruptive. Secondly, in the same respect human psychology resembles that of other animals in dislike or fear of those markedly different from themselves. This is a deep rooted and complex phenomenon. No amount of legal or artificial arrangements can bring about speedy change. It is unfortunate but it is true that racial and cultural differences act as a powerful source of tension, erupting into open hostility on supposed or real grievances, however trivial. So Pakistan is faced with a terrible dilemma. It cannot exist without a strong centre and yet its people are often weakening it. Parochial feelings too are spread to an extent that it ceases to be an effective instrument. How this tangle is going to be resolved is anybody's guess. Perhaps there will be no formal resolution but placid expectation of a virtual state of separation and disintegration. For instance, I am told that Yahya and his associates see nothing wrong in accepting Mujib's Six Points and even if there is any reluctance Mujibur Rahman's pressure tactics will make them surrender completely. Their policy being to take and least line of resistance.

The British amongst others are giving magnificent assistance in the flood affected areas but at the same time their information media like the BBC is highlighting and harping on Bhashani's and Mujibur Rahman's offensive statements against the West [wing] and central government. They maintain that an unfortunate and unhappy alliance between the two wings is probably reaching breaking point. I suppose the Indian radio must be doing the same with a vengeance. They have got a God-sent opportunity. All this is bound to aggravate feelings in East Pakistan and finding a *modus vivendi* which will become with them more and more difficult. Somehow force of circumstances is accelerating the pace of disintegration and favouring those who advocate it.

28 | SATURDAY

📖 Yahya held a press conference in Dacca in which foreign correspondents were also present and answered criticism that is levelled against him and his administration in connection with the relief measures. I think he did a good job. He also announced that elections would be held as scheduled, as certain areas are affected by the cyclone. East Pakistan would have as much autonomy as it wanted in order to conduct its destiny and plan its future and utilize its resources within the framework of Pakistan. This should assuage the Bengali nationalists but I doubt if it would make them any more responsible. The agitation would move on to something else as they have to remain a party of protest. At any rate for the present this announcement would lend further strength to Mujibur Rahman.

📖 Shabbir Ahmed, a senior correspondent of the *Pakistan Times*, came to see me and spoke at length. He seemed more interested in talking than asking me questions. His tenor was that of pessimism about the future. He did not see how separation of the two wings could be avoided and how any form of stability could be maintained. The only hope, he said, lay in Yahya and General Hamid, but the trouble with Yahya was that he was weak and timid and lazy and a debauch.

He said that the Americans were using Bhutto in West Pakistan and Mujibur Rahman in East Pakistan. He said this is a common belief. To what extent is it true, God alone knows.

Shabbir Ahmed complained bitterly of Yahya's unjust treatment of our party. He said if their funds had not been frozen they would have come into the Central Assembly with a strength of at least 100 and would have proved a counter balancing act against the extremists.

Shabbir Ahmed said that in a press conference he covered Air Marshal Nur Khan who said that during eight years of his association with me as the chief of PIA and then as the chief of the air force, I never on a single occasion asked him to do anything irregular. I said not only him but no one in Pakistan could say that I ever put myself under obligation to anybody. This was necessary not only because I am built like that and take special care to protect my self respect, but I had to be in a position to take the hardest decisions against anybody if the occasion so demanded. And unfortunately occasions did occur when I had to remove from service even some of my closest relations. It was painful but I did so without any hesitation, in service for Pakistan.

The honest truth is that my relationship with people has never been personal. It has always been based on efficiency, competence and effectiveness. I have admired those qualities even in my enemies.

He said that some people blame me for being too soft. If I had taken drastic actions the mischief could have been nipped in the bud. I said if I had done that I would have been blamed for causing bloodshed for self-interest. Besides drastic actions, blood-letting, and vote-seeking don't go together.

1 | TUESDAY

📖 Someone confirmed that Yahya has dropped the previous plan of all-out support to Qayyum Khan on finding that he, Qayyum, is not making much headway. Now he and his associates are relying on the hope that mushroom parties, not being able to frame a constitution within 120 days, would then turn to Yahya to give one to them as they would not like to force another election, it being such an expensive hobby. This plan it too simple and naïve. Politicians are no fools. They are well aware of the fact that agreement amongst them is not possible but at the same time they are not going to lose initiative and take the blame unnecessarily. So they are going to manoeuvre in a manner that will pass on the blame to Yahya. Most likely they might well start off with the demand that the assembly be declared as completely sovereign and a fresh government be formed out of the assembly members who would be asked to pilot the constitutional proposals failing which they would boycott the assembly. In the event of acceptance of these proposals Yahya would be rendered powerless. In the case of refusal he will be isolated in the sense that about 1000 elected members of these assemblies, straining at the leash to get into power, will be after his blood exerting all possible pressure which he will find impossible to resist. I would not be a bit surprised if he gives in completely. He has already accepted Mujibur Rahman's Six Points by saying that East Pakistan can have as much autonomy as it wants. Having got him to retreat, the politicians tried to get Yahya on the run. That done, the stage of sharing spoils will come, then the real dogfight for power will start amongst them. What would be the state of the country by then is anybody's guess. And what would follow such chaos lies in the realm of the unknown but prospects are not cheerful.

4 | FRIDAY

📖 People like Mujibur Rahman and Bhashani are thoroughly lacking in scruples. On one side they are complaining of insufficient relief measures and on the other they are doing nothing to help the sufferers even by word of mouth. On the contrary they are holding demonstrations and whipping up feelings against West Pakistan and creating law and order situation for the administration, diverting its energies from relief work and preparation for holding elections.

5 | SATURDAY

📖 Bhashani and his group together with Ataur Rehman[34] and others held a public meeting in Dacca in which they berated the central government and the West Pakistan government and leaders for lack of sympathy for the cyclone sufferers and demanded the implementation of the Lahore Resolution of 1940.[35] In other words, independent and sovereign state of Bengal that was what most of the Bengali nationalists always meant when they talked of complete provincial autonomy but it is the first time they have made an open declaration of their real intention.

Some may say that this demand is made only in pique and in competition with Mujibur Rahman who seems to be drawing too much attention. That too may be right but the real explanation I feel is that having found that Yahya has conceded all the autonomy East Pakistan wants, Bhashani and his associates feel that the time is ripe to make open their real intention so that the constituent assembly does not get involved in a futile attempt to evolve a unified Pakistan. Instead, they should face hard facts of life and plan division of the country. I would not be a bit surprised if this does not spur Mujibur Rahman to go even further than Bhashani. He may well have been waiting for such an opportunity; making independence a common cry of Bengal and turning it into an irresistible movement. I hope we are not witnessing the beginning of the end.

6 | SUNDAY

📖 There is natural and understandable demand for introduction of Islamic laws, *fiqh*, in the country. So far so good, but the trouble arises in the choice of acceptance of *fiqh* as every sect has its own. If Hanfia, the *fiqh* of the majority, is enforced the others would refuse to accept and rebel. Some people have suggested that the answer lies in discarding all the existing *fiqh*s which in any case are based on *Sunnah* and *Shari'ah* that at times contradict the Quran and were compiled about 250 years after the death of the Holy Prophet based on hearsay and perhaps fabrications and a new *fiqh* be drawn up by mutual consultation based on the Quran and in the light of present day circumstances. This is easier said than done. If it were possible for Muslims to be prepared to accept such a solution bitter feuds that arose over the last 14 centuries would have been avoided and unity of the *millat* maintained. The truth is that if no one *fiqh* is universally acceptable an agreed new *fiqh* cannot be evolved. We shall be left with no alternative but to rely on secular public laws for now despite lip service to the contrary. Sectarianism, in which powerful elements have vested interests, has been and will continue to remain the bane of Muslim history. People quote the example of Saudi Arabia for the imposition of *Shari'ah*, little realizing that they are practically all Wahabis, in other words one sect subject to and willing to accept the same code. I suppose this problem would never be solved and therefore the controversy will never end in Pakistan and our politics would continue to be bedevilled by it. So instead of unifying it will be a disintegrating actor like so many other aberrations, such as regionalism, provincialism, linguistic problems, tribalism and individualism, and class hatred that have gripped the people's minds.

7 | MONDAY

📖 Today was the polling day for elections to the central assembly. The results are not yet known.

📖 Bhashani is going about repeating his demand for an independent and sovereign Bengal. The alternative, he says, is to be the slaves of West Pakistan. Some papers have tried to belittle this mischief by describing it as the voice of a frustrated man whose party is in disarray and who has lost influence. This may be so and his may be a solitary voice today, but that does not mean that his slogan will not catch on like the way Mujibur Rahman's Six Points did as it may well touch the inner chord in people's hearts. Separatist tendencies were barely below the surface in East Pakistan. The pressure of exploding population, privations and sufferings due to inflation, floods, and cyclones may well bring these to the surface. People may well be misled and believe that all this is due to the perfidy of West Pakistan and the answer lies in separation from them. This may sound thoroughly unreasonable and illogical but then our people are not famed for being logical. Besides Bhashani is no fool. He is a past master of choosing the right psychological moment to arouse emotions and mislead ignorant and gullible people to win a following.

8 | TUESDAY

📖 Today was a nerve-wracking day. As the results of the election started pouring in it became clear that Mujibur Rahman in East Pakistan and Bhutto in West Pakistan, especially in the Punjab, were scoring landslide victory. The party position is now as follows:

- Awami League 151 seats, all from East Pakistan. Nine seats in the cyclone affected areas where elections will be held later are also bound to go to them.
- Pakistan People's Party 81 seats, 62 from the Punjab, 18 from Sindh and 1 from NWFP.
- Independents, 11 seats including 7 from the tribal areas which should be available to the government in power.
- Ulema of different descriptions about 18 seats.
- The rest a few each.[36]

The meaning of this is that Mujibur Rahman would be able to command the majority, dictate the constitution and form a government on his own. On the other hand, he may form an alliance with Bhutto or if he wants alliance with someone in weak position, he may choose Daultana or Wali Khan with a small following. Of all the combinations the one between Mujibur Rahman and Bhutto would be the most dangerous and disastrous for the country as the former would seek almost separation for his province whilst Bhutto would get busy in forming cells in the army, civil services, leftist elements in the press, lawyers, labourers and others to support his dictatorship should the constitution not be formed or should it break down. He has no interest in democracy and the object of his supporters, at least the communists, can not be fulfilled unless conditions are created which facilitate clamping down of the communist order. They would therefore be seeking to create chaos primarily to enforcing their order. To what extent they would find Bhutto useful at that stage is a moot point. Chances are that they, finding him a hindrance, would eliminate him as he is only a power seeker and no communist at heart.

I can foresee that Bhutto and Mujibur Rahman would soon get together to chalk out a joint plan if possible. In any case they are bound to agree on demanding declaration of the assembly as a sovereign body and forcing their cabinet on Yahya. Bhutto would demand foreign affairs and the defence ministry, particularly the latter, as that would give him free approach to, defence services which is what he is yearning for. And I don't see how Yahya could refuse them these concessions after the staggering backing they have been able to muster in the assembly. Yahya is now like a caged bird in their hands with no room left for manoeuvre.

The staggering victory for Mujibur Rahman in East Pakistan was not wholly unexpected. This was a negative vote not unprecedented. It was based on parochialism and enmity towards West Pakistan which is held responsible for all their ills which are by no means few. It happened in 1954 and has happened again but the motive force behind Bhutto's victory is a new phenomenon. It is the result of strains and stresses and break up of old values produced by the process of development and modernization and resultant class consciousness with socio-economic factors. Not that all those that have been elected are so motivated but the bulk of the voters must have been. Bhutto has not made much headway on the Frontier. The only reason I can think of is that he did not know the Pushto language or the language of the masses.

Mujib and Bhutto's victory would have been of no great concern if they were normal people, but they are not, and especially the latter. He has unbounded ambitions besides being thoroughly unscrupulous with fascist tendencies. If there is any occasion to cause mischief he will not hesitate to do so to promote his interests. Whatever the cost to the country and the people, he may even precipitate a war with India and spoil our relations with countries like America and the Soviet Union. Mujib is no less reckless and dangerous.

If my assessment is any way near correct then 7th December 1970 may well prove to be the darkest day in the history of Pakistan and an unmitigated tragedy.

9 | WEDNESDAY

📖 Mr Suleri, while commenting on the results of elections in *Pakistan Times*, today has expressed satisfaction that Awami League in East Pakistan and People's Party in West Pakistan have come out with clear majorities. He hoped that Mr Bhutto would thus be able to protect West Pakistan's interest. This would be a reasonable expectation if Bhutto's aim was peace and stability in the country or he was interested in seeing parliamentary democracy work. On the contrary he would like to see turmoil and chaos so that he could enforce a totalitarian system of government of which he would be the head. Bhutto believes in extremes. His fate is going to be '*Takht or Takhta*' and nothing in between.

Election results should open the eyes of those who deluded themselves into believing that Bengali nationalism was confined to the urban educated people and did not affect the rural masses who were staunch Muslims and believed in a unified Pakistan.

Someone told me that Yahya was depressed with the election results. He did not expect that Mujibur Rahman and Bhutto would come in with such a sweeping majority, almost eliminating others. He also told me that General Peerzada had the best of both worlds. He had Yahya in the pocket and was also very friendly with Bhutto. There were indications that he kept Bhutto posted with secret information. General Sher Ali too, he thought, was a degenerate and a liability. He could not understand why he was ever engaged and appointed as minister in a sensitive ministry.

The conclusion that can be drawn from these elections is that people have discarded the old politicians and are dissatisfied with the past and are in a desperate mood. Most of them have either been defeated or succeeded with a very small following. In doing so people have voted cutting across family, tribal and local affiliations which was most unexpected and a healthy change. The discarding of old politicians is understandable. They were thoroughly exposed even during my time.

It is now clear that the agitation against me was essentially sparked off and led by Bhutto and then carried on by Asghar Khan. The old politicians had very little public appeal and took a minor part though claiming high credit as far as West Pakistan was concerned. In East Pakistan Mujibur Rahman provided the impetus with Bhashani playing a contributing role.[37] Asghar Khan's defeat has also demonstrated that he was cashing in on Bhutto's following. Once Asghar fell out with Bhutto he lost ground. If the two had remained together, between them they would have formed a formidable combination, and swept the election throughout West Pakistan like the way Mujib did in East Pakistan. But they could not stay together as they are both over ambitious men and cannot bear to be number two to anybody. Where Asghar Khan went wrong was that having gained popularity on the basis of protest he should have remained with the party of protest. Instead he took to advocating status quo to gain popularity with the moderates and lost.

The ulema too have not done too well. For one they were hopelessly divided, and secondly, they had no socio-economic programme worth the name. Their appeal to the people, who were looking for something new, was hackneyed and therefore limited. It did not raise much enthusiasm. The right lesson for them would be to continue to confine themselves to giving people spiritual and moral sermons and refrain from using religion as a vehicle for promoting political ends.

We must not forget that 50 per cent of our population is under 25 years of age. The transistor, the television and the press, mass media, etc. has had a marked effect on their outlook, besides the impact of industrialization, modernization and urbanization. They are yearning for a change—old values carry little consideration with them. So the old appeals have very little relevance especially now that the population is exploding. The economic revolution is not keeping pace with the educational revolution, adding every year a host of educated unemployed to the already large unemployment market and thus increasing frustration.

10 | THURSDAY

📖 Bhashani has kept up his demand for independence and has appealed to Mujibur Rahman to use his preponderant majority for the achievement of the noble cause. He turned this election as a referendum for gaining freedom from domination of West Pakistan politicians, bureaucrats and businessmen. He said at best there could be a loose form of confederation and even an arrangement like the RCD but no more. My view is that he is voicing the inner feelings of his people, right or wrong. This is their thought pattern therefore why should he not be taken seriously. This demand may sound premature today but would become common once Mujib fails to solve the mounting problems of the province, as he is bound to.

Mujib has said that complete autonomy yes, but independence not yet. Meaning thereby that they wanted some more time to milk Punjab and Sindh who have the surpluses and build their economy and then talk of separation. Though these provinces have sold themselves to Bhutto and have no voice of their own left, I wonder if they would not rebel against such an idea. The demand for separation may well start in these provinces once the reality dawns, as it is bound to in course of time, that they are being robbed. This is tolerable in a unified country but not otherwise.

📖 A man who accompanied Yahya on his trip to China and then again went with him to supervise relief work in East Pakistan said things that are unbelievable. For instance, when Yahya returned from China and came to Rawalpindi after a couple of days stay in Dacca a rumour had spread that he returned to Pindi in haste because there had been a military coup. Similarly, when he again went to Dacca and stayed there for some time it was said that he was under arrest in the presidential residence.

This man also visited the cyclone affected areas and saw the havoc caused by it and the relief work and disposal of dead bodies and carcasses. He said that for some days after the initial inrush of sea the whole area was covered by it and there was no way that foodstuff or other materials could be dropped by air. As soon as the water receded, the operation started and the army and the civil relief teams spread out. Help also started coming in from friendly countries. The communications were poor as they were completely disrupted, yet the army relief teams reached every nook and corner. No one died of starvation or cholera though some people suffered from diarrhoea through drinking saline water as all sources of pure water had been polluted. Yet the Dacca press was full of lurid stories of death, deprivation and suffering through starvation and cholera. Government denial and explanation of the truth was given no credence and was deliberately played down as pre-planned mischief. He said from the chief secretary down to the common man in the street blamed West Pakistan for callousness. They blamed West Pakistan for doing nothing whilst the rest of the world was rushing in aid. The fact is that whilst East Pakistan was making no contribution, collection of relief work was taking place all over West Pakistan. This was given no credence. The army was blamed for not sending small observation helicopters which could carry only a couple of people and are no use for carrying heavy loads across India which it had given permission to do so. India radio kept on blaring away lies and poisoning people's minds further.

He said he had never seen such anti-West Pakistan feelings before, all deliberately engineered by the press and the politicians. It was under such circumstances the election took place and Mujibur Rahman took full advantage of it and reaped a unprecedented political harvest.

Another phenomenon which surprised this man was that the local people would not bury their dead. Apparently the custom is that only a certain class of people did the job. So all that was done by the soldiers whilst the locals looked on. The president, on seeing this, was surprised and asked the locals why they did not help. This was translated to them by several officials in Bengali but what the official said was that if you help you would be given money. Eventually they were given rupees ten per body to bury their dead in order to save time and prevent spread of epidemic. Some carcasses were covered with kerosene and burnt. This at once started a howl in that Dacca press that dead were being burnt so the process had to be stopped.

He said there was no congestion of relief materials. Everything was moving smoothly under supervision of the army.

He said Yahya looked very concerned about the results of the elections and seemed to be unhappy with General Peerzada and the intelligence agencies. He must be dissatisfied for not being well informed or misled. The trouble with our intelligence agencies and especially the Director, Intelligence Bureau, is that they tell stories after the event which can be picked up from any newspaper. What they don't do is give advance information which can only be obtained by infiltrating into subversive organizations and finding out their plans. I always had my doubts whether the policemen were the correct people to man such an organization. You need people with much more flexible and subtle minds for a job like that. To achieve that I had appointed a committee under Yahya, but apart from tinkering here and there nothing original came out. This man told me that former General Akbar was the brainchild behind all the planning or establishment of the PPP and conducting their election campaign. I can quite believe that. General Akbar is a great schemer and so were his associates like Major Ishaq and others of the Pindi conspiracy case.[38] They all have communist leanings and must have got together on this venture. They must also be happy on Bhutto's success in the hope that they may well open the way for their lifelong ambition of establishing communist order. There are other hardened communists like Rahim,[39] Mubashir,[40] Rasul Baksh Palejo[41] and Mahmood Kasuri and others too who must have lent a helping hand in evolving theory and action. There is no doubt about it that Bhutto has a substantial number of seasoned and experienced communists behind him apart from large volatile masses of youngsters. But if there is a struggle for power, I would not be a bit surprised if General Akbar makes a bid to supplant Bhutto. The only thing against it is that he is getting on in age, being over sixty years old.

I was also told by this man that the feeling was growing amongst some people that in spite of temporary enthusiasm for the general elections and introduction of parliamentary democracy, the country was bound to slip into fascism. There was no other way to maintain stability, hold it together or govern it. I said this was exactly what Bhutto would like to see happen and was working for it but I can't see any one man ruling both the wings. However, it was quite possible that there would be separate fascists in both the wings or more likely communists.

11 | FRIDAY

📖 It is surprising what little success Wali Khan's party met on the Frontier. They captured only three seats out of 18. He was, of course, powerfully opposed by Qayyum Khan and the mullahs who stole the march over him by capturing 6 or 7 seats. But what probably decisively went against him was his and his father's past impeccable hostility to Pakistan and extra territorial loyalty. Some people in the Frontier, especially in Peshawar and Mardan, did want separate provinces but within Pakistan and not outside it.

12 | SATURDAY

📖 The People's Party victory in West Pakistan has obviously come about because of the people's desire for change in the socio-economic order in which the wealth of the country is equitably divided and gets equal opportunity. They think that Bhutto's promise of socialism provides the answer. I don't think that the concept of socialism is quite clear. They think that others' property and earnings will be divided amongst them and that they will have nothing more to do. This is blissful ignorance. However, one thing is clear: they are not satisfied with the existing state of affairs and they would like to change for the better. So the maintenance of the status quo, however well camouflaged, is not going to give them any satisfaction nor for that matter change to a socialistic order which takes long time to produce results. So many fundamental changes have to be brought about in launching it and make it work. However, one thing is certain that the only type of socialism that can work in this country is the one practiced in the Soviet Union and China. In other words, rigorous regimentation and discipline under an authoritarian rule and no democracy or freedom of speech etc. I don't suppose the bulk of our people, who are illiterate and ignorant, are conscious of this stark reality. If they think that they can have socialism together with freedom then they are living in the world of make believe. On the other hand, such a change may not be so traumatic for them, after all, democracy has never been our historical experience, not for any length of time. As far as the socialists and communists are concerned they would like to keep people in the present state of ambiguity and ignorance until such time that the point of no return is reached. Deception is their well-known tactic and is applied successfully through focusing attention on and highlighting local grievances and inequities to bring about general disinclination on which a communist system can be imposed.

13 | SUNDAY

📖 Mahmud A. Haroon came to dinner and discussed the political situation in the country in consequence of the recent elections. Bhutto's party's success, he said, was quite unexpected. It has brought the country to the threshold of communism. Only a miracle could save us as no individual of any stature was in sight who could resist the situation.

Bhutto himself must be most surprised by his success and indeed embarrassed as he would be expected to redeem his pledges which he knows he could not fulfil, Mahmud said. Sound judgement should tell him to remain in opposition and continue with his posture of protest but being a Sindhi he shall not be able to resist the temptation to get into power by forming a government with Mujibur Rahman and hope that it would lead to his and Mujib's exposure and downfall. He said Yahya would be well advised to dissolve his cabinet as the officials from now on would be looking over their shoulders towards their new masters. I said Yahya may well be forced to do that in any case under the pressure of assembly members. They are bound to demand the formation of a cabinet out of them so as to be able to pilot the constitutional bill. Amongst other considerations, such a demand would be logical and irresistible.

The separation of East Pakistan, he said, was only a matter of time. It was getting nearer every day but the danger was that in the process they would make every effort to destroy West Pakistan too.

In parting, I asked him that is it not the height of tragedy that the fate of the country should be put in the hands of debauches, opportunists and charlatans like Mujibur Rahman and Bhutto? The mere thought of it is revolting and nauseating. Yet our press and other news media gloat over the people's political maturity and want to make it believable that the electorate has acted responsibly and meaningfully. The truth is that the issues are so involved as to be beyond the comprehension of illiterate and ignorant masses. True, they have been able to register dissatisfaction but they also got carried away by false promises incapable of fulfilment. They did not realize that they were being cheated and misled by political opportunists mad after power who would not hesitate to jeopardize the interest of the country to provide their personal ends. Disenchantment would surely come to people, but after a lot of damage has been done. Mahmud A. Haroon commented on the character of our people. He said 99.9 per cent were untrustworthy, self-seekers and opportunists. He disagreed with me when I said that I got so much done by this very material. He said to get that, I carried most of the burden myself and as soon as I left the thing lopped. It was just like a steel girder falling to the ground when the current is cut off from a magnet holding it. He thought that Yahya might be able to cope with the situation if he showed firmness even at this stage. I said for one, he is not built that way. He believes in appeasement and gives in to pressure. Secondly, his position vis-à-vis the elected representatives with such a big following has been very much weakened. He dare not confront them at this stage. He could have done so in the beginning and dealt firmly with some of them and nipped the mischief in the bud, but he chose not to do so and lost the opportunity. I think it was that wrong decision that would go down in history as the undoing of the country.

15 | TUESDAY

📖 Bhutto has given a statement that I and my associates will be tried in an open court when the people's government comes into power. Well, we shall face it when the occasion comes. Bhutto could have been brought to earth if the martial law government had shown any strength of character. But he had succeeded in brow beating and getting them on the run so unless he is handled firmly he shall continue to ride the high horse and be obnoxious. Just heard on the radio that General Sher Ali has resigned and that his resignation has been accepted. He may have done so in the belief that the coming times are going to be difficult and that he had better get out in time. Perhaps people like Bhutto are bound to attack him and it is highly unlikely that Yahya would give him any cover or protection, for Yahya may have found out his immaturity and superficiality and told him to quit. I know that Mahmud Haroon, too, has been feeling uneasy and frustrated in the cabinet. A number of times he has expressed the desire to leave as he did not feel he was doing anything useful. I think he felt that he was not trusted. People like General Peerzada and Qizilbash stole the march over others, being more glib and deceptive.

I am told that in several places people have refused to pay house rent and share of land produce to the landlords in the firm belief that after 17th December, Bhutto would come into power and all this property would become theirs.

16 | WEDNESDAY

📖 I had a haircut this morning. My barber told me that a man told him that he voted for Bhutto because he made certain promises. When told that where was the guarantee that he would be able to fulfil them, the man answered that that did not matter, at least he had made the gesture that others did not. You can see how dissatisfied people are with the status quo and are clutching at any straw that gives them hope for change, however small. Population and inflation are playing havoc with the people but can anybody hope to satisfy their demands?

📖 A knowledgeable person told me that General Sher Ali was made to resign as he bitterly criticized the martial law regime, in the presence of General Hamid, on the conduct of elections and their pampering of Bhutto etc. General Hamid passed it on to Yahya who called for General Sher Ali's resignation. General Sher Ali was also refused an interview by Yahya. Meanwhile, I am told that Yahya has re-established contact with Bhutto probably in response to instinct or self-preservation. This explains why, whilst being critical of everybody else, he has spared Yahya and the regime. A similar approach, I suppose, will be made to Mujibur Rahman as Yahya's future lies in grouping with these people besides getting them to draw up a reasonable constitution.

This man said that whilst Yahya is basically a bad man, he is a lesser evil for the country as well as for me. So his continuance as the president in the present circumstances was necessary.

18 | WEDNESDAY

📖 This morning it was clear that Mujib is sweeping everywhere in East Pakistan. Bhutto is having large majority in the Punjab and a comfortable majority in Sindh. The pattern on the Frontier and Balochistan is not yet clear, but there is no certainty of any party gaining a clear cut majority. Qayyum Khan has however been defeated by Sherpao, a PPP man in Peshawar. This will dampen the style of those who got elected on his ticket in the hope of being suitably rewarded. Lot of voters, especially in Hazara, were influenced by the hope of Qayyum Khan becoming the chief minister and therefore voted for his candidates. If they had any inkling of his fate in Peshawar I am sure they would have acted otherwise. Yahya has declared an amnesty for all the political prisoners who were convicted under martial law regulations. They mostly belong to the People's Party and the Awami League. I don't suppose he has done it from any particular love for them, but it is not bad statesmanship to appease rather than fight or confront rising forces.

19 | SATURDAY

I understand that Qayyum Khan is very worried as he has lost the contest to the provincial assembly from Peshawar and has only got 10 of his followers elected out of a total of 40. That puts him out of the race for the chief ministership of the Frontier on which he was banking upon after having failed to get much of a following in the Central Assembly. His effort will now be to get as many of the splinter groups as possible to join him to secure a majority in the house and also get someone to vacate a seat for him from which he could be comfortably elected. I suppose someone from Hazara might oblige. There is no dearth of sycophants who would be ready to do that, for a consideration, of course.

I am told that Raja George Sikander Zaman,[42] who won the provincial seat against my son, has spent rupees 12 lakhs. It is not easy to believe that but the figure has been quoted by so many knowledgeable persons as not to be ignored. Qayyum Khan alone got rupees 1 lakh in cash and a car worth 97,000 which speaks nothing but a good deal of expenditure on his election, receptions, demonstrations, and processions and motorcades. In return George Sikander Zaman was expecting to be appointed as a minister by Qayyum Khan for Qayyum Khan gave him that hope to scrounge whatever he could out of it. It is surprising the length to which people would go to get an office. Poor George Sikander Zaman must now be crestfallen that there is no hope of Qayyum Khan becoming the chief minister. But George Sikander Zaman is not the only one Qayyum has soaked. I am told that everyone who got his ticket had to cough out a fair amount. Considering the size of Qayyum Khan's belly it needs some filling.

But why single out Qayyum Khan, he is typical of the product of Peshawar city and those that imbibe its spirit. Barring a few honourable exceptions it is the breading ground of devious crooks and cheats.

In my younger days I was at one time Brigade Major of the Peshawar brigade. As such I had many duties—amongst them the protection of water supply which came from Bara and was at that time subject to tribal attacks. Someone told me that Bara water was most wholesome for health. I agreed but added that it also provided the biggest crooks on God's earth and specially those who are the prodigy of provincial civil servants who served their British masters well but thrived and brought their children up on bribery and corruption. The effect is undeniable, most of them have made a success of their lives, but deceit and cunning and treachery is written large on their faces.

The first good news I have heard for a long time. Pakistan has beaten India in hockey in the Asian finals in Bangkok. Both the teams showed superb performance.

There are inspired leaks in the press that the administration is trying to remove all irritants to create a healthy atmosphere for the framing of the constitution. The release of all political prisoners was a move in that direction. Re-institution of the Council of Administration, as was created on imposition of martial law, was removed, and removal of the present cabinet is decided upon. If it means bringing back the three service heads to run the civil administration and contaminate it with politics, then it would be a sad day. Already some good people have been lost and driven into politics where they have made asses of themselves. But the object, I suppose, is to pander to the politicians and specially Mujibur Rahman and Bhutto and give them no cause for complaint. The whole trend is to keep them on the right side. The National Assembly is supposed to be convened in Dacca on February 1st where it will elect the speaker and decide on the voting procedure. Should the constitution be passed on the basis of a simple or two-thirds majority? Mujib's party being in overwhelming majority would naturally opt for the former and probably force it. This might well start a big row, should the West Pakistanis resist. And if Bhutto wants an all out with Mujib, this would be the right occasion to do so by championing the cause of West Pakistan. After these matters are decided or not decided as the case may be, the Assembly is supposed to shift its venue to Islamabad. What a queer and artificial and wasteful arrangement. It is also blissfully hoped that no major party would want to go outside the bounds of the Legal Framework Order.

So it can be seen that the administration, whilst meaning well, is surrendering all along the line and leaving no initiatives in its hands, thus giving the impression of being helpless. Therefore there is no compulsion on the part of the political politicians to behave responsibly or even listen to the president's advice. The president will have to sign on the dotted line unless East and West Pakistanis fall out with each other. He may well be counting on that but that depends very much on Mujibur Rahman and Bhutto not hitting it off, which is not improbable.

The fact is that after these elections and with the emergence of two strong political parties, Yahya has been rendered completely ineffective and neutralized. Even if he wishes to take a strong line people would not take it from him. So *ipso facto* the country's future is at the mercy of Mujibur Rahman and Bhutto. What a fate and tragedy.

I am beginning to feel that Bhutto will not come to terms with Mujibur Rahman and vice versa. It is not that Bhutto does not want a united Pakistan. He does, provided he is the ruler. Since the Bengalis would not accept him, he would be content with the rule of West Pakistan and that can happen only if there is separation of the two wings. So I would not be a bit surprised if he encourages and even drives Mujibur Rahman to extremes. There could be rows over the voting system, second house, division of powers between the centre and the provinces, permanent rule of East Pakistan etc. Mujibur Rahman too would like to use his strength to get the maximum he could for his province and would not like to be sorted out or be dictated to by Bhutto. He would prefer to have the cooperation of West Pakistan leaders with a weak following.

There is suggestion in the press of installing cabinets in the provinces with the concurrence of political parties. I doubt if Mujib and especially Bhutto would accept that as that would at once put their tall election promises on trial. And if the promises can't be fulfilled, as they can't be because of lack of resources, then there is the obvious risk of public disillusionment and frustration setting in. Bhutto certainly and Mujibur Rahman too would not want to run such a risk. They would like to wait till they have complete control at the centre, so as to be able to manipulate things as they wish. But one thing is certain—people are not going to be satisfied with glib talk. They will expect concrete results and quickly, which, in turn, is impossible. So it is a vicious cycle.

These elections have shown that the younger generation, who tend to be leftist, are the decisive factor. It is also clear that this tendency will gain momentum, accompanied by violence, as time goes on. So any thought of peace, calm and stability in the country within the foreseeable future is out of the question as leftism is now an irreversible force. Any effort to divert let alone reverse it is out of the question. No amount of wailing by the older generation can avail, nor a call to old values or religion attract the younger generation. Their outlook is secular, whatever anybody thinks of this or however regrettable it may be.

21 | MONDAY

📖 Gohar and Aurangzeb with their children came from Peshawar for the day.

📖 One man, one vote and breach of parity has given Bengal permanent right to rule over West Pakistan. I doubt if people have quite realized the consequences. Once they do, which may not be too far away, the reaction will be sharp, my fear is that this factor by itself will tend to act as a divisive force.

Rule of Muslim communities by outsiders is not unknown. And even slaves have become rulers, but by merit. But the type of ascendancy which Bengal is now going to get in a democratic setup in a spirit of vengeance would be difficult to sustain and prove durable, especially when they will not be bearing the commensurate burden of running the government. In fact, they will be relying heavily on West Pakistan's resources. Such an unequal partnership often proves fragile and doesn't last. The answer is to bring sense to them and the dangers involved in this situation, but the Awami League leaders, with a heady victory, would be in no mood to listen to reason.

📖 A bunch of People's Party members headed by young lawyers from Manshera came to call. One was the son of a person I knew and looked very bright. He looked concerned. He said that his party had won a thumping victory in the Punjab and Sindh but their leaders have also made tall promises. It remained to be seen whether they could be fulfilled. I said they can't. He felt concerned. He spoke of Qayyum Khan as a most treacherous and untrustworthy man. I agreed but said that others are no different. I know them inside out. He understood what I referred to.

23 | WEDNESDAY

📖 I am told that people like Maududi and Daultana, seeing the dangers involved in the unprecedented success of Mujibur Rahman and Bhutto, are regretting their complicity of taking part in the agitation against me. Maududi especially professes that the approach of communism, present soaring prices and scarcity, might force people to do anything, he thinks. Someone else also said that if the present price level stayed like that for a month or so people would break.

People were expecting that once Bhutto's party won the majority, all the promises he had made would be fulfilled. For instance they were expecting to get a minimum wage raise of rupees three hundred per month, fourteen and a half acres of land free of land revenue each and so many other things like free education, housing etc. Those living in rented houses were promised occupation rights. So were the hired taxi drivers. Some did take over these vehicles and ran away with them but were later caught by the police. It is these promises that swayed the common man in the Punjab in Bhutto's favour.

Bhutto and his party men are now on the defensive. They are going about saying that they would fulfill those promises once they got the power. I think they certainly would do things that cost them nothing, for instance, lower the ceiling giving some land to the tenants, and some measure of industrial and commercial nationalization perhaps without regard to their effect on the economy. These measures may please a few but will hit a large number as production goes down, as it would, and the economy sags further still resulting in widespread discontent. The communists will be happy for the development of such a situation as they are with the present high prices and resultant uneasiness. In fact, they are already busy poisoning the people's mind against the business community and the landowners. No mention is ever made of the economic factors that may well be responsible for the present high price level. I am told that curious people with almost criminal record have got elected on Bhutto's party ticket in the Punjab. For instance, a man called Asghar, a dismissed sub-inspector and Bhutto's pimp in Lahore, is aspiring to become the chief minister. Kardar, an arch intriguer, is another contender. Such people will play havoc with the people and the administration when they get into power.

I see that skirmishing has already started between Mujibur Rahman and Bhutto. In an interview with a foreign correspondent, Mujibur Rahman is supposed to have asked, how could he form an alliance with a man who did not even know his own programme and was so inconsistent? Bhutto, in a speech in the Punjab, retorted that Mujibur Rahman dare not frame a constitution or form a government without his support. However, Bengalis of all shades are united in their aim and objective. West Pakistan and especially Punjab are divided and at the mercy of Bhutto whose sole aim is to use them for his political ends. He has been able to successfully hoodwink them so far and make fools of them.

📖 I have started buying the *Pakistan Observer*, a Dacca-based paper, from today to see what sort of thinking goes on there. In it I came across an interesting letter written to the editor to the effect that so much relief and assistance by the army and civil have been given to the people in his area affected by the cyclone that they have become lazy, dependent and lost all zest for work. So much so that they would not even rebuild their huts. He went on to say that unless the relief was stopped soon people's will to rehabilitate themselves would be destroyed. This was a refreshing contrast to the habitual complaint that enough was not being done for the sufferers of the cyclone.

27 | SUNDAY

📖 I am told that Yahya has ordered that his house, under construction in Peshawar, be completed within three months; that is significant. It means that he has decided to scuttle as soon as the constitution is framed and does not expect to be elected as president. It is doubtful whether Bhutto or Mujibur Rahman would support his candidature.

📖 A person came to see me today. He owns a Chevrolet car which used to be the cheapest make in America. He said so many people stared at him, a bicycle rider refused to give him the right of way shouting that the road belonged to him and as much to anybody else. Several taxi drivers did the same. In one place he was shouted at that the time was fast coming when he would have to part with that car and so on. It seems that class consciousness is developing and class hatred spreading, a sure indication of the pre-revolutionary period. People want to change though they are not clear what should be its shape. However one thing is clear, they will not tolerate class privileges and ostentation any longer. In this respect the rich people should emulate the *Bania*. He never flouted his riches and lived in obscurity.

📖 I saw a flash of Bhutto's procession demonstrating in Karachi on TV. It was fabulous. It is amazing how people get attracted to him without being able to see through him because the man is all froth and no substance.

📖 I see that Indira Gandhi has decided to dissolve the Lok Sabha some fourteen months in advance of its term. Fresh elections will be held early next year. The reason given is that after the split of the Congress Party, her faction does not command absolute majority. As such, she was meeting growing resistance from reactionary elements in pushing through her socialistic legislative measures like the nationalization of banks, taking over of the privileges of the princes etc. Whether measures alone would satisfy the hungry and impoverished masses are doubtful but the call of socialism is attractive and a definite electoral asset. The result of elections in Pakistan too may well have influenced her decision.

29 | TUESDAY

📖 Mr S.M. Zafar, my former law minister, came to call and stayed on for dinner. He said that chances of two wings staying together were remote. He said and thought that 1973 was about the furthest deadline Bhashani was asking for complete and immediate independence. He was probably closer to the inner feelings and was also forcing Mujibur Rahman not to resile from his Six Points. Bhutto, he said, was most anxious to get into power in collaboration with Mujibur Rahman for its own sake and also for keeping his party together which he would not be able to do in opposition. I said but by doing so Bhutto would be alienating hardcore leftists and also his supporters from the Punjab by making major concessions to Mujibur Rahman at the expense of West Pakistan. He said those were no problems because real leftists were not strong enough to be taken too seriously and Punjab representatives were of no consequence as they owed their election to Bhutto. His grip over them was complete. In any case, most of them were of no background or standing and in many cases of notorious character. They were going to play havoc when they came into power. In the provincial sphere drastic land reforms would come, land for the tiller would be the slogan, and better off people would be roughly dealt with. It would be distribution of poverty; there might even be bloodshed and civil war. At the national level banks, insurance and industries would be nationalized. Mujib would be only too glad to go along with that as East Pakistan had nothing to lose. The economy, already stagnating, would be shattered and any standing Pakistan had in the eyes of the world would also be gone. Arrival of chaos if not communism would then be inevitable if there was anything left in the country.

I said in such a state of demoralization and disintegration the army, the only national organization left would be compelled to fill the vacuum again. He said the circumstances of today were different to that of 1958 and 1969. Today, the army stood exposed and discredited as it had proved to be inept, incompetent and not proficient. The old myth that the army had some first class leaders was exposed, therefore, it would take time for the army to be re-establish its prestige. In any case, it was hamstrung because of East Pakistan.

30 | WEDNESDAY

📖 My son, Gohar Ayub visited Lahore and then came to see me. He said Bhutto was very popular in Lahore. Everyone he spoke to turned out to be his supporter. The reception Bhutto received in Lahore was one of the biggest ever given to anybody. He said his party men were determined to go through with their programme of land reforms, and nationalization of industry, including textiles. I said how will they run these things without any hope of maintaining discipline amongst workers and making any profit? He said the way that Nasser did. Gohar Ayub met A.B. Awan in Peshawar after his defeat in elections from D.I. Khan in which he forfeited his security deposit. He complained bitterly of the conduct of the people who stoned and abused him and his wife in places. He made a surprising statement that there is no democracy in this country. Seemed belated awareness on the part of a man who served for 35 years or so in the police in close contact with the people.

DIARY 1971

1 | FRIDAY

📖 Mujibur Rahman, having come in with such a preponderant majority on the issue of hatred against West Pakistan and in a spirit of vengeance, has lost all room for manoeuvre and is under no compulsion to compromise with the West wing on Six Points or other points even if he wishes to, which is doubtful. He is no longer a free agent. He is the prisoner of his vast support. They will accuse him of selfishness and betrayal if he makes any compromise and will not support him as they know what they would have to face on return to Dacca. So I don't see how Mujibur Rahman can resign from the extreme position he has been maintaining. Bhutto may try to compromise with him, but that too can only be up to a point. He would not like to be accused of selling West Pakistan down the drain.

So the net result may be the emergence of two autonomous regions. Though some Bengalis who have a thinking mind would like to be in a position to share the resources of West Pakistan as their own is not enough to keep them going.

However, what every sensible Pakistani should like to see evolve is the ultimate solution, however bitter or unpleasant. We can't go on going through the exercise of constitution-making every other day. My own solution would be to let Bengal and West Pakistan keep their own resources and live on them on account of central and provincial requirements. Khawaja Shahabuddin thought that would not be enough for Bengal. If that be the case then what I asked, is the object of spreading venom against the West and what is all this fuss about?

I think as time goes on this realization will dawn on Bengalis and they will find themselves on the horns of a dilemma. But they will never offer solutions. They will stick to their usual tactics of posing problems.

I said it is curious that the people have put the fate of the country in the hands of Mujibur Rahman and Bhutto. One is educated and sophisticated, the other is an uneducated and crude and uncouth political *goonda*. He said people have not much choice, having lost faith in the old politicians they took their chances on these two. I see there is considerable force in this.

I told Khawaja Shahabuddin that two trends are distinctively visible. One, movement towards disruption and anarchy in the name of socialism and communism, and secondly, estrangement and even separation between the two wings. No amount of effort can reverse these trends. He agreed that class consciousness and an atmosphere of class war is gaining momentum. Apart from the press the mass media like the government controlled radio and television has given it a great boost by publicizing uncontested views and propaganda of certain political leaders. The authorities might have acted in good faith, but in their innocence they have allowed a great amount of harm to be done to unquestioning, gullible and uncritical-minded masses. If they were told what was possible and what was not, the matter would have been different.

3 | SUNDAY

📖 I see there was a conspiracy against the Shah and top Iranian leaders, and also student unrest in Tehran University, which was notorious for ill discipline but remained quiet for several years as did the rest of the country. Iran was lucky in finding more oil resources some of which were diverted to economic development under the Shah's able guidance. Similarly, a number of major irrigation works and industrial projects had been completed and were bearing fruit. As such the country prospered and the people benefited. The rate of progress was visible and phenomenal. Tehran and, I am told, several other cities took on an utterly modern look, motor vehicles and wonder houses increased manifold. Roads, which used to be notoriously bad, improved beyond recognition in many parts of the country. On the whole, Iran was fast becoming a wonder country. But progress is by no means a barrier to convulsion and revolution. The craze for change is great all over the world especially in the developing countries.

4 | MONDAY

□ A mammoth public meeting consisting of over one million people was held under the auspices of the Awami League and addressed by Sheikh Mujibur Rahman after the oath taking ceremony of MNAs and MPAs elected on the party ticket, that they will do everything possible to carry out the party manifesto in letter and spirit to achieve political and economic emancipation and salvation of the people of East Pakistan. Special emphasis was laid on implementation of the Six Points of Mujibur Rahman and the eleven-points of his student supporters emphasizing that they were in no manner negotiable.

All sorts of promises were made to the people and a threat held out that if West Pakistan did not see the advantages of cooperating on his Six Point programme, he had enough strength in the assembly to carry them through on his own. When saying this he seemed to emphasize explicitly his stand and also hoping that some elements in West Pakistan like Daultana and Wali, etc. will see the inevitable of going along with him. He does not seem to rule out acceptance of his terms even by Bhutto. In fact, he foresees a scramble by West Pakistan leaders to get on his bandwagon, of course on his terms. In short, the message he wanted to convey was that West Pakistan had no choice but to accept his East Pakistani dictates and dominance since there was no point in bickering against it so why not swallow it, relax and enjoy.

Look at the strange irony of fate, Pakistan was made to escape the tyranny of an inflexible and hostile Hindu majority and yet a situation is developing within the country where there will be a permanent majority of one wing over the other without bearing a proportionately higher burden or higher liability. How can such an artificial alliance last?

6 | WEDNESDAY

□ I was rung up last night by Raja Sarwar that there was a move to unite the three leagues and a mission of representatives of three factions in Pindi wanted to call on me and get my blessing and guidance. I told him that I was no longer in politics but if they insisted they could send a representative to meet me.

This man, who is a lawyer by profession, turned up and proposed that unless the three leagues got together and formed a united front, the extremists would have a free field and would play havoc with the country. So the representatives of Council Qayyum League in Pindi had agreed to form an alliance and would I persuade the Sarwar brothers to join them. I agreed that it is an excellent idea but for its success he had better persuade the leaders of the three leagues on making a common front and an agreed programme. And that programme should aim at containment of Mujibur Rahman and

Bhutto, in educating people in what is possible and what is not, so that reason may prevail. He said Qayyum was willing but Daultana was hedging. I later discovered that Daultana was hoping to become the president with Mujibur Rahman's blessing, though that would be difficult if Yahya has a tie-up with Mujibur Rahman—then Mujibur Rahman would like to please Yahya to make use of him.

I asked him as to how Qayyum saw the future. He said Qayyum Khan was certain that Daultana was in league with Mujibur Rahman. He was also sure that Mujibur Rahman was not going to be reasonable and flexible on his Six Points demand. Qayyum Khan felt that in that event he would have no alternative but to stage a walkout from the assembly. He also knew that some 28 people were ready to defect from Bhutto's party if the political party's act did not come in their way. Qayyum Khan, he went on to say, felt betrayed by Sobur Khan who deliberately let his seat to an Awami Leaguer and by Wahiduzzaman and Qazi Qadir etc. for making no effort to fight to win. In fact, they all conspired to allow Sheikh Mujibur Rahman to have a big following. This is not easy to believe or swallow because all these men are terribly ambitious. I think Qayyum Khan is using it as an excuse to rationalize his failure in West Pakistan.

There is a general belief that Yahya has an understanding with Mujibur Rahman that he would be retained as president. This accounts for praises that Mujibur Rahman has been showering on Yahya lately in public meetings. Bhutto was supposed to be out of favour for sometime but he too is being wooed again now that he has done so well in the elections in West Pakistan. The price Mujibur Rahman would expect and demand in return would be complete support and acceptance of his Six Point programme which Yahya has already almost conceded, and if these points in any manner clash with the Legal Framework Order, a way would be found to get around them.

The situation, to say the least, is dangerous as the man who has the power of accepting or rejecting the constitution is compromised for personal reasons. He has thus no option left but to play to the tune of Mujibur Rahman and his benefactor.

9 | SATURDAY

📖 According to the news an unsuccessful attempt on the life of Mujibur Rahman was made by a young man as he was coming out of his house in Dacca. The assailant was overpowered and a dagger found on his person. He later confessed that he was hired and there were four other persons armed with pistols to cover him. Political assassinations or violence must be condemned in no uncertain terms but it is surprising that the man chose to use a dagger instead of a pistol, a far more effective weapon at close quarters and also for covering, withdrawal or to get away. If true, it must have been an amateurish attempt.

📖 Two journalists from Lahore came who asked me about Tashkent and if there were any secret clauses as part of it. I told them that there was no secret in that declaration. Bhutto knew that but he had succeeded in making people believe that there was. In doing that his object was to play on the emotions of the people, especially in the Punjab. The Objectives in going to Tashkent and signing the declaration were as follows:

a. The Soviets, for the first time, offered to mediate in a quarrel between two non-communist countries. Their prestige was at stake, besides they are our next-door neighbours and partial to

India. Refusal would have meant a rebuff to them resulting in deepening of their antipathy towards us and greater support to India. It would have been foolish on our part to take such a risk. The Soviet leaders were appreciative.

b. America had stopped military supplies to us. China had assisted but its capacity was limited. So we were anxious to find a new source and that could only be the Soviet. They gave an encouraging reply.

c. Arrange for early withdrawal of troops after the ceasefire in order to re-equip and retrain. If we did not do that we would be in the same position as the Israelis and the Arabs are since 1967. Withdrawal was achieved.

d. Find out if there was any chance of India seeing reason and coming to terms with us. I wanted to present the same sort of arguments to the Indians as Rajagopalachari[1] did the other day. I did not succeed but there was a chance of a forward move if Shastri had lived. He gave me the impression on the day previous to his death that he was sick and tired of the whole thing but he had political difficulties. But he agreed to hold discussions on a ministerial level.

The meeting did take place in Rawalpindi but proved barren. The Indians showed no spirit of compromise. So to all intents and purposes the Tashkent Declaration expired from that day.

The journalists asked me if there was any truth in the statement Nasrullah[2] made at the time that I had inspired Mujibur Rahman's Six Points. I said only a villain would level such a charge and a fool would believe that. Would a man engaged in unifying the people of Pakistan and making a nation out of them do such a thing? I said that some people accuse me of accepting the ceasefire in September '65 either out of sheer mischief or maybe even due to honest but mistaken belief. The truth is that Pakistan can only afford to have a deterrent army against an enemy five times larger in manpower and resources. The relative military budgets of the two countries at any given time would demonstrate this. Besides, our country is split in two halves, separated by a thousand or so miles. That factor further splits our strength. So in these circumstances for any Pakistani to expect that we could march to Delhi against a well equipped and first class fighting human material several times our strength would be the height of folly and ignorance. India of today is different to what it was at the time of Mahmood Ghauri.[3]

In the 1965 war our army put up a magnificent and unprecedented fight against a several times more powerful enemy offensive and brought them to a halt in no time and delivered hard counter blows. Very few such examples exist in military history. So, having blunted the enemy offensive and saved Pakistan, it had accomplished its mission to the utmost limit of its capacity. To expect it to do more would be inhuman. It goes to the eternal glory of the Pakistani soldier to have fought against tremendous odds and we must take our hats off to him. Besides, we had exhausted our reserves while fighting over a front of over 1200 miles. Critical ammunition was running short. India had accepted ceasefire on 15th September and world powers pressure on us was suffocating. Under such circumstances, what alternative did we have other than accepting a ceasefire and getting our army back to re-equip and retrain? We did not get Kashmir but we saved Pakistan and crippled India economically and militarily for its folly. What more was expected from us?

But what a curious fixation the Hindu leaders have that Pakistan is expansionist. Nehru used to speak in the same strain about Kashmir. He used to say if Kashmir was settled, Pakistan would make further such demands.

Now all this is either a fixation with the Hindu leaders or the fear of ghosts of Muslim domination in the past. Or just a subterfuge to maintain a posture of hostility towards Pakistan and not learn to live as good neighbours and reduce the fearful military burden they are carrying and make us do the same.

I should know what Pakistan's intentions are towards India. After all, I had been mainly responsible for making Pakistan's military plans for 19 years.

---

10 | SUNDAY

There is a rumour afloat that the aid to Pakistan consortium has decided to stop giving aid until the country gives itself a stable and reliable constitution and a government. I think there is good deal more to it than meets the eye. Most of them could not have much faith in Mujibur Rahman and Bhutto and probably have doubts about the future of the country. Would it remain one or split up? In other words, they don't want to run the risk of making a bad investment.

Our economy is running down rapidly. Prices are rising, unemployment increasing and production decreasing. The main cause is nervousness on the part of the entrepreneur and uncertainty about the future caused by the pronouncements of political opportunists and demagogues. The only cure is either to accept communism and change over to that system rapidly or to allow the present mixed economic system to function with rough edges, of course, removed. But I don't believe our people are ready to accept communism—not yet—and the politicians wouldn't allow the mixed economy to function. So we are in for a long period of privation, suffering and simple decay. What a prospect.

Mr Daultana was supposed to have made up with Qayyum Khan and they were to jointly address a public meeting in Peshawar on the 8th in support of Yusuf Khattak who is contesting a bye-election from a seat in Peshawar which Qayyum Khan had vacated. Everybody had thought that that was a prelude to all the leagues merging together, but I had my doubts as none of them would yield to so-called leadership of the others. That was what kept them apart and nothing else had happened to make them give up their selfishness. This proved to be right. Daultana, at the last minute, sent a telegram saying that he was suddenly taken ill so he could not come. The implication was obvious. He did not want to be seen in the company of Qayyum Khan and fall out with Mujibur Rahman with whom he has hopes of accommodation.

Qayyum Khan's support of Yusuf Khattak is also surprising. Until a month or so ago, Yusuf Khattak was berating Qayyum Khan day in and day out. The trouble or the 'Virtue' of our politicians is that they can change colours in no time to promote their selfish interests. That comes out of an utter lack of scruples. But it is quite conceivable that Qayyum Khan, whilst contesting and supporting Yusuf Khattak, may in fact be working against him. One of the allergies of Qayyum Khan is that he cannot bear to see an educated man come up on the Frontier in case he turns out to be a rival.

---

11 | MONDAY

A man who visited Dacca, Karachi and Lahore recently and met Mujibur Rahman, Daultana etc. said that the former was not happy with the overwhelming majority he had obtained. He would have been happier with a following of around 100 members from East Pakistan as that would have given him manoeuvrability to compromise with West Pakistan. Now he feels a prisoner of this majority and dare not compromise on Six Points. The student community would also not let him do so.

Mujibur Rahman, he said, had no intention of coalescing with Bhutto. Some 80 members mostly belonging to the People's Party from West Pakistan had already contacted Mujibur Rahman with a view to joining his party.

He said that Mujibur Rahman and his party men were on the horns of a dilemma. On one side, they wanted a weak centre, and on the other, they wanted resources to be transferred from West Pakistan which could only be arranged by a strong centre.

The businessmen and the industrialists in East Pakistan, he said, were very jittery. Some had offered to hand over the keys of their plants to the workers. Others were thinking of migrating.

He also confirmed that there was an understanding between Yahya and Mujibur Rahman that the former would be kept as the president. So Yahya and his Legal Framework Order were completely compromised. Yahya dare not go against Mujibur Rahman's wishes. The fact that Yahya goes all the way to Dacca to meet him instead of calling him here is enough confirmation. It also shows that Yahya is in a weak position and has lost the initiative.

He said that the mood in the Punjab was frightening. People are getting more and more determined to be rid of East Pakistan and they thought that only Bhutto could help them to do so. Bhutto too seemed to have come to the same conclusion, and in fact, had set up a working party of experts to work out the financial and other implications of separation.

A most disturbing news I have heard from several people is that servicemen and civil employees who were given the option to vote by post have done so mostly for Bhutto's People's Party.

The chickens that the smaller provinces had laid in undoing One Unit are coming home to roost. The governor of NWFP[4] announced that the province was running at a deficit of 10 crores on current account only. This does not include the expenditure on the tribal areas. And yet some people had the travesty to say that the smaller provinces were robbed and unfairly treated for economic development. This was all a made up story by the politicians to arouse parochial feeling and create small kingdoms for themselves of their size and stature. What suffering the people would undergo in consequences was no concern of theirs on the Frontier. The chauvinism of Peshawar and Mardan, especially the former, was mainly responsible for creating a separate province. They consider it their birthright to rule over others in the province. I don't think they would ever tolerate a man from other districts to be the head of the administration.

12 | TUESDAY

📖 Today the press was full of news of killings, rioting and rowdy violent demonstrations in several cities, students taking a leading role. Lahore has been put under military control as the People's Party members have taken up the cudgel on behalf of some dismissed journalist and have joined them in a hunger strike with the threat that they would take over the press concerned by force. Meanwhile, Bhashani, in a rally held in Santosh, has repeated his call for complete independence and reunification of the two Bengals. He said Jinnah had tricked them into accepting one Pakistan when the Lahore resolution envisaged two. If it were not for that they would never have supported it. Whilst all this is going on Yahya has decided to visit Larkana for a shoot and accept the hospitality of Bhutto. Fancy identifying himself with that mischief monger at this critical stage. How can that inspire confidence amongst decent and law abiding people who are already so disturbed and worried.

13 | WEDNESDAY

📖 The British High Commissioner, Cyril Pickard, came to convey greetings of Edward Heath, the British prime minister, who is an old friend of mine and was recently on a visit to Pakistan. Edward was very anxious to call on me but Cyril dissuaded him from doing so in case the administration found it embarrassing. Cyril said he had great difficulty in holding him back.

📖 Hassan Amin said that the other night Bhutto gate-crashed into Lt. General Gul Hassan's house, against his protestations through the assistance of Qureshi, and stayed on till after midnight. Lt. General Gul Hassan wanted to talk to him on serious matters but he kept on cutting jokes, mimicking and laughing, keeping everyone amused. I call this a strategy of indirect approach. Win the man's confidence first, find out his complaints against the seniors and then use him for nefarious ends at an appropriate moment.

In doing this Bhutto is looking ahead. He has judged Lt. General Gul Hassan correctly. He is a strong headed man, devoted to his profession with considerable influence with younger people and has strong likes and dislikes. He could be worked up on any serious issue.

Hassan Amin said on one occasion Bhutto told him to look after Lt. General Gul Hassan as he would come in useful one day. I am sure Bhutto's objective was to get Hassan Amin to pass this on to Lt. General Gul Hassan so that he felt obliged to Bhutto. Hassan Amin said that Lt. General Gul Hassan was no fool. He would not allow himself to be made use of. At the same time, he said that Lt. General Gul Hassan regarded Lt. General Hamid, the COAS, completely ineffective, as the man was under the influence of alcohol the best part of the day and night. Besides, he had no power of decision. Lt. General Gul Hassan had also complained against General Yahya for having promoted some useless people to the rank of General. He, that is Lt. General Gul Hassan, said that Musa had one useless Maj. General Nazir, who did so much damage around him whereas Yahya had so many. I told Hassan Amin that this is exactly the sort of thinking that Bhutto will exploit in order to involve and make use of Lt. General Gul Hassan. Hassan Amin said that Mujibur Rahman was no match for Bhutto. Bhutto would twist him around his little finger. I have also heard people say the Mujibur Rahman regards himself no smaller *goonda* than Bhutto. Let us see who twists whom. But one thing is certain, several of Bhutto's elected members have already given their allegiance to Mujibur Rahman. Bhutto, too, is aware of this, so Mujibur Rahman is not sitting idle.

📖 Lt. General Hamid has been promoted to the rank of general. I am told that Yahya rang him up and congratulated him. General Hamid's response was typical. He was not all that thrilled. Presumably he is tired of remaining in suspended animation and not being appointed as the Commander-in-Chief.

14 | THURSDAY

📖 Yahya, on his departure at the airport in Dacca and on arrival in Karachi, gave statements to the press that Mujibur Rahman was the future prime minister. But he would not be there when that happened. When questioned on the deteriorating economic conditions and rising prices, he admitted that the country was badly off and there was no hope of prices falling unless people worked hard. He had no magic wand in his hand to put matters right. He went on to say that he inherited the situation caused by several months of lawlessness, rioting, *gherao*s, *jalao*s, unprecedented floods, devastating cyclones etc. and would hand over to Mujibur Rahman, implying that he would put matters right, as if it would be in his power to do so?

15 | FRIDAY

📖 Quaid-e-Azam's mausoleum has been completed. Yahya carried out the opening ceremony and delivered a speech saying that he and his advisor, Lt. General Peerzada had to make special efforts to complete the work which was going on in a leisurely fashion in the past.

It is good that the mausoleum has been completed. It is also good to hear that Yayha and Lt. General Peerzada took special interest in its completion. But to say that the work was going on in a leisurely manner in the past is nothing but travesty of truth. Every effort was made to hasten its completion but procurement of vast amounts of suitable Pakistani marble and its preparation and fixing action was a major problem and time consuming. The truth is that if it was not for my personal interest, this work would never have started let alone finished.

📖 I was told of an example of Bhutto's dramatics in a public meeting. He said people accuse him of drinking. If he drank it was not people's blood as the imperialists, industrialists and landlords did. There were loud cheers and encouragement to continue with drinking. He said he was accused of carrying alcohol on his person. Thereupon he took off his coat and undid his tie and asked someone to search him, which was done and nothing found on it. Another loud cheer. Then he said he was accused of womanising. Was that not a sign of virility for a young man? Another loud cheer. He said why blame him for sending his daughter to a school in America. Was it not a good thing to get her to know the tricks Americans play and caution the people of this country against them? Another cheer. But one thing he prayed he should not be asked to do. To divulge what was in his attaché case. On that, a few people who had been planted in the crowd insisted that the contents of the case must be divulged. So some of them forced their way onto the stage and opened the case which contained a Mazheri cloth sleeping suit and a copy of the Qur'an. Prolonged cheers. It is with this sort of jugglery, tall talk and impractical promises that he has been able to befool people so completely. His ambitions and methods are truly that of Hitler and Goebbels.

16 | SATURDAY

📖 According to the press, Yahya is going to stay with Bhutto at Larkana for a couple of days. It is extraordinary how the man is making himself so cheap. Ostensibly he will discuss political problems but in reality seeking Bhutto's indulgence more out of fear than anything else. He hopes that these people will treat him kindly when they come to power. How can such a man command anybody's respect let alone inspire confidence. He is utterly shameless, lacking in dignity and self-respect. But someone might well say that that was the way of politics. Adaptability to circumstances and opportunism both needing an easy conscience and disregard of principle. On the other hand, this could be a meeting of two wily men each trying to make use of the other, but chances of Bhutto exploiting things said or unsaid are greater.

22 | FRIDAY

📖 I understand that in the Dacca meeting with Bhutto, Mujib's response was not favourable. He rigidly stuck to his Six Points and refused to make any concessions. And that is not unexpected as he will be on trial as soon as the constitution-making starts. People gave him overwhelming support on Bengali nationalism and they expect him to get it. Nothing less would do. If he falters he is likely to be thrown out. He knows it. Whereas Bhutto can show flexibility in constitution-making. His promises to people don't involve constitutional matters. They relate to administration, the affairs of the government when formed. So his testing time will come much later.

Yahya's meeting with Bhutto in Larkana, I am told, was designed to explore the possibility of using him against Mujibur Rahman and to develop unanimity of approach. But Bhutto is far too shrewd to be used as a tout without extracting a heavy price, knowing the weakness of Yahya's position and his isolation after the elections. Bhutto is supposed to be full of confidence, though not all that satisfied with the election results as Mujibur Rahman still has the majority.

I am told that Bhutto still talks of me with reverence and keeps my paintings and photographs in his drawing room. That may be a pose, but if it is a pose then he is showing a level of decency not common to him. A friend told me that, in spite of a pose to the contrary, Yahya was not a brave man or had any strength of character. He was essentially an unprincipled appeaser given to taking the least line of resistance. Besides, he was born and bred in the streets of Peshawar and was a Qizilbash. Altogether a bad combination. Then he accused me of appointing him as C-in-C. I asked, what was the alternative, to which he said it was too late to give an answer.

23 | SATURDAY

📖 I see that a section of the press has awakened up to reality or has picked up enough courage to say that the answer to people's economic problems is not to rob 22 or 2,200 families, and taking away land from a smaller number, as the politicians have been advocating, but in working hard, maintaining industrial peace and increasing production. If they had done this earlier and told the truth, things would not have got this far. But their main aim is commercial. Anything that helps increase circulation was welcome, whether it led or misled people was of secondary importance. Some deliberately distorted things, fabricated stories or indulged in falsehoods to come into the limelight. Our press has to go a long way to attain maturity and respectability. The real trouble is that there is a great shortage of journalists of calibre, knowledge and integrity.

24 | SUNDAY

📖 Although the government is very shy and reticent of even mentioning the alarming population growth rate in Pakistan, more out of fear of criticism of conservative religious elements, and have relegated family planning to a very low priority, yet an occasional article comes out in the press drawing attention to this menace. The experts estimate that the population of this country has risen to 140 million and the growth rate is 3.3 per cent, amongst the highest in the world. At this rate the population will double itself by the turn of the century and so the process will go on multiplying unchecked, which requir taking very enlightened measures like mass education and bringing awareness to people and even permitting abortions like the way Japan did. Otherwise the prospects for the country are very bleak indeed.

29 | FRIDAY

📖 I am told that Yahya has a draft constitution ready in which the president has been given considerable powers. He tried to sell this idea to Mujibur Rahman when he met him in Dacca recently and also canvassed for presidentship for himself. Mujibur Rahman is supposed to have told him that he could have his presidentship but without any powers, besides, he refused to budge from his Six Points.

This attitude of Mujibur Rahman, together with disturbing information coming from East Pakistan, is supposed to have led Yahya to the conclusion that separation was unavoidable. In fact, there is general talk of eruption of large scale trouble in East Pakistan sometime in February presumably after deadlock in the assembly. So he has switched his attention over to Bhutto. The plan which was discussed with Bhutto at Larkana and alleged to have been agreed to by him is that on separation, West Pakistan would adopt the draft constitution and form a government with Yahya as the president and Bhutto as the prime minister. Could there be a better combination of debauches and perverts. Such an arrangement would suit Bhutto down to the grond as he could, in his own good time, remove and replace Yahya if he finds the presidency more attractive and effective. In any case, he has nothing but aversion for the parliamentary form of government. I am told that Yahya was well satisfied with his talks with Bhutto and came back happy.

All this looks as if the future of the country revolves around loaves and fishes and satisfaction of personal interest of a few individuals. It is sad but I suppose that is how history evolves around human nature, often at its worst.

Yahya is supposed to have blamed Bhutto for misleading labour and the student community. He retorted by saying that he, as a politician, had to say all sorts of things during the pre-election period, but Yahya, as an administrative head, made a great mistake in keeping Nur Khan and allowing him to commit so many absurdities and blunders.

There is no denying that Nur Khan was allowed to do a lot of damage to the country, more out of ignorance and naivety than design, but the damage done by Bhutto is deliberate, incalculable and unforgivable. He is the past master of disruption and agitation. He has shaken the roots of this country by simply posing as a socialist and a friend of the have-nots. And this is believed by an enormous amount of people despite the knowledge that he dresses and lives like a millionaire, drinks like a fish day and night, misbehaves with women, is a mimic, a clown and a liar, unfaithful and thoroughly disloyal. What can you do with people who put their faith in such a man? They will get only what they deserve chaos, deprivation, and suffering.

If the plan mentioned above be true, then Bhutto's current visit to Dacca, accompanied by a large contingent of his party men with a view to having constitutional talks with Mujibur Rahman and his supporters, is designed more to find and enlarge on points of disagreement and demonstrate to the people that East Pakistanis are irreconcilable and rigid on their stand on Six Points, rather than finding accommodation with them. Unfortunately, Mujibur Rahman is likely to take a rigid position and lend support to Bhutto's game. In which case, the ground would be prepared for a public opinion condition for a break when the assembly meets. Bhutto is posing and emerging as a hero and saviour of West Pakistan. Already there is a growing feeling in the West, especially in the Punjab, that East Pakistanis have ceased to be sufferable and the time has come to part company with them. As I see it, the events are moving in that direction. Only a miracle can save the integrity of Pakistan. This can't but be painful for those who served Pakistan to see it united, secure and prosperous. But what about those who created Pakistan. Their bodies must be turning in their graves and lamenting what renegades succeeded them.

📖 Aslam Khattak came to call and discussed the political situation in the country in general and the Frontier province in particular. He was very critical of Yahya and the amount of harm he had done to the country during the last couple of years. I have heard similar views expressed by several of the people. He accused me of having put trust in a Qizilbash. He hinted that the man was privy to agitation against me.

📖 There is a good deal of talk about the devaluation of the rupee as a result of pressure by the World Bank and the IMF. People think that the government has agreed to comply, though no announcement has yet been made. I am told that Yahya checked up with Mujibur Rahman and Bhutto too. They are supposed to have given him the green light, and why should they not, it suits them to get someone else to take the blame for an unpopular decision.

30 | SATURDAY

📖 It is well known that the Ahmadiyya community supported Bhutto's party en bloc. In consequence, over 25 of their people have got elected. Normally not one would have been returned. So they have done well out of the deal. But it also shows that apart from the tribal, family and other such bonds, the sectarian prejudices and barriers have also been broken which is a healthy sign.

📖 According to the press and radio reports, talks between Mujibur Rahman and Bhutto and their representative advisors have terminated, not on any optimistic note. Mujibur Rahman gave an open statement that there was no question of compromise on the Six Points. The advisors too stated their respective points of view but there was no agreement, according to J.A. Rahim and others there, on a socialistic programme and creation of an egalitarian society. J.A. Rahim, of course, is a hardened communist and it is his main obsession. Mujibur Rahman, of course, did say that although he had and absolute majority in the assembly, still he would also like to meet the political leaders in the Frontier province and Balochistan. This may have been thrown as a hint to Bhutto that he was by no means the only mouthpiece of West Pakistan. There were others to be considered and consulted too. Here, of course, he is on a safe wicket, because both Wali Khan and the rabid Balochis agree with his demand for total provincial autonomy and a weak centre.

I noticed that whilst Mujib–Bhutto parleys were going on, Bhashani repeated his demand for an independent Bengal in a public meeting held at Chittagong, and warned Mujibur Rahman that was the mandate given to him by the people who would never forgive him should he resist or compromise. I also have a feeling that Mujibur Rahman is basically in sympathy with this stand and does not need concessions. He is only waiting for a situation and opportunity which may appear.

I don't suppose Bhutto is in the least disappointed with the outcome. He expected it and perhaps wanted it. He did not go there with any hope of countering Mujibur Rahman or even wanting to. He went there to make a show of reasonableness for public consumption and took a further precaution of taking a large number of the West Pakistani contingent to serve as witnesses to Mujibur Rahman and his associates' rigidity and unreasonableness which would serve as material for use against Mujibur Rahman should the stage for separation unhappily come. Bhutto, whilst wanting separation and even encouraging it, would act in such a manner as to put all the blame on Mujibur Rahman, though that would not do any harm to the latter's image. Mujibur Rahman will become a bigger hero in Bengal, at least to begin with, until reality dawns. However, Bhutto's purpose would also be served by having West Pakistan all to himself in conjunction with Yahya. How long he will last, is another matter. I have a hunch that one day this game is bound to come to a sticky end.

It hurt me to see in the press that Mujibur Rahman, when questioned by a foreign correspondent, said that the president could see him should he wish to. It looks like both Mujibur Rahman and Bhutto now take him for granted. And why should they not when the man goes to them as a supplicant? He has sold his self-respect and dignity for the sake of retaining the job.

📖 I see that a martial law order has been issued calling upon officials of the Convention Muslim League to deposit all party funds in their possession in a scheduled bank within a fortnight, and send a copy of bank receipts to the martial law headquarters. Another clause lays down that the chief martial law administrator can cause an inquiry to be made on any expenditure incurred. This seems a permissive clause designed to harass selected individuals and save buddies like Kirmani who is alleged to have indulged in several malpractices. The object of this exercise seems to be to collect all the amounts in banks and then confiscate them so that the party ceases to have the means to exist. This is all done in a spirit of vengeance and crudeness and this party has been singled out for such an unjust treatment whilst others, who are spending crores, perhaps acquired from outside sources, are not touched. There could be no other partiality worse than this and misuse of power as it is now being shown.

31 | SUNDAY

📖 I have had a bad bout of cold during the last few days and had a hard time of it. In fact, it has been recurring every now and then during this winter.

    I am told that Yahya is going to dissolve his cabinet in the near future and also going to make an announcement on devaluation and the date of assembly meeting. In dissolving the cabinet he is particularly concerned about Professor Chaudhary[5] who told him that his life would not be worth living if he returned to Dacca. So he has been given an opportunity to look around for a job in Canada.

2 | TUESDAY

📖 Today is the 44th anniversary of my commission. I was commissioned on 2nd February 1928. In those days getting a king's commission was a rare honour. These long years have been full of events. I have been through so much ups and downs and seen so much that has been the privilege of very few. So I can't complain or regret. It has been a full life and God has been very kind in providing me the opportunity. I don't think merit had all that much to do with it. After all, I am an average person with average capabilities though I do feel for Pakistan with intense sincerity and devotion. My regret is that I failed to make its people a nation. The fault may well be mine but misfortune is certainly of the people because unless and until they make a nation and develop a national outlook they will never get anywhere.

📖 I was horrified and disgusted to hear that at a meal which Yahya gave in honour of the Iranian foreign minister, he drank so much that he was leaking whilst drinking and his trousers were wet throughout. The honoured guest was so embarrassed that he did not know what to say. Eventually he picked up courage and told him, 'Your Excellency, you have spilled something on your trousers, perhaps you would like to go and change them'. There were several Pakistanis present on the occasion too. God knows what they must have felt like.

📖 Bhutto started off his political campaign with a slogan of Islamic socialism and Islamic *musawat*.[6] This was objected to by the communist elements in his party at the conference held at Hala some months ago, saying that socialism had nothing to do with Islam and vice versa and demanded that the word Islam be dropped. After a lot of discussion it was decided that for political purposes it was necessary to use the word Islam which would be dropped after the elections were over. Sure enough, he hardly mentions Islam in his speeches now and has gone on further to say that he stands for a secular state but in order to deceive people adds that no law shall be passed which was against the Quran and the *Sunnah*. This, too, is a hoax and subterfuge and will be dropped when people have been conditioned and get ready but even if he does not, which *Sunnah* and *Fiqh* is acceptable to all the Muslim sects? So he can safely evade this commitment.

4 | THURSDAY

📖 There is no lack of excitement in Pakistan these days. Something unexpected happens every day. For instance, a couple of young Kashmiris hijacked an Indian airliner flying from Srinagar to Jammu and made it land at Lahore. They allowed the passengers to disembark but remained in occupation of the plane saying that unless India released their imprisoned comrades and gave a guarantee of security of their families they would blow up the plane. The authorities made every effort to make them surrender but they refused compliance. And on hearing on the Indian radio that the Indian government had turned down their demands, they blew up the plane. Meanwhile, the passengers were looked after well and sent to India by land route. Despite that, the Indians blamed Pakistan for complicity. Also, several rowdy and violent demonstrations were held against our high commission in Delhi.

Here at home, Mujibur Rahman has condemned the action taken, blaming it on such elements who want to sabotage transfer of political power to the people's representatives, whereas Bhutto has given the action full throttled approval. The object is obvious, one wants to be on the right side of India and the other on the right side of emotional elements in West Pakistan.

The elements Mujibur Rahman has in mind could only be Yahya and Bhutto. I have a feeling that he suspects them as collaborators. This will be further confirmed by a press report that Bhutto, on landing at Karachi airport, went straight to the President's House to see Yahya. Even otherwise Bhutto has been saying that though there were differences between him and the administration and his party was singled out for victimization, all that was now of the past and forgotten. The implication is obvious.

I would not be a bit surprised if Bhutto arranged its publication to ensure Yahya's total commitment to him. Bhutto will continue to make political capital out of this alliance whilst weakening, compromising and isolating Yahya still further and putting him completely at his mercy.

5 | FRIDAY

📖 India has lodged a protest with Pakistan on the destruction of their plane at Lahore airport and held out a threat of strong action and prohibited flights of our military and civil aircraft over their territory. This means that communications between East and West Pakistan will have to be via Colombo and take much longer. Things like this will give a further handle to Mujibur Rahman that in time of trouble two wings were beyond supporting distance of each other. I would not be a bit surprised if this factor did not weigh heavily with India when taking this decision. In fact, they will do everything possible to harden the Bengali attitude at this juncture when the constitution is on the anvil.

6 | SATURDAY

📖 The hijacking of the Indian plane and its destruction has sharpened India–Pakistan animosity but it has also made clear how the Kashmiris in Pakistan, time and again, have played with the emotions of the people of this country and played politics at its expense. They note that there is a large Kashmiri population in West Pakistan. They naturally feel that the people of West Pakistan and especially of Punjab are also emotionally involved. Whenever the occasion arises the Kashmiri leaders take full advantage of it in order to build themselves up. Ibrahim,[7] Khurshid[8] and many others have indulged in this nefarious activity, belittling the tremendous sacrifices Pakistan has made and is making for the liberation of Kashmir. I used to deal with him firmly but he is on the loose again. Bhutto 'too' indulges in the same sort of mischief. The press world has also a large number of Kashmiris who keep on inflaming people's minds adding fuel to fire and exhorting almost extinction of Pakistan for the sake of Kashmir, not admitting that it was the Kashmiri leadership that sold itself to the cunning Brahmins and now put the onus of liberation on us.

Kashmir is indeed a big problem for Pakistan in a number of ways and it can't be given up but its solution, if any, will take a lot of perseverance and patience.

📖 Yahya is supposed to have mentioned somewhere that if Franco could rule Spain for 35 years why could he not do the same in Pakistan. When saying this he forgot that Franco had a strong political and military power base which Yahya has not. Besides, Franco is regarded as a national hero for having fought a bitter civil war and saved the country from falling under communist domination. Furthermore, Franco is known for his bravery and has impeccable character attributes lacking in Yahya.

7 | SUNDAY

📖 Mujibur Rahman has called a meeting of his working committee to review the political situation in the country, specially covering the early convening of the assembly. A threat is held out that if the assembly is not called by the 22nd instant and declaration not made to the effect by the 15th, the Awami League may resort to direct action. I suppose the motive behind this threat is that both Yahya and Bhutto are colluding to delay the meeting unnecessarily and may use the dislocation of air communications with East Pakistan as an excuse. What would be gained by delay is difficult to tell. On the contrary, it may well work to Mujibur Rahman's advantage as many West Pakistani members are quite capable of supporting him for personal gain.

There is also an indication that Mujibur Rahman has decided not to seek the post of prime minister himself and has told his party men to elect another parliamentary leader. A man called Kamruzzaman,[9] who is no better than an animal, is tipped as a probable successor. Mujibur Rahman, I suppose, wants to assume the role of Gandhi in relation to the Congress. He wants to remain out and act as a kingmaker. In making this decision he has shown wisdom far beyond his level. It is going to be no fun accepting the highest responsibility without any hope of satisfying people's expectations thus losing credit with them. Not many politicians in our country realize that a political office is not going to be a bed of roses in future. In our socio-economic circumstances it is the voice of dissent that is going to command attention.

📖 I am told that industry, which was in any case running to partial capacity in the past, is coming to a grinding halt as a result of the credit squeeze put on by the State Bank on the government's instructions. Not only are the commercial banks refusing to give credit but they are also calling back old debts. Meanwhile, labour is agitating for rise in wages.

The insurance companies are languishing as the owners have lost interest because of denial of incentives. They are taking their money out and could not care less if they were nationalized.

9 | TUESDAY

📖 What surprises me is that Yahya indulges in such laxities and debauchery when the country is facing such critical problems. No man with any conscience would do such a thing and yet he seems to be completely unconcerned. I told someone that if this is the way to run the presidency of the country then I had wasted my time working day and night and leading the life of a hermit and ruining my health in the process.

11 | THURSDAY

📖 I see that whereas Mujibur Rahman is critical of the ruling clique and the vested interests for not declaring the date of the assembly meeting and terming it as a conspiracy, Bhutto, who is supposed to be amongst this group, is also blaming the administration for adopting delaying tactics. This is inexplicable. It may well be a pose to show detachment from the administration whilst working closely with them.

12 | FRIDAY

📖 Bhutto came to Pindi and saw Yahya prior to meeting Qayyum Khan, Wali Khan, etc. in Peshawar. This bears out the truth of what I said above.

📖 Some people are very critical of the manner in which the affair of the Indian hijacked plane was handled. They can understand the affair up to landing of the plane at Lahore, but question why asylum was given to the hijackers without surrender of the plane. The trouble, I understand, was that the provincial government could not get a policy decision from the central government. Yahya was just not approachable. Similarly, some mischief makers had been announcing their intention to take the hijackers in a procession in Lahore on the 15th, obviously with the object of creating tension and breach of law and order. The provincial government wanted to ban the procession but could get no confirmation from the central government till the last minute. Obviously the whole thing will end up in a bloody row. The police would just not be able to stop the procession without breaking several heads accompanied by loot and arson. So there is no denying that a weak, unprincipled and vacillating government is a curse and an open invitation to anarchy and chaos.

14 | SUNDAY

📖 It was announced that the assembly session will be held in Dacca at 9 a.m. on 3rd March. This should allay some of the misgivings in the minds of the people. Some thought that the delay in announcement was a deliberate design to sow discord amongst political parties and thus frustrate the formation of a constitution and handing over power to the politicians. I think this was far etched and typically cynical. Having come this far the government has nothing to gain in delaying matters nor has it any room left for fresh manoeuvres and initiatives, even if it had the will, which it has not, to take advantage of any opening.

16 | TUESDAY

📖 There is a bit of a rumpus going on in the press over the transmission of a statement by a news agency that Bhutto accused Yahya, in a conference held in Multan, of having accepted Mujibur Rahman's Six Points. He also threatened to start a movement. This was vehemently contradicted by Bhutto though lately he has been giving indications of disenchantment with him [Yahya]. This is surprising as in the recent meeting in Larkana, he gave the impression that they were hand in glove with each other.

This is a typical case of two card sharpers trying to use each other to promote their selfish interests. So there can be no consistency of faith among them. Their relationship changes with the change of circumstances. It may sound a harsh but unavoidable judgement.

There was welcome news in the press that the police, after thoroughly tear-gassing the squatters in the Valika mills, broke open the gates and drove the inmates out and arrested some of them. Let us hope that the others would take a lesson and this mischief gets nipped in the bud and does not spread.

17 | WEDNESDAY

The papers today were full of Bhutto's and Mujibur Rahman's policy statements which may have far reaching effects on the future of the country. Bhutto said that his party would not attend the assembly session unless Awami League gave prior guarantee of flexibility and adjustment in their Six Points. They had no intention of going there just to endorse a constitution prepared unilaterally by the Awami Leaguers. Besides, he did not want to expose his followers, 82 in number, to the double jeopardy of India's threats and the Awami hostility. Mujibur Rahman, on the other hand, got an endorsement from his working party and the MNAs and MPAs that there shall be no compromise on Six Points nor any retreat. So there is no question of Bhutto's demand being met and presumably no chance of him and his party taking part in the constitution-making.

A situation of deadlock and indeed of confrontation between East and West Pakistan has, therefore, developed. Portents for the future are, therefore, not bright. The point, however, is as to why Bhutto has taken this rigid stand. Basically, Bhutto's stand is logical in view of Mujibur Rahman's uncompromising attitude, but his object is difficult. He wants to pose as the champion of national unity and custodian of the interests of West Pakistan and especially of the Punjab where his greatest strength lies. He also wants to steal a march on the other West Pakistani leaders and put in the wrong those who may wish to collaborate with Mujibur Rahman. Thus assuming for himself the sole leadership of West Pakistan. So he was looking for such an opportunity. This now is very clear and psychologically well timed provided, through Mujibur Rahman's stupidity and arrogance, which Bhutto was waiting for. All that Bhutto has to do now is to sit tight and allow Mujibur Rahman to take the onus and odium of splitting the country of which Bhutto will take full advantage whilst gathering all the credit from West Pakistan.

Constitution-making is, in any case, a time consuming and difficult task at the best of times, but it becomes almost impossible when there is no consensus or agreement on fundamentals and when a community of interest and feeling of common destiny is lacking. God alone knows what would be the outcome. As for now, one sees no silver lining anywhere. The dice for separation are heavily loaded. Meanwhile, the army would be landed with the responsibility of holding the country together. Not an easy task when it looks like effective leadership has failed and there is no consensus between East and West Pakistan.

I see that Mujib has been unanimously elected as a leader of his parliamentary party. This is nothing new. In our country leaders and governments are unanimously elected and just as unanimously discarded. There is a rush for worship of the rising star and an equal abject scuttle when the leader is faced with a difficult situation. The greater parliamentary support does not mean lessening of his burden. It only adds to the dead weight on him in addition to the weight of his responsibilities. At least that was my experience.

As I said earlier, Yahya has no trump card left in his hand nor any bargaining counter. If he had not surrendered on one unit and one man one vote, he could have controlled both Mujibur Rahman and Bhutto. Today they know that Yahya has nothing to offer. So they are under no obligation to listen to him. I would go further and say that if one unit had not been broken, Bhutto would not have emerged as a leader of West Pakistan, certainly not from the Punjab. The reason is simple, he would have certainly sided with Sindhi demands for undoing one unit and thus lost all credit with the Punjabis, who were totally averse to it.

Bhutto has assumed tremendous responsibility in refusing to attend the constituent assembly and therefore wrecking and keeping the country in a state of flux. It may have been an impulsive or pre-planned step. However, he has to justify it in the eyes of the people. I see him embarking on a whirlwind campaign to justify his action and retain public support in West Pakistan. He will hold public meetings, press conferences and employ other gimmicks, spreading poison and vitiating the atmosphere further with East Pakistan beyond point of redemption. Mujibur Rahman, being a limited man lacking foresight and statesmanship, is bound to over-react making accommodation between the two wings impossible. So by putting faith in these charlatans the people of this country have mortgaged their future for disaster and ruination.

📖 One gets the impression that our people are taking Indian threats seriously. For instance, all leaves in the armed forces have been stopped and those on leave recalled, so have been some reservists. In addition, the Horse Show has been cancelled and key approaches from India mined and heavily guarded. The truth is that neither India nor Pakistan can afford to sustain a war, but that provides no guarantee against India's hysterical action and chauvinism. So it is a good thing to be prepared for all eventualities. We are dealing with a wily and a cowardly enemy and can take no chances.

18 | THURSDAY

📖 Reaction to Bhutto's decision is mixed. Even those endorsing it, wished that he had attended the assembly and made his points there instead of wrecking it from the start. His own party men are giving endorsement in the open, but those elected must be doing so with their tongue in cheek as they face losing their membership if not sworn in by a certain date. They could not be relishing the prospect but they dare not rebel until Bhutto's position is weakened which is not in sight. In fact, he may get much greater allegiance of a large number of people of West Pakistan for standing up to Mujibur Rahman. The undercurrent of resentment against Mujibur Rahman and his party and indeed against Bengal is on the increase. The Awami League office in Lahore was burnt. A similar attempt was made in Pindi, but the police saved the place. It looks like East–West confrontation will be on the increase as time goes on. Mujibur Rahman too is helping the process and loses no opportunity to put fuel on the fire. He is attacking everything connected with Muslim culture of West Pakistan and almost taking the Bengalis[…] united Bengal. His theme is that they are Bengalis first and last. Anything else is destructive to Bengalism. No wonder that people here are getting tired of him and may welcome separation, however reluctantly.

I was amused to see Bhutto advancing the argument against going to Dacca, that he did not wish to expose himself and his followers to the double jeopardy of India and Mujibur Rahman's hostility and become their hostages. And yet the man has proclaimed from the house tops that if need be he will fight India for a thousand years, presumably without any risk to himself and hoodlums that make up his party whom the country could well afford to lose. It would be good riddance. One presumes that he wants to do this fighting at the expense of Pakistani soldier's blood from a safe distance. An officer, who had served as my ADC, had recently been in New York. He said a large number of people told him to tell me to take full security measures and not go out unguarded and unescorted. I was surprised to hear that.

I understand Bhutto was called at short notice by Yahya presumably to persuade him to attend the assembly session in Dacca.

---

20 | SATURDAY

📖 Daily *Mashriq* of Lahore has published a baseless and false report to the effect that I have approved and extolled Bhutto's stand vis-à-vis Mujibur Rahman and his decision to stay out of the assembly. I have also called his action as constructive and so on. The fact is that I have never expressed such views at any time. I am having this contradicted but it just shows the depth of degradation of our press. According to the news, Bhutto had a 5½ half hour session with Yahya yesterday. What were they doing so long together, God alone knows. On termination, however, Bhutto held a press conference in which he reiterated his previous stand that unless Mujib shows flexibility on Six Points it would not be possible for him and his party to attend the assembly. He also announced that in the event of anything happening to him Mustafa Khar and a lad called Mairaj would be his successors.

📖 There is a good deal of talk about Indian troop concentrations against West Pakistan border and movement of our troops to the concentration area. People in Lahore think that war is imminent. It would be very foolish if India were to start a war because neither they nor we can afford it and we shall both be ruined.

📖 I am told that Yahya was a president of the dramatic society in college days. No wonder that he acts when dealing with other people and revels in singing and dancing. In some ways he resembles late [Huseyn] Shaheed Suhrawardy though lacking his capacity and calibre.

---

21 | SUNDAY

📖 I was disgusted to hear that General Musa, who was no lover of Bhutto, wrote him a letter during the election that he would do all he could to help his candidate win in Tando Mohammed Khan area where he owns lands. Such a thing could be nothing but the height of sycophancy from a man who is expected to show some strength of character. I am told that Bhutto showed the letter to Yahya during his visit to Larkana and said that he was afraid of two types of people, one, dangerous people like Ayub Khan, and second, sycophants like Musa.

---

22 | MONDAY

📖 Radio news gave out the presidential cabinet had been dissolved with effect from this morning in view of changed political circumstances. I am sure this is meant to be a sop to Mujibur Rahman, particularly to Bhutto who regarded the ministers as a red rag. Bhutto did not want anyone to stand between him and Yahya. Lt. General Peerzada is tolerated as he is a useful confidant and source of information.

I am told that Yahya slipped out, accompanied only by Bhutto, in a car the other night. They obviously went out to debauch somewhere, but the story has gone round that they had come to my house for consultation, which of course is completely baseless. I would not be a bit surprised if such stories are inspired leaks to gain respectability for their plans and activities.

I had a bad day today. Foolishly I ate mango pickle at lunch and enjoyed it. Normally, I do not touch these things. But a couple of hours later I had extreme angina pain and burning sensation which lasted for several hours. I felt almost paralysed, but luckily the pain subsided towards the evening and I had a comfortable night, thanks to treatment by Col. Mohiuddin, who came all the way from Rawalpindi. He, apart from being highly proficient in his profession, is loyal to the core and almost worships me—more, as he sees Yahya and compares with what I used to do.

Bhutto has gone through similar rituals as Mujibur Rahman has in taking an oath on the Quran that he shall under no circumstances compromise on his political stand, then got his followers to take a similar oath and obtained carte blanche to take whatever steps he deemed necessary to obtain party objectives. The support to both of them was unanimous. No one dissented or tried to caution against taking a rigid stand in constitution making. This is the first example of participating democracy so hoarsely shouted about by our politicians. The upshot is that the future of the country is put in the hands of two men, who enjoy no mean notoriety. Yahya is also supposed to be a factor, but with not so much power to influence the future other than the threat of martial law which cannot be expected to provide a lasting solution. So he is a mere spectator than anything else.

23 | TUESDAY

Agha Mohammad Ali, Yahya's brother, came to call and presented me with a prayer carpet. He has recently returned after performing Haj. It is the first time he came to my house and it could not be without a purpose and without his brother's knowledge. Maybe they are worried about the future, especially now that Mujibur Rahman has refused to show any flexibility and Bhutto has declined to attend the assembly unless the former relents on his Six Points. Yahya is faced with an awkward situation and must naturally be in search of a way out. I told Mohammed Ali that Yahya, having lost two powerful trump cards, one unit and parity, had nothing left in his hands to use against these people to get them into a compromising frame of mind. Further, it seems now very difficult to hold the country together as a federation and the best situation would be to withdraw the army from East Pakistan in the best manner that is possible and to think about a confederation, as this seems to be a way in which the country will not be further put through a trauma. Agha Mohammad Ali said, 'Sir, is this your considered view?' and I said, 'Yes, I think so. We have gone beyond the stage of a federation'.

24 | WEDNESDAY

📖 Things I am told keep up the level of intoxication. I saw in the press today that Daultana and his party too have decided not to attend the assembly session unless there was *modus vivendi* between the two majority parties. This was a foregone conclusion though against the inner wishes of Daultana and Shaukat Hayat who are dying to collaborate with Mujibur Rahman and get an office. But it is this fear of unfavourable public reaction which has held them back, at least for the time being. The Hazarvi[10] group of ulema is also having second thought's after meeting with Mujibur Rahman and seeing the trends in West Pakistan. So the indications are that either the assembly would not be held or be off to a bad start.

📖 I have read a certain amount of literature indicating that in America a large number of operations are carried out on cases of coronary blockages of the heart by grafting portions of the blood vessels obtained from another part of the body, allowing the blood to flow beyond the blocked area. Thus, many people have obtained full recovery and vigour. I, too, suffer from angina. I told Mohiuddin to check up with Professor Goodwin in England that I feel that a similar operation might prove effective in my case. He promised to do that but said that this would give rise to all sorts of rumours within the country and it was not beyond the administration to stop my re-entry into the country. I said that such a risk has to be accepted. He said in that case he shall have to consult the Director General, Medical Services, and also inform the president. The latter would be very happy to hear that, as he was frightened to death of my shadow. I said in that case the greater the reason that he should be informed. I would not like to deny him any little occasion to feel happy.

25 | THURSDAY

📖 Mujibur Rahman has reiterated that his party won the elections on the Six Point programme which meant that the people had adopted that programme, as such, he had no authority to retreat an inch from them. But he went on to say that he had no obligation to other provinces having a different relationship with the centre should they so wish. I think this makes sense. I have always been of the view that since a united and strong Pakistan was no longer possible, West Pakistan, because of contiguity of its provinces, common communication and economy should decide on the centre they must have to exist, and then negotiate with East Pakistan as to what extent it wanted to go along with it. That, to my mind, seems to be the only sensible solution, provided there was a leader of stature in West Pakistan to carry through the negotiations. Jokers like Bhutto would not fit the bill and others do not have the mandate and are in any case spent forces. So the danger is that the case of West Pakistan is liable to go by default. The advantage East Pakistan enjoys is that it is talking through one man and if there are any dissenters, which I doubt, they are keeping their mouths shut. If on nothing else East Pakistanis are in unison on opposition to West Pakistan and as such enjoy great advantage over the divided west which has foolishly put its faith in a clown and a jester, an opportunist to the core who will not hesitate to sell them down the drain when it suits his personal ends. The only check on him is the opinion of the public in the Punjab who foolishly, in their ignorance, have become his power base.

1 | MONDAY

📖 Yahya made an important statement at noon in which he said that in view of the fact that since the bulk of West Pakistani members had decided not to attend the assembly session, no useful purpose would be served to hold it on 3rd March. He, therefore, decided to postpone it till such time that there was some sort of consensus amongst the majority leaders representing East and West Pakistan. A constitution, he said, was not like the ordinary law. It was a covenant amongst the people of the country as to how they propose living with each other. So, therefore, a broad consensus was necessary for it to be durable. He hoped that the political leaders would reach this soon in order to take the country out of the serious crises it was facing and so on. The reaction to this in West Pakistan will generally be favourable but it was doubtful if East Pakistan would keep quite. Mujib had announced his intention to see Bhashani, Ataur Rehman, Professor Muzaffar Ahmad,[11] mostly extremists, and announce his reaction in a public meeting on the coming Sunday. One does not have to be a prophet to tell that the reaction of all of them would be violent and they may even hold out a threat of separation. Perhaps they were waiting for such an opportunity.

Meanwhile, there is talk that Yahya's advisors have drawn up a plan visualizing a breakdown in constitution-making and consequent deterioration of law and order, especially in East Pakistan. They proposed tightening up the martial law and curtailing political activity. In other words, greater involvement of the army, and also dealing firmly with the top political leaders who have assumed irreconcilable positions and vitiated the atmosphere for constitution-making. I doubt if such measures would carry conviction with the people at this stage or Yahya has the moral courage to put them through. I doubt also whether the army has much faith in him, either. They have seen him temporise too often, yielding to pressure. So far, he has never taken a stand against the agitators.

2 | TUESDAY

📖 According to today's news all the governors have been given the powers of martial law administrators in their provinces, in addition to their civil duties. Admiral Ahsan has been removed and General Yaqub[12] has taken over from him. This means the government wants to be tough in case the situation deteriorates, which is more than likely to happen in East Pakistan first. Already, there are indications of it yesterday. There was a demonstration of Mujibur Rahman's supporters in front of his house, in which the Pakistan flag was burnt. When Mujib's attention was drawn to this, he made no comment.

Pakistan faces terrible contradictions. It wants unification and democracy, but facts of life are against this combination. East Pakistan is against unification and if democracy is accepted, then East Pakistan has to be given freedom of its choice, secession. The army can hold the country together, but for how long. It can at best be a temporary expediency. If secession is considered unavoidable then the sensible course would be to carry out the process of separation under the cover of martial law to make it a tidy operation. But this would require tremendous moral courage on the part of Yahya. Can he rise to it? He has given no indication of it so far.

What the East Pakistani reaction will be remains to be seen. Chances of it taking a violent turn and even declaring a unilateral declaration of independence are great but then they may decide to lie low and wait for a more suitable opportunity to break away. In any case, separation is unfortunately drawing closer. The Bengalis are doing everything possible to make it do so. Meanwhile, Bhutto, in conjunction with Yahya will do everything possible to accelerate the process.

Some people think that a better alternative would have been to extend the period of constitution-making that would have minimized the danger of eruption of collision in East Pakistan. They also state that indefinite postponement was resorted to, to enable Yahya to stay in power indefinitely. How much truth there is in this contention is difficult to say.

3 | WEDNESDAY

📖 Mujibur Rahman called for a one day *hartal* in Dacca and other places yesterday, which was carried out and led to a good deal of arson and looting. The army clamped down curfew from dusk to dawn for an indefinite period.

Mujibur Rahman, whilst cautioning his people against violence and law breaking, has made a new call for *hartal* for four days affecting every activity of people and the government between the hours of 6:00 a.m. and 2:00 p.m. I would be very surprised if violence, looting and arson does not break out on a large scale. His pious hopes and advice to the contrary, which could not be all that sincerely meant, notwithstanding.

Meanwhile, Bhutto and his henchmen like Mustafa Khar,[13] J.A. Rahim and a few others continued to remain in touch with Yahya. The other day Bhutto was with him for four hours. How can the president of the country afford to waste that much of time with one man is difficult to tell. I suppose most of it was spent in the company of women, a past time dearest to the heart of both of them.

4 | THURSDAY

📖 According to today's news, Mujib has flatly declined to attend the leaders' meeting on the 10th. He asked, how could he do that when Bengalis were being killed day and night? Besides, the meeting was being called under the threat of a gun. This is a foolish decision and may well turn out to be the turning point in the history of Pakistan. He has gone on further that the Bengalis should be ready to face all eventualities unless martial law is lifted immediately and power handed over to them. In other words, he has given an ultimatum for war. He said that he would declare his future course of action on the 7th. Until then *hartal*s must continue. Also for the first time, he mentioned publicly that East Pakistan was determined to secede. He did not say why? The reality is that some people are getting exasperated with a man like him and see no future in getting the Bengalis to make a Muslim nation. So they seem to be prepared to take the bitter pill and separate much against their will.

I think Mujibur Rahman's next step, in conjunction with other Bengali leaders, would be to stir up agitation and prepare for a possible declaration of separation.

If Mujib had any intentions of being reasonable and remaining in Pakistan, a compromise formula could have been easily evolved over his demand for Six Points. The two most controversial points are foreign trade and collection of taxes by the centre. He could have collected as many taxes as he liked leaving a small sphere to the centre to meet its obligations. Similarly, he could have taken all the foreign exchange earned for use in East Pakistan. But he is no mood to listen to reason. The obvious conclusion is that he wants to be out of Pakistan. The profundity of Mujib and those who think like him, and they are many, has become manifest to the people. But they are unclear of Bhutto's real intentions. They are still under his spell and consider that he alone holds the hope for their salvation. They do not realize that the man is selfish to the core, an exploiter and thoroughly insincere, lacking any principles. He has already done a lot of harm to the country and will continue to do so whilst on the loose. Mujibur Rahman's intransigence and Bhutto's open opposition to him has further strengthened his position. So there seems to be little cause for his being found out—not just yet. But his elimination is vital if the country is to be saved from utter chaos, disruption and ruination. In the final analysis, he is the real enemy but would this dawn on the people? At present, they do not see it that way and are in no mood to listen to anything against them.

I heard on the radio Nurul Amin has also declined an invitation to attend the leaders' conference saying that the answer was to convene the assembly. The conference would serve no useful purpose. I think he has done this more out of fear of *goonda* elements in the Awami League than anything else and so has the representative of the Jamaat-e-Islami in Dacca. The people of our country are getting, and will continue to get, what they ask for. They have no one else to blame except themselves. The law of God will take its course. People get what they deserve. The course of history, like the mainstream of a river, does not change in a hurry.

6 | SATURDAY

I see that East Pakistani politicians are vying with each other in eulogizing their unchallenged leader Mujibur Rahman and what he stands for and blaming West Pakistanis for being unreasonable. This has been my view. Basically they all agree on the substance of Six Points and animosity and jealousy towards Pakistan, even though they may personally dislike Mujibur Rahman. Their present policy seems to be to line up behind Mujibur Rahman to grab whatever they can for East Pakistan, putting their differences with him in cold storage for the time being to gain the main objective. Once that is done, there would be time enough for dealing with Mujibur Rahman. In any case, he would have committed so many blunders by then that he would put himself out of favour with the people. The Bengalis may be secretive but he is relentless in pursuing his political objectives, however short sighted or unreasonable and even damaging to himself. Rational approach to him on these matters cuts no ice.

Yahya, in his broadcast, enumerated his sincere effort at handing over power and giving politicians every opportunity to frame a sensible and workable constitution and how his efforts were frustrated at every turn. He lamented the recent rejection of Mujibur Rahman and Nurul Amin to attend the leaders' conference to iron out differences and save the assembly. Not only was his gesture, he said, misunderstood or deliberately flouted, but Mujibur Rahman did not even agree to meet him despite his repeated requests. Instead he launched a movement to disrupt life, bringing insecurity and privation to law-abiding people, thus forcing the hands of the administration to shoot down members who robbed and were vandals, and so on and so forth. He said he could not wait indefinitely, so he had decided that the session of the assembly would be held on 25th March. Why 25th March, perhaps because that is the second anniversary of his takeover.

Let us see how Mujibur Rahman reacts to it. He is due to make his policy statement tomorrow. Chances are that he will be difficult and repeat his demand for immediately lifting martial law and establishment of the civil government. Failing which he may hold out all sorts of threats like boycotting the assembly, demanding that the two wings should make separate constitutions, or even threatening to declare independence. Bhutto too has been put in a dilemma. Will he be able to overcome his previous resolution of boycotting the assembly if Mujibur Rahman shows no flexibility in his stand? If Bhutto stood by his resolution, there is a possibility that some of his supporters may revoke the mandate thus bringing about an open cleavage in the party. This act alone may force him to change his position and agree to attend the session.

Let us hope that these people realize the gravity of the situation and desist from taking the country over the precipice but, knowing these people, I doubt if they are capable of rising to such an occasion, so the future seems dim.

Another danger that faces the country is the amount of poison and hatred that Mujibur Rahman and others have been able to spread against West Pakistan, which is beginning to have repercussions here too. It is doubtful whether people like Bhutto can safely stay there, and Mujibur Rahman in West Pakistan. I do not think it would be possible to ensure Mujibur Rahman's safety here, if he becomes prime minister. In such an unfortunate situation created by a few politicians, how would it be possible to keep the country together and establish any measure of mutual trust and understanding? The tragedy is that in this state of mistrust everything that is happening whether consciously or unconsciously is widening the gulf between the two wings and we are moving fast in creation of disintegration.

In this sorry state of affairs, I keep on reassuring people that Yahya may yet be able to save the situation, but it does not seem to stick. Nobody believes that he is up to it, applies his mind and makes any effort. A friend compared him to a mythical Hindu ruler who slept for six months and kept awake during the other six, recuperating in enjoyment and merrymaking. So he had no time left to attend to anything serious in life. In the case of Yahya, he said, he keeps busy in enjoyment till three to four in the morning. The resultant hangover inevitably takes the best part of the day to pass over. He has to have some sleep too. So where is the time for attending to anything serious? All he can do is to sign anything that his subordinates like Lt. General Peerzada put before him and you know what sort of mentality that man has.

According to the TV news, Bhutto has announced his intention to attend the assembly session and Lt. General Tikka Khan has been appointed as the governor of East Pakistan. Why Tikka, is difficult to understand. He has no experience of that province and knows nothing about it. Tikka is a nice and a simple man, but comes from the Punjab. This is bound to be misunderstood by the mischievous elements in Bengal and will be used as a proof of Punjabi domination etc.

7 | SUNDAY

At about 4:30 p.m. started feeling pain and burning sensation in the chest, which grew in intensity to such an extent that I was in agony for several hours. Taking a large number of tablets, which normally give relief, proved of no avail, so sent for Col. Mohiuddin, who brought me to the hospital where they examined me and said that it was just a severe attack of angina. That was reassuring, but it made me go through hell all the same.

I am not afraid of death, but terrified of life in such a condition. So I am trying very hard to get to Britain or America where they are doing a lot of heart surgery in reopening closed arteries of blocked vessels. In case of success, a man gets almost a new lease of life.

According to the radio, Mujib announced his conditions in a public meeting for attending the assembly session on 25th. He asked for lifting of martial law, handing over power to the civil government, causing an inquiry into the killing of Bengalis during the riots, and payment of compensation to the bereaved families. He went on to say that if these conditions were not fulfilled he would call for prolonged and total *hartal* including non-payment of government dues and taxes. In other words, he is talking of a province-wide struggle and non-cooperation instead of seeking and offering cooperation for formulation of the constitution. This is the last thing he would have done if his intentions were honest. Under the circumstances, how would Yahya be able to hold the assembly session, and that in Dacca, is difficult to say and how many West Pakistanis would be willing to go and live there?

As I see it, there are only two alternatives before the country, some sort of accommodation in maintaining one entity which would depend on the price West Pakistan would be called upon to pay. Chances are that it would be exorbitant therefore unacceptable. Secondly, separation, but would it be tidy and well planned? I doubt it. It suits Bengalis to separate in a huff to escape payment of their share of internal and external debt. Therefore they will try and create a situation of utter confusion and breakdown in the province, so that separation could be presented as a panacea. Meanwhile, I pity the lot of West Pakistanis there. My fear has been that even the army may have to fight its way out. I wonder if the commanders on the spot have visualized and catered for such a contingency.

Taking a general view of the situation, feelings between East and West Pakistan are similar to those that obtained between the Hindus and Muslims at the time of partition. There seems to be no way out of this unfortunate and tragic impasse. The hatred in East Pakistan is too deeply burnt into the bones and souls of the people. The politicians, in their perfidy, have seen to it. Meanwhile, feelings of aversion are growing fast in West Pakistan, however divided. Psychologically they too seem to be ready to part company with unreasonable and insufferable companions, though much against their will, for want of anything else or any other choice.

Bhashani holds out dire threats in case Bengal is not given independence. Mujib calls for total strike even affecting government offices and non-payment of taxes. Bhutto threatens to set the country on fire from Khyber to Karachi if his party is ignored in constitution-making. The least their conduct can be called is sedition, if not treason. This is happening during the martial law and yet no notice is taken of it. The trouble is that men running the martial law are by now well known for lack of guts, moral courage or principles. So no political *goonda* takes notice of them or has any respect for them, let alone fear. If they had any moral courage they should have firmly dealt with the above mentioned people to set an example to others. Mercy is a laudable virtue, but not at the cost of maintaining the law of the land and dealing with those who are bent upon subverting and disrupting society. A government that condones or overlooks such crimes either through cowardice or for promotion of personal interest is unworthy of any country that lays claim to even a modicum of civilization.

8 | MONDAY

The government, through a press note, indicated that a number of casualties were suffered during the weeklong disturbances in East Pakistan. In all, 172 people were killed and 358 wounded, including 23 dead and 26 wounded by the army. The rest were killed or wounded either by the police or the

East Pakistan Rifles who were attacked in a number of places and had to open fire in self defence, or through mutual fights amongst the civilians, which means Bengalis and non-Bengalis. All this was accompanied by looting, arson and attacks on several government installations and the railways. The army too suffered one officer killed and one wounded. Meanwhile, I suppose movement of goods has come to a halt and so has business and what little production there was in the industrial concerns. Naturally, prices will rise still further adding to the suffering of the middle class and the common man. So the country owes no small debt of gratitude to Mujibur Rahman and his ill plans. This is happening when they are out of power. God alone knows what misfortunes await the country once they get in.

At present West Pakistan appears to be calmer, but that is an illusionary and deceptive situation. Mr Bhutto and his communist friends must also be engaged in contingency planning should things not go their way.

I am told that Mujibur Rahman has held out a threat to the contractors in East Pakistan not to supply anything to the army units. He has also threatened to cut off their water supply, power etc.

In a confused situation like this, it is difficult to say what is the correct solution. The choice lies between so many evils. Some shooting might well be a lesson and more effective answer. This may sound hard hearted and callous, but a large majority of people who are law abiding are entitled to protection from the *goondas* which only the state can and must provide.

Mujib has declared that his civilian disobedience movement will continue until such time that martial law is lifted and power handed over to his party, which is in majority. In other words, it is an ultimatum to Yahya and the army to abdicate their responsibilities before the constitution is framed. Just imagine the confusion that will ensue should such a suggestion be foolishly accepted.

9 | TUESDAY

📖 Admiral Ahsan's military secretary, who was at one time on my staff, asked the bank where his wife's jewellery was deposited for its return before returning to Karachi with Admiral Ahsan who had been relieved of governorship of East Pakistan. The bank refused to comply unless permission was obtained from Mujibur Rahman. This officer was puzzled, but went to Mujibur Rahman and obtained the jewellery after his intercession. It is obvious that the government in that province has ceased to be effective and is replaced by Mujibur Rahman's brigands. Bangladesh is beginning to be established.

All bank transactions are now virtually controlled by Mujibur Rahman ostensibly to prevent what he chooses to call 'flight of capital' to West Pakistan. But very soon it will become a means of extracting money and bribe taking. It is unbelievable, but true that the Awami League when in power prior to October 1958 had passed a law that operation of industry big or small was subject to yearly renewal of license.

It was confirmed that the chief justice of East Pakistan[14] refused to administer oath of office to Tikka Khan as Sheikh Mujibur Rahman had made a call for boycott of courts until martial law was lifted and civilian government introduced. Anybody can tell that this is no judicial decision. The man has acted on political considerations more out of fright of Mujibur Rahman than anything else. Wild rumours are afloat about the state of affairs in East Pakistan and are being fanned by the Indian radio and also the BBC which is more objective. However, what is very obvious is, according to them

Mujibur Rahman has repeated that until such time that martial law was lifted and he is handed over power, civilian disobedience would continue. In consequence Mujibur Rahman is a virtual ruler and everybody takes orders from him. The authority of the central government extends to the military cantonments and no more.

Yahya intends going there presumably to appease Mujib. The politicians and the businessmen never yield unless they have some compulsions and Mujibur Rahman has none. He has been given East Pakistan majority on a platter and has thundering support from the people. So unless Yahya is prepared to completely surrender, I doubt if Mujibur Rahman would yield an inch.

I am told that PIA flights to Dacca have now to refuel at Colombo as they are not sure of getting that done at Dacca. Some flights have to turn back to Colombo from half way to Dhaka through deliberate lack of response from the control tower there. West Pakistanis and East Pakistanis are naturally anxious to get out to save their skins and so are the foreigners. But curiously enough the Americans feel secure to stay on and have shown no concern at the turn of events. The conclusion is obvious. They must have an equation and understanding with Mujibur Rahman. In fact, Mujibur Rahman must be relying heavily on their support, especially economic.

12 | FRIDAY

📖 Apparently the army, despite so many provocations, is acting with great restraint. At times their supplies, water, power etc. have been cut off and their small detachments prevented from moving from one place to another. How long can they take these things lying down is incomprehensible and shows the measure of the administration's helplessness. I think the agitators will get bolder as they become aware of it.

📖 Bhashani and Mujibur Rahman have now joined hands in liberating the Purba[15] Bangladesh. In a joint public meeting in Dacca, Bhashani proclaimed full support to Mujib's programme calling him his son and called upon the Bengalis to support his civil disobedience and non-cooperation movement until success was achieved. He also called upon the people to prevent entry of foreign troops, meaning West Pakistanis, through Chittagong and Chalna. There is also a rumour that either he or Mujibur Rahman proclaimed that they were not helpless. If need be, he could call upon friendly troops to come to their assistance.

13 | SATURDAY

📖 Just heard that Lt. General Yaqub has resigned. He was accused of being too close to Mujibur Rahman. I feel sorry for him as well as for the army because he was the only general qualified to be the commander-in-chief. I would not be a bit surprised if some ambitious generals close to Yahya conspired against him to get him out of the way. Tikka's appointment is highly resented in Bengal especially after Yaqub's and Ahsan's removal who were liked by the people. I am told that Mujibur Rahman may not have taken such umbrage if he was consulted on the change of date for assembly meeting or the meeting had been announced along with postponement. Due to the omission he felt slighted and took a hard line. Besides, he had to do this to appease the hardliners in his party. I am told that the sympathies of the Bengali troops are with the movement. They were not used in the recent turmoil as a precautionary measure. This was a wise precaution. Meanwhile, the CSP and the PSP association in East Pakistan has pledged their complete loyalty to the Sheikh. Meaning of that is clear; they would take no action against law breakers unless cleared by Mujibur Rahman. So Mujib is the ruler of East Pakistan in substance if not in form. The common cry in Bengal is that they want blood—whose blood? Presumably of non-Bengali Muslims, not Hindus, who exploited and drained away their resources to West Bengal.

Yahya has not announced when he would be going to Dacca. Someone suggested that his life may not be all that safe in the President's House.

15 | MONDAY

I am told that Mujibur Rahman is under great pressure from the younger elements to announce a unilateral declaration of independence. In fact, they expected and very much wished him to do so the other day in the public meeting held at Dacca.

Yahya reached Dacca this afternoon presumably to meet Mujibur Rahman. I doubt if he will get any change out of Mujibur Rahman unless he is prepared to surrender completely. Mujibur Rahman is under no obligation or compulsion to concede anything nor has Yahya any power to make him do so.

Bhutto also held a public meeting in Karachi yesterday, in which he indulged in his usual jugglery of words and tried to explain the reasons why he declared to boycott the assembly if Mujibur Rahman did not give prior guarantee of flexibility on certain points. This was a reply to some people who were accusing him of sabotaging the assembly. Bhutto agreed that Mujibur Rahman's party be allowed to form a government in East Pakistan, as well as the majority parties in the provinces of West Pakistan. He hinted that let Mujibur Rahman be the master in East Pakistan and he in West Pakistan. In other words, that the country be divided as there was no hope of keeping it together. He also termed Mujibur Rahman's financial demands on West Pakistan absurd and baseless.

16 | TUESDAY

Mujibur Rahman has issued 35 detailed directives under which different institutions, departments, and government and semi-government organization will or will not be run. The object seems to be to cripple the central government financially and extinguish its authority, sever all connections and transactions with West Pakistan and gain control of the administration, social, and political and economic life of the province. He has largely succeeded in doing so. I don't suppose these are his personal efforts. He must be backed up by strong political, administrative and economic teams. Whilst this is going on, the martial law administration is presumably sitting as helpless spectators. Mujibur Rahman has, in fact, launched a constitution based on Six Points rendering the assembly superfluous.

17 | WEDNESDAY

Mujibur Rahman had a two-hour meeting with General Yahya yesterday. He is to meet him again today. Mujibur Rahman has already established his Six Points, including non-payment of central taxes and Bhashani, Ataur Rehman and others have given him full throated support. So what does he care for the assembly unless it meets on his terms and those would include causing as much disruption in West Pakistan as possible. His philosophy is based not so much on the love of Bengal, as enmity towards West Pakistan. The more he can damage it, the happier he would be. And there are enough fools or opportunists here to be beguiled by him. A year or more ago, I had stated that the time had come to shed emotions and make believe and face facts. And facts are that East Pakistan either does not want a centre, and if it does, it wants it to be next to useless, whereas West Pakistan cannot do without an effective centre. Under the circumstances, therefore, it was no use finding a compromise centre, which would be completely unsatisfactory for both. Thus, the answer was to evolve a centre for West and then let East negotiate to what extent it wanted to partake in it. If they don't want to do so, they should be free to make their choice. It would be a painful decision, but there is no other way out. We have failed to appease the Bengalis for 23 years. The more they were appeased the more disgruntled and dissatisfied they became. I can say this with authority as I had tried this policy with all sincerity and what was the outcome? More dissatisfaction and enmity. We have to recognize the fact that they feel different to, and uneasy, with us. They want to be left alone and run their show on their own, good or bad. The answer is to let them do so with our prayers for success. Otherwise, they will finish themselves, as well as us.

Mujibur Rahman has met Yahya again. I don't suppose they could have got very far, as Mujibur Rahman, on coming out, told the pressmen that the Bengali struggle for emancipation would continue until the final goal was achieved. The meaning of that is clear. He does not wish to budge an inch from his stand and why should he? He holds all the trump cards in his hands.

I don't know whether to laugh or cry but I have heard that Yahya when drunk, which happens particularly every night, makes water on everything looking upright. Once he did that with a policeman who was on sentry duty close by. His habits are also well known. He drives out in a car at night with an odd man. On occasion he comes to Islamabad to see a plot of land which, he had bought. That has given rise to rumours that he comes to consult me at the dead of night, which of course, is completely false.

18 | THURSDAY

📖 Bhutto was apparently invited to join the president for discussions with Mujibur Rahman on the 19th. He held a meeting with his party men and decided not to go as according to him there was no flexibility in Mujibur Rahman's stand. The truth is that he is frightened of a hostile reception in Dacca with the possibility of being done in. Feelings against him are running high in Bengal.

20 | SATURDAY

📖 Mujibur Rahman had another meeting with Yahya yesterday and looked cheerful on coming out. They arranged for a team of their experts to meet and thrash out certain things. Yahya's team consisted of Lt. General Peerzada, Justice Cornelius and one Col. Hassan of the JAG (Judge Advocate General Department) branch. None of them have any knowledge of the political, social or economic problems of East Pakistan so I would not be a bit surprised if the interests of this zone are sold down the drain to appease Mujibur Rahman. Meanwhile, Bhutto has held out a threat that he would launch a civil disobedience movement if the interests of this wing were sacrificed. I think what he means is that there would be trouble unless he and his men are not accommodated. He is afraid of Daultana and others joining Mujibur Rahman and forming a government. It is not for the love of West Pakistan so much as jeopardy to his personal interest that is probably making his heart bleed. According to a military statement, people have acquired a large number of weapons through dealers and otherwise and are using them freely. The local press community puts the blame on the army for any shooting that takes place.

My fear is that in the event of withdrawal of West Pakistan military personnel from Bengal either through separation or even in a tenacious and troubled relationship they may well have to shoot their way out under pressure. Such a withdrawal is difficult even over the land route when accompanied by women, children, and vast amounts of baggage, but it poses formidable problems when communications are poor, water obstacles innumerable and has to be effected to a port for embarkation on vulnerable ships which have to negotiate narrow waterways before entering the high seas. I hope the local commanders have contingency plans ready just in case events take an ugly turn.

Mujibur Rahman had another meeting with Yahya in the presence of their representative advisors. It seemed that Yahya has given in to Mujibur Rahman in a big way. Meanwhile, Bhutto is intending to proceed to Dacca accompanied by a contingent of 20 advisors. This is supposed to be in response to Yahya's request and after getting satisfaction for some points he had raised. Brohi, too, has been sent for. Wali Khan, Daultana, and Mufti Mahmood are already there. Shaukat Hayat has also made haste to join. He does not want to be left behind. His anxiety is to secure a job before anybody else gets it.

If Yahya makes a disastrous compromise or fatal mistake at this juncture, it would be due to the fact that he has allowed the executive, that is the martial law executive, to be enfeebled to the point of impotence. The politicians have got the measure of him. They cannot only dictate terms, but also paralyse the central authority and indeed run a parallel government, as Mujibur Rahman is doing in East Pakistan or Bangladesh according to the new jargon. In consequence, the army too is demoralized and on the defensive. It has to be apologetic even when acting in self-defence. It has lost all initiative to restore sanity other than trying petty shopkeepers and sundry criminals at the behest of the civil administration who are making fools of them. In East Pakistan, movement of troops is becoming more and more difficult. They encounter roadblocks and mob attacks now with firearms. Such things are not difficult to deal with, but a howl is raised all over the province if they take any counteraction. The administration at once gets cowed down and promptly yields. In consequence, the army's prestige, morale, and reputation has suffered a great setback, due mainly to the weak and irresolute top leadership.

21 | SUNDAY

I see that Bhutto and his party men have reached Dacca. Special security precautions were taken for him as, in the eyes of Bengalis, he is responsible for the initial postponement of the assembly and being hostile to Mujibur Rahman. According to the press reports, pro-Bhutto slogans were shouted at the airport and he exhorted not to allow the country to be divided. They must have been non-Bengalis, but there was also a hostile demonstration at the hotel, obviously arranged by Mujibur Rahman. Bhutto had an hour long chat with the passengers at the airport waiting to catch the plane to Karachi to find out the state of affairs privately in the province. They could not have painted a rosy picture, as non-Bengalis were brutally treated during the disturbances. They must be fleeing for their lives. I think Bhutto must be collecting such material for use in West Pakistan to whip up an agitation should it become necessary.

Bhutto was to be lodged in the cantonment, but on his instance, he was put up in a hotel. This was one of the points he insisted upon. The other was an assurance that Mujibur Rahman would at least give him a hearing, however brief. The president was able to assure him on both the points. Hence, he said, he felt satisfied and was prepared to go to Dacca.

This sounds like raising lame and childish excuses. What he really wanted was an assurance that he would be taken into the provisional government should one be formed and Mujibur Rahman would not ignore his party in framing a central government later. The rest was a hoax in befooling West Pakistanis that he was championing the national and West Pakistan's cause. Someone told me the intelligence has lost faith in Bhutto. They regarded him as a self-seeker and an opportunist, but the common man still believed in his promise. A couple of years of Bhutto rule might bring disillusionment. I asked, what would be left of the country by then? As to intelligentsia, I said, they are only good for making mischief. To expect them to do anything positive was wishful thinking.

---

23 | TUESDAY

📖 Today is the Pakistan Day. There are not going to be any celebrations. I suppose with the country being in such a mess nobody is in the mood to celebrate anything.

Yahya, in his Pakistan Day message, stated that the stage has now been set for elected representatives to work together for the common goal, accommodating both East and West wings in a smoothly working and harmonious system. The details of the system are not yet divulged. The press reported Bhutto's meeting with Mujibur Rahman in the presence of Yahya, when Mujibur Rahman explained the arrangements that had been agreed upon between him and Yahya, Bhutto then had a long meeting with his advisors lasting the whole night and part of the day. He then sought an interview with Lt. General Peerzada. No further meetings took place with Mujibur Rahman nor did they call at each other's residences. All this indicates that Bhutto is not quite satisfied with what has being agreed to by the president, nor has bitterness between him and Mujibur Rahman been removed. I understand that Mujibur Rahman stated at one time that he would rather see the country divided than have anything to do with Bhutto. So I would not be a bit surprised if Bhutto raises difficulties over having been slighted by Mujibur Rahman and not treated at par with him. If so, he will use the cover of unfair treatment to Sindhis and Punjabis and work up agitation.

📖 Today, *Jang* was full of photographs of Bhutto and his associates in an obvious effort to appease him. I think the proprietor has been successfully brought to heel by Bhutto's men who tried to set fire to *Jang* installations for not towing the line. These activities are the responsibility of ex-general Akbar Khan who is the organizer of the so-called People's Party volunteers, in other words, local bad hats and hot-headed students. Similar people rough handled Air Marshal Asghar Khan who tried to address the Multan Bar Association the other day. And there is some indication that they wanted to set fire to Maududi's house in Lahore. I think such activities will henceforth become common and especially when People's Party men takeover the administration in the Punjab and Sindh. The police would be told to lay off and let the *goondas* have a free hand.

24 | WEDNESDAY

📖 I understand that a shipload of people, which reached Karachi from Chittagong the other day, were mostly those who are wounded or sustained injuries during the rioting. They suffered terribly and have lost all their belongings. They were even searched at the time of embarkation so that they should not bring out anything worthwhile.

The government has wisely suppressed the news as otherwise there would have been reprisals in West Pakistan. Even otherwise Bengalis in the West wing are jittery. They are trying to flee by air. The ones in Islamabad are even getting threats through anonymous letters and telephone calls and are naturally scared. They avoid going out of their houses.

Another piece of information is that a small naval base in Chittagong, which has now become the centre of Naxalite type of people, was attacked by a mob of 40 to 50,000 people. The timely arrival of an army contingent saved the situation, otherwise the place would have been overrun and all the inmates killed. Even so some were killed though they inflicted causalities on the attacking mob.

The army is supposed to be demoralized presumably because they are not allowed to deal with the situation firmly. Feelings between them and the people are also tense, mostly through the efforts of the local press, which continus to fabricate stories and spread poison against them.

Bhutto is staying on presumably because he has not had the satisfaction he hoped for. He and his advisors met the president's aide again. Mujibur Rahman's advisors are also going to meet them so Bhutto's hope for direct talks with Mujibur Rahman and his advisors has not materialized. Their talks have mostly been indirect, through the president's aide. I suppose Bhutto is staying on in the hope that they may yet be able to establish an equation with Mujibur Rahman and get better terms from him.

When relations between the two zones have been vitiated to such an extent, who in his senses can be sure of smooth running of the assembly either from Dacca or Islamabad? Furthermore, which Bengali can rule from Islamabad or West Pakistani from Dacca. In such circumstances, the chances of formation of a joint ministry between the two wings seems extremely remote due to vitiation and poisoning of relationships by Mujibur Rahman and his associates. I think the point of no return has long since been crossed. Yahya's effort at reconciliation, however laudable, may well turn out to be an exercise in futility.

It was painful to know that there were only three places where the Pakistan flag was put up on March 23rd in Dacca. This was at the President's House, Government House, and the cantonment. The rest of the place was covered with the flags of Bangladesh and the day was celebrated as the 1940 Resolution Day or Liberation Day. In places, Pakistan flag was forcefully hauled down and burnt. This is the sure indication of Bengali determination to run a separate country and yet we are dreaming of running a common country. The trouble is that everyone with commonsense knows that separation is unavoidable and some Bengalis are saying so openly, but no one in West Pakistan has the moral courage to admit it in public. If they had done that sometime back, things could not have got so bad. The extremist Bengali may rein up before the precipice if his bluff is called in time and he is told to get off our necsk and run his affairs in the manner he likes. The silence of people here has given him the impression that we cannot exist without him. So, regarding us as vulnerable he has been constantly pushing up his claim to the limits of absurdity and now there is no holding him back. The only answer is to face the situation and accept hard facts of life apparent in the mood of people. It is a waste of time quoting scriptures and past history and resolutions. They no longer cut any ice. This is the sad, but plain truth.

The country faces tremendous problems of social and economic reconstruction. The quicker people, especially in Bangladesh, are made to face these problems instead of living on political blackmail, the better. The time for artificial make believe has long gone past. People don't realize that unwilling partnerships can never be satisfactory or lasting. If the country was contiguous, the present separatist tendencies would have been contained, even dealt with. But since there is over a thousand miles of hostile territory between, application of force is no answer. So we have no other way but to go by the will of the people or those that call themselves their representatives. It is like a civil marriage that is terminable by either party at so much notice.

Our radio made no mention but BBC announced that there had been clashes between the army and the mob in Chittagong, Rangpur and perhaps in one or two other places. At least 35 people were killed and over a 100 wounded. In Chittagong, the trouble arose because the mob tried to prevent unloading of ammunition from a ship. Mujibur Rahman has called for a complete *hartal* on Saturday. That, I am sure, would lead to further trouble. There would be looting and arson and killing by the *goonda* elements, leading to more shooting and aggravation of the situation, affecting and perhaps nullifying the talks Yahya has been having for resolution of constitutional deadlock. This is most unfortunate. Mujib's demand for autonomy, which verges on sovereignty, is likely to be louder. The extremists will become more strident.

In West Pakistan, too, there have been large scale riots in Lyallpur resulting in looting and arson of government property like the police station, municipal office, and government buses. This was engineered by Bhutto's party men just to test out their capacity in case they had to repeat what the Awami League was doing in East Pakistan. Meanwhile, the army has been called in to assist the police. Curfew has been imposed, according to the BBC. Some factories have also been burnt and looted.

26 | FRIDAY

Yahya returned to Karachi last night, but Bhutto is still there. It is obvious that no final settlement acceptable to Mujibur Rahman, Bhutto and Yahya on the formation of an interim government or the shape of the future constitution has taken placed.

Yahya is giving a radio address in half an hour's time. We will know little more what is the form, but 5:00 p.m. news depicted a dark picture of the situation in East Pakistan and announced certain stringent measures that the martial law authority has intended taking. It is the first time that this administration has spoken with firmness. Let us see to what extent they intend acting in that spirit. If they are serious about the business then they will have to deal with arch conspirators, Mujibur Rahman, Bhashani and others. Tikka may well wish to do that, but it is doubtful if Yahya would give him the necessary backing for any length of time. He is quite liable to back out any moment. He is incapable of withstanding any political pressure.

Force and resistance has never been able to kill an idea that is widely believed. So it looks like all these ugly events and measures are hastening the move towards separation. Fantastic casualty figures are rumoured and have been inflicted by the army in the recent disturbances in East Pakistan.[16] They vary from 25,000 to 50,000. In Dacca, tanks were also used, including gunfire against students using firearms from the university premises. Apparently Iqbal Hall was flattened. It is quite possible that the situation needed strong action, but there was also a psychological element. Soldiers were subjected to taunts and abuse for a long time and they were getting tired of it. Also, they saw gruesome atrocities committed on non-Bengalis. The Bihari colony[17] in Mirpur was attacked by the locals with the assistance of the police. The army arrived in time and saved them, at the same time, delivering hard blows to the police. There is talk that Mujib's son, who turned out to be a bigger *goonda* than his father went to Iqbal Hall to instigate the students. In the ensuing firing he and a notorious student leader were killed. Similarly, Tajuddin and Moazzam Ali[18] were shot dead while resisting arrest. If this much was done, then I wonder why a number of leading scoundrels were not dealt with in the same fashion. The province would have seen some peace for some time.

Yahya's attitude toward Bhutto is not understandable. Either he is relying on Bhutto's political support for the future, which would prove a delusion, or he is waiting for a suitable opportunity in the same manner as he dealt with Mujibur Rahman. Every sensible person hopes that Bhutto and his leading henchmen are dealt with in a drastic measure to save the country from being wrecked. Yahya is a wily and cunning man and is an expert at concealing his intentions. I would not be a bit surprised if he has such a plan at the back of his mind. Bhutto, too, is no less cunning. He would waste no time in enlarging his cell in the army and strike at Yahya when he is vulnerable or the army loses faith in him. Already, Yahya's habits are drawing a lot of criticism in the services. I have a feeling that the apparent collaboration between the two is marriage of convenience and both must be watching each other like hawks. They would not hesitate to strike at each other whenever the opportunity arose.

India is taking undue interest in Pakistan's troubles. The East Pakistan situation was discussed in the Indian parliament and by a special cabinet meeting. I am told that Mujibur Rahman and a dozen or so others arrested with him, including Masihur Rehman, have been brought over to West Pakistan. Others arrested with him, including Masihur Rehman, have been lodged in Attock fort. Someone said that Mujibur Rahman has shown willingness to sign any constitutional arrangement the government wants. I do not believe that for a moment. He cannot do that if he wants to maintain his leadership or even to be able to live in Bengal. Besides, he is a prisoner of the students and the extremists. He dare not do anything without their consent. In fact, during the parleys with Yahya they dictated what he would say, and of course their dictat was extremist.

I got a more accurate account of what happened at Iqbal Hall in Dacca University and the reason why tanks were used, from an official who happened to be in Dacca at that time.

Apparently Iqbal Hall was a centre of the extremist student community's, subversion activities and the were armed to the teeth. It was naturally the first target of the martial law to be neutralized. So a company of infantry was detailed to occupy it. They put in an attack and on being fired at used their weapons and returned fire. The place was occupied after inflicting some casualties in which Mujibur Rahman's son, who was busy instigating the students, was killed and so was a notorious student leader named Tofail,[19] amongst others. There is some talk that one or two of Mujibur Rahman's daughters, busy instigating the students, were also killed. On search, the place was found full of weapons, including automatics and explosives. The tanks, on the other hand, were used to destroy the sources through which the venom was spread. The building and presses of two notorious pro-Awami papers *Ittefaq* and *People* were burned. The army meted out similar treatment to the police station and its inmates that had joined the locals in killing refugees in Mirpur. The reserve police located in Lal Qila in Dacca was also set upon for being openly hostile to the non-Bengalis and for being anti-Pakistan.

31 | WEDNESDAY

📖 I am told that there were some desertions in the Bengali units in East Pakistan. In consequence, the East Pakistan Regiment has been disarmed as a precautionary measure. What is bothering the authorities are 47,000 rifles belonging to the Ansars and deposited with the police. Their falling into wrong hands will pose a serious problem.

Somebody said that Mujibur Rahman and his party are held in custody in Quetta and not at the Attock Fort. Most likely it is the Mach Jail. I wonder what they are going to do with them? After having accused him of being a traitor and the enemy of the country, they would have to put him on trial.

People in West Pakistan feel relieved heartened that after all the government has taken a resolute decision. They also feel that a similar operation should have been launched here, too. The inner circles, on the other hand, feel that until recently the administration was playing with Mujibur Rahman. It was only the pressure of the army that had forced a change of mind on them. Now Bhutto had become a blue-eyed boy and has found popularity in army circles. This is a trend fraught with great danger.

1 | THURSDAY

📖 I have heard that the army, instead of taking similar action against West Pakistan politicians as they did in the East[...] which politicians other than Bhutto and Asghar and their kind matter? But for that they have to have an ostensible excuse. So it all depends on whether Bhutto and his party would give them a chance. They might well lie low for a time and bide their time. The only thing against it is Bhutto's impatience. How long can he wait without power?

There are also a lot of rumours that Bhutto told Yahya that Lt. General Peerzada was partial to Mujibur Rahman and was passing on all the secret information to him. It is quite possible that Lt. General Peerzada has changed loyalties. He is an opportunist and overambitious and must be on the lookout to like his fortunes to the rising star. I am told that he is aspiring to become the next Commander-in-Chief.

The situation in East Pakistan is supposed to be improving except at Chittagong where only Bengali troops were available and who did not have their heart in the job. This is not surprising. I have always been of the view that at the time of internal stress they will be influenced by political considerations and would not be able to stand the strain.

There is a talk of Indian armed men infiltrating into East Pakistan. I hope they can be brought to battle and delivered hard blows and destroyed. This infiltration is quite possible considering that both the houses of the Indian parliament have passed a resolution openly identifying themselves with the secessionists in East Pakistan.

Another rumour is that another division is being dispatched to East Pakistan. I wonder if it is true. Chances are that certain units are being sent to replace Bengali units who cannot be much use in that province.

2 | FRIDAY

📖 According to Altaf Gauhar, who came to call, Yahya successfully cheated us. We could not tell his real intentions till the last minute. In reality, he, Lt. General Hamid, Lt. General Peerzada and Razvi, the Director, Intelligence Bureau, had planned the takeover after my illness in 1968 and General Yahya had been encouraging some politicians to start an agitation for my removal—and yet he kept on assuring us that he would destroy any element that opposed me. That was all a bluff. If it was not for his treachery the agitation could have been controlled. Altaf Gauhar then touched on Yahya's private life, which is all known, but he also mentioned big corruption which was being carried on by him through Alvi of the Standard Bank. Alvi was tipped off in advance of any government policies which have a bearing on prices. In consequence, the Alvi brothers have lately being speculating in a big way in cotton and other things.

Altaf Gauhar talked about the situation in East Pakistan and wondered how long the army could remain in a state of confrontation. It was costing the country so much, apart from creating international complications. Besides, it was a single-ended tunnel as far as any political settlement was concerned. Whom will the army negotiate with in the end? He did not seem to have much respect for Bhutto. And I was surprised to hear that Bhutto openly talked ill of Yahya. He went about telling people, including army men, that Yahya was like an old woman and unfit to be a leader. That bears out my contention that Bhutto would be working on younger army elements to replace Yahya and other senior officers and assume their leadership.

I was told that Bhutto and Mujibur Rahman were, of course, heavily financed by the industrialists in the elections, but Yahya's men also collected large sums in cash. For instance, the two oil companies and the refineries alone contributed 30 lakhs each to Maj. General Umar. Yet our party, which kept its accounts meticulously, is still the target of official wrath.

3 | SATURDAY

📖 I see that the British are pulling out of East Pakistan en bloc and so are the Americans. Now that Mujibur Rahman is under arrest they do not seem to be so sure of themselves and their safety. Previously, even their president was confident that the Americans had nothing to fear.

I hear that Bengali elements in Yahya's headquarters are not trusted and will probably be replaced. Lt. General Peerzada, too, is regarded with suspicion and of being partial to Mujibur Rahman and has therefore being pushed into the background. It is a mystery then as to who is carrying on the work because Yahya does very little himself.

There is so much talk of Six Points, secession etc. and an impression that none of this would have come about if Mujib had not been freed from the Agartala case. He is held responsible for all this. This is one erroneous impression and a mistaken belief. The fact of the matter is that from the day Pakistan came into being, Bengali nationalism also took birth and Muslim nationalism began to be regarded as a deadly poison for it. The agitations like that on the language question and others issues were only a camouflage to cover this feeling and to show hostility to West Pakistan and non-Bengali Muslims on any pretext. So in reality they are not Six Points but only one-point. They had no intention of making a Muslim nation and living with West Pakistan. Today, hostility towards Muslim culture and connections is openly encouraged and past regimes are accused of distorting the Bengali culture. I wish the people in the country understood this and faced up to harsh reality. West Pakistan, other than the Punjab, is bedevilled by sub-nationalism and that is why this urge for separate provinces.

Some Bengalis are critical over the manner in which Sheikh Mujibur Rahman was treated and discriminated against. He fought elections and won on the basis of Six Points which are no different to what he is saying now. He was then called the future prime minister of Pakistan by Yahya and now he is called a traitor. Whereas Bhashani goes about openly preaching independence and is not called a traitor and is not touched.

They failed to see however that whilst Bhashani's activities are seditious and objectionable, Mujib openly rebelled by setting up a parallel government leading to a reign of terror, murder and arson against non-Bengalis, paralysing the administration, and the authority of the central government was completed flouted.

📖 Our foreign office and the ambassador in Washington have been very good in getting in touch with a heart surgeon in Cleveland, Ohio, about my possible heart surgery. He has seen my papers and expressed an opinion that I am a fit case to be examined. He, being a very busy man, has asked me to be there either on the 4th or 11th instant, which of course, is impossible. So I have asked for a date to be given in the month of May. I shall probably get Gohar to accompany me. But the charges they have quoted are exorbitant. It will cost about one lakh rupees between the two of us. However, it would be worth it if they can do me some real good.

4 | SUNDAY

📖 India mounted a well planned and massive vicious propaganda campaign against Pakistan, and the situation in the eastern wing which was believed and echoed by the rest of the world. Knowing that India would lose no opportunity in striking against us whenever vulnerable, we should have foreseen and forestalled this. But, we have always been weak in two things, public relations and intelligence, arts which require a lot of skill, imagination and vision.

We have been poor at public relations. We either over-do or under-do it, forgetting the subtle approach for carrying conviction and making an effort. Our internal intelligence is equally bad, being in the hands of policemen using crude methods. They content themselves with telling stories about the events, forgetting that their main task is to find out the thinking, intention and plans of the subversive elements by infiltrating their organizations. The need, therefore, is for a different type of people to man the central intelligence. I will, however, say one thing in favour of public relations people. The policy makers hardly ever put them in the picture in advance and give them time to plan out their line of action. Hence, they are often caught short. Besides, the policy makers do not realize that this world, through speed of communication, has shrunk. The news travels fast and the first story often sticks and is believed. Besides, the big powers, interest's get involved and they give credence and publicity to what is said in their proximity and for their purpose. Morality, ethics and truthfulness have no place in it.

I said earlier that the emergence of Bengali nationalism, in spite of what the Hindus did to the Muslims in the past and the sub-nationalism in West Pakistan, has been the bane of our political life. Another factor which had a debilitating effect was that East Pakistan, apart from being so far away and difficult to approach because of the hostile intervening territory, contains the majority of population which includes about 20 per cent culturally advanced Hindu population. They used all methods possible that the Bengalis should not be drawn towards Muslim nationalism. However, I feel that in spite of these handicaps, if the Bengali population was smaller than West Pakistan, politically thinking and ambitious, things might have been different and the events might have taken a different turn. I do not say that they would have been any happier in the company of West Pakistan, but an acute form of Bengali nationalism would not have emerged. It might well have stopped at the level of sub-nationalism. East Pakistan might then have been called Purbo Pradesh and not Purbodesh.

5 | MONDAY

📖 I see that the Congress Parliamentary Party in India has passed a resolution offering sympathy and support to the secessionist movement in Bangladesh. A special committee has been set up to supervise these matters. India has made an open declaration that India cannot remain a passive spectator when so much is happening in East Bengal. Foreign powers like USA, Russia, the UN and others have been approached to intervene. Swaran Singh has refused to accept this as the internal problem of Pakistan. Some troop movements have also been ordered in that direction and infiltrators encouraged to go in with arms. Thus, so far, India is doing everything possible short of war to support the secessionists, to ensure that the movement does not die down. And even if it does they want to put them under permanent obligation as having proved as friends in need that can be counted upon in the future too. So in one way or the other India has reaped a rich harvest and established the right to meddle in Pakistan's internal affairs. But this could not have come about all of a sudden. There must have been a prior tie up between India and the secessionists. Beside, the situation in East Pakistan must have come as a Godsend to India to divert the attention of the Marxist government in West Bengal from internal turmoil.

6 | TUESDAY

📖 Mr Podgorny has written a long letter of protest to Yahya about the situation in East Pakistan in a polite form, but towing the Indian line. The Russians may have been prompted to do so on India's behest with the threat of Chinese interference thrown in. Also due to their concern for peace in the subcontinent. Another factor may well be looming into power of the pro-Moscow communists in West Bengal. The Russians would not mind seeing them dominate East Pakistan and possibly Assam as a rebuff and counter to Chinese form of communism.

As I said earlier, it is surprising how internal matters assume international proportions especially when you have unscrupulous neighbours like India which excels in the art of spreading lies and misleading others. Yahya's reply was firm and assertive.

📖 Major General Rafi, who was my military secretary and was given a division to command on my retirement, came to call. He was suspected and harassed by telephone taping and letter censorship since I left. Why they regard him as a danger, I cannot understand. Now he is being retired almost prematurely as a measure of victimization. I feel sorry for the poor man as he is suffering because of me.

Major General Rafi was talking about the situation in East Pakistan. He said two infantry divisions have been dispatched from here. Another division is being raised to fill the gap. All East Pakistani troops, he said, proved unreliable, some deserted, some were disarmed and the ones in Chittagong played havoc with the non-Bengalis. Now that fresh troops have reached Chittagong, they have taken to the hills with their weapons and ammunition. His view was that it was a futile effort keeping Bengal in Pakistan. The quicker we separate the better chances of keeping West Pakistan intact.

Major General Rafi said that Tikka was only a front man in Dacca. All the rough stuff was being done by Mitha,[20] who was at one time the commander of the Special Services Group and a buddy of Yahya.

He said the things did not work out the way Yahya wanted. His plan was to play to the tune of the politicians so long as they let him stay as the president and did not interfere in his debauchery. What happened to the country was no concern of his.

Rafi thought that Lt. General Hamid had Yahya in his pocket. He had all the Punjabi generals behind them and could winkle out Yahya anytime he wished, but he had no intention of doing so. Why should he be landed with the headache of resolving formidable political tangles? If Lt. General Hamid's mind is working on these lines then I say that he is very shrewd and farsighted man.

Major General Rafi said that he was astounded at Yahya's ungratefulness and faithlessness to me. As a Qizilbash, he should have been loyal as they were imported by an Afghan king from Iran for being trustworthy chowkidars. I was amused to hear that.

A number of East Pakistanis like Nurul Amin, Farid Ahmed, Hamidul Haq have given insipid statements more in criticism of India than cautioning their own people of the dangers of their conduct and behaviour. They know that their throats will be slit if they did that and would be regarded as renegades and traitors. That is the trouble in Bengal. Right thinking people dare not open their mouths and give true guidance to people.

7 | WEDNESDAY

The Chinese embassy in Delhi has lodged a strong protest with the Indian government for interfering with the internal affairs of Pakistan, and accused the Indian government of supporting the secessionists. The Chinese also protested over the Indians staging a provocative demonstration in front of the Chinese Embassy. The Indian officials refused to accept the protest.

I always thought that the Chinese were not going to sit idle whilst India was mounting a malicious and false campaign directed against the internal affairs of Pakistan, especially after the Russians had protested to Pakistan for towing the Indian line, which, in fact, was in support of Moscow-oriented communists in West Bengal; people who are no friends of China. But some people were doubtful of China's sympathies due to Yahya's attitude which is very much influenced by the Shah of Iran who tows the American line.

There is also talk that the Chinese have concentrated nine divisions on the NEA front. I suppose they were there already to deal with the Khampa[21] rebellion. Also, Chinese communications must have improved considerably for ease of maintenance.

8 | THURSDAY

There is a rumour that Indians have infiltrated about a division's strength in East Pakistan and a large number of Bengali deserters are also operating. The local population must also be supporting them. If this is true, then the task of the army in dealing with them could not be easy in any area where there is so much cover and mobility would be much reduced soon due to arrival of the monsoons.

Our radio admitted that the Pakistan air force was used in support of the army in dealing with road blocks and a motor convey of arms and ammunition sent by India. However, the Indian infiltration is probably continuing and the Indians would leave no stone unturned to disrupt Pakistan. Mujibur Rahman and his associates have given them a God sent opportunity to do so.

Whilst the country is facing a grave situation, one shudders to hear some of the things Yahya does. The other day, he attended a dinner party at the Chinese embassy and got so drunk that he had to be dragged to the car. Now what sort of impression would he have left on the Chinese, on whose support we will have to heavily rely in the event of war with India.

10 | SATURDAY

📖 Indian leaders continue to ride the high horse and indulge in offensive statements against Pakistan. A few days back Swaran Singh, the Foreign Minister of India, had stated that happenings in East Pakistan can no longer be regarded as the internal affairs of Pakistan. India repeated this yesterday by saying that the upheaval in East Pakistan was a danger to the security of India and in spite of some setbacks India would succeed in her aims. The aims, I suppose, being to bring about the separation of that province and establish dominance over it. They seem confident that Mujibur Rahman will not change his stance whatever happens, and furthermore, West Pakistan may well get tired of holding that province by force and give it up as a bad job. Meanwhile, they are encouraged by the support given by the Soviet Union and even the USA. Besides, their expansion of the armed forces and re-armament programme is now complete. They are in a position to flex their muscles and give an impression to Pakistan that from now on it must regard itself as a satellite and subservient to India. We shall thus be constantly faced with this threat and India's open endeavour to take full advantage of Pakistan's vulnerability. I doubt if reckless and subversive elements in Pakistan are conscious of this danger. In fact, they must be happy that they have willing friends close by who would lend a helping hand for the asking.

12 | MONDAY

📖 The Chinese have repeated their previous stand that India was interfering in the internal affairs of Pakistan in collaboration with two powers Russia and America. China would certainly help Pakistan in maintaining its integrity and sovereignty.

I think India and its collaborators were banking on a quick victory by the so-called freedom fighters, with their assistance, but they little realized the speed with which reinforcements arrived and went into action followed by a rapid collapse of the resistance. It is always dangerous to overrate the sting power of so-called freedom fighters. Once they are brought to battle and delivered hard blows, they crack up in no time and the front of enthusiasm and offensive spirit evaporates rapidly. The real well-trained guerrillas are different. They believe in hit and run and harassing tactics in a difficult area. They never present themselves as targets to superior force or firepower and therefore fight on indefinitely, especially in a wooded country. Vietnam and to a certain extent Nagaland are classic examples. But it is also true that guerrillas can't win wars by themselves until they are strong enough in manpower, weapons and a sound logistic system to help fight concentrated battles.

I am told that the Awami League had enough funds to run the province for a complete year. Meanwhile, Raschid,[22] who is a Bengali and the governor of the State Bank, was transferring more funds to Dacca. This was discovered in time and stopped. Raschid, I am told, has been put under arrest and the Awami funds frozen. The rumour is that most of these funds were provided by India and also a large military force to help in their elections and to neutralize the Pakistan army. In the event of any resistance, America may also have helped with money.

It is tragic that bitterness between the West Pakistani troops serving in the East wing and the Bengalis has become acute. It can be measured from a letter sent by a West Pakistani soldier serving in East Pakistan to his relatives here. He said he was not sure of coming back but as long as he was alive he would miss no opportunity in avenging the terrible atrocities committed on the defenceless non-Bengalis, especially women and children.

I am told that Mujibur Rahman, on being brought to West Pakistan, was moved from place to place for fear of being kidnapped or rescued by helicopter. I think this was too far fetched. Now he is supposed to be lodged in Dargai Fort.

13 | TUESDAY

The British press has become blatantly hostile. It is not prepared to accept anything Pakistan says and swallows everything India puts out. For instance, they don't believe that the infiltration of Indian infantry companies in Jessore sector, reported to have been destroyed, could be true, but they believe the Indian story that Indian soldiers were kidnapped by Pakistan from Indian territory. Also, they ignore the provocative nature of what India, her associates, the press and the radio have been saying. Their one theme is that West Pakistan soldiers should stop holding East Pakistan and allow it to separate. This, too, is the American theme, of whom the British are the mouthpiece and faithful hirelings.

Major General Mitha reached Dacca on the 23rd and returned a couple of days ago. He planned most of the commando operations including the arrest of Mujibur Rahman. Mujibur Rahman asked permission to go to England and promised to return whenever required by the president. It is said that Mujibur Rahman was getting ready to disappear for a time one hour after the arrest. He must have got the scent of what was coming. At least one-third of the population is supposed to be solidly behind Mujibur Rahman. Best part of the police, East Pakistan Rifles and units of the Bengal Regiment defected, some with arms. Not all of them have been disarmed. However, some action was taken against the Bengal Regimental Training Centre. Large numbers were killed or wounded. Some ran away and took to the hills. However, the arms they carry are of Chinese make. So, India would not be able to replenish their ammunition. Resistance continues in several places. Economic life is said to have been severely disrupted. It will take a long time to regain normalcy at an enormous cost. Continuance of martial law for at least two years is anticipated.

A high level conference was to be held at GHQ today to review the situation and determine what should be done in West Pakistan. Some people think that whereas Mujibur Rahman was playing for high stakes. Yahya was also playing his hands with no less dexterity. His plan was to soft-pedal with Mujibur Rahman in the hope of winning him over. So he sent Ahsan and Yaqub to East Pakistan to make friends with Mujib. But, as soon as he realized that his plan had failed and was bearing no fruit, he threw these two men out unceremoniously and replaced them with Tikka and others.

There is a rumour in the town that Yahya is, for the last four days, staying in a private house with a woman and would not come back home despite entreaties from his son and wife. If this be true, then all one can say is that the man has no soul and is devoid of any sense of responsibility. A truly loathsome creature.

The Bengalis blame others for harming and exploiting them, but they don't seem to realize the amount of damage their own power hungry leaders have done to them and brought so much misery and privation on their heads.

14 | WEDNESDAY

📖 I received an intimation from the chest specialist that he would like me to appear in his clinic at Cleveland, Ohio, on the 1st or 2nd of May. So it means that I shall have to leave on the 24th or so, stay for a few days in England and then move on to the USA. The cost, however, is going to be enormous, 25,000 dollars. Unless I am given this at par, it will cost me 225,000 rupees and that too because half would be at par and half on bonus vouchers. That is the new government rule but I am asking for relaxation as I was entitled to pension in sterling, which I drew in rupees, and was also entitled to go abroad on several occasions, which I never availed of.

📖 I am told that commando troops have been in East Pakistan for over three months. They and the army were told to avoid reacting to whatever provocation was put before them. This state of affairs lasted for over three weeks during which people showed open disgust and scant regard for them. People jeered and spat on them and desecrated the Pakistan flag in their presence. A number of officers and men were hacked to death during this period. This passivity and inaction probably emboldened Mujibur Rahman and his associates to declare a unilateral declaration of independence. They got the impression that West Pakistani troops were on their way out. In any case, they considered that Bengal Regiment units, the East Pakistan Rifles, the police and the Indian infiltrators would be more than enough to deal with them. But it seems that Mujibur Rahman had no controlling organization to coordinate their activities. So when the crackdown came, it was a great shock for them. Now the fight is between West Pakistan units and Bengali armed personnel and their Indian supporters.

People blame Ahsan and General Yaqub for inactivity and failure to suppress the rebellion in time. I wonder if they were entirely to blame. They were probably heavily controlled by GHQ and stopped from suppressing the rebellion in time.

Another difficulty people say, was that there was no secrecy of information. All orders about Bengali units and personnel were passed on to them by Bengali officers at different levels. The same was the case in the president's office. Mujibur Rahman knew in advance what questions he was going to be asked in his meetings with the president.

Another story is that when Yaqub was corps commander, the troops at one stage had only one and a half day's reserve of ration and very little ammunition. Meanwhile, the Bengali contractors had ceased supplying vegetables etc. Their water supply and power were also cut off. At one stage water and vegetables had to be flown in from West Pakistan. I think it was the strong feeling of the troops which finally forced Yahya's hand and strong action was ordered. If he had not done that, there was every probability of the troops turning against him and the senior officers acting on their own.

16 | FRIDAY

📖 The situation in East Pakistan seems to be improving in the sense that the army is in control of most of the cities and towns. Chuadanga, which, according to Indian radio, was headquarters of the provisional government of so-called Bangladesh, has also been occupied and no traces of such a government found. The Indian infiltrators have also withdrawn to their frontiers together with Bengali deserters and hard core Awami Leaguers, who escaped arrest.

The BBC reported today that the Indian Deputy High Commissioner in Dacca, together with his Bengali staff, declared allegiance to the republic of Bangladesh.

There are different and exaggerated versions of the casualties suffered by the army and the Bengali personnel in East Pakistan. Bengali casualties are put in the hundreds and thousands. This must be a gross exaggeration, unless there were pitched battles. Why should the army have to shoot that number?

As regards the future, it is quite possible that pockets of resistance in the form of terrorist gangs may continue to operate for some considerable time and keep the army engaged and add to the already heavy defence expenditure, besides making political settlement difficult. There is no knowing if things may flare up in West Pakistan either.

I heard one or two people say that the Chinese have agreed to equip two divisions recently sent to East Pakistan with weapons, because the one already there has the Chinese weapons, and in fact the ordinance factory installed there will also be producing ammunition of Chinese calibres. Chinese weapons are light, rugged, highly mobile and deadly accurate. For instance their equivalent of 2 inch mortar has the fantastic range of 1150 yards and is as accurate as a machine gun.

20 | TUESDAY

📖 The Cleveland Hospital in Ohio has told me to reach there on 2nd May, Sunday evening. They have proposed that I should be admitted there. They propose to examine me on 3rd and 4th and carryout the bypass operation on 4th or 5th should they decide to do so.

21 | WEDNESDAY

📖 Conflicting news is coming from Bengal, but by and large things are quieting down. In the evening Agha Mohammed Ali, the brother of General Yahya, came to call and asked as to what the solution in East Pakistan would be. I repeated my previous answer to him that it is now impossible to keep Pakistan as a federation and our troops should be withdrawn from East Pakistan and a confederation worked out with Mujibur Rahman who is today a prisoner in West Pakistan. Agha Mohammed Ali said, 'Sir, is this is your final view.' I said, 'Yes, kindly convey it to the president.'

23 | FRIDAY

📖 Flew down to Karachi in the evening en route to the USA and stayed at Gohar's house. A large number of people came to call. Several said that not only they but even my bitterest enemies were openly confessing that what I had said about their demands and the future of the country was coming true. They all seem very uncertain and apprehensive of the future.

25 | SUNDAY

📖 Malik Qasim, who had just returned from a visit to East Pakistan, came to call. He repeated some of the harrowing tales that one had heard, but he did not think that there was any organized Indian military infiltration. The fight was now confined to deserters from the Bengali armed forces and their

Awami supporters and the army. Some of the leading Awami personalities like Colonel Osmany[23] had crossed over to India. The stories of large scale killing by the army, he said, were not true. They only acted against those that had put up resistance.

Qasim went to Chittagong to see Fazlul Qader Chaudhary who escaped Awami wrath. They had every intention of killing him. The port, he said, was working, but was short of labour who were afraid to return to work. Most of the West Pakistanis in the Pakistan Air Force observer corps on the border were killed by their Bengali comrades, and so were the officers and men in the East Pakistan Rifles and East Bengal Regiment. They were mostly shot in the back. He then described incidents and happenings in Jessore. He said that when West Pakistani units were busy controlling the city, a battalion of the Bengal Regiment located in the cantonment revolted. So they had to come back and disarm them. Having done that they returned to the city and surrounded a large crowd that was resisting or defying. A large number of people were supposed to have been killed on the occasion.

26 | MONDAY

📖 Left Karachi at midnight accompanied by Gohar Ayub, for London, reaching there early morning. The Pakistan cricket team was also in the same plane. The Bangladesh supporters had gathered at Heathrow airport to demonstrate against them, but the authorities took the team out by a different route. I had a bad night in the plane and even during the day had recurrence of chest pains and angina, at times severe and distressing. I am staying at the Selsden Park Hotel near London. It is an old-fashioned place and somehow a resort for old people, but outside the city, in beautiful green country surroundings. No road noises other than big jets flying over. This amenity is not easy to get inside the city centre in London. The BBC invited me to give a talk on the situation in East Pakistan, I declined the offer as I have so little knowledge of the sad affairs but there is no doubt about it that we getting very bad publicity in this country over this matter. The theme here is that the military junta, having given the people the right of free vote, are now trying to stop them by using West Pakistani troops to suppress the people mercilessly.

A good deal of this may well be true and wilful and deliberate but the government too has brought it on itself by not giving out the whole, and the true, story. As usual, our lack of interest in public relations is chiefly to blame. Even our embassy here was not told anything of the unfortunate happenings for some three weeks. And they had to face not only the British public, but a very anxious Pakistani community amounting to over 3 lakhs. So they are being fed on rumours and the hostile British information media. The anxieties, especially of those from East Pakistan whose relations and homes might be involved, can be well imagined.

30 | FRIDAY

📖 Mr Arshad Hussain is on a roving visit to different European countries to explain the government's point of view. He has been to Moscow, France, and is awaiting to see Douglas Hume, who is on a visit to Turkey. He said the French were courteous and understanding, but Kosygin was very cross and unhappy. His fear was that Bhutto was being helped to get into power and should that happen war between India and Pakistan might well be precipitated. He accused us of genocide and an unduly harsh reaction to the situation in East Pakistan.

Whether this is right or not is a different matter, but the Russian reaction is not based on purely humanitarian grounds. They have political motives. They consider support to India and the Bengali communists essential to the objectives of their policy on the subcontinent. Besides, they consider Mujibur Rahman a lesser evil than Bhutto.

When in Karachi I heard disturbing news from an air force officer that all Bengali personnel had been grounded on the suspicion of indulging in a conspiracy. And one of their aircraft had crashed due to sabotage. Some Bengali personnel was suspected of foul play. He had a Bengali pilot in his unit. He was told to keep an eye on him. The only way he could do that was to fly with him, armed. It shows that the extent of suspicion amongst Bengalis and non-Bengalis in the services is now acute. To re-establish which would be a formidable task, if at all.

2 | SUNDAY

📖 Flew from London to New York by a TWA jumbo jet. It is a monster of an aircraft capable of carrying some 300 passengers. They are talking of building even bigger ones. The flight was very comfortable. Was met by Agha Hilaly and Agha Shahi[24] together with the representative of the State Department[25] at Kennedy airport. Yusuf Haroon and his wife also came. Yusuf then kindly accompanied us to Cleveland. At the airport a helicopter was awaiting to take us to the clinic which is some 25 miles away. The chairman of the trust that runs the hospital flew the helicopter and landed on top of the hospital building. The object was to save a long drive and also for security reasons especially as we have a bad press over East Pakistan affairs and Bengalis had been demonstrating.

The State Department man had brought a letter from President Nixon expressing warm regards. Lord Cromer, the British ambassador, also wrote. I had met him when he was the head of the Bank of England. On arrival in the hospital the doctors immediately started their medical examinations, x-ray etc.

A nurse came to tag my name on my wrist. I have been given the name Joseph Kahn. Security is being carried to an absurdity, but I suppose the hospital people don't want to take any chances and have been so advised by the State Department.

5 | WEDNESDAY

📖 During the last few days I have been in hospital they have carried out several blood, urine, culture tests and x-rays, the major ones being angiography. Doctor Soanes, the head cardiologist, carried them out himself. The normal practice is to carry it out through the right arm. Apparently it is easier and simpler to reach the heart that way, but in my case he found that there was blocked bifurcation around the shoulder and the tube could not enter the proper vein. So he tried it on the left arm and carried out the examination. He said that he found the phenomena of bifurcation on the right in one case in 300 or 3000, I have forgotten which.

Doctor Soanes was obviously unhappy at having to puncture both my arms and so was the staff. The head nurse told me that whenever they took special precautions, something unexpected happened.

In the evening Doctor Soanes came and gave me the result of his examination. He said my right artery was blocked as a result of the heart attack I had in 1968, but subsidiary blood vessels had opened up and were supplying blood. The main artery on the left hand, however, had developed an obstruction and it became blocked. The consequences could be very dangerous indicating that heart surgery was necessary. The chest surgeon Doctor Efler, who carries out the operation, also came to see me. Both these men are regarded as top notches in their line and highly respected. I have been having low-grade fever and irregularity of heartbeat for the last few days. This may be due to catheterisation. They have developed an ingenious technique—when the x-ray camera is looking at the heart, the picture is also reflected on a TV set. Sometimes it is visible to the patient also.

6 | THURSDAY

📖 Was rung up by President Nixon from Washington inquiring about my health. He also expressed concern over the state of affairs in Pakistan and assured me that there shall be no interference by the USA in the internal affairs of Pakistan.

Our ambassador Hilaly had also told me that the State Department had pressed very hard to intervene, but Nixon refused to accept their advice.

I was told by Doctor Efler that they had decided to carry out chest surgery, a bypass, on me on Monday. He said there was always an element of risk in surgery, but the risk to do nothing was greater. Out of the three arteries one was already blocked, the left one was functioning well, but the middle one was beginning to get blocked from its inception. The consequences would be very serious if it got blocked and then there was every chance that it would. He said so far they had done a good job beforehand and built up a reputation. So he could promise their best effort. He said that he would like me to take a couple of alcoholic drinks every evening. He knew Muslims were forbidden to take alcohol, but his Turkish patients used to tell him that it would be perfectly all right if he prescribed it as medicine. So he had prescribed it for me.

An American railway engineer who served in Pakistan and had met me once or twice is also hospitalised here with the same complaint as mine, came to call. He had the heart surgery done and had five bypasses in his heart arteries, only a few days ago. He was bubbling with life and energy and said that he never felt so well. He could not walk more than 50 yards previously prior to the operation, but now he roamed all over the hospital. He talked of this new treatment of the heart as miraculous. But he said, 'Boy, do they cut you up. However, you do heal up soon.'

I stayed in the hospital up to 6th [May] and moved to the hotel. I am still running low-grade fever and suffering from terrible depression. I was told that this happened with most people after this operation. I left the hotel on 2nd June for a hotel called Somerset Inn on the outskirts of Cleveland in more open surroundings, but my fever still continued and I had no appetite for food but did eat a certain amount by force to maintain vitality. During this period the hospital staff became more friendly and showed a lot of kindness. Doctor Efler entertained us on several occasions and one Ms Peters used to take us for long drives everyday.

Earlier in America, Gohar Ayub stayed with me and then Tahir Ayub replaced him on 29th June. They both acted as a sort of nurse and secretary and worked ceaselessly in taking care of me. I was naturally deeply moved by their feelings of loyalty and prayed for their better future.

After the operation President Nixon rang up to inquire after my health and President Johnson asked me to stay with him in Texas, but I was in no condition to undertake such a long and arduous journey. The State Department, too, constantly kept my family informed of my condition. Our embassy staff also did all they could to help.

One thing that galled one was a very adverse press on Pakistan in America and in fact in the whole world on account of the happenings in East Pakistan. The exodus of refugees aggravated the situation. The few Pakistanis who came to see me were very depressed. Some told me that they had no intention of returning home. Things became so bad that our ambassador told me that responsible American officials even refused to see him.

The Indians were very active and successful in using the East Pakistani personnel, officials and non-officials against Pakistan. Our ambassador told me that his Bengali personnel met the Indians daily and openly to take instructions. A worse state of affairs could not be imagined.

At times I had discussions with the doctors as to how effective the operation they had done on me was. They could not commit themselves, but Efler, the surgeon, said that if he did not see me hale and hearty after ten years he would consider his time wasted on me. This may be mere speculation but he showed great confidence in his art.

16 | WEDNESDAY

They held a medical board on me and decided that I could go back home. They thought that my recovery would be speeded up by living in my normal environment.

17 | FRIDAY

Left Cleveland for New York and stayed with Jalil of the Pakistan National Oil at his apartment in 5th Avenue, which was palatial. Shoaib, Hilaly, and others also turned out with Professor Chaudhary from East Pakistan. It was natural that the situation and their problems should come under discussion. Some people felt that the time had to come to call it a day and separate. After all that had happened in East Pakistan living together was impossible and all talk of conversion of Bengali attitude was futile and wishful thinking. twenty-three years experience should prove that.

19 | SATURDAY

Flew to London and stayed at Selsden Park Hotel outside London. The weather was foul, rainy and foggy.

21 | MONDAY

Flew to Amsterdam and took a PIA flight to Islamabad.

22 | TUESDAY

Reached Islamabad an hour in advance of time. I am told that a lot of people that wanted to receive me missed the chance, but the crowd at the airport made my approach to the car almost impossible. People not only wanted to shake hands with me, but embraced me, little realizing that my chest wounds were still tender. A pressman asked me if I had noticed the emotions of the nation. I said I did, what I did not tell him was that it does not take long for our people to be misled and changed.

Demonetisation of 500 and 100 rupee notes was probably justified, but it has hit poor people hard. Their lifelong hoarded savings have been lost, as some in remote areas did not get the information or did not know what to do. The effect of this action was visible in other ways too. You hardly see any goods traffic moving on the roads. The money supply would undoubtedly be reduced, but I doubt if the prices would come down. How can they in the face of reduced production?

23 | WEDNESDAY

Mr Bottomley, who was at one time the Commonwealth Secretary of State in the Labour government and who is now on a fact finding mission to East Pakistan, came to call. He discussed the problem of East Pakistan and asked me what he could do to help. He was obviously against dismemberment of Pakistan, but at the same time did not see how Mujibur Rahman could be bypassed. He did not think that any settlement would be durable unless it was affected through Mujibur Rahman. I agreed, but he said General Yahya considers him a scoundrel and would have nothing to do with him. I agreed again, but political circumstances have put him in a key position at least for the present. He said he was sure that a good deal of this would have been avoided if I were there, but he said you can't have two Ayub Khans. Then he asked me if I had influence with Yahya. I said none whatsoever.

25 | FRIDAY

There is news of extensive Indian firing on East Pakistan's borders. The object seems to be to give cover and encouragement to Bengali terrorists and keep our army engaged in a war of attrition. The Indians are also threatening to go to war once the refugee problem further increases. They would not send them back unless the government of their choice was established, which means Mujibur Rahman and his party. A responsible official told me that the Americans and the Soviets had warned the Indians against starting any aggression, but one could never be sure. The Indians are also apprehensive of Chinese reaction.

India is also talking of preparations for carrying out underground nuclear explosions for peaceful purposes. This is nothing but a subterfuge for the production of an atomic bomb. I suppose they have enough material, plutonium from the Trombay reactor, to make several bombs. These, when made, will undoubtedly pose a very serious threat to Pakistan.

26 | SATURDAY

I am told that great security precautions are taken for Mujibur Rahman. The army is afraid that he may be whisked away by a helicopter etc. to India by Bengali personnel. The Americans seemed to be anxious to know his whereabouts. There is also talk that he may be tried. That would be a waste of time and make him a bigger hero. He himself wishes to be allowed to go to England and presumably make it his base for agitation as there are a large number of Bengalis in that country. I was also told that he got very attached to a parrot in the place he is in. He was apparently deeply disturbed when the parrot was killed by a cat.

I was also told about a Bengali officer who carried out atrocities on West Pakistanis, was wounded and captured in an encounter with the army and brought to West Pakistan presumably for trial. Presently he is undergoing treatment in a hospital. When questioned he is supposed to have said that he killed West Pakistani men, women and children and would do so again if he got a chance. One can see how deep the bitterness has gone.

18 | SUNDAY

📖 Kissinger, President Nixon's advisor, visited this country and went to stay in Nathiagali under cover. From there he is supposed to have slipped across to visit Peking and obtain an invitation for Nixon to visit Peking. This may bring about a major political change in Asia, but the obstacles are formidable. The future of Taiwan would prove a major obstacle. The Chinese would insist on it being regarded as a part of China.

📖 The Indian utterances are becoming more bellicose. They continue to talk of war over the situation in East Pakistan. We shall have to be very watchful from November onwards when the monsoons cease and the ground becomes hard and dry and fit for campaigning.

📖 My fever stopped on return from the USA, but started again when in Abbottabad. It makes me feel depressed and miserable when on. My doctor insists on eating more protein—at least one pound of meat a day, I tried but it is not easy.

📖 Neville Maxwell[26] of the *Times*, also came. He wants to write a book on the 1965 war and asked for my assistance. I told him that I could be of no help as I had kept no notes of that period. GHQ and the foreign office could help best as they were in possession of all the information. I said to him that you want to write about the 1965 war but I am looking at a 1971 war.

📖 The latest news about Kissinger's trip to Peking is that he flew straight from Rawalpindi in the early hours of the morning. The trip to Nathiagali by some of his staff was a cover move. Even they did not know what Kissinger was up to.

📖 I understand that the Indians are training a large number of guerrillas. The incidents of sabotage, sniping and ambush one hears of in the border areas in East Pakistan are carried out by them. The shelling carried out by the Indians is probably in support of these parties when they get into difficulties.

23 | FRIDAY

📖 Pir of Sarsina[27] came yesterday looking very worried. He has been the target of attack of the extremists and many attempts have been made on his life. He implored me to come back to politics little realizing that for one, the elections are over, and secondly, in the changed circumstances I can do very little good. He said that if I did not come back the religious and nationalist elements would be wiped out. Captain Zaidi of Pabna also spoke in similar strains.

It is now crystal clear that, apart from the political and moral support, India is now giving all manner of military support to the Bangladeshis. Training camps have been opened in several places where these people are given guerrilla training. They are then launched across the border to carry out sabotage, lay ambushes, disrupt communications etc. How enthusiastic these people are is difficult to tell but one thing is clear, that they, together with deserters from East Pakistan Rifles etc., will constitute a large uncontrolled force and are bound to become a headache for their politicians. I have no doubt that close association would have convinced them that the politicians are a pretty poor lot and not fit to govern the country. So I would not be a bit surprised if they take over the province at the first possible opportunity once the Pakistan army is withdrawn. Even otherwise, they will make politicians' life pretty miserable.

India keeps on hurling threats to Pakistan. She may or may not go to war, but by establishing guerrilla camps for Bangladeshis, they have made certain that a large amount of Pakistan army will remain deployed to deal with guerrillas and also there will always be insecurity in the province affecting administration and production thus bleeding Pakistan white in course of time.

26 | MONDAY

Attempts are being made to unite the three factions of the Muslim League. The administration wants it, especially to bring Qayyum to the forefront, but is not taking any active part. Meanwhile, Yahya is busy parleying with Bhutto and his motley crowd. Who is trying to cheat whom is difficult to say. Perhaps both are playing the same game. Bhutto is in a hurry to get into power and Yahya cannot hand over to him for his own safety and unless an understanding is reached with East Pakistan and the constitution framed which politicians are not capable of doing.

Reports about East Pakistan are discouraging. The tea industry has almost been destroyed, being on the border with India. Incidents of sabotage are continuing. Rail and road communications are still disrupted. Some 343 bridges were destroyed, obviously by the Indian sappers, and very few jute mills and other concerns are in operation through lack of labour. So East Pakistan is a white elephant and added burden to West Pakistan. How long can this erroneous burden be borne?

31 | SATURDAY

Air Marshal Nur Khan came to call. Though he operated against me when in power, I did not make any mention of it and treated him with all courtesy. He has fabulous ideas on labour and student problems beyond the capacity of this country, but he is very sore that those were not accepted. He has now fallen out with his party and relinquished any office he had held.

I was told that a Bengali major who was on the staff of a striking brigade on the Sialkot front has crossed over the border into India with all the plans and maps. Similarly, two senior Bengali air force officers who went to perform *Umra* have disappeared. Even if it is possible to stay together, which is doubtful, it has become impossible and positively dangerous to trust the Bengalis in the armed forces. This fact alone makes the running of a united country impossible.

4 | WEDNESDAY

📖 Yahya's long interview with the foreign correspondents was telecast. They asked why no action was taken when EPR and EBR were being subverted. The answer is that Yahya, to retain his job, was bending backwards not to displease Mujib.

6 | FRIDAY

📖 Yahya went to Karachi en route to Dacca, but changed his mind and returned home. He was told that a visit to Dacca would be dangerous. An attempt might be made on his life. He might be hijacked and might even be attacked in the air by the Bengali pilots who had defected to India. It is difficult to form a judgement without knowing full facts, but on the face of it looks like a bad decision. Arrangements could have been made to secure his protection. He should have gone there and faced the situation.

9 | MONDAY

📖 Gromyko, the Russian foreign minister, paid a surprise visit to New Delhi. The outcome of his meeting with the Indian leaders was a treaty of friendship. Attack on one will be regarded as an attack on the other. Nobody is going to attack India, but it might well be a warning to China and Pakistan and perhaps a move to steady India. The Russians are probably also worried that if China and America come to terms India may well drift towards them. This would mean complete alienation of Russian influence from Asia. Be as it may, India has scored a big point against us, America and China and they must be gloating over it. What would be the American reaction remains to be seen? Normally they should regard it as a dangerous move, but in their present state of psychological and hysterical exhaustion they would probably take it lying down. Still any rift between America and Russia is to our advantage. Let us hope it turns out to be so.

11 | WEDNESDAY

📖 Heard on the radio that the Americans had given a stiff warning to India on 31st July that India will have to pay a fearful price beyond their capacity if they launched an attack against East Pakistan. I admire this action of the Nixon administration at a time when American public opinion is so much against us. Also, one would like to know what they mean by this statement. Are they going to come to our help or give us more equipment? Both these things would be difficult to sell to the American public in the present circumstances.

It is quite possible that Russia has countered the American threat to India by signing a pact of mutual defence. They also hope that it would be ahead of any threat by China to India.

📖 I see that the trial of Sheikh Mujibur Rahman and several others has started. I wonder how much good it will do despite his unforgivable perfidy. It will only be exploited by our enemies within and abroad.

14 | SATURDAY

📖 Today is the 27th anniversary of Pakistan. Normally it should be a day of rejoicing but I wonder how many people feel that way. The idea that had brought Pakistan into being can never lose validity, but its spirit has lost attraction, certainly for the generation below the age of 30 who form the bulk of the population. Regionalism and provincialism has supplanted it, specially so in East Pakistan. We have no constitution and there is no consensus as to what it should be like. East Pakistan is on the point off breaking off. What will happen in West Pakistan remains to be seen. People like Bhutto have already got their plans ready. The only binding force left is the army. It has the formidable task of holding the country together and meeting the threat of Indian aggression, which is getting ever louder and provocative. Since the '65 war India has doubled its military budget and is now armed to the teeth. It thinks that the time is ripe for having a go at Pakistan when the country is so badly divided and leaderless.

16 | MONDAY

📖 My son, Gohar Ayub, flew in from Karachi yesterday. He happened to meet Lt. General Gul Hassan, the CGS, who was returning from a visit to East Pakistan. He [Gul Hassan] was very pessimistic about the situation in Bengal. He said the administration had ceased to exist, violent resistance, even in the interior of the province, was on the increase. A large number of guerrillas were being trained in 138 centres established by the Indians around the province. They not only operated close to the border, but went to the villages in the interior and were given protection by the people either willingly or through fear. He saw the situation deteriorating as time went on. He said that those who were cooperating and called themselves peace committees asked constantly for military protection. They could not face the people. Time, he said, was running out. We must come to a final decision, but who will? There was no one of any stature in the province.

📖 Someone said that India does not have to go to war against Pakistan. It is achieving its disruption even otherwise with much less effort.

23 | MONDAY

📖 Nazir Ahmad[28] and Aziz Ahmad,[29] both ex-CSP, came to call. Aziz Ahmad is thinking of writing a book on the 1965 war and asked if I could provide some material, especially on how the war started. I very nearly told him that it was his persistence as foreign secretary that was the main cause. However, I told him to get GHQ permission before he started on such as project.

24 | TUESDAY

📖 I see that Dr Malik[30] has been appointed as Governor of East Pakistan. He will be allowed to have a civilian cabinet under the cover of martial law. Malik is a patriot, but utterly spineless and indecisive. His main task apparently will be to conduct the bye-elections. I wonder if these could be held. Even those who have been cleared of any stigma have demanded and been promised military protection. They and those that would fight the bye-elections on non-Awami ticket will surely become the target of the Mukti Bahini.[31]

For the present the task of the Mukti Bahini seems to be to disrupt communications, and intimidate workers so as to wreck the economy. They have succeeded in this to a large extent.

7 | WEDNESDAY

Yahya has built a house in Peshawar cantonment financed by the Alvi brothers of Standard Bank. Its opening ceremony took place the other day followed by several days of orgy, drinking and womanising. On one occasion dancing of women and men went on for hours on the lawns of the house which was surrounded by some 300 security police. Then Yahya sat down with two women on his lap and Lt. General Hamid had one, whereupon a policeman got so furious that he wanted to shoot them.

There is a good deal of talk of war. Some foolish military men are supposed to have suggested that we should go in for a pre-emptive war. This will be the most fatal and foolish thing to do. It will endanger the survival of Pakistan.

11 | SATURDAY

Yahya has gone down to Karachi on the way to Tehran to see the Shah. I wonder what could this meeting be about? Most likely, the future of Mujibur Rahman and East Pakistan or about the Indian war threat. In both cases the American initiative is probably operative.

14 | TUESDAY

Yahya visited the Shah of Iran for two days and returned. He looked very glum whilst meeting the Shah on arrival at Tehran airport. It is quite possible that he may ask to see the Shah for a loan of military equipment should India attack or the Shah may have invited Yahya about the constitution arrangements on behalf of the Americans.

We now see the reason why there is so much prejudice against the Punjabis both in East and West Pakistan. Given the opportunity, the Punjabi surpasses all of them in every field. Though Karachi has benefited most and made great industrial progress in my times. The Punjabi has made a big leap forward in agriculture and small scale industries. Today he is at a standstill as he is not sure of the future and is scared of political instability.

India is waging an undeclared war on East Pakistan's borders. Guerrillas in large numbers are being trained for use in the province for sabotage and large scale raiding parties are sent into the interior under the cover of artillery fire. Men are also being trained to intimidate loyal elements and carry out acts of sabotage. The object is to maintain a state of lawlessness, disrupt the economy, communications and so on and the distribution of food. Some people apprehend famine conditions setting in soon. Someone told me that in spite of the trial and tribulations Pakistan is going through, Yahya seems to show no concern and is full of confidence. This is a good thing, but I wonder how much of it is justified.

27 | MONDAY

📖 I gather that Lt. General Hamid is unhappy over General Yahya hanging on to two jobs. He thinks that he has been tricked. But Lt. General Hamid is a silent and patient man. I do not think he will kick up any fuss.

📖 Sir Fredrick Bennett, MP, who is a very good friend of Pakistan, called on me with his wife. He was genuinely unhappy over the present state of affairs in Pakistan. He said November to March was a critical period. India may well launch an attack against Pakistan, sure in the knowledge that the Himalayan passes will be closed and the Chinese will not be able to assist. If there is anything they are afraid of, he said, it was the Chinese.

29 | WEDNESDAY

📖 Our armed forces seem to be aware of Indian intentions and of this situation and making necessary preparations. They think they have never been so close to war as today. The apprehension is that India will try to occupy certain portions of East Pakistan where they can settle the refugees. That is eye wash and an excuse to grab East Pakistan. But whatever their intentions, such a move will inevitably lead to general war both in East and West Pakistan. India has a weak government with a woman at the head. If she gets an opportunity, she is bound to show off to prove she is as good as a man.

Kosygin is supposed to have criticized Pakistan at a luncheon party given in his honour by Indira Gandhi in Moscow, but also said that under no circumstances will they allow war to break out in the subcontinent.

5 | TUESDAY

📖 Abdul Hameed, Qayyum Khan's brother, came to call. He apologized for having sided with his brother in the elections in Haripur in 1970 against Sardar Bahadur Khan. He said he was forced to do this because of his brother, but he never uttered a derogatory word against me during the whole campaign and so on. Hameed is the man I had appointed as the President of Azad Kashmir.

12 | TUESDAY

📖 It seems that India has come to the conclusion that war with Pakistan over Bangladesh is unavoidable. They always had this intention but have now found a strong argument for world consumption: that without a war the establishment of a government in Bengal sympathetic to refugees and have them repatriated is not possible. The Russian attitude makes this apparent. They have unleashed propaganda against Pakistan to prepare public opinion for them to side with India should the war breakout. So the period of semblance of good relations between Pakistan and Russia are over. This reminds me of what Chou En-lai, the premier of China, had once told me, 'you will find that the Russians are thoroughly unreliable'.

Russian hostility against Pakistan is becoming more blatant. The American attitude towards us is also dubious. Although the administration tries to look friendly, there are powerful forces in the State Department who are convinced that Pakistan cannot remain one and emergence of Bangladesh is inevitable. They are also believe in giving full support to Bangladesh when it comes into being.

14 | THURSDAY

📖 In Iran, the 2500th anniversary of the monarchy is being celebrated at the site of the old capital Persepolis. Heads of governments and states of a large number of countries have come. I am told fabulous arrangements have been made for the reception and stay of the guests. I wonder if the Shah was wise in going into such an artificiality. Celebrations of monarchy do not go well with the times, especially in developing countries where there is so much poverty. I would not be a bit surprised if the Shah invites trouble.

📖 I had shocking news this morning, former Governor Monem Khan was shot in the stomach in his house and died later in the hospital. A couple of rascals pretended to have a talk with him about something. Then suddenly one of them pulled out a pistol, fired at him, and I have no doubt that they made good their escape. Obviously, Monem Khan was alone at the time.

📖 News from Bengal is that holding of by-elections there is almost impossible. Nobody would come to vote, in that 90 per cent of the people, especially in the rural areas, have turned Bangladeshi. Nationalist elements are the major target of the Mukti Bahini. A number have been killed. In any case, the by-elections would produce no different results. Most Bengali parties demand the same as Mujibur Rahman. Even Nurul Amin is saying the same thing.

Although the border clashes get the headlines, the interior is no less disturbed as armed Mukti Bahini have managed to get back to their villages and are intimidating people. The army does chase them, but it cannot be everywhere. The border clashes are gaining in intensity, but it is not a one-sided affair. Our people also chase the Hindus. The rumour has it that in one case 24 Indian artillery pieces were captured and brought back. However, our infiltrators are at a disadvantage. They cannot go far into the interior because of the Hindu population.

21 | THURSDAY

War hysteria is gaining momentum. Our people are worried. Indian leaders' statements are getting more bellicose, stringent and threatening. Troops from both sides are getting closer to battle positions. Any aggressive move on the part of India would spark off a major conflict.

There is a rumour that a major incident may occur on the 24th or 25th of this month. The unfortunate thing is that if the war comes, it would not be a popular war. People or even the armed forces do not show any enthusiasm for it. They have no faith in political and military leaders like Yahya or even Lt. General Hamid sordid personal life is becoming too well known. So one can only pray that Pakistan will survive the ordeal. The trouble is that there is no one to galvanize the scattered people together.

Russia, though pretending to be friendly, is becoming more and more hostile. Their press, which is controlled, is freely writing articles against Pakistan. I notice that the Chinese are keeping silent. At least I have not seen anything in the press from them.

People keep on asking me to stage a comeback. I keep telling them that I could do no good at this juncture as I am not a healthy man. After surgery I am living on a borrowed heart. Besides, so many people have betrayed me that it would be difficult to forget their perfidy and trust anyone.

23 | SATURDAY

Heard the first good news after a long time. Our team beat the Spaniards by one goal to nil and won the world hockey gold cup. Apparently the match was hotly contested. It looks like the standard of hockey in many Europeans countries is rising to first class level.

26 | TUESDAY

Colonel Mohiuddin is normally very tongue-tied but when he gets over-frustrated and disgusted with Yahya's conduct, he blurts out things, even to me. He told my brother Sardar Bahadur Khan today that I may or may not have made other mistakes but appointing Yahya was a great blunder. He said God would never forgive me for that. I said what else was the answer at that time. He went on to say that the situation in Pakistan is so complicated that there seems to be no answer to many problems and that is why someone else in the army has not taken the plunge and replaced this man. He was so far safe because of that realization.

📖 I understand that people living in and on the Lahore and Sialkot front, are moving out. They are thinning out from these cities for fear of bombardment from long range Russian guns that the Indians have.

📖 I am told that Asghar Khan speaks well of me these days. I do not understand what has brought about this change.

8 | MONDAY

📖 I have not been in the writing mood during the last fortnight or so, because every bit of news was more depressing than the last. Everyone who comes to me asks me whether there will be a war and how I see the future. War threat is, of course, real. Indian military build-up is enormous and complete. The indication is that the Russians had given them the added cover of a defence treaty. In consequence, they are getting more bellicose and aggressive. The shelling and the limited attacks on the border villages of East Pakistan are a daily occurrence. Their object must be to provoke us into staging a major counteraction so that they can use that as a cover to launch an offensive against Pakistan. So far our people have shown great restraint and retaliated on a small scale. This is the right policy as the world would never forgive us if we are the aggressors, which India would like us to be.

📖 Indira Gandhi is touring western capitals presumably to get clearance for aggression against Pakistan. According to the press, the British were noncommittal. The Americans warned her of the dangers of war. They naturally do not want to queer the pitch for Nixon's visit to Peking by having trouble in Asia. To what extent she will be influenced by that remains to be seen but she cannot afford to ignore American warnings, if seriously given. But meanwhile, the Russians are giving Indians all encouragement. Several important personalities and delegations have visited New Delhi lately and a vast amount of military material is being flown in from Russia.

📖 Criticism of Yahya's private life and public decisions have become common. He commands very little respect in the eyes of the people and even in the armed forces. Wherever he goes heavy security precautions are taken, but nothing seems to dampen his lust for gay life and merrymaking.

📖 Zulfiqar Ali Bhutto was sent as the head of a mission to Peking. The Chinese have given an encouraging statement of support in the event of war with India. This will build Bhutto's image further and he will become a bigger monster for Yahya. I wonder if he has taken this factor into consideration. Bhutto will sadly use it to his political advantage, and if need be, against Yahya.

📖 Mujibur Rahman's trial, I am told, is being held in Lyallpur jail. On entering the courtroom, he gives a call of 'Jai Bangladesh'. He has also said that the President had declared him a traitor. So why hold a trial. Why not proceed in spite of so many tragedies perpetrated by his followers and of the poisons spread by him. There is not concrete evidence against him. Mujibur Rahman apparently was given a briefing on the latest situation in East Pakistan. He was very happy that things were going according to plan. Mujibur Rahman also wanted to know if Bhutto had not gone mad yet, because his sole aim is to gain power. He cannot live without it.

11 | THURSDAY

📖 A reliable person told me that Yahya's son's betrothal was fabulous; a lot of jewellery was given to the girl and a vast amount of gifts accepted. Merrymaking went on for days. People could not make out why all this was happening whilst East Pakistan was on fire. He also told me that:

1. Before proceeding to Dacca in March, Yahya and Bhutto had agreed that it was no longer possible to retain East Pakistan. Separation was unavoidable. Bhutto did not want to say that openly. He wanted Yahya to take the responsibility. Yahya desisted at the last moment and fell out with Mujibur Rahman. Previous to that there was an understanding between Mujibur Rahman and Yahya. But Mujibur Rahman would only offer him a presidency of the Indian type. Yahya refused. It was then that he started hobnobbing with Bhutto again with a view to securing his position.

2. Yahya was anxious to hand over power to the public representatives provided he could retain his position with considerable powers.

3. Whilst the situation in East Pakistan is deteriorating, nobody amongst the junta seems to be concerned. In fact, they seemed very confident.

4. The thinking is that Yahya will remain the president, Nurul Amin as the prime minister and Bhutto is demanding to be appointed as the vice prime minister. He does not like the word deputy.

5. Bhutto will not hesitate to remove Yahya as soon as he gets the chance. They have very little faith in each other.

6. Lt. General Peerzada is with Bhutto. His ambition was to replace Yahya or become commander-in-chief of the army with the help of Bhutto. Lt. General Peerzada keeps Bhutto well posted with secret information.

7. Mohammad Ali, Yahya's elder brother, has very little influence over him. He comes and talks about the public criticism of his private life. Yahya does not see such people. He probably thinks that he knows more about his private life than anybody else. Such stories are no news to him.

8. He said the radio and television etc. give out correct figures of enemy casualties. They are mostly Mukti Bahini, whom the Indians use as cattle fodder. Our casualties are five to ten daily.

9. A young officer who has been brought to the CMH Rawalpindi for mental treatment is supposed to have killed nearly 14,000 people. The mere thought of this gives him convulsions and nightmares.

10. In the earlier stages, the Hindus carried out a lot of atrocities. Now they are shot at sight. No questions are asked.

11. The army is not happy over the amnesty given to those who killed their comrades. Now they don't send who are caught in action up those for trial. They are just shot.

12. Ahsan and Lt. General Yaqub had both separately recommended that the mood in which the Bengalis were in only a political situation had any chance of success. They did not see how their demand for almost separation could be bypassed. Lt. General Yaqub pointed out the futility of military action and was removed, and so was Admiral Ahsan.

12 | FRIDAY

📖 I understand that people are getting desperate of Yahya and the future. They foresee Pakistan going under Indian domination in course of time. They think that the only one who can save the situation is me. This is sheer myth. Things have gone too far to be rectified whilst the Indian military threat is constant.

17 | WEDNESDAY

📖 Aurangzeb came from Swat where he had met the American ambassador[32] who told him that there will be no war. There is no doubt about it that the Americans are exerting a lot of pressure on the Indians to desist from rashness.

21 | SUNDAY

📖 I was so ashamed to see a passage in *Time* magazine quoting a diplomat: 'Pakistan is a drowning dog. India does not have to push its head under.' I am told that a very damaging article has come out in the *Newsweek*, banned in Pakistan, on the private life of Yahya. It talks of his ten girlfriends and their doings and the influence they command.

📖 Just heard on the TV that the Indians have launched a two-brigade attacks on the Jessore front. Does it mean the start of the war?

23 | TUESDAY

📖 According to radio and press, the Indians have launched a major offensive on the Jessore, Sylhet and Chittagong Hill Tracts fronts. The offensive on the Jessore front consisted of two divisions supported by armour. The battle started on Sunday and is still going on. It looks like the Indians will open other fronts too to cause disruption of our forces. I hope our people would be able to hold them, at least beat them back, but the odds against them are tremendous.

26 | FRIDAY

📖 Gohar Ayub, who came here for a few days, has left for Karachi.

📖 I could not believe my ears when told that the administration in Dacca thinks that Monem was murdered by his relatives because of some property dispute. The trouble was that he took no care of his safety. He did not even have a watchman. Nevertheless, this story sounds too far-fetched. I think this was a case of political murder. He had far too many enemies.

📖 Indian attacks on East Pakistan have intensified. Several fronts have been opened. But so far they have made no appreciable progress. They have been halted everywhere and in most places beaten back. Meanwhile, pressure by some generals on Yahya to commence hostility in the West is mounting, but he is not agreeing; which to my mind is wise for several good reasons.

📖 A few days back American personnel were evacuated from Lahore, but now they have been told to go back again. This is significant. Of course, one knows that the Americans are making diplomatic efforts to halt the conflict.

📖 There is a persistent rumour that corruption has entered the army in East Pakistan and there have been cases of rape and looting by the soldiery. This is sad if true. Our soldiery had a clean record in the past in these respects.

28 | SUNDAY

📖 A foreign correspondent reported some time ago that the Indians are planning to launch a major offensive on the 28th. It did not happen and the Indians launched major attacks on a dozen places or so around East Pakistan. So far they have not got far. The intention seems to be to occupy Jessore, Khulna, a bit of the northern districts like Dinajpur, Bogra, etc., and isolate Chittagong, cutting off communications to it. Our troops are fighting valiantly as usual, with what faith one does not know.

30 | TUESDAY

📖 Indira Gandhi, in a show of Brahamanic arrogance, has invited Pakistan to withdraw its troops from Bengal. She has suggested that is the best solution to this problem.

1 | WEDNESDAY

📖 A man who has been in military intelligence for a long time, and probably still is in their pay, came to call. I have known him for a long time. The impression I got was that he was more interested in giving me the news rather than getting information. This was probably due to the great concern with which the average person in Pakistan has begun to view the situation. One gets that impression from every strata of society. He said the following:

1. People of all descriptions, including those who agitated against me, now want me back. They openly admit that they had made a great mistake in agitating against me. Some people, however, blame me for letting Mujibur Rahman out of jail.
2. People are anxious and puzzled about the future. The man who should put them in the picture is Yahya. He says nothing. In my time, they used to get regular information through my monthly broadcasts apart from the occasional statements I used to make on public functions. This is the period in which the president should say something occasionally to keep up people's morale.
3. Why does Yahya not go around to see troops in the front line? He should have gone and seen them in East Pakistan where they are so hard pressed. Instead, he is busy drinking himself into a stupor and playing with women.
4. There is some rumour of a coup.

I do not think coups are a probability, but general dissatisfaction against Yahya is increasing. People think he is incapable of giving true guidance.

3 | FRIDAY

📖 I heard in the evening that the Indian advance forces supported by air and artillery had opened the second front all along West Pakistan. Our air force retaliated by attack on nine forward airfields extending from Srinagar to Rajasthan and deep down to Agra. This, I think, is a remarkable feat to get in against extensive enemy radar screens and Russian SAMs. I have a feeling that the Indians were caught unaware. They did not expect such extensive attacks to come so soon.

📖 There were several air raid alarms last night. There must have been extensive air activity. When the first alarm went, little Tania, my granddaughter, was the first to awake and tell every body else to take shelter.

6 | MONDAY

📖 The Security Council has taken up the question of Pakistan-India conflict in an effort to bring about a ceasefire, but their efforts have been frustrated by Russia. They have vetoed everything reasonable.

7 | TUESDAY

American policy seems to have taken a pro-Pakistan turn. They have condemned India as the aggressor and stopped all developmental aid. This is some gain for us. It may bring home to India that they are in no position to engage in a sustained war just as Pakistan can't. We are both ruining ourselves in a negative effort. But what can we do. India would not see reason.

Up to last evening, the Pakistan Air Force scored kills. The number of Indian losses has gone up considerably. I wonder what could be wrong with them. Either their training is defective or they have not their heart in the war or they consist of soft bania human material. On the ground, however, their troops have made a better showing.

India has recognized the Bangladesh government. In consequence, Pakistan has severed diplomatic ties with India. There is no great disadvantage in this step. We should not get the amount of intelligence we used to about India.

8 | WEDNESDAY

Nurul Amin and Bhutto have been appointed as the prime minister, and the deputy prime minister and foreign minister respectively. I hope it does not prove to be the darkest day for Pakistan as this man Bhutto is capable of creating untold problems. Whilst he is alive and living in this country there will be no peace. Nurul Amin and even Yahya are no men to control him. Bhutto has been sent to the United Nations to represent Pakistan. He may do that, but his effort will be to build himself.

Since the war started nights and even the days had been pretty hectic due to enemy air raids, but last night was peaceful. They come in ones or twos and drop bombs and strafe aimlessly, killing and wounding a lot of civilians.

The news from East Pakistan is not too good. We seem to have been pushed back in several areas, but our troops are fighting valiantly.

The UN General Assembly has passed a resolution by overwhelming majority calling upon Pakistan and India to ceasefire and withdraw their troops to their respective territories. What affect will this have remains to be seen. Perhaps not much as India is in no mood to listen to reason.

10 | FRIDAY

Nurul Amin's appointment seems artificial. Whom does he represent? I do not think he would be able to put his nose in Bengal as Yahya and Bhutto cannot. However, he is a good administrator, but now too old, 74 years. To make any positive contribution, I believe he and his relations have evacuated Bengal knowing that they cannot live there.

Our troops in East Pakistan are fighting valiantly, but they are heavily out-numbered and out-weaponed. They are also blockaded by the Indian navy which means that no reinforcements or replenishments can reach them. They literally have to fight with their backs against the wall among a hostile population. I am told that Bengalis' attitude has not changed in the least in spite of Indian aggression.

It was hoped that the offensive in the West would relieve pressure in the East. That has not happened except a few squadrons of the air force have been withdrawn by the Indians and brought over to the west where their air had a thorough beating at the hands of the Pakistan Air Force who have done a magnificent job. So the chances of saving Bengal and that magnificent army seems bleak, unless a miracle happens.

Heaven forbid Bengal falls. Repercussions in the West would be terrible. I do not think this government would last in spite of martial law. The army itself may be compelled to do something. That would be disastrous and make West Pakistan vulnerable to heightened Indian military pressure.

Somebody said that appointment of Nurul Amin and Bhutto does not mean sharing of power, but finding scapegoats to share blame. But they are clever enough to see that the blame falls squarely where it belongs. Leading people in politics in our country may not be politicians let alone statesmen but they are past masters in agitation. They would twist anything to suit their end. Look at how they have befooled people and loosened the roots of this country and yet nobody blames them. Such is the ignorance of our people. I particularly blame the educated people who have not the moral courage to expose these rascals.

12 | SUNDAY

📖 Last couple of days, the news media has been trying to emphasize what a formidable array of force our small army in Bengal is facing. The enemy is superior in man and material. Lately, he has been using helicopters to ferry troops. A para-brigade was dropped some 60 miles north of Dacca. It looked as if they were preparing the people for the worst. Tragic and heartbreaking. All this has been brought about by the Bengalis on themselves in collusion with the Indians. The hymn of hate against non-Bengalis, West Pakistan and especially Punjabis is now beginning to bear bitter fruit. Their misfortune is that they cannot distinguish between friend and foe. For this lapse they will have to pay dearly for centuries. Meanwhile, the situation in the country will get more and more complicated, perhaps beyond repair.

📖 Heard sad news yesterday, Maj. General Iftikhar Janjua,[33] one of our gallant officers, died in a helicopter crash. He was directing operations of his division in Chhamb Sector. Even in the 1965 war he, as a brigade commander, personally conducted a counterattack by companies and battalions.

13 | MONDAY

📖 President Nixon is supposed to have sent a stiff letter to Indira Gandhi demanding a ceasefire. There is also a hint that they could even intervene under a treaty obligation, presumably CENTO and SEATO. Somebody also suggested that the Americans and Chinese were consulting each other as to how to support Pakistan. Meanwhile, a Russian high powered mission is sitting in New Delhi and a similar Indian mission has gone to Moscow. Apparently, the Russians were unhappy at the pace at which Indians were progressing in East Pakistan. The Russians want Dacca to be occupied and the Bangladesh government to be installed by the 15th instant so that they do not have to use their veto again in the Security Council. Indira bemoaned, in a public meeting in Delhi, lack of support from the world community which has branded India as the aggressor and so on and warned that difficult days lie ahead for India. She also revealed that they had suffered heavy losses in the battles.

I wonder how seriously President Nixon's words are meant. It is possible that they are worried about the Russian hold over India and would not like to see Pakistan dismembered, but the Americans are psychologically, morally, physically and economically, a tired and exhausted nation. It is doubtful they would take on any new military commitments at this stage. The best they could do was to send a part of the Seventh Fleet[34] to the Bay of Bengal and that too after some understanding with the Chinese that they will not take any offensive action against Formosa.

14 | TUESDAY

📖 The Russians again vetoed the American resolution in the Security Council for bringing about a ceasefire. My fear is that after this the Americans will cool off and if their fleet is moving to the Bay of Bengal it would not be used. This is the Indian estimate. They think that the Americans are just showing their anger. I am inclined to agree with it. The Indians are now getting daring. They have refused to answer the American query whether they have any intention of attacking Azad Kashmir or West Pakistan. The trouble with the American administration is that, apart from their inhibitions described earlier, they have to face a hostile and pacifist Congress who have very little use for alliances. They regard them as an unnecessary burden and irritant, especially CENTO and SEATO, and therefore do not support the president who has an election ahead of him.

📖 The last few days have been most depressing. The news from East Pakistan is bad. The enemy is attacking all the major towns around the periphery and dropped a parachute brigade at Tangail some 40 miles north of Dacca. Another brigade was heli-bound and there are rumours of a column moving from the East. The enemy air is in complete command and is attacking all sorts of targets, civilian and military, with impunity. The Government House was attacked and set on fire. Our radio and press continued to give reassuring news that the enemy is firmly held and contained, but British sources maintain that the noose around Dacca is tightening and the fighting has reached the suburbs. They managed to get this information on the telephone and claim to have heard noises of gunfire and other weapons.

15 | WEDNESDAY

📖 A dispatch from Singapore indicated that the American carrier *Enterprise,* accompanied by seven more ships, passed through the straits of Malacca and is heading towards the Bay of Bengal. Later news confirmed this and said that they might well be going towards Chittagong. What their intention is, is not known. This force has considerable power, but I doubt if it is going to be used to reverse the situation in Bengal.

📖 Midday news gave a hint of the worsening situation around Dacca. In the evening it was openly admitted that fighting was taking place around Dacca in all directions and the ring was tightening. A number of enemy columns were converging on it. It is heartbreaking news. It seems to be the beginning of the end of East Pakistan, but this is what some foolish people, blinded by parochial feelings, worked for without realizing its consequences. If they wanted separation, it could have easily been obtained in a peaceful manner.

16 | THURSDAY

📖 Just heard that Niazi[35] in East Pakistan has surrendered and fighting has ceased and the Indian troops are marching into Dacca. The Mukti Bahini took active part in softening Dacca by mortar and other types of fire. They are busy butchering the nationalist and Jamaat-e-Islami types. The Indians have declared that the Bangladesh government will be sworn in today since it has been liberated. Indira Gandhi has announced that since their objective has been achieved, they will unilaterally cease fire by 7:30 p.m. tomorrow. The object, I suppose, is to deceive world opinion by their changed peaceful intentions and to gain time to bring troops over to West Pakistan, although there is some evidence that the Indians have lifted them from Bengal and taken them to the Chinese border. In actual fact, the Chinese don't have to do much. A few demonstrations of force on the Himalayan border would make India commit considerable forces, and relieve the pressure against West Pakistan. So it was a dark day for Pakistan, entailing not only the loss of a province and 6.5 crore Muslims going under Indian influence, but loss of our magnificent divisions and some air and naval forces. How we would extricate them will present a big problem. The Indians will demand big consideration for releasing these hostages.

The separation of Bengal, though painful, was inevitable and unavoidable. The majority of those people had been duped into believing that West Pakistan was their enemy. I wish our rulers had the sense to realize this in time and let the Bengalis go in a peaceful manner instead of India bringing this about by a surgical operation.

I suppose the Hindu morale is now very high. It is the first victory they have had over the Muslims for centuries. It would take us a long time to live this down. But the Indian jubilation will soon come to an end. The problems they will have to face are formidable. Maintenance of law and order in Bangladesh would require at least four divisions. The communications, rail, road and river, which have shattered, will have to be restored. The refugees will have to be rehabilitated. Food shortages will have to be looked into and three million tons will have to be made good otherwise there will be large-scale starvation and famine. War damage to the property will be made good and the shattered industry rehabilitated and so on. The bill would be formidable. I don't see India being able to cope with it. The Bengali too will soon realize that he has bought liberation from Pakistan very dearly.

Our forces would have been able to hold on longer, but the Indians managed to produce helicopter lift capability to the extent of one brigade at a time. They brought in large number of troops like that and that is how Dacca was surrounded. The expectation is that Mujibur Rahman's Awami League won't last long. They will be superseded by the communists who will soon join hands with Naxalites and other communists in West Bengal.

17 | FRIDAY

📖 I understand that the Bengalis in Islamabad and Pindi were jubilant on the surrender of our forces and distributed sweets. They will soon find that these sweets have a poisonous core.

📖 Yahya was to announce the outline of the new constitution at 7:15 p.m. Everybody was wondering what relevance the constitution, which postulated a united Pakistan, has in the present context. This dawned on somebody at the last minute and the talk was cancelled, though I am told copies of the constitution are widely distributed and its details are known. Yahya gave a pep talk on the fall of Bengal. It left people dumbfounded and totally dissatisfied. They were not at all impressed.

It is understood that there is complete confusion in Dacca and in the other places where Indian troops are stationed. The Mukti Bahini are on the rampage and shooting at random at all and sundry. Besides, I am told that a large portion of the army has not surrendered. They are fighting on.

There were large scale demonstrations in Karachi, Lahore, and Rawalpindi against the ceasefire. People are abusing Yahya and the political leaders for bringing the country to such an impasse. I am also blamed for handing over to Yahya. What else could I do, he was the C-in-C of the army. I am told alcoholism changes a man's personality.

There were wild rumours that Yahya has been deposed and his new house in Peshawar burnt. I don't think there is any truth in them.

There is widespread scare and consternation throughout the country that the 50 rupee note has been demonetised. People started saying that this government has robbed them before by tricking and ruined them and they would not hesitate in doing so again. But the government has a case too. They have to do something to protect the currency now that Bengal has been occupied. The most sensible thing to do would be to issue new notes of all denominations and allow people to exchange old notes. Anything else would rob people of any purchasing power they have, which is precariously little because of the failures of several crops and economic stagnation.

19 | SUNDAY

📖 It was confirmed by the press that Yahya's house and its furniture was burnt by an agitated mob. This is very sad and a bad precedent. There is also an indication that Yahya may have to resign. Pressure on him is mounting. The people are also shouting against Bhutto. They think that he and Yahya wanted to shed Bengal. Finding it difficult to do so politically, they hoped that India would do this for them by military action. Thereby they risked the magnificent army for their selfish ends.

It was pronounced through the news media that Yahya would hand over power to a civil authority and resign. Meanwhile, he told Bhutto to return home immediately.

20 | MONDAY

📖 Bhutto returned to Islamabad this morning. Yahya appointed him as the president, and curiously, chief martial law administrator as well.[36] How will the army take this remains to be seen. I suppose it will remain quiet in its present state of shock from East Pakistan. Bhutto will see to it that they remain so. The older politicians must also be demoralized. Bhutto will make every effort to chase them out of politics so as to have a free rein for himself. The circumstances favour him in that. Is it not a great misfortune that the fate of the country lies in the hands of this opportunist and rascal? What happens to Yahya is not known. His stay in the country would be very difficult. It is also not known whether he has given up the job of C-in-C. He will find it very difficult to hang on to it. General Peerzada, who is the poisonous snake in the grass and should have been got rid of, will probably stay on. He is a buddy of Bhutto and constantly worked for him against Yahya's interest.

📖 Just heard that Lt. General Gul Hassan has been appointed as the C-in-C of the army. Bhutto must have a big hand in it. His aim would be to use Lt. General Gul Hassan for promotion of his personal ends and make his cells in the army.

I would have been happier to see a Punjabi commanding the army. Lt. General Gul Hassan too is no high flier, but perhaps he is better than others. He has a certain amount of go in him, though crude and unrefined.

21 | TUESDAY

📖 In spite of Yahya's betrayal and disloyalty to me I feel sorry for him and the manner and circumstances under which he had to go. The people rose against him and so did the officer corps. I believe that at a GHQ weekly meeting Lt. General Hamid was heckled and almost threatened with physical violence. This was unthinkable in the past, but the mood and the tempo of the people has changed, especially due to the present strain and stress and the debacle in Bengal where the army has been humiliated, for which the higher command is blamed. As such takeover by Bhutto was not normal. It was almost the acceptance of an abject surrender. This suited his dramatic stance and gave him a flying start as a conqueror. From there he moved fast, sacked seven generals who were the associates of Yahya and took two other important decisions like lifting the ban on the Awami League, releasing prisoners, etc. Things like these don't cost anything, but have an impact on the public mind. I feel sorry for Yahya also that he took so many major wrong decisions to please certain politicians to secure his position.

22 | WEDNESDAY

📖 Bhutto has appointed Sherpao,[37] Mustafa Khar and Mumtaz Bhutto[38] as governors of NFWP, Punjab and Sindh, respectively, in place of army generals who have been retired. From this we can see the shape of things to come and hollowness verging on recklessness with which Bhutto is moving. I have a feeling that he will either come a cropper or change the whole set of values. In any case his government will be that of the *goondas*, for the *goondas*.

📖 Look at the profundity of some people. Qayyum Khan was the first man to denounce Yahya as a traitor after retirement, though Yahya was his staunch supporter and bread giver.

📖 On Bhutto's takeover, a person remarked how unfortunate we were. We had moved from one curse to another. I asked someone what was the reaction to Bhutto's takeover. He said some people thought that he would prove the worst dictator. Others thought that the change might bring good, and my view is that the former is most likely to happen.

23 | THURSDAY

📖 Mustafa Khar, after being sworn in as Governor, stated that the land reforms would be given top priority. They would be carried out in two stages: stage-I would be given effect now and stage-II when the constitution is framed.

📖 Bhutto announced a ten member central government and ministers.[39] They are to be inducted later. All ten, most of them, are communists. It is obvious that they are going to play havoc with the country and the economy. Incidentally, they were sworn in at 3:00 a.m.

📖 Nurul Amin has been appointed as the vice president by Bhutto. Does it mean that he wants to revert to a presidential form of government? His personal choice was always in favour of it.

📖 I am told that Bhutto goes to bed at 4:00 a.m. and is ready for work again at 8:00 a.m. It may be due to pressure of work, but this was his normal habit. He can't sleep for more than three hours.

📖 The government announced through the news media that there will be no holiday on the Quaid's birthday. Then all of a sudden this was changed and a holiday was ordered. The lapse was blamed on the previous government, a blatant lie.

25 | SATURDAY

📖 Yahya, I am told, is still in the President's House. Bhutto is living in the Government House. Meanwhile, a commission has been set up under the Chief Justice of Pakistan to inquire into the causes which led to the surrender in East Pakistan and ceasefire in West Pakistan.[40] The reasons are obvious but the object is to get at Yahya. A couple of lawyers in Lahore have also filed suits against Yahya for murder, treachery etc. The High Court has allowed the cases to be admitted. This will lead to lot of mudslinging and bring the army into disrepute.

I am told that the younger elements in the army are feeling hurt over the manner in which fifteen generals have been summarily retired and their experience lost. Some are also unhappy over non-appointment of a Punjabi as a C-in-C. The appointment of inexperienced governors has also aroused their feelings and resentment is growing. Some feel that Bhutto and his associates should be got at.

28 | TUESDAY

📖 When the present agitation started it was directed against Yahya as well as Bhutto. They were both jointly blamed for having conspired to be rid of Bengal even though Indian aggression aided the Bengali resistance. In consequence, Bhutto's followers remained in hiding for the first few days, but they were clever enough to deflect the blame from Bhutto and put it on Yahya.

Bhutto has started an extensive scale of victimization on the basis of personal enmity and against those who were close to Yahya. For instance, apart from removal from service, several have been put under house arrest. People like General Habibullah, General Sher Ali, Vice Admiral U. Saeed, Durrani, the two Alvi brothers and a few others are given this treatment.

📖 One hears shocking stories about the army. For instance, the newly raised units are short of equipment, weapons and clothing. They looked more like rebel than fighting units. What is shocking is that in this cold, they only have one blanket each. Even those who have been sent to heights like Titwal are no better off. How they have survived so far is a marvel. I was told that in Abbottabad the men slept nights leaning against walls. It was too cold to lie down on a *charpoy* in one blanket. This is scandalous and shows poor planning and utter lack of foresight. One shudders to think what they will do when they get into a fight. With what spirit will they do so?

📖 It came out in the press that a man who runs a bakery has lodged a suit in a court that Yahya and several others are responsible for the tragedy in Bengal. I am included for handing over power to Yahya who abrogated the 1962 constitution etc. I have no doubt this is inspired.

29 | WEDNESDAY

📖 I understand that PPP people have inspired this case and hired a lawyer who, though briefless, is a big mischief-maker.

30 | THURSDAY

📖 Later information indicated that the lawyer's wife happens to belong to Abbottabad. When she heard of the case against me she made a big row and told her husband that if he did not withdraw the case she would seek a divorce. People of the locality also threatened the man so he withdrew the case in spite of communist remunerations to the opposite.

DIARY 1972

1 | SATURDAY

 📖 Bhutto and his party have made a lot of tall promises to people. How will they be able to fulfil them remains to be seen. The fact is that they cannot and in the process they will ruin the economy, which is already in shambles.

 I have heard some people say that if India had also taken over West Pakistan, their agony would have been cut short. I think they are saying this in desperation and also to be saved from Bhutto. They regard him as highly emotional and capable of indulging in recklessness.

 There is no doubt that the separation of East Pakistan is an unmitigated tragedy not from the material angle but the fact that a large number of non-Bengali Muslims were butchered. Yet it may prove a blessing for West Pakistan in the economic sphere. It could make rapid progress given a stable government and freedom from threat from India. These are big ifs and highly problematic.

 Yahya, I am told, was allowed to stay in the President's House pending transfer to his own house in Lalazar Colony in Rawalpindi. I have a feeling that he would find it difficult to stay anywhere in Pakistan. The feeling against him is running high amongst the people and especially amongst those whose relatives are taken prisoner in Bengal. The Hindus are not going to let them free in a hurry. They are going to make impossible demands and humiliate us to the maximum extent possible.

 The press has started talking about Yahya's personal life, his contacts with women and general moral laxity. They are most unprincipled people. Why did they not level these charges when the man was in office? Now they talk about him when he is not in a position to reply or hit back. This is the character of people. One blames the politician but how are the people any better.

2 | SUNDAY

 📖 According to the press, Yahya's family members were almost mobbed as they went to inspect the house in Lalazar Colony. Most of them were local *goondas* and the students.

 📖 All the news media are trying to sell Bhutto very hard as a great leader and a saviour. His acrobatics at the Security Council meeting recently are repeated time and again on television. Some people are getting tired of seeing them. His hand waving, mimicking and prancing at the public meetings are also oft repeated. To anyone with a grain of commonsense he looks a buffoon, a joker, a clown, but the common man in this country gets impressed by such conduct. His [...] are so childish and immature that any juggler can make a fool of him. He has not the capacity to distinguish between something genuine and fake.

1 | WEDNESDAY

 📖 The finance minister has announced taking over under state control of certain industries. The first announcement said that the list was final and exhaustive. But later it was said that the government may well take over certain other industries. This counter-statement is probably due to communist pressure. Meanwhile, the government has taken away the right of the management to declare a lockout. Consequently *gheraos* have become the order of the day in Karachi and production probably

is at a standstill. This is the direct outcome of popular government coming into power and foretaste of things to come.

📖 People are critical of General Habibullah being put under house arrest and Mumtaz Bhutto being made the governor. They regard these as glaring instances of victimization and nepotism. One keeps on hearing of patriotic elements being brutally murdered in Bengal. The figure of 70,000 or more is quoted. Individuals like Maulvi Farid, Fazlul Qader Chaudhary[1] have, of course, been murdered, but Sobur Khan apparently was skinned alive first and then hacked to pieces, how tragic.

5 | WEDNESDAY

📖 Yahya apparently left the President's House yesterday and went to Lt. General Hamid's place. Thereafter his whereabouts are unknown. Someone said that he went in the direction of Jhelum in which case he will probably stay in Kharian or Mangla, which contained purely military garrisons. In spite of his major failings I feel so sorry for the man. He cannot be denied the right of citizenship.

8 | SATURDAY

📖 The Shah of Iran came, stayed for six hours and flew back. He may have come on his own or was possibly sent by the Americans to caution Bhutto against extremism. He too must be worried about the socialist views spreading to Iran.

📖 Heard on the radio last night that Yahya and Lt. General Hamid have been put under house arrest. This was a great shock in spite of their misdeeds as it is a further blow to the prestige of the army, which is already low. I wish somebody could put it right and stop this charlatan Bhutto from playing with the self-respect of people.

📖 Mujibur Rahman has been set free and flown to London. Bhutto must be happy as that completes the process of separation and leaves him free. The British received him with due consideration. In his press conference, he showed delight that their struggle for establishment of Bangladesh had succeeded and that he was selected as the president. He thanked India for the support given and said he was looking forward to being back in Dacca as soon as possible. Meanwhile, the Indians have placed a plane in London to fly him back via Delhi where Indira is anxiously waiting to meet him. So that is that as far as Bengal is concerned. Permanent separation is complete and anybody in West Pakistan who thinks otherwise, is living in a fool's paradise.

9 | SUNDAY

📖 In the evening, pictures of some of Yahya's girlfriends who had obtained industrial licenses were telecast with great relish. The press, too, is slinging mud at Yahya and the army, stating that the rule of the army was an unmitigated tragedy. Some of this is undoubtedly justified but the present vilification campaign is designed to convince people that under no circumstances must military rule come back again, whatever the degree of mess the country may be. This is a wonderful and unexceptional proposition and would be welcome most by the soldiers but what are they expected to do when political mismanagement reaches unbearable limits. People themselves would yell for their intervention.

📖 Mujibur Rahman was reported to have left England by a Royal Air Force plane and supposed to have reached Delhi. The British are taking a lot of interest in him and even supported his movement to the hilt.

10 | MONDAY

📖 Mujibur Rahman was given a rousing reception in Delhi. The president and Indira went to receive him. Later, he addressed a public meeting thanking the Indians for the help they had given him and for the liberation of Bangladesh. After a three hour stay in Delhi, Mujibur Rahman flew on to Dacca where he was given a grand reception. In a public meeting, he declared that all ties with Pakistan were snapped and that Bangladesh was a free and sovereign state. The separation of Bengal is now complete. What the future holds in store for the Bengalis is not difficult to guess.

11 | TUESDAY

📖 The TV and radio are being deliberately prostituted by the regime for their nefarious ends. Plays and dialogues encouraging class hatred are being shown and staged. Derogatory scenes of political opponents are shown and special effort is being made to expose the army to ridicule. For instance, a film on the surrender scene of Dacca was shown from our TV stations. Similarly, photos of Yahya's girlfriends were telecast and so was General Habibullah's entry into jail.

📖 I am told that ten more generals are being retired. This is inexplicable and is not going to do any good to the morale of the army. Nobody is going to be sure of his future.

13 | THURSDAY

📖 I am told that some tried to get at Yahya in the place of confinement. So he has been shifted elsewhere, probably into a prison. This, if true, is sad. I mentioned this to someone who blamed me for having appointed him as C-in-C.

16 | SUNDAY

📖 The government has taken over eleven more industries and abolished all managing agencies. Let us see what will be the net result of it. My own feeling is that efficiency already low and will deteriorate still further and production will suffer. Who will work with any enthusiasm when there is no incentive? But I suppose some such steps had to be taken as public opinion demanded it.

25 | TUESDAY

📖 Yesterday Bhutto announced the release of Ahmed Dawood, Valika and General Habibullah as a token of goodwill to the industrial community. Their arrest, of course, was purely on personal pique to demonstrate how powerful he was. It is a typical dirty trick played in Sindh by those in authority to show their strength and over awe opposition. But times have now changed and such tricks are seen through and looked down upon. For instance, Habibullah's arrest has caused lot of resentment in the Frontier. That is why he was taken down to Karachi for release. The authorities probably thought that his release in Haripur might cause an ugly scene.

📖 The process of cutting off diplomatic relations continues. Relations with Yugoslavia have been cut off because of recognition of Bangladesh by that country. Today Russia and Czechoslovakia have also recognized Bangladesh. So our ambassador is being withdrawn from Moscow. I think we have put ourselves in a vicious circle and terrible predicament. By this process, we are playing India's game and isolating ourselves from the rest of the world. What a stupid policy, the affect of which is that whilst Bangladesh is getting recognition by the world, we are getting ourselves de-recognized by our own short-sighted policy. We have to recognize the fact that whilst the world, as demonstrated by the veto in the UN General Assembly, condemned India for aggression, they never denied the Bengalis the right to determine their own future. The recognition of Bangladesh is the inevitable outcome.

28 | FRIDAY

📖 Some people think that in spite of deprivation and civil commotion and Indian aggression, the future of Bengal is brighter than West Pakistan, because it is likely to have more political stability there. They think that there is a movement in Sindh to join India and in Balochistan and NFWP to be independent or be part of Afghanistan. India will undoubtedly encourage these trends.

30 | SUNDAY

📖 Our government has decided to quit the Commonwealth with immediate effect as Britain, Australia and New Zealand are going to recognize Bangladesh in a day or two. I have heard of animals biting themselves when wounded. Our behaviour in the present crisis is not dissimilar.

The common man, though groaning under the economic strain, still hopes that his lot will be improved under Bhutto. The thinking man, on the other hand, feels disenchanted with him. His vindictive and unjust actions against certain individuals has put them off. They are also getting apprehensive of growing class hatred fanned by Bhutto's party and general demoralization of administration which is being rundown by the government. Meanwhile, private armies are being raised by his party. What a mess they will make of law and order and put a fearful strain on an already debilitated administration. Meanwhile, the Indian army is waiting along our borders to take advantage of any opportunity to destroy West Pakistan. I am told that Bhutto and his ministers are conscious and fearful of Indian intentions and are worried about the situation on the Frontier and Balochistan. But ministers have blind faith in Bhutto. They think he will be able to manage things. This is understandable as they have no personal backing. It is only Bhutto's backing that got them elected.

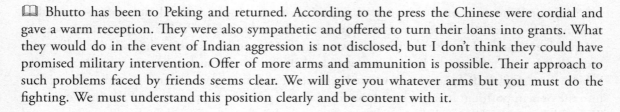

3 | THURSDAY

📖 Bhutto has been to Peking and returned. According to the press the Chinese were cordial and gave a warm reception. They were also sympathetic and offered to turn their loans into grants. What they would do in the event of Indian aggression is not disclosed, but I don't think they could have promised military intervention. Offer of more arms and ammunition is possible. Their approach to such problems faced by friends seems clear. We will give you whatever arms but you must do the fighting. We must understand this position clearly and be content with it.

📖 Several blackguards like Shaukat Hayat and Bhutto have exploited the Tashkent declaration calling it a surrender. Now let us see how they achieve withdrawal of troops facing each other on the frontiers and how they evacuate occupied territories and return of prisoners etc. The Indians are going to rub Mr Bhutto's nose hard before they come to any agreement. Rumour has it that they are demanding retention of a post overlooking Kargil, and surrender of Azad Kashmir failing which acceptance of the ceasefire line in Kashmir as an international boundary. I saved Pakistan all this by having an innocuous agreement at Tashkent, yet some of our malicious people blame me to this day.

4 | FRIDAY

📖 Some of our papers published a statement purported to have been made by the famous dacoit Mohammad Khan, convicted to death on five murder charges, that I had intended to engage him to murder Ghulam Jilani of Lahore and a few others, but he refused the offer, whereupon I had engaged professional murderers from India and used my son to bring them to Lahore and take them back to India. This is all a concoction and utter lie. But Mr Daultana, regarding it as a great opportunity, tried to get Jilani to make a statement and launch a case. Jilani refused, saying that he knew this to be utterly false, as the truth of the murder plot against him is fully known to him. Certain other articles vilifying me have appeared in the Karachi evening gutter press. I would not be a bit surprised if all this is inspired by the government to counter people's feelings and a certain amount of affection for me. They get very jittery when people recall my days with nostalgia.

5 | SATURDAY

📖 Heard on the radio last night that Altaf Gauhar, who is now the chief editor of *Dawn*, has been arrested. He has been writing very sensibly but exposing Mr Bhutto's pretensions in an oblique way. This could not have endeared him to Bhutto who wants to listen to nothing but praise of himself.

Bhutto and his henchman have been saying that henceforth there will be freedom of the press. Presumably, freedom to fulminate against those out of power and no more. Freedom of the press has a curious meaning in our country. The press understands it and it is in their nature to hit those who are not in a position to hit back. Those in power are presented as angels until they are ousted.

6 | SUNDAY

📖 Mujibur Rahman is on a visit to Calcutta where he met Indira Gandhi and addressed a public meeting. He stated that there was no question of any ties with Pakistan. Bangladesh was an independent country. Friendship with India was eternal. On another occasion, he had stated that since independence his aim was to have an independent Bengal. That much for those who live in make believe that Mujibur Rahman never wanted separation and that it was later events that forced him into the present position. It is also stated that Bengal gave powerful support to the Pakistan movement. Then what was it that made them change their minds? We all know that The Bengali national movement took birth at the time of partition of India. Dacca University was its centre. It very quickly pervaded the Bengali mind and overwhelmed pro-Pakistan elements. Their approach was simple and clear. Resist anything that savoured of identification and unification with West Pakistan and its economy, embrace everything that led to division. They went to the extent of saying that Islam was forced upon them. They had a perfectly good religion and culture and could do without Islam. These ideas took root and gradually became a powerful and dominant force, which culminated in the bloody and tragic separation.

9 | WEDNESDAY

📖 The Indian army in Bangladesh was very cautious and on its best behaviour. They wanted to demonstrate how different they were from Pakistani troops and real friends of the people. From now on India will move very cautiously, starting with a cultural conquest followed by an economic conquest. The latter has already started with the opening of borders and unhindered flow of goods, for instance, a good deal of spare food has been smuggled out of India.

21 | MONDAY

📖 I have not been writing lately, not because there was nothing to write about, but I was disgusted with the growing irregularities committed by the administration and resultant deepening frustration and disenchantment of the people. The feeling is growing that the crisis in the country is deepening.

22 | TUESDAY

📖 There is a police strike in Peshawar extending to other districts. Their demand is that Sherpao, as the head of the People's Party in the province, should submit a written apology on behalf of his party men who have misbehaved with them. They are going about attacking the party offices, colleges etc. and beating up people and commandeering vehicles. A reign of terror prevails in the province. This is the inevitable harvest of what Bhutto has sown. Certainly the country and even he will have to pay for it dearly.

📖 Mr Nixon reached Peking yesterday and started talks with the Chinese leaders. Let us hope they come to some understanding, though the Chinese are so very cool.

📖 The Americans have decided to resume aid to Pakistan. What sort of aid is not yet known.

2 | THURSDAY

Bhutto announced land reforms. The ceiling has been drastically reduced and tenants given certain concessions. The approach is basically political. Economics and production have been given scant attention. Unless cooperatives are enforced in the country, effective land utilization is not possible.

Wali Khan maintains that if it was not for his criticism and fear, Bhutto would have indulged in many excesses by now. This might well be true. On the other hand, Bhutto has told someone that if martial law were lifted prematurely, the NAP on the Frontier and Balochistan would secede. They would be most foolish to take such a step.

4 | SATURDAY

The story is that Lt. General Gul Hassan was removed because he refused to use troops against police in Lahore. For one, the troops were sitting in trenches facing the Indians, and secondly, Lt. General Gul Hassan did not want a situation like the one in East Pakistan to develop here. Even otherwise, Lt. General Gul Hassan has been saying that it was impossible to serve Bhutto. Why Air Marshal Rahim[2] went is not known.

9 | THURSDAY

I cannot believe it but it is said that Altaf Gauhar is prepared to tender any form of apology to Bhutto, but the latter wants his nose rubbed hard. Meanwhile, Bhutto is putting pressure on the Supreme Court to delay disposal of Altaf's case. The court is obliging as the Chief Justice Hamood-ur-Rahman, being a Bengali and not sure of his future, is kowtowing to Bhutto. It is a sad state of affairs when the highest court in the land cannot feel it is possible to act in accordance with law.

The government is considering re-establishment of diplomatic relations with those countries that had recognized Bangladesh. The world would laugh at us. And why should they not when we do not know how to behave like adults.

10 | FRIDAY

I am told Yahya attempted suicide twice but his brother, who lives with him, managed to save him in time. His son was serving with an oil company. They removed him the day Yahya left.

12 | SUNDAY

The Indian army is supposed to have withdrawn from Bengal. The BBC called it a withdrawal in triumph and popularity, as was their arrival. Mujibur Rahman took the parting salute; over one hundred thousand people witnessed the parade.

The Americans, after having given us some verbal support, have now declared that they have no intention of giving arms and even spares to Pakistan. They have always avoided coming to our assistance in difficult times. In the present context their attitude is not understood. Having surrendered to the Soviets in India they do not consider it necessary to build up their influence in Pakistan. One does not understand the logic of this unless they have decided to wash their hands off this part of the world. If they go on like this, very soon Russia will lay its hands on West Pakistan and Iran. Afghanistan is already in their pocket. They will have a free run from Burma to the borders of Western Europe and dominate the Arabian Sea, and especially the Persian Gulf, a very sensitive area and unguarded area now that the British have left.

13 | MONDAY

There are a few scoundrels in Karachi who produce lurid and fabricated stories in the evening papers. Several have come out about me. The latest is that I have made up with Bhutto and he has offered me the presidency. There is no truth in it whatsoever. The last thing I want to do is to be seen in the company of Bhutto and dependent on his support. Someone reproduced this story in Pindi in the form of a news sheet. I am told they were sold in the thousands. Also, people kept on ringing my house. My servants told me that they had hardly any sleep.

16 | THURSDAY

Thousands of innocent people have been done to death in Khulna and surrounding areas. The government is under pressure to bring these people, some two million or more, to West Pakistan. There was a demonstration in front of Bhutto's house in Karachi. Police had to use force to disperse the crowd. In consequence, all schools and colleges have been closed for ten days. But one is surprised at the extent of the Bengali brutality and bestially. It does not seem to end.

Bhutto is on a visit to Moscow. He took an entourage of 58. He has obviously gone there to persuade the Russians to bail him out, but the Russians will only repeat what the Indians and Bengalis are saying about the prisoners, evacuation of occupied territories etc. They will also expect Pakistan to join their anti-Chinese Asia security arrangement. Bhutto must be praying hard for someone to arrange another Tashkent for him. It is quite common to hear people say nowadays that the best investment lies in buying arms. They obviously expect a class war and civil commotion in the near future.

Indira Gandhi is supposed to be visiting Dacca tomorrow. Consultations with Mujibur Rahman are only going to harden their attitude towards Pakistan's future of prisoners, etc.

The Red Cross people gathered from their counterparts in India that our prisoners, by and large, are treated well. The officers are kept in separate camps. Their routine is bed-tea in the morning, some PT followed by good breakfast. Then they are taken for several hours of lectures and schooling before lunch. These lectures are disguised to brainwash them so that they are good propagandists for India on return home.

18 | SATURDAY

📖 Bhutto returned to Lahore after a three day visit to Moscow. There he had talks with the Soviet leaders on conclusion of which a joint communiqué was issued. It talked mostly of economic aid and technical assistance etc. The Soviets, though desiring peace on the subcontinent, had very little to give hope that they will persuade India to return our prisoners or agree to a troop withdrawal. That means that they have no intention of doing anything against the Indian or Bengali will. If anything, they will expect us to make sacrifices. I also now know that the Soviet leaders have an intense dislike for Bhutto. They regard him as undependable and unreliable so they are not going to help in resolving his political problems. Meanwhile, Indira Gandhi has returned from Dacca after making a promise to Mujibur Rahman that anyone required by him as a war criminal from amongst our prisoners will be returned to Dacca. This is ominous. She will encourage this stunt to humiliate Pakistan.

23 | THURSDAY

📖 Today is Pakistan Day, the day on which the Pakistan resolution was passed. I happened to go to the other end of Rawalpindi to see my son. En route I saw the Pakistan flag only on a couple of private buildings. No enthusiasm was noticeable amongst the people. I naturally felt sorry. It looked as if that enthusiasm and fire of earlier days had gone out of the souls of the people. I think uncertainty about the future and high cost of living has killed their spirit.

📖 I understand that there is a growing feeling in the country that I should return to power to put things right, failing which let Indira's flag fly. A horrible thought.

5 | WEDNESDAY

Someone who was a member of the press on Bhutto's entourage on the trip to Moscow told me that the Russians were very blunt with Bhutto. They asked him in what capacity had he come to see them, as the Chairman of the People's Party, as the Chief Martial Law Administrator or as the President. On the question of repatriation of prisoners they said how did he expect them to help. Had he forgotten his behaviour after Tashkent? He had nothing but abuse for them. No, he should go back and square the score with the Indians. As I said some time earlier, no country in the world trusts Bhutto and they are not going to do anything which gives him political support. The Russians especially have a great dislike for him and would welcome his ouster.

I am told that Gromyko asked some members of Bhutto's entourage who had accompanied him to Moscow, as to why had they accompanied that man Bhutto. They felt slighted, but replied that they had brought Bhutto to him. It demonstrates how the outside world regards him. This is also obvious from the casual manner in which the aid consortium has treated Pakistan's development requirements. Some other government actions are also causing concern. For instance, Hafeez Pirzada[3] visited North Vietnam, China and North Korea. On the other hand, we are begging America for food, aid, arms, etc. These contradictory moves are signs of immaturity and irresponsibility and are noticed by the outside world, if not by our own people. There are elements in the country who expect assistance from America and yet delight in giving senseless pinpricks to them. This is considered smart.

10 | MONDAY

A reliable person told me that Bhutto has started making money. Ahmed Dawood has been squeezed. Also, though Qayyum Khan does not command a majority in the province, it has been arranged that four opposition members would be unseated through election petitions pending against them and then pro-Qayyum Khan members be elected. If that fails then the NAP government could be harassed through withholding of food grain and other essential commodities. You could not think of more soulless and wicked people than Bhutto and Qayyum Khan. They are capable of conjuring up any perfidy.

12 | WEDNESDAY

S.M. Zafar, who had been helping Wali Khan in negotiations with Bhutto for framing a draft constitution, on the other hand, had a different story to tell. He said that Bhutto had very cleverly parleyed with Wali Khan and come to an agreement, which he had no intention of fulfilling, in order to gain time and prevent any movement being started against him, retaining martial law before the assembly meets. Wali Khan fell into the trap and foolishly gave Bhutto the opportunity to back out of the agreement. Bhutto also, by his publicity, made Wali Khan blameworthy in the eyes of the people. This has had disastrous effects in the Punjab and Wali has lost considerable ground.

14 | FRIDAY

📖 The assembly session was convened. Bhutto was given an overwhelming vote of confidence and appointed speaker. This I don't understand. Why does he want to grab every job? I suppose he wants to follow the footsteps of Quaid-e-Azam who was a Governor General, Head of Cabinet, the Muslim League President and the leader in the assembly. Though nobody objected because of his dominant personality, several people thought that it was not a good example.

Bhutto has also distributed a draft of the interim constitution. One of the articles appoints him as president for five years. He has assumed power of the viceroy, chief martial law administrator and any powers that were given to the president under my constitution. Fundamental rights have not been made justifiable. Also, until the constitution is passed in August 1973, the assembly will not act as a legislature. He has announced if this constitution is passed, he will lift martial law on 21st instant. This, I think, is a clever inducement to members to pass his constitution.

17 | MONDAY

📖 The interim constitution was passed in the assembly.[4] Let us hope it brings some peace and stability in the country.

18 | TUESDAY

📖 I am told that the Supreme Court was threatened by Bhutto that if they gave a judgment in Altaf Gauhar's case before the dispersal of the assembly, they would be dismissed. He obviously was expecting an adverse judgment.

20 | THURSDAY

📖 I am told that the Russians gave a clear warning to Bhutto that in the event of any military action taken against any portion of India from West Pakistan, the history of Bangladesh would be repeated. The Afghans also threatened that they will give all possible support to the Pukhtoons if they were suppressed.

21 | FRIDAY

📖 The Supreme Court has given a judgment in the Ghulam Jilani and Altaf Gauhar cases. They have held the assumption of power by Yayha as usurpation, illegal and unconstitutional. They have ruled that actions other than those taken in the public and administrative interest as not legal. This will open the flood gate of litigation.

25 | TUESDAY

📖 Mr Daultana has been appointed as the high commissioner to London. Fancy a man of his standing accepting such a job at this stage of life and in such a bad state of health. His wife also is a heart case. But that is the trouble with our people. A job means everything to them. They will not hesitate to sells their soul to get it. On occasion Mr Daultana was vehemently accused by his opponents of seeking the same job. He said the president was aware of the type of reply I would get in humiliating him in such a manner.

3 | WEDNESDAY

Yahya's son Ali called in the evening. He said his father and the rest of the family were shifted to Abbottabad. He was very critical of Bhutto. Said that on termination of the Security Council meeting, which Bhutto was attending, he lingered on in New York though a special Boeing plane was sent to bring him back. Then he broke journey in Rome without anybody's knowledge. I think his object must be to gauge public opinion on accepting the ceasefire and let any adverse criticism be directed on to Yahya. Bhutto goes about saying that he never agreed to the ceasefire while the truth is that he advised in favour of it from New York, saying that Russians were openly hostile and determined to veto any resolution against Indian aggression. The boy said that it was Bengali pressure led by Nurul Amin which made Yahya surrender to Bhutto.

I am told that Nurul Amin has turned a new leaf and looks hale and hearty. He is a vehement defender of Bhutto's policies.

I see the old fox Bhashani is active again. He held a rally in Dacca criticizing all and sundry. Of course, he has always been dead against Mujibur Rahman. He criticized India for interfering in the internal affairs of Bangladesh. He said they did not shake off Rawalpindi's rule to allow India to boss over them—noble thoughts but belated. India has not invested so much in Bangladesh for nothing. They want a return and they will get it.

9 | TUESDAY

A reliable person told me that the reason why Lt. General Gul Hassan and Air Marshal Rahim Khan were removed was that both refused to shell and bomb the trouble-making policemen in Peshawar and Lahore. Also, Bhutto could not bear that they were responsible for putting him on the throne. The reason why they were now accepting ambassadorial jobs was that they were expecting trouble in the country within a few months; they prefer to be out or they would be blamed for all sorts of things.

11 | THURSDAY

The Pakistani rupee has been devalued. Its price has been decreased from 4 rupees and 75 paisa to 11 rupees to a dollar. The bonus voucher scheme has been abolished. The IMF and the World Bank had been demanding this for a long time. In my time, we resisted the pressure. The present finance minister, a miserable creature called Mubashir,[5] claims credit for having done so and blames the previous government for not doing so. This is not going to help much. We have no surpluses to dispose of. All that will happen is our traditional exports like cotton, which were in any case selling, will fetch less foreign exchange, our imports will be more costly and our debt servicing more expensive. Why the fools don't admit this fact is incomprehensible. Another virtue he has claimed for this step is that people will have no incentive left to keep their money out. Even the blithering idiot knows that rate of exchange has very little to do with keeping money out. They do so when they are not sure of the value of their currency and lack of political stability, childish economic policies of government.

14 | SUNDAY

The Kabul government has been carrying on virulent propaganda against Pakistan in support of Pakhtoonistan. This must obviously have been at the behest of Russia and with the connivance of India. Bhutto sent his wife and Mir Afzal of Mardan[6] as a special emissary with a letter to King Zahir Shah presumably asking him to drop their hostile propaganda. This is the height of wishful thinking that the ruling family in Kabul will change its anti-Pakistan stance in a hurry. These tries have been made before and failed. The royal family considers this stunt as a factor in their survival.

On return Begum Bhutto and Mir Afzal gave glowing accounts of their trip. But one thing was significant, Zahir Shah gave no written reply to Bhutto's letter. Kabul and Afghans are past masters in the art of diplomacy. Nobody can surpass them in this art. Our people who come into contact with them get taken in by their smooth language and behaviour and take them on face value. This is the height of folly. We have to accept the bitter truth that Kabul will always be hostile to us and that the only relationship we can hope to have with them is that of armed neutrality.

Incidentally, Bhutto does not understand the Pathan mentality. Sending women as emissaries does not go down well with them and they regard it as a sign of weakness as the woman is regarded as [...]. I wonder who advised him on this move. Probably no one. He acted on his own impulse.

22 | MONDAY

Nawabzada Nasrullah Khan, who has been my bitter opponent, turned up in the evening. He looked very depressed and pessimistic about the future of the country. He apprehended the disintegration of West Pakistan drawing close. He has no faith in Bhutto or his associates. Because of a lack of scruples on Bhutto's part he did not think anybody's life, property or honour is safe. He also said political murders are going to be a common phenomena in this country. Also, no government has become so unpopular as this one in such a short time. Nawabzada Nasrullah is an Ahrari, opposed to Quaid-e-Azam and Pakistan. He has also opposed each and every government. Whether he is a sadist or a frustrated visionary is difficult to say.

24 | WEDNESDAY

Someone told me that hardened communists like J.A. Rahim think that West Pakistan has received a mental shock in separation of Bengal, but it needs a physical shock to turn communist. So they are hoping that India will launch an attack on West Pakistan and destroy the morale of the people completely thus preparing them to accept communism as an alternative to their wretched existence. After all, this idea is not so far fetched. Even Lenin encouraged the Germans to defeat the Russian army and he went to Moscow with their connivance whilst the war was still on. He also said Russian influence was increasing amongst trade unions and the labour class as a whole.

I am told that during Princess Ashraf's, the sister of Shahinshah of Iran, visit to Quetta anti-Shah posters were put up. They were printed abroad either in Russia or in Iraq.

30 | TUESDAY

📖 I have not written for the past few days or so. I am staying with Gohar in Abbottabad. His house is situated on a hilltop and commands a gorgeous view, the distant snowy mountains are also visible, and the water here is very hard as such I get a disturbance in my stomach. It feels like bursting any moment, though I am getting treatment.

📖 The Sindhis intend passing a resolution in the assembly making Sindhi the official language. This has perturbed a large number of the Urdu-speaking refugee population in Sindh and a couple of million non-Sindhis working or settled in Karachi. This short-sighted measure is bound to lead to confrontation embittering further inter-regional feeling. I am told that even otherwise feelings against Bhutto in Karachi are growing. Some people think that he won't last after July, especially after his visit to India where he will either have to surrender or come back empty handed. Some predict attempt an on his life.

📖 There is hope of getting 223 million dollars aid from consortium countries. They have also agreed on a short moratorium on payment of debts.

10 | SATURDAY

📖 On Bhutto's departure abroad, the diplomatic corps was asked to turn up with their wives at the airport. They did, but when Mrs Bhutto arrived she got straight into the aeroplane without meeting these ladies. Next time when asked to turn up, they just refused to go.

📖 An Arab diplomat, when questioned on the effect of Bhutto's tour, said we have great regard for Pakistan, but not for this man who is thoroughly untrustworthy and unreliable.

12 | MONDAY

📖 It is reported that Sheikh Abdullah has accepted Kashmir's accession to India. It is undoubtedly a measure of lack of confidence in Pakistan, but he has also portrayed opportunism and superficiality of character. This is a poor ending to the long suffering he underwent for the cause of his people. But it must not be forgotten that he was the one who sold his people to the Hindus initially.

19 | MONDAY

📖 Bhutto is preparing to go to Delhi for talks with Indira Gandhi. The critical points in the talks will obviously be recognition of Bangladesh—though I don't see why should we settle in Delhi. After all it is a matter that needs settlement between Bangladesh and Pakistan, and acceptance of the status quo in Kashmir. Bhutto is calling different types of people to gain acceptance on his point of view. He is trying to sell the idea that we should accept Bangladesh and refuse change of stance on Kashmir. Meanwhile some people, especially in Lahore, are whipping up feelings against recognition of Bangladesh. They hope that on his return from Delhi the ground would have been prepared for a rising against Bhutto. I doubt whether this would succeed as there is no one to spearhead such a movement. Nevertheless, feelings against Bhutto are growing. High cost of living, and unemployment and disillusionment with the administration are the curse. Bhutto is posing that everything is going his way and is riding a high horse in an endeavour to conceal nervousness.

📖 Wali Khan's recent visit to Kabul was not so innocent. He was sent for by the Kabul government who said that they had made considerable investment in them for a purpose, to weaken Pakistan. He should, therefore, not give statements that will discourage Bhutto from accepting Indian terms. So on return to Pakistan Wali Khan got Arbab Sikandar[7] to give an encouraging statement in favour of Bhutto, while saying nothing himself, keeping his options open.

📖 Bhutto, when questioned, told someone that Pakistan had no chance of survival if India attacked. And yet he used to talk about fighting for a thousand years. Someone said that Bhutto has started talking of using a surgical instrument and carrying out surgical operation against those who oppose him. Rumour has it that on return from India, he is going to crackdown on communists and Wali Khan. A crackdown against communists might be all right, but it won't be so against Wali Khan. The internal and external reaction would be violent.

📖 Bhutto stated on an occasion, that the Chinese and the Americans made a show of support to Pakistan during the war with India with their teeth dug in their lips. In other words, they were lukewarm.

📖 Several political murders have taken place during the last month or so. The victims are leading political figures in the Jamaat-e-Islami. The suspicion is that General Akbar's cutthroats have done this at Bhutto's behest. The Jamaat, though non-violent, considers that *Kasaas*[8] is permitted by Islam. They think that if revenge has to be taken then the man to go for is Bhutto. They have fanatics amongst them. They are quite capable of carrying out such an operation and sacrifice themselves. Besides, Bhutto is seeking a violent end the way he is going. I am told that his arrogance and behaviour with people is atrocious and abominable.

21 | WEDNESDAY

📖 The linguistic and racial rivalry in Sindh is becoming acute. Whilst recognizing Urdu as a national language, Sindhi has been made the official language thus eliminating Urdu-speaking people, which comprise nearly half the population there, from the current of life. This is obviously unjust and cannot be sustained, but Sindhis are going on with this madness and cowardly action. The basic reason, I think, is that they cannot match with the Urdu-speaking in their intelligence and industry and are trying political gimmicks to keep them suppressed. Meanwhile, G.M. Syed came out with a call for re-establishment of Sindhu Desh which, he says, existed since 5,000 years ago. I would not be a bit surprised if this has the blessing of Bhutto. He has not said a word against this traitor. I think Bhutto's plan is that if ever he slipped at the centre, he would at once spearhead the Sindhu Desh movement. Besides, he wants to keep Syed in hand in Dadu for use against Hamid Jatoi[9] with whom he has fallen out. Incidentally, Hamid Jatoi has come out of jail after repeated incarcerations by Bhutto. The High Court held his repeated internments as illegal.

28 | WEDNESDAY

📖 Bhutto flew to Chandigarh and then went by helicopter to Simla. The paper said the reception was cool and no gun salute etc. which Bhutto loves. He is reported to have taken an entourage of 91 people with him. The Indians are supposed to have said that they prefer smaller parties with whom they can do business. But I suppose Bhutto thinks that is one way of conquering India. I noticed during my office that the more bogus the man, the bigger the party he carried with him. That is why perhaps countries like America lay down the number of people you take with you.

Indira Gandhi asked to see Bhutto separately after the initial meetings. He agreed but asked to have two advisors with him. The wily Hindu could not have failed to notice that the man did not have the confidence of his people, hence insistence on the presence of two witnesses. Yet I am sure he will not fail to talk to her at some function should he be looking to make a private deal.

2 | SUNDAY

Bhutto complained in a press conference in Simla that the Indian press made personal attacks on him and his character. Of course, it is bad form to disgrace a guest, but the trouble is that he is too well known in the world.

What the reaction of this agreement[10] will be at home is too early to tell. My view is that many people will feel relieved. The prisoners families will, however, be unhappy, but they are so scattered that they cannot prove much of a problem to the government. Individual anger and the decision to satisfy it is a different matter. I hope this agreement proves fruitful. Past experience does not encourage it. Many agreements were arranged but they soon lost impetus and became dead later. The reason is obvious, there is no desire on the part of India to coexist with us. Our presence on their flank is anathema to them and they want to break our power for good. It is only then that they could have decisive influence in the Middle East.

The news media has been turned on full blast to convince people that Bhutto has made great achievements in Simla. This will go on for a week or more to brainwash people and keep them confused.

4 | TUESDAY

Bhutto is a great actor, or more appropriately, a clown. After delivering a speech to the crowd at Lahore airport, he moved forward to shake hands with them. He then took off his coat and threw it at them. They promptly tore it to bits and kept pieces as souvenirs.

9 | SUNDAY

The province of Sindh has been on fire for the last few days. There have been protest meetings, demonstrations and bloody clashes by the Urdu-speaking people with the police. Sukkur, Hyderabad and Karachi have been chiefly affected. Several have been killed, wounded and arrested. The whole trouble has arisen over passage of a bill in the provincial assembly making Sindhi the official language without any regard for Urdu when over 40 per cent of population in Sindh is Urdu-speaking. The object, I suppose, was to humiliate non-Sindhis and put them in their place. This hasty and crude step has been taken at the behest of Bhutto and his cousin, Mumtaz Bhutto, knowing full well what the consequences would be.

10 | MONDAY

There are reports of more rioting, killing and arson from a number of cities in Sindh. Karachi and Hyderabad had been handed over to the army and a 24-hour curfew imposed. Meanwhile, Bhutto called several old and new Sindhis for consultation and finding a solution. A man from Sindh thought that the matter has got out of government control. Also, in a number of places people are shouting slogans in my favour. They are saying that Bhutto promised them food, cloth and shelter instead they are getting bullets, coffins and graves.

12 | WEDNESDAY

📖 Bhutto and his cousin, Mumtaz Bhutto, have been saying that if they were thrown out of office they would see to it that Pakistan ceases to exist. This supports my fear that Bhutto is quite capable of making a deal with India on the future of Sindh. So I would not be a bit surprised if the current troubles in Sindh were continued by him to prepare the ground for separation. Otherwise, where was the need for ugly haste in passing a highly controversial language law?

I was told that Bhutto has collected a lot of money from businessmen and deposited it in the banks in his personal account. I do not quite believe that he would do such a stupid thing. He is too wily for that.

15 | SATURDAY

📖 Bhutto went to Karachi yesterday on a tour of Sindh to explain his policy on the language question. Meanwhile, he has announced his compromise formula. Whether it is going to satisfy Urdu-speaking people is doubtful. Meanwhile, he has started attacking and vilifying me in a most vulgar form. He has got alarmed over stringent voices being raised in Karachi demanding his removal and my return.

18 | TUESDAY

📖 Bhutto was attacking me in the National Assembly. He was hysterical but tremendously arrogant. It is this, I hope, which will get him down one day. Basically being a petty man, he cannot absorb power. He also said that he was Sindhi first and Sindhi last. No one in the house had the courage to get up and say that then why was he sitting as the President of Pakistan.

Some persons told me that Bhutto had not touched me so far, not out of love or affection. It was the fear of public reaction which was him holding him back. This might well be true. He also said that people were putting up posters and writing slogans on the walls in my favour even though the intelligence people remove them every day.

20 | THURSDAY

📖 Urdu and Sindhi-speakers have come to an agreement of sorts based on which an ordinance has been issued guaranteeing that for 12-years Urdu-speakers will not be discriminated against for employment etc. This has cooled the rioting and curfew etc. It has been relaxed and lifted in many places. But this does not mean the return of goodwill. That will depend on the large-heartedness shown by the people and especially the government of Sindh.

26 | WEDNESDAY

📖 As I said earlier, posters have been appearing all over Karachi, Lahore and Pindi etc. in my favour. This has angered Bhutto and he has started fomenting against me. I believe a pamphlet against me and my family is under preparation. There is also a plan to assassinate me.

1 | TUESDAY

📖 I have not written for a week, not because nothing new has been happening in the country but it has been of a repetitive nature. General dissatisfaction with Bhutto, posters and demonstrations especially in Lahore. Bhutto has been on a tour of Sindh. He visited several places mostly by helicopter and addressed people in town halls etc. which were heavily guarded. He tried to justify passage of the language bill in Sindh and also had some softening words for the Urdu-speaking people. I heard Bhutto say that nobody, not even anybody's grandfather, can remove him from his chair. But should he be compelled to leave, he shall see to it that Pakistan goes up in flames. Sensible people told me that there will be a real class-war by September. Bhutto wants it. The man must be mad if this is so. After all, he is in power. What more does he want? I should have thought that it would be in his interest to have peace and calm in the country. I hear Bhutto has become very allergic to my name. He goes mad when he hears it. The fool does not realize I have no more political ambitions.

2 | WEDNESDAY

📖 Heard that Asghar Khan's house in Abbottabad was burnt down. Whether it was a deliberate act of political vandalism or accident is not yet known but it is not beyond General Akbar and people like that who happened to be in Abbottabad that day to have indulged in such foul play. He had held meetings with his party workers in Hazara the day before.

4 | FRIDAY

📖 Abdullah Khan Rokhri came to give Wali Khan's message to the same effect as Ali Asghar Shah had given that I should take more precautions about my safety as Bhutto, in conjunction with Khar, had decided that I should be bumped off. He said opposition to Bhutto and his party was growing. He said it was pathetic to see the type of men that represent the People's Party in the provincial assembly. He said that intensity of protest against Bhutto in the Punjab is growing. Yesterday the lawyers carried out a bare-foot march against him in Lahore.

5 | SATURDAY

📖 Apparently Bhutto is well assured of the loyalty of the army which is how it should be. He could not, of course, find a better goof than General Tikka Khan. But the army has never been a threat to any politician until they make a mess of the country. Then it becomes a survival and rescue operation, and if the survivors are incapable of carrying it out some junior will take the jump. This is the common experience of most new countries.

I understand that Bhutto sent for General Tikka Khan and told him that he had concrete evidence that he was planning to overthrow him. General Tikka Khan said before he, Bhutto, went any further he would give him the true story. Some politicians had approached him with the proposal to remove Bhutto. His answer was that the army was not interested in any such thing but he wanted also to make it clear that the army would not shoot down peaceful demonstrators.

I understand General Tikka Khan flew to Nawabshah to receive Bhutto. On arrival the crowd showered him with flower petals. They must have been Urdu-speakers.

I am told that former Major General Akbar Khan of the Rawalpindi conspiracy fame sees the Russian ambassador every other day. I am sure he must be seeking their assistance for his plans. He has also caused a lengthy proforma to be filled by every army officer to ascertain his connections and political reliability. Why the Army chief is allowing this, I cannot understand. Intelligence anticipates that the country would almost be in a state of civil war by the end of the year.

8 | TUESDAY

📖 I hear that the burning of Asghar Khan's house was an act of sabotage. It has been burnt down completely and is a total loss. On hearing the news of burning, Bhutto rang up the deputy commissioner and told him to issue a statement saying that the loss was negligible, worth about 15,000 rupees. The deputy commissioner checked up with the governor who told him to refrain from doing any such thing. The police investigation is continuing. I understand Bhutto is preparing a speech of six and a half hours for the assembly due to meet on the 14th.

12 | SATURDAY

📖 A confidant of Bhutto, who is the Chairman of the Press Trust, which is completely under government control, is going about selling the idea that in Kashmir, India should get Jammu, Pakistan Azad Kashmir, and the valley to become independent. Then the valley, Pakistan, India and Bangladesh, should form a confederation. He might well be voicing Bhutto's views.

14 | MONDAY

📖 Today is Independence Day, normally a day of rejoicing and merry making, but with what face can we do that when the country is in shambles due mainly to the perfidy of Bhutto and his associates. Our policies are destructive, socially we are disorganized and economically in ruins with no hope of recovery as investors are reluctant to invest and workers unwilling to work through ruinous government policies. We have no credit left in the outside world. India and Russia's shadow is looming large over us. They are ready to take advantage of our weaknesses and disorganization. So, instead of rejoicing we should seriously engage in introspection as to what has gone wrong with us and what should we do to put it right, but I doubt if we would do that. Certainly our rulers won't be motivated by honest and sincere intentions.

18 | FRIDAY

📖 I have heard today that the National Security Council under General Akbar has said that my name is coming too much in the intelligence reports and too many opposition people and journalists were meeting me. So there was need for surveillance over me. A friend heard this from a reliable source and passed the information on to me. I have told my staff to take precautions against bugging my house. According to today's news both Major General Sher Ali [Pataudi] and Shorish Kashmiri have been arrested. Major General Sher Ali on the charge of sedition for giving an innocuous speech and Shorish under Defence of Pakistan Rules. These, like many others, are glaring cases of victimization. The impression one gets is that in Karachi 90 per cent of people are against Bhutto.

21 | MONDAY

I am told that Bhutto is calling upon members of his party in the assembly to hand over undated letters of resignation to him so that undesirable or difficult ones could be eliminated at will. This he did after having failed to have a bill passed that if a party passed a vote of no confidence in a member, he should automatically lose his seat in the assembly. If any of these measures succeed, the assembly would be reduced to a sham and be completely paralysed, being at the mercy of one man of mercurial, vindictive and dictatorial temperament. He has a big majority in the house. Most of these owe their seats to him. True, there are some non-conformists amongst them and they open their mouths, but there would always be such people in any party. I suppose he has the jitters where they are concerned and wants to see them out by hook or by crook, but he does not realize that this would be another nail in his coffin.

6 | WEDNESDAY

📖 President Sukarno's daughter, who is on visit to Pakistan, came to call. She is a very well mannered and sweet girl and looks very much like her father, who is such a dear friend of mine.

📖 The Chinese deputy foreign minister has been on a visit to Pakistan. He came on his own without an invitation. He moved about here and met people in a very relaxed and jovial fashion so uncommon to the Chinese. They have also offered to tarmac and to blacktop the Karakoram road with their own personnel. All this has shaken and made suspicious some of our officials. I believe the Chinese were advised by some Pakistani friends that by endorsing the Simla Agreement they were strengthening Indian and Russian hands against Pakistan and encouraging Bhutto to maintain complete submission to them. The Chinese veto in the Security Council and their deputy foreign minister's visit to Pakistan, both unasked for, was meant to warn all concerned that they have a strong interest in Pakistan and they would not like Pakistan to submit to India beyond a certain limit. They certainly want to keep Bhutto in check.

23 | SATURDAY

📖 Zahoor Elahi,[11] an MNA, was sent for by Bhutto, embraced and told that they would be friends in future. But as soon as Zahoor Elahi's back was turned Bhutto rang up the governor and told him to sit on Zahoor Elahi. Zahoor Elahi, being an ex-policeman, soon discovered what Bhutto had done. So he complained to him on the next meeting. Whereupon Bhutto said he had to tell lies and cheat to hold his position. Politicians are known for dishonesty, at least in our country, but this man surpasses all of them and all bounds. How can any good come to this country under such a character?

30 | SATURDAY

📖 Both Mahmood Kasuri and Ghulam Mustafa Jatoi have withdrawn their resignations. In our country a fellow would much rather lose his life, honour and everything than give up a job. The face saving device Mahmood Kasuri has produced is that the constitution of this country shall be federal and parliamentary, the executive being answerable to the legislature. I think Bhutto can still have his way in this framework. Ghulam Mustafa Jatoi has said that a search of his house took place without Mumtaz Bhutto's knowledge, Mumtaz has given a written apology and was prepared to make amends in any manner desired. He had therefore decided to withdraw his resignation and stand shoulder to shoulder with his leader. In other words, he has taken a sigh of relief at having been able to retain his job.

📖 My doctor, who also attends to Bhutto, used to be very critical of him but lately he has become an admirer. He must have been given satisfaction in some way. So he has become very reticent. However today he said I am heavily watched as my name is on everybody's lips and that jitters the rulers.

1 | SUNDAY

The cracks in the People's Party higher echelon are appearing and widening. Governor Mustafa Khar criticized Mahmood Kasuri and Ghulam Mustafa Jatoi for resigning from the cabinet. He termed it an act of sabotage. Mahmood Kasuri hit back in strong terms. His rejoinder is aimed at Khar, though meant for Bhutto.

3 | TUESDAY

Heard a horrible news. Six of our prisoners of war were killed and nineteen wounded by Indians in a camp in Madhya Pradesh. The Indian explanation is that one of the prisoners snatched a bayonet from a policeman and wounded another. Thereupon the Indians opened fire on the unarmed, unfortunate prisoners. Mere show of force would have brought the unarmed prisoners under control.

7 | SATURDAY

Altaf Gauhar's writ petition against detention is being heard in the Karachi High Court. So far the government has been able to bring forward various childish allegations against him. Great stress is being laid on one or two intercepted letters which he wrote to a girlfriend in Dacca. The object being to tarnish his image.

8 | SUNDAY

Mahmood Kasuri's resignation has been accepted after all, on which he has gone and given a press statement to which Bhutto replied. He then issued a long rejoinder exposing Bhutto's misdeeds, misrule, tyrannical and arbitrary actions and ruinous economic and other policies, and for ruining the services. Someone said that Mahmood Kasuri was looking for leadership in the Punjab. So what if he did, but I don't think he could succeed.

According to the press the Council and the Convention Muslim Leagues have decided to merge. I hope the process goes through smoothly because Bhutto and all the old opportunists would do everything possible to see that the effort fails. If the effort succeeds, Bhutto's position in the Punjab and even in Sindh would be seriously challenged, of which he is naturally afraid.

If we want to regain our reputation, we have to somehow regenerate our moral and spiritual values based on the spirit of Islam and we have to become Muslim nationalists. All this seems too tall an order in the present circumstances. Only a leader dedicated to these ideas can rekindle them. Unfortunately today none is in sight. Hence our predicament is going to be long drawn out and painful.

17 | TUESDAY

📖 There was welcome news that leaders of all parties have unanimously agreed on the framework of the constitution. I hope this unanimity continues till the bill is passed. In accordance with this framework, the centre has been given adequate subjects and powers and provinces too have been given considerable autonomy. Bhutto has shown flexibility here through force of circumstance and pressure of the opposition, but he could not be very happy with it. He would have preferred the presidential form and something akin to the French constitution. His unhappiness is apparent on his face appearing in the media and also the fact that he let his law minister announce the decision instead of doing it himself. If he had considered this a creditable achievement, he would have made the announcement himself. He never misses an opportunity to get kudos on the slightest pretext if it is to his liking.

18 | WEDNESDAY

📖 There had been another shooting incident of our prisoners of war in a camp at Allahabad. Six prisoners are reported to have been killed. It is difficult to know how to avenge these repeated atrocities. Shooting their prisoners in our hands would be seen as a cowardly act. But I would not be surprised if one day our guards lose their heads and mow them down. There is a limit to human forbearance.

📖 The constitution committee is now in session. The controversial points are two. The opposition's demand is full provincial autonomy and superiority of the prime minister at the centre. They are opposed to the French type of constitution which Bhutto wants. If he is wise he should meet the opposition half way. In that case the constitution would not be advancing the cause for which Pakistan was demanded and made, but it will have some chance of working, as those in power at the centre and provinces have never been in sympathy with the spirit of Pakistan. Such elements represent the lowest denominator of Muslim nationalism. To expect anything more from them would be a folly.

📖 On resignation from the law ministry and the chairmanship of the constitutional committee, Mahmood Kasuri has been implicated in a murder case which took place some months ago. This is the style of government. As soon as a man falls from favour he is subjected to terror and victimization. This is how democracy works here.

21 | SATURDAY

📖 A young army officer, who happens to be related to me and at present is undergoing an aviation course, came to call. He looked tense and under considerable pressure. I do not know him well, but it is the first time I have seen him like that. He asked if it was safe to talk in the place? I said as far as I could tell it was, though means of bugging have become very sophisticated. He said he had been commissioned to come to me. All the squadrons in the air force except two were ready to strafe Bhutto. The young officers in the services were fed up to the teeth with him and had lost confidence in their senior officers who had been promoted for loyalty to Bhutto instead of professional merit. They behaved as clowns and set bad examples to others. Bhutto was a man lacking in conscience and patriotism. There was a danger that we might well lose the country if he remained in office for any length. His elimination, and of a lot of others, was essential. I said it was wild and highly dangerous talk for the country. Today we had no credit left in the world. A military coup would pull us out of the pall of civilization. Internally, too, a military takeover would not be acceptable. People would demand civil rule even without Bhutto. Besides, a constitution was in the process of being made. It was essential that the process reached its logical conclusion. Thus there was every indication that people at large were losing faith in Bhutto. Their patience and sufferings were increasing. Another six months would tell whether they were ready to put up with all that or if they seek Bhutto's removal. Then they might well look to the army for assistance. He said all that was known. Their fear was that by then they might not be in a position to do anything. He said that a lot of us would then resign and go. He said that if I had not left in spite of the agitation against me, the country would not have come to this pass. I explained my difficulties. Then he turned around and asked if I would not back them? I said not if they did anything against the interests of the country. He left not very satisfied.

I told him not to talk in such a brazen manner. He said it was an open secret and was common talk in the officer's messes. The intelligence knew that. That was why the military secretary at general headquarters was told by Bhutto to produce a list of passed-over officers. There were 2000. Bhutto thinks that criticism of him emanates from these people. When I said that the armed forces had no one to sell to the people, he said even young officers like Gaddafi succeeded. I said conditions in Libya were different, a small population, assured of enormous oil royalties. Mistakes can be made there without any serious ill effects because of this economic cushion.

I hope I have staved off any rashness, but from the look of the man it appeared that unless Bhutto changed considerably and behaved in a humane manner and ceased to play about with the armed forces, his days are numbered, as it would not be possible to hold back these young men for any length of time if they are really thinking the way this man described.

24 | TUESDAY

Went to the burial of Father Byrne, a Catholic missionary, who had rendered great service to Pakistan in the educational field. He had died of heart failure. I had helped him to be treated by Professor Goodwin, who is a friend of mine and the best cardiologist in England. I believe Professor Goodwin suggested heart surgery, but Father Byrne balked.

3 | FRIDAY

📖 I understand the army is very short of essential equipment, especially for the newly raised divisions. The Chinese have not as yet supplied them the material promised. This is surprising as they are very prompt in keeping their promises. Apparently, tank casualties were heavy. Some 120 tanks were lost and our people were unable to recover them. The Chinese supply has been tardy. Only 50 tanks have been received so far though another shipload is expected. But they have supplied some 130 mm and a large number of 122 mm guns. The former are long range and the latter, field guns. Both are deadly accurate and effective.

At the time of the 1965 war Bhutto asked me as to why we could not raise another two divisions. Now it must be dawning on him as to what it means to raise even one. The initial cost would be around 200 crores if one can purchase weapons and equipment.

6 | MONDAY

📖 There was an apprehension that because of general discontent, frustration and specially the burden of inflation and reduced production through labour troubles, there will be an uprising by the student community, who are mainly controlled by the Jamaat-e-Islami, and the labour, who are in the hands of the communists supported by the urban population, in October, on the opening of the schools and colleges. Luckily this has not happened so far except for the labour troubles in Karachi where there has been a good deal of violence and shooting. I think the reason is that they have come to the conclusion that the People's Party should be given the chance to rule the country for its term of five years. This decision may be based on patriotism or the feeling that the only way to discredit the People's Party is to let it remain in office and make mistakes. Wali Khan too has adopted a conciliatory tone towards the People's Party. Whatever may be the real intentions, let us hope that this spirit continues and a reasonable constitution is framed. The country cannot afford another turmoil.

📖 To be trustworthy and acceptable a ruler must have the following minimal qualities:

1. Refrain from doing anything which demolishes people's self respect.
2. Not make false promises. If he has made a promise then he should be candid and explain to people his compulsions and difficulties.
3. Refrain from being vindictive and harassing his opponents. This reminds one of Nawab of Kalabagh's saying on becoming the governor. He told his opponents that there was no more enmity between them from that day. However, they could resume status quo ante on his retirement. Whereas Bhutto is:
    a. Haughty, abusive and intolerant.
    b. Makes false promises knowing they cannot be fulfilled.
    c. He is busy concocting false and flimsy cases against his political opponents or anybody else who had differences with him at any time. He is thoroughly vindictive.
4. Law of God is untenable. What fate such people meet, is well known.

📖 I understand that some time during or after my elections in 1965, the communists saw danger in consolidation and economic progress under me. I became the target of their attack. A meeting was held in Bombay in which the following decisions were taken to pave the way for communism to come in:

a. Make me, the constitution and the administration the target of attack and demolish my image.
b. No attack should be made on the Quaid or Islam. Keep the religious leaders humoured.
c. Attack our economic policies and belittle whatever progress has been made in this field. Slogans of rich are getting richer and poor getting poorer should be propagated.
d. Use the labour, student community, dissatisfied elements specially in urban areas for this purpose.
e. Propagate the theory of so many nationalities in Pakistan. Thus cutting people off from their ideological moorings.
f. Later when Bhutto came in the field, it was decided to support him to use his platform.

So the communists have a plan and they are busy in implementing it. Some of the activities of their administration and certain individuals in high position are a great help to them.

8 | WEDNESDAY

📖 Eid-ul-Azha was celebrated today. A large number of people came to call on me. They complained of the deteriorating law and order and the economic situation. It has become a common cry. In the arid areas, the distress is especially acute. Three successive crops have failed. The farmers are selling their cattle for a song for lack of fodder but they are being fed on rosy promises by the government. Promises which are far beyond the resources of the country and there is no hope of their fulfilment. The general feeling of lack of peace of mind, uncertainty of the future and hopelessness amongst the people is very disturbing.

📖 In order to understand the Hindu mentality you have to read a book called *Arthashastra*, written by the renowned Hindu political philosopher called Chanakya[12] who was born in ancient times. Though his name was Chanakya, he was proud to call himself Kautilya, and so he is known up to this day. The meaning of Kautilya is 'a deceitful trickster'. He laid down the following basic principles for foreign relations:

1. The desire for territorial expansion must never be allowed to freeze.
2. The immediate neighbours must be regarded and treated as enemies.
3. Have good relations with distant states.
4. Keep self-interest uppermost even with those who are friends and use every stratagem and deviousness in diplomacy with them.
5. Keep the fire of rivalry burning in the hearts and use every means to keep up the warlike spirit. War should be fought ruthlessly and no notice should be taken of the sacrifices and sufferings that your own people may have to undergo.

6. To keep the people of the other countries confused and off balance, carry out vigorous propaganda savouring of disruption whilst creating a fifth column amongst them.

7. Bribe and buy freely people in other countries and carry out economic warfare against them.

8. Never think of peace even though the whole world presses you to do so.

The modern world blames Machiavelli for political deviousness and devilry because they have not heard of Kautilya. I am told Pandit Nehru used to keep a copy of *Arthashastra* on his bedside table.

14 | TUESDAY

A friend told me that Bhutto had engaged a journalist to write a book to prove that it was due to my mishandling the Agartala case that Mujibur Rahman got such prominence. Bhutto had no hand in it. All sorts of secret files had been shown to that man to select material. The object is to clear himself and demolish my image.

The same man told me that whereas people in the Punjab had lost confidence in Bhutto, they had no confidence in the opposition members either. They were all petty and small men of no consequence. The slogan that 'if not Bhutto then who else' was coined and circulated by the Jamaat-e-Islami. The opposition, he said, was not consistent. Their attitude changed from day to day and people had taken note of that, which meant that the opposition was also regarded as opportunist.

20 | MONDAY

Bhutto has started an eleven-day tour of the Frontier. According to the press and radio he is getting a good reception. It is difficult to tell whether it is genuine or based on curiosity. I never believed in the loose talk that gave him two, four or six-months. He has come to stay for five or ten years barring some accident or other forces of economic pressure and other strains and stresses for which he will put the blame on others. He is a past master in the art of hoodwinking.

I am told that King Faisal of Saudi Arabia has gone back on his promise of paying the cost of the Faisal Mosque in Islamabad.[13]

21 | TUESDAY

According to the press, India is in the throes of a serious economic crisis. Exports and production have gone down because of stagnation in the private sector. Too much talk of socialization has had a paralysing effect. The government has failed to define the industrialist's role like in our country. Here, of course, the government has gone further and encouraged a class war, consequently, nobody wants to invest and nobody wants to work. Also, there is a shortfall in food production by 19 million tons due to failure of monsoon rains in some areas and excessive rain in others. In traditional dry areas like Rajasthan and Bihar there is a serious shortage of drinking water and fodder. There is a danger of cattle dying in millions. We face a similar situation in our vast arid areas. And yet India refuses to have peace with us and insists on keeping an enormous army, forcing us to do the same. It is surprising with what little wisdom the world is run and how most of the miseries of mankind are of their own making.

📖 I was shocked to hear that poor Doctor Malik,[14] the last governor of East Pakistan, has been sentenced by an inquisition court of Mujibur Rahman to a life sentence for allegedly collaborating with the Pakistan army. This is a most vicious and barbarous act against a patriot and a humane person. All his life he served the cause of labour and the poor. Many others like him are rotting in jails and will presumably be given similar treatment.

📖 I stated earlier that Bhutto, irrespective of his perversity and wickedness, had come to stay. Someone said that, that was rational deduction. The mass mind, however, when subverted did not work on reason. How, for instance, in my time did a rumour spread like wild fire that I was causing school boys to be injected with something that would castrate them as a family planning measure. Similarly, no one read the university ordinance which was based on the pattern of Oxford and Cambridge and yet caused a howl amongst the students and indeed throughout the country. Nobody bothered to reason and find out the truth. Similarly, recognition of Bangladesh could become an issue of that nature especially in Punjab at this juncture when people are finding the cost of living unbearable and unemployment is on the increase. Under such circumstances any little spark could cause an explosion. This reasoning is basically valid provided there was a credible man to lead. No such man is in sight. That is why Bhutto is so suspicious of me. He thinks that people may drag me out.

A reliable friend confirmed today that a team of special police had been set up to go into my, and even my distant relatives' financial transactions under orders from Bhutto. The Central Board of Revenue had been told to tax us at least one crore. If we paid it up it would break our backs. If we did not then we should be put in jail. In this connection, I was told that the IG Special Police, who was recently appointed, has been transferred because he called on me for eid greetings.

24 | FRIDAY

📖 Air Marshal Asghar Khan held a public meeting in Rawalpindi. The gathering was large; he criticized the government vehemently and called for fresh elections. However, his meeting was disturbed several times by people using firearms. They were obviously organized by the People's Party as one of the ministers, Khurshid Hassan Mir,[15] was seen at a nearby petrol pump watching or directing the operations. Several people received bullet wounds. The police made a feeble attempt to make a few arrests. I suppose these people would be let off soon. Asghar continued with his speech despite these interruptions. After the meeting, he held a press conference. Very little of what he said at the meeting and the conference was allowed to come out in the press but he was supposed to have said that if he was assassinated, people with whom he served for decades were not going to take it lying down. I don't think he gave an idle threat.

26 | SUNDAY

📖 Most of the big business families are splitting and acquiring interests abroad. The intention is to have an alternative base to go to should conditions deteriorate and become unbearable in this country.

I am told that the Russians are active, especially in Karachi. Most of the labour troubles are financed by them. Recently three shoe-making firms who have business connections with them have been caught. They were used as a channel to finance the labour trouble. The Russians are not interested so much in spreading communism but strengthening their communist friends to bring about a government of their liking in Pakistan; and that means a government which is not so pro-Chinese and anti-Indian. Their global interest in these regions demands that.

27 | MONDAY

Bhutto goes about saying that I sent him word to be careful of Governor Khar as he was a snake in the grass. This is an utter lie. Never has such an idea entered my mind. But this is not a solitary instance. Lying is his main stock and trade to bamboozle people. He abuses and slanders his opponents in public knowing that they either can't reply or won't stoop down to his level.

30 | THURSDAY

The People's Party is holding its convention today in the army stadium. Why this, is incomprehensible? However, some 3000 delegates have been invited. They are handpicked and say they will have no hesitation in rubber-stamping whatever Bhutto desires.

* * * *

After this date the Field Marshal stopped recording his diary due to his ill health. Field Marshal Mohammad Ayub Khan died on 20 April 1974, of a heart attack, and was buried the following day at his ancestral village, Rehana. He was survived by his widow, Zubaida Khatoon, four sons and three daughters. (See *New York Times*, 20 April 1974, p. 53.)

Appendix 1

From: Field Marshal
       Mohammad Ayub Khan, N.Pk., H.J.   24th March, 1969

My dear General Yahya,

It is with profound regret that I have come to the conclusion that all Civil administration and Constitutional authority in the country has become ineffective. If the situation continues to deteriorate at the present alarming rate, all economic life, indeed, civilized existence will become impossible.

I am left with no option but to step aside and leave it to the Defence forces of Pakistan which today represent the only effective and legal instrument, to take over full control of the affairs of this country. They are by the grace of God in a position to retrieve the situation and to save the country from utter chaos and total destruction. They alone can restore sanity and put the country back on the road to progress in a civil and constitutional manner.

The restoration and maintenance of full democracy according to the fundamental principles of our faith and the needs of our people must remain our ultimate goal. In that lies the salvation of our people who are blessed with the highest qualities of dedication and vision and who are destined to play a glorious role in the world.

It is most tragic that while we were well on our way to a happy and prosperous future, we were plunged into an abyss of senseless agitation. Whatever name may have been used to glorify it, time will show that this turmoil was deliberately created by well-tutored and well-backed elements. They made it impossible for the Government to maintain any semblance of law and order or to protect the civil liberties, life and property of the people. Every single instrument of administration and every medium of expression of saner public opinion was subjected to inhuman pressure. Dedicated but defenceless Government functionaries were subjected to ruthless public criticism or blackmail. The result is that all social and ethical norms have been destroyed and instruments of Government have become inoperative and ineffective.

The economic life of the country has all but collapsed. Workers and labourers are being incited and urged to commit acts of lawlessness and brutality. While demands for higher wages, salaries and amenities are being extracted under threat of violence, production is going down. There has been [a] serious fall in exports and I am afraid the country may soon find itself in the grip of serious inflation.

All this is the result of the reckless conduct of those who, acting under the cover of the mass movement, struck blow after blow at the very root of the country during the last few months. The pity is that a large number of innocent but gullible people became victims of their evil designs.

I have served my people to the best of my ability under all circumstances. Mistakes there must have been but what has been achieved and accomplished is not negligible. There are some who would like to undo all that I have done and even that which was done by the Governments before me. But the most tragic and heart-rending thought is that there are elements at work which would like to undo even what the Quaid-e-Azam had done, namely, the creation of Pakistan.

I have exhausted all possible civil and constitutional means to resolve the present crisis. I offered to meet all those regarded as the leaders of the people. Many of them came to a Conference recently but only after I had fulfilled all their pre-conditions. Some declined to come for reasons best known to them. I asked these people to evolve an agreed formula. They failed to do so in spite of days of deliberations. They finally agreed on two points and I accepted both of them. I then offered that the un-agreed issues should all be referred to the representatives of the people after they had been elected on the basis of direct adult franchise. My argument was that the delegates in the Conference who had not been elected by the people could not arrogate to themselves the authority to decide all civil and constitutional issues, including those on which even they are not agreed among themselves. I thought I would call the National Assembly to consider the two agreed points but it soon became obvious that this would be an exercise in futility. The members of the Assembly are no longer free agents and there is no likelihood of the agreed two points being faithfully adopted. Indeed, members are being threatened and compelled either to boycott the session or to move such amendments as would liquidate the Central Government, make the maintenance of the armed forces impossible, divide the economy of the country and break up Pakistan into little bits and pieces. Calling the Assembly in such chaotic conditions can only aggravate the situation. How can anyone deliberate coolly and dispassionately on fundamental problems under threat of instant violence?

It is beyond the capacity of the Civil Government to deal with the present complex situation, and the Defence forces must step in.

It is your legal and constitutional responsibility to defend the country not only against external aggression but also to save it from internal disorder and chaos. The nation expects you to discharge this responsibility to preserve the security and integrity of the country and to restore normal social, economic and administrative life. Let peace and happiness be brought back to this anguished land of 120 million people.

I believe you have the capacity, patriotism, dedication and imagination to deal with the formidable problems facing the country. You are the leader of a force which enjoys the respect and admiration of the whole world. Your colleagues in the Pakistan Air Force and in the Pakistan Navy are men of honour and I know that you will always have their full support. Together the armed forces of Pakistan must save Pakistan from disintegration.

I should be grateful if you would convey to every soldier, sailor and airman that I shall always be proud of having been associated with them as their Supreme Commander. Each one of them must know that in this grave hour they have to act as the custodians of Pakistan. Their conduct and actions must be inspired by the principles of Islam and by the conviction that they are serving the interests of their people.

It has been a great honour to have served the valiant and inspired people of Pakistan for so long a period. May God guide them to move toward greater prosperity and glory.

I must also record my great appreciation of your unswerving loyalty. I know that patriotism has been a constant source of inspiration for you all your life. I pray for your success and for the welfare and happiness of my people.

Khuda Hafiz,

Yours sincerely
[signed]
Field Marshal Mohammad Ayub Khan

Appendix 2

My dear countrymen,

Assalam-o-Alaikum,

This is the last time I am addressing you as president of Pakistan. The situation in the country is fast deteriorating. The administrative institutions are being paralysed. Self-aggrandisement is the order of the day. The mobs are resorting to gheraos at will and get their demands accepted under duress. And no one has the courage to proclaim the truth.

The persons who had come forward to serve the country have been intimated into following the mobs. There is none among them who can challenge this frenzy. The economy of the country has been crippled: factories are closing down and production is dwindling every day. You can appreciate the feelings which overwhelm at this moment. The country, which we nourished with our sweat and blood, has been brought to a sad pass in within a few months.

I had once suggested to you that the national problems should be settled in the light of reason and not in the heat of emotions. You have seen that the fire of emotions once kindled has rendered every man helpless.

I have endeavoured to serve you to the best of my ability. I firmly believe that the people of Pakistan are endowed with the blessings of an eternal faith and they have the capacity to overcome every difficulty. All that our people need is patience, discipline and unity.

On February 21st, I had announced that I would not contest the next elections. I had hoped that after this announcement people would try to find a suitable solution to the country's political problems in a dispassionate mood. I thought that personal hatred would vanish and once again we would devote ourselves to the progress of the country.

Unfortunately, the conditions continued to deteriorate from bad to worse. You are aware of the result of the Round Table Conference. After weeks of deliberations the representatives of various parties could agree only on two demands. And I accepted both of them. I had suggested that the issues over which there was no unanimity should be referred for a decision to the directly elected representatives of the people.

But this proposal was not acceptable to the political leaders. Every one of them was insisting for the immediate acceptance of their demands without even waiting for the election of the people's representatives.

Some people suggested to me that if these demands were accepted, peace would be restored to the country. I asked them 'in which country?' For the acceptance of these demands would have spelled the liquidation of Pakistan. I have always told you that Pakistan's salvation lay in a strong Centre. I accepted the parliamentary system because in this way also there was a possibility of preserving a strong Centre.

But it is being said that the country be divided into two parts. The Centre should be rendered ineffective and in a powerless situation. The Defence Services should be crippled and the political entity of West Pakistan be done away with.

It is impossible for me to preside over the destruction of our country. It grieves me to see that a great desire of my life could not be realised. It was my desire to establish the tradition that the political power should continue to be transferred in a constitutional manner.

In the conditions prevailing in the country, it is not possible to convene the National Assembly. Some members may not even dare to attend the Assembly session. And those who would come would not be able to express their real opinion because of fear. There is also the danger of the National Assembly becoming the scene of bloody conflicts.

The integrity of the country takes precedence over everything. The fundamental and basic constitutional issues can only be settled in a peaceful atmosphere when people's representatives can deliberate on these calmly.

Today such an atmosphere does not exist. As soon as conditions improve someone stokes the fire of mischief. It is also painful that people are bent upon destroying all that has been achieved in the last ten years, or even during the previous regimes. There are some who would like to destroy the country established by the Quaid-e-Azam.

It hurts me deeply to say that the situation now is no longer under the control of the Government. All Government institutions have become victims of coercion, fear and intimidation.

Every principle, restraint and way of civilized existence has been abandoned. Every problem of the country is being decided in the streets. Except for the Armed Forces, there is no constitutional and effective […] to meet the situation.

The whole nation demands that General Yahya, the Commander-in-Chief of the Pakistan Army, should fulfill his constitutional responsibilities. The Pakistan Navy and the Air Force are with them and the entire nation has faith in their valour and patriotism. They always keep in view the welfare of the people and their every action should [be] in conformity with the principles of Islam.

The security of the country demands that no impediments be placed in the way of the Defence Forces and they should be enabled to carry out freely their legal duties.

I am conscious of your sentiments. Have faith in the Almighty and do not abandon hope. I am very grateful to you that you not only conferred on me the honour of being the President of Pakistan for ten years but also participated in the work of national reconstruction with courage and perseverance. Your achievements will be written in history in letters of gold, I also thank the Government servants who at difficult moments displayed courage and selflessly served the nation in every way. Some of my close associates have been subjected to bitter and uncalled for criticism. But unmindful of all this they have worked day and night for the betterment of the country with humanity and dedication. The Almighty will reward them. My dear countrymen, my parting request to you is to appraise the delicate situation and assist your brethren in the Defence Forces in every conceivable manner to maintain law and order.

Every soldier is your own brother. He is animated by love for the country and his heart and head are illuminated by the light of Islam.

I pray to God for the speedy and complete establishment of harmony and peace so that we continue to march towards progress and prosperity along the path of democracy.

Aameen. Khuda Hafiz. Pakistan Paindabad.

Appendix 3

- Ayub delegates all powers to Fazlul Qader Chaudhry. Early elections of new PML president urged. From Shabbir Hussain, our special correspondent.

- Field Marshal Ayub has surrendered all functional authority including financial powers as president of the Pakistan Muslim League to the party's vice president Mr Fazlul Qader Chaudhry. In a letter addressed to Mr Chaudhry, the Field Marshal had said that henceforth you will perform all functions and exercise all powers and carry out all duties and responsibilities attached to this office.

- This virtually amounts to the Field Marshal's complete retirement from politics and from any functions connected with the Pakistan Muslim League. He has been wanting to be relieved of the presidentship for long, but did not find it legally possible to resign. This course has enabled him to remain completely away from the party responsibility. He has expressed the hope that the party elections would be held soon to induct the new president under the other Muslim League constitution.

Appendix 4

My Dear Fazlul Qader,

As you know, I have always been insisting on Muslim League leaders that as I have retired from politics I want to be relieved of the presidentship of Pakistan Muslim League. After having legal advice, you all have been telling me that I could only be replaced by a process of election, as there is no provision in the constitution that if I formally resign who should step in my shoes, but there is a provision that I could transfer my powers and responsibilities and accordingly, I delegate all my powers and responsibilities as president of the Pakistan Muslim League to you. Hence forward, you will perform all functions and exercise all powers and carry out all duties and responsibilities attached to this office under the constitution of Pakistan Muslim League. All concerned have been instructed to that effect.

You would agree, it would be in the best interest of the organization that the party elections be held quickly and a new president and other office bearers be inducted under the constitution. I know that you all are making every effort to finish the election soon, but it is unfortunate that some of our friends for reasons known to them put impediments in holding elections. I could only hope and pray that they would also understand that immediate elections would result in the interest of the organization.

We had differences in the past, but at this critical hour of our national life, I appreciate that you have come forward to shoulder this responsibility. My blessings should attend the efforts of all of you in the service of the nation. I am sure, you will get cooperation of all sincere Muslim Leaguers and I also appeal to them to rally around you in the struggle to strengthen the cause of Pakistan.

May God bless you all.

Notes

AUTHOR'S NOTE

1. Mohammad Ayub Khan, *Friends not Masters: A Political Autobiography* (London: Oxford University Press). See also: Altaf Gauhar, *Ayub Khan: Pakistan's First Military Ruler* (Lahore: Sang-e-Meel, 1994); Lawrence Ziring, *The Ayub Khan Era: Politics in Pakistan, 1958-1969* (Syracuse: Syracuse University Press, 1971); and Herbert Feldman, *Revolution in Pakistan: A Study of the Martial Law Administration* (Karachi: Oxford University Press, 1967).
2. The diary was impounded for more than thirty years. Just before starting to write this diary, on 31 August 1966, Mohammad Ayub Khan reconstituted his cabinet. The following were the members:

Altaf Hussain	Commerce and Industries	Retained from the former cabinet, but resigned in 1968 and replaced by Ajmal Ali Chowdhury.
Ghulam Faruque	Commerce	Retained from the former cabinet, but resigned in 1967 and replaced by Nawabzada Abdul Ghafoor Khan of Hoti.
N.M. Uqaili	Finance	Retained.
Khawaja Shahabuddin	Information and Broadcasting	Retained.
Sharifuddin Pirzada	Foreign Affairs	Retained from the former cabinet, but resigned in 1968 and replaced by Mian Arshad Hussain.
Abdus Sobur Khan	Communications	Retained.
Vice Admiral A.R. Khan	Defence	Retained from former cabinet. Given additional portfolio for Kashmir Affairs on 11 December 1966, on the resignation of Ali Akbar Khan.
S.M. Zafar	Law	Retained.
Kazi Anwarul Haque	Education	Retained.
A.H.M. Shams-ud-Doha	Food and Agriculture	Retained.

Source: Lawrence Ziring, *The Ayub Khan Era: Politics in Pakistan, 1958-1969* (Syracuse: Syracuse University Press, 1971), pp. 3–4, 199–201.

DIARY 1966

September 1966

1. Malik Amir Mohammad Khan, Nawab of Kalabagh, (1900–67), was a major landholder in Kalabagh, Mianwali District. He was associated with the National Unionist Party—a party that was opposed to the partition of India. In spite of the fact that after independence he was not active in politics, he was appointed Governor of West Pakistan in 1960. After leaving his post in 1966, he returned to his lands. He was killed by his son over a family dispute over land on 26 November 1967.

2. EBDO (Elective Bodies Disqualification Order) was an order instituted in August 1959 that disqualified a substantial number of politicians from the pre-Ayub period from electoral activity for a period of seven years. It ended on 31 December 1966. As will be noted later, a substantial number of politicians returned after the expiry of this order.

3. Zulfiqar Ali Bhutto, (1928–79), was the son of Sir Shahnawaz Bhutto, a politician in the province of Sindh. Bhutto was educated at the University of California, Berkeley, and Oxford University and was a barrister. He was included in the cabinet of Ayub Khan formed on 28 October 1958 and held several portfolios including that of commerce. The sudden death of Mohammad Ali Bogra in 1963 propelled Bhutto to the rank of Foreign Minister. When war began between India and Pakistan on 6 September 1965 and ended seventeen days later, Bhutto opposed the Tashkent Declaration brokered by Aleksei Kosygin between Ayub Khan and Lal Bahadur Shastri which led to the withdrawal of military forces to pre-war locations without any further progress in the negotiations. Bhutto left the cabinet and along with politicians from West and East Pakistan, launched a campaign against Ayub. In 1967, he formed the Pakistan People's Party. On 25 March 1969, Ayub decided to step aside and hand over power to General Agha Mohammad Yahya Khan. The latter tried to crush the anti-Pakistan movement in East Pakistan but the Pakistan army was defeated and the East wing seceded to establish Bangladesh. Bhutto supported Yahya in the secession. On 20 December 1971, Yahya left the presidency and Bhutto took over as President and first civilian Chief Martial Law Administrator. Bhutto assumed the mantle of Prime Minister on 14 August 1973, upon adoption of the Constitution of 1973. He was unable to settle differences with the opposition and was deposed by the military on 5 July 1977 and was subsequently tried and convicted in a murder case. He was executed on 4 April 1979. See Stanley Wolpert, *Zulfi Bhutto of Pakistan: His Life and Times* (New York: Oxford University Press, 1993); Zulfiqar Ali Bhutto, *If I Am Assassinated?* (Delhi: Vikas, 1976); and *The Myth of Independence* (London: Oxford University Press, 1969); and Shahid Javed Burki, *Pakistan Under Bhutto, 1971–77* (London: Macmillan, 1980). In documents Bhutto's first name is spelled as either Zulfiqar or Zulfikar.

4. The Indonesian diplomat and politician, Dr Subandrio, (1914–2004), was President Sukarno's foreign minister, second deputy prime minister and chief of intelligence from 1960 to 1966.

5. Walter Patrick McConnaughy, Jr., (1908–2000), was the US ambassador to Pakistan from 1962 to 1966.

6. The Regional Cooperation for Development (RCD) consisted of Pakistan, Iran, and Turkey.

7. Mirza Muzaffar Ahmed, (1913–2003), was a key economic planner, the vice chairman of the Planning Commission and a key adviser to Ayub Khan. He was later employed by the World Bank. Muzaffar was the grandson of the founder of the Ahmadiya movement, Mirza Ghulam Ahmad. See references to the Ahmadiya movement in the entries for Sir Muhammad Zafarullah Khan (Diary 1966, note 39) and Muhammad Munir (Diary 1967, note 66).

8. These Six Points of Ayub Khan's Muslim League are not the Six Points put forward by the Awami League in 1966. The latter were the platform upon which the Awami League contested the 1970 election.

9. The Majlis-i-Ahrar was formally established in 1930. It stood for rigid adherence to Muslim doctrine, and was especially opposed to the Ahmadiyas. This opposition was displayed during anti-Ahmadiya rioting in 1953. The Ahrars were also active during anti-Sikh riots at Shahidganj in 1935. See Syed Nur Ahmad (translated by Mahmud Ali and edited by Craig Baxter) *From Martial Law to Martial Law* (Boulder, Colorado: Westview Books, 1985), Chapter 29; Wilfred Cantwell Smith, *Muslim Islam in India* (Lahore: Ashraf, 1946), pp. 252–257, and *Report of the Court of Inquiry constituted under Punjab Act II of 1954 to Enquire into the Punjab Disturbances of 1953* (Lahore: Superintendent of Government Printing, 1954).

10. Maulana Syed Abul Ala Maududi, (1903–79), founded the Jamaat-e-Islami in 1941. A noted scholar, he brought together a devoted following that was dedicated to the study and propagation of Islamic culture. He opposed the partition of India as he felt that the leaders of the Muslim League were not in favour of an Islamic state but to a form of secular state. He saw the leadership of the League as a body of persons trained in the law of the British. He believed that the creation of Pakistan would cause the citizens of Pakistan to put the interest of the state above the demands of religion. The Jamaat-e-Islami strongly opposed the Ahmadiyas, who were also opposed by the Ahrars. The Ahmadiyas

were a sect founded by Mirza Ghulam Ahmad in 1889 in Qadian, Punjab. Ghulam Ahmad claimed that he was a prophet and therefore denied the finality of the prophethood of Muhammad (PBUH) that is a basic tenet of Islam. For the anti-Ahmadiya riots of 1953 see note 9 (above) pertaining to the Ahrars. The Ahmadiyas have been declared non-Muslims by the Jamaat and the other groups. See Abul Ala Maududi, *Political Theory of Islam* (Lahore: Islamic Publications, 1960), and *Short History of the Revivalist Movement in Islam* (Lahore: Islamic Publications, 1963). See also Syed Vali Reza Nasr, *The Vanguard of the Islamic Revolution: The Jama'at-i-Islami of Pakistan* (Berkeley: University of California Press, 1994).

11. The Deoband School was founded in 30 May 1866 in the town of Deoband, Saharanpur District, Uttar Pradesh. The school, Darul-uloom-Deoband, described its curriculum as Islamic science and Islamic studies. Those associated with Deoband included Maulana Shabbir Ahmed Usmani (1885–1963) who was educated at Deoband and taught there. He entered politics in 1919 and was involved with the Khilafat movement. He founded the Jamiat-i-Ulema-i-Islam (JUI) and campaigned for Muslim rights and was chosen by Jinnah to raise the Pakistani flag on 14 August 1947 at Karachi. Expansion of the JUI took place primarily in the North West Frontier Province (NWFP) and Balochistan. The leader of the JUI was Maulana Mufti Mahmood (1909–81) who was succeeded by his son, Maulana Fazlur Rahman (b.1953). In 1969 a small group led by Maulana Ghulam Ghaus Hazarvi (Diary 1971, note 10) split from the party; this group merged with the Pakistan People's Party in 1977. Currently the JUI is split into two factions, one led by Maulana Fazlur Rehman (JUI-F) and another by Maulana Samiul Haq (b.1937).

A separate organization is the Jamiat-i-Ulema-i-Pakistan (JUP) which was headed for many years by Maulana Shah Ahmad Noorani who died in 2003. His son, Maulana Anas Noorani, has not yet been confirmed as his successor. The JUP is associated with the Barelvi group and is not part of the Deobandi JUI. The JUI factions, the JUP and the Jamaat-e-Islami operate *madrassas* (also known as *madaris*). Estimates of the number of *madrassas* vary widely. The total number as stated by Khurshid Ahmad, a senator from the Jamaat-e-Islami, is between 6,000 and 7,000 (*The Economist*, 21 May 2005, p. 45), but others estimate much higher numbers. The JUI *madrassas* are said to be more radical than other groups and have been associated with the Taliban. 'The State of Sectarianism is Pakistan,' published by the International Crisis Group (Asia Report No. 95, 18 April 2005), a comprehensive study on the subject estimates the number of *madrassas* at about 13,000.

The three parties, the JUI (both factions), JUP and Jamaat-e-Islami entered into an electoral alliance for the 2002 elections calling themselves the Muttahida Majlis-i-Amal (MMA). This electoral alliance controls the legislature in NWFP and is part of a coalition in Balochistan.

See Barbara Daly Metcalf, *Islam Revival in British India: Deoband, 1860–1900* (Princeton, NJ: Princeton University Press, 1982); Ziaul Hasan Faruqi, *Deoband School and the Demand for Pakistan* (New York: Asia Publishing House, 1963); and Sayyid A.S. Pirzada, *Politics of the Jamiat-ul-Ulema Pakistan, 1971–1977* (Karachi: Oxford University Press, 2000). See also http://darululoom-deoband.com. For a more recent study of the Islamic groups see Sumita Kumar, 'The Role of Islamic Parties in Pakistani Politics,' in *Strategic Analysis*, XXV:2, a journal of the Institute of Defence Studies and Analyses, published by Jawaharlal Nehru University. This covers the JUI and JUP and also contains information on the Jamaat-e-Islami.

12. Sir Syed Ahmed Khan, (1817–98), was an Islamic scholar and a government official. He was aware of the lack of education among Muslims and the consequent dearth of employment opportunities. To overcome these shortcomings he founded the Anglo-Oriental College in 1877. The college was subsequently renamed the Aligarh Muslim University. He also founded the All-India Muhammadan Education Conference in 1886 to enable Muslims to adapt to the intellectual and political changes accompanying Western rule. See Hafeez Malik, *Sir Sayyid Ahmad Khan and Muslim Modernization in India and Pakistan* (New York: Columbia University, 1980); Shah Mohammad (ed.), *Writings and Teaching of Sir Syed Ahmad Khan* (Bombay: Nachiketa Publications, 1972); and Sir Syed Ahmad Khan, *The Causes of the Indian Revolt*, with an introduction by Francis Robinson (Karachi: Oxford University Press, 2000).

13. Mohammad Ali Jinnah, (1876–1948), was the principal leader of the movement that led to the partition of British India and the independence of Pakistan. He was born in Karachi and read law in London. Jinnah was called to the Bar in 1895, moved to Bombay in 1897 and began to practice law. He soon became active in politics and joined the Indian National Congress. He moved over to the Muslim League in 1913. Jinnah spoke principally on Muslim affairs even as a member of the Imperial Legislative Assembly. However, he became disenchanted as religious themes asserted themselves in political debates and went back to London where he continued his legal practice. He returned to India in 1935 and once again began active participation in politics, heading the Muslim League as the party moved toward a separate state for Muslims in India. On 23 March 1940, the Muslim League passed the 'Lahore Resolution', demanding a separate homeland for the Muslims. Pakistan became an independent state on 14 August 1947 with

Karachi as its capital. Jinnah became its first governor general. He died on 11 September 1948. A number of books have been written on Jinnah including: Stanley Wolpert, *Jinnah of Pakistan* (New York: Oxford University Press, 1984); Sharif al Mujahid, *Quaid-e-Azam Jinnah: Studies in Interpretation* (Karachi: Quaid-e-Azam Academy, 1981); and Ayesha Jalal, *The Sole Spokesman: Jinnah, the Muslim League and the Demand for Pakistan* (London: Cambridge University Press, 1985).

14. Allama Sir Mohammad Iqbal, (1877–1938), was a noted poet-philosopher of Islamic India. He wrote in English, Urdu, Arabic and Persian. His doctoral dissertation from Munich was written in German. Iqbal studied at Lahore and Cambridge and taught in Lahore and London. He published many of his philosophical concepts in *Reconstruction of Religious Thought in Islam* (London: Oxford University, 1934). See also Hafeez Malik (ed.), *Iqbal: Poet-Philosopher of Pakistan* (New York: Columbia University Press, 1971).

15. Before the outbreak of war between Pakistan and India on 6 September 1965, there was infiltration during the summer by Pakistanis into Indian-occupied Jammu and Kashmir. This was named 'Operation Gibraltar'. The intention was to initiate rebellion by the Muslims in Jammu and Kashmir against those termed as occupiers of this former princely state which had a majority Muslim population.

16. Muhammad Musa, (1915–91), was born in Balochistan and was a Naik (junior officer) in the Hazara Pioneers. He then attended the Indian Military Academy in Dehra Dun and graduated with the first batch of the Indian commissioned officers. He took part in the Waziristan Operations (1936-1938) before the Second World War and later served in the war in North Africa. Musa opted for the Pakistan Army after independence and rose quickly in the ranks. As a major general, he succeeded Ayub Khan as commander of forces in East Pakistan in 1950. Other assignments followed before he took over as the commander-in-chief when Ayub declared martial law in 1958. He retired in 1966 and replaced the Nawab of Kalabagh as governor of West Pakistan and held that post until March 1969. Recalled from retirement, Musa was appointed governor of Balochistan in 1986 and served until 1990. He is the author of his memoirs titled *Jawan to General: Recollections of a Pakistani Soldier* (New Delhi: ABC Publishing House, 1985).

17. The Islamic Research Institute was founded in the 1950s. It was incorporated into the Islamic University in Islamabad in 1980.

18. Khan Abdul Ghaffar Khan, (1890–1989), hailed from the North West Frontier Province. He founded the Khudai Khidmatgar organization that worked for the betterment of the people of the province. To a great extent, his programme was similar to that of Gandhi and he was thus referred to as the 'Frontier Gandhi'. He opposed the creation of Pakistan and did not have a liking for Jinnah. He campaigned for autonomy for the Pathans in Pakistan and for a closer relation with the Pathans (known as Pakhtuns) in northeast Afghanistan, in the area surrounding Jalalabad. He spent much time in prison in Pakistan. He did not oppose the Soviet invasion of Afghanistan in 1979. A stroke in 1987 greatly disabled Ghaffar Khan. He died in Pakistan, but at his request he was buried in Jalalabad. See also the entry for his son, Wali Khan (Diary 1969, note 30).

19. Hamood-ur-Rahman, (1910–81), was a lawyer in Calcutta (now Kolkata) and moved to Dhaka following partition in 1947. He held a number of positions: advocate general of East Pakistan, 1953–4; judge in the Dhaka High Court, 1954–60; judge of the Supreme Court, 1960–8; and Chief Justice of Pakistan, 1968–75. He was also chancellor of Dhaka University, 1958-60. He was the head of the Commission on Education in 1966.

20. Public Law 480 of the United States provided for the sale of American agricultural crops to developing states for local currencies that would be used for economic development projects.

21. General Agha Mohammad Yahya Khan, (1917–80), was born in the North West Frontier Province. He joined the British Indian Army but opted for Pakistan at the time of partition. He rose in the ranks and succeeded General Musa as commander-in-chief in September 1966 when the latter became governor of West Pakistan. At this time Ayub was facing challenges to his rule. The Combined Opposition Parties nominated Fatima Jinnah to challenge Ayub. He defeated Miss Jinnah in January 1965 presidential elections, but the contest weakened him. In December 1968, the opposition challenged Ayub through the Democratic Action Committee. A conference between Ayub and his opponents was initiated, but before the conference was concluded Yahya and the army forced Ayub's hand and he had to hand over power to Yahya on 25 March 1969. Yahya's control was contrary to the rule of the Constitution which required the Speaker (Abdul Jabbar Khan) to become acting president until a new election for the presidency could be held. Yahya dissolved the One Unit of West Pakistan in July 1970 and restored the provinces of Punjab, Sindh, Balochistan, and the Frontier. Yahya also ended the allocation of seats in the legislature by parity, i.e. the two wings of Pakistan were allotted 150 seats each. Yahya allotted seats based on population to each wing. This meant 162 seats for East Pakistan and 138 to West Pakistan. In the ensuing elections in December 1970, the Awami League won 160 seats, a clear majority of the total of 300, although the party won no seats in West Pakistan. Civil war began in East Pakistan

and ended with the secession of East Pakistan, now Bangladesh, with the surrender of Pakistani forces to the Indians on 16 December 1971. Yahya resigned and handed over power to Zulfiqar Ali Bhutto. See: Fazal Muqeem Khan, *Pakistan: Crisis in Leadership* (Rawalpindi: National Book Foundation, 1973); Richard Sisson and Leo E. Rose, *War and Secession: Pakistan, India and the Creation of Bangladesh* (Berkeley: University of California Press, 1990), Craig Baxter, *Bangladesh: From a Nation to a State* (Boulder, Colo.: Westview Press, 1997); Hasan Zaheer, *The Separation of East Pakistan: The Rise and Realization of Bengali Muslim Nationalism* (Karachi: Oxford University Press, 1994); and Ayesha Jalal, *Democracy and Authoritarianism in South Asia* (Cambridge: Cambridge University Press, 1995); columns titled 'General Agha Mohammad Yahya Khan' by Ardeshir Cowasjee in *Dawn* from August–September 2000 published the text of Yahya's journal written in 1976.

22. Arshad Hussain, (1910–1987), was a career diplomat who served as ambassador or high commissioner in a number of posts including New Delhi. He was foreign minister, 1968–77. His brother, Azim Hussain, served in the Indian Foreign Service and the brothers once concurrently served as ambassadors in Beirut. Their father, Mian Sir Fazl-i-Husain (1877–1936), was the leading member of the National Unionist Party, a party that ruled Punjab until independence in 1947. A sister married Sheikh Manzur Qadir (Diary 1968, note 28). Azim Hussain wrote a biography of his father, *Fazl-i-Husain* (Bombay: Longmans Green, 1946) which was a major study of the Unionists. See also Syed Nur Ahmad, *Mian Sir Fazl-i-Husain* (Lahore: Punjab Educational Press, 1936).

23. Air Marshal Nur Khan, (b.1927), was the second Pakistani to command the Air Force. Before he took command of the Air Force in 1965, he headed the national airline, Pakistan International Airlines. He took command of the air force just before the outbreak of war in 1965 and remained in this post until 1969. Nur Khan served in the Yahya cabinet from 1969 to 1970, when he was named governor of West Pakistan. He resigned in June 1971 after disagreements with Yahya. He was elected to the National Assembly in 1977. He was briefly the head of a commission on education in 1970.

24. The Wali of Swat at the time was Miyangol Abdul Haqq Jahanzib, (1908–87). He reigned from 1949 to 1969 when the state was terminated on 28 July 1969 on its absorption into the North West Frontier Province as a district.

25. The Wali's father was Miyangol Golshahzada Abdul Wadud, (1882–1971). He reigned from 1917 to 1949.

26. Altaf Gauhar, (1923–2000), was a member of the Civil Service of Pakistan and the biographer of Ayub Khan. His longest period of service was as Information Secretary and during that time he became a close associate of Ayub. On leaving the civil service in 1969, he became editor of *Dawn* where he had differences with Bhutto, who was chief martial law administrator, and who twice put Altaf in prison. On release from prison, he left *Dawn* for London where he was editor of the *Third World Quarterly*. He returned to Pakistan in 1991 and became editor of *The Muslim*.

October 1966

27. Lieutenant General Habibullah Khan, (1916–96), was a senior general when Ayub's coup took place. Habibullah's daughter, Zebunissa, married Ayub's second son, Gohar (b.1937). Habibullah left the army and invested in industry. With assistance from General Motors, he developed Ghandhara Industries for the assembly of automobiles and trucks. Gohar Ayub was associated with his father-in-law in the business. Habibullah was arrested by Bhutto and Ghandhara Industries was nationalized. Habibullah became minister of industries under Ziaul Haq for a short period before Zia appointed political ministers. See an interesting article in *Saudi Aramco World*, March/April 2005 about the elaborate paintings on Bedford trucks formerly built by Ghandhara Industries, 'Masterpieces to Go: The Trucks of Pakistan.'

28. Ambassador Eugene Murphy Locke (1966-67).

29. Qudratullah Shahab, (1920–86), had already taken office as Secretary of Education when Ayub wrote this note in his diary. A member of the Civil Service of Pakistan, Shahab had served earlier as private secretary to President Mirza and President Ayub. Shahab wrote several books in Urdu, but only one in English titled *Pathans* (Karachi: Pakistan Publications, n.d.).

30. The members of the Central Treaty Organization were the United Kingdom, Turkey, Iran, and Pakistan. The United States was a sponsor but not a member.

31. N.M. Uqaili was Pakistan's minister of finance from January 1965 to March 1969. Before becoming minister, he had been managing director of the Pakistan Industrial Credit and Investment Corporation (PICIC). After leaving office when Ayub resigned as president, Uqaili served as a consultant with international organizations including a mission in Indonesia.

32. Abdul Monem Khan, (1899–1971), was elected to the National Assembly in 1962 and became minister of health, labour and social welfare. However, before the end of 1962 he was replaced by Rana Abdul Hamid and appointed Governor of East Pakistan (1962–69) in place of Ghulam Faruque. He was assassinated in 1971 during the civil war.

33. Ishtiaq Hussain Qureshi, (1902–80), was a distinguished historian. He received a doctorate from Cambridge University in 1939 and was professor of history and later also dean of the faculty of arts at Delhi University. After partition in 1947, he was a member of the Constituent Assembly of Pakistan and Minister of Education. He later taught at Columbia University and Karachi University. He was the author of a number of historical works including *Muslim Community of the Indo-Pakistan Subcontinent, 610-1947* (Karachi: Ma'aref, 1977), *Struggle for Pakistan* (Karachi: University of Karachi, 1969) and *Ulema in Pakistan* (Karachi: Ma'aref, 1972.

34. Orville L. Freeman was Secretary of Agriculture, (1961–69), in the Kennedy and Johnson presidencies.

November 1966

35. The writings of Turabi, (1908-73), were almost exclusively written in Urdu. At least one was published in English: *The Ways of the Enlightened* (publishing information is not available).

36. The Talpurs, a Baloch tribe, established a state in Sindh in the eighteenth century that in periods included Hyderabad and Karachi. In 1843, Sindh was annexed by the British except Khairpur, a state founded in 1783, which was recognized by the British in 1843. The princely state of Khairpur was ruled by the Talpurs. It acceded formally to Pakistan in 1955 and now is a district in Sindh. The negotiations that led to the incorporation of Khairpur into West Pakistan are recounted in Wayne Ayers Wilcox, *Pakistan: the Consolidation of a Nation* (New York: Columbia University Press, 1963).

37. Son-in-law of President Ayub Khan.

38. Ghulam Faruque, (1899–1992), was an industrialist and politician. Faruque founded the Pakistan Industrial Development Corporation and headed Pakistan Ordnance factories and the Water and Power Development Authority. He was governor of East Pakistan (1962) and federal minister of commerce, (1965–7). He also served as defense advisor (1965–6). Faruque was general manager of Eastern Railways before independence, 1945–7.

39. Chaudhary Sir Muhammad Zafarullah Khan, (1893–1985), was educated in law in Lahore and London and practiced principally in Lahore. He was a member of the Punjab Legislative Council from Sialkot, 1926–35, and a member of the Executive Council of the Governor General, 1935–42. Zafarullah Khan was appointed a judge of the Federal Court of India, 1942–7. At independence, he was named foreign minister of Pakistan, 1947–53. He was a justice of the International Court of Justice at the Hague, 1954–72. He also served as the president of the United Nations General Assembly, l962–3. He was a member of the Ahmadiya sect and was removed from the foreign ministry on the demands of the anti-Ahmadiya rioters in 1953. Zafarullah's memoirs were published in *Forgotten Years: Memoirs of Sir Muhammad Zafarullah Khan*, edited by Ashiq Hussain Batalvi (Lahore: Vanguard, 1991). He also wrote *Servant of God: A Personal Narrative* (Zurich: Indo-Oriental Publishers, 1958[?]). The anti-Ahmadiya demonstrations of 1953 were reported in the study known as the Munir Report (see Diary 1967, note 66). A balanced study of the movement is by Spencer Lavan, *Ahmadiya Movement: a History and a Perspective* (Delhi: Manohar Book Service, 1984).

40. Ashiq Hussain Batalvi, was born in 1907, and studied at the School of African and Oriental Studies in London and taught there as well as in Lahore. His writings, except that listed in the previous note, were published in Urdu. Much of his work was on the pre-independence period.

41. Vice Admiral S.M. Ahsan, (1920–90), was appointed Commander-in-Chief of the Pakistan Navy in 1966. When Yahya deposed Ayub, Ahsan was asked to remain in his position and was named deputy martial law administrator. He became governor of East Pakistan in August 1969 but resigned in 1971, possibly forced as a result of his opposition to the policy on East Pakistan espoused by Yayha.

42. Altaf Hussain was minister of industries, 1965–68. He was previously editor of *Dawn*.

43. The Habib Bank was issued a charter in Mumbai on 25 August 1941. The bank was promoted by the Habibs, a trading family from Mumbai. The bank was established through motivation of Mohammad Ali Jinnah to encourage the Muslim community as in India, banking at the time was almost exclusively in the hands of British and Hindu bankers. After independence, the Habib family expanded in Karachi by going into manufacturing and were among the principal industrial combines in the late 1960s. The government of Zulfiqar Ali Bhutto nationalized the bank and other concerns controlled by the Habibs in the 1970s.

44. The Dawood family is, like the Habibs, a major economic power in Pakistan. They are Memons who migrated from India to Pakistan at the time of partition. Their enterprises include extensive holdings in textiles, leather goods, food, construction materials and paper products. The last was made in East Pakistan by an investment in the Karnaphuli Paper Mill. Among other investments in East Pakistani was the Dawood Rayon and Cellophane Industries in the Chittagong Hill Tracts. All investments in East Pakistan were nationalized by the government of Bangladesh. In 1971, Zulfiqar Ali Bhutto began a programme of nationalization that also led to a decline of the Dawood wealth. However,

the family later revived its industrial enterprises and remains among the largest family concerns in Pakistan, although divided into three groups: Ahmad, Sadiq and Suleman groups.

45. Mohammad Shoaib, (1906–74), was a career member of the Pakistan Accounts Service and was Vice-President of the International Bank for Reconstruction and Development (World Bank). He was named finance minister by Ayub Khan in 1961 and served until 1967. He rejoined the World Bank in 1967.

December 1966

46. Ayub Bakhsh Awan was a member of the Police Service of Pakistan and director of the Intelligence Bureau. He was defeated from the North West Frontier Province in the 1970 election.

47. Ghulam Faruque was defence advisor.

48. Sharifuddin Pirzada, (b.1923), graduated from Bombay University in 1945. He was involved in the practice of law and in the Muslim League in Mumbai before moving to Karachi in 1947. He succeeded Zulfiqar Ali Bhutto as foreign minister on 20 July 1966 and remained so till 1968. He then became minister of law and parliamentary affairs and Attorney General, 1977–84. Among his books are *Evolution of Pakistan* (Lahore: All-Pakistan Legal Decisions, 1963), and *Quaid-i-Azam Muhammad Ali Jinnah and Pakistan* (Islamabad: Hurmat Publishers, 1989).

49. The Rann of Kutch is a barren area of salt marshes and mud flats. It is a part of the former princely state of Kutch, but the area of the Rann has been the subject of a dispute between India and Pakistan. The two nations fought over it, among other issues, in 1965 during the larger India–Pakistan war. The British and the United Nations intervened diplomatically to end that war. In 1968, the International Court of Justice awarded 90 per cent of the territory of the Rann to India and the remainder to Pakistan. The award to Pakistan amounted to about 380 square miles of its claim of about 3500 square miles. However, the award agreed to on 4 July 1969 remains a point of contention by Pakistan. An area known as Sir Creek is the locus of the continuing dispute.

50. Hakim Muhammad Saeed, (1911–98), founded the Hamdard foundation that funded research in *tibbi* medicine. Hakim Saeed served as governor of Sindh from 1993–4. He was assassinated on 17 October 1998.

51. A comprehensive study of Mohenjodaro and other sites in the Indus basin by Jonathan Mark Kenoyer and Kimberley Heuston is titled, *The Ancient South Asian World* (New York: Oxford University Press, 2005. See also Kenoyer and Richard H. Meadow, 'Fifty-five Years of Archaeological Research in Pakistan: The Prehistoric Periods,' in Craig Baxter (ed.), *Pakistan on the Brink: Politics, Economics and Society* (Lanham, Maryland: Lexington Books, 2004), pp. 191–219.

52. Malik Khuda Bakhsh Bucha, former Secretary of Agriculture in West Pakistan and later Minister of Agriculture in the province, was president of the West Pakistan Muslim League in 1966.

53. Nasreen, daughter of Inspector General of Police Alamgir Kabir, married Humayun Kabir (no direct relation) about one month prior to the dinner referred to by Ayub. Humayun was a member of the Pakistan Foreign Service and later of the Bangladesh Foreign Service and was serving as permanent representative to the United Nations and ambassador to the United States.

54. A.H.M. Shams-ud-Doha served as minister of food and agriculture, the last to hold that position in the Ayub period. Doha had been a member of the Police Service of Pakistan. His son, A.R.S. Doha, was foreign minister from 1982–4 in the Ershad regime in Bangladesh.

55. Maulana Ather Ali was a leader of the Nizam-i-Islam party.

56. S.M. Zafar, (b.1930), is a distinguished lawyer. He was minister of law in the Ayub cabinet from 25 March 1965 until he resigned on 21 March 1969. He was also deputy leader of the National Assembly during that time. He was elected Senator from March 2003 till 2006 and was re-elected in March 2006 till 2011. He is also the Chancellor of Hamdard University. Presently, he is Chairman, Human Rights Society of Pakistan. He is the author of several books including *Dialogue on the Political Chessboard* and *Through the Crisis*.

57. Gohar Ayub, (b.1937), is the second son of Ayub Khan. His connection with Ghandhara Industries is mentioned in the entry for General Habibullah Khan. Gohar received military training at the Pakistan Military Academy and at Sandhurst. He was elected to the National Assembly in 1965, 1977, 1985, and in 1990 was also elected speaker. Gohar was also elected in 1997 and became foreign minister and later minister of water and power in the Nawaz Sharif government.

58. Mian Mumtaz Mohammad Khan Daultana, (1916–95), was a prominent Punjabi politician as were several of his relatives. He was the son of Mian Ahmad Yar Khan Daultana who was a member of the Punjab Legislative Council from 1921–3 and 1926–37 and a member of the Punjab Legislative Assembly from 1937 until his death in 1940, when he was replaced by a relative, Mian Allah Yar Khan Daultana (d.1947). Mumtaz was also a nephew of Chaudhry Sir

Shahabuddin (d.1946). Shahabuddin was a member of the Central Legislative Council (1921–3), a member and president of the Punjab Legislative Council (1923–36) and member and speaker of the Punjab Legislative Assembly (1937–45). Mumtaz succeeded Shahabuddin in the Assembly and was a member of the cabinet headed by Nawab Iftikhar Hussain Khan of Mamdot (q.v.). Mumtaz succeeded Mamdot as chief minister in 1951 and resigned in 1953 in connection with the anti-Ahmadiya riots. He was minister of defense in the Chundrigar central cabinet in 1957. He was 'EBDOed' in 1960, but when this expired, Mumtaz headed the Council Muslim League in opposition to Ayub. He became a member of the National Assembly in 1970, but resigned in 1972 to become High Commissioner to the United Kingdom, a post he held until he retired in 1978.

59. Qazi Mohammad Isa, (1913–76), was the representative from Balochistan to the working committee of the Muslim League from 1940 to 1951. He had been chief adviser to the government of Balochistan, essentially chief minister, as Balochistan did not yet have full province status. He served as ambassador to Brazil, 1951–6, and became general secretary of the Muslim League in 1956. Later, he headed the Muslim League (Qayyum) in Balochistan in 1970 but did not contest the 1970 election.

60. Sardar Amir Azam Khan, (1912–76), was a minister in the Suhrawardy, Chundrigar and Noon cabinets. He was also chairman of Orient Airways, a predecessor of Pakistan International Airways. He was in the housing construction industry which generally built low cost apartments.

61. Qazi Fazlullah Obaidullah, (1902–87), was from the Larkana District. He entered the Sindh assembly in the second election of 1946 from Larkana and remained a member of the cabinet from 1947 to 1950. In 1951, when he was chief minister he was dismissed by Governor Din Muhammad under the Public and Representative Offices Disqualification Act. Obaidullah was a member of three West Pakistan cabinets. He was 'EBDOed' by Ayub, but was the first one to be restored when he was appointed a minister in the Musa cabinet in 1967. He remained in the cabinet until 1969. He contested the 1970 election as a candidate of the Convention Muslim League for the National Assembly and was defeated by Mumtaz Bhutto.

DIARY 1967

January 1967

1. Syed Ahmed Saeed Kirmani was a long time member of the Muslim League and was often a member of the assemblies of either Punjab or West Pakistan. He was minister of information in the Musa government in West Pakistan. Being an attorney, he was president of the bar association of the Lahore High Court in 2005. Kirmani was involved in the anti-Ahmadiya riots in 1953 and has been mentioned in brief in the Munir Report. He became a member of the Muslim League Nawaz faction when it was formed and in 2005 remains in opposition to the ruling party.

2. Khan Abdul Qayyum Khan (1908–81) was a major figure in the politics of the North West Frontier Province. He was educated at the London School of Economics and called to the bar from Lincoln's Inn. Qayyum Khan began his political career by supporting Khan Abdul Ghaffar Khan but later strongly opposed him. He was a member of the Central Legislative Assembly from 1934–46, as a member of the Congress Party, but he then changed his affiliation to the Muslim League. Qayyum Khan was elected to the Frontier Assembly in 1946 and became chief minister in 1947. He held that position until he joined the Bogra central cabinet in 1954. He was 'EBDOed' and when that ban was lifted he and Daultana were rivals for the leadership of the Council Muslim League. Qayyum Khan then split the Muslim League to form his own faction and successfully contested the 1970 central election. His party joined the coalition led by Bhutto and Qayyum became Home Minister in 1972. The coalition broke in 1977.

3. Allahbakhsh Karimbakhsh [A.K.] Brohi (1915–87) was a member of the Bogra cabinet. While drafting the 1956 Constitution, Brohi favoured a strong central government as, in his view, the geographic separation of the wings of Pakistan could lead to a complete separation. He was a senior advocate in the Supreme Court and lower courts. Among his works are *Islam and the Modern World* (Lahore: Islamic Book Foundation, 1981). As his name indicates, he was a member of the Brahui-speaking community based in Balochistan.

4. Sardar Bahadur Khan, (1908–76), was a member of the Legislative Assembly of the North West Frontier Province in the period 1939–46, and speaker during 1943–6. He was member of the cabinet of Pakistan, 1949–54; chief minister, North West Frontier Province, 1955; minister in the West Pakistan government, 1955–1956; and leader of the opposition, West Pakistan Legislative Assembly, 1956–8. Sardar Bahadur Khan was Agent to the Governor General in Balochistan and leader of the opposition from 1962–4.

5. Khawaja Shahabuddin, (1898–1977), was a member of the family of the Nawab of Dhaka and was the younger brother of Khwaja Sir Nazimuddin (1894–1964). He was a member of the Bengal Legislature and a member of the Nazimuddin cabinet of Bengal, 1943–5. He was governor of the North West Frontier Province (1951–4) and a member of the Pakistan cabinet (1954–5). Shahabuddin served in several diplomatic posts and was minister of information (1965–9) under Ayub. He earned some notoriety when he banned the works of Rabindranath Tagore from Pakistan radio and television, an action that was reversed in the face of heavy criticism in East Pakistan. He remained in Pakistan, after the independence of Bangladesh, until his death.

6. The princely state of Bahawalpur was established in 1690 and was referred to as a Rajputana state. It acceded to Pakistan on 7 October 1947. The state was terminated on 14 October 1955 as the united West Pakistan was formed on 30 September 1955. Bahawalpur was divided into three districts: Bahawalnagar, Bahawalpur and Rahim Yar Khan. The details of the negotiations on the Bahawalpur controversy are recounted in Wayne Ayers Wilcox, *Pakistan: The Consolidation of a Nation* (New York: Columbia University Press, 1963). See also Syed Hassan Mahmood, *A Nation is Born* (Lahore: privately printed, 1958).

7. Justice Syed Mahbub Murshed, (1911–79), was a barrister. He was appointed to the Dhaka High Court in 1955 and was named chief justice in 1964. He resigned to enter politics in 1968 and was a member of the Democratic Action Committee that negotiated with Ayub in 1969. In the planned 1969 elections, that were never held, Murshed had announced that he would run for the presidency. He was a nephew of Maulvi Abul Kasem Fazlul Haq (1873–1962).

8. The Khan at the time of this meeting was the holder of the title but exercised no official power. The Khan was Ahmad Yar Khan, (1904–79). Kalat was one of the four Baloch states: Kalat, Kharan, Las Bela and Makran. The latter three states listed delayed their accession to Pakistan until 17 March 1948. Kalat acceded a short time later, on 31 March 1948. The four states formed the Balochistan States Union on 3 October 1952. The union was terminated on 14 October 1955 as the unified province of West Pakistan was formed. The negotiations for the Union and West Pakistan are detailed Wayne Ayers Wilcox, *Pakistan: The Consolidation of a Nation* (New York: Columbia University Press, 1963). For a study of later developments in Balochistan see Selig S. Harrison, *In Afghanistan's Shadow: Baluch Nationalism and Soviet Temptations* (Washington: Carnegie Endowment for International Peace, 1981).

9. The Pir Sahib of Dewal Sharif often gave Ayub solicited and unsolicited advice. One comment on the pir is contained in *lokpunjab.org*, 30 March 2004, 'An Intellectual King of Sialkot,' by Shafaq Tanvir Mirza: 'Ayub Khan never sought the advice of the really wise men of his era. Rather, he collected the so-called wise men and asked them to form a writers' guild for the regimentation of the intellectuals of both wings of the country…The real consultant was the Pir of Dewal Sharif.'

10. The document was not attached.

11. The present Makhdoom of Hala is Makhdoom Amin Fahim. Presently he is chairman ARD (Alliance for the Restoration of Democracy) and president of the Pakistan People's Party Parliamentarians (PPPP), which is loyal to Benazir Bhutto and in opposition to the present Musharraf government. In the 2002 elections, the PPPP won the second-largest number of seats in the parliament of Pakistan.

12. Jam Sadiq Ali Junejo (1932–92) was close to the Pir of Pagaro as the scion of the wealthiest family in Sindh, and elected PPP member of central Sindh's Sanghar district. He associated himself with Zulfiqar Ali Bhutto and was appointed as a senior cabinet minister by the chief minister of Sindh, Ghulam Mustafa Jatoi (1973–7). When Bhutto was deposed by General Ziaul Haq, Jam Sadiq Ali exiled himself from Pakistan and lived in England. During Benazir Bhutto's 20-month government, he served as an adviser but eventually resigned because of differences. After the dismissal of Benazir Bhutto's government in 1990, Jam Sadiq Ali was appointed chief minister of Sindh (1990–92), heading a minority government which was ruthless in suppressing opposition.

13. Fazal Ellahi Chaudhary, (1904–82), was defeated when he contested as a Unionist from Gujrat in 1937, but was elected as a Muslim Leaguer to the Punjab Legislative Assembly in 1946 and 1951. He was briefly a member of the Mamdot cabinet in 1948. Fazal Ellahi was elected to the West Pakistan Assembly in 1955 and was elected as speaker by the Republicans. He was elected to the National Assembly in 1962 and 1965. He left the Muslim League (Convention) and joined the Pakistan People's Party and was elected speaker in 1972. He became the President of Pakistan in 1973 and on the expiry of his term in 1978 was succeeded by General Ziaul Haq.

14. Fatima Jinnah, (1894–1967), was the sister of Mohammad Ali Jinnah. Although trained as a dentist, she devoted much of her life to her brother. Her only foray into active politics was when she was a candidate for president representing the Combined Opposition Parties against Ayub Khan in 1965 and was defeated.

15. Chaudhary Ghulam Abbas, (d.1967), worked to attain the accession of Kashmir to Pakistan. He did not play a significant role after independence. He seems to have been closely associated with Shorish Kashmiri (see Diary 1969, note 12).

February 1967

16. The Saigol industrial group began in 1890 with a shoe shop that became the Kohinoor Rubber Works. The group used the name Kohinoor in some other enterprises as well. Like with other industrial groups, much of their property was nationalized by the Bhutto regime including the United Bank. Rafique Saigol was one of the few scions of industrial groups who entered active politics and was secretary of finance of the PML. Z.A. Bhutto made him chief of the Pakistan International Airlines.

17. Malik Sir Mohammad Feroz Khan Noon, (1893–1970), was a member of the Punjab Legislative Council, 1921–36, and a minister, 1931–6. He was the High Commissioner to London, 1936–41, and a member of the Executive Council of the Governor General, 1941–5. He campaigned for the Muslim League in the 1946 election and was a member of the Constituent Assembly, 1947–58. Sir Feroz was governor of East Pakistan, 1950–3. He became chief minister of Punjab in 1953, serving until 1955. He was foreign minister of Pakistan, 1956–7, and was prime minister in 1958. He then retired from holding office. His autobiography is entitled *From Memory* (Lahore: Ferozesons, 1966). Noon's second wife, Viqarunnisa, was instrumental in developing tourism in Pakistan.

18. Inamullah was the chief justice of the Lahore High Court, 1965–7.

19. The All-Pakistan Women's Association (APWA) was founded under the leadership of Begum Ra'ana Liaquat Ali Khan (Diary 1967, note 53) in 1949. Its aim is to see the furtherance of the moral, social and economic welfare of the women and children of Pakistan. The organization is non-profit and non-political. It has its headquarters in Karachi with branches in urban and rural areas of the country.

20. Major General Akbar Khan, (1920–94), was the leader of the Rawalpindi conspiracy in 1951 in an attempt to overthrow the Liaquat Ali Khan government. Akbar and others were convicted and sentenced to long prison terms. Earlier Akbar led the Pakistani forces in Kashmir against India. After being out of politics for many years he was named minister of state for defence by Zulfiqar Ali Bhutto in early 1970 and served for a short time.

21. Maulana Kausar Niazi, (1934–94), was a political maulvi who first joined the Jamaat-e-Islami. He joined the National Democratic Alliance, a party that worked with the Pakistan People's Party led by Zulfiqar Ali Bhutto and later by Benazir Bhutto. He became minister of information and broadcasting in Z.A. Bhutto's cabinet and remained a member until that cabinet fell in 1977. He headed the Council of Islamic Ideology in 1994. Niazi wrote many books, mainly in Urdu. His *Last Days of Premier Bhutto* (Lahore: Jang Publications, 1991) presents Niazi's views of that time.

March 1967

22. Habibullah Khan had served in the cabinet in the North West Frontier Province before independence under Sir Abdul Qayyum Khan (not the same Qayyum Khan who was chief minister after independence and held many political positions). Habibullah was also home minister in the West Pakistan cabinets headed by the Nawab of Kalabagh and Musa.

23. Sir Khizr Hayat Khan Tiwana, (1900–75), was the son of Nawab Sir Umar Hayat Khan Tiwana (1874–1944) and was one of the leading landlords in Punjab. Khizr became minister of public works in the Unionist ministry headed by Sir Sikandar Hayat. Khizr replaced Sikander on his death in 1942 and headed the cabinet until the time of partition. The cabinet comprised the Unionist Party, the Congress and the Akali Dal. With partition the coalition ended and the Muslim League formed a post-partition cabinet. Khizr did not take part again in active politics, but he remained a leading personality especially in Punjab and was the patron of the famous Lahore Horse Show. See Ian Talbot, *Khizr Tiwana: The Punjab Unionist Party and the Partition of Pakistan* (Surrey: Curzon, 1996).

24. Nawab Sir Muzaffar Ali Qizilbash, (1908–82), was head of the premier family of Lahore District and a leader of the Shia community. The extended Qizilbash group includes many prominent persons such as General Agha Mohammad Yahya Khan. Muzaffar Qizilbash was elected to the Punjab Legislative Assembly in 1937 as an independent and in 1946 as a Unionist. He was elected to the second Constituent Assembly in 1956, became a central minister in the Suhrawardy cabinet in 1957. He became chief minister of West Pakistan in 1958. He next held the portfolio of finance in the Yahya cabinet, 1970–1. He was appointed as ambassador to France in 1972, remaining there until 1976.

25. Brother-in-law of Major General Shahid Hamid.

26. Ghulam Ishaq Khan, (1915–2006), was from the North West Frontier Province and was inducted into the provincial service in 1938. In the ensuing period he held increasingly important positions. He was a member of the Land Reform

Commission and then chairman of the West Pakistan Water and Power Development Authority. In 1962, Ishaq became secretary of the Finance Ministry and later was named governor of the State Bank of Pakistan. He was cabinet secretary, in 1971. He returned to the central government in 1975 as secretary of the Ministry of Defence. He had a number of positions as economist under Ziaul Haq and was subsequently elected to the Senate and became its chairman. When Zia was killed in an aircraft accident, Ishaq, in accordance with the Constitution, became president and held that position until May 1993. During his presidency, Ishaq dismissed the government of Prime Minister Benazir Bhutto in August 1990 and Prime Minister Nawaz Sharif in April 1993.

27. Mian Ghulam Moinuddin Riaz was a retired civil servant who served as secretary of the Ministry of Fuel, Power and Natural Resources. His son, Mian Ghulam Fariduddin Riaz, married Qudsia Begum, (1946–89), who was the youngest daughter of Sajida Sultan, Begum of Bhopal, (1915–95), and the sister of Nawab Mansur Ali Khan of Pataudi, a noted cricketer. Qudsia's daughter, Sara, married Faiz, son of Shaharyar Khan who is the son of Abida Sultaan, (1913–2002), elder sister of Sajida Sultan. The two sisters were daughters of Nawab Hamidullah Khan of Bhopal who died in 1960. Abida moved from India to Pakistan in 1950 thereby relinquishing her role as heiress-presumptive of her father and Sajida was confirmed as Begum of Bhopal by the Government of India in 1961. Princess Abida Sultaan was a member of the Pakistan Foreign Service and her memoirs were published posthumously as *Memoirs of a Rebel Princess* (Karachi: Oxford University Press, 2004). The book was edited by Shaharyar Khan, a former foreign secretary of Pakistan. Mansur Ali Khan of Pataudi married the actress Sharmila Tagore, the grandniece of Nobel Laureate Rabindranath Tagore.

28. The Anjuman Himayat-i-Islam was founded in 1884 to assist needy Muslims including orphanages and widow's homes. It is active in education and founded the Islamia College in Lahore in 1892 and later the Islamia College for Women. Many of its leaders were involved in politics and public service, including the former chief justice Dr Nasim Hassan Shah (b.1929), the current president of the Anjuman. Dr Shah owns a press that publishes books on secular and religious topics.

29. Mohammad Khan Junejo, (1930–93), was elected to the West Pakistan assembly in 1962. He resigned the seat to join the West Pakistan cabinets of the Nawab of Kalabagh and General Mohammad Musa, holding the posts until the imposition of martial law by Yahya Khan on 25 March 1969. Following a non-party election, Junejo became prime minister on 23 March 1985. He was dismissed by Zia on 29 May 1988.

30. A.R. Cornelius, (1903–91), studied at Allahabad and Cambridge and joined the Indian Civil Service in 1926. In 1947, he was appointed to the Supreme Court of Pakistan. He became chief justice in 1960. See Ralph Braibanti, *Chief Justice Cornelius of Pakistan: An Analysis with Letters and Speeches*, (New York: Oxford University Press, 1999), with foreword by Chief Justice Nasim Hasan Shah.

31. Tofazzal Hussain (Manik Mian), (1911–69), was the founder and editor of the newspaper *Ittefaq*. He had been in the civil service but left in the late 1930s. He was a follower of Huseyn Shaheed Suhrawardy in the Muslim League and later in the Awami League. The newspaper became the *de facto* mouthpiece of the Awami League. The newspaper was banned and Manik Mian spent some time in jail during the Ayub regime. The newspaper did not support the authoritarian steps by Mujibur Rahman after the independence of Bangladesh and was again proscribed for a period.

32. Yusuf Ali Choudhry (Mohan Mian), (1905–71), was a pre-independence member of the Bengal Legislative Assembly as a Muslim Leaguer. He was dismissed from the Muslim League in 1953 and joined the Krishak Sramik Party of A.K. Fazlul Haq. He was a member of the National Democratic Movement aimed at ousting Ayub Khan. Mohan Mian was opposed to the independence of Bangladesh.

33. Abdul Jabbar Khan, (1902–89), was the speaker of the Constituent Assembly, 1968–9. He was president of the East Pakistan Muslim League, 1963–5, and was elected to the National Assembly in 1965. He left his post as speaker when Yahya Khan proclaimed Martial Law in 1969. Jabbar Khan did not return to politics and lived a retired life in Bangladesh. He had a number of children who were active in Bangladesh politics and government service. Enayatullah (d.2005) was a left wing journalist and was the founder and editor of the weekly *Holiday*. Another son, Rashid Khan Menon, is the leader of the Workers Party, a small left wing party. A third son was the late Obaidullah Khan.

34. A.K.M. Fazlul Qader Chaudhary, (1919–73), was a leading member of the East Pakistan Muslim League. He was a member of the Ayub Khan cabinet in 1962 and was speaker, 1963–6. He opposed the liberation of Bangladesh and spent some time in jail after it took place. However, his son, Salahuddin Qader Chaudhary, is a member of the Bangladesh Nationalist Party and has been a member of Parliament.

35. A few migrants from West Bengal used Urdu, although most from Bihar did.

36. 'The Begum Dacca' who is referred to by Ayub is properly known as the Nawab Ayesha Begum of Dacca. The title Begum Nawab was given to the wife of the Nawab of Dacca. Ayub erred in that the wedding was not that of a son (she had no sons) but was that of the Nawab Begum's younger daughter, Nawabzadi Asmat Bano to K.M. Omer. Nawab

Ayesha Begum was born in 1917, the daughter of the Maharaja of Chhota Udaipur (who converted to Islam). As a widow she is now known as the Dowager Nawab. She was the wife of Nawab Habibullah and the daughter-in-law of Nawab Salimullah (1866–1915) who was among the founders of the Muslim League who met at Ahsan Manzil, the nawab's palace in Dhaka in 1906. Like most of the family of the nawab she moved to Pakistan after the founding of Bangladesh and now lives in Karachi. Source: www.nawabbari.com, Official Web Site of the Dhaka Nawab Family.

April 1967

37. Syed Amjad Ali, (1907–97), was a scion of a prominent Muslim business family in the Punjab involved in industry and related businesses and also a noted political figure. He was a member of the Punjab Legislative Assembly, 1937–45, and junior minister in the cabinets of Sir Sikander Hayat Khan and Sir Khizr Hayat Khan Tiwana. He was a member of the Indian Constituent Assembly, 1946. Amjad Ali was ambassador to the United States, 1953–5; minister of finance of Pakistan, 1955–8; and Pakistan representative to the United Nations, 1964–7. The Islamic Institute in New York was established with its headquarters on Third Avenue between 96th and 97th Streets.

38. Sardar Shaukat Hayat Khan, (1915–98), was the son of Sardar Sir Sikander Hayat Khan (1892–1942) who was the first prime minister of the Punjab after the enactment of the Government of India Act, 1935. He entered the Punjab Assembly in a by-election after the death of his uncle, Nawab Muzaffar Khan. After Sikander's death a new cabinet under the leadership of Malik Sir Khizr Hayat Tiwana was formed. Shaukat was included in the cabinet that was dissolved at the time of independence. He was also a member of the short-lived post-independence Punjab cabinet headed by the Nawab of Mamdot. He then joined the Azad Pakistan Party briefly, but then was inactive in politics until he was elected to the National Assembly in 1970. See Shaukat Hayat Khan, *The Nation that Lost its Soul: Memoirs by a Freedon Fighter* (Lahore: Jang Publications, 1995). Shaukat's sister, Tahira, married Nawab Muzaffar Khan's son, Mazhar Ali Khan (1917–93), a left leaning editor of the *Pakistan Times* published by Progressive Papers (see Diary 1970 note 21). He later edited *Dawn* and was the editor and publisher of the weekly *Viewpoint* (1975–92). *Viewpoint* carried a chronology each week that is useful for research. See Mazhar Ali Khan, *Pakistan: The Barren Years, Editorials and Columns of Mazhar Ali Khan, 1975–1992* (Karachi: Oxford University, 1998).

39. Sharifuddin Pirzada.

40. Canadian dollars.

41. Locke left Pakistan to become deputy ambassador in South Vietnam.

42. Darul Uloom means a place of learning where the learning is based on Islam, although some institutions also emphasize other subjects. Another term is madrassa.

43. Sheikh Mujibur Rahman, (1921–75), was a student member of the Muslim League in the 1940s. He was a founding member of the Awami League with Huseyn Shaheed Suhrawardy in 1949 and the principal organizer of the party in East Pakistan. Mujib was minister of commerce in East Pakistan, 1956–7, but his skills were devoted principally to party matters. Among these matters was the attainment of parity between the two wings. In 1966, he declared the Six Point Programme for the Awami League and led it in the 1970 election. The League won 170 of 172 seats in East Pakistan in the National Assembly (no seats were won in West Pakistan) and won 288 of 300 seats in the provincial assembly. In early 1971, negotiations among Mujib, Bhutto and Yahya on the issue of parity were unsuccessful and in March of that year, the Pakistan army acted in East Pakistan to stop any move for independence for East Pakistan. Mujib was arrested and held in West Pakistan. The independence movement, aided by the Indian army, led to the surrender of the Pakistani forces in December 1971. Mujib was released and returned to Dhaka, capital of Bangladesh, with stops in London and New Delhi. The government of Bangladesh was first a parliamentary system led by Mujib, but was poorly run. Then Mujib obtained approval of the parliament for establishment of a presidential system with him as the president. He also formed a single party system. Mujib was assassinated on 15 August 1975. See Moudud Ahmed, *Bangladesh: Era of Sheikh Mujibur Rahman* (Dhaka: University Press, 1983); Craig Baxter, *Bangladesh From a Nation to a State* (Boulder, Colorado: Westview Press, 1997); and Richard Sisson and Leo Rose, *War and Secession: Pakistan, India and the Creation of Bangladesh* (Berkeley: University of California Press, 1990).

44. Fazlur Rahman Malik, (1919–88), was a major and significant scholar of Islam and founded the Islamic Research Institute (now attached to the International Islamic University) in Islamabad in 1960. One fellow researcher described Fazlur Rahman as 'probably the most learned of the major Muslim thinkers in the second-half of the twentieth century, in terms of both classical Islam and Western philosophical and theological discourse.' His father, Maulana Shahab al-Din, was a scholar at Deoband. Fazlur Rahman received his doctorate from Oxford University and taught at Durham University and McGill University before returning to Pakistan to set up the Islamic Research Institute. He left the

institute as a result of political opposition to his views on the modern study of Islam. He then went to the University of California, Los Angeles, and thence to the University of Chicago where he produced his major work, a widely accepted textbook *Islam* (Chicago: University of Chicago Press, 1979). A major work is his interpretation of Islam in *Islam and Modernity: Transformation of an Intellectual Tradition* (Chicago: University of Chicago Press, 1982). A posthumous publication edited by Ebrahim Moosa, is *Revival and Reform in Islam: a Study of Islamic Fundamentalism* (Oxford: Oneworld Publications, 1999).

May 1967

45. Prince Sadruddin Khan, (1933–2003), was the younger son of Aga Khan III (q.v.). He was the United Nations High Commissioner for Refugees (1965–77).

46. Dir was one of four princely states in the region of the North West Frontier Province. The other three were Amb, Chitral and Swat. Each of the states came under the suzerainty of Pakistan in 1947. The states, except for Amb, were incorporated into Pakistan on 28 July 1969. Royalty was abolished in Amb in 1973 and it was also incorporated into Pakistan, but its territory did not become a separate district as did Chitral, Dir and Swat. Later Dir was divided into Upper Dir and Lower Dir districts. The state of Hunza had been under the suzerainty of the Maharaja of Kashmir and Jammu since 1891. Its territory is under the control of Pakistan following the conflict between India and Pakistan, 1947–9. Hunza became a part of the Northern Territories of Pakistan on 25 September 1974. The small state of Nagar was also incorporated at the same time as Hunza. The Northern Territories are not a part of the area that is described as Azad Kashmir and is often referred to as Gilgit–Baltistan. See Wayne Ayers Wilcox, *Pakistan: The Consolidation of a Nation* (New York: Columbia University Press, 1963). There are also two classical studies of the Pathans: Sir Olaf Caroe, *The Pathans* (New York: St. Martin's Press, 1958) and Fredrik Barth, *Political Leadership Among the Swat Pathans* (London: Athlone Press, 1959). Some of the residents of the Northern Areas have demanded that the territory either become the fifth province of Pakistan or be autonomous like Azad Kashmir. See *Dawn*, 3 September 2005.

47. Pakistan Democratic Movement was a group of political parties opposed to the continuance of Ayub in office. Most parties in the opposition were formal members of the Movement. These included the Pakistan People's Party of Zulfiqar Ali Bhutto and the Awami League led by Mujibur Rahman. A new grouping using the name Pakistan Democratic Party was formed in May 1969. This comprised the Nizam-i-Islam Party led by Chaudhary Mohammad Ali, the Awami League (Nawabzada Nasrullah Group), National Democratic Front led by Nurul Amin and the Justice Party led by Asghar Khan. The party was short-lived as the Justice Party withdrew and Chaudhry Mohammad Ali retired from politics for reasons of ill health by November 1969. However, the name was kept on by the group led by Nasrullah.

48. Nurul Amin, (1897–1974), was elected to the Bengal Legislative Council in 1942 and the Bengal Legislative Assembly in 1946 as a Muslim Leaguer. He succeeded Nazimuddin as chief minister of East Bengal in 1948 when the latter became governor general of Pakistan. Nurul Amin and the Muslim League were defeated by the United Front (a coalition principally of the Krishak Sramik Party and Awami League) in the 1954 provincial election. Nurul Amin was elected to the National Assembly in 1965 and played a role in the negotiations that led to the resignation of Ayub Khan in 1969. He strongly opposed the creation of Bangladesh He won one of the two seats won by the opposition in East Pakistan for the National Assembly in the 1970 election. Nurul Amin moved to Pakistan and remained here becoming vice president in 1971 in the Bhutto regime. He held the office until 1973 when the new parliamentary constitution took effect.

49. Nawabzada Abdul Ghafoor Hoti was appointed minister of commerce in July 1967 in succession to Ghulam Faruque. From 30 December 1985 to 13 April 1986 he was governor of North West Frontier Province. Hoti was close to Ayub Khan as is evident from the many entries in the diary. He served as railways minister under Mohammad Khan Junejo in 1985. He was a member of an important family based in Mardan and had served in the British Indian and Pakistan armies, retiring in 1953.

50. Colonel Mohammad Amir Hoti, (1919–2005), was commissioned from Sandhurst and served in North Africa during the Second World War. He and others in his family established industries in the Mardan area including the Charsadda Sugar Mill (since closed) and Charsadda Paper Mill. He also served as ambassador of Spain.

51. Khan Mohammad Khan Hoti is a cousin of Ghafoor and Amir. He was minister of education in the West Pakistan cabinet of the Nawab of Kalabagh.

52. George David Woods, (1901–82), was president of the International Bank for Reconstruction and Development (World Bank), January 1963–March 1968. See Robert W. Oliver, *George Woods and the World Bank* (Boulder, Colo.: Lynne Rienner, 1995).

53. Begum Ra'ana Liaquat Khan, (c.1905–90), was the second wife of Liaquat Ali Khan and worked with her husband in the Pakistan movement. She strongly supported women's rights and created the All-Pakistan Women's Association (APWA). Raana was not involved in politics after the assassination of Liaquat Ali Khan in 1951. However, she accepted an appointment as governor of Sindh (1973–6). Before her marriage to Liaquat Ali Khan her name was Irene Pant and she was the granddaughter of Tarachand Pant of Nainital who had embraced Christianity.

54. Vice Admiral A.R. Khan, (1921–83), was appointed minister of defence on 7 October 1966 in succession to Ayub who had held that portfolio since 1958. Khan had been commander-in-chief of the navy. S.M. Ahsan (see Diary 1966, note 41) succeeded Khan to the post.

55. General Azam Mohammad Khan, (1908–94), was appointed as administrator of Martial Law Zone B (West Pakistan except Karachi) when Ayub Khan became chief martial law administrator in 1958. He also served as minister of refugees and rehabilitation. In 1960 he was appointed governor of East Pakistan where he was popular with the people. His popularity in this role was seen by Ayub Khan as a possible threat to his rule and he was removed in 1962. Azam supported Fatima Jinnah against Ayub Khan in the 1964 elections and thereafter led a retired life.

56. Said Hassan was the Permanent Representative of Pakistan at the United Nations, 1960–1.

57. The Six Points were announced in Lahore in November 1966 by Sheikh Mujibur Rahman and formed the basis of the manifesto of the Awami League in the 1970 election. These points were: (1) a federal parliamentary government with free and regular elections; (2) federal government to control foreign affairs and defence; (3) a separate currency or separate fiscal accounts for each province to control movement of capital from east to west; (4) all power of taxation at the provincial level with the federal government subsisting on grants from the provinces; (5) each federating unit could enter foreign trade agreements on its own and to control the foreign exchange earned; (6) each unit could raise its militia. These points were in part based on the 21 points programme of the United Front (primarily the Awami Party and Krishak Sramik Party) formed to contest the 1954 election for the East Pakistan Legislative Assembly. Prior to the election of 1970, Yahya Khan issued a Legal Framework Order on 20 March 1970 (see Diary 1970, note 14). It is not clear what the Eight Points were. It is possible the reference is to the Seven Point Programme of the Council Muslim League issued on 25 August 1966.

June 1967

58. Shah Mohammad Aziz-ur-Rahman, (1925–88), was general secretary of the All-Muslim Students Federation, 1945–7. He also served as joint secretary and secretary of the East Pakistan Muslim League, 1947–58, but joined the Awami League in 1964. Rahman was the deputy leader of the Awami League in 1969, but was not involved in the Bangladesh war, and became active when the Bangladesh Muslim League was permitted to operate in 1976. In 1979, he was elected to Parliament as a member of the Bangladesh Nationalist Party and became prime minister until 1981. He was expelled from the party in 1985 for 'disciplinary reasons.'

59. Ahmed Mian Soomro was the deputy speaker of the West Pakistan Assembly and was later a senator. He began the Senate committee system. His son, Mohammad Mian Soomro, (b.1950), was governor of Sindh, 2000–2, and is the chairman of the Senate of Pakistan (2006).

60. Rhodesia gained independence and was renamed Zimbabwe in 1980.

61. Mian Mushtaq Ahmed Khan Gurmani, (b.1905), was a member of the Punjab Legislative Council, 1930 and 1932–6 and of the Punjab Legislative Assembly 1937–46. He served as a parliamentary private secretary in the cabinets of Sikander Hayat and Khizr Tiwana. Gurmani was prime minister of the state of Bahawalpur, 1947–8, and a member of the central cabinet, 1949–54. He was named governor of Punjab, 1954, and of West Pakistan, 1955–7.

62. Begum Zari Sarfarz, (b.1923), came from a business and political family of Mardan. Her brother Mir Afzal (see Diary 1972, note 6) once served as chief minister of the North West Frontier Province. She was a legislator in the province and at the centre. Zari was head of the Pakistan Tuberculosis Association, president of a children's village in Dera Ismail Khan, chairwoman of APWA, a member of the Human Rights Commission of Pakistan as well being the head of several industrial concerns in the Frontier.

July 1967

63. Information on the Indian plans is expected to be included in a forthcoming book by Gohar Ayub, son of Mohammad Ayub Khan.

64. Biafra.

65. Sir Cyril Pickard.

66. Mohammad Munir, (1895–1981), became a justice of the Punjab High Court in 1942 and was chief justice, 1949–54. He was a justice of the Federal Court in 1947 and was chief justice, 1954–60. Munir is best known for his role in the anti-Ahmadiya riots in 1953 and authoring of the report on the riots: *The Report of the Inquiry into the Punjab Disturbances of 1953*. The report is often referred to as the 'Munir Report'. He retired in 1962, but served as law minister in the Ayub cabinet, 1962–4. Munir espoused a state that was based on secular legal concepts which he saw as the principles of Jinnah and opposed the stance of Ziaul Haq who supported an Islamic state. These ideas were presented in *From Jinnah to Zia*. (Lahore: Vanguard, 1979).

67. Major General Iskander Mirza, (1899–1969), was born into a Shi'a family in Mumbai that traced its early history to the Murshidabad District of Bengal. His family included the family of the Nawab of Bengal who was defeated at Plassey in 1757. In 1919, he was the first Indian cadet from Sandhurst. He transferred from the army to the Indian Political Service, but retained his military commission. Almost all of his service was in the North West Frontier Province. Mirza was named military secretary of Pakistan in 1947, governor of East Pakistan in 1954 and a central minister the same year. He became governor general in 1955 and president the following year. He proclaimed martial law in October 1958 and was replaced as president by Ayub Khan, whom Mirza had declared as chief martial administrator. Ayub retained both positions. Mirza was exiled and spent much of his remaining years in London. He is buried in Mashhad, Iran. See Humayun Mirza, *From to Plassey to Pakistan: The Family History of Iskander Mirza, the First President of Pakistan*, (Lanham MD: University Press of America, 2002).

68. Mohammad Ayub Khuhro, (1901–80), was from Larkana District, Sindh. He was a member of the Bombay Legislative Council, 1924–36, the Sindh Legislative Assembly 1937–56, and the West Pakistan Legislative Assembly from 1956 until it was dissolved in 1958. He was chief minister of Sindh three times between 1947 and 1954 (16 August 1947–24 April 1948, 25 November–29 December 1951, and 9 November 1954–13 October 1955) but he was disqualified each time under the Public and Representative Offices Disqualification Act (PRODA). Khuhro was Minister of Defence in the Noon cabinet in 1958. He contested the 1970 election for the National Assembly but was defeated by Zulfiqar Ali Bhutto. See Hamida Khuhro, *Mohammad Ayub Khuhro, a Life of Courage in Politics*, (Lahore: Ferozsons, 1998) and Mohammad Ayub Khuhro, *Suffering of Sind*, (Karachi: Lateef Adabi Academy, 1993), second edition, edited by Hamida Khuhro.

69. Syed Hassan Mahmood was a key official of the Bahawalpur government.

August 1967

70. Chaudhary Khaliquzzaman, (1889–1973), graduated from Aligarh and entered politics as a member of the Congress. He became a member of the Muslim League in the United Provinces and then moved to Karachi. Khaliquzzaman was the president of the League and served as governor of East Pakistan, 31 March 1950–31 March 1953. He also served in the Musa cabinet in West Pakistan. He wrote *Pathway to Pakistan* (Karachi: Longmans, 1961).

71. Ziauddin Ahmad Suleri, (1913–99), was a noted political writer and editor. He wrote a number of well-received books including *Politicians and Ayub: a Survey of Pakistani Politics From 1948 to 1964* (Lahore: Lion Art Press, 1964). His books also include those on Jinnah and Liaquat Ali Khan. His daughter, Sara Suleri Goodyear, has written a memorial to her father, *Boys will be Boys: a Daughter's Elegy* (Chicago: University of Chicago Press, 2003).

72. Dr Abdus Salam, (1926–96), was the Chief Scientific Advisor to the president, 1961–74. He hailed from Jhang, and studied physics at Cambridge University. Dr Salam worked at Cambridge and Trieste. He was awarded the Nobel Prize in physics in 1979.

73. Roger Revelle, (1909–91), proposed a major project to alleviate the onset of salinity in the Indus plain. While British and Pakistan engineers provided for the distribution of irrigation water, they had not made arrangements for drainage with the result that much of the land was subject to salinity and had become barren. Revelle led a team that was formed following a meeting between Ayub and President Kennedy. His proposal was contained in a paper written by him and R. Dorman and H. Thomas, 'Waterlogging and Salinization in the Indus Plain, some basic considerations,' *Pakistan Development Review*, 5(3): 331–70. The programme was dubbed the Salinity Control and Reclamation Project (SCARP).

74. Syed Fida Hassan served as Ayub Khan's private secretary. He also served as the president of the Board of Control for Cricket. His wife, Zeenat, was a legislator.

75. Vaseem A. Jaffrey, (b.1927), served in a number of posts as economist in West Pakistan and then moved to the central government before becoming governor of the State Bank. Jaffrey left the State Bank and was named economic advisor to the prime minister, Benazir Bhutto, in 1988, and returned in 1993 to the post during the second Benazir Bhutto administration. He left the government when the second Benazir Bhutto government was dismissed in 1996.

76. Benjamin H. Oehlert, Jr. served as American ambassador 16 August 1967–17 June 1969.

77. Hakeem Ahmad Shuja (1893–1969) was an Urdu poet and playwright. The catalogue of the Library of Congress lists no English publications.

78. Abdul Sobur Khan, (1910–82), was a member of the Muslim League and a minister in Ayub's government, 1962–9, holding the communications portfolio. The Muslim League was banned in 1971 in Bangladesh, but he was permitted to return to political activity in 1976. Sobur was elected to Parliament as a Muslim Leaguer in 1979.

79. Sufi Zulfikar Haider was a Bengali author and poet. None of his works in English, if any, are listed in the catalogue of the Library of the Congress. He was born in 1899. The date of his death has not been reported in any of the works consulted for this book.

80. Junagarh (also spelled Junagadh) was previously a princely state located at the base of the Girnar Hills on the Kathiawar Peninsula. Junagarh is the site of Buddhist caves, dating from the 3rd century BC, Ashokan edicts and Hindu temples. The state was incorporated into India over the objection of Pakistan.

81. Manavadar was a tiny princely state located in the current state of Gujarat in India. The rulers were from the family that also ruled Junagarh.

September 1967

82. The Khudai Khidmatgar ('Servants of God' movement) was formed in the 1930s. Its goal was the achievement of some level of autonomy for the Pathans of the North West Frontier Province. The Khidmatgars wore red uniforms which earned them the nickname 'Red Shirts.' The movement mobilized landless peasants and low paid workers against the British. They also opposed the landed aristocracy in the province. Although the movement was predominantly Muslim, because of the anti-British aspect, members were also drawn to the Indian National Congress and to Gandhi. The most important leaders were the Khan brothers, Dr Khan Sahib and Abdul Ghaffar Khan. Khan Sahib (1882–1956) received a medical degree from the University of London and practiced medicine briefly before entering politics. His coalition of the Khudai Khidmatgars won offices in the province in both the 1937 and 1946 elections and Dr Khan Sahib led the provincial governments. The Khidmatgars had supported an unpartitioned India. But when a referendum was held on the single question of whether the Frontier should join India or Pakistan upon independence the Khudai Khidmatgars boycotted it. Consequently, the referendum's low turnout gave a result in favour of joining Pakistan. Dr Khan Sahib was removed from the chief minister's post by Jinnah. He returned to politics as a minister of the cabinet headed by Mohammad Ali Bogra in 1953 and in 1955 became chief minister of the unified province of West Pakistan. Dr Khan joined with others, including Iskander Mirza, to join the Republican Party in opposition to the Muslim League. He was assassinated in 1956. The younger brother, Abdul Ghaffar Khan (1890–1989), known as the 'Frontier Gandhi', worked mainly to better the conditions of the Pathans. He did not support the concept of an independent Pakistan and was not supportive of Jinnah. Ghaffar Khan supported autonomy for the Pathan province, although this stand was taken to mean the creation of an independent state for the Pathans who lived in both Pakistan and Afghanistan to be called Pukhtunistan. He spent a number of years in prison, but would not support Pakistan. On his death, he refused to be buried in Pakistan and was buried in Jalalabad, Afghanistan.

83. J.F.C. Fuller, (1878–1966), *The Generalism of Alexander the Great* (London: Eyre and Spottiswoode, 1958).

84. Major General Shahid Hamid, (1910–93), recounted his career in *Autobiography of a General* (Lahore: Ferozsons, 1988). He had earlier written *Disastrous Twilight: A Personal Record of the Partition of India* (London: L. Cooper, 1986) with a foreword by Philip Ziegler. Hamid was private secretary to Field Marshal Sir Claude Auchinleck during 1946 and 1947 and a member of Ziaul Haq's cabinet.

85. Sir James Charles Napier, (1782–1853), was the British conqueror of Sindh, winning the battle of Miani in 1843. He is known for his use of Latin in his alleged dispatch to the governor general, the Earl of Ellenborough: 'peccavi.' Translated it means 'I have sinned'. Napier's victory ended the rule of the Talpurs in Sindh and Mirpur, but they continued to rule Khairpur. See William Napier, *The History of General Sir Charles Napier's Conquest of Scinde* (Karachi: Oxford University Press, 2001, introduction by Hamida Khuhro.)

86. Capital Development Authority (CDA) was established on 14 June 1960, first by an executive order issued on 24 June 1960 entitled the Pakistan Capital Regulation, to be superseded by the CDA ordinance issued on 27 June 1960. The Capital Development Authority was charged with the construction of the city of Islamabad. The plan was designed by Doxiadis Associates, a Greek firm. See Orestes Yakas, *Islamabad: the Birth of a Capital* (Karachi: Oxford University Press, 2001).

October 1967

87. This memorandum was either misdated or was an earlier memorandum and was an enclosure to the letter.

88. Field Marshal Kodandera Madappa Cariappa, (1899–1993), was a Coorgi. In 1949 he became the first Indian to be the commander-in-chief of the Indian army. At the time of independence in 1947 he was designated general officer commander-in-chief of the Western Command. See Chandra B. Khanduri, *Field Marshal K.M. Cariappa: a Biographical Sketch* (Delhi: Dev Publications, 2000).

89. Sheikh Mohammad Abdullah, (1905–82), known as the 'Lion of Kashmir,' struggled for the independence of India and, within India, autonomy for the state of Jammu and Kashmir. The state at the time was ruled by Hari Singh, Maharaja of Kashmir, as a princely state and with other states was assimilated to India (although some states were incorporated into Pakistan). Abdullah founded the Kashmir Muslim Conference in 1932 and changed the name in 1948 to National Conference so others such as the Hindus resident in Jammu and Kashmir could participate in the movement for autonomy. Abdullah spent time in jail or detention for opposing the Indian government. But he was recognized as chief minister of the government of Jammu and Kashmir, 1948–53 and 1975–82. For much of his time from 1953 to 1964 he was in jail. In 1971, Abdullah and Indira Gandhi signed an agreement under which he accepted the accession of Jammu and Kashmir to India. Eventually, some time after this agreement, in 1975, Abdullah returned to the post of chief minister. He put forth his views in 'Kashmir, India and Pakistan,' in *Foreign Affairs*, April 1965. See also Alastair Lamb, *Kashmir: A Disputed Legacy, 1846–1990.* (Hertingord, England: Roxord Books, 1991). Afzal Baig was a long time associate of Abdullah, although at times they disagreed.

90. Aga Khan III, see Diary 1968, note 30.

November 1967

91. Professor Dr Amir Hasan Siddiqui was the founder-Head of the Department of Islamic History, University of Karachi. He was chair of the department till 1967. He died of shock over the fall of Dhaka.

92. Bahaullah (1817–1892) was a Persian who founded the Baha'i faith.

93. Aftab G.N. Kazi, after his service as the head of the Water and Power Authority, was later finance secretary and deputy chairman of the Planning Commission.

94. Mangla Dam on the Jhelum River was the first major dam constructed under the Indus Waters Treaty signed in 1960 among Pakistan, India and the World Bank. Envisaged also was a dam at Tarbela on the Indus River and extensive canal and barrage construction that would greatly extend the system of canals. The history leading to the treaty and the first years of its implementation is studied by Aloys A. Michel, *The Indus Rivers: The Effects of Partition* (New Haven: Yale University Press, 1967). As Ayub notes at several places in his diary, much more work is required for fully developing the river system as well the systems of storage and delivery of the waters. For a current survey see Khaleeq Kiani, 'WB Ready to Invest in Large Dam: 10-fold Raise in Funding Promised,' *Dawn*, 20 September 2005. The article notes the opposition to the Kalabagh Dam. But it is also pointed out that the present storage capacity in Pakistan is 150 cubic metres per capita as compared with the per capita storage capacity in Australia and in the United States which is 5,000 cubic metres and China which has 2,200 cubic metres.

95. Liaquat Ali Khan, (1895–1951), was educated in Aligarh, Allahabad, Oxford and London and took part in the deliberations before partition. He was a member of the United Provinces Legislative Council, 1926–40, and general secretary o the Muslim League 1936–47. In 1946, he was a member of the interim government as a Muslim member of the cabinet headed by Jawaharlal Nehru. On 14 August 1947, Liaquat Ali became the first prime minister of Pakistan. He was assassinated on 16 October 1951. See Muhammad Reza Kazimi, *Liaquat Ali Khan: His Life and Work* (Karachi: Oxford University Press, 2003).

96. Bashir Qureshi was a member of the Pakistan Civil Service. His valuable assistance for the Lahore Museum renovation was on a voluntary basis.

December 1967

97. Sultan Mohammad Khan was a career member of the Foreign Service serving as ambassador to China and was secretary of the Foreign Ministry during the Yahya regime. He is the author of *Recollections and Reminiscences*, London: Centre of Pakistan Studies, 1997.

98. Mirza Nurul Huda, (1919–91), was an educator, civil servant and economist. He was the son-in-law of Maulvi Tamizuddin Khan (d.1963), speaker of the first Constituent Assembly. He was finance minister of East Pakistan, 1965–9, and was briefly governor in 1969. He was a member of the Muslim League and participated in the roundtable conference held by Ayub. Nurul Huda returned to teaching during the regime of Mujibur Rahman but became finance

and planning minister of Bangladesh during the government of Ziaur Rahman, 1975–80. He served as vice president briefly in the Abdus Sattar government in 1982.

99. Qazi Mohammad Qadir, (1913–2002), was an office-bearer in the East Pakistan Muslim League and was Minister of Food, Agriculture, Fisheries and Cooperation, 1962–5, in East Pakistan. He remained in Bangladesh after independence and was elected to the Bangladesh Parliament as a Muslim League candidate in 1978. He was president of the Bangladesh Muslim League, 1982–2002.

100. The book to which Ayub refers is Raghu Pati Kapur's, *Revolution and Dictatorship?* (Delhi: R.K. Printers, 1967).

101. Mashiur Rehman, (1928–79), began his career as a member of the Muslim League, but in 1957 joined the National Awami Party founded by Maulana Abdul Hamid Khan Bhashani who had withdrawn from the Awami League that year. Mashiur Rehman was elected to the National Assembly in 1965, but resigned in 1969. During 1971, he left for India and opposed the Bangladesh movement. Returning to Bangladesh he was jailed. After the death of Bhashani, he became president of the National Awami Party in 1977. However, he left the party and joined the Bangladesh Nationalist Party led by Ziaur Rahman and became a senior minister in the Zia cabinet. In 1979, he was returned to Parliament and was expected to become prime minister. He died suddenly and Shah Azizur Rahman was named prime minister.

102. For a history of the Farakka Barrage dispute see Ben Cook, *Sharing the Ganges* (New Delhi: Sage, 1995). A treaty between Bangladesh and India on the sharing of the waters was signed on 12 December 1996 for a term of thirty years. However, differences between Bangladesh and India over water sharing have not abated.

103. Nur Ahmad Etamadi, (1921–78), was prime minister of Afghanistan, 1967–71. He was executed in 1978 by the new government led by Noor Mohammad Taraki.

104. Sardar Mohammad Daud Khan, (1909–78), was a cousin of King Mohammad Zahir Shah who was deposed by him in 1973. Daud was subsequently deposed and killed by the army in 1978. Afghanistan then came under the control of the Marxist government of Noor Mohammad Taraki. See Ralph H. Magnus and Eden Naby, *Afghanistan: Mullah, Marx and Mujahid* (Boulder, Colorado: Westview Press, 2002).

DIARY 1968

January 1968

1. The present Pir of Zakori Sharif, Dr Mohammad Khalid Raza, is a senior vice president of the Pakistan Muslim League and also president of the Ittehad-ul-Ulama-wa-Mashaikh Pakistan. His seat is in Dera Ismail Khan. The pir has referred to his predecessor as 'one of the closest friends of the Quaid-i-Azam.' A statement by the present pir in the Jang newspaper on 6 August 2005 reads, '... the present difference between the Islamic World and the West, is due to lack of understanding. This lack of understanding on the part of Muslims is due to scarcity of education, while the lack of understanding on the part of the West is due to lack of knowledge about the true teachings of Islam.' The pir is of the Brelvi school of thought.

2. The Tashkent Declaration was signed by Ayub Khan for Pakistan and Lal Bahadur Shastri for India on 10 January 1966 in the capital of Uzbekistan where the two leaders had been invited by Aleksei Kosygin, the Soviet Prime Minister. Kosygin acted as a mediator between the two states. Ayub was opposed by the then foreign minister, Zulfiqar Ali Bhutto. Despite Bhutto's opposition, Ayub joined Shastri in signing the document. The two countries agreed to withdraw their troops to the boundaries existing before the conflict. The usual clause to work toward the peaceful settlement of their disputes was agreed to, a clause that has had no positive effect.

3. Economic Committee of the National Economic Council.

4. An air base at Peshawar used by the United States Air Force. Ayub Khan had allowed the CIA to establish a massive electronic intelligence-gathering facility at Badaber, near Peshawar, in 1963. The United States used that site to monitor nuclear tests and other events in the Soviet Union and China until 1968, when Ayub Khan succumbed to Soviet pressure and closed the base. Among its uses was that by the U-2 spy aircraft. One of the aircrafts piloted by Gary Powers was shot down by the Soviets. Powers was rescued and eventually returned to the United States. See Michael Beschloss, *May Day: Eisenhower, Khrushchev, and the U-2 Affair*, New York: Harper and Row, 1986.

5. Nirad Chaudhuri, (1897–1999), wrote in both English and Bengali, although his best known works are in English. His most noted work is *Autobiography of an Unknown Indian* (New York: Macmillan, 1951) of which several editions have been published. Among his other works is *Continent of Circe, Being an Essay on the Peoples of India* (New York: Oxford University Press, 1966).

April 1968

6. See Diary 1968, note 26.

7. Sudhir Ghosh, (1916–67), was a member of the Rajya Sabha, 1960–6. His book is titled *Gandhi's Emissary* (Boston: Houghton Mills, 1967).

May 1968

8. J. William Fulbright, *Arrogance of Power* (New York: Random House, 1967).

9. The region called Iraq-El-Ajam was the area ruled by Media (Medes) in ancient times and later was the Umayyad and Abbasid province of Jubal. The term is translated 'foreign Iraq,' now modern northwestern Iran.

10. Rashtriya Swayamsevak Sangh (RSS), (lit: National Voluntary Service), was founded in 1925 by Keshav Baliram Hedgewar, (1889–1940), to inculcate Hindu ideas into the minds of Hindu male youth, although those who joined when young often continued membership of it when they were older. Hedgewar's successor and the best known leader was 'Guruji' Madhav Sadashiv Golwalkar (1906–73). The RSS was the precursor to the Bharatiya Jana Sangh. See Walter K. Andersen and Shirdar D. Damle, *The Brotherhood in Saffron: The Rashtriya Swayamsevak Sangh and Hindu Revivalism* (Boulder, Colo.: Westview Press, 1977).

11. The Hindu Mahasabha was founded in 1915 to propagate Hindu ideas in the politics of India under the leadership of Vinayak Damodar Savarkar, (1883–1966). It operated mainly in Bengal. Here it campaigned to preserve the unity of Bengal. It has no significant following currently. See Joya Chatterji, *Bengal Divided: Hindu Communalism and Partition, 1932–1947* (New York: Cambridge University Press, 1994).

12. Bharatiya Jana Sangh has been known as the Bharatiya Janata Party since 1980. The party was founded in 1951 under the leadership of Shyama Prasad Mukherjee (1901–53). He was a member, as part of the Hindu Mahasabha, of the first cabinet led by Jawaharlal Nehru in 1947. Such strength as the party had in the early period was concentrated in north and western India, but in the 1990s gained additional strength. Atal Bihari Vajpayee was prime minister of India, 1998–2004, heading a coalition in which the dominant party was the Bharatiya Janata Party. See Craig Baxter, *Jan Sangh: a Biography of an Indian Party* (Philadelphia: University of Pennsylvania, 1969), and G.D. Graham, *Nationalism and Indian Politics: The Origins and Development of the Bharatiya Jan Sangh* (Cambridge: Cambridge University Press, 1990).

13. Documents and works on Ayub Khan use 14 May 1907 as the birth date.

14. Quintin Hogg, Baron Hailsham of St. Marylebone, (1907–2001), was a British politician and often a Conservative member of Parliament and a Tory minister.

June 1968

15. Fazl-e-Akbar served as chief justice from 4 June 1968 to 17 November 1968.

16. Naseem Hussain proposed the formation of the Society for Promotion of Peace in Asia. It is not known whether it was actually established.

July 1968

17. Begum Khudeja G.A. Khan was the founder of the Girl Guides movement in Pakistan in 1947. She was a member of the Punjab Legislature, 1951–5 and was re-elected from the Muslim Women, outer Lahore seat. She served as a deputy minister in the West Pakistan government, 1956–8.

18. Begum Zeenat Fida Hassan served in the Punjab Assembly, 1951–5, as a representative from Rawalpindi City Women's seat.

19. Amjad Ali Chaudhry was killed in 1971. ·

20. Akhtar Hameed Khan, (1914–99), resigned from the prestigious Indian Civil Service in 1945 to devote himself to the uplift of the poor. In 1950, he migrated to Pakistan and was appointed as the principal of Victoria College, East Bengal, where he served until 1958. In 1960, he became the director of what is now called the Bangladesh Academy of Rural Development at Comilla, where he remained for eleven years. In the 1970s he served in the Peshawar Rural Development Academy (PRDA). In April 1980, he initiated an urban development project, the Orangi Pilot Project in Karachi, and served as its director. He was a recipient of the Magsaysay Award, the Sitara-i-Pakistan and the Hilal-i-Imtiaz. During the last years of his life, he continued to work on the extension of his community development model to a number of different areas in Pakistan.

21. Shaista Suhrawardy Ikramullah (1915–2000) was the daughter of Dr Sir Hasan Suhrawardy (1884–1946), a prominent physician. Sir Hasan had also served as the vice chancellor of Calcutta University and as a member of the legislative

bodies in Bengal and at the centre. She was the niece of Huseyn Shaheed Suhrawardy (1893–1963), an important political leader and prime minister of Pakistan (1956–7). She earned a Ph.D. from London University. She married M. Ikramullah, who later became the foreign secretary of Pakistan. Her youngest daughter, Sarvath, married Prince Hassan bin Talal of Jordan, a brother of the late King Hussein and the uncle of the present king, Abdullah II. Her eldest daughter, eminent human rights activist Barrister Salma Sobhan (d.2003), married Rehman Sobhan, a noted (then Pakistani and now Bangladeshi) economist. Shaista Ikramullah was the first woman in the Pakistan Constituent Assembly (joined later by Begum Jahanara Shah Nawaz). She served as ambassador to Morocco and as a delegate to the United Nations. Among her books were *From Purdah to Parliament* (Karachi: Oxford University Press, 1998, revised edition) and *Huseyn Shaheed Suhrawardy* (Karachi: Oxford University, 1991). She died in Karachi at the age of 85.

22. Philip J. Noel-Baker was awarded the Nobel Prize for Peace in 1959.
23. Paul VI.

August 1968
24. Pakistan Institute of Nuclear Science and Technology.
25. Khan Abdus Salam Khan Achakzai, (1907–73), is sometimes referred as the 'Baloch Gandhi.' although he was a Pathan from the region north of Quetta. He worked for the independence of Balochistan and when this was unattainable his goal was a major role in Pakistan for the Pathans in Balochistan. He opposed one-unit. He was a member of the National Awami Party until 1969 when he formed the Pakhtoonwada National Awami Party. He was elected to the Balochistan Legislative Assembly in 1970. He was assassinated on 2 December 1973.
26. Mahbubul Haq, (1934–98), was a distinguished economist who played a major role as planner in Pakistan as well as internationally. He was noted for his book *The Strategy of Economic Planning: A Case Study of Pakistan* (Karachi: Oxford University Press, 1963). He also identified the twenty-two families that especially benefited during the Ayub period. Haq was in the World Bank, 1968–81, devoting his work to the alleviation of poverty. He was finance minister during the presidency of Ziaul Haq, and then joined the United Nations Development Programme. While there he initiated the annual *Human Development Report* that is still published.
27. In the Agartala Conspiracy case thirty-five individuals, including Mujibur Rahman, were accused of 'plotting to deprive Pakistan of its sovereignty over a part of its territory by an armed revolt with weapons, ammunitions and funds provided by India.' It was alleged by the Pakistan government, in an announcement on 2 January 1968, that the plot was hatched in Agartala, the capital of the Indian state Tripura. It was alleged that an officer of the Indian High Commission in Dhaka was involved. As stated in the following note, the trial was never completed as the charges were dropped when Ayub resigned the presidency and martial law was imposed by Yahya Khan.
28. Sheikh Manzur Qadir, (1913–74), was a leading lawyer and served as foreign minister in the first Ayub ministry, 1958–62. He was the chairman of the committee for drafting the constitution of 1962 and served as chief justice of the West Pakistan High Court, 1962–3. Manzur Qadir led the government's case against Sheikh Mujibur Rahman in the Agartala conspiracy case in 1969, a case that was defaulted when Ayub resigned the presidency. He was the son of Sheikh Sir Abdul Rahim, (1874–1950), who was a minister in the Punjab Legislative Council and later a member of the Council of State. 1934–7. Sir Abdul Rahim was a close associate of Mian Sir Fazl-i-Hussain. Manzur Qadir was married to a daughter of Sir Fazl-i-Hussain.

September 1968
29. The Library of Congress catalogue does not list a book by P.T. Lenine.
30. Aga Khan III (Sir Muhammad Sultan Khan, 1877–1957) was the spiritual leader of the Nizari Ismaili sect of Shia Muslims. He was the head of the Muslim delegation to Lord Minto in 1906 and was a founder of the Muslim League earlier that year. He served several terms as the president of the Muslim League. The Aga Khan was leader of the Indian delegation to the League of Nations and was president of the League in 1937. He had the status of an Indian prince although he ruled no territory. See the Aga Khan's memoirs: *World Enough and Time* (New York: Simon and Schuster, 1954). See also Ghulam Ali Allana, *His Highness Aga Khan III, a Brief Survey of His Life and Work* (Karachi: Hamdard National Foundation, 1973). He had two sons, Prince Aly Khan (1911–60) and Prince Sadruddin Khan (q.v.). Aga Khan III was succeeded by his grandson, son of Aly Khan, Prince Karim (b.1936). Prince Karim, i.e. Aga Khan IV heads the Aga Khan Development Network and associated agencies. Much of this work is centred in the Northern Areas and the North West Frontier Province.
31. Nawab Salimullah of Dhaka, (1866–1915), was one of the founders of the Muslim League in 1906 and his palace, Ahsan Manzil, is where the founding session was held. He was also a founder of Dhaka University.

32. Wahiduzzaman, (1912–76), was a successful businessman. He entered politics in association with Abul Kasem Fazlul Haq and was elected to the Bengal Legislative Assembly in 1942. After independence, he joined the Muslim League and was a member of the Constituent Assembly, 1951–5. He was minister of commerce in the Ayub cabinet, 1962–5. He left the Muslim League in 1969 and campaigned for the restoration of democracy.

33. Fakir Abdul Mannan, (1901–94), seems not to have had further activity in politics. His son, Brigadier (retired) Abdul Hannan Shah, was minister of jute in the first cabinet of Khaleda Zia, 1991–6.

34. Maulana Muhammad Akram Khan, (1870–1968), was a founding member of the Muslim League in 1906. He founded the daily *Azad* in 1936 that was a firm supporter of the Muslim League. Akram Khan served as the president of the provincial Muslim League and as vice president of the central Muslim League. He was given Pride of Performance in Literature award by the Government of Pakistan. He disapproved of the movement for a confederation for Pakistan and opposed even more firmly independence for what was East Pakistan at the time of his death in 1968. The newspaper took this view as well.

35. Abul Hashim (referred to as Hashimuddin in the diary, 1905–74) was a member of the Bengal Legislative Assembly, 1937–47. He joined the Muslim League in 1937 and was a general secretary of the League in Bengal. He remained in India till 1950 during which time he was the leader of the opposition in West Bengal. In East Pakistan, he became president of the language movement for Bengali, and general secretary of the East Pakistan Muslim League. He was the first director of the Islamic Academy in Dhaka. His son Badruddin Umar, has written a number of books on Bengal from a leftist point of view. In English he wrote *The Emergence of Bangladesh: Class Struggles in East Pakistan (1947–1958)* (Karachi: Oxford University Press, 2004) and *Emergence of Bangladesh, Vol. 2: The Rise of Bengali Nationalism (1958–1971)* (Karachi: Oxford University Press, 2006).

36. The last name was spelled Siddiky in court documents and by the Red Cross (see Diary 1971, note 14).

37. Qammar-ud-Din Ahmad-ud-Din, (1912–82), is most often known as Kamruddin Ahmad, the form of his name used when he was writing. He was a lawyer and, as Ayub notes, he was ambassador to Burma, 1958–61. Ahmed was a member of the Muslim League, but then joined the Awami League in 1954 and was associated with Huseyn Shaheed Suhrawardy. He was a founder of an organization now called the Bangladesh Institute of Law and International Affairs (BILIA). The headquarters of BILIA is in the former home of Suhrawardy in Dhaka. Kamruddin Ahmad's major work is *A Social History of Bengal* (Dhaka: Progoti Publications, 1970).

38. The report by Hamood-ur-Rahman was a survey of education. His better known report was on the conduct of the 1971 war that resulted in the creation of Bangladesh.

39. Khwaja Hasan Askari, (1921–84), was the last Nawab of Dhaka during the Pakistan period. He was the eldest son of Nawab Khwaja Habibullah. He was an officer in the British Indian Army serving in Burma during the Second World War and remained in the Pakistan army until 1961. Askari became a member of the Pakistan National Assembly in 1962 and later became communication minister of East Pakistan. He opposed the independence of Bangladesh and remained in Pakistan until his death.

40. Kazi Nazrul Islam, (1899–1976), was a Bengali poet, dramatist and journalist. He served in the British Indian Army in the First World War and used his experiences to express his opposition to the British occupation of India. He wrote mainly from 1919 to 1941. His political views were very much to the left. Islam was a co-founder of the Bengal Workers and Peasants Party that was later absorbed into the Communist Party. He lived in Calcutta but moved to Dhaka at the end of his life where he is buried. Although Nazrul Islam held many views that might be considered left leaning, he was also a close friend and associate of Rabindranath Tagore. (It might also be noted that Tagore wrote the poetry that became the national anthems of both India and Bangladesh.)

October 1968

41. Shah Waliullah, (1702–63), flourished as the Mughal empire began to decline. He wrote on Islamic subjects in an effort to revive the Mughals, but his work was hindered by the rise of the Sikhs. He is said to have been the first person to have translated the Quran into Persian. See Saeeda Iqbal, *Islam Nationalism in the Sub-continent with Special Reference to Shah Waliullah, Sayyid Ahmad Khan and Allama Muhammad Iqbal,* (Lahore: Islamic Book Service, 1984).

42. Giuseppe Tucci (1894–1984).

43. Maulana Abdul Rashid Tarkabagish, (d. 1986), was a prominent member of the Muslim League, but opposed the League's stance on East Pakistan and joined the Awami League. He became president of the East Pakistan Awami League in 1957. He relinquished the presidency to Mujibur Rahman in 1963. In 1976, Tarkabashi formed the Gana Azad League (People's Freedom League) that attracted little attention.

44. Agha Hilaly, (1911–2001), was born in Bangalore. He entered the Indian Civil Service. During the conflict between West and East Pakistan in 1971, Hilaly was ambassador to the United States. Among other diplomatic assignments, he was High Commissioner to New Delhi. He was the elder brother of Agha Shahi.

45. The Nawab of Junagadh, (1922–89), Nawab Muhammad Dilawar Khanji, was the son of the previous nawab, Sir Muhammad Mahabat Khanji (d.1959), who was the ruler of the state in 1947. Junagadh was one of three princely states ruled by Muslims (the others were Hyderabad and Manavadar). It, as well as Manavadar, was located in the area that was to become Indian (in the current state of Gujarat). It was inhabited by a substantial majority of Hindus. The Nawab acceded to Pakistan. A rising of the Hindu residents, abetted by India, succeeded in driving away the Nawab along with his family and retainers from Junagadh. His *diwan* (prime minister) Sir Shahnawaz Bhutto (father of Zulfiqar Ali Bhutto) also left with him on 24 October 1947. Nawab Muhammad Dilawar Khanji served as governor of Sindh, 1976–7. He was appointed governor by Zulfiqar Ali Bhutto.

46. Kazi Anwar-ul-Haq, (1909–2001), was an officer of the Indian Police Service, becoming inspector general in 1959 and then chief secretary of East Pakistan in 1961. He served as a member of the cabinet of Ayub, 1965–9. After the independence of Bangladesh he served in the cabinets of Abu Sadat Muhammad Sayem, Ziaur Rahman and Abdus Sattar.

November 1968

47. Air Marshal Muhammad Asghar Khan, (b.1921), served as the first Pakistani Commander-in-Chief of the Pakistan Air Force, from 1957 until leaving that post following the 1965 India–Pakistan war. He served as the head of Pakistan International Airlines. On entering politics, Asghar Khan was active in the deposition of Ayub in 1969. He contested and lost in the 1970 election, and was also defeated in 1977, although he aided in the organization of the Pakistan National Alliance in opposition to Zulfiqar Ali Bhutto. Asghar's opposition, along with others, led to the fall of Bhutto and the assumption of power by General Ziaul Haq on 5 July 1977. After Zia's assumption in 1977, Asghar Khan remained associated with the opposition and spent some time under house arrest. He formed the Tehrik-i-Istiqlal which was part of the Movement for Restoration of Democracy. The Movement was ineffectual. Following the death of Zia in an aircraft accident in 1988, politics was highlighted by the contest between the Pakistan People's Party of Benazir Bhutto and the Muslim League led by Nawaz Sharif. Asghar Khan left politics in 1996. He has written several books including *Generals in Politics: Pakistan, 1958-1982* (New Delhi: Vikas, 1983), *Pakistan at the Cross-Roads* (Karachi: Ferozsons, 1969), and *We've Learnt Nothing from History—Pakistan: Politics and Military Power* (Karachi: Oxford University Press, 2004).

December 1968

48. Huseyn Shaheed Suhrawardy, (1893–1963), hailed from a prominent Muslim Bengali family, many of whose members were civil servants, politicians and scientists. After his education at Oxford and in the Inns of Court, he was elected to the Bengal Legislative Council from 1921 to 1936 and the Bengal Legislative Assembly from 1937 until 1947. Suhrawardy served in the cabinets of Fazlul Haq and Khwaja Nazimuddin. He was also deputy mayor of Calcutta (now Kolkata) in addition to service in the Legislative Council and Assembly. His group defeated Nazimuddin in 1946 and he was elected prime minister of Bengal serving until the partition of India in 1947. He was a key organizer of the Awami League. In 1954, Suhrawardy's Awami League and Fazlul Haq's Krishak Sramik Party formed the United Front that severely defeated the Muslim League in East Pakistan. Suhrawardy moved from provincial politics to the national stage, leaving Ataur Rahman Khan (1907–91) in charge of East Pakistan politics. Suhrawardy was a member of the cabinet headed by Mohammad Ali Bogra, 1954–5, and was prime minister, 1956–7. After Ayub declared martial law in 1959, Suhrawardy worked for the restoration of democracy. He died in Beirut on 5 December 1963.

49. Maulana Abdul Hamid Khan Bhashani, (1885–1976), though a Bengali, was a leader of the Muslim League in Assam. After independence he returned to Bengal and was a founder of the Awami League. Although holding the Islamic title *maulana*, he was seen as a left wing politician. Bhashani espoused the cause of the peasants and opposed the elitist politics of many in East Pakistan. He often supported the views of China and was at odds with the West. He broke with Suhrawardy in 1956 as he felt Pakistanis were too close to the United States. He and his associates formed the National Awami Party in 1957. He opposed the signing of the India–Bangladesh Treaty in 1972 by Sheikh Mujibur Rahman.

DIARY 1969

March 1969

1. The usual definition of *hartal* is 'general strike' to put forward grievances that can be political, labour issues and other matters and are directed against the government. *Hartals* are often associated with violence.

2. The Democratic Action Committee (DAC) was formed in December 1968 by a group of eight parties to demand the removal of Ayub's strictures on political activity. Among the demands were the establishment of a federal parliamentary government, the restoration of civil liberties, and the release of Bhutto, Mujibur Rahman, Khan Abdul Wali Khan and others who were detained in prison. Ayub proposed a round table conference between his government and the DAC. The discussions between the parties had not yet begun when Ayub was removed from office on 25 March 1969. It must be noted, however that on 13 March 1969 Ayub had agreed to accept the form of parliamentary government and direct elections rather than through the Basic Democrats. The DAC did not continue when martial law was invoked by Yahya.

3. The text is contained in Altaf Gauhar, *Ayub Khan: Pakistan's First Military Ruler* (Lahore: Sang-e-Meel Publications, 1994), pp. 478–80. Gauhar's account shows that at the time Yahya recorded his speech on 25 March in his response to Ayub's speech on the same day he was accompanied by some civilian officers (not named) and Generals Hameed, Peerzada and Gul Hassan. As the civilians left, Yahya is reported to have said, 'I don't know about you fellows, but I definitely deserve a drink.' See Gauhar, p. 478. The theme of drinking and other activities become a frequent subject of Ayub's diary entries. Yahya abrogated the Constitution of 1962 and declared martial law, with himself as martial law administrator. The National Assembly and the Provincial Assemblies were dissolved. He also announced that elections would be held.

4. Yahya assumed the presidency on 31 March 1969.

April 1969

5. The Awami League demanded 56 per cent seats in the national legislature as the population of East Pakistan was 56 per cent of the total population of Pakistan. The existing seats in the legislature were shared equally between East and West Pakistan.

6. On 23 April 1969, Yahya met members of the opposition: Chaudhary Mohammad Ali of the Nizam-i-Islam Party, Mumtaz Khan Daultana of the Council Muslim League and Nawabzada Nasrullah of his branch of the Awami League. The three then went to Dhaka on 25 April 1969 to meet with Mujibur Rahman of the Awami League, Hamidul Haq Chaudhary of the Krishak Sramik Party and Mashiur Rahman of the National Awami Party (Bhashani was ill at the time). On 1 May 1969, the group met Bhutto of the PPP and on 4 June 1969 met Asghar Khan of the Tehrik-i-Istiqlal Party.

May 1969

7. Major General S.G.M.M. Peerzada, (1918–93), was military secretary to Ayub until 1964. He had a severe heart problem and had to be hospitalized several times due to which Ayub Khan had him sent back to the GHQ. Writing in his diary on 1 December 1969, he said about Peerzada 'he is shallow, hasty and verbose, besides being petty and vindictive.' There are other comments by Ayub on Peerzada in the diary. In Yahya's regime Peerzada was principal staff officer to the president and chief martial law administrator and a member of the Council of Administration (i.e., the cabinet). The appraisal by G.W. Choudhury in *The Last Days of United Pakistan* (London: C. Hurst, 1974) p. 67, 'Both Peerzada and Omer were totally incompetent in handling external problems.' In Ayub's diary 'Omer' is spelled 'Umer.' Umer was a member of the National Security Council.

8. Ghulam Ali Allana was a poet and author. His works include *Quaid-i-Azam Jinnah: The Story of a Nation* (Lahore: Ferozsons, 1967) and *His Highness Aga III: A Brief Survey of Life and Work* (Karachi: Hamdard National Foundation, 1973).

9. The Library of Congress catalogue does not contain a book titled *The History of the Muslims in Bengal*.

10. Chaudhary Shamsur Rahman, *Why Pakistan* (Dacca: Society for Pakistan, 1970).

July 1969

11. Chaudhary Mohammad Ali, (1905–80), was born in Jullundur, Punjab, and educated in Lahore. He entered the Indian Audit and Accounts Service in 1928. He was an adviser to Liaquat Ali Khan when the latter was finance minister in the provisional government. After independence he became secretary general to the government of Pakistan. Mohammad

Ali became finance minister in 1951 and prime minister in 1955, resigning in 1956. During the Ayub period, he was adviser to the National Bank of Pakistan and later chairman of the Pakistan Industrial Credit and Investment Corporation. He resigned in 1962 to become the leader of the Nizam-i-Islam Party which aligned with the Democratic Action Committee in opposition to Ayub. He is author of the book *The Emergence of Pakistan* (New York: Columbia University Press, 1967).

12. Agha Shorish Kashmiri, (1917–75) was a prolific writer in Urdu and a journalist. Many of his items support the anti-Ahmadiya movement. An early book has been heralded as a study of prostitution in Pakistan, especially in Lahore. Only one of his books was translated into English: *India Partitioned: The Other Face of Freedom* (New Delhi: Lotus Collection, 1995, edited by Mushirul Hasan).

13. Malik Ghulam Mohammad, (1895–1956), a Khakazai Pathan from Jullundur, was the first Muslim appointed to the Indian Audit and Accounts Service. He left the government to first become a director of Tata Iron and Steel and later a partner in Mahindra and Mohammad (later Mahindra and Mahindra). After independence, Ghulam Mohammad became finance minister of Pakistan until he was appointed governor general in 1951 succeeding Khwaja Nazimuddin who relinquished the governor generalship and replaced Prime Minister Liaquat Ali who had been assassinated. Ghulam Mohammad retired in 1955 and was succeeded by Iskander Mirza as governor general.

August 1969

14. On 4 August 1969, Yahya Khan appointed a civilian cabinet whose members are listed below:

- Abdul Muttalib Malik, Health, Labour, Family (see Diary 1970, note 26).
- Sardar Abdul Rashid, Home, formerly chief minister of the North West Frontier Province, 1953–5, and chief minister of West Pakistan, 1957–8.
- Abdul Khair Mohammad Hafizuddin, Industries and Natural Resources, former inspector of police in East Pakistan and ambassador to Switzerland.
- Nawab Muzaffar Ali Khan Qizilbash, Finance (see Diary 1967, note 24).
- Mohammad Shamsul Haq, Education, former vice chancellor of Rajshahi University, later foreign minister of Bangladesh.
- Nawabzada Mohammad Sher Ali Khan Pataudi, Information and Broadcasting, retired major general, former high commissioner to Malaysia and ambassador to Yugoslavia and Switzerland.
- Ahsan Haque, Commerce, former ambassador to Indonesia and Romania.
- Mahmud Haroon, Agriculture and Works, added 13 August 1969 [see note 17 below].
- A.R. Cornelius, Law, added 17 September 1969 [see Diary 1967, note 30].
- G.W. Choudhury, Communications, added 8 October 1969 [see Diary 1971, note 5].

15. Syed Shah Mardan Shah, Pir Pagaro VII, (b.1928), heads the Hur (free and brave men) movement. His father, Pir Syed Sabghatullah Pagaro, the sixth pir, led a Hur rebellion against the British in Sindh and was hanged by the British in 1943. The current pir has been quoted as saying that his party (Pakistan Muslim League [Functional]) takes its orders from the GHQ. He states that he plays a role in army recruiting. In 2005, he left the Pakistan Muslim League (Functional) as a mark of opposition to Prime Minister Shaukat Aziz, a former bureaucrat. The name is also spelled Pagara. The seat of the family is at Pir Jo Goth in Khairpur District.

16. The Adamjee group of companies is one of the oldest groups in Pakistan. Adam Dawood founded the business in 1896. His family came from Jetpur in Kathiawar, but did business in Burma and then in Kolkata. After Partition the company operations were relocated in Pakistan, primarily Karachi. Among the important industries was the Adamjee Jute Mills in Narayanganj, East Pakistan. Labour problems often curtailed production, especially in 1954. After Bangladeshi independence, the mill was nationalized and then was closed in 2002. Other industries in which the Adamjees are involved include engineering, insurance and pharmaceuticals. The family also founded the Muslim Commercial Bank. During Bhutto's regime, a number of firms were nationalized including the Muslim Commercial Bank. Also lost to the family was the Adamjee Insurance Company. The family retains extensive industries including sugar and cotton mills.

September 1969

17. Mahmud Abdullah Haroon, (b.1920), was a member of the Sindh and West Pakistan Legislative Assemblies from 1946 to 1958 with a gap between 1953 to 1956. He was elected to the National Assembly in 1965, but resigned to accept a place in the Kalabagh cabinet in West Pakistan. He, along with others, supported an opposition candidate in a contest for a seat in the National Assembly and was asked to resign from the cabinet in 1966. He was asked to resign for helping to defeat Habibullah Paracha for a provincial seat at the behest of the Nawab of Kalabagh. Kalabagh and Paracha had old scores to settle dating to 1932 over money matters in a colliery. Mahmud Haroon was High Commissioner to London, 1968–9. He also served in the cabinets of Yahya and Ziaul Haq. He is the son of Sir Abdullah Haroon (1880–1942) and the brother of Yusuf Haroon (see note 20 below). Sir Abdullah was the founder of the Haroon business enterprises, including the firm that publishes *Dawn* and associated publications. Sir Abdullah also served as a member of the Sindh Legislative Assembly. His wife, Nusrat Khanum (1886–1966) was involved in women's causes. For a recent appreciation of Sir Abdullah see Sharif al Mujahid, 'Abdullah Haroon and his Two-Nation Theory,' *Dawn,* 27 April 2005 and *Haji Sir Abdullah Haroon* by Doulat Haroon Hidayatullah (Karachi: Oxford University Press, 2005).

18. Hamidul Haq Chaudhary, (1903–92), was a lawyer, politician and newspaper owner. He owned the *Pakistan Observer* that was renamed the *Bangladesh Observer* after the independence of Bangladeshi. He was elected to the Bengal legislature in 1937 and 1946, serving after Partition in the Nurul Amin cabinet, 1947–9. He was disqualified in 1949 under the Public and Representative Office Disqualification Act (PRODA). Chaudhary had been elected to the Constituent Assembly in 1946 and was elected again in 1955 despite his disqualification. He was foreign minister in the cabinets of Chaudhary Mohammad Ali and Feroz Khan Noon. He was again barred from politics by Ayub Khan in 1969, but was a member of the Combined Opposition Parties opposing Ayub. He opposed the separation of East Pakistan and lived in Karachi for several years but returned to Dhaka where his properties were restored including the newspaper. See Hamidul Haq Chaudhary, *Memoirs* (Dhaka: Associated Printers, 1989).

19. Chaudhary Rehmat Ali, (1897–1951), while a student at Cambridge University, founded the Pakistan National Movement and proposed a Muslim state in northwest provinces of India. He designated this state 'Pakistan'. The letters in the name stood for Punjab, Afghania (i.e. North West Frontier Province), Sindh and 'tan' applied to Balochistan. He visited Pakistan shortly after independence, but returned to Cambridge where he died.

October 1969

20. Yusuf Haroon, (b.1917), was the son of Haji Sir Abdullah Haroon who built one of the major concentrations of industrial power in pre-independence Sindh and it became one of the largest groups in Pakistan. An important investment is the Herald Group that publishes *Dawn, Herald* and other periodicals. Yusuf was elected to the Central Legislature in 1942 and re-elected in 1946. He had been the president of the Sindh Muslim League and was chief minister of Sindh, 18 February 1949–7 May 1950 and was then named High Commissioner to Australia and New Zealand, a post he held until 1954. Yusuf Haroon was a central minister in the Chundrigar cabinet for a brief period of time in 1957. He was 'EDBOed' but supported his brother, Mahmud Haroon. He was also governor of West Pakistan for a few months, 20 March–1 September 1969. Since 1971, he has lived in New York. See also note 17 above for notes on his father, Sir Abdullah Haroon.

21. The Karakoram (or KKH) highway connects Pakistan and China, passing through the Khunjerab pass (15,750 feet or 4,700 meters). The KKH ends in China at Kashgar, Xinjiang. In Pakistan, the highway passes through Abbottabad, Mansehra, Gilgit and Hunza. The road is about 800 miles (1,300 km) long. It crosses the Indus River and for a distance follows the Hunza River. Air transportation is available from Islamabad to Gilgit, a frequent destination for tourists. The KKH can be best described as an engineering miracle. Lives were lost during the construction and the constant maintenance is a continuing problem.

22. Dur Mohammad Usto (or Osto) was a member of the West Pakistan Assembly, 1962–5, and of the Sindh Assembly, 1972–7. He was Minister of Commerce and Works in the West Pakistan Assembly and Minister for Education in Sindh, 1972–4.

23. Nawab Iftikhar Husain Khan of Mamdot, (1906–69), entered active politics in 1942 following the death of his father, Nawab Sir Shah Nawaz. At that time, Iftikhar became the president of the Punjab Muslim League and a member of the Provincial Assembly. He led a successful campaign to remove the Unionist ministry headed by Sir Khizr Hayat Tiwana at the time of independence in 1947. Mamdot became chief minister in 1947, but there was dissidence in the party and he left the office in 1948. In 1950 he formed the Jinnah Muslim League and a year later renamed the party

the Jinnah Awami League and associated it with the Awami League of Suhrawardy. He was governor of Sindh in 1953. After the formation of the One Unit he joined the Republican Party and became a minister in West Pakistan.

November 1969

24. G.M. Syed (Syed Ghulam Murtaza Shah), (1904–99), believed that Muslim interests could best be served by a loose confederation of Indian states. He and some others opposed the centralizing position taken by Jinnah and the Muslim League. However, Syed became a member of the Muslim League and was a co-sponsor of the 'Pakistan Resolution' in 1940. After independence, he worked in sponsoring moves that put himself on the side of strengthening provincial government, principally in Sindh, but these positions also favoured the other provinces. Syed opposed the One Unit. He spent long periods in jail as a result of the propagation of his views. He referred to Sindh as 'Sindhudesh.' See his English work *Struggle for a New Sind* (Karachi: Sind Observer, 1949).

25. The Shatt-al-Arab, a river course formed by the confluence of the Tigris and Euphrates, serves as the disputed area between Iran and Iraq. Conflict between the two states began in September 1980 when Iraq invaded Iran in an attempt to assert its sovereignty over the waterway. The conflict continued until August 1990 when the two states agreed on joint sovereignty of the waterway.

26. Mir Ghous Bakhsh Bizenjo (d.1989) was a politician who at times was opposed to the government and at other times was with it. At the time of independence and partition he was chief *wazir* of the Khan of Kalat, a ruler who tried to assert independence. Bizenjo advised the khan to agree on accession to Pakistan in a document signed by Jinnah in March 1948. It has been reported that the khan had earlier, before independence, agreed to join India through a letter to Nehru who did not reply. Bizenjo was a member of the National Awami Party through which he gained membership of the National Assembly in 1970. He was appointed by Bhutto as governor of Balochistan, 1972–3.

December 1969

27. Nawab Mohammad Akbar Bugti, (1927–2006), was the chief of the Bugti tribe with his seat in Dera Bugti in the Bugti Hills at the western end of the Sulaiman mountain chain. He was Governor of Balochistan from 14 February to 31 October 1973. The pre-eminent resource in the barren region is the Sui gas field. Gas was discovered in 1950–1. The producing firm is government owned, but the tribe receives royalties from the wells. Frequent disturbances still occur. In January 2005, the region was placed under the command of the Frontier Corps. For reading on Balochistan see Akhtar Husain Siddiqui, *Baluchistan (Pakistan): Its Security, Resources and Development* (Lanham, Maryland: University Press of America, 1998) and Muhammad Usman Hasan, *Baluchistan in Retrospect* (Karachi: Royal Book Co., 2002).

28. Lt. Gen. Gul Hassan Khan, (1921–99), served in Burma during the Second World War. At the time of the Bangladeshi war of independence he was chief of the General Staff and was later appointed Commander-in-Chief of the Army in December 1971 by President Bhutto. This posting was brief and he was asked by Bhutto to resign in March 1972. He was not active in politics or public roles after his resignation. He is the author of *Memoirs of Lt. Gen. Gul Hassan Khan* (Karachi: Oxford University Press, 1993).

29. In the process of the partition of India, the district of Sylhet in the province of Assam was divided through a plebiscite in which the sub-divisions of the district voted separately to determine whether each sub-division would either remain in India or accede to Pakistan. In the result, the sub-divisions of Sylhet, Sunamganj, Moulvi Bazaar and Habiganj chose to join Pakistan. Sir Sa'adullah was the prime minister of Assam.

30. Khan Abdul Wali Khan, (1921–2006), the son of Abdul Ghaffar Khan, followed the Pathan patriotism of his father. He entered politics in 1942 and was associated with the Quit India movement of Gandhi. Wali, Khan along with Ghaffar Khan and his uncle, Dr Khan Sahib, spent long periods in jail for their views. He joined the former National Awami Party (NAP) along with Maulana Bhashani and won several seats in the assemblies of the North West Frontier Province and Balochistan. With the end of Martial Law, the NAP formed short-lived coalition governments in the NWFP and Balochistan. The Zulfiqar Ali Bhutto regime prosecuted Wali Khan and others for standing against the integrity of the state; the Supreme Court upheld this decision. Wali Khan formed the Awami National Party (ANP) in 1986. After the death of Ziaul Haq in 1988, he joined hands with the Pakistan Muslim League headed by Nawaz Sharif. In 1995, Wali Khan turned the presidency of the NAP over to his wife, Nasim Wali Khan. The obituary in *Dawn*, 27 January 2006, gives Wali Khan's age as eighty-nine at the time of his death.

31. Pir Ali Mohammad Rashidi, (1905–87), was born in Sindh and pursued careers in journalism and politics. He was deputy speaker of the Constituent Assembly and later served as ambassador to the Philippines and to the People's

Republic of China. See Pir Ali Mohammad Rashidi, *Sindh: Ways and Days—Shikar and Other Memories* (Karachi: Oxford University Press, 2003).

32. Ghulam Mustafa Jatoi, (b.1934), entered Sindh politics in 1956 as a member of the West Pakistan Assembly. In 1962, he entered the National Assembly. He joined the Convention Muslim League of Ayub Khan, but left with his associate Zulfiqar Ali Bhutto. In 1968, he joined Bhutto's Pakistan People's Party. Jatoi joined the central cabinet in 1971 and was chief minister of Sindh from 25 December 1973 to 5 July 1977. He left the PPP and formed the National People's Party in 1986, which was defeated in the 1988 election. Jatoi was caretaker prime minister following the dismissal of the Benazir Bhutto government from August to December 1990 and was replaced by Nawaz Sharif.

33. Mohammad Yasin Khan Wattoo, (d.2002), was elected to the West Pakistan Assembly in 1963 and was named minister of local government and basic democracies. He was selected for cabinet during the regime of Ziaul Haq and held portfolios of finance and planning, yielding the latter when the ministry was split and Mahbub-ul-Haq became planning minister. He served with Prime Minister Mohammad Khan Junejo, with whom he had worked earlier in the West Pakistan cabinet. Wattoo was killed in an auto crash.

34. General Khalid Mahmud Sheikh, (b.1910), was Home Minister in Ayub's cabinet, 1958–62. He served as minister in several ministries as a concurrent charge. Later he became ambassador to Turkey and then was chairman of the Capital Development Authority, 1967–70.

35. Nasrullah Khattak was chief minister of the North West Frontier Province, 3 May 1975 to 9 December 1977.

36. Sahibzadi Memooda Begum was a member of the Punjab Assembly, 1951–5, from Rawalpindi, Sargodha Division, women's seat.

DIARY 1970

January 1970

1. Santosh in Tangail District served as Bhashani's headquarters.
2. The Valika family controlled a number of concerns principally in the textile industry. The late Fakhruddin Valika was the head of the companies.
3. Sir Ghulam Hussain Hidayatullah, (1879–1948), was the first prime minister of Sindh, (23 April 1937–23 March 1938), following the 1937 elections He served again as prime minister, 14 October 1942–14 August 1947. At independence in 1947, he was appointed governor of Sindh and served until his death on 4 October 1948. His wife, Sughra Begum, (1904–85), was active in Muslim League affairs before and after independence.

February 1970

4. General Mohammad Attiqur Rahman, (1918–96), went to school in England and then joined the Indian Military Academy, Dehra Dun, where he was commissioned in 1940 and joined the Frontier Force Regiment where he saw action in Burma and was awarded the Military Cross. At Independence, he joined the Pakistan Army as Chief Instructor at the Military Academy, Kakul, after which he was given command of his own regiment. During Yahya Khan's martial law, he was appointed Martial Law Administrator and Governor of West Pakistan. After the break-up of one unit, he took over as Governor of Punjab. He retired from the army and as Governor in 1971. In 1977, General Ziaul Haq appointed him Chairman, Federal Public Services Commission (1977–85). His memoirs titled *Back to the Pavilion* were first published by Ardeshir Cowasjee in 1989 and reprinted by Oxford University Press, Pakistan in 2005.

5. Maulvi Farid Ahmed, (1923–71), resigned from government service to support the language movement in 1952 as a member of the Nizam-i-Islam Party. He was elected to the Constituent Assembly in 1955 and to the National Assembly in 1962. As a candidate of the Combined Opposition Parties, he was elected to the National Assembly in 1964. Farid Ahmed joined the movement against Ayub in 1969. He opposed the independence of Bangladesh and as a member of the Peace Committee set up by the Pakistan government he opposed the Mukti Bahini, the force organized to support Bangladesh. He was killed in 1971. He was a staunch opponent of the Ahmadiya movement, as he expressed in his book *The Sun Behind the Clouds* (Dacca: Zaman Kitab Mahal, 1971).

6. See Diary 1967, note 57 for the Six Points as described by the Awami League.

March 1970

7. Amir Abdullah Khan Rokhri was a leading political figure in Mianwali District. He served as a member of the Provincial Assembly and National Assembly and as a senator. He founded a major trucking company called New Khan.

8. Sayed Jamaluddin Afghani, (1838–97), was a noted Islamic scholar. He travelled more extensively in India, the Middle East and Europe than in Afghanistan. In Europe he visited England, France and Russia. He is perhaps best noted for the time he spent in Egypt where he, in association with Egyptians such as Abduh, proposed political reforms. In 1944, his remains were reburied in Kabul. See Nikki R. Keddie, *Sayed Jamaluddin Afghan: A Political Biography* (Berkeley: University of California Press, 1972). Muhammad Abduh (1849–1905) was a jurist, religious scholar and a founder of Islamic modernism. He was exiled from Egypt, 1882–8, but returned to serve as a judge and to propagate his ideas of changes in the medieval Islam as he thought they should be.

9. Sir W.H. Morrice James (Lord St. Brides), (1916–89), recorded his stay in Pakistan as British High Commissioner in *Pakistan Chronicle* (New York: St. Martin's Press, 1993) with Prologue and Concluding Section by Peter Lyon.

10. Shiromani Akali Dal was founded in 1926 to represent the interests of the Sikhs. Those Sikhs in the areas that were colonized by the British in the western portion of the province of Punjab fervently opposed the partition of India. The key leader in this movement was Master Tara Singh (1885–1967). After the partition, the areas occupied by the proposed Punjabi Suba demanded a state and sought the partition of the Indian state of Punjab. That partition on 1 November 1966 created the Punjabi-speaking Punjab and the Hindi-speaking Haryana. A radical wing of the Akali Dal demanded a strict religious regimen for Punjab. This turned violent in a standoff at the Golden Temple in Amritsar in 1984 led by Sant Jarnail Singh Bhindranwale (1947–84). The Indian forces took the Golden Temple by Force and Bhindranwale was killed. The radical Sikhs retaliated and Prime Minister Indira Gandhi was assassinated by two Sikhs who were members of her guard on 31 October 1984. See Kaldeep Kaur, *Akali Dal in Punjab Politics: Splits and Mergers* (New Delhi: Deep and Deep, 1999).

11. Dravida Munnetra Kazhagam (Dravidian Progressive Federation) was founded in 1949 by C.N. Annadurai to represent the interests of the people of the state of Madras, now Tamil Nadu. Annadurai's views were opposed to the 'Hindu chauvinism,' as he described it, of the north and also the domination of the Brahmins in Tamil Nadu. The movement did not constitute a challenge to the unity of India. The party was later divided into the DMK and the Anna DMK. See Robert L. Hardgrave, Jr., *The Nadars of Tamilnadu: Political Culture of a Community in Change*, (Berkeley: University of California Press, 1960).

12. Syed Ghiasuddin Ahmed was described as defence adviser in 1971. Yahya appointed an Emergency Committee on 27 November 1971 of which Ghiasuddin was convener. On the same day, Yahya issued a Proclamation of Emergency and decreed a Defence of Pakistan Ordinance. Ghiasuddin held positions such as food secretary for East Pakistan in 1961.

13. Nazir Ahmad Razvi was a member of the Police Service of Pakistan. He was the head of the Intelligence Bureau. He authored the book *Our Police Heritage: Saga of the Police Services of Pakistan and India* (Lahore: Police Service of Pakistan, 1961).

14. The Legal Framework Order issued on 31 March 1970, contained the following points: (1) Pakistan must be based on Islamic ideology; (2) the country must have a democratic constitution providing free and fair elections; (3) Pakistan's territory must be upheld in the constitution; (4) the disparity between the wings, particularly in economic development, must be eliminated by statutory provisions to be guaranteed by the constitution; (5) the distribution of power must be made in such a way that the provinces enjoy the maximum of autonomy consistent with giving the central government sufficient power to discharge its federal responsibilities, including the maintenance of the country's territorial integrity. Hamid Khan, *Constitutional and Political History of Pakistan* (Karachi: Oxford University Press, 2001), p. 421.

15. Hamid Nizami, (d.1962), founded *Nawa-i-Waqt* in 1940 which became a leading Urdu newspaper. The firm publishes other periodicals including the daily English *The Nation*. Another member of the family, also Hamid, interviewed Ayub.

April 1970

16. The Internet source '*World Statesmen*' lists the governors of the ex-West Provinces as on 1 July 1970: (1) Balochistan: Ghous Bakhsh Raisani, (2) North West Frontier Province, Khwaja Muhammad Azhar Khan, (3) Punjab, Muhammad Attiqur Rahman, (4) Sindh, Rehman Gul. The new provinces were initiated on 1 July 1970. It appears that Ayub entered 'Riaz' rather than 'Raisani' (d.1987), who was governor of Balochistan, 1970–2. However, an article entitled 'How Intelligence Agencies Run Our Politics,' by Altaf Gauhar, in *The Nation*, 18 August 1997, states '...during the 1965 war with India. At that time the Inter-Services Intelligence (ISI) was under Brigadier Riaz Hussain who later became the Governor of Balochistan.'

17. The eleven-point programme was issued by the East Pakistan Students' All-Party Committee of Action on 5 January 1970. In summary, the points were: (1) reorganization of the college and university education system; (2) parliamentary democracy on universal franchise, (3) federal system of government and the federal government limited to defence, foreign affairs and currency; (4) sub-federation of Sindh, Balochistan and the North West Frontier Province; (5) nationalization of most firms; (6) reduction of taxes for peasants; (7) fair wages for workers; (8) flood measures for East Pakistan; (9) withdrawal of emergency and similar orders; (10) withdraw from CENTO, SEATO and US-Pakistan pacts; and (11) release all political prisoners including those accused in the Agartala conspiracy. See also Diary 1967, note 57 for Six Points. CENTO was formed as the Middle East Treaty Organization in 1955 and was often referred to as the Baghdad Pact. The members were Turkey, Iraq, Iran, Pakistan, the United Kingdom and the United States. Iraq withdrew in 1959 and Iran withdrew in 1979. The organization was terminated in 1979. SEATO, also formed in 1955, had a much larger group of members: Australia, France, New Zealand, Pakistan, Philippines, Thailand, the United Kingdom and the United States. Pakistan withdrew in 1968. The organization was disbanded in 1977. A major project funded by SEATO in Pakistan was the International Cholera Research Institute in Dhaka.

18. Pethidine is an opioid analgesic, a pain reducer, most often known as Demorol, although other commercial trade names are also used.

19. Ibn Khaldun (Abdur Rahman Waliuddin Muhammad ibn Khaldun), (1332–1406), was probably the first historian who studied universal history (as well as he understood the then world). He was for a time the principal of Al Azhar University. His works were compiled in *Arab Philosophy of History, Selections from the Prolegomena of Ibn Khaldun,* translated by Charles Issawi (London: Murray, 1950). Also see Franz Rosenthal, editor, *The Muqaddima: An Introduction of History* (Princeton: Princeton University Press, 1967, three volumes). A contemporary of Ibn Khaldun was the geographer and traveller Ibn Battuta (Abu Abdullah Muhammad ibn Battuta) (1304–69). See *Travels in Asia and Africa, 1325–1954,* edited by Sir Hamilton Gibb (London: Routledge and Kegan Paul, 1958).

20. General Wajid Ali Burki, (1899–1989), was a medical officer in the British Indian Army and the Pakistan Army. In 1955, he was appointed director general of the Medical Corps. He joined the cabinet when Ayub took control and had the portfolios of labour and social development in addition to health. Burki served as deputy to Ayub in the cabinet from 1960 to 1963. He was appointed ambassador to Sweden in 1963. After retirement, he devoted his life to medical development including the setting up of the Jinnah Postgraduate Medical College in Karachi.

21. Progressive Papers was founded by Mian Iftikharuddin, (1907–62), who had joined neither the Unionist Party nor the Muslim League but was elected in 1936 on the ticket of the Congress to the Punjab Legislative Assembly. He was jailed, 1942–9, and on his release he joined the Muslim League. He served briefly in the Mamdot cabinet in Punjab after independence. Iftikharuddin founded the English-language *Pakistan Times* and the Urdu *Imroze*. He and his press challenged the policies of the Muslim League and he was expelled from the party in 1951. He founded the Azad Pakistan Party and then merged the party into the National Awami Party led by Maulana Abdul Hamid Bhashani, a left wing politician from East Pakistan (see Diary 1968, note 49). Progressive Papers was dissolved and the two newspapers were nationalized in 1958 under the martial law of Ayub. Among the editors of *Pakistan Times* were Faiz Ahmed Faiz (1911–84), a noted poet who received the Lenin Peace Prize from the Soviet Union, and Mazhar Ali Khan. See Diary 1967, note 38 for entry on Shaukat Hayat Khan for additional information on Mazhar Ali Khan.

22. Ismet Inonu Pasha, (1884–1973), was the principal lieutenant of Mustafa Kamal Ataturk in the revolution in Turkey against the caliph and the establishment of the Turkish republic. Inonu was prime minister of Turkey, 1923–38. On Ataturk's death in 1938, Inonu succeeded him as president and held the office, 1938–50.

May 1970

23. Javid Iqbal, (b.1924), a noted jurist, is the son of Allama Sir Mohammad Iqbal. He was named a judge of the Lahore High Court in 1971 and was chief justice of the Punjab High Court, 1982–6. He became a justice of the Supreme Court of Pakistan in 1986, retiring in 1989. Among his publications are *Concept of the State in Islam* (Lahore: Iqbal Academy, 2000), *Islam and Pakistan's Identity* (Lahore: Vanguard Books, 2003), and *Encounters with Destiny: Autobiographical Reflections—A Translation of Apna Grebaan Chaak* (Karachi: Oxford University Press, 2006).

24. A.Z.M. Obaidullah, (d.2001), a son of Abdul Jabbar Khan, was a member of the Civil Service of Pakistan and after 1971 served in Bangladesh. He was minister of agriculture in Bangladesh and was Bangladesh ambassador to the United States.

July 1970

25. Mohammad Aslam Khattak (b.1908) first held office when he was elected to the West Pakistan Assembly in 1962 and 1965 and to the North West Frontier Province Assembly in 1970. He was governor of the province, 15 February 1973 to 24 May 1974. He then served as ambassador to Iran, Iraq and Afghanistan. Khattak was a member of the National Assembly in 1985 and appointed interior minister. He has published *Pathan Odyssey* (Karachi: Oxford University Press, 2004) with a foreword by James W. Spain. He is a half-brother of Lieutenant General Habibullah Khan (see Diary 1966, note 27).

26. Tikka Khan, (1915–2002), joined the Army in 1937. He was the administrator of Martial Law Zone-A, i.e. East Pakistan in 1971 in Yahya's regime. He administered the province during the most violent period of the civil war. He was replaced later in the year (1971) by Abdul Muttalib Malik as governor. Tikka Khan was appointed Chief of the Army Staff in 1972 by Zulfiqar Ali Bhutto and completed his term in 1976. He joined Bhutto's Pakistan People's Party and became the general secretary of the party. He remained in the party during the Ziaul Haq period. Prime Minister Benazir Bhutto appointed him governor of Punjab and he retired when her government was dismissed in 1990.

27. Vengalil Krishnan (V.K.) Krishna Menon, (1897–1974), studied at the London School of Economics and joined the bar from Middle Temple. As a result of his studies he became a socialist, and a member of the Labour Party [UK]. He served in local offices in local government. Menon represented the Congress in London and became Indian High Commissioner in London in 1947. He was a member of the Lok Sabha, 1953–74, and was Minister of Defence, 1957–62.

28. Lal Bahadur Shastri, (1904–66), was born in Mughalsarai, Uttar Pradesh. He abandoned his studies to take part in the non-cooperation movement started by Gandhi in 1921 and began studying philosophy at the nationalist, Kashi Vidyapeeth. In 1926 he was given the title *Shastri* (scholar). Following independence, he held several important posts like minister of police, minister of railways, general secretary of Lok Sabha, minister for transport, and home minister. When Nehru died, Lala Bahadur Shastri emerged as the consensus candidate in the midst of party warfare and was unanimously chosen as the leader of the ruling Congress party. He became prime minister on 9 June 1964. His term is best known for introducing measures to make India self-sufficient in food production. In 1965 Pakistan attacked India on the Kashmir front and Lal Bahadur Shastri responded in kind. In January 1966 Shastri and Pakistani President, Mohammad Ayub Khan, attended a summit in Tashkent organized by the Soviet premier, Kosygin, and signed an agreement known as the Tashkent Declaration which formally brought an end to the 1965 Indo-Pak war. Lal Bahadur passed away in Tashkent before returning home. He was posthumously conferred with the Bharat Ratna Award and a memorial was built for him in Delhi.

August 1970

29. Malik Ghulam Jilani was a member of the civil service. He opposed the move by Ayub Khan to gain control of Pakistan and resigned from the Civil Service. It has been reported that Jilani hosted a dinner honouring Mumtaz Daultana, who opposed Ayub and had been 'EBDOed'. Jilani was imprisoned and allegedly the target of a shooting incident at his Lahore residence. Jilani has two daughters who are lawyers: Asma Jehangir and Hina Jilani, who each specialize in human rights litigation. Asma Jehangir is chairperson of the Human Rights Commission of Pakistan. She was awarded the Magsaysay Award in 1995.

September 1970

30. Sardar Khair Bakhsh Marri was associated with Mengal (see below) in opposition to the concept of a Punjabi-dominated Pakistan. His views are expressed in a chapter in Tariq Ali, *Can Pakistan Survive?* (New York: Penguin, 1983). Marri was elected in 1970 to the National Assembly as a candidate of the National Awami Party.

31. Sardar Ataullah Mengal was a leader of the nationalist and separatist movement in Balochistan and the head of the Mengal tribe. Immediately after the independence of Bangladesh in 1971, Mengal and Khair Bakhsh Marri and their followers rose in revolt against Punjabi dominance in Pakistan. Bhutto used the Air Force and troops to suppress the revolt and Mengal was rewarded by becoming chief minister of Balochistan, 1972–3. Mengal again raised the flag of revolt and was dismissed from his position as chief minister. The demand of the Mengal and Marri tribesmen and some other tribesmen was an independent Balochistan comprising the territories in Pakistan and also in Iran. Mengal took refuge in 1975 in Britain and obtained support from the Soviet Union. See Selig Harrison, *Afghanistan's Shadow: Baloch Nationalism and Soviet Temptations* (Washington: Carnegie Endowment for International Peace, 1991).

32. Nabi Bakhsh Zehri was a marble quarry owning entrepreneur in Balochistan. He had supported regimes in Islamabad probably in return for favourable consideration of applications for quarrying licenses. See Harrison, op. cit., pp. 163–4.

October 1970

33. Maj. Gen. Ghulam Umer was secretary, National Security Division in 1971.

December 1970

34. Ataur Rahman Khan, (1907–91), was an original member of the Awami League. He acted as president of the East Pakistan Awami League for several terms when Bhashani was jailed. When the Awami League joined the Krishak Praja Party in the United Front, Ataur Rahman served as chief minister of East Pakistan during most of the period from 1956 to 1958. After the death of Huseyn Shaheed Suhrawardy in 1963, Ataur Rahman and Mujibur Rahman contested for the leadership of the Awami League resulting in him forming the Pakistan (later Bangladesh) National League. Ataur Rahman and his party were shut out in the 1970 elections. He won a seat in the 1973 election and became leader of the opposition. He was prime minister in the Ershad government, 1984–5.

35. The Lahore Resolution was passed 23 March 1940. It is often called the Pakistan Resolution although the word Pakistan is not in the resolution. The resolution stated that if the conditions of the Muslims in India did not improve, the Muslim League would call for independent *states* in the eastern and north-western areas of India. In 1946, the Muslim League modified the call to that for a single state comprising the eastern and north-western areas. The Cabinet Plan proposed in 1946 by three British ministers led by Sir Stafford Cripps called for a 'three tier' government: a central government, three zonal governments and the provincial governments. The zonal areas were to be essentially the same as those envisaged in the Lahore Resolution. The Cabinet Plan was accepted by the Muslim League in essence, but rejected by the Indian National Congress notably by Nehru in what has been described his 'unfettered' speech in which he declared that India would not be bound (i.e., fettered) by statements by the British. Nehru was criticized by the leading Congress member Maulana Abul Kalam Azad (1888–1958) for failure to consider it as the Cripps plan might have provided a chance, however slim, to keep India united. Azad expressed these views in his book *India Wins Freedom* (Bombay: Orient Longmans, 1959).

36. The official results of the National Assembly were:

East Pakistan:	Awami League 160, Pakistan Democratic Party 1, Independent 1	Total 162
Punjab:	Pakistan People's Party 62, Council Muslim League 7, Jamiat-i-Ulema-i-Islam 4, Convention Muslim League 2, Pakistan Muslim League (Qayyum) 1, Jamaat-e-Islam 1, Independents 5	Total 82
Sindh:	Pakistan Peoples Party 18, Jamiat-i-Ulema-i-Islam 3, Jamaat-e-Islam 2, Pakistan Muslim League (Qayyum) 1, Independents 3	Total 27
North West Frontier Province:	Pakistan Muslim League (Qayyum) 7, Jamiat-i-Ulema-i-Islam 6, National Awami Party 3, Pakistan People's Party 1, Jamaat-e-Islam 1, Independents 7	Total 25
Balochistan:	National Awami Party 3, Jamiat-i-Ulema-i-Pakistan 1	Total 4

37. Most observers maintained that Bhashani had little or no influence in the outcome of the election in East Pakistan. See Craig Baxter, 'Pakistan Votes—1970,' *Asian Survey*, XI:3 (March 1971), pp. 197–218; David Dunbar (pseudonym), 'Pakistan: The Failure of Political Negotiations', *Asian Survey*, XII:5 (May 1972), pp. 444–61; and Robert LaPorte, 'Pakistan in 1971: The Disintegration of a Nation,' *Asian Survey*, XII:2 (February 1972), pp. 221–30.

38. The Rawalpindi Conspiracy was formulated in 1951 among senior officers with the goal to dismiss the government of Liaquat Ali Khan and replace this by a cabal of senior officers. Some civilians who had left wing political views were a part of the conspiracy such as Faiz Ahmed Faiz, the renowned poet and journalist, and Syed Sajjad Zaheer, a member of the Communist Party (one of Sajjad's brothers, Syed Ali Zaheer, was a member of the interim cabinet headed by Jawaharlal Nehru before independence and served in the cabinet of Uttar Pradesh). The principal conspirator was Major General Akbar (Diary 1967, note 20) and a key person was a major named Ishaq. Many were sentenced to prison terms; most were released in 1955. Faiz (1911–84) had been the editor of the *Pakistan Times* when the paper was founded (see Diary 1970, note 21 for entry on Progressive Papers). Sajjad was permitted by Nehru to move to India, where his brothers, including Ali, lived. This was an exception to the Indian rule that those Muslims from India who

chose Pakistan at the time of Partition were not allowed to move back to India. See Hasan Zaheer, *Times and Trial of the Rawalpindi Conspiracy, 1951: The Coup Attempt in Pakistan* (Karachi: Oxford University Press, 1998).

39. J.A. Rahim, (1900–87), served successively in the Indian Civil Service, the Pakistan Civil Service, and the Pakistan Foreign Service, in the last as foreign secretary. He worked with Zulfiqar Ali Bhutto when the latter was foreign minister in Ayub's government, 1963–6. Rahim left the Foreign Service in 1967. He was among the founding members of the Pakistan People's Party and it's secretary general. He was minister of production in Bhutto's cabinet in 1972, but was dismissed in 1974 when, in Rahim's view, Bhutto moved the party to the right.

40. Mubashir Hasan, (b.1920), was an engineer by training but a politician by avocation. He was a key founder of the Pakistan People's Party and was the principal drafter of the party's Foundation Papers. He was named minister of finance in 1970 and contributed to the programme of nationalization of industries and banks. He introduced a labour policy to the benefit of industrial workers. These steps angered many and led Bhutto to drop him from the ministry in 1974. He did not play a major role thereafter. His departure decreased the ideological base of the party's policies.

41. Rasul Bakhsh Palejo, from Sindh, was a close associate of Bhutto in the Pakistan People's Party. He left that party and joined the Awami National Party and led a faction of that party called the Sindhi Awami Tehrik.

42. Raja George Sikandar Zaman Khan was acting chief minister of the Frontier, 12 November 1996–21 February 1997.

DIARY 1971

January 1971

1. Chakravarti Rajagopalachari, (1879–1972), was the first and only Indian to hold the post of governor general, 1948–50 (his successor, Rajendra Prasad, became president). Rajagopalachari was prime minister of Madras, 1937–9 and chief minister, 1947–8. He and his followers opposed Nehru and created the Swantantra Party, a party of the right centre. Rajaji, as he was known, wrote extensively, including for children's accounts of the *Mahabharata* and *Ramayana*.

2. Nawabzada Nasrullah Khan, (1922–2003), was a member of the Majlis-i-Ahrar, but joined the Awami League after its formation. He left the party when Mujibur Rahman put forward the programme of autonomy for East Pakistan. Nasrullah Khan opposed what he called the rule of the military and was a member of the Combined Opposition Party that fought Ayub in the 1964 presidential election. He cooperated with Zulfiqar Bhutto in supporting the constitution of 1973, but withdrew when he saw that Bhutto, in his opinion, had rigged the 1977 election. He opposed the military regime of Ziaul Haq, but supported Benazir Bhutto in 1993.

3. Ayub apparently meant Mahmud of Ghazni, (971–1030), who led the Muslim forces into north-east Iran and north-western India from his small base in Afghanistan in a series of battles against Hindu rulers based in Punjab and the area of Delhi. The Hindu Jaipal ruler was defeated in a battle near modern Peshawar. Mahmud's raids gained extensive treasures from Hindu temples, most notably from Somnath in Gujarat. However, he also supported the arts and literature. In his reign the Persian poet Ferdausi composed the *Shahnameh*. Nonetheless, to the Hindus, Mahmud was seen as a conqueror. See S.M. Ikram and Percival Spear, *The Cultural Heritage of Pakistan* (New York: Oxford University Press, 1955).

4. General Khwaja Muhammad Azhar Khan was governor 1 July 1970 to 25 December 1971.

5. G.W. (Golam Wahid) Choudhury, (1926–97), was a professor at Dhaka University and a noted scholar. He was appointed during Yahya's regime to be head of the research division of the Ministry of Foreign Affairs and was made a minister in the cabinet concerned principally with constitutional developments. His experiences in the role are described in his book *The Last Days of United Pakistan* (Bloomington: Indiana University Press, 1974). After the conflict, he taught at North Carolina Central University and later retired and lived in Dhaka.

February 1971

6. The term *musawat* is translated as 'equality.'

7. Sardar Mohammad Ibrahim Khan, (1915–2003), was a leader in the Muslim Conference with others including Sheikh Mohammad Abdullah before independence. He was from Poonch. He authored *Kashmir Saga* (Mirpur, Kashmir: Verinag, 1990, second edition).

8. K.H. Khurshid, (1924–88), was Jinnah's secretary from 1942 until Jinnah's death. He wrote *Memories of Jinnah* (Karachi: Oxford University Press, 1990). Khurshid was president of Azad Jammu and Kashmir, 1949–75, when he was dismissed by the Bhutto government of Pakistan.

9. A.H.M. Kamaruzzaman, (1926–75), served in the first provisional cabinet in Bangladesh and served in the Mujib cabinet as commerce minister. He was killed in the Dhaka jail killings.

10. Maulana Ghulam Ghaus Hazarvi, (d.1981), was a leader of the Jamiat-ul-Ulema-i-Islam (JUI). The party split in 1969 as Hazarvi led the leftist faction and the bulk of the party continued under the leadership of Mufti Mahmood. The Hazarvi faction merged with the Pakistan People's Party in 1977.

March 1971

11. Muzafar Ahmed, (d.1972), was the leader of the pro-Soviet wing of the National Awami Party. Very early on, after independence of Bangladesh, he proposed that new elections be held. He maintained that the circumstances of the 1970 election meant that independence should be confirmed through a new election in Bangladesh.

12. Sahibzada Yaqub Khan, (b.1920), was born in the United Provinces (Uttar Pradesh) as a member of the royal family of Rampur and joined the British Indian Army. He then opted to enter the Pakistan Army and followed a successful career. On 2 March 1971 he was appointed governor of East Pakistan and commander of Pakistan's forces in the province. He did not believe that force was the means to settle the issue of East Pakistan and resigned shortly after taking up his East Pakistan military assignment. He was replaced by General Tikka Khan on 7 March 1971, but remained as governor until November 1971. He was appointed ambassador to the United States by Ziaul Haq and was later named foreign minister, 1982–7, and remained in the position when Benazir Bhutto became prime minister. Yaqub Khan retained the post of foreign minister (1988–91) during the caretaker administration that followed Benazir Bhutto's first dismissal. He was again nominated foreign minister, 1996–7 during Benazir's second term. He also served as ambassador to France and the Soviet Union. He wrote *Strategy, Diplomacy, Humanity* (Islamabad: International Forum, Takshila Research University, 2005).

13. Mustafa Khar, (b.1932), was a founding member of the Pakistan People's Party. He served Bhutto as governor of Punjab, December 1971–February 1973 and briefly in March 1975–July 1975. He joined the Pakistan Muslim League as senior vice president after Bhutto's execution. He was a minister in Benazir Bhutto's government in 1993.

14. The chief justice who refused to administer oath to Tikka Khan was Badruddin Ahmad Siddiky (1915–91). He was appointed chief justice of East Pakistan on 16 November 1967 and served until the independence of Bangladesh. Siddiky continued as chief justice of Bangladesh after independence. He was also president of the Red Cross of Pakistan and later of Bangladesh. The Bangladesh unit was renamed Bangladesh Red Crescent in 1984. He was the permanent representative of Bangladesh at the United Nations, 1986–8. In some documents his last name is spelled Siddiqui.

15. *Purba* means 'east'.

16. The operation (Operation Searchlight) of the Pakistan Army in East Pakistan began on the evening of 25 March 1971. Indian troops moved into East Pakistan on 16 November to join the Mukti Bahini (Liberation Army). On 16 December, the Pakistan Army surrendered to Lt. Gen. Jagjit Singh Aurora, the commander of the Indian forces.

Four books in particular, among many others, detail the events that led to the division of Pakistan: Hasan Zaheer, *The Separation of East Pakistan: The Rise and Realization of Bengali Muslim Nationalism* (Karachi: Oxford University Press, 1994); G.W. Choudhury, *The Last Days of United Pakistan* (Bloomington: Indiana University Press, 1975), Siddiq Salik, *Witness to Surrender* (Karachi: Oxford University Press, 1979) and Herbert Feldman, *The End and the Beginning, 1969–1972* (Karachi: Oxford University, 1972).

The United Nations and many states were involved in efforts to end the conflict and some also endeavoured to preserve the unity of Pakistan. The record of the United States has been made available in the relevant volumes on the foreign affairs of the Nixon–Ford Administration that were released in 2005. These documents are recorded in Volume XI: *South Asia Crisis* and Volume E-7: *Documents on South Asia, 1969–1972*. These volumes can be accessed on the Internet: http://www.state.gov/r/pa/frus/nixon/ They can also be purchased from the United States Government Printing Office.

Opinion was not universal on the position taken by the United States government. Differences of opinion were expressed by Foreign Service Officers in both Dhaka and Washington. Although the documents containing these expressions of views were not published in the referenced volumes, they were represented in Archer K. Blood, *The Cruel Birth of Bangladesh: Memoirs of an American Diplomat* (Dhaka: University Press, 2002). Blood was the American consul general in Dhaka. In June 1971, he was replaced by Herbert D. Spivack, who became chargé d'affaires when the United States recognized Bangladesh diplomatically.

17. Bihari is the term used for Urdu-speaking refugees from India at the time of partition, most of them originally from the Indian state of Bihar.

18. Tajuddin Ahmed, (1922–75), was not killed in 1971. He was the head of the provisional government of Bangladesh until the return of Mujibur Rahman. He had worked with Mujib in negotiations with Yahya and held a number of portfolios in the post-independence government led by Mujib. Tajuddin favoured close relations with the Soviet Union, a stance that was not favoured by Mujib who urged close relations with the United States. Tajuddin was one of the four leaders killed in the Dhaka jail murders. No information on Moazzam Ali is available.

19. Tofail Ahmed was a leader of the Bangladesh independence movement in 1971 and then became the political secretary to Mujibur Rahman, 1972–5. He was a minister in the cabinet of Sheikh Hasina Wajid (the daughter of Mujibur Rahman), 1996–2001.

April 1971

20. Major General Abu Bakr Osman Mitha, (1923–99), was a specialist in military intelligence and commanded the Special Forces Group. He was implicated in the failure of the 1971 war, but was cleared in the Hamoodur Rahman report. He was retired after the war for Bangladeshi independence and stripped of his medals and pension. See Abu Bakr Osman Mitha, *Unlikely Beginnings: A Soldier's Life* (Karachi: Oxford University Press, 2003) which was published posthumously.

21. The Khampa is a Tibetan tribe that often opposed the Chinese Communist regime. Many had settled in Nepal and India. The most noted Khampa was Tensing Norgay (1914–86) who accompanied Edmund Hillary in the conquest of Everest in 1953.

22. Mahboob Ullah Raschid became deputy chairman of the Planning Commission (1970–1) according to the Commission's internet site that lists all those who were deputy chairmen. It is unlikely that he followed this post by becoming governor of the State Bank as that would have been demotion. No information is available that might indicate that, being a Bengali, he might have gone to Bangladesh.

23. Muhammad Ataul Ghani Osmany, (1918–84), was retired as a colonel from the Pakistan Army in 1967. He was elected to the National Assembly in 1970 as a member of the Awami League. He commanded the Mukti Bahini during the conflict in 1971. Osmany was promoted to general and was made commander-in-chief of the Bangladesh Army, a post he held until April 1972. He was then made a member of the cabinet. He resigned his parliamentary seat in protest against Mujib's creation of a single party, the Bangladesh Krishak Sramik Awami League (BAKSAL). He stood for the post of president in the elections held in 1978 and 1981 and was defeated each time.

May 1971

24. Agha Shahi, (1920–2006), was the Pakistani representative to the United Nations during the civil war between West and East Pakistan in 1971. He was born in Bangalore and was initially a member of the Indian Civil Service. He was foreign secretary, 1973–7, and foreign minister, 1977–82. In 2005, he was chairman of the Institute of Strategic Studies. Agha Hilaly was his elder brother.

25. The representative of the State Department was William F. Spengler, later consul general in Lahore.

July 1971

26. There is no record in the Library of Congress catalogue that Maxwell wrote a book on the 1965 war. Maxwell published *India's China War* (Garden City, N.Y.: Anchor Books, 1972).

27. Hazrat Pir Sarsina Sharif Amir of Hizbullah, Dhaka, is an important religious leader. It was reported that he was an adviser of former president of Bangladesh, Hussain Muhammad Ershad (born 1930). Ranking with Sarsina is the Pir of Atroshi who also involves himself in politics. See U.A.B. Razia Akhter, *Islam in Bangladesh* (Leiden: Brill, 1992).

August 1971

28. Nazir Ahmad, a member of the Civil Service of Pakistan, was defence secretary under Ayub. His recollections are mentioned in Gauhar, op. cit., page 17, as being unpublished. No source is given for publication other than the reference by Gauhar. His son Salik Nazir Ahmed was chief secretary of Sindh.

29. Aziz Ahmad, (1906–1982), appointed by Ayub in 1958 was secretary general and deputy martial law administrator. He was ambassador to the United States and foreign secretary during the terms of Bogra and Bhutto as foreign ministers. He played a role in Operation Gibraltar in 1964 with Bhutto in an effort, unsuccessfully, to free Kashmir and retained the post as foreign secretary during the 1965 war with India and the Tashkent negotiations. He left the foreign secretary post in March 1966 when he became chairman of the Press Trust. He returned to the Foreign Ministry as secretary general during Yahya's regime and served as foreign minister briefly in 1977.

30. Abdul Muttalib Malik, (1905–77), became a minister in the Yahya cabinet when he was appointed special assistant to the president for Displaced Persons and Relief and Rehabilitation Operations in East Pakistan, July–September 1971. He was appointed governor of East Pakistan in November 1971 in an effort by Yahya to civilianise the government of the province. His role ended on 16 December 1971 when Pakistani forces surrendered. By training, Malik was an ophthalmologist but entered politics as a member of the Bengal Legislative Assembly, 1937–47, and later was a cabinet member in Pakistan and an ambassador. He played no role in independent Bangladesh.

31. The Mukti Bahini (literally, Freedom Force) was formed after March 1971 the beginning of the conflict in East Pakistan. Members were mainly drawn from Bengali personnel in the Pakistan Army, the East Bengal Rifles and the East Bengal Police along with many Bengali civilians.

November 1971

32. Joseph Simpson Farland (b.1914) US Ambassador to the Dominican Republic, 1957–60; Panama, 1960–3; Pakistan, 1969–72; Iran, 1972–3, and New Zealand 1973–6.

December 1971

33. General Iftikhar Janjua, (d.1971), was a brigadier in the Kutch war. He was the first general officer killed in conflict.

34. A section of the Seventh Fleet passed through of Strait of Malacca and into the Bay of Bengal on 13 December 1971. See Henry A. Kissinger, *The White Years* (Boston: Little Brown, 1979), pp. 911–2. See also Kissinger's Chapter XXI, 'The Tilt: The India–Pakistan Crisis of 1971' in its entirety. Zaheer states the fleet arrived in the Bay of Bengal on 15 December and notes that it had no 'immediate political or military impact on events in South Asia,' p. 400. He quotes Christopher Van Hollen, 'The Tilt Policy Revisited: Nixon–Kissinger Geopolitics and South Asia,' *Asian Survey*, XX:4 (April 1980).

35. Lieutenant General Amir Abdullah Khan Niazi, (1915–2004), was an officer in the British Indian Army. He fought in Burma during the Second World War and was awarded the Military Cross. He was assigned to command Pakistani troops in East Pakistan in April 1971. Although in command, he was junior in rank to General Tikka Khan who was then governor. Tikka ordered an offensive against Bengali intellectuals and other civilians, a tactic opposed by Niazi. The combination of the Bengali Mukti Bahini and Indian troops forced Niazi to surrender on 16 December 1971. His troops were taken prisoner. He was the last prisoner to be released after which he was deprived of his rank and his pension. He requested a trial by court martial but this was denied. Niazi wrote *The Betrayal of East Pakistan* (Karachi: Oxford University, 1998). In this book, that was well received, Niazi blamed Yahya and Tikka for the debacle in 1971.

36. Under pressure from senior officers of the army, Yahya resigned the presidency and appointed Bhutto president and chief martial law administrator. Bhutto dismissed General Abdul Hamid Khan, General S.G.M.M. Peerzada, Major General Ghulam Umar Khan and Lieutenant General Abdul Gul Hassan from the cabinet.

37. Hayat Muhammad Khan Sherpao, (1935–75), was from the North West Frontier Province. He was appointed governor of the province on 25 December 1971 by Zulfiqar Ali Bhutto, and served until 30 April 1972 and then became a member of the central cabinet when the PPP ministry in the North West Frontier Province lost power while retaining it at the centre. He was assassinated on 8 February 1975.

38. Mumtaz Bhutto, (b.1936), is a cousin of Zulfiqar Ali Bhutto and was active in the Pakistan People's Party. He was briefly in the central cabinet when Z.A. Bhutto became president and chief martial law administrator in December 1971. He was governor of Sindh, 24 December 1971–20 April 1972, and when a parliamentary system of government was installed, he became chief minister of Sindh from 1 May 1972 to 20 December 1973. He was replaced by Ghulam Mustafa Jatoi. Mumtaz Bhutto left for London after Z.A. Bhutto's execution in 1979. After the death of Ziaul Haq in

1988, President Farooq Leghari named Mumtaz Bhutto caretaker chief minister of Sindh on 7 November 1996 and he served until 22 February 1997. He strongly opposed, Benazir Bhutto in the election of 1997.

39. Bhutto's cabinet, as sworn in on 24 December 1971, was:
   - Zulfiqar Ali Bhutto, President
   - Nurul Amin, Vice President
   - Mubashir Hasan, Finance, Economic Affairs, Development
   - Jalaluddin Abdur Rahim, Presidential Affairs, Culture, Town Planning, Rural Affairs
   - Mian Mahmud Ali Qasuri, Justice, Parliamentary Affairs
   - Faizullah Kundi, Public Services
   - Muhammad Rashid, Social Affairs, Health, Family Planning
   - Raja Tridev Roy, Minorities
   - Ghulam Mustafa Jatoi, Political Affairs, Communications, Natural Resources
   - Malik Meraj Khalid, Food, Agriculture, Underdeveloped Regions
   - Abdul Hafeez Pirzada, Education, Information and Radio
   - Muhammad Hanif, Labour, Local Administration, Public Works
   - Dr Abdus Salaf (added 20 January 1972), Science and Technology, Production

Vacancies: Commerce, Industrial, Kashmir, Tribal Affairs

(Qasuri resigned 26 September 1972, accepted 10 October 1972.)

40. The report was prepared by a commission appointed by Bhutto in 1972 and led by Chief Justice Hamoodur Rahman. Rahman was a Bengali but chose to remain in Pakistan. The report was withheld by the government of Pakistan. A purported text of the report was published in *India Today*, December 2000. Then what is said to be the complete text was released by the Government of Pakistan although there is speculation that some secret documents had been withheld. The text was published as *The Report of the Hamoodur Rahman Commission of Inquiry into the 1971 War as Declassified by the Government of Pakistan* (Lahore: Vanguard, 2001). The report is highly critical of the military leadership for strategic and tactical errors and misjudgements and for its treatment of the Bengali population. It also criticized Bhutto's concept of two majorities in Pakistan: that of the PPP in West Pakistan and of the Awami League in East Pakistan. The commission stated that Bhutto's concept might be fit for a confederalist system, not a federalist one. It also noted that the Awami League held a majority in the assembly with the power to impose a constitution for Pakistan. The commission suggested that Yahya and his associates such as Tikka Khan should be tried for illegal usurpation of power from Ayub Khan, but no trials were held.

DIARY 1972

January 1972

1. Sobur was not killed; he died in 1982 (see Diary 1967, note 78). A.K.M. Fazlul Qader Chaudhary died in 1973; his son, Salahuddin Qader, is a leader of the Bangladesh Nationalist Party (see Diary 1967, note 34). Khwaja Khairuddin, (d.1993), who was a member of the Peace Committee opposing the liberation of East Pakistan went to Pakistan after 1971 and was active in Muslim League politics. In 1981, Khairuddin led his faction of the Muslim League into the multi-party Movement for the Restoration of Democracy (MRD) in opposition to President Ziaul Haq. He was a member of the family of the Nawab of Dhaka. Maulvi Farid was killed in 1971 (see Diary 1970, note 5).

March 1972

2. Air Marshal Abdur Rahim, (1925–90), was commander-in-chief of the Pakistan Air Force, 1969–72.

April 1972

3. Hafeez Pirzada was an early associate in the Pakistan People's Party with Zulfiqar Ali Bhutto. He teamed with Bhutto and Kausar Niazi in an attempt to reach an agreement with the Pakistan National Alliance following the 1977 election. The failure contributed to the imposition of martial law by General Ziaul Haq on 5 July 1977. Pirzada was on the left wing of the PPP. In 1985, he broke with the PPP-led party of Benazir Bhutto, along with Mumtaz Bhutto, Ataullah Mengal, Afzal Bangash and others to form the short-lived Mazdoor Kisan Party (MKP).

4. Although the interim constitution was passed on 17 April 1972, the final constitution was passed by the assembly on 31 December 1972 and became effective on 14 August 1973.

May 1972

5. See Diary 1970, note 41.

6. Mir Afzal Khan of Mardan was twice chief minister of the North West Frontier Province. He held the post from August 1990 to July 1993 and again during the caretaker central government headed by Moeen Qureshi. He negotiated an agreement between the NFWP and Balochistan on the management of waters in the two provinces. His family was involved in industry including sugar refining in the province. His sister, Begum Zari Sarfaraz was a legislator and a social worker. See her entry.

June 1972

7. Arbab Sikandar Khan Khalil, (d.1982), was governor of the North West Frontier Province, 30 April 1972–11 February 1973. He was assassinated in 1982.

8. *Kasaas* can be translated as 'obligatory revenge.' In pre-Islamic times, tribes practiced the revenge killing of persons who were killers and the revenge killing extended to succeeding generations. In Islam, the practice often means 'blood money' as goods are paid to assuage the damage to the heirs who do not demand the death penalty. The penalty no longer passes from generation to generation.

9. Abdul Hamid Khan Jatoi died 11 January 2004 at the age of 85. He was a former member of the National Assembly.

July 1972

10. The Simla Agreement, signed 3 July 1972, was agreed at a meeting of the foreign secretaries of India, Pakistan and Bangladesh. The signatories of the major element of the agreement were Indira Gandhi and Zulfiqar Ali Bhutto. The major component was the release of the more than 90,000 Pakistani military personnel from Indian custody. It was agreed that the ceasefire line in Jammu and Kashmir would become a 'Line of Control' and that the two countries would settle their disputes peacefully, a concept that was hardly original under the circumstances. India returned to Pakistan the land that it had occupied during the conflict. The main text of the agreement is contained in Hamid Khan, *Constitutional and Political History of Pakistan* (Karachi: Oxford University Press, 2001), pp. 454–5. Bangladesh was not formally recognized by Pakistan until 22 February 1974.

September 1972

11. Chaudhary Zahoor Elahi, (d.1981), was a constable in the police force, as Ayub notes. After independence, he set up a textile factory in his home district, Gujrat. He held a number of central ministerial posts. His son, Chaudhary Shujaat Husain, has served in the National Assembly and held party positions including as head of the ruling Pakistan Muslim League and Prime Minister from 30 June 2004–28 August 2004. Chaudhary Zahoor Elahi's nephew, Chaudhary Pervez Elahi, became chief minister of Punjab in 2002. Chaudhary Zahoor Elahi was assassinated on 25 September 1981.

November 1972

12. Kautilya (also known as Chanakya) lived around 300 BC. He was a Brahmin and was educated at Taxila in one of the major early institutions often described as universities. A companion school was at Nalanda in Bihar and both centres contain Buddhist artifacts. Kautilya composed the *Arthasastra*, an early treatise on politics and government. It seems to have been written during the Mauryan dynasty founded by Chandragupta Maurya. The latter's grandson was Ashoka.

13. Ayub was not correct. The mosque was funded and was opened in 1986. Housed in the same area is the International Islamic University that opened in 1980.

14. Malik was not sentenced to imprisonment, but died at home in 1977.

15. Khurshid Hassan Mir, (b.1925), was among the founders of the Pakistan People's Party headed by Bhutto. He defeated Asghar Khan in the 1970 elections. Mir was a member of Bhutto's cabinet, but was dismissed in December 1974 along with several other ministers including J.A. Rahim. Mir and many of the left-wing PPP supporters felt that Bhutto was moving to the right following the extensive nationalization in industry and trade.

Bibliography

Ahmad, Syed Nur, *From Martial Law to Martial Law: Politics in the Punjab, 1919-1958*. Translated by Mahmud Ali. Edited by Craig Baxter. Boulder, Colorado: Westview Press, 1985.

Baxter, Craig and Syedur Rahman, *Historical Dictionary of Bangladesh*. Lanham, Maryland: Scarecrow Press, 2003, third edition.

Biographical Encyclopedia of Pakistan. Research Institute of Historiography, Biography and Philosophical, 2002.

Burki, Shahid Javed, *Historical Dictionary of Pakistan*. Lanham, Maryland: Scarecrow Press, 1999, second edition.

Choudhury, G. W., *The Last Days of United Pakistan*. London: C. Hurst and Company, 1974.

Cohen, Stephen P., *The Pakistan Army*. Berkeley: University of Press, 1984.

Gauhar, Altaf, *Ayub Khan: Pakistan's First Military Ruler*. Lahore: Sang-e-Meel Publications, 1994.

Harrison, Selig S., *In Afghanistan's Shadow: Baluch Nationalism and Soviet Temptations*. Washington: Carnegie Endowment for International Peace, 1981.

Khan, Hamid, *Constitutional and Political History of Pakistan*. Karachi: Oxford University Press, 2001.

Magnus, Ralph H. and Eden Naby, *Afghanistan: Mullah, Marx and Mujihid*. Boulder, Colorado: Westview Press, 2002.

Mahmood, Safdar, *Pakistan: Political Roots and Development*. Karachi: Oxford University Press, 2000.

Malik, Hafeez and Gankovsky, Yuri V., editors, *The Encyclopedia of Pakistan*. Karachi: Oxford University Press, 2006.

Pakistan: From 1947 to the Creation of Bangladesh. Keesing's Research Report 9. New York: Charles Scribner's Sons, 1973.

Talbot, Ian, *Pakistan: A Modern History*. New York: St. Martin's Press, 1998.

Wasti, Syed Razi, *Biographical Dictionary of South Asia*. Lahore: Publishers United, 1980.

Wilcox, Wayne Ayres, *Pakistan: The Consolidation of a Nation*. New York: Columbia University Press, 1963.

Zaheer, Hasan, *The Separation of East Pakistan: The Rise and Realization of Bengali Muslim Nationalism*. Karachi: Oxford University Press, 1994.

Ziring, Lawrence, *The Ayub Khan Era: Politics in Pakistan, 1958-1969*. Syracuse: Syracuse University Press, 1971.

Index

Note: references to notes are given by page number and note number. Such citations have been italicised.

A

Abbas, Chaudhary Ghulam, 53, *560 n. 15*
Abdullah, Sheikh, 165, 195, 200, 202, 274, 318, 529, *567 n. 89*
Achakzai, Khan Abdus Salam Khan, 247, *570 n. 25*
Adamjee, 327, *574 n. 16*
Afzal, Mir, 527, *587 n. 6*
Aga Khan III, 256, *570 n. 30*
Agartala conspiracy case, 239, 250, 251, 261, *570 n. 27*
Agricultural Development Corporation, 158
Ahmad, Aftab, 259
Ahmad, Aziz, 54, 84, 157, 491, *585 n. 29*
Ahmad, Professor Muzaffar, 457, *583 n. 11*
Ahmad, Qammar-ud-Din (Kamruddin), 260, *571 n. 37*
Ahmadiyya, 445
Ahmed, M.M., 4, 54, 71, 105, 128, 132, 143, 230, 231, 237, 238, 254, 370, 371, 372, 376, 384, 386, *552 n. 7*
Ahmed, Maulvi Farid, 98, 362, 476, 514, *577 n. 5*
Ahmad, Nazir, 491, *585 n. 28*
Ahmed, Syed Ghiasuddin, 374, *578 n. 12*
Ahmed, Tajuddin, 470, *584 n. 18*
Ahmed, Tofail, 470, *584 n. 19*
Ahrars, 5, *552 n. 9*
Ahsan, Admiral S.M., 26, 376, 386, 403, 462, 463, 478, 479, 499, *556 n. 41*
Ahsan, Hakim, 230
Ahsan-ud-Din, Pir, 333
Akalis, 369, *578 n. 10*
Akbar, Brig., 222
Akbar, General, 241, 242, 335, 374, 422, 530, 533
Ali (Aly) Khan, Prince, 167
Ali, Agha Mohammad, 338, 378, 386, 455, 480, 499
Ali, Chaudhary Rehmat, 332, 368, *575 n. 19*
Ali, Choudhury Mohammad, 100, 297, 298, 299, 302, 306, 322, 378, *573 n. 11*
Ali, Jam Sadiq, 50, *559 n. 12*
Ali, Maulana Ather, 36, *557 n. 55*
Ali, Moazzam, 470
Ali, Syed Amjad, 47, 78, 297, *562 n. 37*
Allana, Ghulam Ali, 315, *573 n. 8*

Amer, Marshal (of Egypt), 33, 34
Amin, Hassan, 441
Amin, Nurul, 94, 100, 268, 299, 362, 459, 476, 495, 499, 503, 504, 509, 526, *563 n. 48*
Anjuman Himayat-i-Islam, *561 n. 28*
Anwar-ul-Haq, 281
APWA, 64, *560 n. 19*
Arab-Israeli War 1967, 102, 103, 104, 105 106, 107
Arif, President Abdul Rahman, 109
Aryana, General, 201
Ashraf, Princess, 527
Askari, Nawab Khwaja Hasan, 258, 265, *571 n. 39*
Aslam, Sardar, 258
Atomic energy stations, 48-49
Aurangzeb, Naseem, 28, 166, 209, 268, 269, 311, 320
Awami League, 101, 136, 268, 343, 376, 419, 420, 426, 428, 436, 450, 452, 459, 462, 469, 477, 506, 508, *573 n. 5*
Awan, Ayub Bakhsh, 32, 431, *557 n. 46*
Ayub Agriculture Research Institute (Lyallpur), 16
Ayub, General, 383
Azhar, Maj.-Gen., 376
Aziz-ur-Rahman, Shah Mohammad, 106, *564 n. 58*

B

Badaber, 46, 223, 224, 235, 242, 251, 274, *568 n. 4*
BANGSAM, 122
Bahaullah, 173, *567 n. 92*
Bahawalpur, *559 n. 6*
Balochistan, 14, 228, 247, 343, 372, 408
Bashir, Mian, 383
Batalvi, Dr Ashiq Hussain, 25, 368, *556 n. 40*
Bennett, Sir Fredrick, 494
Beria, Lavrenty, 155
Bhashani, Maulana A.H.K., 288, 289, 300, 305, 308, 310, 312, 328, 330, 333, 334, 342, 343, 357, 363, 364, 373, 374, 376, 377, 384, 386, 401, 404, 414, 416, 417, 418, 420, 421, 430, 440, 446, 457, 463, 465, 469, 473, 526, *572 n. 49*
Bhinder, Anwar, 345
Bhutto, Mumtaz, 508, 514, 531, 532, 536, *585 n. 38*
Bhutto, Nusrat, 527, 529

Bhutto, Zulfiqar Ali, 3, 15, 29, 33, 36, 43, 44, 58, 61, 69, 73, 75, 84, 99, 125, 168, 181, 239, 255, 263, 266, 281, 282, 284, 290, 291, 297, 300, 302, 307, 310, 318, 324, 331, 334, 336, 344, 345, 346, 348, 357, 360, 361, 373, 374, 375, 382, 386, 399, 406, 409, 410, 435, 436, 437, 440, 449, 455, 458, 459, 460, 462, 468, 469, 470, 471, 472, 473, 482, 489, 491, 504, 513, 514, 526, 528, 535, 536, 540, 541, 544, *552 n. 3*; 1970 Elections and aftermath, 419-429; Accuses Yahya of accepting the Six Points, 451; Agreement with Yahya on the impossibility of retaining East Pakistan, 499; Announces land reforms, 520; Announces release of Ahmed Dawood, Valika, and Gen. Habibullah, 516; Announces ten-member central government, 509; Appointed deputy prime minister and foreign minister, 503; Appointed president and CMLA, 507; Appointed speaker of assembly, 524; Arrested under Defence of Pakistan Rules, 283; Assets in India, 111; Attacks General Sher Ali and Yahya Khan, 367; Cabinet members, *586 n. 39*; Calls upon party members to handover undated resignations, 535; Confronts Gen. Tikka Khan, 533, 534; Cracks in PPP, 537; Declines to join Yahya-Mujib discussions, 465; Dramatics in a public meeting, 442; Election tour of the Frontier and Punjab, 358; Eleven-day tour of the Frontier, 542; Engages journalist to write book on Agartala case, 542; Fascist, 344; French type of constitution, 538; Gate-crashes into Lt.-Gen. Gul Hassan's house, 441; Government of and for *goondas*, 508; Happy with instability, 340; Head of a mission to Peking, 498; Hunger strike, 299; Indian demands for return of POW, 517; Letter to Iskander Mirza, 407; Lt.-Gen. Gul Hassan appointed as C-in-C, 508; Meeting with Ghulam Faruque, 121; Meeting with Mujib, 443, 445, 446, 445; Meeting with Yahya Khan, 370, 378, 443, 444, 454, 458; Meetings with lawyers, 324; People losing faith, 539; Plan to create instability, 405; Policy on language question, 532; Political murders, 530; Public meeting in Karachi, 464; Quits Commonwealth, 516; Refuses to attend assembly session, 452, 453; Responsible for ousting Ayub Khan, 326; Sends Nusrat Bhutto to Kabul, 527; Simla Agreement, 531; Slogan of Islamic socialism, 448; Starts victimization, 510; Talks with Indira Gandhi, 529, 530; Threatens civil disobedience, 465, 466; Tour of central Punjab, 402; Tour of Sindh, 533; Victimization of Ayub Khan's family, 543; Visit to Dacca, 445, 466, 467; Visit to Lahore, 431; Visit to Moscow, 521, 522, 523; Visit to Peking, 517; Yahya-Mujib-Bhutto meeting, 467
Bizenjo, Mir Ghous Bakhsh, 47, 340, *576 n. 26*
Bolkov, 220, 222
Bonny, Jack, 135
Bowles, Chester, 122, 126, 221

Brezhnev, Leonid, 149, 152, 153, 155, 174, 214
Brohi, A.K., 43, 388, 389, 409, 466, *558 n. 3*
Brown, George, 29
Bucha, Malik Khuda Bakhsh, 34, 63, 92, 229, 265, 318, 339, *557 n. 52*
Bugti, Akbar, 343, 408, *576 n. 27*
Burki, General Wajid Ali, 381, *579 n. 20*

C

Capital Development Authority, 365, *566 n. 86*
Cargil, Mr, 282
Cariappa, General, 29, 164, 165, *567 n. 88*
CENTO, 16, 19, 87, 89, 112, 130, 170, 212, 239, 504, 505, *555 n. 30*
Chagla, M.C., 29, 32, 204
Chaudhary, Fazal Ellahi, 52, 331, *559 n. 13*
Chaudhary, Fazlul Qader, 76, 329, 347, 350, 352, 357, 358, 359, 365, 373, 378, 390, 396, 397, 403, 408, 481, 514, *561 n. 34*
Chaudhary, Hamidul Haq, 330, 476, *575 n. 18*
Chaudhry, Amjad Ali, 238, *569 n. 19*
Chaudhuri, Nirad, 209, 380, *568 n. 5*
Chavan, Y.B., 124, 146, 153, 165, 220
Chen-yi, 97, 115, 168, 181, 185, 247
Chiang Ching, 96
Chou En-lai, 64, 97, 141, 181, 182, 185, 247, 495
Choudhury, G.W., 447, 486, *582 n. 5*
Cornelius, A.R., 75, 203, 465, *561 n. 30*

D

DAC (Democratic Action Committee), 299, 300, 302, 304, 305, 306, *573 n. 2*
Dacca, Begum of, 77, *561 n. 36*
Dara, Dastoor, 366
Daultana, Mian Mumtaz, 39, 43, 44, 78, 79, 94, 100, 297, 302, 304, 310, 320, 331, 341, 344, 360, 363, 364, 381, 389, 390, 396, 397, 401, 403, 404, 405, 406, 407, 413, 419, 428, 436, 437, 439, 456, 466, 466, 517, 524, 525, *557 n. 58*
Dawood (family), 27, *556 n. 44*
Dawood, Ahmed, 92, 280, 372, 516, 523
De Gaulle, General Charles, 22, 30, 31, 107, 111, 167, 168, 179, 238, 314, 316, 412
Demirel, Suleiman, 88, 89, 170, 171, 292, 293, 336
Deoband group, 5, *553 n. 11*
Desai, Morarji, 67, 95, 153, 156, 164, 165, 220, 235
Dewal, Pir Sahib of, 48, 84, 200, 280, 366, *559 n. 9*
Dir, 91, 92, *563 n. 46*
DMK (Dravida Munnetra Kazhagam), 369, *578 n. 11*
DPR (Defence of Pakistan Rules), 203, 283, 300, 535

E

East Pakistan Rifles, 461, 478, 479, 481, 488

East Pakistan: Agartala conspiracy case, 261; American interests in, 123, 124; Army in control of most cities and towns, 479; Bengali nationalism, 473, 474; Casualties suffered in weeklong disturbances, 461; Clashes between the Army and the mob, 469; Clashes between Urdu speaking refugees and Bengalis, 337; Communist, 357; Cultural situation in, 262; Cyclone, 14, 35, 219, 241, 412, 414, 415, 421, 422; Deterioration of law and order, 305; East-west relations, 260; Economic situation, 261; Effects of leftist government in West Bengal, 79; Facing ruination, 337; Farraka barrage, 262, 271; Flags of Bangladesh, 468; Floods, 261, 271, 281, 401; Growing disparity in GNP, 187; Hindu influence, 281; Language question, 148; Leaders of opposition parties, 88, 90; Leftism and communism, 330; Neglect of agriculture, 376; Officialdom behind Mujib's demands, 365; Political situation, 260; Private sector, 210, 376; Rate of development, 143, 175; Report by the military intelligence, 136; Separation of Bengal, 506; Session of the Central Assembly, 182; Student community on rampage, 358; Student leaders in Dacca University, 333, 334; Student problem, 263

EBDO (Elective Bodies Disqualification Order), 3, 8, 39, 40, 43, 44, 54, 552 n. 2

Eight Point programme, 96, 100

Eisenhower, President David Dwight, 22, 168, 310

Elahi, Chaudhary Zahoor, 536, 587 n. 11

Eleven Points, 376, 436, 579 n. 17

Elizabeth II, Queen, 28, 29, 31

EPIDC, 159

Etamadi, Nur Ahmad, 194, 568 n. 103

F

Faisal, King (of Saudi Arabia), 14, 24, 33, 89, 144, 149, 207, 211, 243, 308, 331, 334, 336, 542

Farland, J.S., 585 n. 32

Farraka Barrage, 225, 262, 276, 568 n. 102

Faruque, Ghulam, 24, 44, 45, 54, 110, 113, 121, 122, 326, 556 n. 38

Fawzi, Mahmoud, 149

Fazl-e-Akbar, Justice, 227, 264, 569 n. 15

Fazlullah, Qazi, 39, 40, 61, 110, 112, 121, 136, 180, 272, 558 n. 61

Firyubin, Nikolai Pavlovich, 12

Freeman, Orville L., 18

Friends not Masters, 52, 121, 315, 322, 326

Fulbright, J. William, 217, 569 n. 8

Fuller, J.F.C., 566 n. 83

G

Gandhi, Indira, 11, 67, 75, 95, 108, 124, 131, 154, 165, 188, 213, 214, 220, 221, 369, 402, 430, 494, 498, 501, 504, 506, 518, 521, 522, 529, 530

Gauhar, Altaf, 13, 17, 24, 46, 53, 85, 91, 123, 128, 154, 157, 201, 222, 237, 250, 251, 264, 301, 306, 308, 315, 374, 388, 401, 409, 472, 517, 520, 524, 537, 555 n. 26

Ghosh, Sudhir, 216, 569 n. 7

Goodwin, Professor, 208, 243, 456, 539

Grechko, Marshal, 306

Gromyko, 490, 523

Gul, Maj.-Gen. Rehman, 376

Gurmani, Mushtaq, 110, 113, 121, 229, 564 n. 61

H

Habib Bank, 27, 556 n. 43

Haider, Sufi Zulfikar, 138, 566 n. 79

Hala, Makhdoom of, 559 n. 11

Hamid, Maj.-Gen. Shahid, 350, 566 n. 84

Hamid, General, 51, 146, 150, 220, 338, 361, 366, 378, 414, 425, 441, 475, 493, 494, 496, 508, 514

Hamood-ur-Rahman, 284, 520, 554 n. 19, 571 n. 38; commission, 586 n. 40

Haq, Mahbubul, 248, 570 n. 26

Haq, Maulvi Abdul, 258, 259

Haq, Kazi Anwar-ul-, 281, 572 n. 46

Haroon, Mahmud, 125, 329, 335, 343, 359, 364, 373, 386, 390, 401, 424, 425, 575 n. 17

Haroon, Yusuf, 290, 307, 335, 339, 340, 344, 483, 575 n. 20

Harriman, William Averell, 22, 177, 178

Hasan, Mubashir, 422, 526, 582 n. 40

Hasan, Sahibzada Faizul, 5, 59, 75

Hashimuddin, 259, 329, 330, 571 n. 35

Hassan, Begum Zeenat Fida, 237, 569 n. 18

Hassan, Fida, 132, 141, 166, 194, 218, 246, 271, 372, 565 n. 74

Hassan, Said, 99, 564 n. 56

Hazarvi, Maulana Ghulam Ghaus, 456, 583 n. 10

Hidayatullah, Ghulam Hussain, 360, 577 n. 3

Hilaly, Agha, 269, 270, 483, 484, 486, 572 n. 44

Hindu Mahasabha, 221, 569 n. 11

Hogg, Quintin, 225, 569 n. 14

Hoti, Abdul Ghafoor Khan, 94, 110, 113, 125, 146, 149, 180, 183, 270, 283, 312, 313, 327, 328, 329, 563 n. 49

Hoti, Col. Amir Muhammad Khan, 397, 563 n. 50

Hoti, Mohammad Ali, 94, 563 n. 51

Hoveida, Amir Abbas, 19, 211

Huda, Dr Nurul, 187, 305, 308, *567 n. 98*

Hume, Douglas, 481

Hussain, Altaf, 26, 194, 206, 326, *556 n. 42*

Hussain, Amjad, 257, 301

Hussain, Arshad, 11, 34, 217, 219, 239, 247, 310, 481, *555 n. 22*

Hussain, Naseem, 233, 234, 243, 350, *569 n. 16*

Hussein, King (of Jordan), 27, 28, 104, 105, 144, 150, 206, 207, 208, 240, 251

I

Ikramullah, Begum Shaista, 240, *569 n. 21*

Inamullah, Chief Justice, 64, *560 n. 18*

Iqbal, Allama Sir Mohammad, *554 n. 14*

Iqbal, Javid, 386, *579 n. 23*

Isa, Qazi Mohammad, 39, 408, *558 n. 59*

Inter Services Intelligence, 274

Islam, Kazi Nazrul, 265, 267, *571 n. 40*

Islamic Research Institute, 6, 90, 253, *554 n. 17*

J

Jaffery, Vaseem A., 132, 271, 292, *565 n. 75*

Jamaat-e-Islami, 63, 66, 67, 272, 357, 403, 459, 530, 540, 542

James, Sir Morrice, 369, *578 n. 9*

Jamiat-ul-Ulema of Pakistan, 291

Jana Sangh, 221, 331, 369, *569 n. 12*

Janjua, Maj.-Gen. Iftikhar, 504, *585 n. 33*

Jatoi, Ghulam Mustafa, 344, 536, 537, *577 n. 32*

Jatoi, Abdul Hamid Khan, 530, *587 n. 9*

Jinnah, Fatima, 53, 78, 79, 96, 128, 173, 315, 316; death, 114; funeral of, 115-116; *559 n. 14*

Jinnah, Mohammad Ali, 315, 316, 319, *553 n. 13*

Johnson, President Lyndon B., 3, 15, 22, 46, 80, 82, 105, 107, 108, 134, 135, 143, 144, 151, 153, 154, 168, 170, 191, 192, 193, 206, 209, 213, 214, 223, 224, 242, 248, 274, 281, 484

Junagadh, Nawab of, *572 n. 45*

Junagarh (Junagadh), *566 n. 80*

Junejo, Mohammad Khan, 75, *561 n. 29*

K

Kalabagh, Nawab of, 134, 179, 312, 346, 347, 363, 540, *552 n. 1. See also* Malik Amir Mohammad Khan

Kamruzzaman, 450, *583 n. 9*

Karakoram highway, *575 n. 21*

Karim, Prince, 166, 167

Kashmiri, Shorish, 292, 322, 534, 535, *574 n. 12*

Kasuri, Mahmood, 422, 536, 537, 538

Kaunda, Kenneth, 107

Kazi, Aftab, 175, 193, *567 n. 93*

Kennedy, President John F., 269

Kennedy, Robert, 228

Khairuddin, Khawaja, 299

Khalil, 122, 124

Khaliquzzaman, Chaudhary, 128, 173, 191, 241, *565 n. 70*

Khan of Kalat, 47, 247, *559 n. 8*

Khan, Abdul Ghaffar Khan, 7, 370, *554 n. 18*

Khan, Abdul Jabbar, 76, 201, 203, 387, *561 n. 33*

Khan, Abdur Rehman, 244

Khan, Abdus Sobur, 137, 201, 210, 257, 290, 301, 325, 329, 330, 333, 337, 350, 414, 437, 514, *566 n. 78, 586 n. 1*

Khan, Adam, 360

Khan, Admiral A.R., 97, 98, 283, 308, 405, *564 n. 54*

Khan, Air Marshal Rahim, 520, 526

Khan, Akhtar Hameed, 238, *569 n. 20*

Khan, Asghar, 284, 286, 290, 291, 297, 299, 310, 324, 326, 342, 344, 346, 348, 351, 360, 362, 386, 390, 406, 420, 467, 472, 497, 533, 534, 543, *572 n. 47*

Khan, Ataur Rehman, 417, 457, 465, *581 n. 34*

Khan, Begum Khudeja G.A., 237, 238, *569 n. 17*

Khan, Begum Nasim Wali, 397

KHAN, FIELD MARSHAL MOHAMMAD AYUB

- 1970 Elections and aftermath, 419-429
- 2500th anniversary of Iranian monarchy, 495
- 27th anniversary of Pakistan, 491
- 44th anniversary of commission, 448
- 7th RCD ministerial meeting, 130
- Abrogation of the constitution in 1958, 116-117
- Accused of encouraging communists, 382
- Address to: press editors, 237, 263; the conference of inspectors general, 139, 140; West Pakistan High Court Bar Association, 62; a *jirga*, 91
- Advocating cause of the Arabs, 113, 117
- Agreement on the framework of the constitution, 538
- Ahmed Dawood's dinner party, 280
- Aid to Pakistan, 237, 238; consortium, 439
- All squadrons except two ready to strafe Bhutto, 538, 539
- Amendment of Article 98 of the constitution, 288
- America: condemns India as aggressor, 503; withdraws support, 521
- American: and British pull out of East Pakistan, 473; carrier *Enterprise* heading towards Bay of Bengal, 505; espionage work, 125; warning to India, 490; fanning discontent in the country, 310
- Armed forces' pension code, 218, 238, 239, 247

– Arms: deal with Russia, 232, 239, 240; manufacture capability, 176; new American policy on supply, 80; supply to Pakistan, 275

– Asghar Khan: house burnt down, 533, 534; intentions to join politics, 284; retirement from politics, 345, 348

– Assassination: attempt by Hashim, 283, 325; plot, 97, 98, 532

– Assessment of: G.M. Syed, 367; Pir of Dewal, 366

– Ayubia, 116

– Badaber, 274

– Benevolent fund and group insurance, 232

– Bengali attitude, 234

– Bhutto making money, 523

– Bhutto-Wali Khan parleys, 523

– Birth control, 245

– Birthday, 223

– Blamed for two martial laws, 335

– Break up of One Unit, 395

– Briefing at GHQ, 255

– Briefing to General Musa, 7-8, 272

– Budget 1968-1969, 229

– Cabinet meeting, 54, 96, 100, 114, 141, 177, 206, 223, 229, 235, 250, 307, 309

– Call assembly to carry out necessary amendments to the constitution, 306, 307, 308

– Canadian aid, 80

– Causes of political maladies, 311

– Chinese protest Indian interference in Pakistan, 476, 477

– Commercial aims of the press, 443

– Communism, 541

– Concern of the intelligence agencies, 291

– Concise version of Mujib's Six Points, 362

– Conspiracy to bring about independent Bengal, 192, 200, 201, 203, 207

– Corruption of army, 501

– Criticism of Dr Fazlur Rahman, 253

– Cultivation of crops, 48, 164, 228, 229, 273

– Curfew, 299

– Cutting off diplomatic relations by Bhutto government, 516

– Daultana resigns presidency of Council Muslim League, 406

– Death of de Gaulle, 412; Iskander Mirza, 339, 340

– Debate on budget, 231

– Decade of reforms, 222

– Decision not to contest next elections, 301, 304

– Demand for introduction of Islamic laws, 418

– Demonetisations of 100 and 500 rupee notes, 486

– Demonstrations and protests against the government, 298, 299, 305

– Destruction of a hijacked Indian plane at Lahore, 448, 449, 451

– Deterioration of law and order in Dacca, 301

– Devaluation: of the pound, 176, 209; of the rupee, 445

– Direct elections and parliamentary federal government, 306

– Discussions: on textbooks, 46-47; with governors and ministers, 26; with Justice Fazal-e-Akbar on Supreme Court's problems in Dacca, 264; with King of Nepal, 85; with King Zahir Shah, 58-59, 60; with Mahmoud Fawzi, 149; with Mian Arshad Hussain, 219, 220; with Mr Harriman and Mr Locke, 22-23; with President Kenneth Kaunda, 108; with President Sunay, 16, 17, 18; with Prime Minister Suleiman Demirel, 88, 89, 292; with Shah of Iran, 70, 72, 293

– Division of waters of the Ganges, 398

– Eastern rivers' waters, 225

– Economic crisis in India, 542

– Economic development in underdeveloped countries, 322, 323

– Economization in manpower and weapons in defence, 271

– Elections on the basis of direct adult franchise, 312

– Emergence of two autonomous regions, 435

– Explosive situation in East Pakistan, 333

– Extracts from de Gaulle's writings, 316

– Failure of system, 331

– Falsely accused: of attempting to murder Ghulam Jilani, 517; of extolling Bhutto, 454

– Feels sorry for Yahya Khan, 508, 514

– Fight with the mullahs/ulema, 48, 49, 63, 79, 85

– Food, 18, 35, 45, 49, 66, 121, 339

– Foreign exchange, 45, 206, 287

– Foreign visits by government officials, 267

– Freezing of Muslim League funds, 396, 397

– Future of: agriculture, 221; Dir state, 91, 92; refugees and new settlers in Sindh, 329; political prospects, 317

– General Hamid's report on the Jordanian forces, 150, 151

– General Niazi surrenders, fighting ceases in East Pakistan, 506

– Genesis of turmoil in the country, 303

– Gist of talk between M.M. Ahmed and McNamara, 230

– Gloomy: picture of East Pakistan, 330; prospects for Pakistan, 311, 312

– Gohar Ayub: assessment of Asghar Khan's announcement for retirement, 351; visit to China, 97; meeting with Lt.-Gen. Gul Hassan, 491

– Gossip, 402, 403

– Governors given powers of martial law administrators, 457
– Governors' conference (discussions), 9, 35, 66-67, 158, 159, 160, 161, 162
– Greatest: achievement, 321; influence on thought and action, 256
– High level conference at GHQ, 478
– Hindu mentality, 541, 542
– Hostility of: Kabul government, 271, 272, 527; Russian Press, 496; the British Press, 478
– How to teach your mind to think, 90
– Ideas to discuss with Yahya Khan, 117-119
– Illness and treatment, 208, 376, 377, 380, 383, 384, 385, 386, 387, 395, 396, 446, 455, 460, 473, 479, 480, 483, 484
– Income Tax Returns of relatives, 352, 357
– India as member of the Muslim Summit, 331; Pakistan delegation boycotts conference, 332; India debarred from attending conference, 332
– India: declares allegiance to Bangladesh, 480; giving military support to Bangladeshis, 488, 489, 491, 493; launches major offensive, 500, 501; recognizes Bangladesh government, 503; supports secessionist movement in East Pakistan, 474, 475, 487
– Indian army infiltrating in East Pakistan, 472, 476
– Indian: economy, 225; general elections, 67; plans of attack, 112, 177, 211, 222, 241
– Indo-Pak relations, 81, 83, 94, 145, 146, 152, 153, 156, 164, 165, 187, 188, 289, 399, 400
– Industrial matters, 318
– Interview to Hamid Nizami of *Nawa-e-Waqt*, 375
– Invasion of Czechoslovakia, 249, 250
– Iran-Turkey relations, 273
– Islamabad University, 73, 244, 247
– Jalil Ahmed's assessment of the political situation, 346, 347
– Karakoram Highway, 215, 336
– Kashmir, 449
– Kissinger's trip to Peking, 488
– Kosygin unhappy with East Pakistan situation, 481, 494
– Labour and student community, 232
– Labour troubles financed by Russians, 544
– Leftists, 334
– Letter on the future of Commonwealth, 93
– Letter to Agha Hilaly, 270
– Letter to governor of West Pakistan, 229
– Mahmud Haroon's observation of the political situation, 359-361, 364, 373, 390, 401, 424
– Martial law order to Convention Muslim League, 446
– Meeting of the defence committee of the cabinet, 133, 134, 287

– Meeting with: A.K. Brohi, 388, 389; A.K. Sumar, 409; Asghar Ali Shah, 403, 404; Aslam Khattak, 397, 445; Begum Ra'ana Liaquat Ali Khan, 410; Bottomley, 486, 487; Chancellor Kiesinger, 179, 180; Charles de Gaulle, 167, 168; Fida Hassan, 372; fruit experts, 255; General Khalid Sheikh, 365-366; Ghulam Jilani Malik, 405; Giuseppe Tucci, 268; Khawaja Shahabuddin, 407, 408; law minister, 128; M.M. Ahmed, 370-372, 384, 386; Maj.-Gen. Rafi, 475, 476; Maulvi Abdul Haq, 258; Monem Khan and dissident Muslim Leaguers, 290; N.M. Uqaili, 410; Nawabzada Nasrullah, 527; Rashidi, 344-345; S.M. Zafar, 430; Shabbir Ahmed, 415, 416; Shah of Iran, 243; Sheikh Mujibur Rahman, 302; the DAC, 305, 306; the opposition, 304; the Shah of Iran and the Turkish Prime Minister, 126; Yahya's brother, 455; Yusuf Haroon, 225, 290, 291, 339, 340
– Message from Kosygin, 214
– Minimal qualities of a ruler, 540
– Mobile banks, 246, 251
– Murder of: Monem Khan, 495, 500; Nawab of Kalabagh, 179, 192, 347, 368
– Muslim culture, 268
– Mutual trade over land routes, 321
– Newly raised army units short of equipment, weapons, clothing, 510, 540
– News media trying to sell Bhutto as a great leader, 513
– Nuclear: armament race, 55; power plant, 132
– Nur Khan's resignation, 362, 363; visit to China, 181
– Objectives in going to Tashkent, 437-439
– Opening of Mangla Dam, 178
– Pakistan army out-numbered, 504
– Pakistani community in Britain, 244
– Pakistani rupee devalued, 526
– Paper on the problem of agriculture cooperatives, 183, 184, 185
– Passivity and inaction of the army, 479
– Pep talk to editors and senior journalists, 176
– Points for talks to the senior officers in Dacca, 188, 189, 190
– Police demoralized, 333
– Police strike in Peshawar, 518
– Population growth, 254, 322, 444
– Power generation, 6
– POWs killed in Madhya Pradesh, 537; Allahabad, 538
– Précis of talk with Kosygin, 212, 213, 214
– President Nixon demands ceasefire from Indira Gandhi, 504
– Problems of East Pakistan, 132
– Protest against merger of Swat, 324
– Protests by Chinese Charge d'Affaires, 141, 149
– Public sector, 233
– Railway strike, 57

– Reaction by Iranian foreign minister on trivial matters, 274
– Rebuttal of Suleri's false allegations, 315
– Recruitment of armed forces on 50:50 basis from East and West Pakistan, 359
– Relinquishment of presidency of Muslim League, 330
– Remains of Chaudhary Rehmat Ali, 332, 368
– Report by Chester Bowles, 221
– Resignation from the Muslim League, 357
– Resignation of Lt.-Gen. Yaqub Khan, 463
– Retirement, 311, 313, 319
– Review of: *A Short History of Pakistan*, 145, 147; *Arrogance of Power*, 217; *Gandhi's Emissary*, 216; *Through the Crisis*, 378, 379, 380
– Revolution Day television talk, 275, 276, 277, 278, 279
– Rice production, 256, 265
– Rights of citizens trampled upon, 398
– Route permit system, 285
– Rumours of making up with Bhutto, 521
– Rumours of stroke, 61
– Rumours, 337, 338
– Russia-China relations, 64, 68
– Russia-India treaty of friendship, 490
– Russians blunt with Bhutto, 523
– Russians support India in 1971 war, 505
– Security Council's effort to bring about ceasefire in India-Pakistan conflict, 502
– Separation of East Pakistan, 306
– Sharing of the Ganges water, 292
– Sheikh Abdullah accepts Kashmir's accession to India, 529
– Shorish Kashmiri's writ petition, 292
– Sindhi as official language, 528, 530, 531, 532
– Sindhi MNAs on the warpath, 300
– Sindhism 180
– Sir Morrice James talks about the situation in India, 369
– Situation of deadlock/confrontation between East and West Pakistan, 452, 453
– Situation of lawlessness in the country, 287, 288
– Six points for the Muslim League, 4, 552 *n. 8*
– Skeleton staff provided by government, 391
– Socialism, 339
– Steel mills project, 326
– Stepping aside for General Yahya Khan, 308, 309
– Strikes, 382
– Student community, 267
– Sugar, 273
– Supreme Court judgments in Altaf Gauhar and Ghulam Jilani cases, 524
– Surprise visit by Chinese deputy foreign minister, 536

– Suspension of 303 civil officials, 347, 366
– Taking over of industries by Bhutto government, 513, 515
– Talk: at opening ceremony of High Court building in Dacca, 258, 259; to GHQ officers, 81-83; to Manpower Commission, 248, 249; to Muslim League assembly party, 96, 102; to Muslim League Party, 217, 218; to the central government secretariat, 85-88; with King Hussein of Jordan, 207
– Tank demonstrations, 256
– Tank population in the army, 199
– Tank-infantry cooperation, 269
– Tarbela Dam: ground breaking ceremony, 282; Tender for, 181, 193
– Thoroughfares and streets named after prominent personalities, 334, 335
– Thoughts on emergence of new nations and problems they face, 391-393
– Three hurdles faced by constitution makers, 404
– Treatment of POWs by Indians, 521
– Tribal belts, 368, 369
– Trouble between Pathan and non-Pathan students, 242
– UN General Assembly passes resolution calling upon Pakistan and India to ceasefire, 503
– Under surveillance by the National Security Council, 534
– Unification of North Korea, 109
– Views: of former ADC on Yahya's government, 342, 343; on anti-Chinese riots in Burma, Nepal, and India, 115; on Chinese pressure on Hong Kong, 115; on East Pakistan, 100; on India, 157; on Romanian progress, 169; on situation in the Middle East, 115, 120; on ulema, 5
– Visit to: East Pakistan, 36-37, 76, 78, 137, 138, 182, 183, 184, 185, 186, 187, 188, 257, 288, 289, 290, 299; England, 28-30; France, 31, 166, 167; Iran, 18, 20, 171; Jordan, 27-28; Russia, 152, 153, 154, 155, 156; Turkey, 170
– Visitors while hospitalised at CMH: Maj.-Gen. Rafi, 381; General Wajid Burki, 381; Mian Bashir, 383
– Wali Khan and the Red Shirts, 370; visit to Kabul, 529
– War with India unavoidable, 494, 495, 496, 498
– War with India, 453, 454
– Widespread scare on the fall of Dacca, 507
– Worsening situation in East Pakistan, 505, 506
– Yahya's treachery, 472
Khan, General Azam, 98, 286, *564 n. 55*
Khan, General Khwaja Muhammad Azhar, *582 n. 4*
Khan, General Tikka, 397, 398, 460, 462, 463, 475, 478, 533, 534, *580 n. 26*

Khan, General Yahya, 10, 14, 69, 97, 98, 99, 117, 135, 165, 203, 211, 220, 232, 239, 240, 255, 256, 269, 304, 308, 309, 310, 312, 317, 318, 319, 321, 324, 326, 331, 332, 335, 348, 350, 352, 358, 361ff, 370ff, 378, 381, 382, 396, 397, 398, 402, 411, 441, 455, 458, 461, 462, 463, 470, 472, 473, 476, 478, 479, 487, 489, 490, 494, 496, 499, 508, 515, 524, *554 n. 21*, *574 n. 14*; 1970 Elections and aftermath, 419-429; Accused by Bhutto of accepting Six Points, 451; Announces assembly session to be held on 25th March, 459; Army operation in East Pakistan, 470, 471; Attempts suicide, 520; Ayub-phobia, 393; Cold shouldering Qayyum and his associates, 413, 417; Constitutional plan/matters, 338, 341, 344, 351, 374; Damaging article in *Newsweek* on private life, 500; Dissolves cabinet, 447; Draft constitution, 444; Drinking and womanising, 329, 338, 350, 363, 366, 377, 385, 450, 493, 502; Facing suits for murder and treachery, 509, 510; Family members mobbed, 513; Family shifts to Abbottabad, 526; Forms special board to look into corruption, 313; House burnt by mob, 507; Interview with Asghar Ali Shah, 403; Legal Framework Order, 374; Letter of protest from Podgorny, 475; Losing faith in people, 409; Meeting with Bhutto, 440, 442, 443, 444, 454, 458; Meeting with Mujib, 464, 465, 466; Opening ceremony of Quaid-e-Azam's mausoleum, 442; Pakistan Day message, 467; Pep talk on the fall of Dacca, 507; Playing a curious game, 386; Policy statement, 399; Postponement of elections, 405; Postpones assembly session, 457; Presidential cabinet dissolved, 454; Press conference in Dacca, 415; Radio address, 469; Reference to Franco's rule in Spain, 449; Son's betrothal, 498; Statement to press, 442; Under house arrest, 514; Understanding with Mujib, 437; Visit to Dacca, 464; Visit to Iran, 493; Visit to Russia, 390, 393, 394, 395; Visit to the UN, 410; Visit to Turkey, 384, 389; Wets trousers at an official dinner, 448; Yahya-Mujib-Bhutto meeting, 467
Khan, Ghulam Ishaq, 70, 132, 385, *560 n. 26*
Khan, Gohar Ayub, 39, 44, 97, 209, 227, 238, 246, 339, 351, 404, 405, 431, 481, *557 n. 57*
Khan, Gul Hassan, 343, 361, 367, 441, 491, 508, 520, 526, *576 n. 28*
Khan, Habibullah, 11, 69, *560 n. 22*
Khan, Khan Abdul Ghaffar, 143
Khan, Liaquat Ali, *567 n. 95*
Khan, Lt.-Gen. Habibullah, 14, 510, 514, 515, 516, *555 n. 27*
Khan, Maj.-Gen Mohammad Rafi, 24, 54, 97, 104, 115, 381, 475, 476
Khan, Maj.-Gen. Akbar, 64, 467, 534, *560 n. 20*
Khan, Malik Amir Mohammad, 3, 9, 10, 47. *See also* Nawab of Kalabagh

Khan, Maulana Muhammad Akram, 258, *571 n. 34*
Khan, Monem, 17, 35, 37, 56, 66, 76, 78, 79, 100, 107, 137, 177, 185, 187, 188, 207, 228, 255, 257, 258, 259, 264, 281, 282, 305, 308, 329, 330, 387, 495, 500, *555 n. 32*
Khan, Nawabzada Nasrullah, 299, 300, 302, 305, 438, 527, *582 n. 2*
Khan, Nur, 11, 109, 112, 181, 182, 254, 275, 313, 321, 338, 340, 342, 343, 362, 363, 468, 371, 403, 408, 414, 444, 489, *555 n. 23*
Khan, Qayyum, 43, 44, 58, 78, 290, 325, 343, 344, 344, 345, 346, 352, 358, 363, 364, 365, 370, 373, 378, 381, 386, 390, 391, 396, 397, 398, 401, 402, 403, 406, 407, 408, 413, 417, 423, 425, 426, 428, 437, 439, 451, 489, 523, *558 n. 2*
Khan, Ra'ana Liaquat Ali, 96, 410, *564 n. 53*
Khan, Sahibzada Yaqub, 457, 463, 478, 479, 499, *583 n. 12*
Khan, Sardar Amir Azam, 39, *558 n. 60*
Khan, Sardar Bahadur, 43, 495, 496, *558 n. 4*
Khan, Sardar Mohammad Daud, 194, *568 n. 104*
Khan, Sardar Mohammad Ibrahim, 449, *582 n. 7*
Khan, Sarwar, 242
Khan, Shaukat Hayat, 78, 381, 456, 466, 517, *562 n. 38*
Khan, Sir Syed Ahmed, *553 n. 12*
Khan, Sultan, 185, *567 n. 97*
Khan, Wali, 283, 302, 344, 358, 360, 370, 386, 396, 403, 413, 419, 423, 436, 446, 451, 466, 520, 523, 529, 533, 540, *576 n. 30*
Khar, Mustafa, 454, 458, 508, 509, 537, 544, *583 n. 13*
Khattak, Aslam, 397, 445, *580 n. 25*
Khattak, Nasrullah, 351, 352, *577 n. 35*
Khattak, Yusuf, 439
Khrushchev, Nikita, 99, 155
Khudai Khidmatgar, *566 n. 82*
Khuhro, Ayub, 121, 319, 320, 341, 344, *565 n. 68*
Khurshid, K.H., *583 n. 8*
Kiesinger, Kurt Georg, 179, 180
Kirmani, Ahmed Saeed, 17, 43, 54, 227, 237, 241, 246, 345, 346, 347, 446, *558 n. 1*
Kissinger, Henry, 488
Knudson, Morrison, 135
Kosygin, Aleksei, 11, 12, 20, 21, 64, 89, 107, 108, 110, 152, 153, 54, 155, 156, 174, 206, 209, 211, 212, 213, 214, 218, 220, 230, 240, 248, 260, 306, 395, 481, 494
Kohistan (newspaper), 92, 120, 125, 312

L

Lahore Resolution, *581 n. 35*
Legal Framework Order, 374, 377, 427, 437, 440, *578 n. 14*

Lenine, P.T., 256
Liu Shao-chi, 96, 129, 141
Locke, Eugene Murphy, 14, 22, 23, 80, 89, 105, *555 n. 28, 562 n. 41*

M

Mahendra, King (of Nepal), 84, 85
Mahmood, Hassan, 396, *565 n. 69*
Mahmood, Mufti, 466
Malik, Dr Abdul Muttalib Malik, 491, 543, *585 n. 30, 587 n. 14*
Malik, General Akhtar, 367
Malik, Ghulam Jilani, 405, 406, *580 n. 29*
Mamdot, Nawab Iftikhar Husain, 336, *575 n. 23*
Manavadar, *566 n. 81*
Mannan, Fakir Abdul, 258, *571 n. 33*
Mangla Dam, 178, *567 n. 94*
Mao Tse-tung, 20, 64, 65, 96, 129, 141, 149, 152, 154, 155, 215, 247, 271
Marri, Khair Bakhsh, 408, *580 n. 30*
Maududi, Maulana, 5, 14, 48, 59, 65, 75 79, 85, 98, 357, 404, 407, 428, 467, *552 n. 10*
Maxwell, Neville, 81, 488
McConnaughy, Walter Patrick, Jr., 122, 126, *552 n. 5*
McCormack, James, 239
McNamara, Robert, 168, 230, 254, 284
Mehmooda Begum, Sahabzadi, 353, *577 n. 36*
Menderes, Adnan, 171
Mengal, Sardar Ataullah, 408, *580 n. 31*
Menon, Krishna, 3, 399, 400, *580 n. 27*
Mian, Manik, 76, 100, *561 n. 31*
Mian, Mohan, 76, 100, *561 n. 32*
Mir, Khurshid Hassan, 543, *587 n. 15*
Mirza, Iskander, 116, 117, 339, 340, 370, 407, *565 n. 67*
Mitha, Maj.-Gen. Abu Bakr Osman, 475, 478, *584 n. 20*
Mohammad, Malik Ghulam, *574 n. 13*
Mohammadi, General, 135, 154, 156, 176, 222
Mohiuddin, Col., 208, 338, 377, 384, 393, 394, 395, 455, 456, 460, 496
Mohyuddin, 194
Moinuddin, G., 53, 74, 75, *561 n. 27*
Mosib-ur-Rehman, 373
Muhammad, Hanif, 128
Mukti Bahini, 491, 495, 496, 499, 506, 507, *585 n. 31*
Munir, Justice Mohammad, 116, 117, 246, *565 n. 66*
Murshed, Justice, 45, *559 n. 7*
Musa, General Muhammad, 6, 7, 10, 11, 13, 14, 34, 57, 91, 97, 98, 111, 127, 165, 169, 179, 219, 227, 237, 242, 272, 285, 291, 300, 307, 322, 346, 361, 405, 441, 454, *554 n. 16*

Muslim League, 4, 25, 36, 43, 78, 176, 227, 238, 240, 241, 257, 258, 270, 283, 285, 286, 302, 317, 319, 325, 326, 345, 347, 348, 352, 362, 489
Muslim Summit Conference (Rabat), 331, 332, 334

N

NAP (National Awami Party), 136, 408, 520, 523
Napier, Sir Charles, 147, *566 n. 85*
Nasser, Gamal Abdel, 70, 102, 103, 104, 105, 106, 107, 109, 120, 126, 129, 144, 150, 151, 165, 172, 207, 431
National Democratic Front, 100
National Economic Council, 34, 35, 95, 175, 187, 217, 282, 389
NATO, 170
Nawaz, Major General Haq, 38
Nazir, Maj.-Gen., 441
Nehru, Pandit Jawaharlal, 19, 146
Nehru, R.K., 75
Niazi, A.A.K., 506, *585 n. 35*
Niazi, Kausar, 64, 65, 200, *560 n. 21*
Nikolayevich, 155
Nixon, Richard, 84, 213, 246, 270, 280, 282, 284, 285, 325, 409, 483, 484, 488, 490, 498, 504, 505, 519
Nizami, Hamid, 375, *578 n. 15*
Noel-Baker, Philip J., 243, *570 n. 22*
Noon, Feroz Khan, 47 64, *560 n. 17*

O

Obaidullah, A.Z.M., *579 n. 24*
Oehlert, Benjamin H., Jr., 134, *566 n. 76*
Operation Gibraltar, *554 n. 15*
Operation Searchlight, 470, *583 n. 16*
Osmany, Col. 481, *584 n. 23*
Oxford University Press, 17, 253

P

Pagaro, Pir, 326, *574 n. 15*
Pakhtunistan, 7, 230, 527
Pakistan Democratic Movement, *563 n. 47*
Pakistan Industrial Corporation, 158
Pakravan, Hassan, 4, 329
Palejo, Rasul Baksh, 422, *582 n. 41*
Paracha, Habibullah, 47
Pasha, Ismat Inonu, 131, 384, *579 n. 22*
Pataudi, Sher Ali Khan, 345, 350, 365, 367, 373, 406, 420, 425, 510, 534, 535
PDP, 359, 362
Pearson, Lester, 254

Peerzada, General S.G.M.M., 315, 338, 340, 342, 366, 367, 374, 374, 381, 390, 398, 409, 420, 422, 425, 442, 455, 460, 467, 472, 473, 499, 508, *573 n. 7*

Philip, Prince (Duke of Edinburgh), 28, 31

Pickard, Sir Cyril, 337, 441

PIDC, 159

PINSTECH, 247, *570 n. 24*

Pirzada, Hafeez, 523, *586 n. 3*

Pirzada, Sharifuddin, 19, 29, 32, 88, 99, 107, 130, 142, 144, 168, 170, 194, 217, 280, *557 n. 48*

Podgorny, Nikolai, 109, 152, 153, 154, 174, 214, 390, 475

Pompidou, Georges, 167

PPP (Pakistan People's Party), 181, 419, 420, 422, 423, 426, 428, 440, 467, 468, 540, 543, 544

Progressive Papers Limited, 382, *579 n. 21*

Public Law 480 (United States), 10, 14, 15, *554 n. 20*

Q

Qadianis, 407

Qadir, Manzur, 251, 294, 300, 306, 308, 375, *570 n. 28*

Qadir, Qazi, 188, 257, 258, 259, 330, 331, 347, 348, 437, *568 n. 99*

Qasim, Malik, 328, 329, 330, 333, 336, 345, 346, 348, 350, 352, 358, 365, 368, 385, 396, 397, 398, 480, 481

Qizilbash, Muzaffar, 69, 329, 358, 365, 373, 386, 390, 396, 398, 401, 425, 443, 445, 476, *560 n. 24*

Qureshi, Bashir, 180, *567 n. 96*

Qureshi, Dr Ishtiaq Hussain, 18, 145, 147, 173, 315, *556 n. 33*

R

Rahim, Brig., 357

Rahim, J.A., 422, 445, 458, 527, *582 n. 39*

Rahman, Chaudhary Shamsur, 316, *573 n. 10*

Rahman, Dr Fazlur, 90, 253, *562 n. 44*

Rahman, Sheikh Mujibur, 88, 100, 124, 239, 251, 261, 302, 304, 305, 306, 310, 312, 320, 326, 328, 330, 333, 334, 337, 341, 342, 344, 348, 357, 358, 359, 360, 361, 362, 363, 365, 367, 372, 374, 389, 390, 396, 397, 401, 402, 403, 404, 405, 407, 410, 413, 414, 416, 417, 418, 430, 435, 438, 441, 448, 449, 469, 472, 473, 476, 477, 478, 479, 482, 487, 495, 499, 502, 506, 522, 526, 542, 543, *562 n. 43*; 1970 Elections and aftermath, 419-429; Adverse comments on LFO, 376, 377; Announces conditions to attend assembly session, 461; Arrested and brought to West Pakistan, 470, 471, 478, 487; Assassination attempt, 437; Attacks West Pakistan Muslim culture, 453; Calls for *hartal*, 458; Calls meeting of working committee to review political situation, 450; Civil disobedience movement, 461, 462, 463; Controlling bank transactions, 462; Exploiting parochialism, 364; Future prime minister, 442; Indian army withdraws from Bengal, 520; Indira Gandhi visits Dacca, 521, 522; Issues 35 detailed directives, 464; Mammoth public meeting, 436; Meeting with Bhutto, 443, 445, 446; Meeting with Yahya, 444, 464, 465, 466; No compromise on Six Points, 452; Not happy with overwhelming majority, 439-440; Plans for secession, 336; Refuses to attend 10 March 1971 meeting, 458, 459; Reiterates victory to Six Points, 456; Rousing reception in Delhi, 515; Set free and flown to London, 514; Trial, 490, 498; Under pressure to declare independence, 464; Understanding with Yahya Khan, 437; Visit to Calcutta, 518; Yahya-Mujib-Bhutto meeting, 467

Rajagopalachari, Chakravarti, 438, *582 n. 1*

Rann of Kutch, 32, 375, *557 n. 49*

Raschid, Mahboob Ullah, 477

Rashidi, Pir Ali Mohammad, 344, 345, *576 n. 31*

Rawalpindi Conspiracy, *581 n. 38*

Razvi, Nazir Ahmed, 374, 378, 386, 401, 407, 409, *578 n. 13*

RCD (Regional Cooperation for Development), 4, 19, 70, 89, 130, 131, 178, 267, 277, 292, 293, 421, *552 n. 6*

Rehman, General Attiqur, 362, 376, *577 n. 4*

Rehman, Manibur, 192

Rehman, Mashiur, 192, 470, *568 n. 101*

Rehmatullah, Ibrahim, 247

Revelle, Dr Roger, 132, 133, *565 n. 73*

Riaz, Maj.-Gen., 376

Rokhri, Abdullah Khan, 368, 533, *577 n. 7*

Round Table Conference, 389

RSS (Rashtriya Swayamsevak Sangh), 221, *569 n. 10*

Rusk, Dean, 122, 168, 170

S

Sabri, Ahsan, 130, 131, 320

Sadruddin, Prince, 91, *563 n. 45*

Saeed, Commander, 377

Saeed, Hakim Muhammad, 32, *557 n. 50*

Saigol, Rafique, 63, *560 n. 16*

Salam, Dr Abdus, 132, 133, 244, *565 n. 72*

Salimullah, Nawab (of Dacca), *570 n. 31*

Sandys, Duncan, 244

Sarfraz, Begum Zari, 110, *564 n. 62*

Sarsina, Pir of, 488

Sayed, Shaukat, 208

Schmidt, Professor, 49

Seaborg, Dr Glen, 48

SEATO, 87, 504, 505

Shah of Iran, 4, 18, 19, 20, 23, 33, 70, 71, 72, 106, 109, 123, 126, 149, 165, 169, 170, 171, 204, 211, 230, 234, 235, 239, 243, 254, 273, 277, 292, 293, 338, 340, 435, 493, 495, 514, 527

Shah, Asghar Ali, 403, 404, 533

Shah, King Zahir, 58, 59, 60, 70, 527

Shahab, Qudratullah, 15, 46, 206, *555 n. 29*

Shahabuddin, Khawaja, 44, 49, 113, 137, 145, 200, 201, 203, 204, 206, 281, 283, 290, 297, 298, 299, 300, 304, 325, 337, 339, 357, 358, 363, 407, 435, *559 n. 5*

Shahi, Agha, 483, *584 n. 24*

Shams-ud-Doha, A.H.M., *557 n. 54*

Shastri, Lal Bahadur, 400, *580 n. 28*

Shehu, Mehmet, 166

Sheikh, General Khalid Mahmud, 349, 365, 366, *577 n. 34*

Sherpao, Hayat Muhammad Khan, 425, 508, 518, *585 n. 37*

Shoaib, Mohammad, *557 n. 45*

Shuja, Hakeem Ahmad, 136, *566 n. 77*

Siddiky, Badruddin Ahmad, 259, *571 n. 36, 583 n. 14*

Siddiqui, Dr Amir Hassan, 173, *567 n. 91*

Sihanouk, Prince, 204

Sikandar, Arbab, 529, *587 n. 7*

Simla, 531; Agreement, 536, *587 n. 10*

Singh, Swaran, 19, 34, 474, 477

Six Points, 100, 304, 359, 362, 363, 367, 376, 377, 379, 413, 415, 417, 430, 435, 436, 437, 438, 440, 443, 444, 445, 451, 454, 455, 456, 458, 459, 464, 473, *564 n. 57*

Smith, Arnold, 93

Soekarno (Sukarno), 73, 166

Soomro, Ahmed Mian, 107, *564 n. 59*

Stalin, 155, 166, 214

Stewart, Michael, 286

Stoica, Chivu, 169

Subandrio, Dr, 3, 168, *552 n. 4*

Suharto, Haji Mohammad, 102, 121

Suhrawardy, Huseyn Shaheed, 288, 302, 335, 454, *572 n. 48*

Sui gas, 6

Suleri, Z.A., 129, 148, 253, 311, 315, 316, 326, 365, 420, *565 n. 71*

Sumar, A.K., 54, 409

Sunay, President Cevdet, 16, 17, 18, 336

Swat, Wali of, 12, 268, 311, 322, 323, 325, 328, 337, *555 n. 24*

Syed, Col. Shaukat, 383

Syed, G.M., 337, 340, 344, 345, 360, 336, 413, 530, *576 n. 24*

T

Talpurs, *556 n. 36*

Tarbela dam, 17, 269, 282, 365, 371, 389

Tarkabagish, Maulana, 268, *571 n. 43*

Tashkent Declaration, 202, 375, 438, 517, *568 n. 2*

Thant, U, 83, 84

Tito, Marshal, 202, 204, 205, 249

Tiwana, Khizr Hayat, 69, *560 n. 23*

Toochi, 268

Trading Corporation of Pakistan, 247

Tuania, General, 201

Turabi, Maulana Rashid, 23, *556 n. 35*

U

Umer, Maj.-Gen., 409, 473, *581 n. 33*

Uqaili, N.M., 17, 53, 69, 132, 133, 215, 219, 241, 410, 411, *555 n. 31*

Usmani, Dr, 29, 30, 48

Usto, Dur Mohammad, 336, *575 n. 22*

V

Valika, Fakhruddin, 359, 516, *577 n. 2*

Vietnam, 22, 46, 80-81, 95, 178, 222, 247, 248

Volkow, Herr, 176

W

Wahiduzzaman, 258, 259, 299, 301, 302, 325, 330, 331, 333, 336, 347, 348, 358, 396, 437, *571 n. 32*

WAPDA, 92, 158, 175, 191, 193, 219

Wattoo, Yasin, 347, 352, 396, 397, *577 n. 33*

Waziristan, 368, 369

Wilson, Harold, 29, 107, 337

Woods, George, 94, 95, 128, 269, *563 n. 52*

Z

Zafar, S.M., 37, 378, 379, 380, 408, 430, 523, *557 n. 56*

Zafar-ul-Haq, Raja, 334

Zafarullah, Chaudhary, 25, 63, *556 n. 39*

Zahedi, Ardeshir, 131, 204, 211, 273, 340

Zakori, Pir, 200, 351, *568 n. 1*

Zaman, Raja George Sikander, 426, *582 n. 42*

Zehri, Nabi Bakhsh, 408, *580 n. 32*